BUILDING BACARDI

BUILDING BACARDI
Architecture, Art & Identity

ALLAN T. SHULMAN

Foreword by
TERENCE RILEY

RIZZOLI
NEW YORK

New York · Paris · London · Milan

The author wishes to thank the many individuals, archives and lending institutions who assisted in the research for this book, especially Raul Alvarez; The Bacardi Archive and Bacardi U.S.A., with special thanks to Aura Reinhardt; Francisco Brennand; Hilario Candela; Ignacio Carrera-Justiz; Juan Ignacio del Cueto Ruiz-Funes; Ermina O. Equilior; Armando Molina Garcia; Enrique Gutierrez; Angela Pedrao; Roberto Segre, V'Soske and Enrique Vivoni.

First published in the United States of America in 2016 by
RIZZOLI INTERNATIONAL PUBLICATIONS, INC.
300 Park Avenue South, New York, NY 10010
www.rizzoliusa.com

ISBN-13: 978-0-8478-4748-8
Library of Congress Control Number: 2015953983

Distributed to the U.S. Trade by Random House, New York

Front cover: Bacardi Building, Havana, Cuba. Lobby. Esteban Rodriguez-Castells and Rafael Fernández Ruenes, architects, 1930. Photograph by Kenneth Treister, 1997. Courtesy of The Bacardi Archive and Kenneth Treister.

Page 2: Bacardi Building, Havana, Cuba. Parapet detail. Esteban Rodríguez-Castells and Rafael Fernández Ruenes, architects, 1930. Photograph by Kenneth Treister, 1997. Courtesy of The Bacardi Archive and Kenneth Treister.

Back cover: Rumbera. Advertisement. Rafael Lillo Bonet, artist, 1949. Courtesy of The Bacardi Archive.

Designed by Aldo Sampieri

Printed and bound in China

2016 2017 2018 2019 2020 / 10 9 8 7 6 5 4 3 2 1

CONTENTS

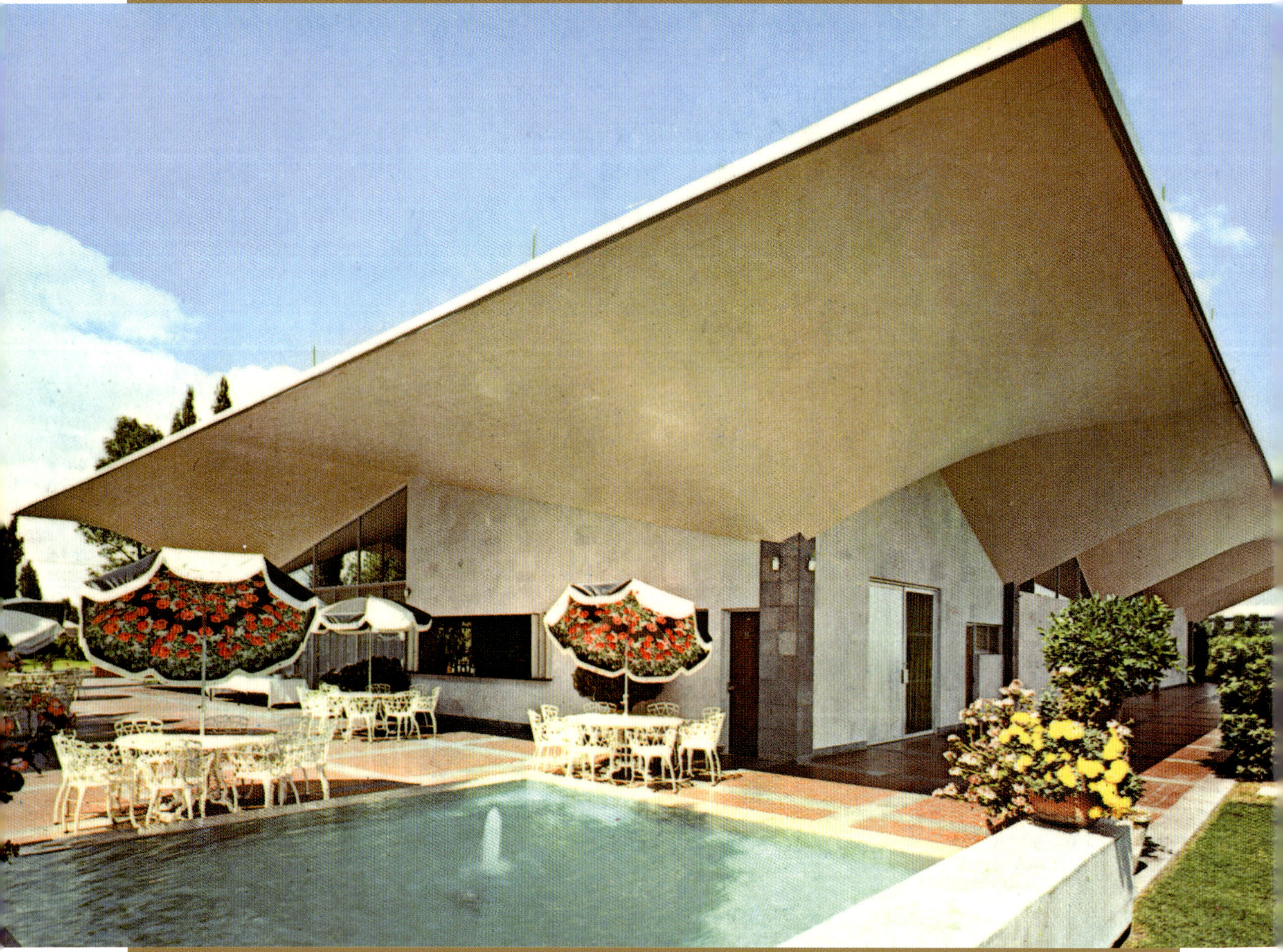

FOREWORD

Terence Riley

Building Bacardi traces the history of the Cuban distiller's use of visual and spatial strategies to create associations with their award-winning rum. In its earliest days, Bacardi adopted the now famous bat logo as a purely visual emblem, as merchants have done for centuries. Nonetheless, the company was an early adaptor when it came to modern marketing and played a unique role amongst corporate patrons of architecture.

An early nineteenth-century promotional image shows factory sheds and chimneys billowing smoke—the universal icon of industrial progress. Those factories did indeed bring Bacardi great success, which is more than evident in the 1928 designs for their grand high-rise headquarters in Havana.

In the first decades of the twentieth century, Bacardi was certainly not the only industrial enterprise that favored rationalized modern architecture for manufacturing and more ornate settings for its headquarters. *Building Bacardi* tells the fascinating story of how, over time, the modernity of its factory architecture begins to be the dominant theme that the company wished to express in its representational buildings as well.

Bacardi cannot be said to have been "purists" when it came to their patronage of modern architecture. When, in the 1930s, the company began establishing itself in New York City, they turned to such architects as Morris B. Sanders—a modernist in the mold of Howe & Lescaze. Jose "Pepin" Bosch, who led the company from 1944 until 1976, commissioned another New York architect, Philip Johnson, to design a house for him in Cuba in 1956. Bosch also commissioned a house in Puerto Rico from Henry Klumb who had briefly worked for Frank Lloyd Wright before moving to San Juan.

Nonetheless, two figures—Felix Candela and Mies van der Rohe—developed long-lasting relationships with Bacardi. Candela was educated as an architect in Spain, worked in an engineering office in Germany and emigrated to Mexico where he pioneered lightweight concrete shell construction. The climate of Bacardi's field of operations—Cuba, Puerto Rico, and Mexico—was suited to Candela's vaulted structures, which were often open-air canopies rather than enclosed buildings. Bacardi's ongoing patronage undeniably contributed to Candela's ability to refine his singular methods for calculating the structural requirements for his elegant paraboloid structures.

Bacardi commissioned Mies van der Rohe to design its headquarters in Santiago de Cuba in 1957, just as the German-born architect was finishing an office tower in New York for another famous distiller—Joseph E. Seagram's and Sons. Although never completed, Mies' design for a glass pavilion supported by eight exterior columns can be considered as the basic research for this type of structure, which Mies favored and was able to realize ten years later in the Neues Nationalgalerie in Berlin.

Bacardi turned to Mies for one more commission: the administration building in Tultitlan, outside Mexico City, an example of Mies's ongoing development of structurally rational, minimal glass pavilions that he designed and built in the 1950s. While it may seem in retrospect that Mies' stature as one of the leading modern architects in the world was assured by that point in time, the importance of the Bacardi commissions in consolidating his reputation should not be underestimated. As the work of this volume illustrates, the promotion of spirits and design often went hand in hand.

Bacardi y Compañía, S.A. Bottling Plant, Tultitlán, Mexico. Canteen. Félix Candela (Cubiertas Ala), architect, with SACMAG and Luis Torres Landa engineers, 1960-61. Courtesy of The Bacardi Archive.

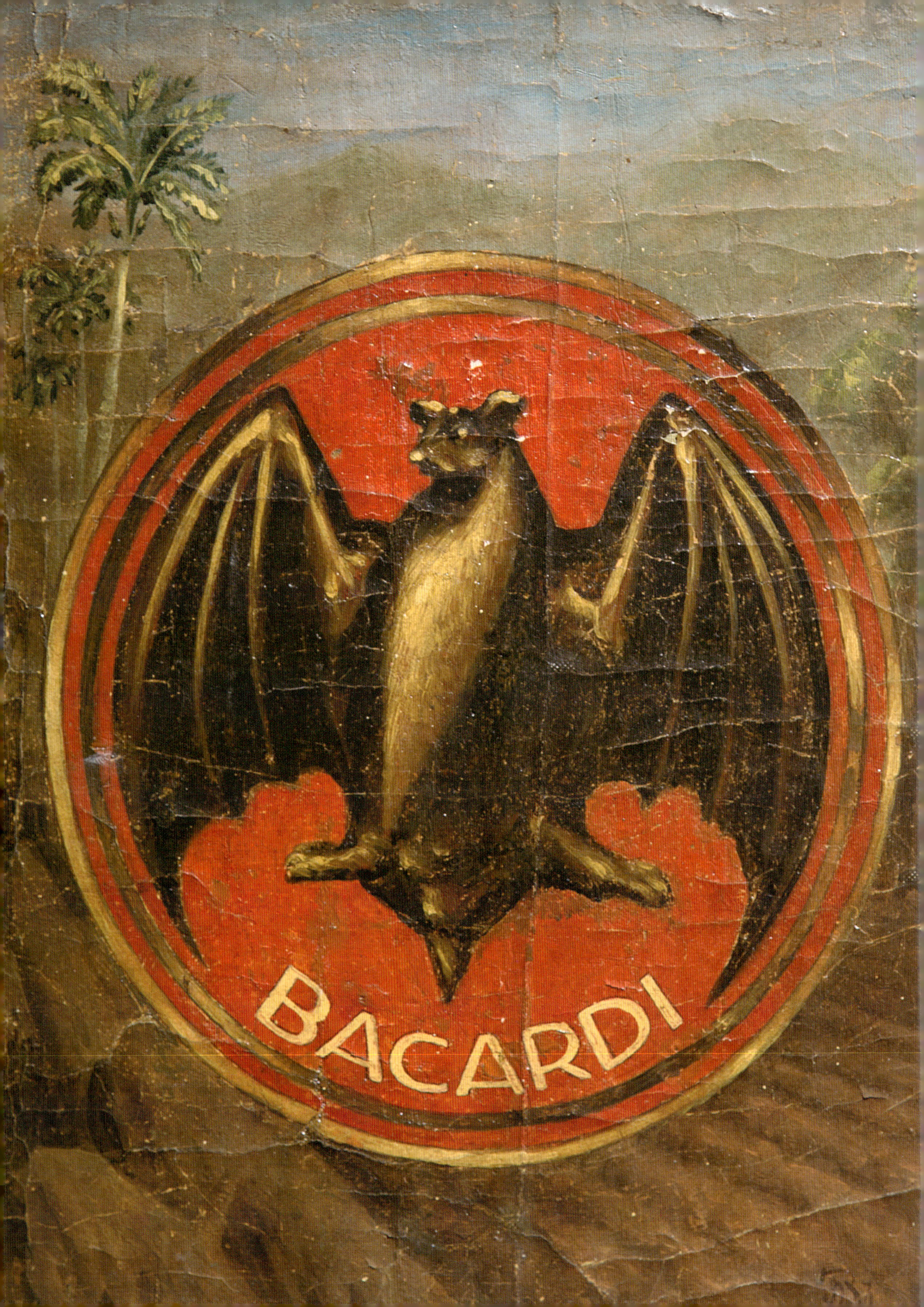
BACARDI

BUILDING BACARDI

Architecture, Art & Identity[1]

INTRODUCTION: A BRAND DISTILLED IN BUILT FORM

About an hour south of London, in the countryside of Hampshire, England, an adventurous synthesis of industry, architecture and brand identity has taken shape. The Distillery at Laverstoke Mill, recently completed for gin maker Bombay Sapphire, might at first be taken for the bucolic vestiges of an earlier industrial era. Victorian brick buildings ramble along the verdant banks of the River Test; only the faceted prisms of two new greenhouses peeking from this pastoral landscape predict something new and extraordinary. Upon closer investigation, state-of-the-art mechanical and environmental systems weave carefully into restored brick buildings, whose white, loft-like interiors contain polished high-tech equipment. Tourists also weave through the complex, following a circuit that allows them close-up contact with the production. The landscape and buildings are part of a carefully curated, holistic sensory experience designed to educate, and above all deliver a long-lasting impression of Bombay Sapphire. As such, all the elements of the brand—its botanical ingredients, its distilling process, its signature cocktails, as well as the evidence of its institutional support of creative industries and its place in the environmental consciousness of the early twenty-first century—are assembled here. The distillery is a communications system premised on the power of design and aesthetics as a crucial medium of product identification. As a place to explore, to think and feel, the plant stimulates experiences designed to transform functional vocations into the embodiment of desire.

Laverstoke Mill is the latest product of its parent company, Bacardi Limited, best known for its trademark rum—and its red and black bat logo. A powerhouse in the spirits industry, the family-owned enterprise today sells more than 200 brands, produced in 29 facilities around the world. Much has been written about Bacardi, but the company's role in the history of modern corporate architecture is less examined. Yet for more than 100 years Bacardi has been a prodigious builder of distilleries, bottling plants, corporate offices, bars, and museums. Through striking acts of architecture, the company has promoted its corporate identity and especially its "brand," the roughly intangible quality that Anna Klingmann has argued imparts an "aura of meaning" around a product. [2]

In architectural histories, Bacardi is celebrated for having commissioned iconic modernist structures by prominent architects like Ludwig Mies van der Rohe and Felix Candela. However, the continuous and ongoing architectural record of the company tells a more compelling story. The way Bacardi has used the medium of design to define itself is a window into architecture's capacities and limits; it shows how architecture can unfold in multi-dimensional ways, and acquire multiple meanings. It supports the idea that architecture has the power to represent and influence, to negotiate and communicate; in short that architecture is an expressive act. In this inventory of work, notions of synthesis, pluralism, flexibility, respect for heritage, and the importance of myth and play comingle with functional necessities. The role of iconic designers comingles with the work of indigenous architects whose partnership with Bacardi produced novel and contextually grounded designs.

Bat Device, oil on leather, c. 1890s. Courtesy of The Bacardi Archive.

This book explores the record of Bacardi's many identities, its evolving brand, in four terrestrial paradigms: local, national, global and ultimately regional. In the flow between these various paradigms, it becomes evident that while Bacardi sought to identify effective strategies, these strategies were subject to continuous adjustment, refinement and even abandonment.

From the company's beginning, architectural expression has been a key component of the Bacardi business plan. Born in eastern Cuba, Bacardi distilled a strong local and national identity from the cultural alchemy of this tropical region. As a provincial rum distiller in Santiago de Cuba, Bacardi established itself as an institution while erecting monuments in its hometown to translate its growing success into civic engagement. "Bacardi is Santiago and Santiago is Bacardi," notes a tourism pamphlet of the 1930s.[3]

When the distiller grew to be a national icon, Bacardi represented the nascent Cuban nation both at home and abroad. After World War II, Bacardi's Cuban identity was the essential platform for its global expansion as a Pan-American entity. Bacardi buildings simultaneously manifested Cuban identity and a globalized modernity, consolidating the brand and expanding it. The development of numerous new homes, standardized in function but each considered as a unique cultural landscape, emblematized an increasingly international corporation.

The Cuban Revolution uprooted Bacardi, reinforcing the company's Cuban identity in exile, while accelerating its internationalization (and revealing a well-marked penchant for turning political predicaments into new horizons). Ultimately, as Bacardi has expanded beyond the tropics, the company has claimed a series of "brand homes" to establish relevance for acquired spirits concerns whose heritage lies in territory ranging from the Scottish Highlands to the French countryside. The imperative for regional authenticity reflects the contemporary multi-brand nature of Bacardi Limited.

Bacardi is such a compelling study because it both engages and challenges established ideas about corporate architecture. The company has employed the most important commercial building types of the twentieth century, from office towers to corporate campuses. It has developed new, commissioned structures, but it has also inhabited existing structures, sometimes selecting buildings of great meaning and adapting them for its own purposes. In spite of its size and global position, the company never codified its architectural ambitions or created parameters for a recognizable Bacardi style. Eschewing sameness, Bacardi has experimented with approaches from rationalist to expressionist, from everyday to exotic, and from purist monumentality to hybrid works of artistic synthesis. At the same time, the company has developed recurrent forms and ideas that are embedded in its collective memory and that transcend everyday concerns; Bacardi today is the sum of these ideas, a culture constructed in the crucible of modern world history.

Bacardi facilities are best understood as allegories, manifesting corporate values as diverse as civic pride, cultural engagement, political conviction, technical ingenuity, hygiene, scientific know-how and cultural authenticity. Identity management has always functioned at the top level of the company, not through consultants or lower-

Top: Bacardi y Compañía S.A. Distillery, La Galarza, Matamoros, Puebla, Mexico. Featured in *Nuevo Orgullo de Bacardí* (Bacardi's New Pride). From *Bacardi Grafico* 6 (July 1957): 12–13. Courtesy of The Bacardi Archive.

Bottom: Collage of Bacardi buildings. *97 Años Cubanos... ¡97 Años Creando!* (97 Cuban Years... 97 Years of Creating!), *Bacardi Grafico* 12 (January 1959): Front and back covers. Courtesy of The Bacardi Archive.

Nuevo Orgullo de Bacardí

En un cálido y hermoso valle a 192 kilómetros de la capital se encuentra ubicada la hacienda "La Galarza", asiento de la nueva destilería Bacardí en México. Alrededor se extiende la fecunda campiña mexicana salpicada de pintorescas ruinas coloniales. En la línea del paisaje se confunden el pasado, con sus tradiciones y recuerdos, y el presente con su dinámica de progreso diariamente renovado.

Tres horas en automóvil desde la ciudad de México por la moderna carretera Panamericana, conducen hasta el bello paisaje de la sierra de Puebla. La silueta funcional de La Galarza se ofrece a la vista con todos los atributos de la arquitectura moderna, marcando un contraste con las edificaciones de piedra.

Una bóveda de pañuelo cubre los cinco fermentadores de 235,000 litros de capacidad. La bóveda constituye una audacia arquitectónica, con 24 metros de distancia entre las columnas.

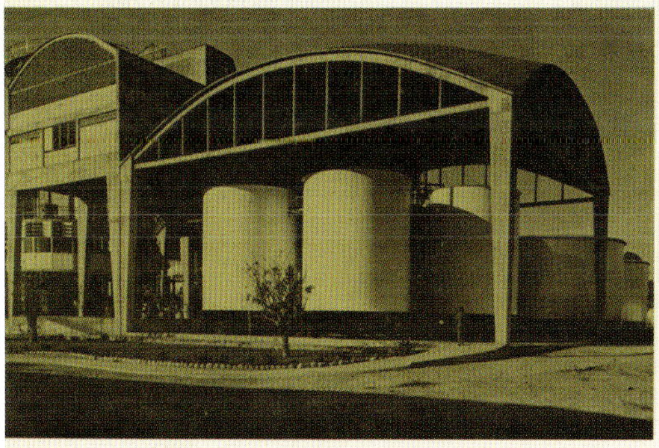

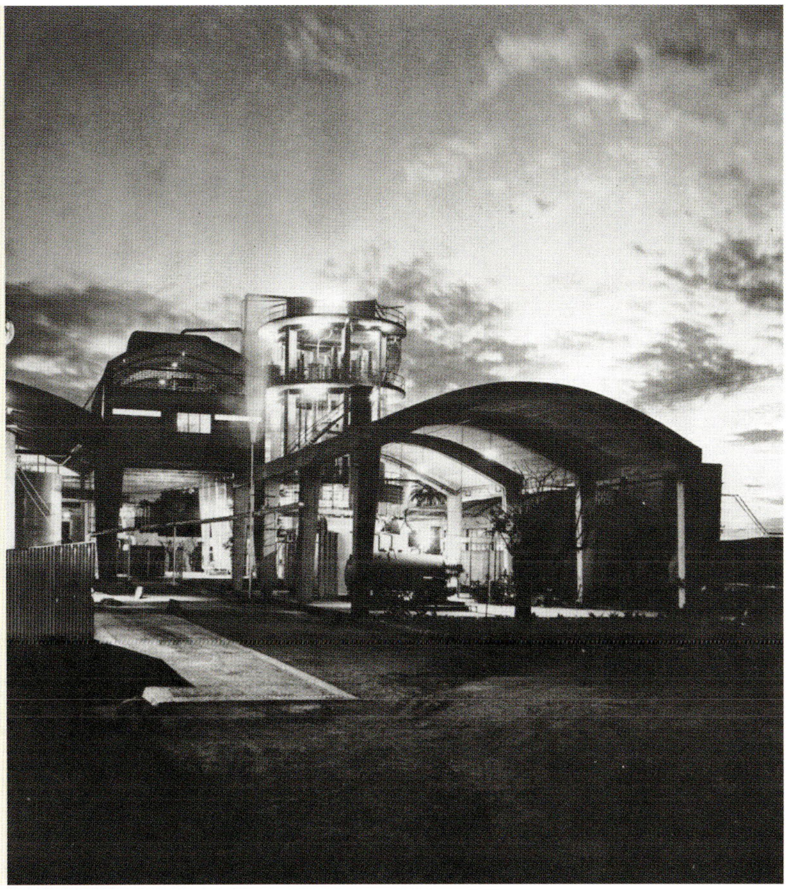

11

FEBRERO 4

97 Años Cubanos... ¡97 Años Creando!

Con orgullo de cubanos libres, la Casa Bacardí conmemora hoy sus 97 años de fundada, inaugurando una nueva destilería en Santiago de Cuba.

Inquebrantablemente hemos estado al lado del Pueblo Cubano. Nuestra historia en el 95, en el 30 y ahora, así lo demuestran. Siempre lo estaremos.

Con esta confianza, y sabiendo que nuestros productos cumplen una misión de calidad y cubanía en el mundo entero, seguiremos creando y creyendo; y no perderemos ninguna oportunidad de cumplir con este maravilloso pueblo que tanto ha hecho por nosotros.

1862-1959

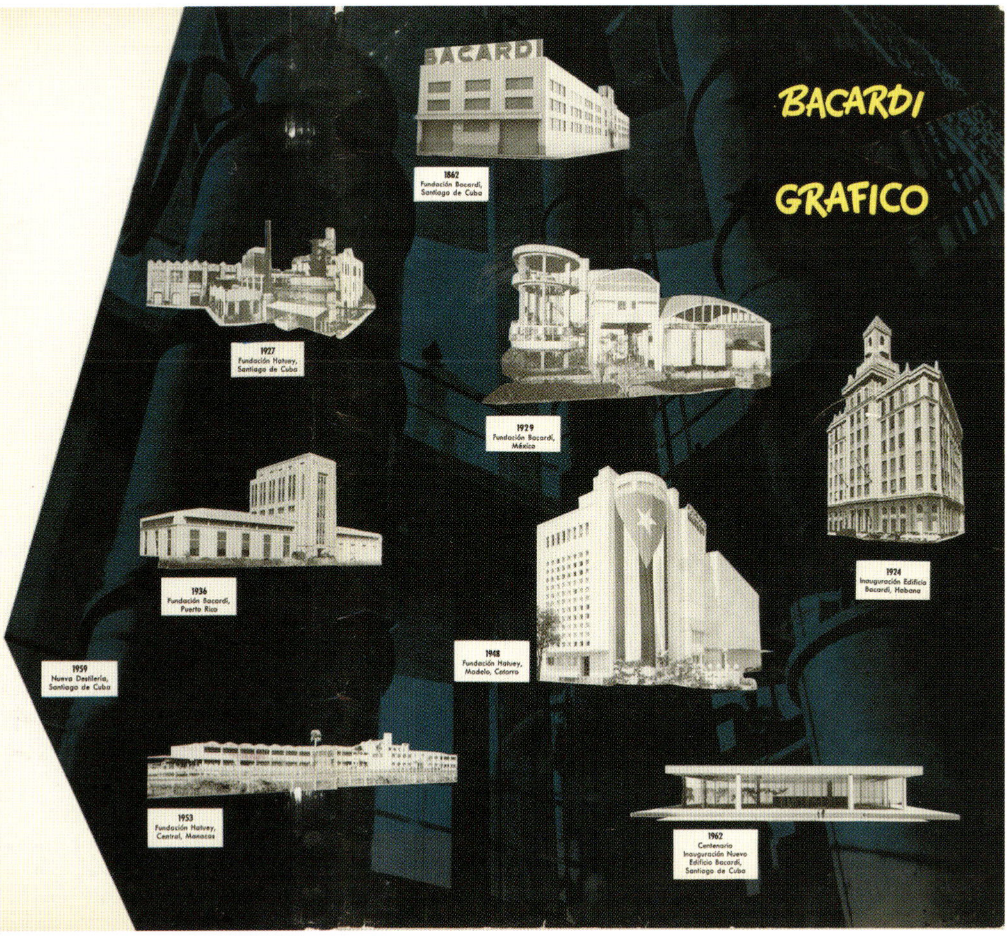

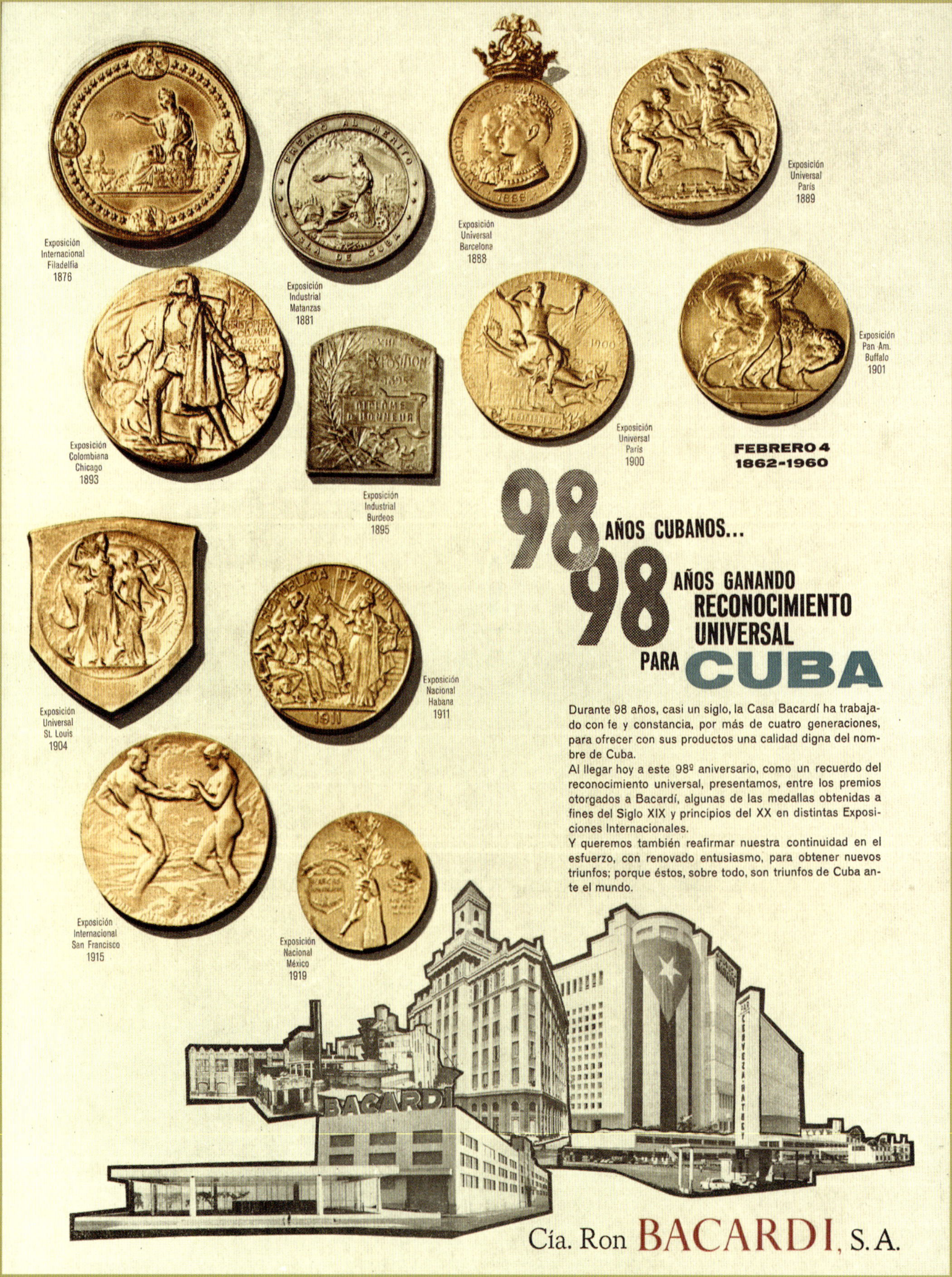

Exposición Internacional Filadelfia 1876
Exposición Industrial Matanzas 1881
Exposición Universal Barcelona 1888
Exposición Universal París 1889
Exposición Colombiana Chicago 1893
Exposición Industrial Burdeos 1895
Exposición Universal París 1900
Exposición Pan Am. Buffalo 1901
FEBRERO 4
1862-1960
98 AÑOS CUBANOS...
98 AÑOS GANANDO RECONOCIMIENTO UNIVERSAL PARA CUBA
Exposición Universal St. Louis 1904
Exposición Nacional Habana 1911
Durante 98 años, casi un siglo, la Casa Bacardí ha trabajado con fe y constancia, por más de cuatro generaciones, para ofrecer con sus productos una calidad digna del nombre de Cuba.
Al llegar hoy a este 98º aniversario, como un recuerdo del reconocimiento universal, presentamos, entre los premios otorgados a Bacardí, algunas de las medallas obtenidas a fines del Siglo XIX y principios del XX en distintas Exposiciones Internacionales.
Y queremos también reafirmar nuestra continuidad en el esfuerzo, con renovado entusiasmo, para obtener nuevos triunfos; porque éstos, sobre todo, son triunfos de Cuba ante el mundo.
Exposición Internacional San Francisco 1915
Exposición Nacional México 1919
BACARDI
Cía. Ron BACARDI, S.A.

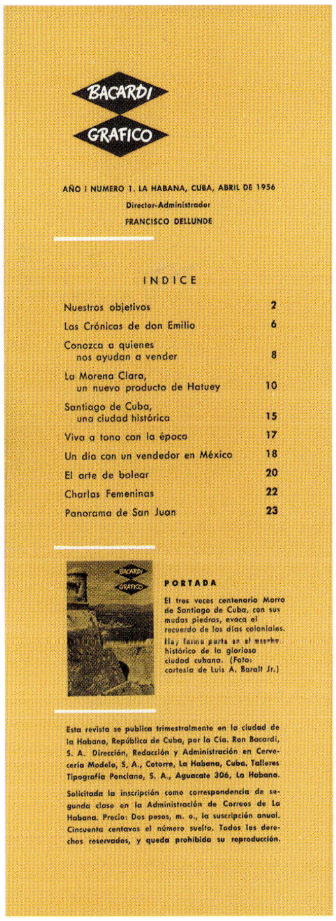

BACARDI GRAFICO

AÑO I NUMERO 1. LA HABANA, CUBA, ABRIL DE 1956

Director-Administrador

FRANCISCO DELLUNDE

INDICE

PORTADA

El tres veces centenario Morro de Santiago de Cuba, con sus mudas piedras, evoca el recuerdo de los días coloniales. [illegible] histórico de la gloriosa ciudad cubana. (Foto: cortesía de Luis A. Barait Jr.)

Esta revista se publica trimestralmente en la ciudad de la Habana, República de Cuba, por la Cía. Ron Bacardí, S. A. Dirección, Redacción y Administración en Cervecería Modelo, S. A., Cotorro, La Habana, Cuba. Talleres Tipografía Ponciano, S. A., Aguacate 306, La Habana.

Solicitada la inscripción como correspondencia de segunda clase en la Administración de Correos de La Habana. Precio: Dos pesos, m. o., la suscripción anual. Cincuenta centavos el número suelto. Todos los derechos reservados, y queda prohibida su reproducción.

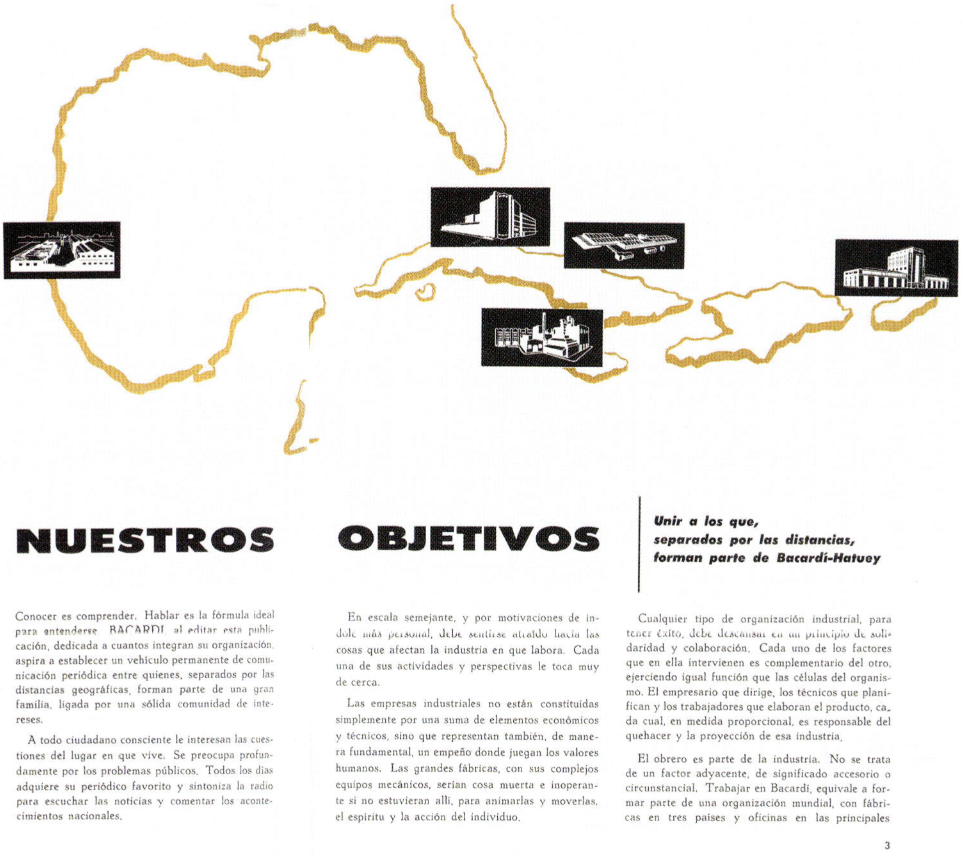

NUESTROS OBJETIVOS

Unir a los que, separados por las distancias, forman parte de Bacardí-Hatuey

Conocer es comprender. Hablar es la fórmula ideal para entenderse. BACARDI, al editar esta publicación, dedicada a cuantos integran su organización, aspira a establecer un vehículo permanente de comunicación periódica entre quienes, separados por las distancias geográficas, forman parte de una gran familia, ligada por una sólida comunidad de intereses.

A todo ciudadano consciente le interesan las cuestiones del lugar en que vive. Se preocupa profundamente por los problemas públicos. Todos los días adquiere su periódico favorito y sintoniza la radio para escuchar las noticias y comentar los acontecimientos nacionales.

En escala semejante, y por motivaciones de índole más personal, debe sentirse atraído hacia las cosas que afectan la industria en que labora. Cada una de sus actividades y perspectivas le toca muy de cerca.

Las empresas industriales no están constituidas simplemente por una suma de elementos económicos y técnicos, sino que representan también, de manera fundamental, un empeño donde juegan los valores humanos. Las grandes fábricas, con sus complejos equipos mecánicos, serían cosa muerta e inoperante si no estuvieran allí, para animarlas y moverlas, el espíritu y la acción del individuo.

Cualquier tipo de organización industrial, para tener éxito, debe descansar en un principio de solidaridad y colaboración. Cada uno de los factores que en ella intervienen es complementario del otro, ejerciendo igual función que las células del organismo. El empresario que dirige, los técnicos que planifican y los trabajadores que elaboran el producto, cada cual, en medida proporcional, es responsable del quehacer y la proyección de esa industria.

El obrero es parte de la industria. No se trata de un factor adyacente, de significado accesorio o circunstancial. Trabajar en Bacardí, equivale a formar parte de una organización mundial, con fábricas en tres paises y oficinas en las principales

3

Left: Collage of Bacardi buildings. *98 Años Cubanos... 98 Años Ganando Reconocimiento Universal para Cuba* (98 Cuban Years...98 Years Gaining Universal Recognition for Cuba), *Bacardi Grafico* 16 (March 1960). Courtesy of The Bacardi Archive.

Above: Nuestros Objetivos (Our Objectives), *Bacardi Grafico* 1 (April 1956): 2-3. Courtesy of The Bacardi Archive.

level brand managers, putting aesthetics in the hands of its entrepreneurial leaders. The buildings and sites discussed in this book illustrate the hybrid motives of a company navigating overseas expansion and global identity.[4] These works are a public stage where the company's ambitions have confronted powerful economic, social, and political forces.

Memory is everywhere, featured in the continuous recall of built landmarks as symbols of corporate success. Bacardi has frequently represented its identity in single advertisements, lithographed corporate letterheads, photomontages, collages, and murals by assembling the company's geographically distant and stylistically eclectic buildings. These surrealist assemblages, with their turbulent collisions, suggest a fantasy Bacardi portrait that is true to the BACARDI rum motto, "the mixable one."

Bacardi's built work embraces a hybridity as Creole[5] as the company's Caribbean roots, and as diverse as the company's global presence. Provincial, Cuban, modern, exiled, global, whether distilling rum, gin, or vodka, or brewing beer, Bacardi has employed a constantly shifting concept of "home" and erected or adapted a series of buildings that make the company at home everywhere. This adaptability makes the company a compelling case study, not just in the history of global corporate architecture but in the story of architecture generally.

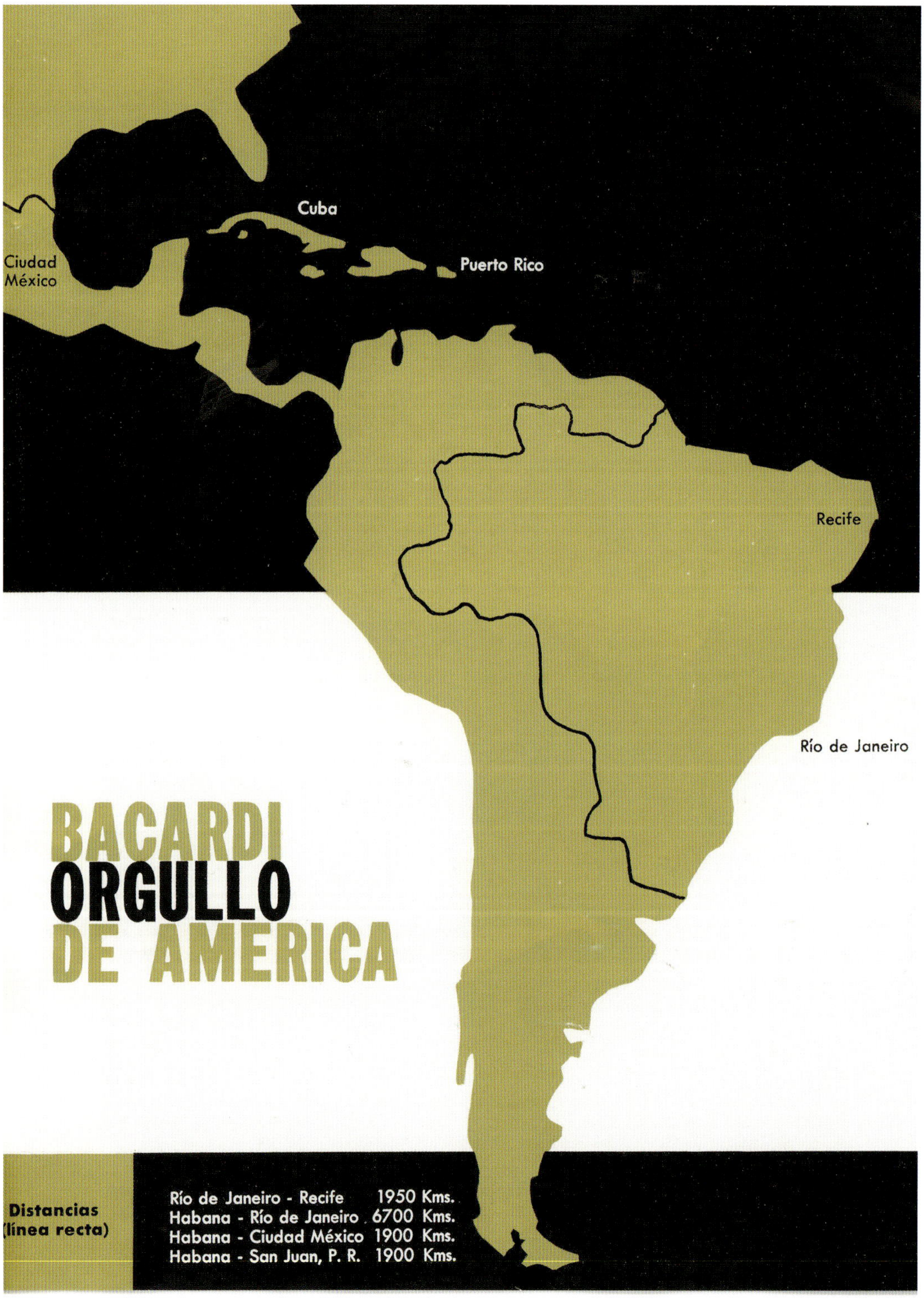

Above; Bacardi Orgullo de America (Bacardi, America's Pride), *Bacardi Grafico* 9 (April 1958): 6. Courtesy of The Bacardi Archive.

Right: Bacardi en el Mundo (Bacardi in the World), *Bacardi Grafico* 14 (September 1959): 15. Courtesy of The Bacardi Archive.

BACARDI en el MUNDO

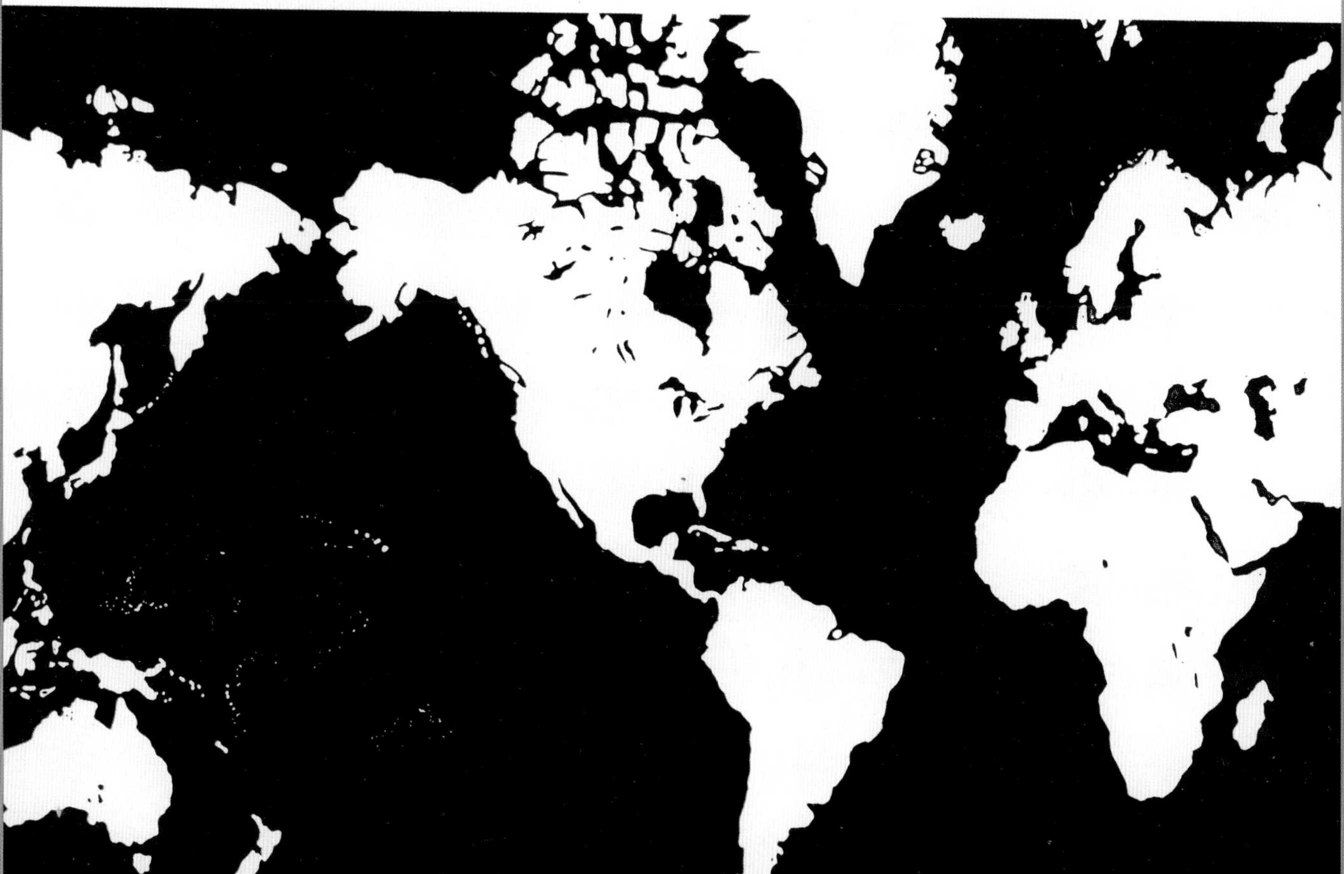

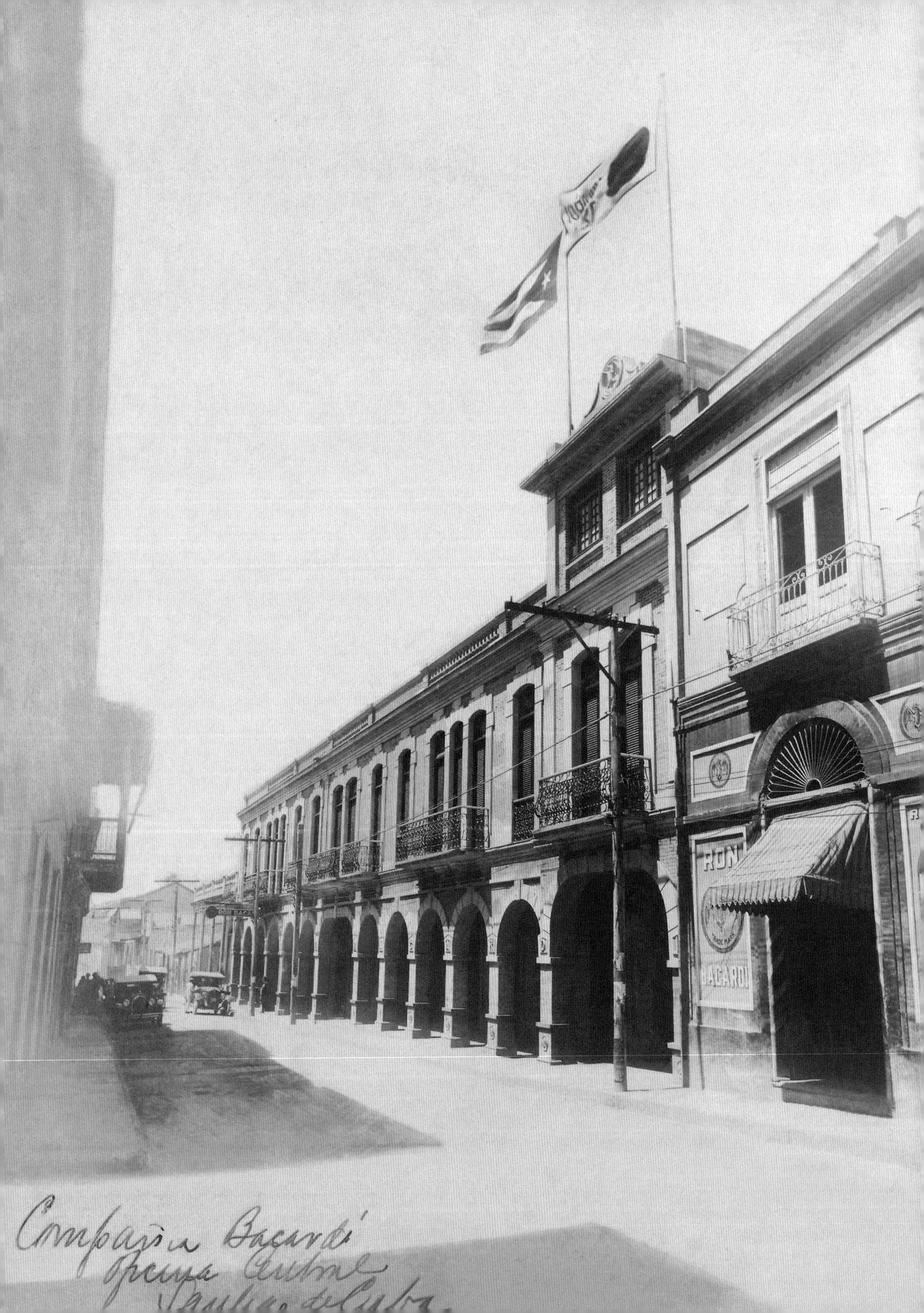
RON
TRADE MARK
BACARDI
Compañía Bacardí
Oficina Central
Santiago de Cuba

PRIDE OF SANTIAGO

The formula for Bacardi's global expansion was discovered along with the formula for distilling clear rum. Don Facundo Bacardí Massó, a Catalan immigrant, developed a technique for turning native raw materials into an especially refined and consistent clear spirit.[6] This technique revolutionized rum distilling, creating new markets that slowly built Bacardi. The company then advanced chemical technology to the point where Bacardi's specific taste profiles could be reproduced in other regions, using other sugars. This unprecedented development in the spirits industry would have extraordinary consequences, as Bacardi soon diversified production and administration overseas, amalgamating its own traditions with those found in new territories.

Long before its worldwide expansion, Bacardi's character was forged in Santiago de Cuba, where the company was founded in 1862. The Caribbean port is Cuba's second city, a Creole center built on colonial trade networks. Sugar played an important role in the colonial economy, so that by the middle of the nineteenth century it had become Cuba's principal commodity and Cuba its primary producer; the development of a rum industry was a natural by-product.[7] Bacardi y Compañía (as the company came to be known) used Santiago's position and, after 1898, an influx of Americans, to launch a global enterprise. The Spanish American War (1898), followed by the U.S. military occupation and the establishment of the Cuban Republic (1902), tied the U.S. and Cuba together in numerous ways. In 1933, the end of U.S. Prohibition (1919–33) along with President Franklin Roosevelt's Good Neighbor Policy, which emphasized reciprocal hemispheric trade, only strengthened the association, celebrated through the lens of cocktail culture in the BACARDI rum advertisement: "The Good Neighbors are good mixers."[8] In Cuban–American relations, Bacardi found fertile ground for the development of a culturally and economically transnational company. Architecturally this idea was translated in the importation and exportation of building types, architects, and manifestations of modernism.

In the wake of the Spanish American War, Santiago was the evocative backdrop for Bacardi's first advertising campaign.[9] A set of postcards distributed to American troops paints a portrait of regional trade and commerce: the harvesting of sugarcane, the smoking chimneys of its industry, the arcaded shop fronts on Calle de la Marina (where Bacardi had its offices), and tin-roofed wood sheds like the one that housed the first Bacardi distillery, on Matadero Street near the old port. That humble shed, and *El Coco* (the inaugural coconut tree planted by Don Facundo's son Facundo Jr.), has formed the sentimental grounding of the company, commemorated in illustrations and bronze casts.

By the first decades of the twentieth century, Bacardi was the economic heart of Santiago.[10] Under a new corporation, Compañía Ron Bacardi, S.A., the rum distilling and bottling complex on the north side of the colonial city grew into a powerful machine. A new distillery built in 1922 joined other distilling components, including a bottling plant and ice plant, numerous warehouses for aging rum, tank farms, and a 30,000 gallon water tower shaped like a bottle of rum. The facilities sprawled from the Matadero Street distillery, the cradle of Bacardi distilling operations, along the railroad corridors that fed the complex, to the San Pedrito district, where the old Santiago Brewing Company stood. Here, in 1927, Bacardi started brewing its signature beer, Hatuey.

The distillery complex included prototypes for the company's later development of gardens and a public café, Casa Bacardi, where tourists were refreshed with free cocktails. Here began the idea of enriching production facilities by designing the ways in which they were open and visible to the public, in the process transforming technical facilities into multi-dimmensional spaces. The soon famous gardens and café, early adventures in exploiting everyday activities as acts of placemaking, moved the company toward a more complex understanding of architecture.

Ron Bacardi headquarters and distillery on Calle de la Marina (baja), Santiago de Cuba. Courtesy of The Bacardi Archive.

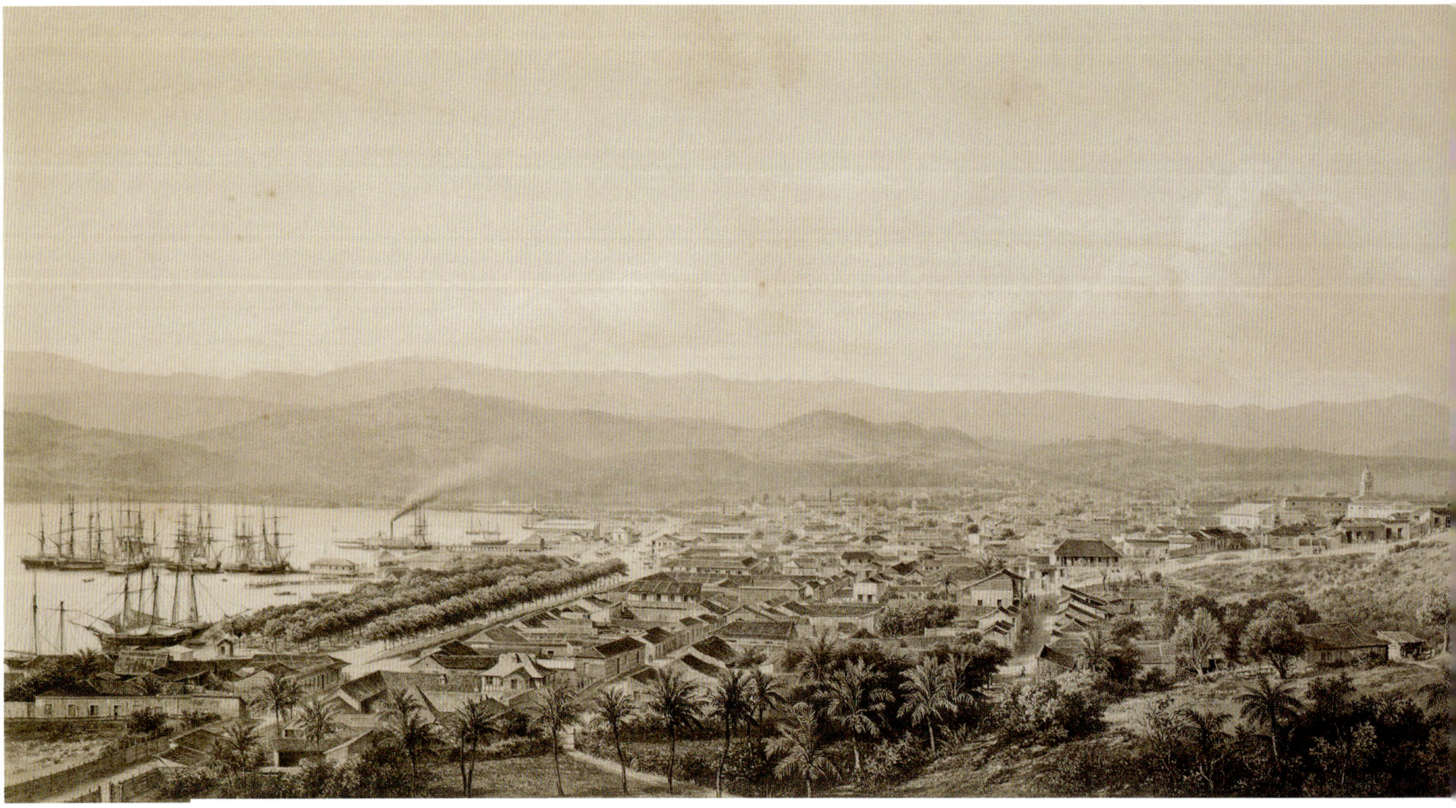

VISTA PANORÀMICA DE SAN-IAGO DE CUBA
TOMADA DE LA LOMA DEL GAZOMETRO.

Vista Panoramica de San-iago de Cuba Tomada de la Loma del Gazometro (Panoramic view of Santiago de Cuba taken from the gas storage tank hill). Lithograph. c. 1880s. Courtesy of The Bacardi Archive.

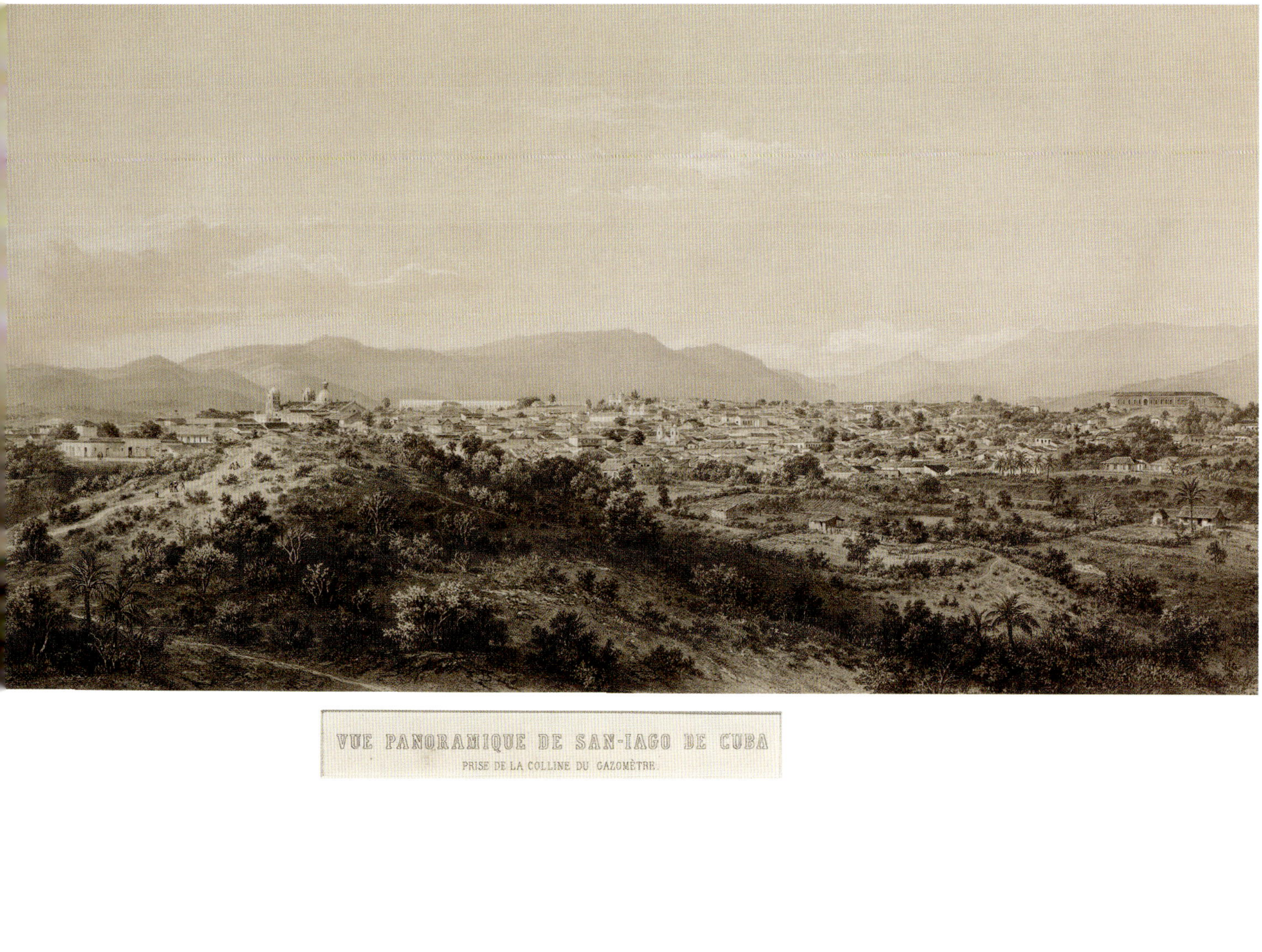

VUE PANORAMIQUE DE SAN-IAGO DE CUBA
PRISE DE LA COLLINE DU GAZOMÈTRE

In the same measure, Bacardi began to consider the iconography of its plants. In 1915, the company replaced its first distillery, the Matadero Street shed, with a new plant conceived to dignify the enterprise. Its classically inspired facades borrowed the grandeur of the contemporary Panama-Pacific International Exposition, where BACARDI rum won several medals. Following on models of the exposition, the building was a paean to the power and majesty of industry. More importantly, it was an acclamation of the company's own identity: the C-shaped building featured prominent bat iconography and paid homage to the site by preserving and honoring *El Coco,* the inaugural palm tree, in its center court. Almost as much as the atavistic bat, the tropical tree became a privileged icon of the company.

An even richer and more complex hagiography monumentalized the life of the company's first president, Emilio Bacardi, who played multiple roles in his home city of Santiago de Cuba: corporate leader, independence activist, writer, politician and chronicler of the life of the city. From 1898 to 1906, under American occupation, Bacardi was the mayor of Santiago. In this capacity, he oversaw the modernization of the city, building schools, libraries, and parks, and founding cultural institutions like the provincial museum and library (the first museum in Cuba, completed in 1899), as well as the Academia de Bellas Artes (1902).[11] The Museo Emilio Bacardi Moreau, initiated postmortem by Bacardi's widow, Elvira Cape, crystallized the merger of corporate patronage with civic construction. Designed by Santiago architect Carlos Segrera Fernández and completed in 1927, it appropriately took the form of a temple, or republican shrine. The building featured a grand staircase that stretched across the street front and rose to a deep front portico. Grouped around its interior colonnaded court were a library, art gallery, and a museum whose collection spanned from an Egyptian mummy to artifacts of the independence movement in Cuba. It was instantly Santiago's most prominent institution.[12] A counterpoint to the humming industrial campus growing just outside of the city, the museum associated the Bacardi name with the promotion of high culture. As the company later developed and built museums at its many plants, the strategy was inverted, embedding Bacardi industry in its own cultural milieu.

Santiago was no company town, but the combination of Bacardi industry and corporate patronage transformed the city. The political dimension of the company's activities reached an apotheosis under Emilio Bacardi, in whose person any distinction between corporate and civic purposes was blurred. They soon reached another in the 1920s, as Bacardi became Cuba's most important industry, in fact one of the top native industries in Latin America.[13] By 1928, Bacardi employed more than 1,500 workers in its hometown, many of whom lived in housing built by the distillery in suburbs it created.[14] Until 1960 Santiago remained the industrial base and administrative center of Bacardi's increasingly far-flung network of production, distribution, and management.

Ingenio BACARDI (Bacardi plant) and *Vista parcial* (partial view). Postcard series, c. 1898. Courtesy of Bacardi & Company Limited.

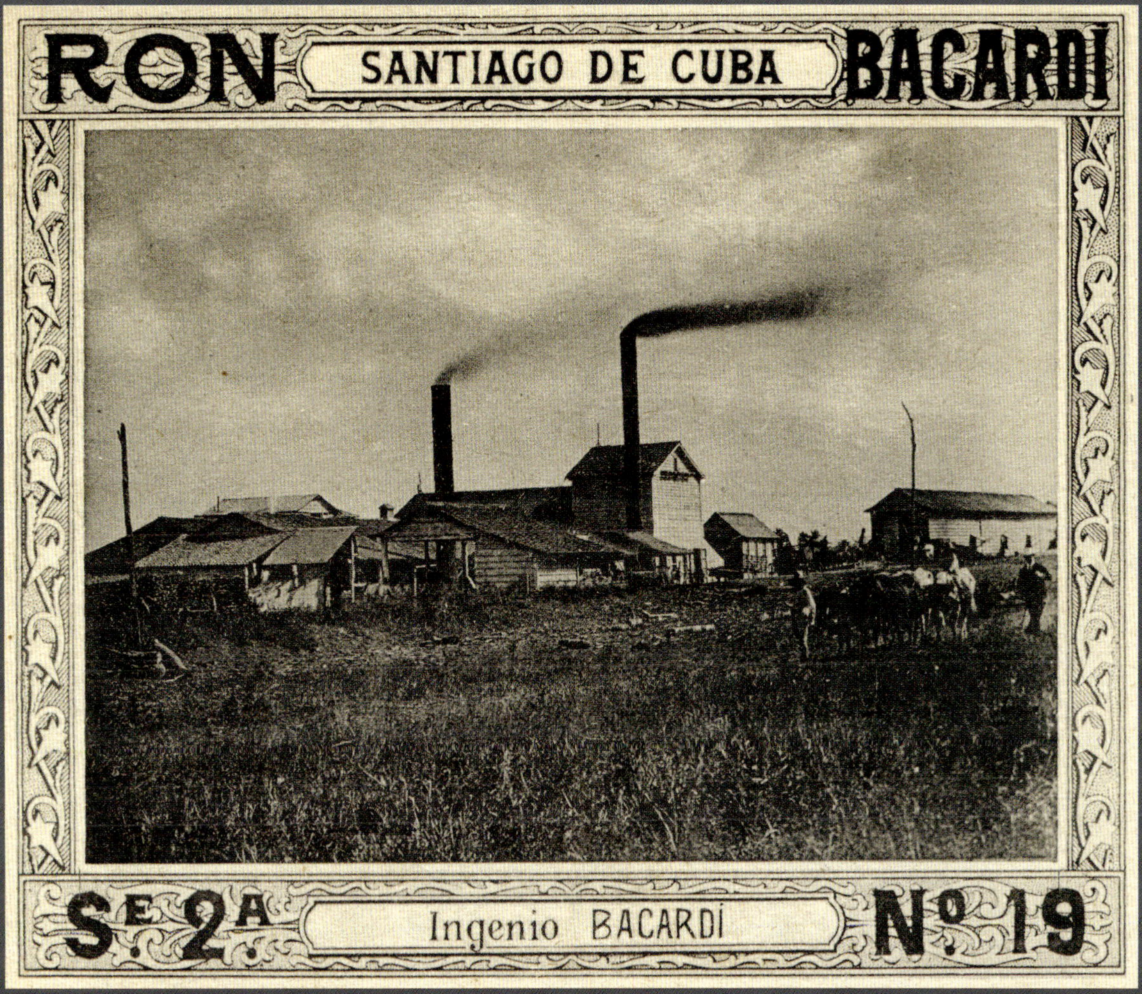
RON
SANTIAGO DE CUBA
BACARDI
S.E 2A
Ingenio BACARDI
Nº 19

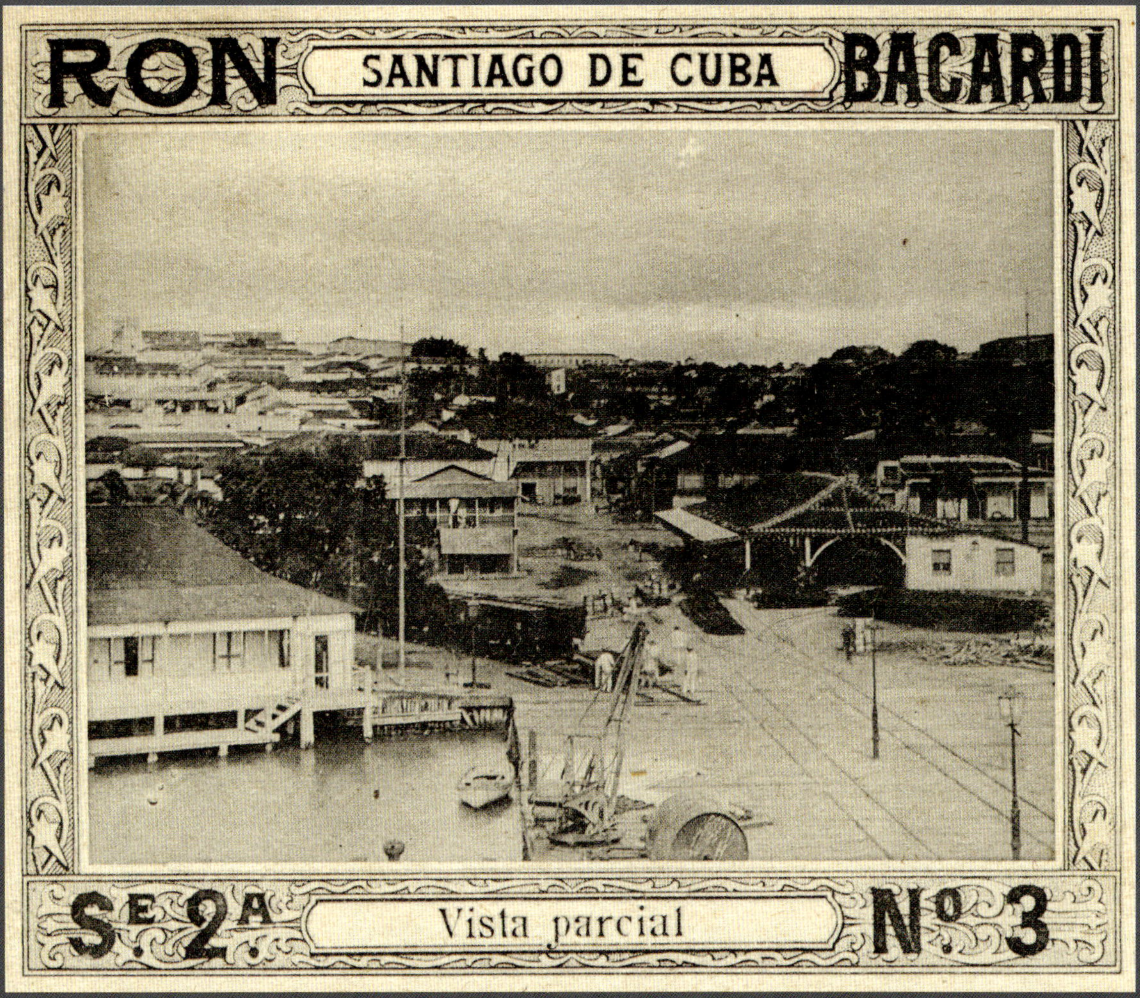
RON
SANTIAGO DE CUBA
BACARDI
S.E 2A
Vista parcial
Nº 3

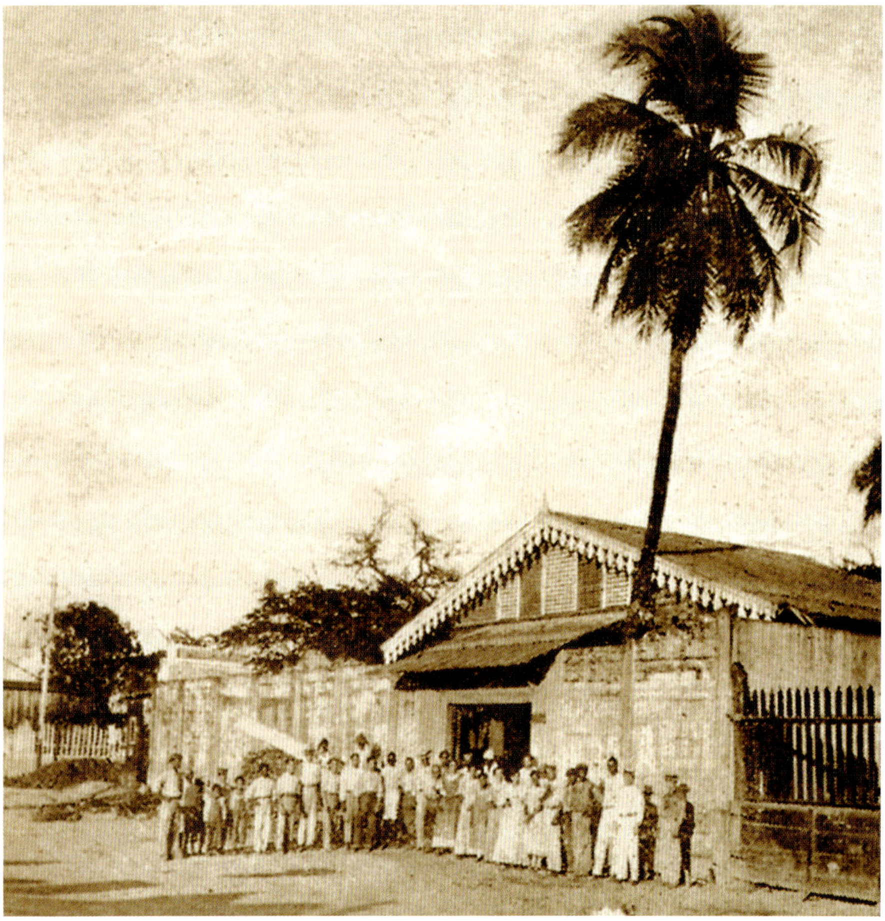

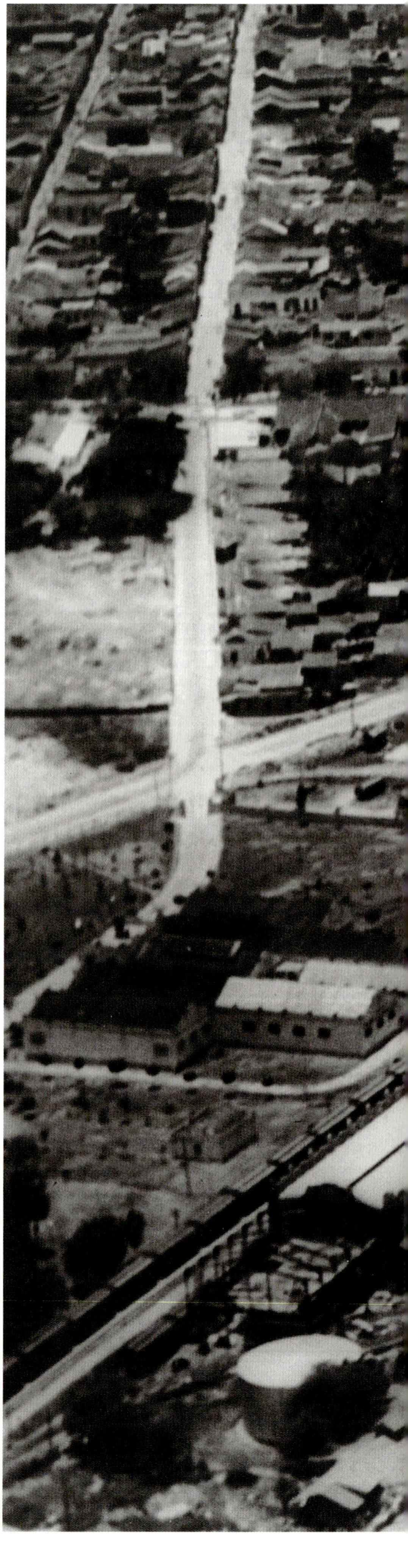

Above: Ron Bacardi distillery on Matadero Street, with *El Coco*, Santiago de Cuba, c. 1830s. Courtesy of The Bacardi Archive.

Right: Aerial view of the Bacardi-Hatuey industrial site, Santiago de Cuba, c. 1930. Courtesy of The Bacardi Archive.

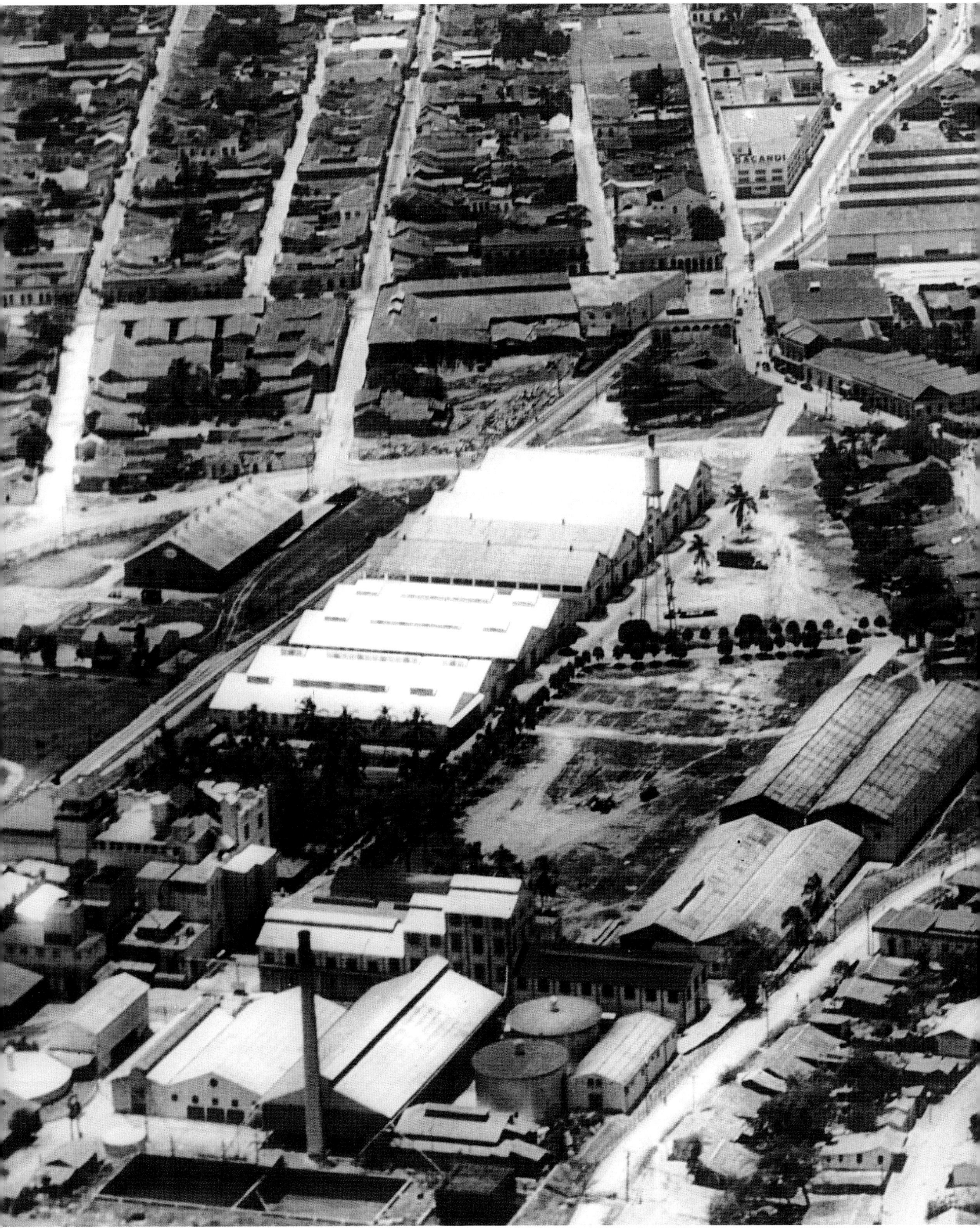
BACARDI

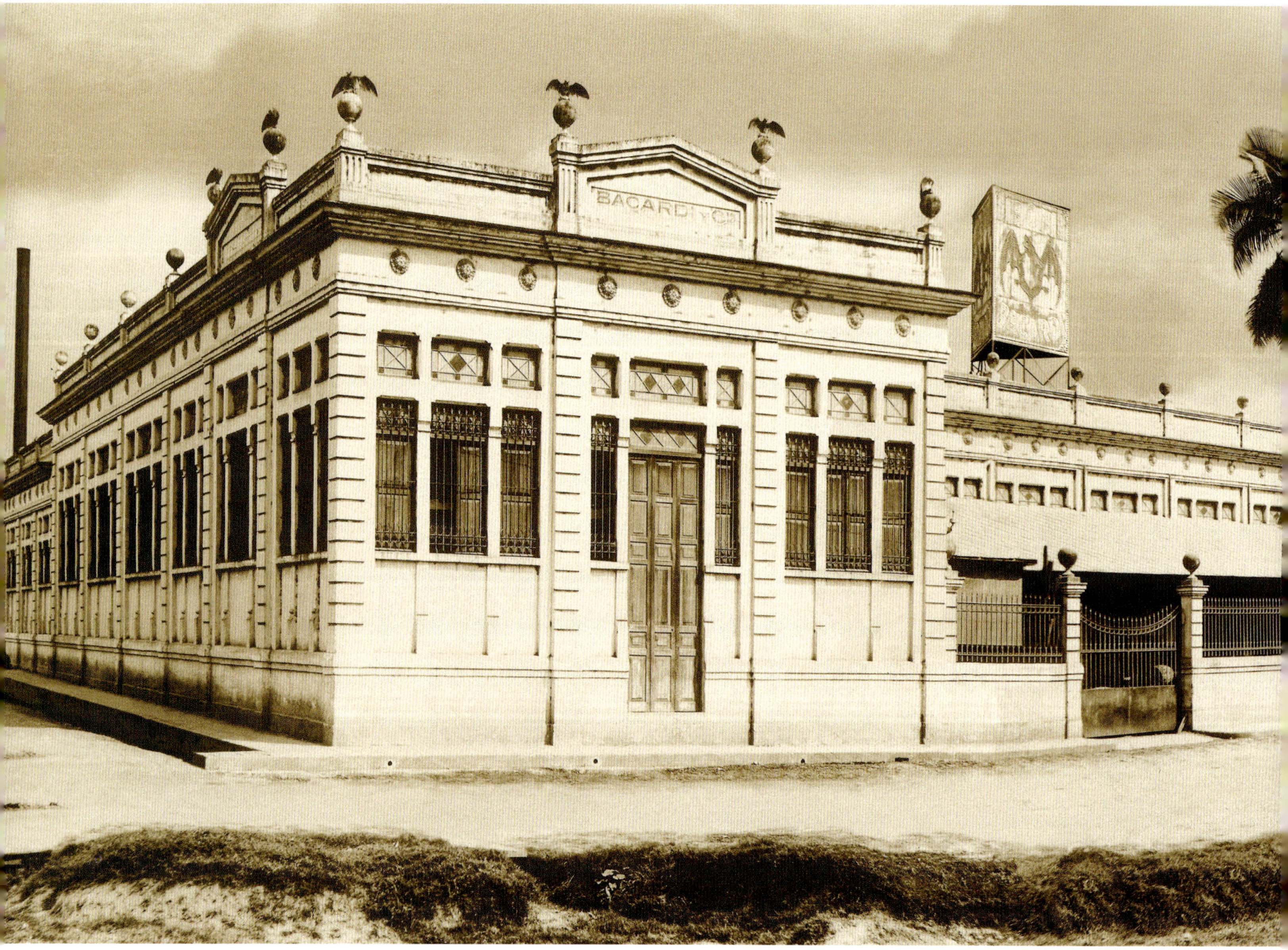

Above: New Ron Bacardi plant on site of original Matadero Street Distillery, with *El Coco*, Santiago de Cuba.
Gerardo Vega Wright, master builder, c. 1915. Courtesy of The Bacardi Archive.

Right: Water tower at the Ron Bacardi distillery, c. 1920s. Courtesy of The Bacardi Archive.

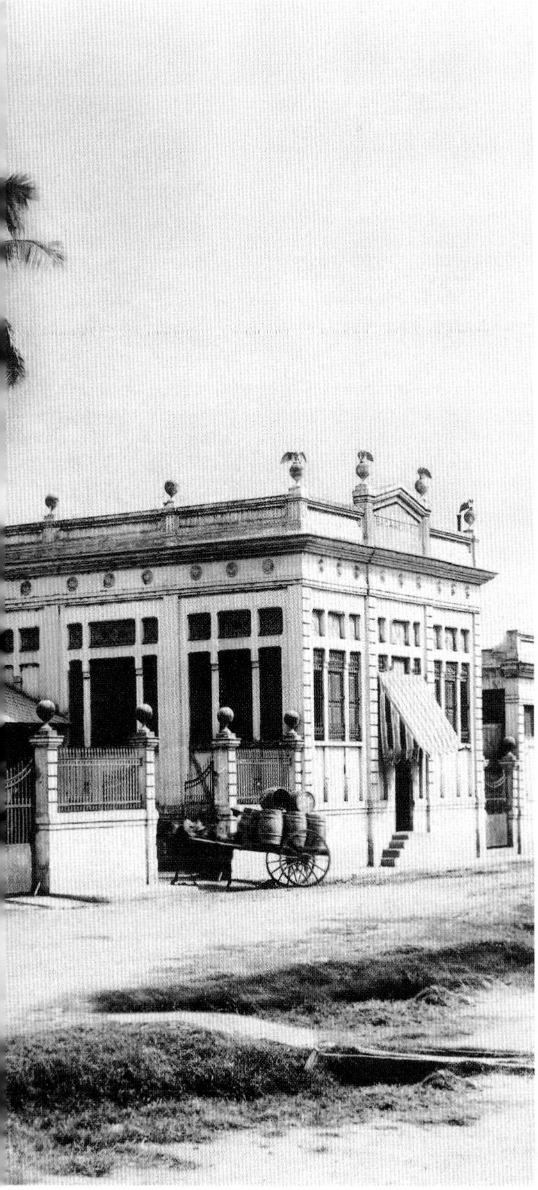

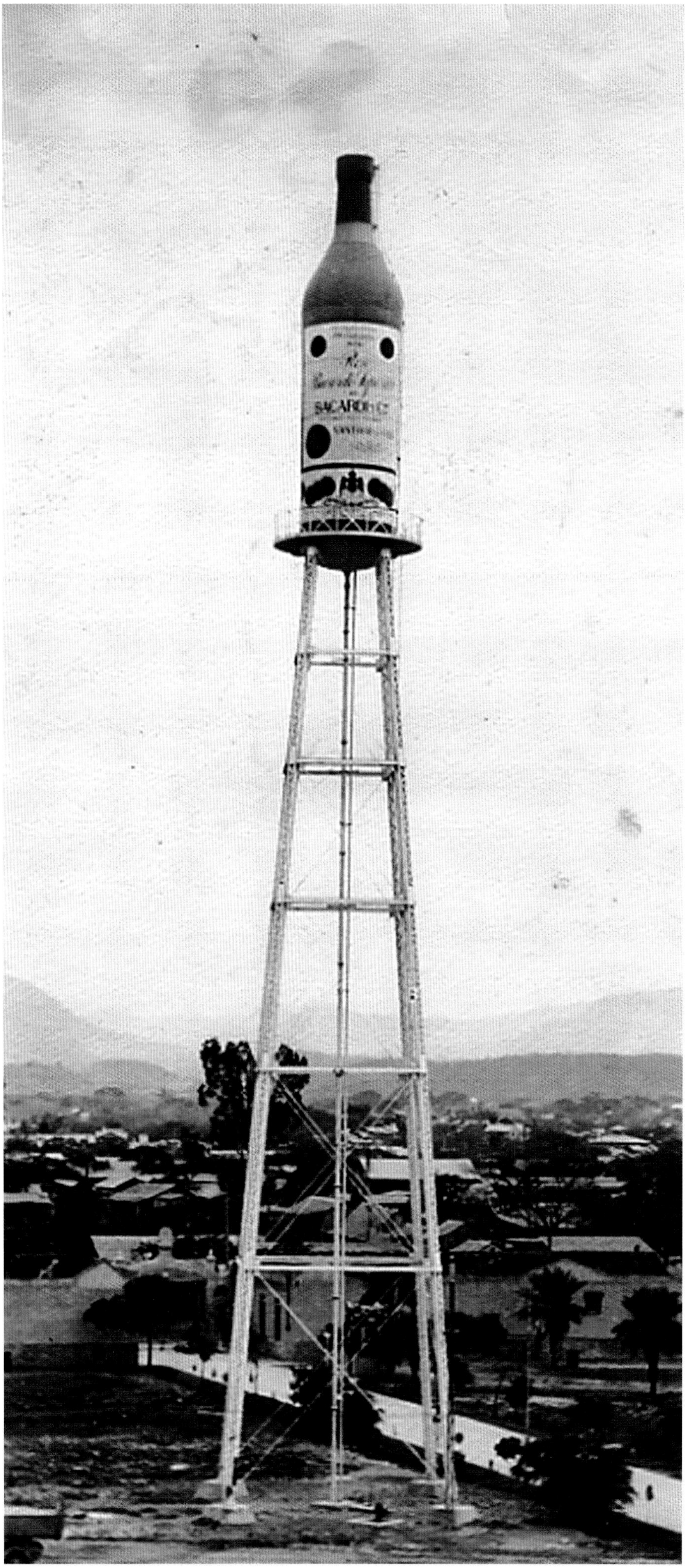
BACARDI

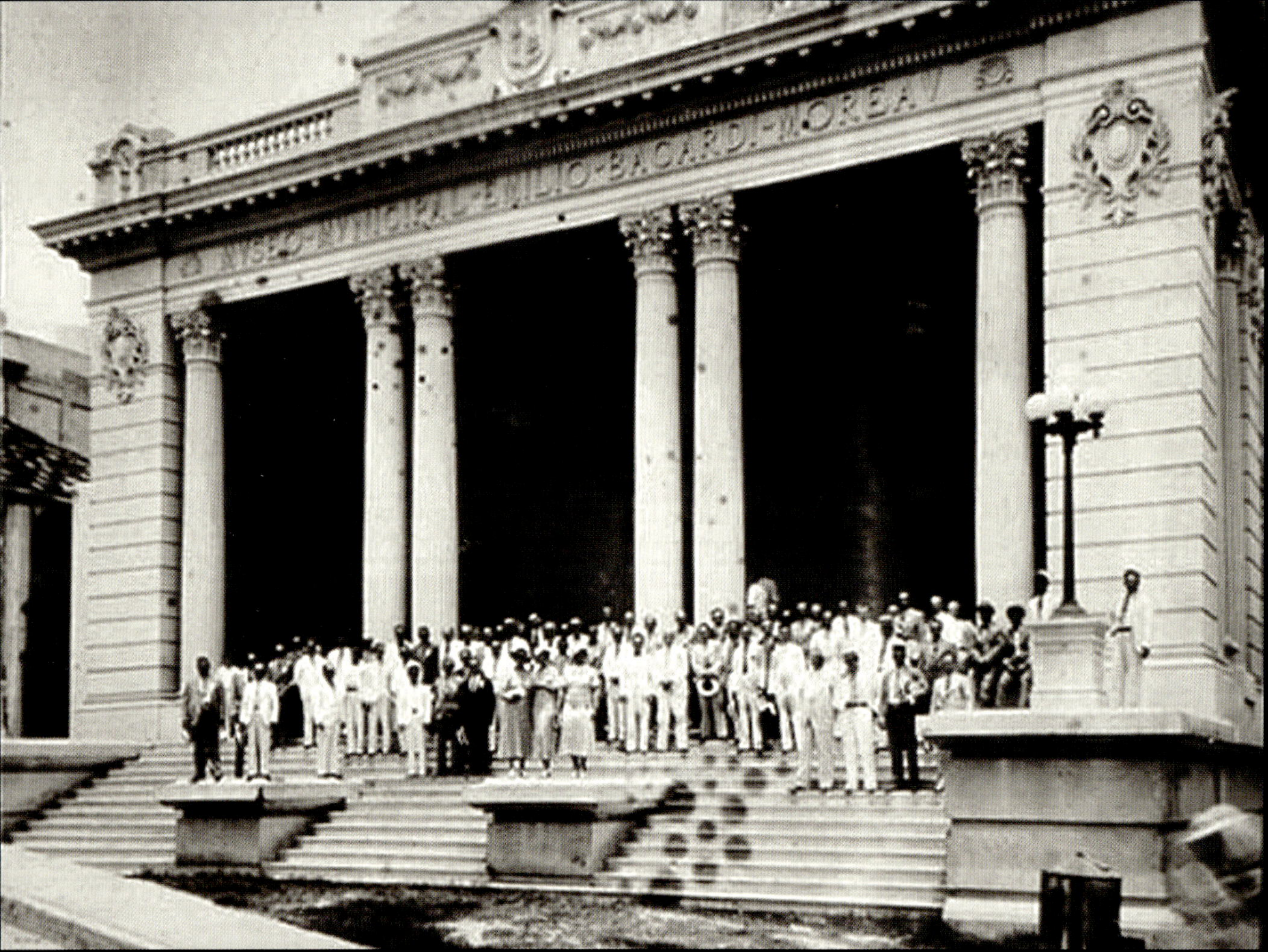
MVSEO·MVNICIPAL·EMILIO·BACARDI·MOREAV

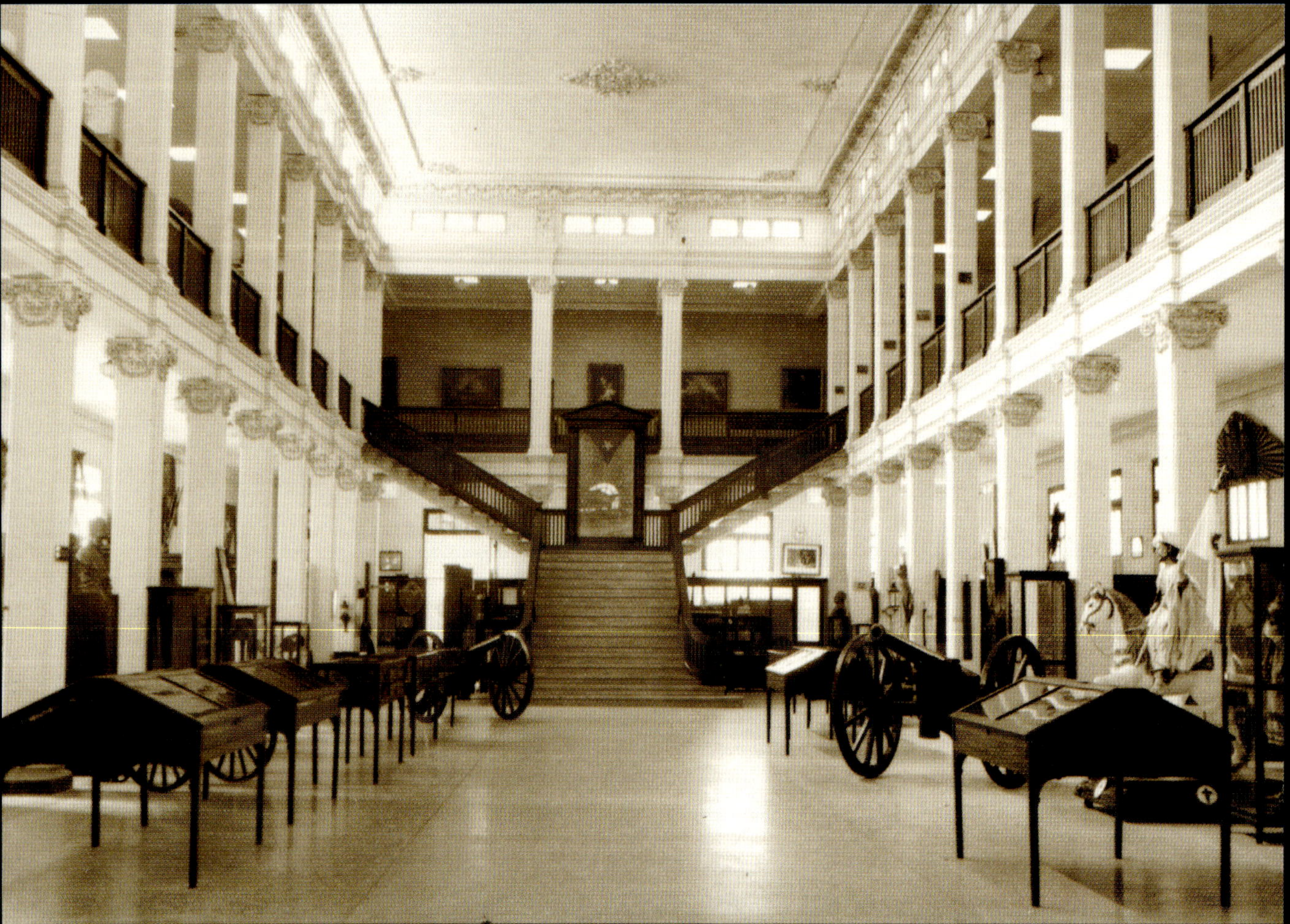

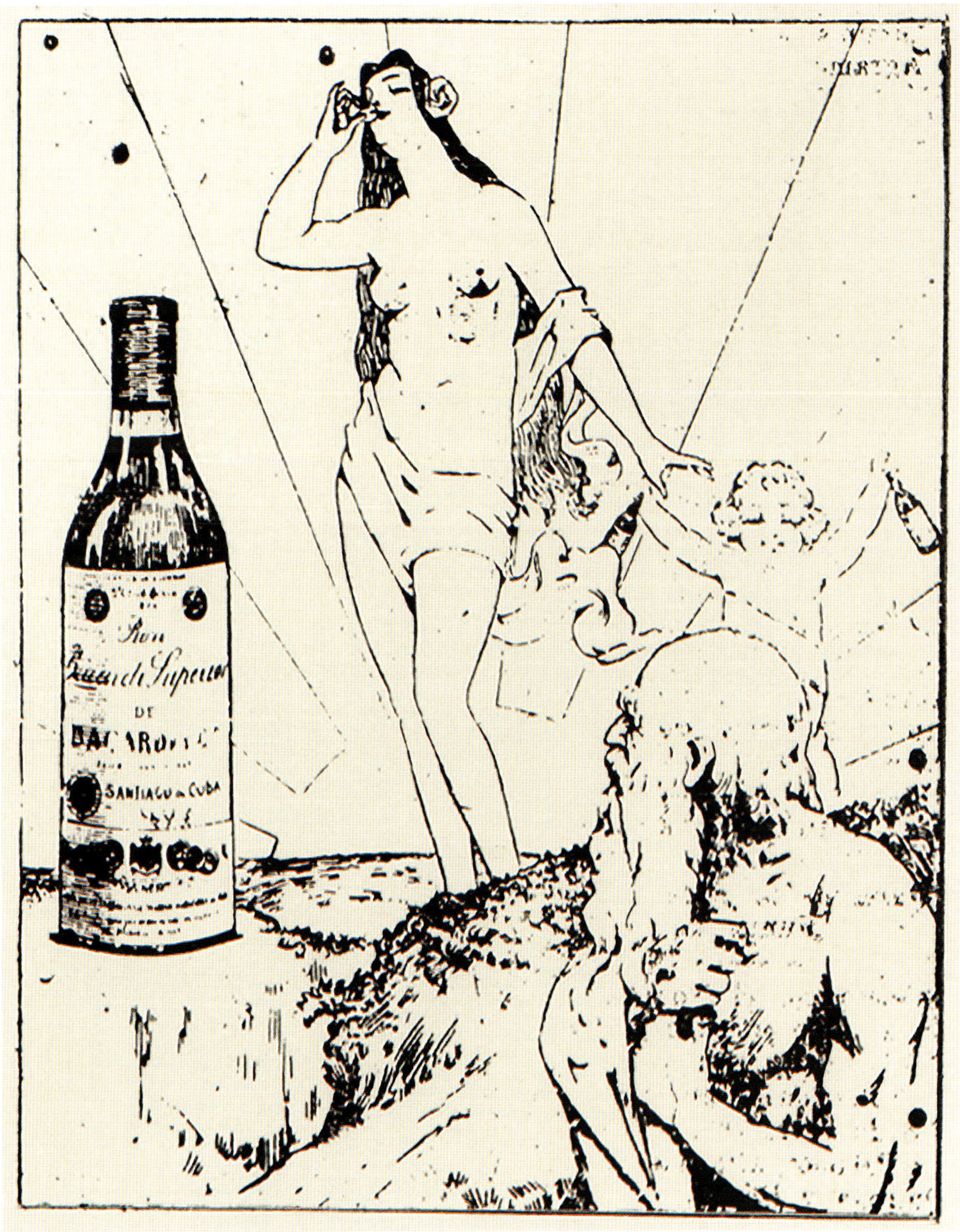

Top Left: Emilio Bacardi Moreau Museum, Inauguration day, January 20, 1928, Santiago de Cuba.
Carlos Segrera Fernandez, architect, 1927. Courtesy of The Bacardi Archive.

Bottom Left: Emilio Bacardi Moreau Museum, Santiago de Cuba, 1928. Interior view.
Carlos Segrera Fernandez, architect, 1927. Courtesy of The Bacardi Archive.

Above: Advertisement, c. 1910. Courtesy of The Bacardi Archive.

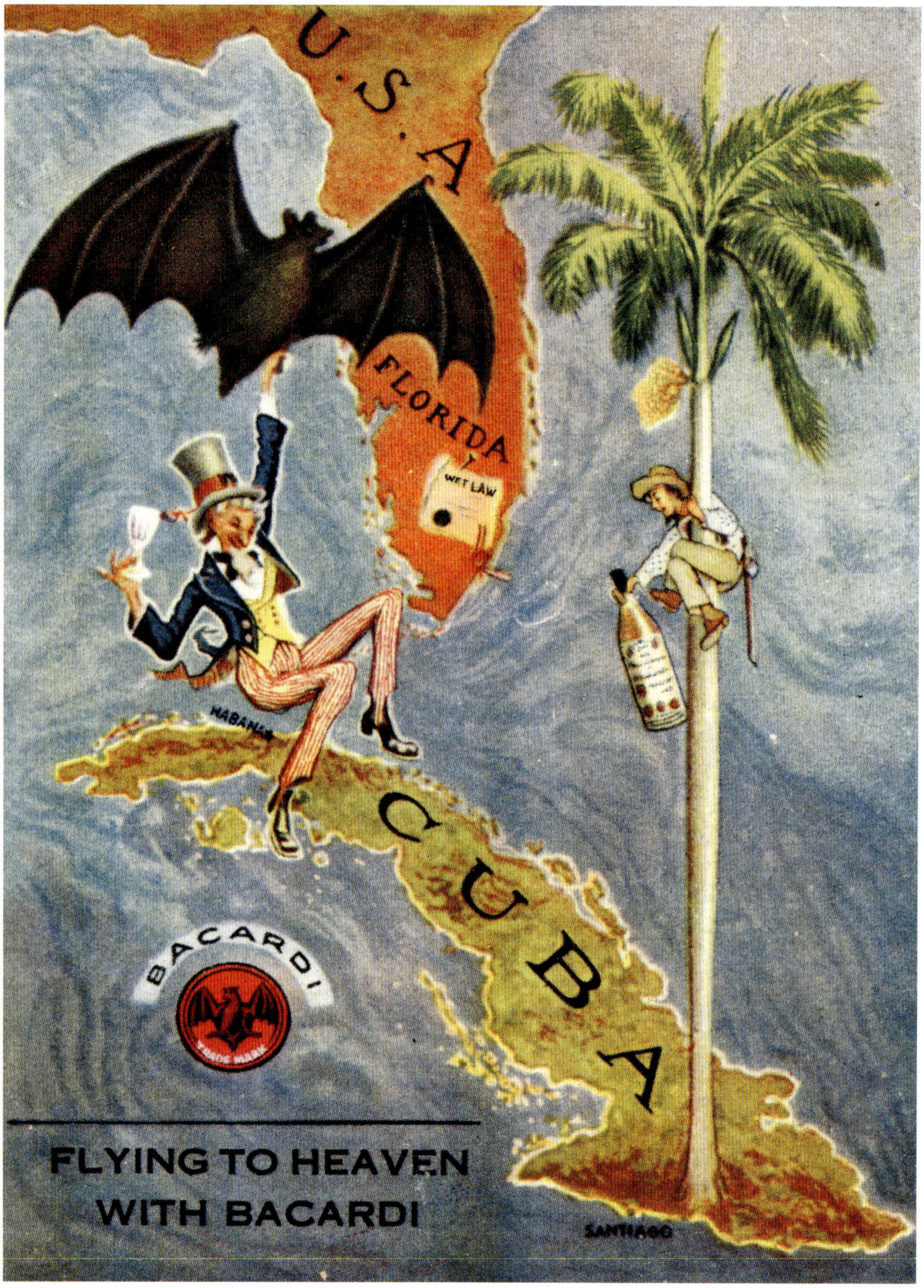

Flying to Heaven with Bacardi. Advertisement, 1920s. Courtesy of The Bacardi Archive.

CUBAN ICON

When American tourists landed in Havana during the Prohibition, the gilded bat atop the Bacardi Building led them to one of the city's most famous landmarks. The building loomed not just above the skyline, but also in the imagination of American tourists eagerly "flying to heaven with BACARDÍ."[15] Like fine cigars, guayaberas, and the rumba, BACARDI rum was part of an idealized vision of Cuba. The company encouraged this association, playfully using the imagery of the rumbera in its advertisements. The Bacardi Building was a banner for the pleasure principle of the cocktail age, of which Havana was a capital.

The Bacardi Building also possessed another meaning. A leading exporter, and by 1927 the island's largest industrial enterprise, Bacardi was at the forefront of changing the narrative about Cuba, from colony and battlefield to modern, republican state. Bacardi represented a new national identity—a Cuban icon. As Bacardi patronage took on a national dimension, the company became a symbol and protagonist of cultural transformation in Cuba.[16] The Bacardi Building symbolized the new landscape of the Republican state: the ascendance of powerful mercantile forces, modernity, and an international outlook. The double meaning—North American symbol of play, Cuban symbol of metropolitan progress—made this singular tower an emblem of the company, the city, and the era.

Henri (Enrique) Schueg y Chassin, Bacardi's second president, found meaning in contemporary social behaviors and fashions, and cultivated these to launch a new era of design for the company. In particular, Schueg focused on the spirit of the cocktail that, culturally and artistically, was an important motif of the period and of Bacardi. Once considered a bastard concoction, the cocktail was remixed in the 1920s and '30s as a symbol of urbane sophistication, with Bacardi as an iconic, if exotic ingredient. [17]

As Bacardi assimilated the spirit of the cocktail, it also exploited two of the most important Jazz Age American motifs: the skyscraper and the cocktail bar. These two motifs were bound together in function and style at the Bacardi Building. Its tower soared above the colonial structures of the Cuban capital as an advertisement, while the swank Bacardi Bar, the building's main event, drew tourists from the street.

The Bacardi Building was intended to represent the Bacardi family and its interests in the modern nerve center of the Cuban capital.[18] The site on Avenida de Bélgica was purposefully located at the edge of the colonial heart of Havana, near the recently renovated Paseo del Prado and only a block from the new Parque Central (as well as the neoclassical Capitol building, then still under construction). These urban projects, led by the French landscape architect Jean Claude Nicolas Forestier, were the first phase of a program to "transform the colonial image of the city into a metropolitan vision in tune with the ambitions of the Republic," as Jean-François Lejeune has noted.[19] The Bacardi Building would be a symbolic shell, since most of the space in the tower was to be rented; the company required only a bar and exhibition hall, as well as modest office and storage spaces. As symbol, the building also would capture, as it turns out, the transition to architectural modernism in the Cuban capital.

Bacardi stirred public and professional interest, by announcing an invited competition to design the building.[20] Its results were eclectic, "a thermometer of the durability of traditionalists in the profession," as Roberto Segre notes. [21] Establishment Cuban architects, friends of the company, participated as competitors and jurors.[22] The winning entry, by architects Esteban Rodríguez Castells and Rafael Fernández Ruenes, with engineer José Menendez, featured a Renaissance Revival-style commercial block crowned by a tower whose stepped pyramidal roof was topped by the gilded bronze bat. The scheme recalled a memorable design prepared five years earlier for the city's first cooperative apartment building, the Edificio Cooperativo de la Habana, by architects Francisco Centurión and Félix Cabarrocas.[23] Like that design, which mixed "Yankee proportions" with "an agreeable Spanish air,"[24] the Bacardi competition winner echoed a generation of North American towers inspired by the iconic Giralda tower of Seville's cathedral (for instance, Schultze and Weaver's Biltmore Hotel in Coral Gables, Florida, 1926). Paradoxically, the Giralda-influenced tower transported the North American Hispanofilia of the 1920s into Republican Cuba.

In fact, all of the competition finalists employed tower forms to represent the power and metropolitan character of the modern corporation. The second-place entry by architects Manuel Copado and Manuel de Tapia Ruano, inspired by the recently completed Chicago Tribune Building (John Mead Howells and Raymond Hood, 1925), sought to convey the imposing power of the company in the guise of a gothic cathedral.[25] If the competition results evinced strong currents of North American commercial architecture, they also revealed the expanding civic authority of the tower. The skyscraper, as Francisco Mujica observed, could be understood as a true and representative pan-American type. The Bacardi Building resonated so impressively because it used the tower to synthesize the company's commercial prowess and incipient hemispheric identity with Havana's emergence as a capital city.[26]

Before the completion of the steel structure in 1930, Rodríguez-Castells and Fernández Ruenes modernized the building's revivalist facades and interior spaces, a metamorphosis attributed to influences from the 1925 *Exposition internationale des arts décoratifs et industriels modernes* in Paris. Rich polychromatic effects already planned for the building, including the lavish use of foreign-sourced stones and ceramics (likely inspired by Catalan Modernismo), now came to life in stylized geometric Art Deco form.[27] Classical features were flattened into surfaces of color, suggesting the influence of the important English-American colorist Leon Victor Solon in New York.[28] Richly saturated decorative terra cotta friezes crowned the building, pairing organic forms and playful human figures. Reputedly designed by the American illustrator Maxfield Parrish, the friezes anticipated the extraordinary postwar integration of ceramic and glass art in the development of Bacardi's architecture.

An ecclectic, hybrid spirit pervades all aspects of the building. Red granite and burnt umber brick are offset by glazed terra-cotta in colors ranging from ocher and sienna to white, yellow and cobalt blue. Modern decorative expressions contrast with the building's original Renaissance Revival delineation. Also intriguing, the architects employed vernacular Cuban building elements, like geometrically patterned leaded glass, fretwork grilles, wood persianas (louvered windows), and iron grilles. Traditional, modern and vernacular, the Art Deco landmark exposes the complexity at the heart of the company.

The variegated splendor of the building's facades was matched in the suite of public rooms on the ground floor. Veined marble, polished metal, and patterned plaster in the lobby yielded to muted colors, precious woods, gilded bas-relief, mirrors, and gold leaf in the exhibition salon. The unrestrained use of materials and colors was designed to astonish visitors to the tower's legendary bar, integrated as a mezzanine overlooking the ground floor salon. For its largely American clientele, the bar suggested the Prohibition-era conventions of a speakeasy[29]—discreet and cozy, with a gold-hued club-like atmosphere. The floors were patterned in black, gold and white terrazzo, and the wood paneled walls were richly endowed with curios, mirrors and celebrity photographs. The black lacquer bar, accented in gold and vermilion

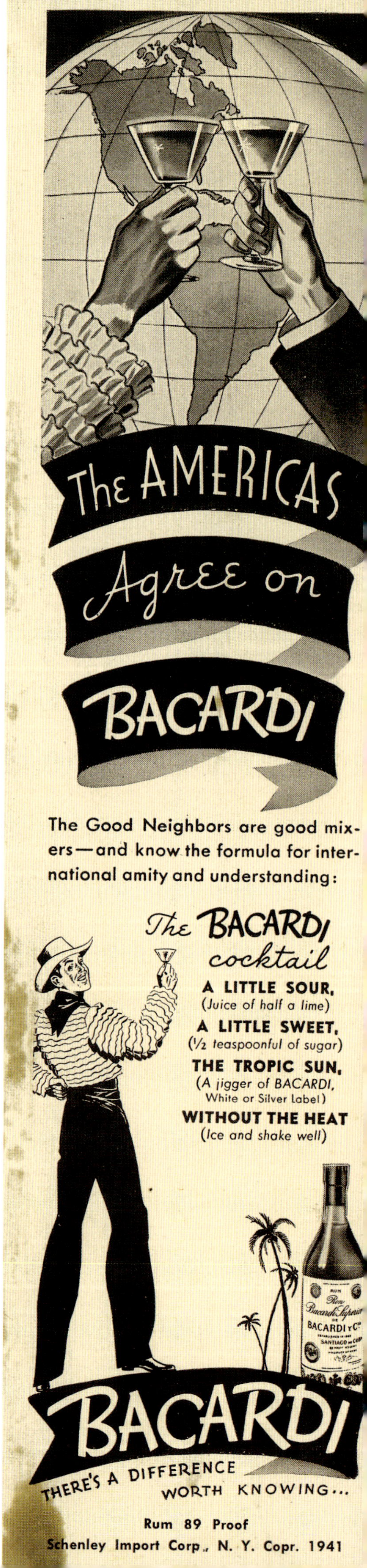

and Bacardi bottles, highlighted the white-coated barman who stood prominently at the symbolic center of the enterprise.

The cocktail bar, indeed the whole tower, was a corporate showcase for the development of Bacardi's brand.[30] It advanced the model of Casa Bacardi (the company's open exhibition bar in Santiago) by adding a gloss of smart styling and opulence to cocktail demonstrations. Moreover, a prime attraction in Havana, the building physically embodied the Bacardi slogan, "The One That Has Made Cuba Famous." The same indispensible message was reiterated in Cuban illustrator Conrado Massaguer's stylized 1936 ad: "Cuba is Great—there is a reason: Bacardi."[31]

Bacardi set a high tone for the representation of spirits, one that would soon be assimilated by American distillers.[32] When U.S. Prohibition ended in 1933, liquor brands installed themselves in prominent quarters in New York City, especially the upper reaches of the recently completed Chrysler Building and Empire State Building.[33] Like the Edificio Bacardi in Havana, these towers translated physical grandeur and sumptuous Art Deco styling into emblems of commercial power and modern taste. In these new quarters, tasting bars such as Bacardi had developed in Havana in 1930, served as semi-official homes for distinguished brands. Bacardi opened two such bars in New York, using them for receptions, bartender training and *guateques* (parties). In each of these bars, the company synthesized modern design with traditional motifs, allegorical artwork representing the Cuban experience, and of course mixed drinks.

The first New York Bacardi Bar was located in the headquarters of the Schenley Import Company, one of the four major liquor conglomerates that emerged in the U.S. and Canada after Prohibition.[34] In 1933 Schenley president Lewis Rosenstiel catapulted the company from small Pennsylvania whiskey distiller into a national corporate giant,[35] acquiring as its home the venerable clubhouse of the defunct New York Club, a limestone, brick and terra-cotta palazzo designed in 1907 by Henry Hardenburgh.[36] The Club's legendary ground-floor taproom was immediately re-fit by architect Percival Goodman as an Art Deco–styled whiskey bar. Only a year later, when Rosenstiel burnished Schenley's reputation by assembling a collection of foreign liquors in 1934, architect Morris B. Sanders remodeled the whiskey bar as a Bacardi Bar.[37]

The Schenley Bacardi Bar offered a club-like and Cuban-themed complement to the company's bar in Havana. The space was bathed in dark colors and rich textures, including tropical wood paneling and black, beige and vermilion leather furniture. The focal point was the curved white leather bar, retained from Goodman's earlier design. The bar's centrality was reinforced by a linear channel, also blocked in white leather, that ran down the center of the room's vaulted, gold-leafed ceiling. On either side, murals by the social-realist painter William Gropper provided what the *New York Times* called "appropriate pictorial notes" for the sumptuous modern room.[38] Gropper amusingly juxtaposed scenes of Cuba with towns and vineyards in southern Europe and, in a satirical touch, the faces of Schenley executives.[39] In Gropper, Sanders chose a caricaturist with an inclination for social protest and political satire.[40] However, *New Yorker* architectural critic Lewis Mumford saw in the Bacardi murals the artist's

The AMERICAS Agree on BACARDÍ.
Advertisement, 1941.
Courtesy of The Bacardi Archive.

ability to transcend political advocacy with a profound humanist sensibility: "He is a realist and a Surréaliste, and a fantasist and an objectivist and a satirist and an idyllist."[41] As collaborations with Conrado Massaguer and other illustrators in Cuba would prove, Bacardi was adept at using political satirists to convey the company's identity in apolitical ways.

Photographs by Russell C. Aikins for *Fortune* make plain the luscious, full-toned character of the Bacardi Bar,[42] a striking contrast with the cool commercial styling of the executive bar at Schenley competitor Joseph E. Seagram & Sons in the Chrysler Building, designed the same year by Morris Lapidus of Ross-Frankel Inc.[43] Lapidus, considered by many a guru of modern retail design, conveyed machine-age aesthetics with repetitive curves, a perforated cheese-hole display wall, and the use of new materials like plywood paneling and rubber flooring. The distinction of the Schenley Bacardi Bar, which deployed what architect Robert Stern has labeled "unlikely combinations of vernacular and folkloric themes,"[44] becomes all the more apparent. Bacardi and Schenley created their image not by emphasizing modernity, but by integrating modern motifs into archetypal traditional spaces.

The Bacardi Room[45] at the Empire State Building, designed by Franklin Hughes and inaugurated on Cuba's independence day in 1938[46] went further, transmitting the company's Cuban identity in a chimerical space, activated by myth and whimsy. Hughes, a popular club designer, conceived the new home of Bacardi in the United States as a private lounge on the 35th floor of the tower, a location for "Rumberos Americanos."[47] The unusual bar delivered chic amusingly through evocations of the Cuban countryside. The centralpiece was Cuban artist Antonio Gattorno's wall-sized mural *Waiting for Coffee,* a pastoral scene of *guajiros*—country people—in the cane fields. Around the room, a hand-adzed wooden screen veiled Manhattan views through the tower's windows, and Cuban cowhide–covered circular couches and low-backed chairs in vivid tropical colors (that matched the mural) were scattered in conversation groups.[48]

Waiting for Coffee plunged the viewer into the artistic sensibility of the Cuban *vanguardia*, a representation of an authentic *Cubanidad* through tropical landscapes, pastoral rural scenes, and Cuban peasants. At the center is the romantic figure of the white goat, the model for which, named *El Señor*, hilariously went missing in the 1,200-foot-tall tower, according to legend and public relations copy.[49] Gattorno was championed for the project by the American writer Ernest Hemingway, whose understanding of Cuba was reaffirmed in the Cuban artist's modern primitivism.[50] Similarly, in promoting both the artist and the vision, Bacardi wrapped its own identity in exoticism and *Cubanisimo.*

In Havana, the company had romanticized North America's passion for brash towers and sophisticated cocktail bars. Contrastingly, in New York, Bacardi's exotic re-affirmation of *lo Cubano* stood at the heart of the city's newest skyscraper, symbol of American spirit and global capital. The company had situated itself in the space between globalization and the affirmation of a vernacular *Cubanidad*. Soon, this delicate balance would shift as growth propelled Bacardi's function and status as a global corporation.

Top Right: Bacardi Building Competition, first place entry. Rendering. Esteban Rodríguez-Castells and Rafael Fernández Ruenes, architects. From *Concurso para el Edificio Bacardi*, *El Arquitecto* 3:22 (January 1928): 69. Courtesy of New York Public Library, Manuscripts and Archives.

Bottom Right: Edifício Cooperativo de La Habana. Cover illustration from sales catalogue. Instituto de Artes Graficas, Habana, c. 1920s. Courtesy of The Bacardi Archive.

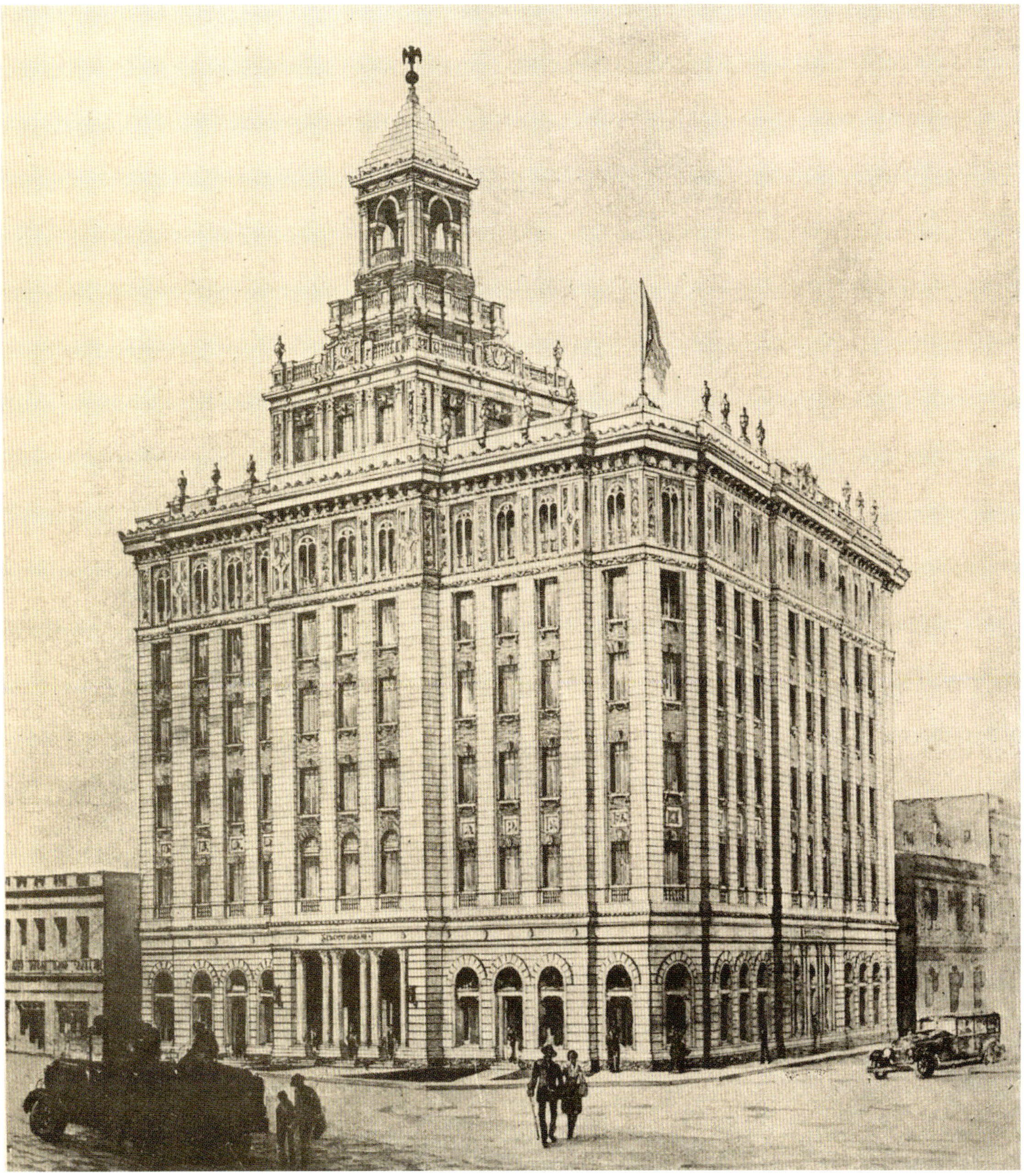

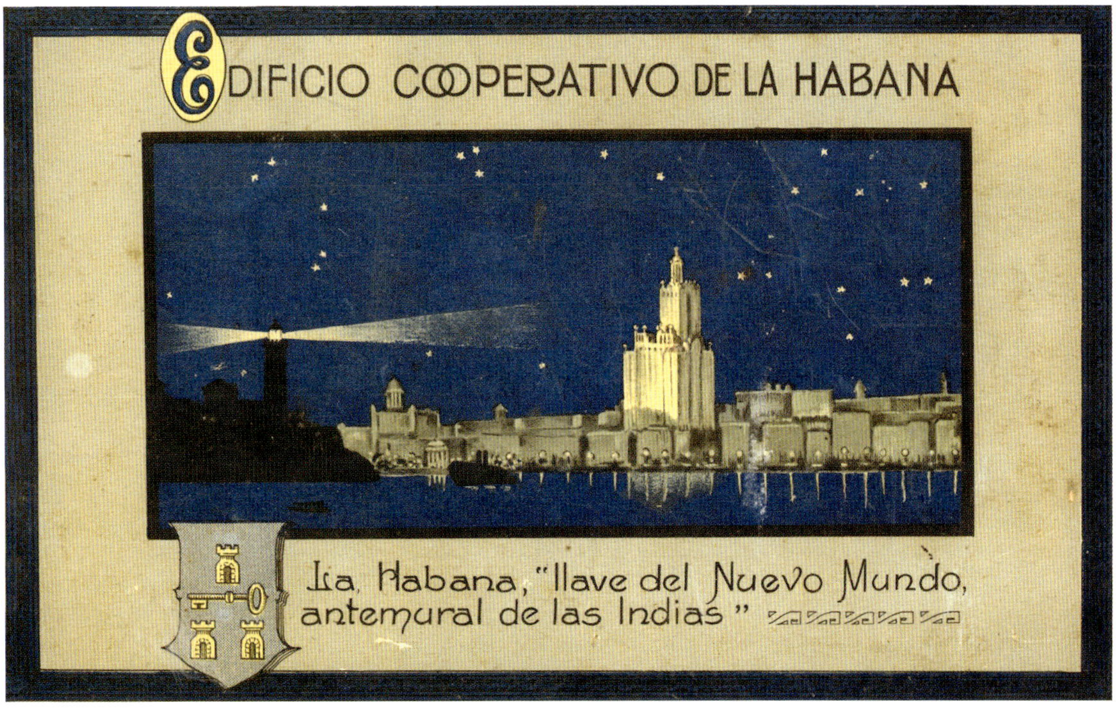
EDIFICIO COOPERATIVO DE LA HABANA
La Habana, "llave del Nuevo Mundo, antemural de las Indias"

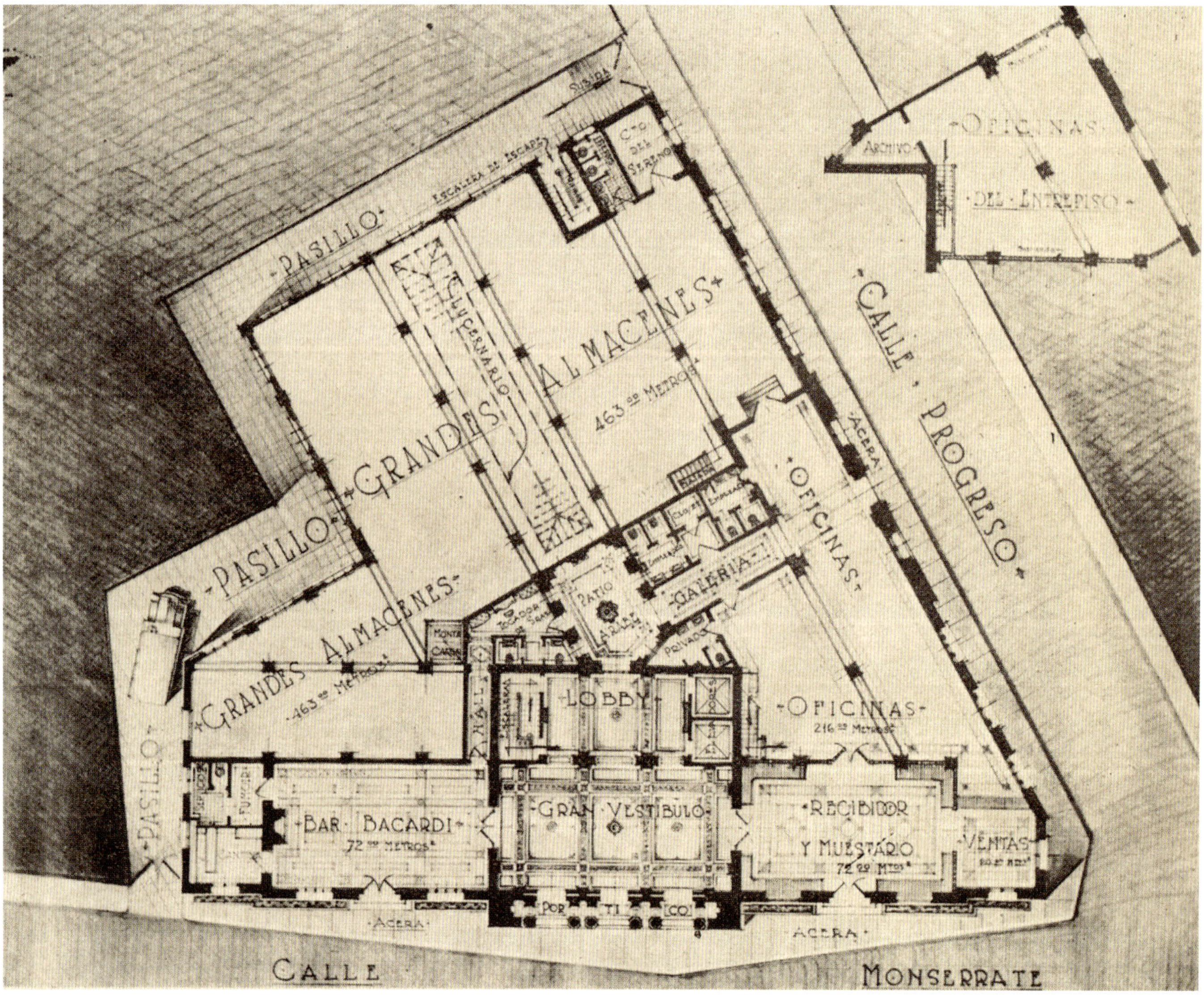

Above: Bacardi Building Competition, first place entry. Floor plan. Esteban Rodríguez-Castells and Rafael Fernández Ruenes, architects. From *Concurso para el Edificio Bacardi*, *El Arquitecto* 3:22 (January 1928): 67. Courtesy of New York Public Library, Manuscripts and Archives.

Right: Bacardi Building Competition, first place entry. Section. Esteban Rodríguez-Castells and Rafael Fernández Ruenes, architects. From *Concurso para el Edificio Bacardi*, *El Arquitecto* 3:22 (January 1928): 68. Courtesy of New York Public Library, Manuscripts and Archives.

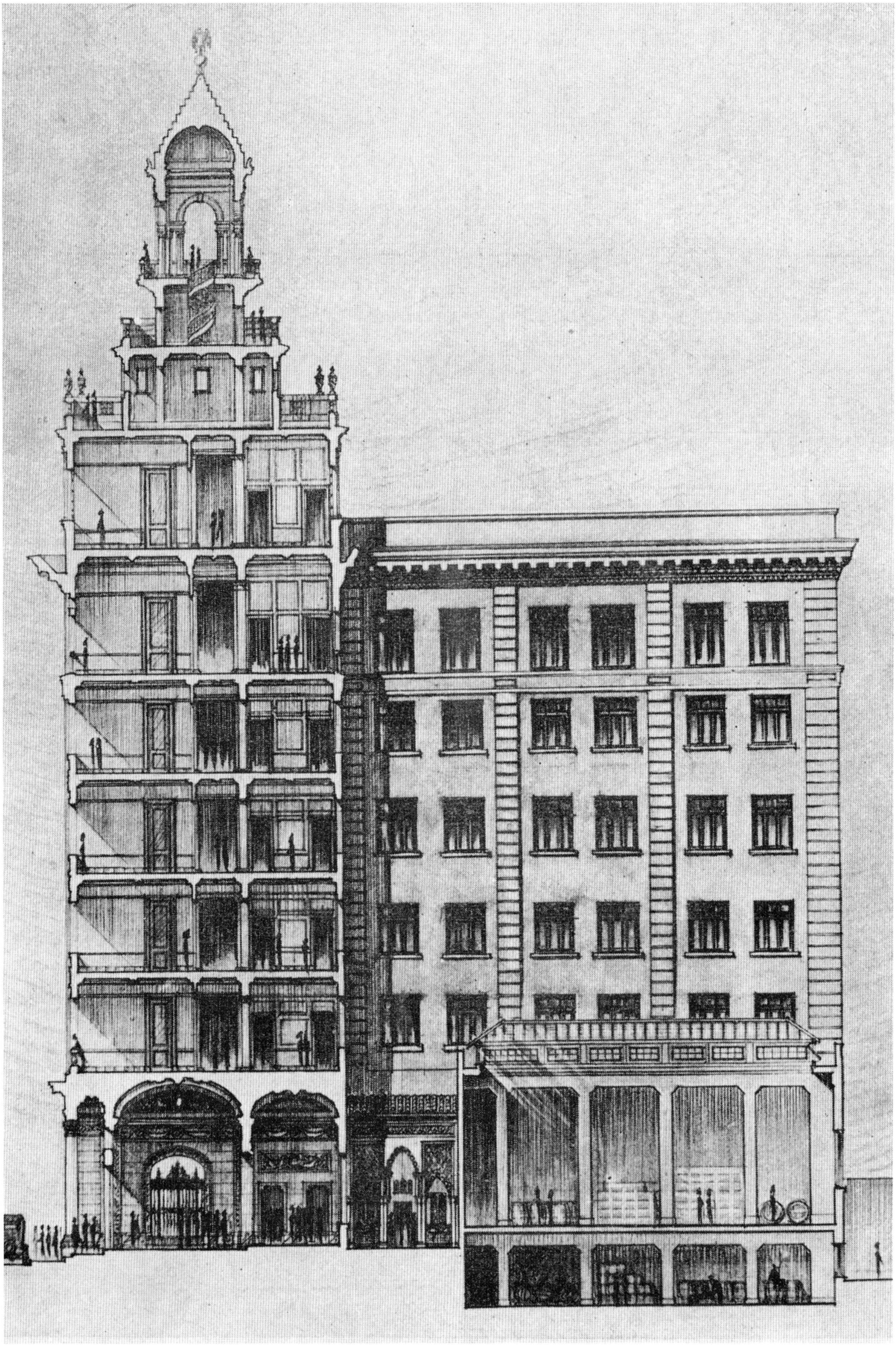

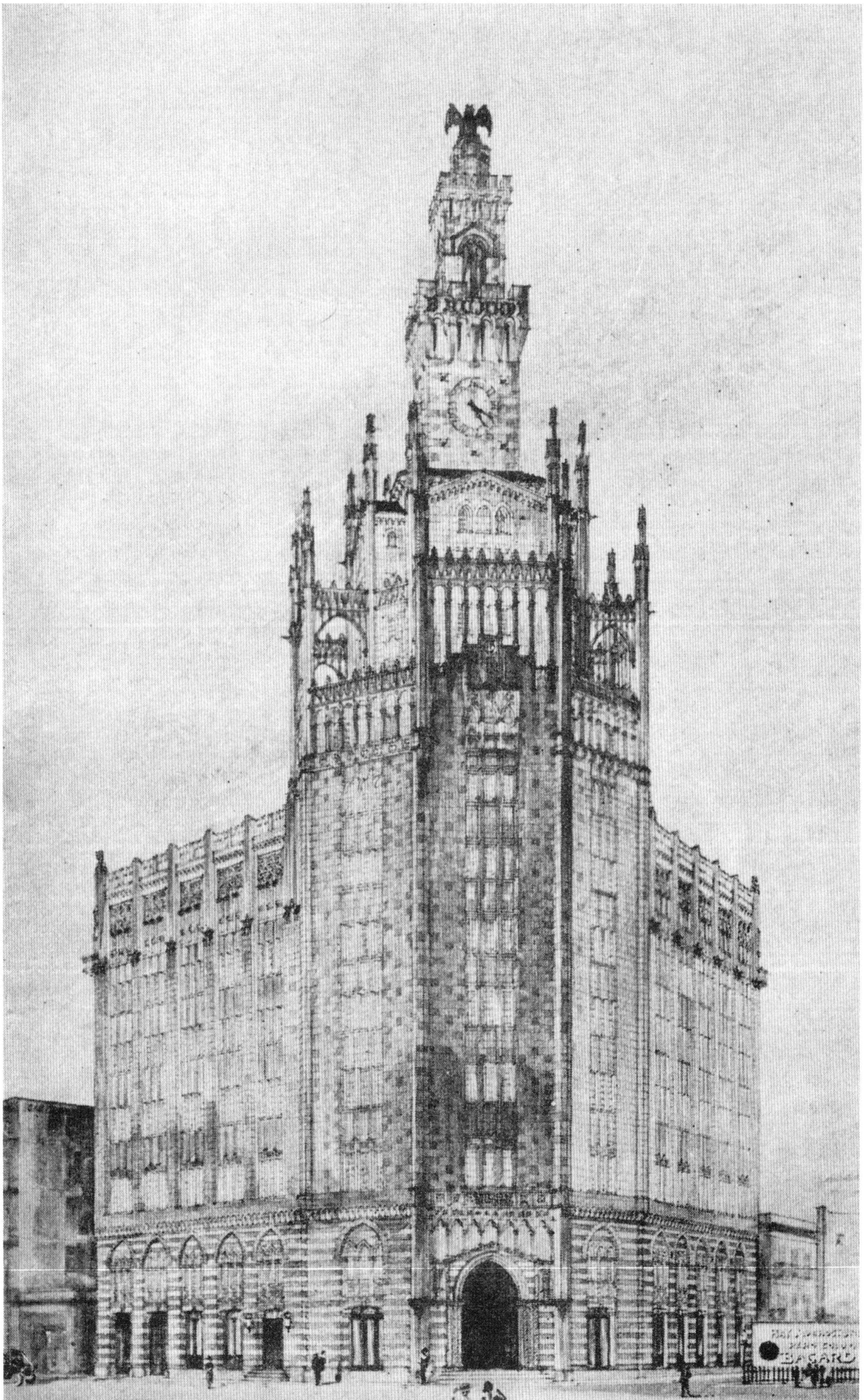

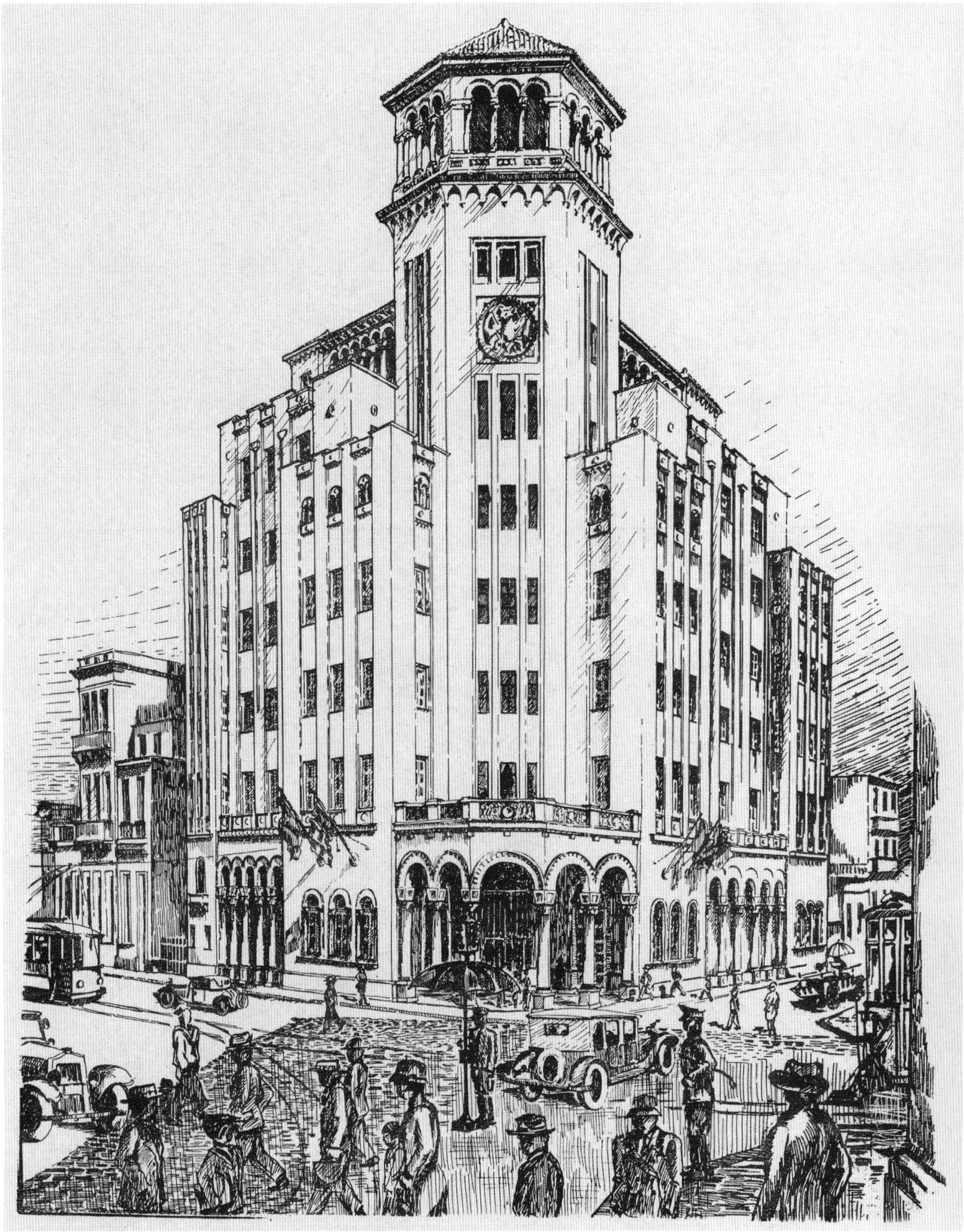

Left: Bacardi Building Competition, second place entry. Rendering. Eugenio Cosculluela, architect. From *Concurso para el Edificio Bacardi*, *El Arquitecto* 3:22 (January 1928): 73. Courtesy of the New York Public Library, Manuscripts and Archives.

Above: Bacardi Building Competition, third place entry. Rendering. Rafael de Cardenas. From *Concurso para el Edificio Bacardi*, *El Arquitecto* 3:22 (January 1928): 73. Courtesy of the New York Public Library, Manuscripts and Archives.

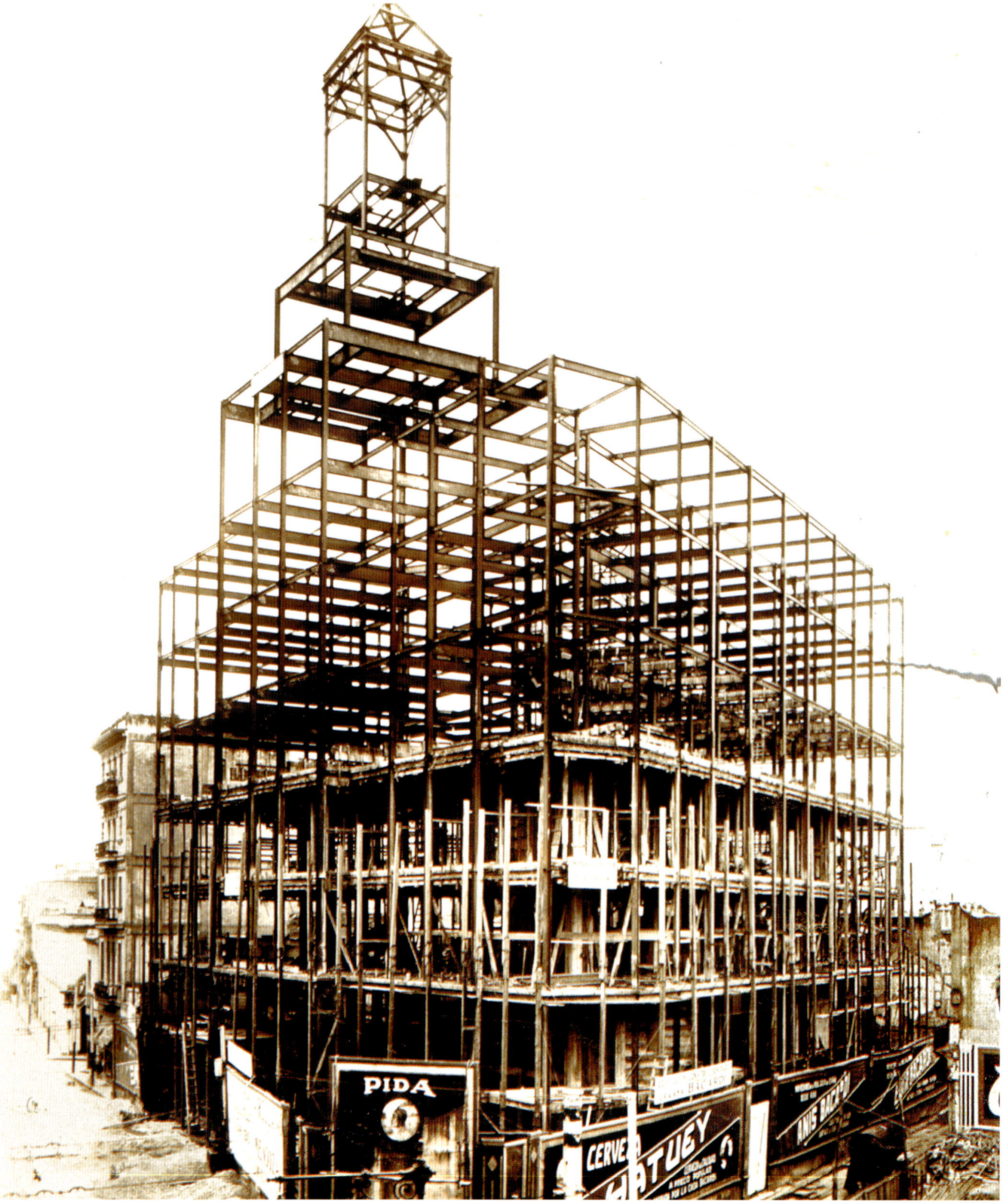

Above: Bacardi Building under construction, Havana, c. 1929. Esteban Rodríguez-Castells and Rafael Fernández Ruenes, architects. Courtesy of The Bacardi Archive.

Right: Nearly completed Bacardi Building, Havana, c. 1930. Esteban Rodríguez-Castells and Rafael Fernández Ruenes, architects. Courtesy of The Bacardi Archive.

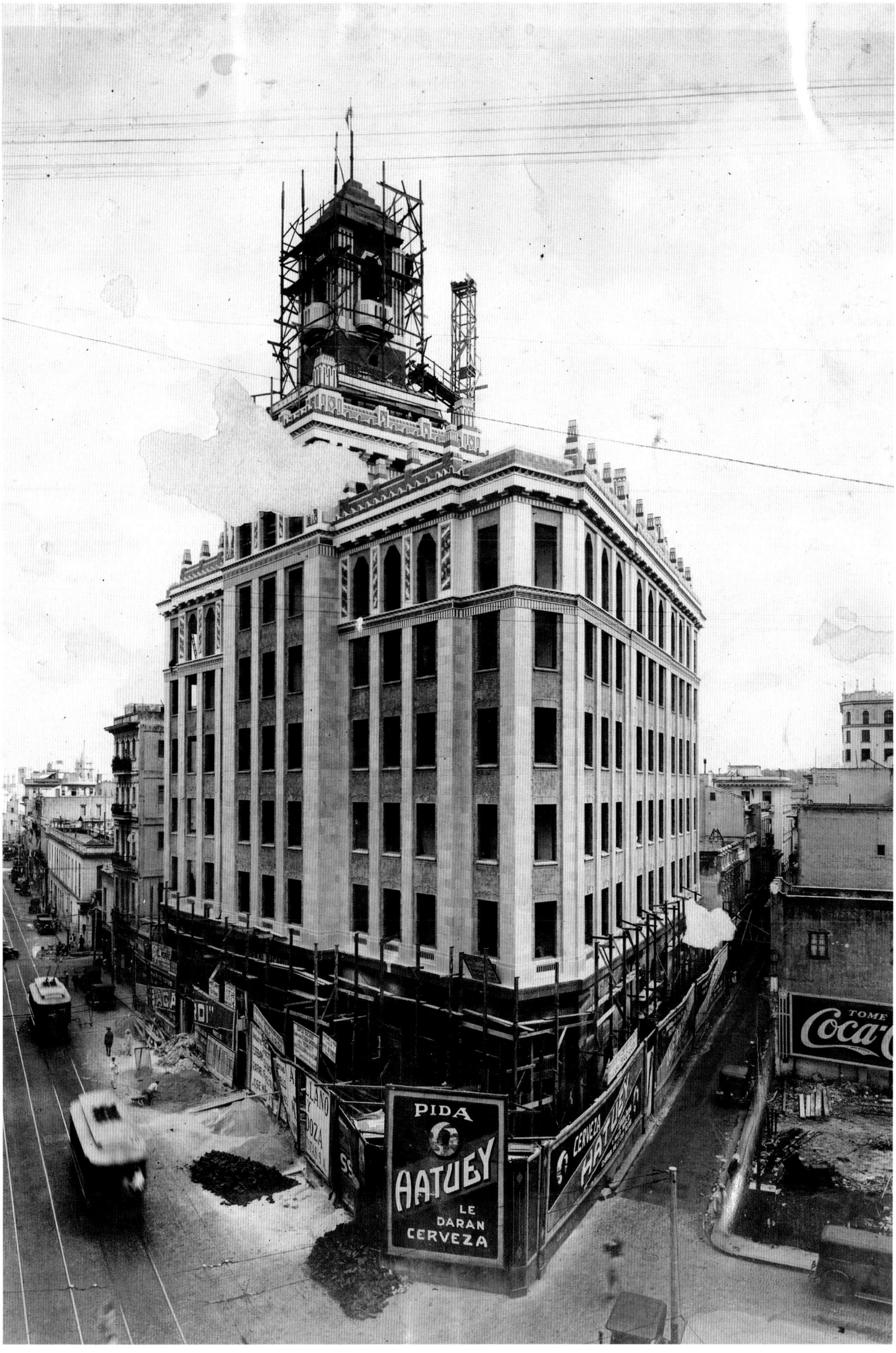
PIDA
HATUEY
LE
DARAN
CERVEZA
CERVEZA
TOME

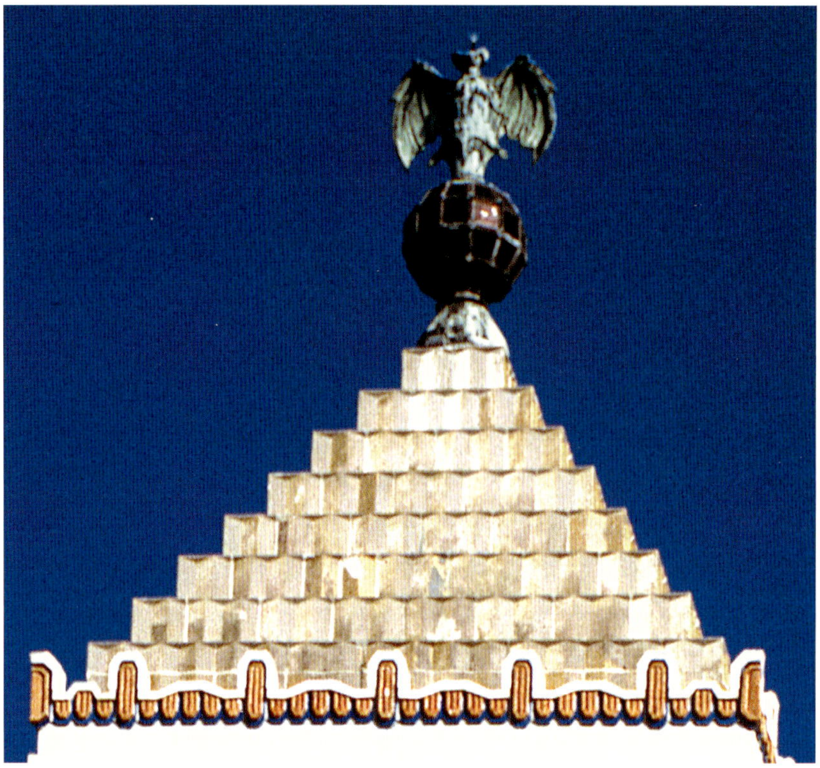

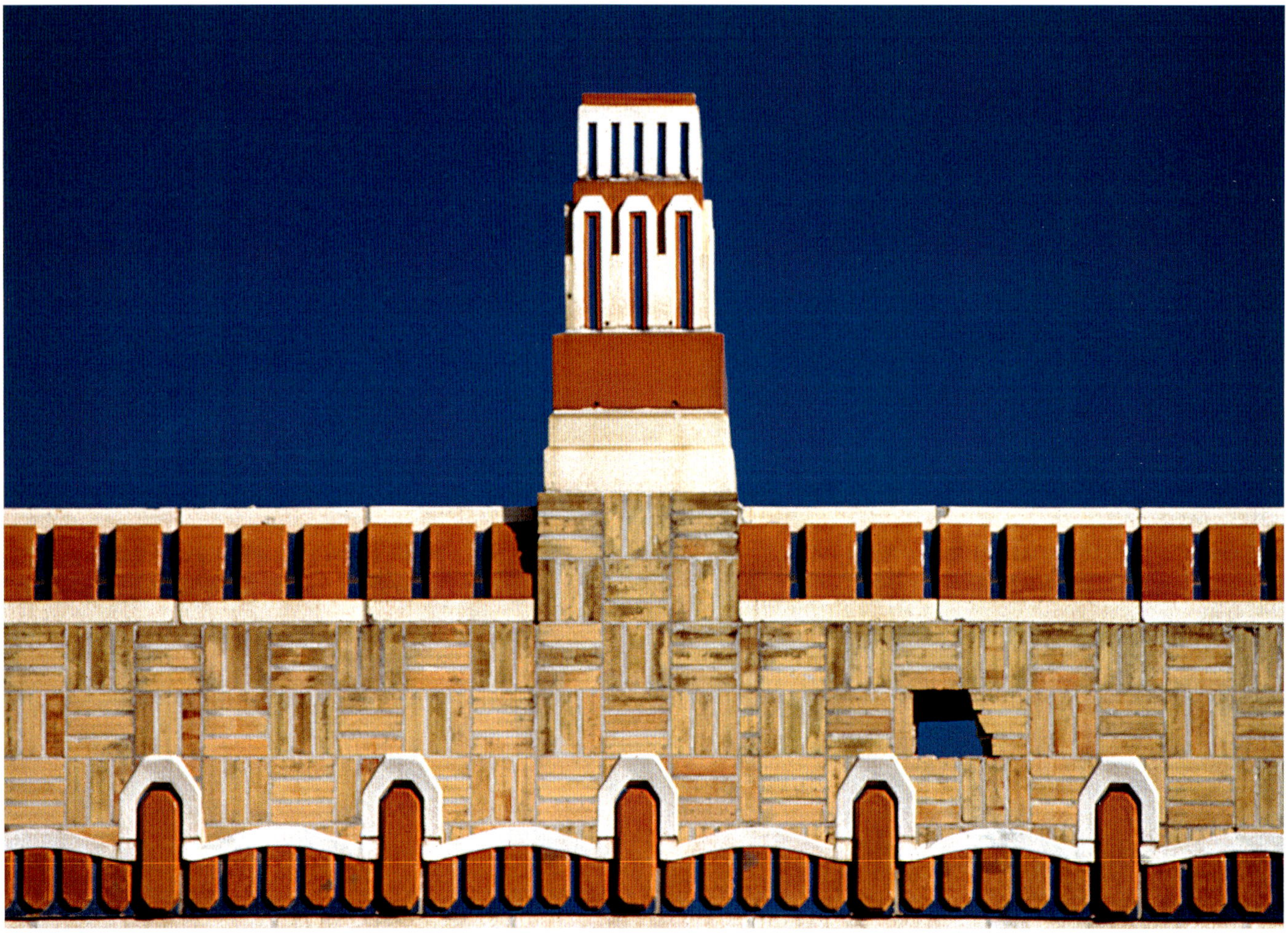

Top: Bacardi Building, Havana. Detail of the pyramidal crown and bat. Esteban Rodríguez-Castells and Rafael Fernández Ruenes, architects, 1930. Photograph by Kenneth Treister, 1997. Courtesy of The Bacardi Archive and Kenneth Treister.

Bottom: Bacardi Building, Havana. Parapet detail. Esteban Rodríguez-Castells and Rafael Fernández Ruenes, architects, 1930. Photograph by Kenneth Treister, 1997. Courtesy of The Bacardi Archive and Kenneth Treister.

Right: Bacardi Building, Havana. Detail of terra-cotta frieze attributed to Maxfield Parrish. Esteban Rodriguez-Castells and Rafael Fernández Ruenes, architects, 1930. Photograph by Kenneth Treister, 1997. Courtesy of The Bacardi Archive and Kenneth Treister.

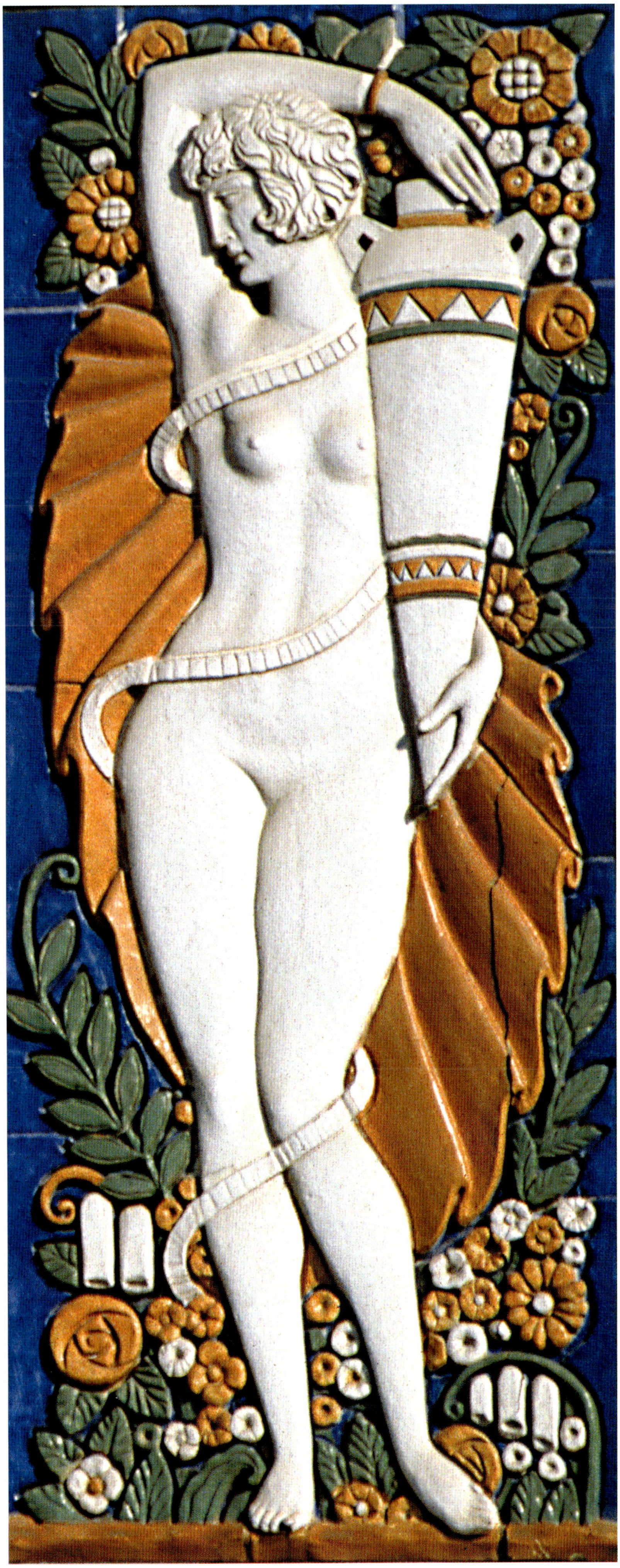

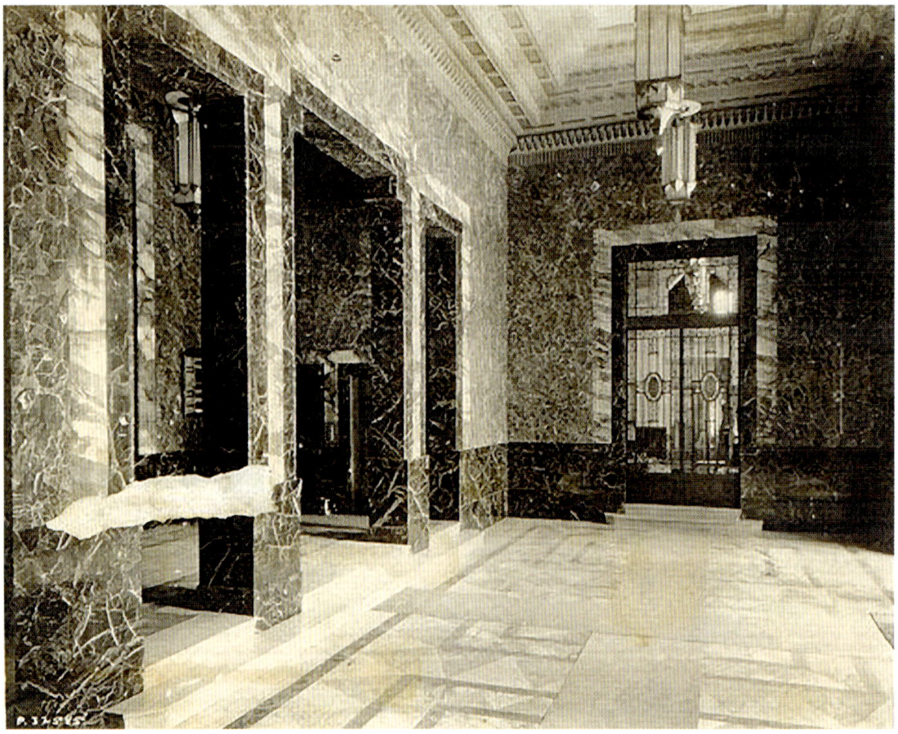

Above: Bacardi Building, Havana. Lobby. Esteban Rodríguez-Castells and Rafael Fernández Ruenes, architects, 1930. Courtesy of The Bacardi Archive.

Right: Bacardi Building, Havana. Lobby. Esteban Rodríguez-Castells and Rafael Fernández Ruenes, architects, 1930. Photograph by Kenneth Treister, 1997. Courtesy of The Bacardi Archive and Kenneth Treister.

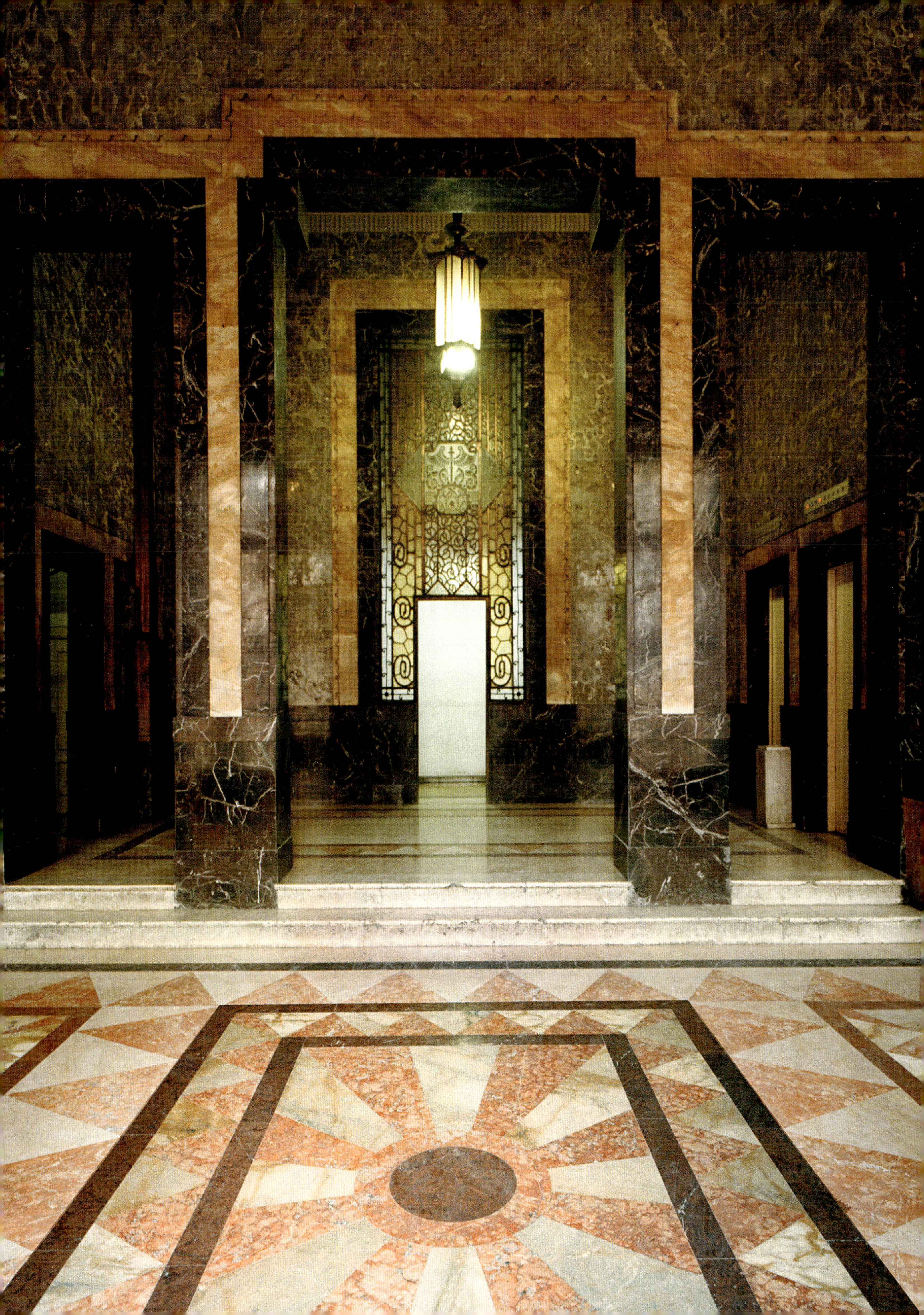

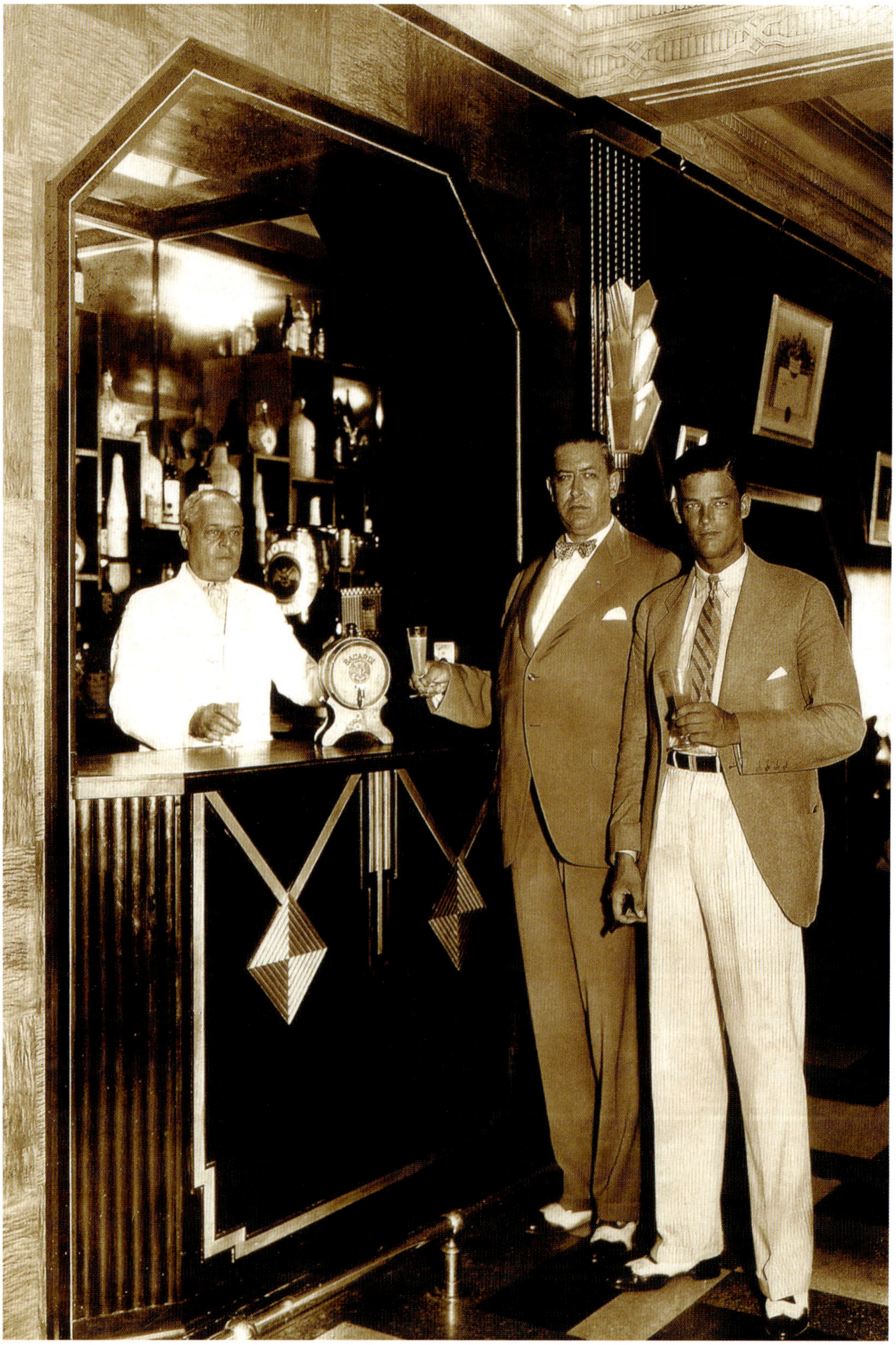

Above: Florida policeman and son served by brand ambassador Rafael "Pappy" Valiente at the bar of the Bacardi Building, Havana, 1930s. Courtesy of The Bacardi Archive.

Right: Cuba is great. There is a reason. BACARDÍ. Advertisement. Conrado Massaguer, artist. From *Havana Yacht Club*, 1936. Courtesy of The Bacardi Archive.

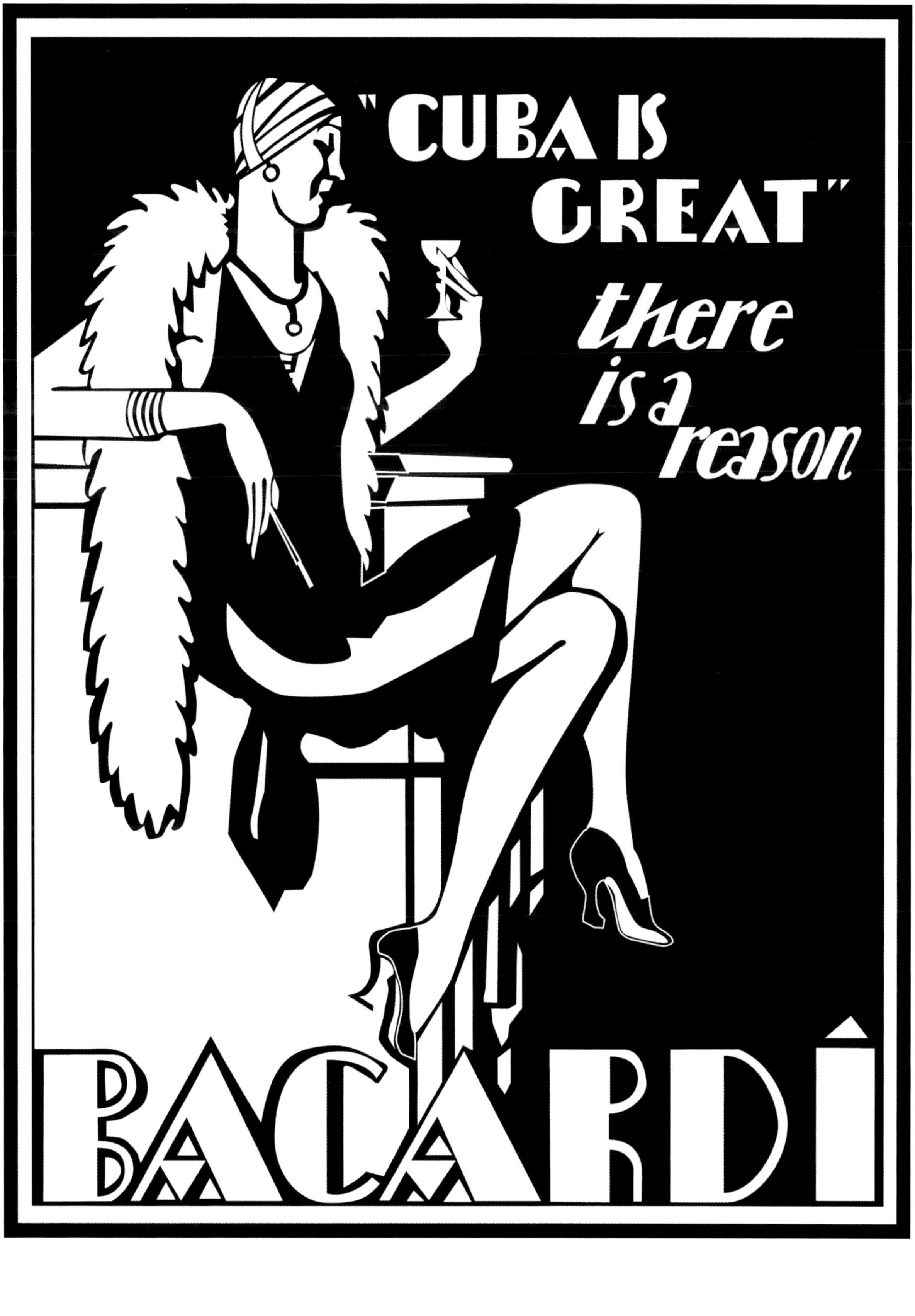
"CUBA IS GREAT"
there is a reason
BACARDI

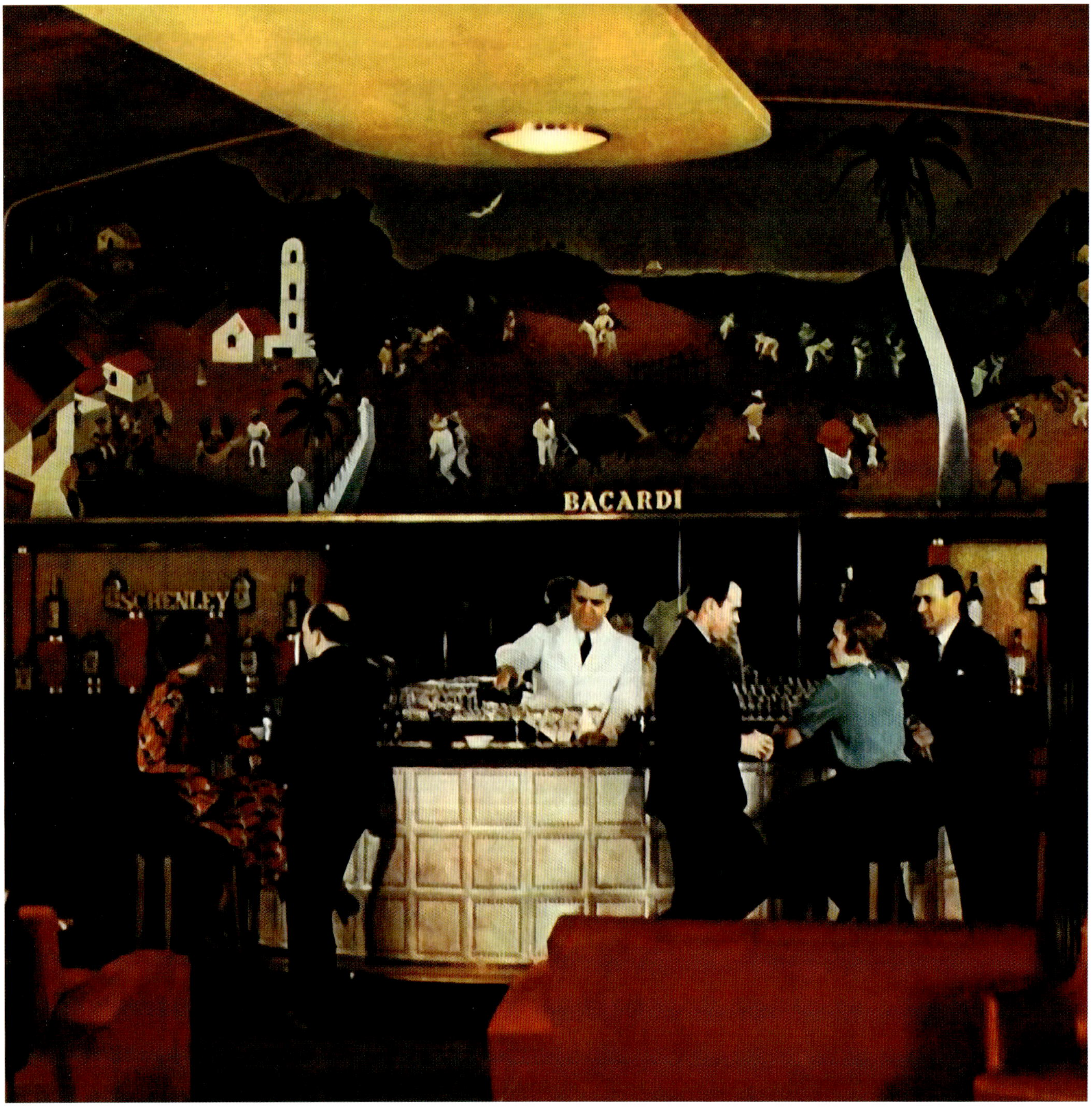

Above: Bacardi Bar at Schenley Import Company headquarters (former New York Club).
Morris B. Sanders, interior designer; William Gropper, muralist. Photograph by Russell Aikins.
From "Name, Schenley; Age, Three: Bacardi Pays the Bartender," *Fortune* 13 (May 1936): 102-103.

Right: Bacardi Bar at Schenley Import Company headquarters (former New York Club). Morris B. Sanders, architect and William Gropper, muralist. Photograph by Richard Garrison. Courtesy of The Bacardi Archive.

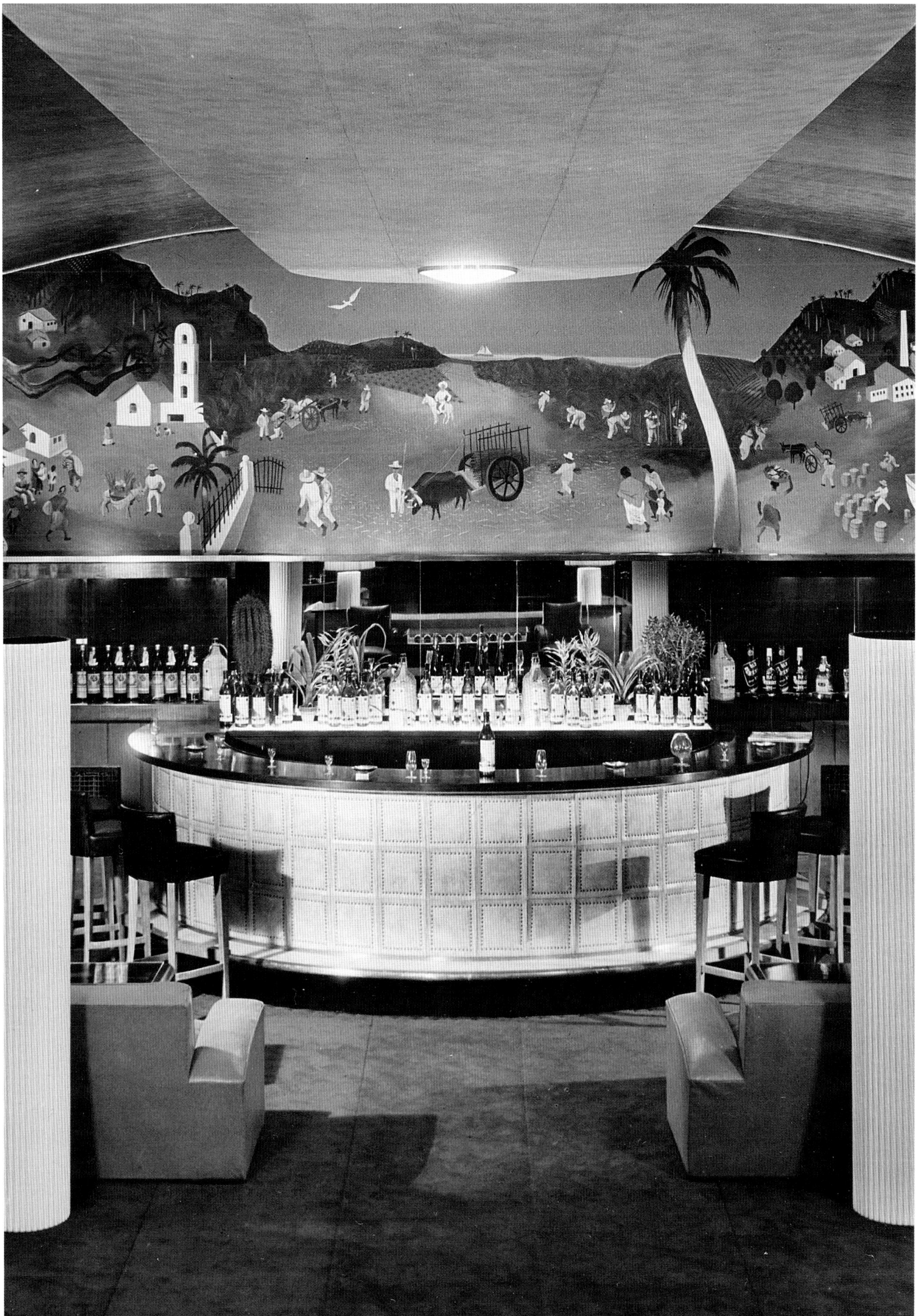

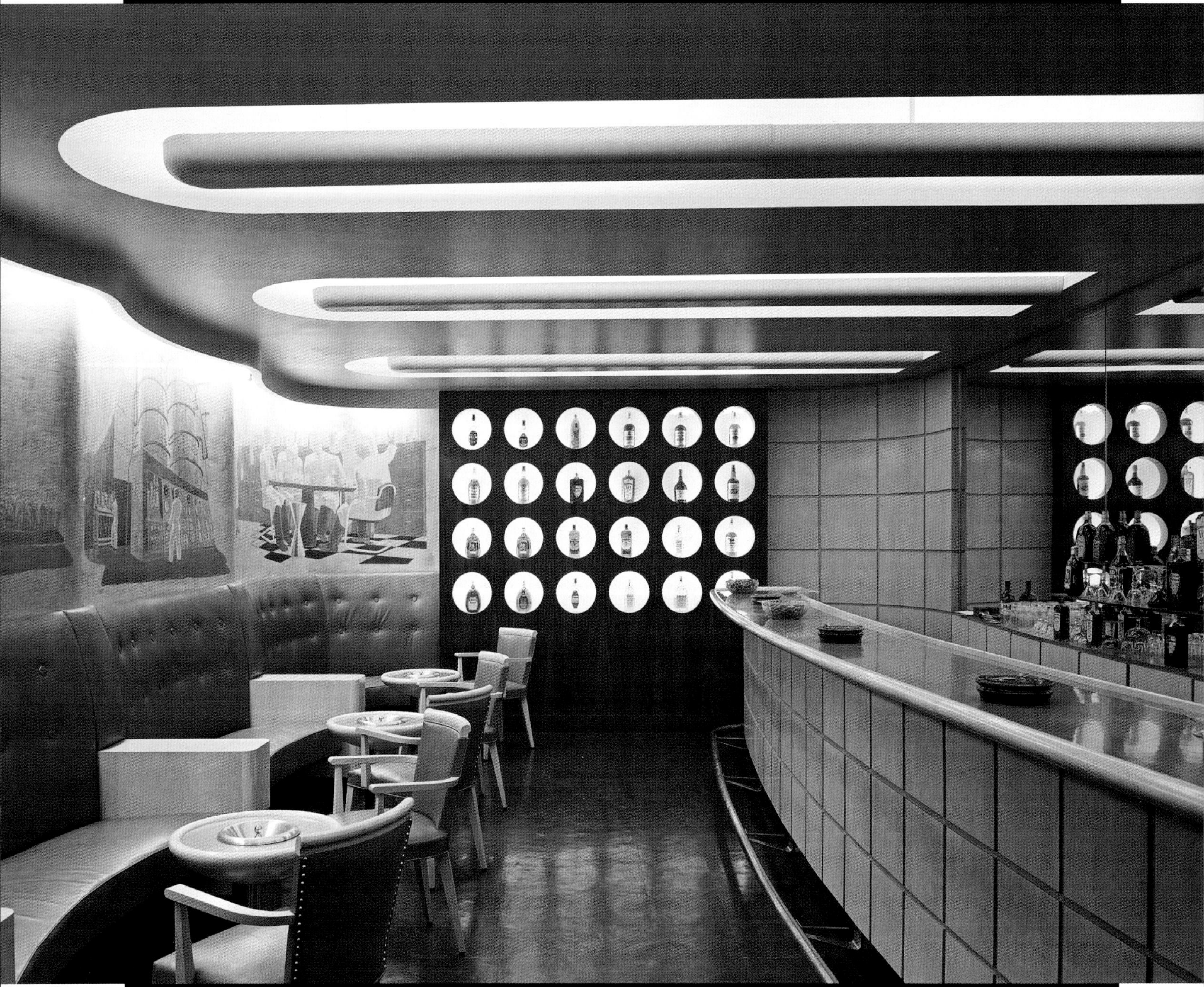

Above: Seagram Executive Bar in the Chrysler Building, New York. Ross Frankel, Inc. and Morris Lapidus, interior designer, 1936. Photograph by Samuel Gottscho. Library of Congress, Prints & Photographs Division, Gottscho-Schleisner Collection.

Right: Bacardi Room at the Empire State Building, New York. Franklin Hughes, interior designer and Antonio Gattorno, muralist, 1937. Photograph by Kurt Schelling. From "Entertaining at Your Private Club," *Arts & Decoration* 47-48 (June 1938): 20-21.

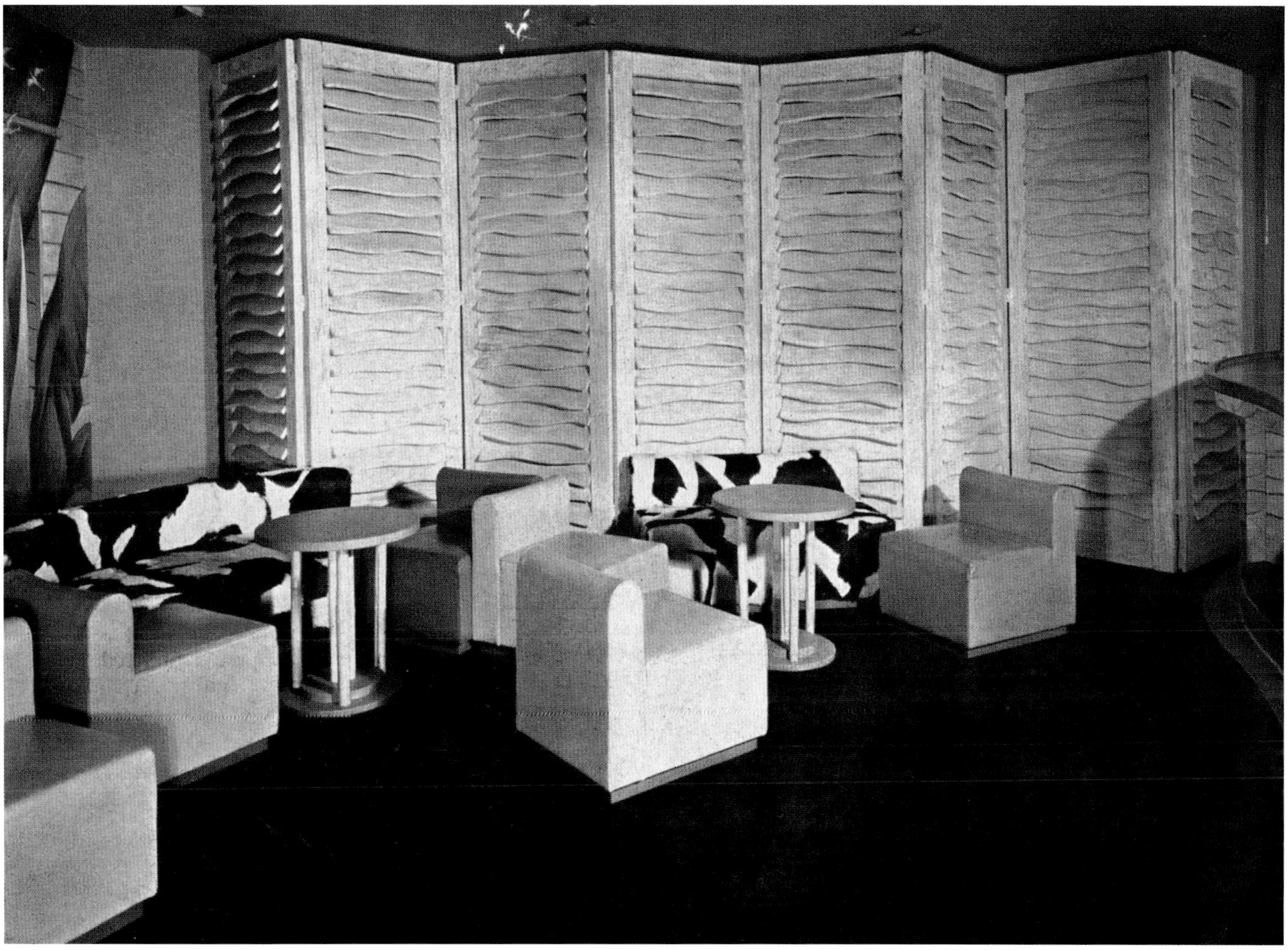

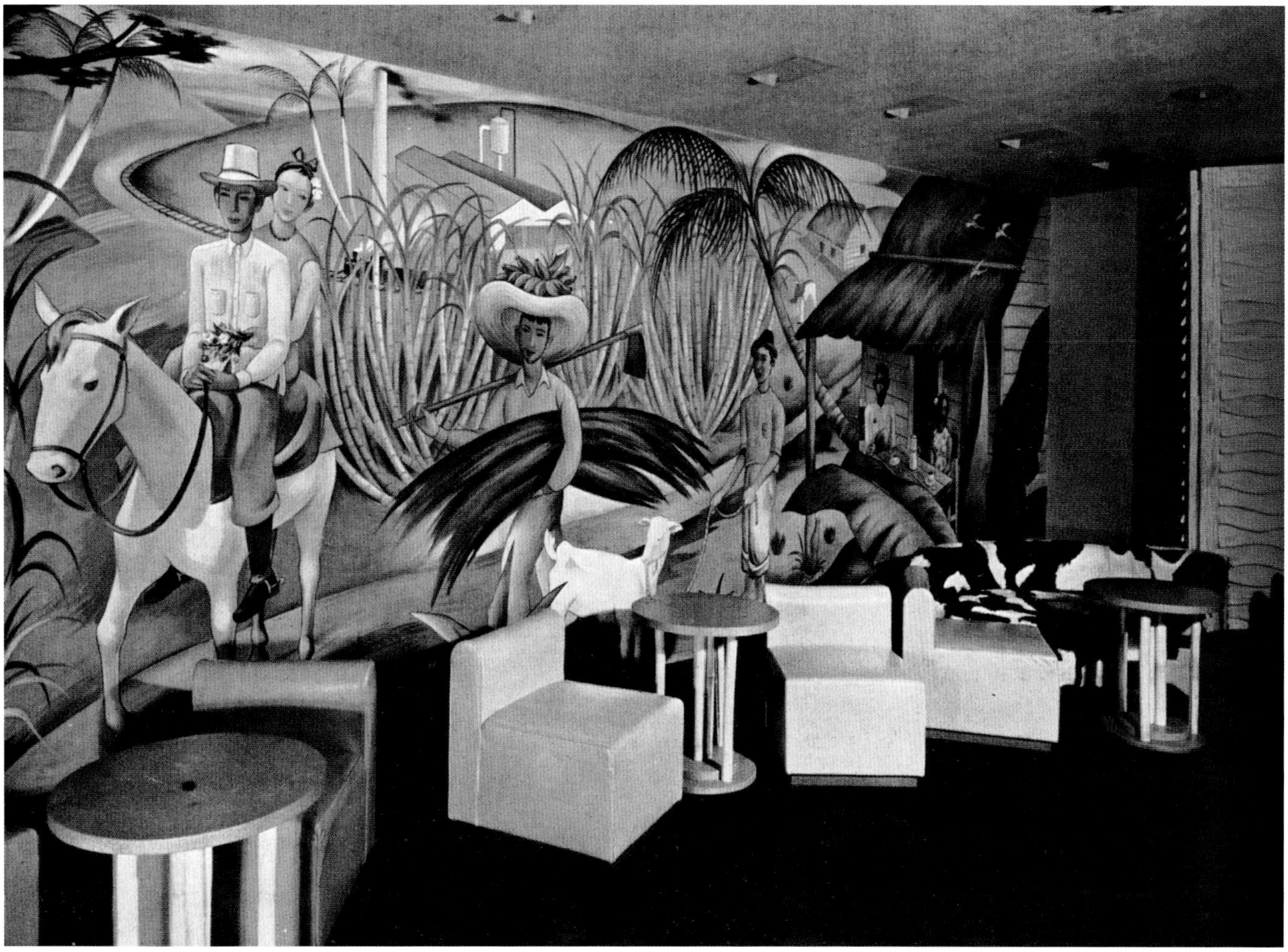

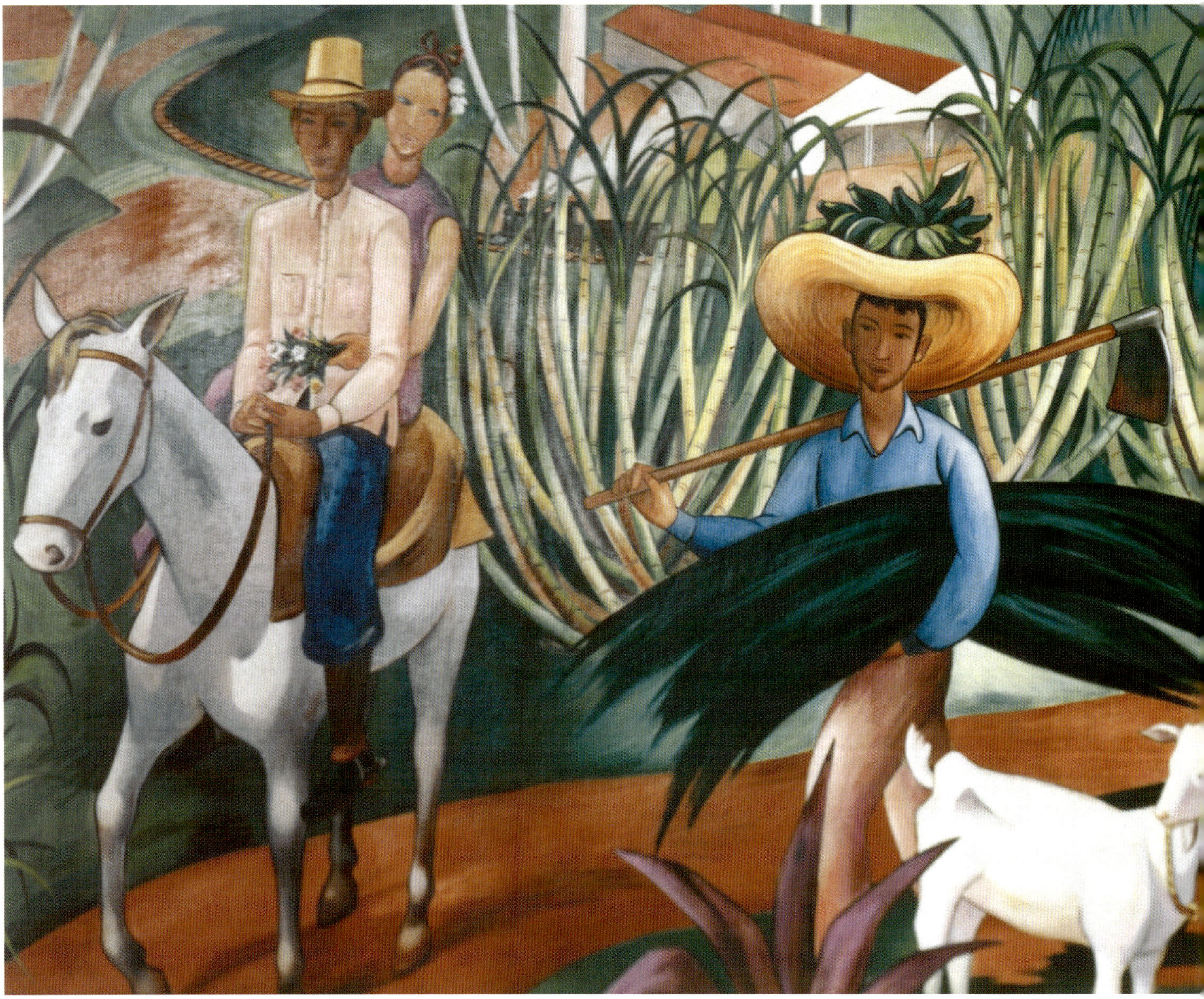

Waiting for Coffee (partial panel), Antonio Gattorno, muralist, 1937. Courtesy of The Bacardi Archive and the Gattorno Foundation.

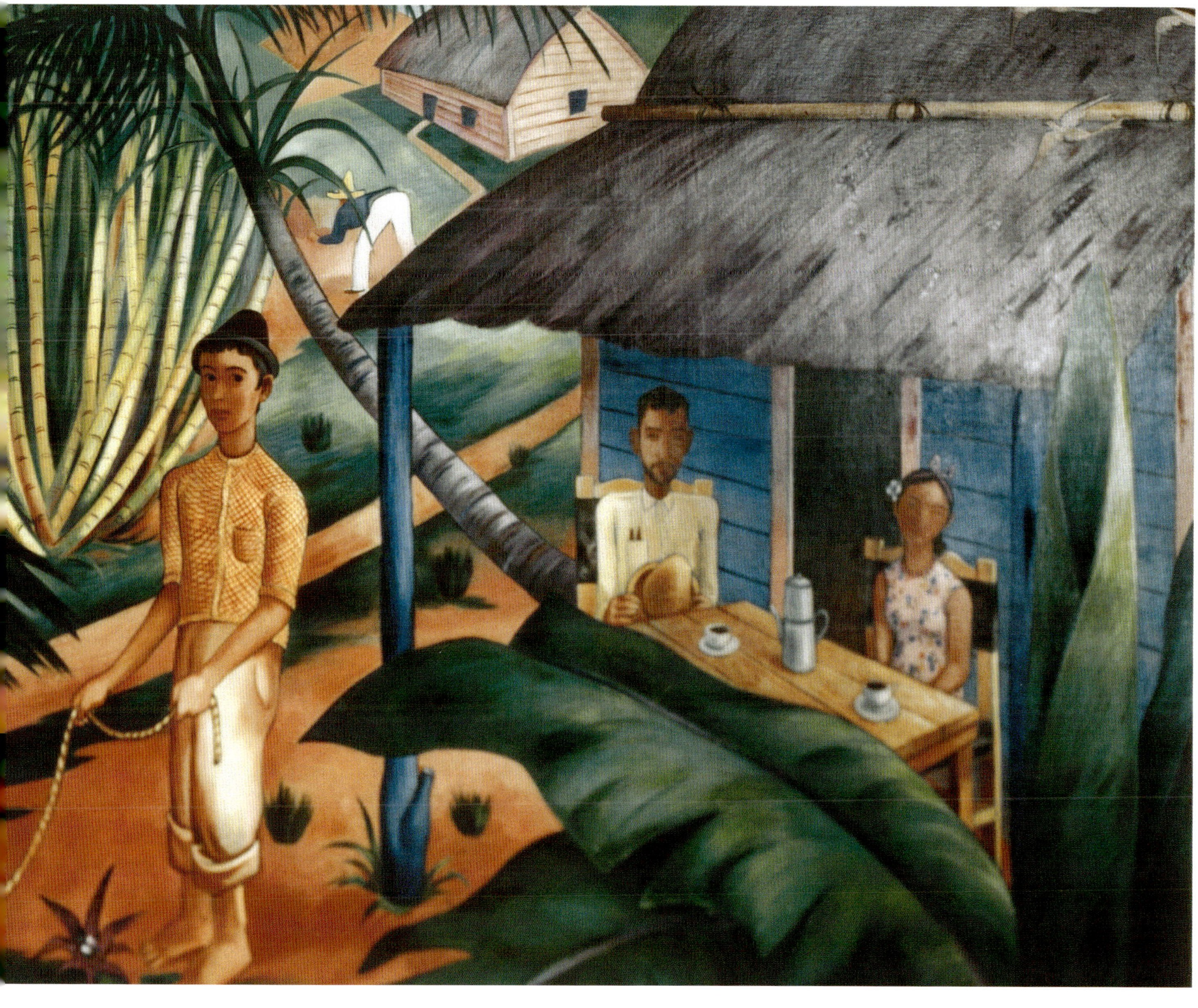

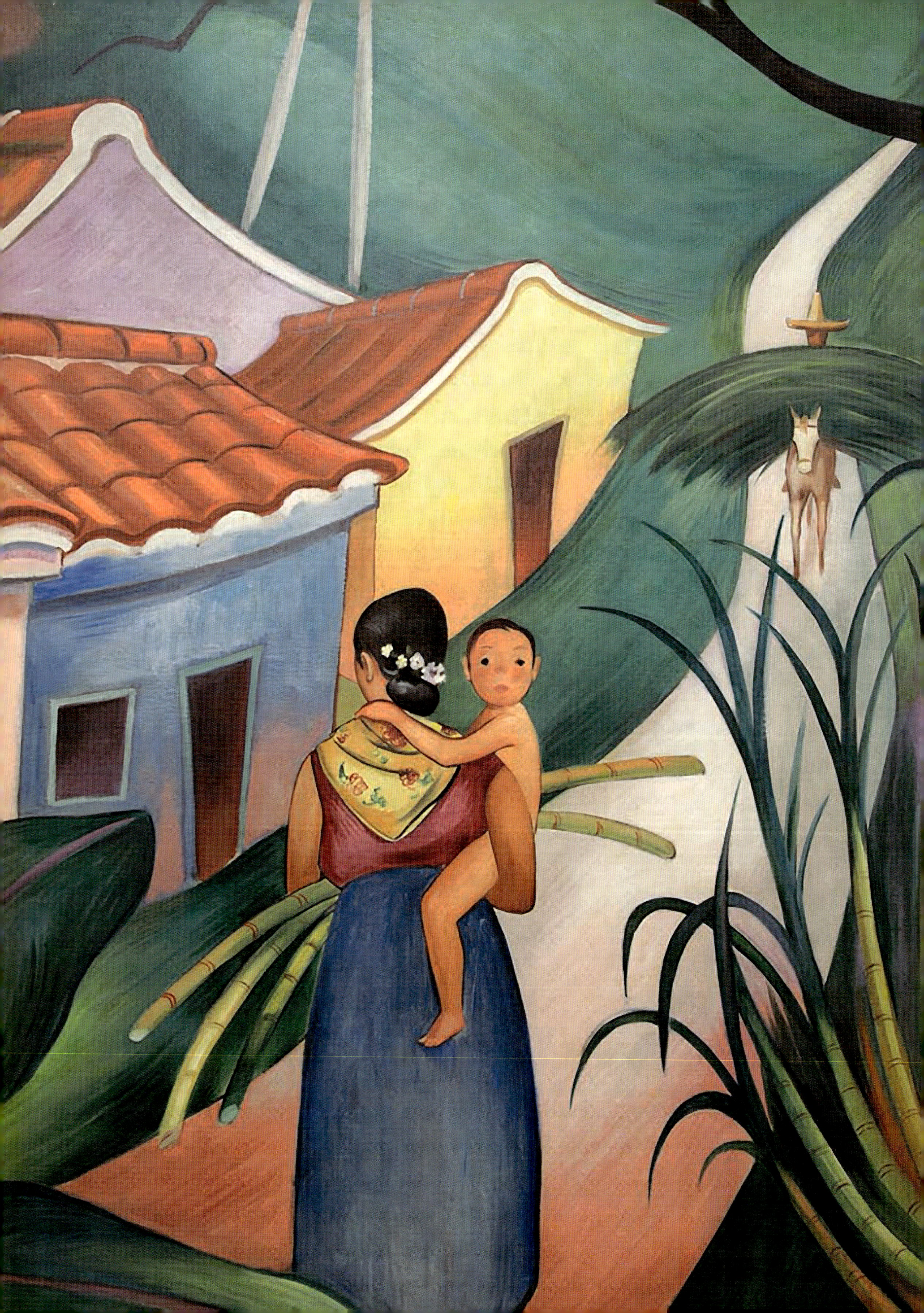

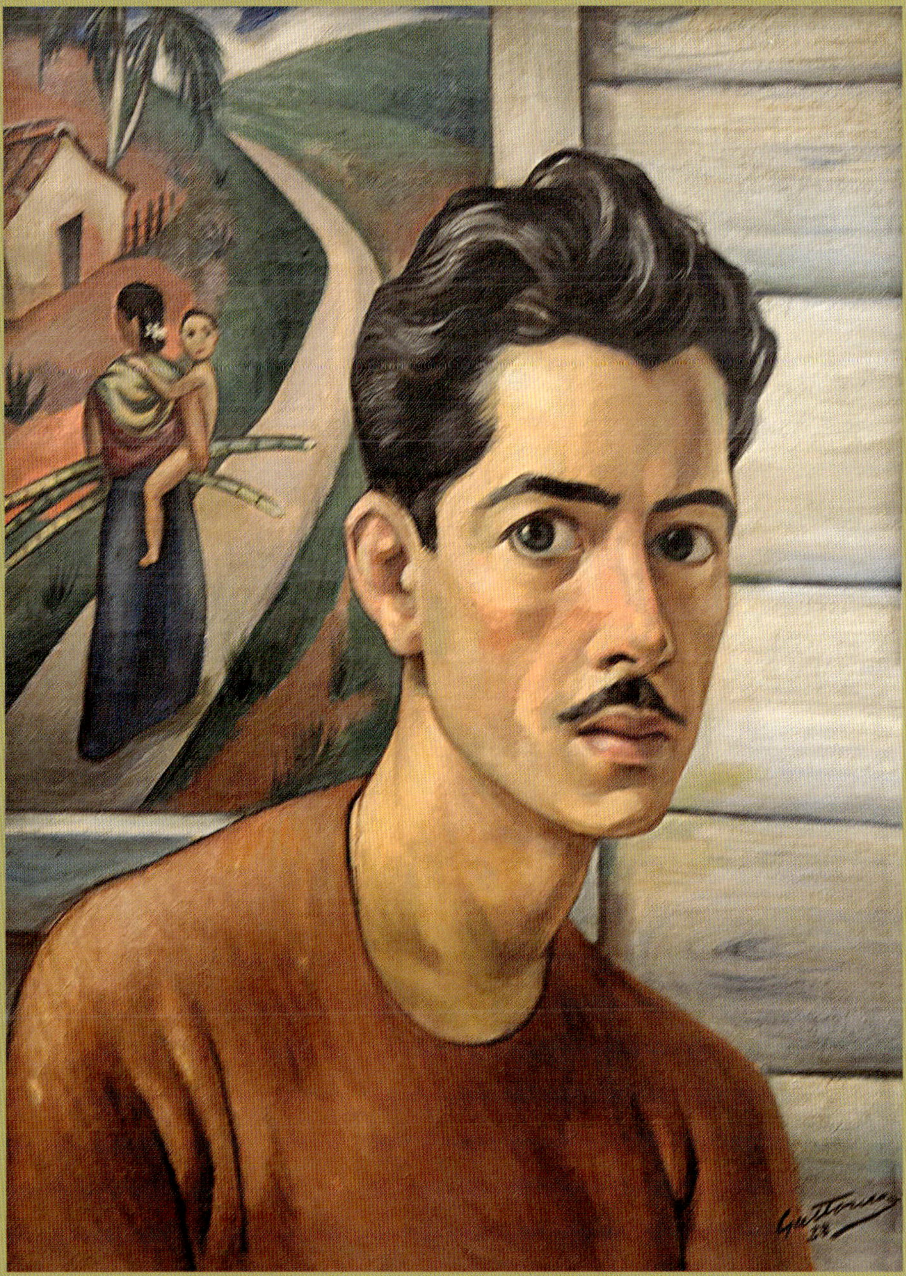

Left: Waiting for Coffee (separated panel). Antonio Gattorno, muralist, 1937. Courtesy of the Gattorno Foundation and the Rudman Family.

Above: Untitled (self-portrait). Antonio Gattorno, 1937. *Waiting for Coffee* and the Bacardi Room's wood screen form the backdrop. Courtesy of the Gattorno Foundation and the Rudman Family.

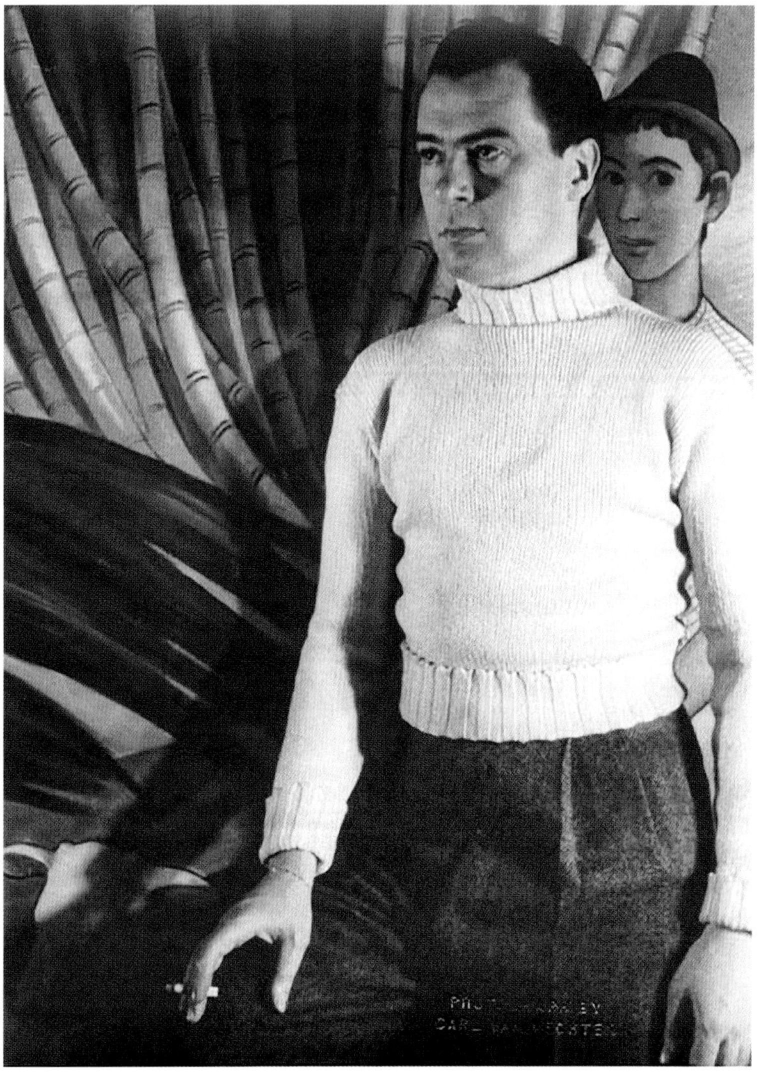

Above: Designer Franklin Hughes in the Bacardi Room, 1938. Photograph by Carl Van Vechten, 20 April 1938. Courtesy of The Yale Collection of American Literature, Beinecke Rare Book and Manuscript Library and the permission of the Carl Van Vechten Trust.

Right: SEÑOR, Only BACARDI Has It. Advertisement. G. de Zayas, artist, 1937. Courtesy of Bacardi & Company Limited.

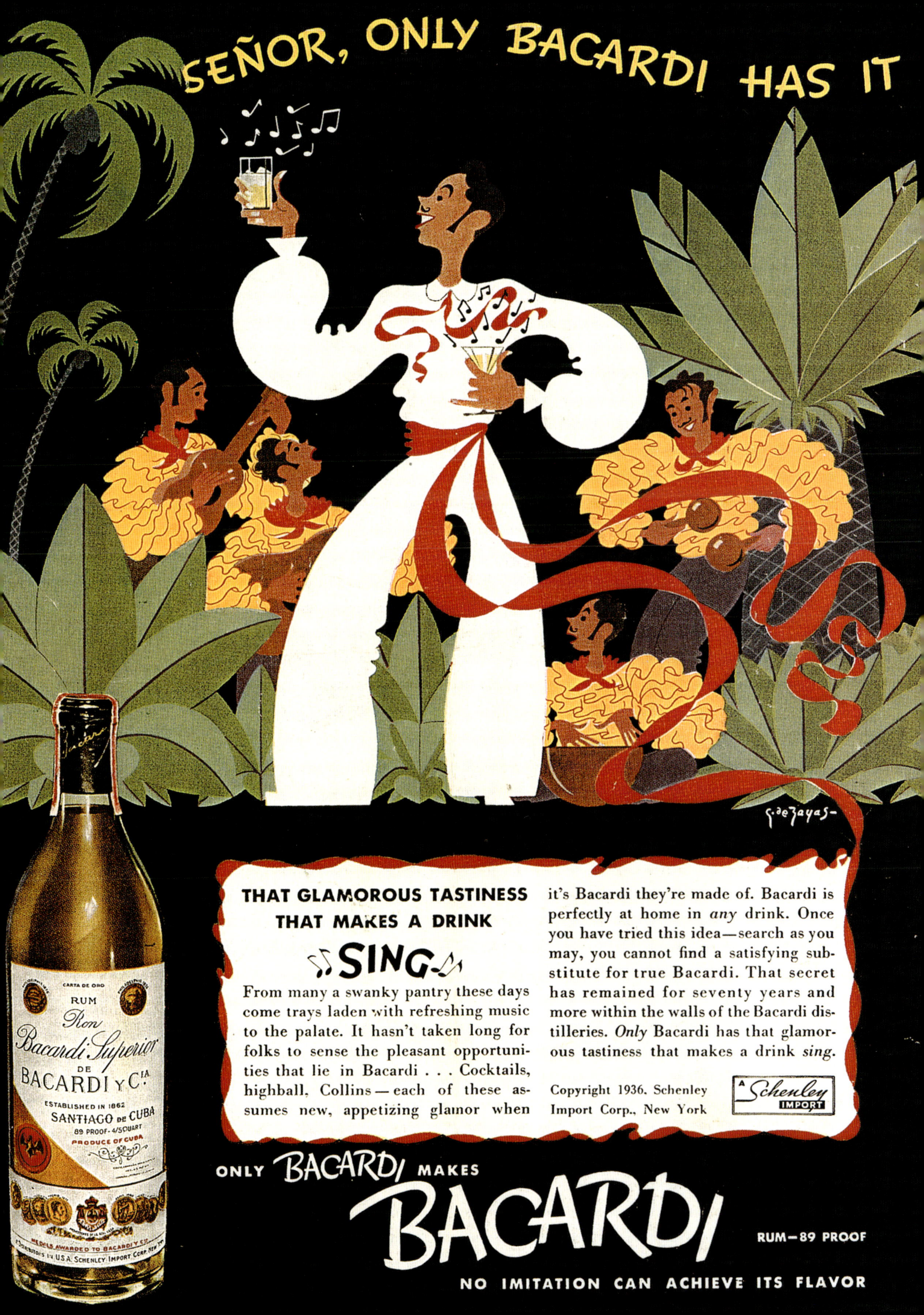

SEÑOR, ONLY BACARDI HAS IT
G. de Zayas
CARTA DE ORO
RUM
Ron
Bacardi Superior
DE
BACARDI Y Cia
ESTABLISHED IN 1862
SANTIAGO de CUBA
89 PROOF - 4/5 QUART
PRODUCE OF CUBA
THAT GLAMOROUS TASTINESS THAT MAKES A DRINK SING
From many a swanky pantry these days come trays laden with refreshing music to the palate. It hasn't taken long for folks to sense the pleasant opportunities that lie in Bacardi . . . Cocktails, highball, Collins — each of these assumes new, appetizing glamor when it's Bacardi they're made of. Bacardi is perfectly at home in *any* drink. Once you have tried this idea — search as you may, you cannot find a satisfying substitute for true Bacardi. That secret has remained for seventy years and more within the walls of the Bacardi distilleries. *Only* Bacardi has that glamorous tastiness that makes a drink *sing*.
Copyright 1936, Schenley Import Corp., New York
A Schenley IMPORT
ONLY BACARDI MAKES BACARDI
RUM — 89 PROOF
NO IMITATION CAN ACHIEVE ITS FLAVOR

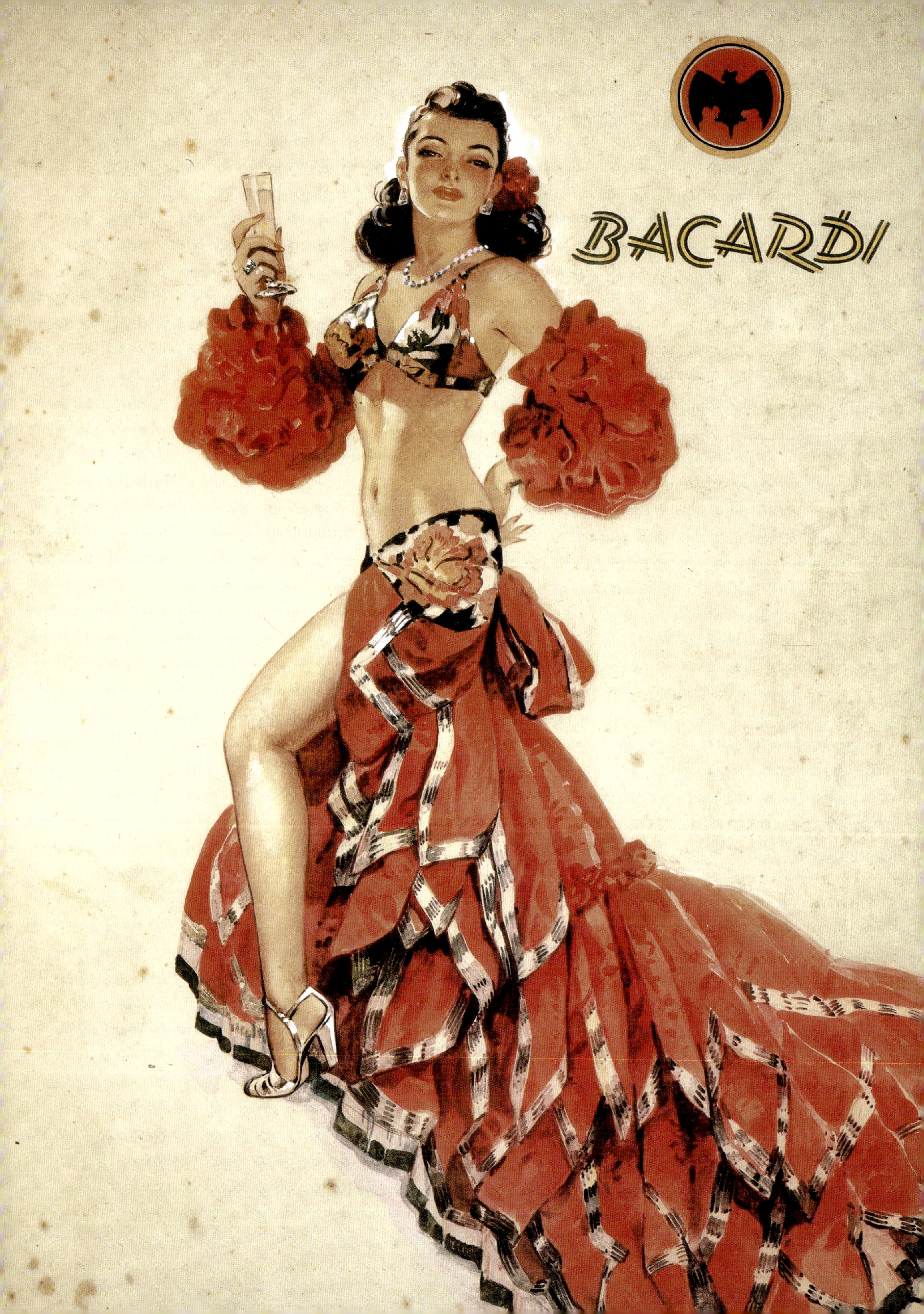
BACARDI

A COCKTAIL MODERNITY

The Distilled Spirits Exhibit at the 1939 New York World's Fair crowned the prewar efforts of spirits companies to remake their collective image in the wake of Prohibition. Beneath the marquee that depicted the agricultural products used in distilling, and past the infographic murals, visitors arrived beneath the exhibit's dome. Here, the exhibit's 35-foot high "theme spiral" brought to life the products and processes of the industry, ascending from farms to factories, silos and offices buildings; harvesters, tractors and trucks circulated at its base, and a freight train wound up the spiral to its summit. Designed by Ross Frankel, Inc. and Morris Lapidus, with Morris Sanders as architect (the duo that designed stylish demostration bars for Seagram and Bacardi), the exhibit depicted the role of spirits woven into American life—not through the lens of glamour, sociability and urban sophistication, but rather in terms of science, industry and commerce. The spirits industry's emphasis on enterprise and economic opportunity predicted profound changes at the heart of American culture that found full expression after WWII in the form of ascendant corporate culture. The essence and symbolic power of the modern corporation dominated the postwar global economy to which Bacardi increasingly belonged.[51] Under the leadership of José Mario "Pepín" Bosch, company president from 1944 to 1967, Bacardi operations were reorganized through the symbol of the corporate institution.[52] Bosch envisioned an iconic new corporate headquarters in Santiago de Cuba, a quintessential example of modern architecture, to symbolize the international and highly integrated corporate nature of Bacardi operations.

In the postwar era, the certainties of chemistry and international commerce drove business growth. "There is no secret in the manufacturing of rum," Bosch once noted. "The main thing is the scientific control of distillation and maturation."[53] The Bacardi president also took a view of the business increasingly less centered on Cuban identity, a hedge perhaps against political instability in Havana. Spurred by the globalization of rum production that Bosch helped mastermind, Bacardi deepened its roots in adopted lands, engaging local affairs as well as local architects for striking new plants in Puerto Rico and Mexico. Bosch shuttled ceaselessly around the Americas on *El Murciélago* (the bat), the Bacardi plane, as he directed the company's outward expansion.

Manifestations of Bacardi's emerging international profile were offered quarterly in the pages of *Bacardi Grafico*, the company's internal magazine. Designed by Bosch's cousin, the designer and illustrator Abril Lamarque, *Grafico* was published from 1956 up to the Cuban Revolution. The journal celebrated the company's numerous architectural exploits, connecting them with corporate principles and social values. It specifically used these principles and values to link Bacardi across its many lands, drawing its workers into a greater corporate family.

Cuba remained an important field of operations in the 1940s-50s. When Bosch sought to modernize Bacardi's well-established Santiago operations, he engaged Cuban modernist architects like Enrique Luis Varela, Ermina Odoardo-Ricardo Eguilior Arquitectos and SACMAG. In these projects, he indulged a passion for cleanness and naked function in architecture, but also for striking imagery and potent gestures. Varela, director of the journal *El Arquitecto* and an outspoken voice for monumentalizing Cuba's rise as a modern nation,[54] designed the distiller's new technical offices and laboratories in 1948. The austere industrial block had sky-signage that spelled "BACARDI" and an entrance that recalled a theater marquee. Odoardo, one of the earliest female architects in Cuba, and Eguilior designed an addition to Bacardi's Matadero Street plant that carefully inserted into the building's courtyard and integrated its eminent palm tree, *El Coco*. The façade was an open filagree of concrete columns and pre-tensioned concrete beams conceived to stabilize the failing walls of the now aging plant.[55] Playfully, this latticework placed *El Coco* in a "picture frame," and produced a tropicalist screen that threw shadows along the walls of the new addition.

Rumbera. Advertisement. Rafael Lillo Bonet, artist, 1949. Courtesy of The Bacardi Archive.

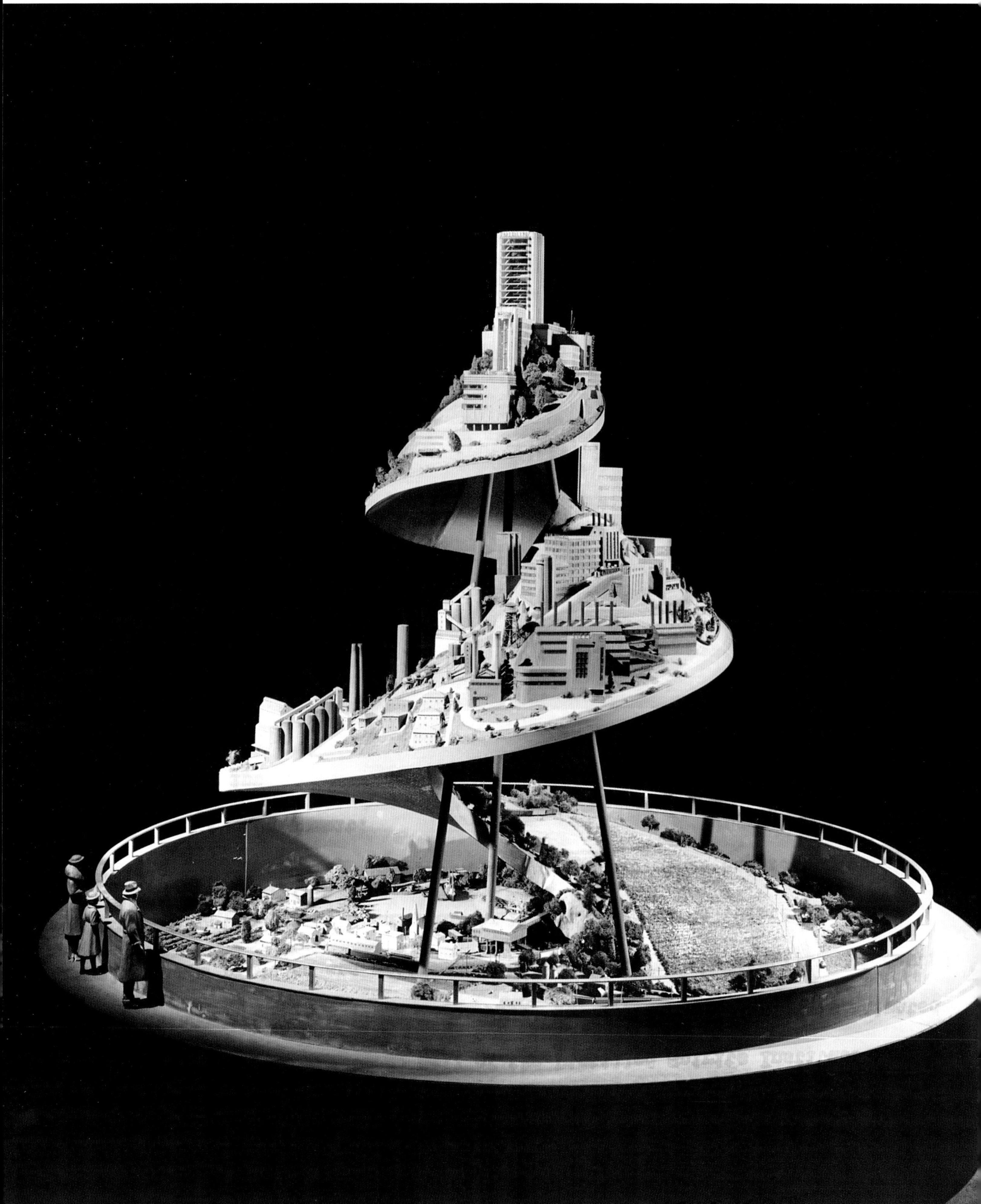

Saenz-Cancio-Martin (later SACMAG), a Cuban firm of engineers and architects, was at the heart of many postwar Bacardi projects. [56] SACMAG was singular in Cuba in promoting a corporate face similar to large American architectural firms; fluent in the language of business and modern architecture, the company combined architecture and engineering disciplines, and employed modern styles of project documentation and delivery.[57] Engineer Luis P. Saenz, a respected professor at the University of Havana, led the firm and forged a reputation for structural virtuosity. In 1957, the firm grew with the addition of Raúl Alvarez and Enrique Gutiérrez, young architects celebrated for their collaboration with Richard Neutra and Roberto Burle Marx on the Schultess Residence in Havana (1956). SACMAG's 1959 Bacardi warehouse on the Via Blanca in Havana notably comprised a corrugated concrete roof supported on V-shaped columns that spanned 100 feet of column-free space.

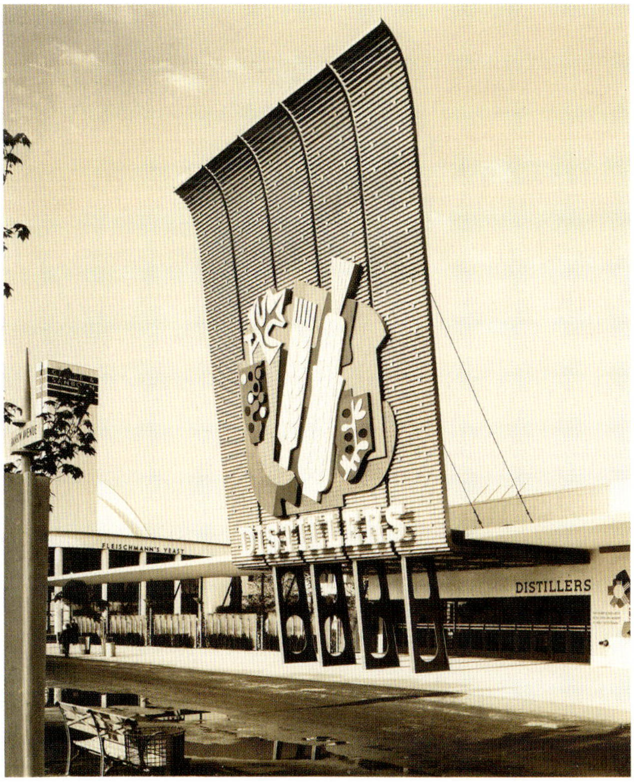

Left: Distilled Spirits Institute Pavilion, New York World's Fair. Model of the 35-foot tall theme spiral. Morris Sanders, architect and Ross Frankel, Inc. and Morris Lapidus, interior designer, 1939. Courtesy of New York Public Library, Manuscripts and Archives.

Right: Distilled Spirits Institute Pavilion, New York World's Fair. Marquee. Morris Sanders, architect and Ross Frankel, Inc. and Morris Lapidus, interior designer, 1939. Courtesy Wurts Brothers Photography Collection, Museum of the City of New York.

Starting in 1955, Bosch spread his patronage in another way, exploiting the cultural impact of Bacardi's new initiatives by commissioning prestigious international architects, whom he paired with SACMAG as architect of record. These included Philip Johnson, the former director and curator of Architecture and Design at New York's Museum of Modern Art, who designed Bosch's vacation home; the German émigré architect Ludwig Mies van der Rohe, who designed Bacardi's new headquarters in Santiago de Cuba and Mexico City; and the Spanish émigré Félix Candela Outeriño, who designed the new Bacardi distillery near Puebla and bottling plant in Mexico City.

International recognition came quickly for these conspicuous works, which captured the spirit of the age and provided some of its most alluring imagery. By June 1959, *Architectural Record*'s Jeanne Davern inquired about the surge of prominent designs: "I am curious to know what has produced Bacardi's sudden interest in architecture."[58] Bosch replied that the development of Bacardi's headquarters in Santiago "gave me the opportunity of looking into the work of many architects," adding, "I may want to mark my tenure of office with indelible marks that to my successors would create a definite necessity to work for the greater success of our enterprise."[59] Undeniably, the prominence of Mies and Candela lent credibility and legitimacy to Bosch's ambition, and publicity value to the company's projects. Mies was particularly successful at wielding the power of modern architecture and personality to attract global publicity.[60] Mies's authority was enhanced by his contemporary work, with Philip Johnson, for Joseph E. Seagram & Sons, the Canadian distiller whose new bronze-clad tower rising on Park Avenue in New York (1954–1958) had recast the company as a business frontrunner.

As it turned out, Johnson, Mies and Candela all developed ideas for flexible open spaces. Whether for a home, factory or administration building, there appeared the same imperative for column-free spatial sweep and amplitude. Of course, each work reflected the discrete and personal ideological positions of their architects; together they were a picturesque collage. Herein lies a fascinating paradox:

Bacardi engaged the ideological leaders of the age without precisely ascribing to any one ideology. Bosch was indeed a pragmatist, generally against the moralizing arguments of modern architecture, yet open to its idealized spaces, forms, and structures.

The unusual beach house designed by Johnson for Bosch in Varadero, a resort east of Havana, is one of the Bacardi president's least-known projects. It resembled a concrete birdcage, variously octagonal or twelve-sided, with slender columns that rose to a sculpted umbrella made of conical vaults.[61] Johnson here adapted the transparent house formula he had executed so well in New Canaan, Connecticut to a Caribbean climate. The enclosed ground floor of the home contained its bedrooms and service areas. From this plinth, a corkscrew stair emerged into an airy upper living space, nearly 60 feet across and 30 feet tall, beneath the birdcage structure's concrete firmament. Below the sculptural roof vaults, the walls of the open air living area were to have been a textile screen of brises-soleils, a tropicalist approach that insightfully echoed Cuba's traditional *persianas*.

Bosch may have come in contact with Johnson in 1956, while the latter was designing the Hotel Monaco, a never-built casino hotel planned for Havana's Malecón. As in that hotel project, Johnson revealed here his interest in the form-making possibilities of concrete, in particular the influence of formalist architects like Pier Luigi Nervi and Felix Candela, and his increasing distance from the parameters of the International Style that he earlier helped promote. [62] The home's unusual spatial conceit and geometric clarity sprung from its use of concrete in a classically inspired yet modern way.[63] The unbuilt home was certainly a "folly," but it highlighted Bosch's penchant for architectural drama that combined structure, form and expressive skin. [64]

It was only a small jump from this private folly to a larger novelty. By late 1956, Bosch engaged Mies van der Rohe, whose work had already helped define postwar architecture, to design Bacardi's new headquarters building in Santiago.[64] Like his colleagues Eero Saarinen, Eliot Noyes, Charles Eames, and Skidmore, Owings & Merrill, Mies had translated corporate building form into iconic terms. Bosch intended the new headquarters to design to provide just such an iconic, state-of-the-art corporate face for Bacardi in time to celebrate the company's upcoming centennial.

Even before it began working with Mies, Bacardi had identified the type of modern corporate structure it desired. In 1954, Saenz-Cancio-Martin's Georgina George developed the comprehensive program for an efficient and modern new office complex with touristic potential, gardens as an aide to productive working, and a suburban location with access to factories, housing, and major highways. [66] The arrangement adopted the postwar strategy of prominent North American corporations in leaving the city center for greener suburban pastures. Business leaders like General Motors and IBM used the modern architecture of a suburban campus to demonstrate modern planning, and communicate progressive ideas about corporate form.[67] These campuses captivated Americans by validating the confluence of corporate thinking, modern aesthetics and technology.[68] Bacardi acquired a prominent open site along the national highway that, while not pastoral at all, prioritized urban detachment, visibility, and mobility.[69]

Crear es la Palabra de Pase de Este Siglo (Creation is the Watchword of This Century). Advertisement, 1953. Courtesy of The Bacardi Archive.

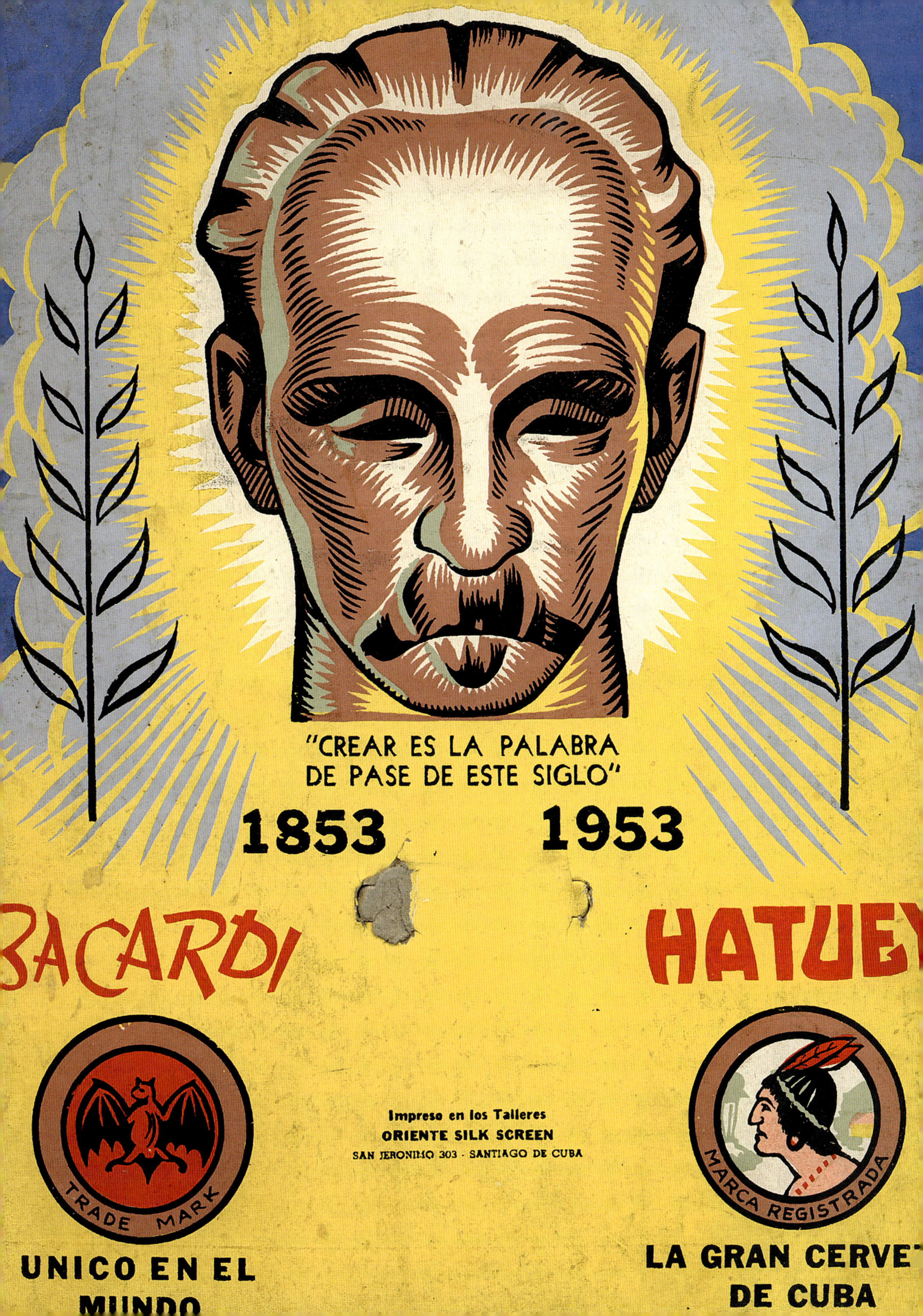

"CREAR ES LA PALABRA
DE PASE DE ESTE SIGLO"
1853
1953
ACARDI
HATUE
TRADE MARK
UNICO EN EL
MUNDO
Impreso en los Talleres
ORIENTE SILK SCREEN
SAN JERONIMO 303 - SANTIAGO DE CUBA
MARCA REGISTRADA
LA GRAN CERVE
DE CUBA

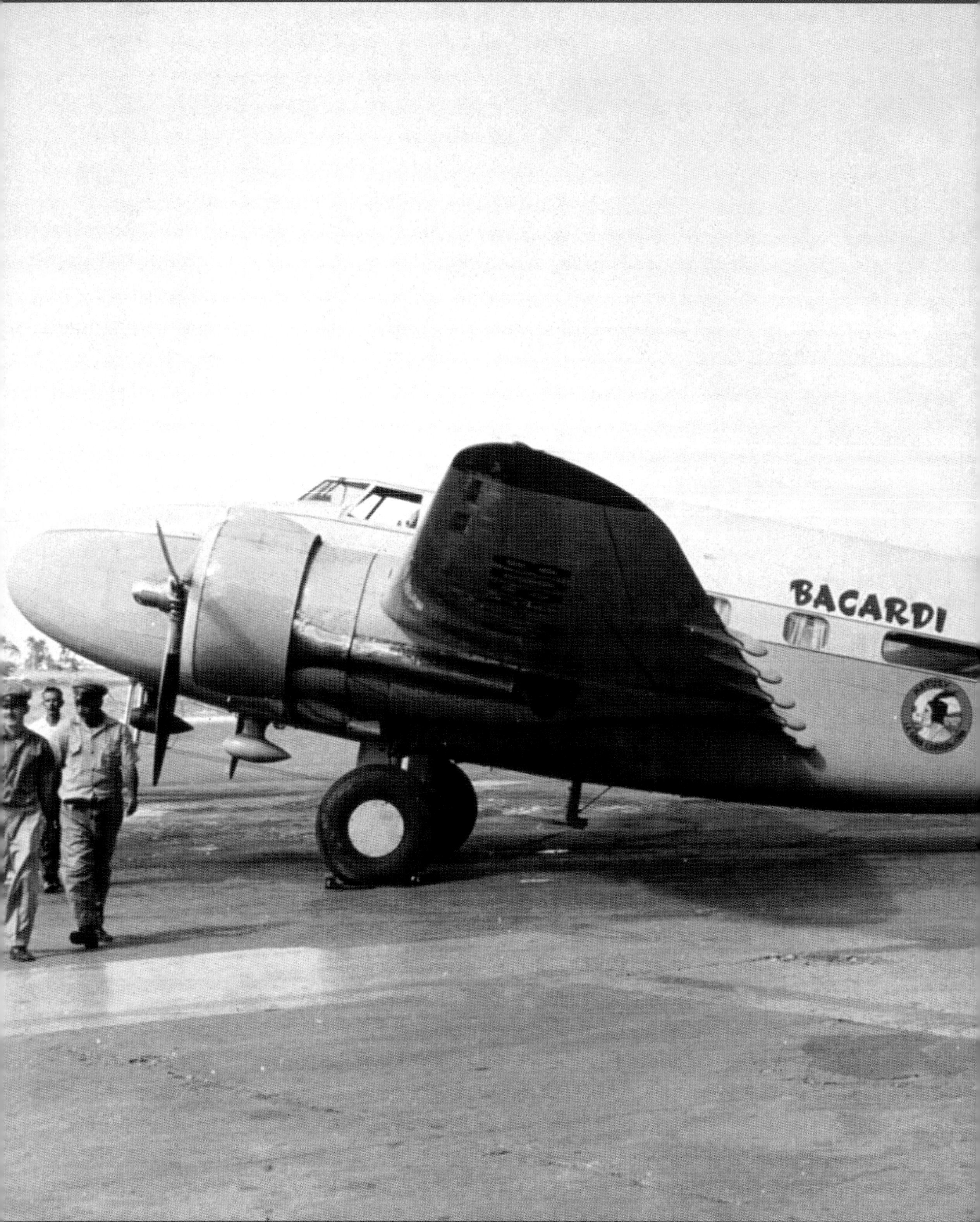
BACARDI

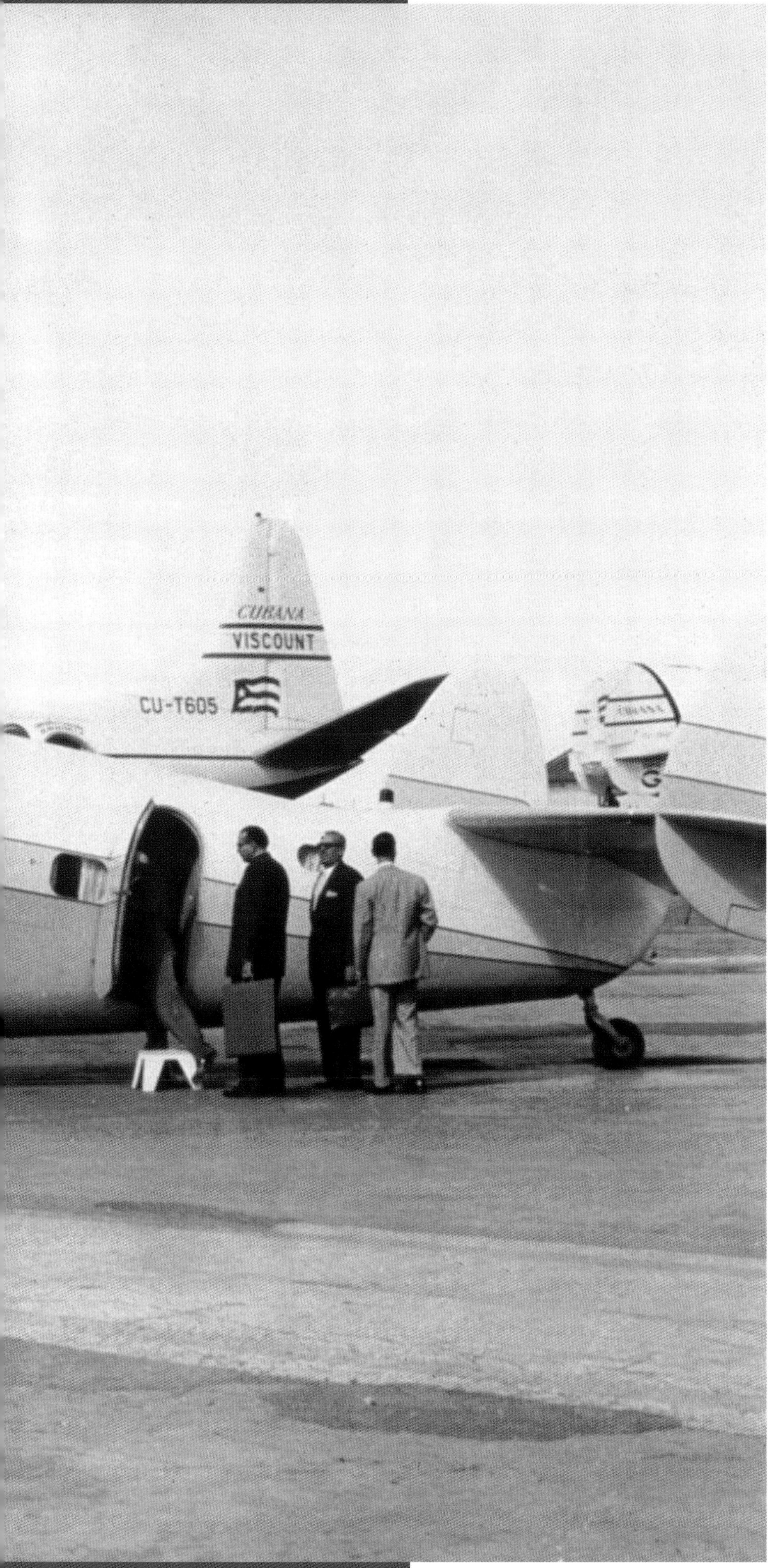

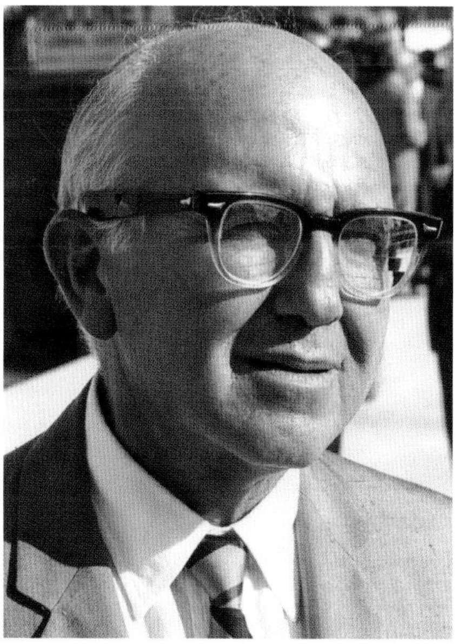

Left: El Murciélago (The Bat), Bacardi airplane, 1954. Courtesy of Bacardi & Company Limited.

Above: José "Pepin" Bosch. Undated portrait. Courtesy of The Bacardi Archive.

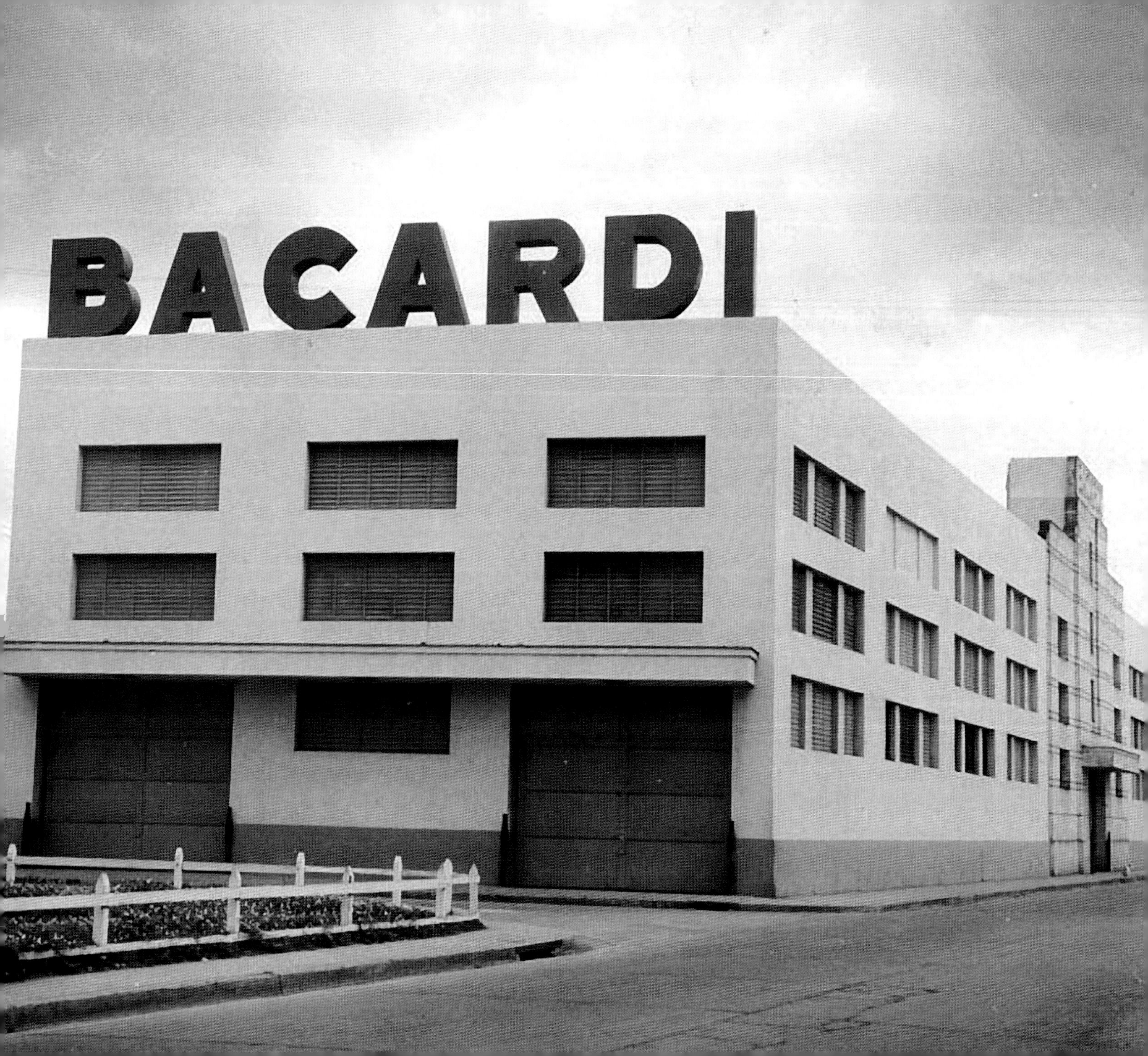
BACARDI

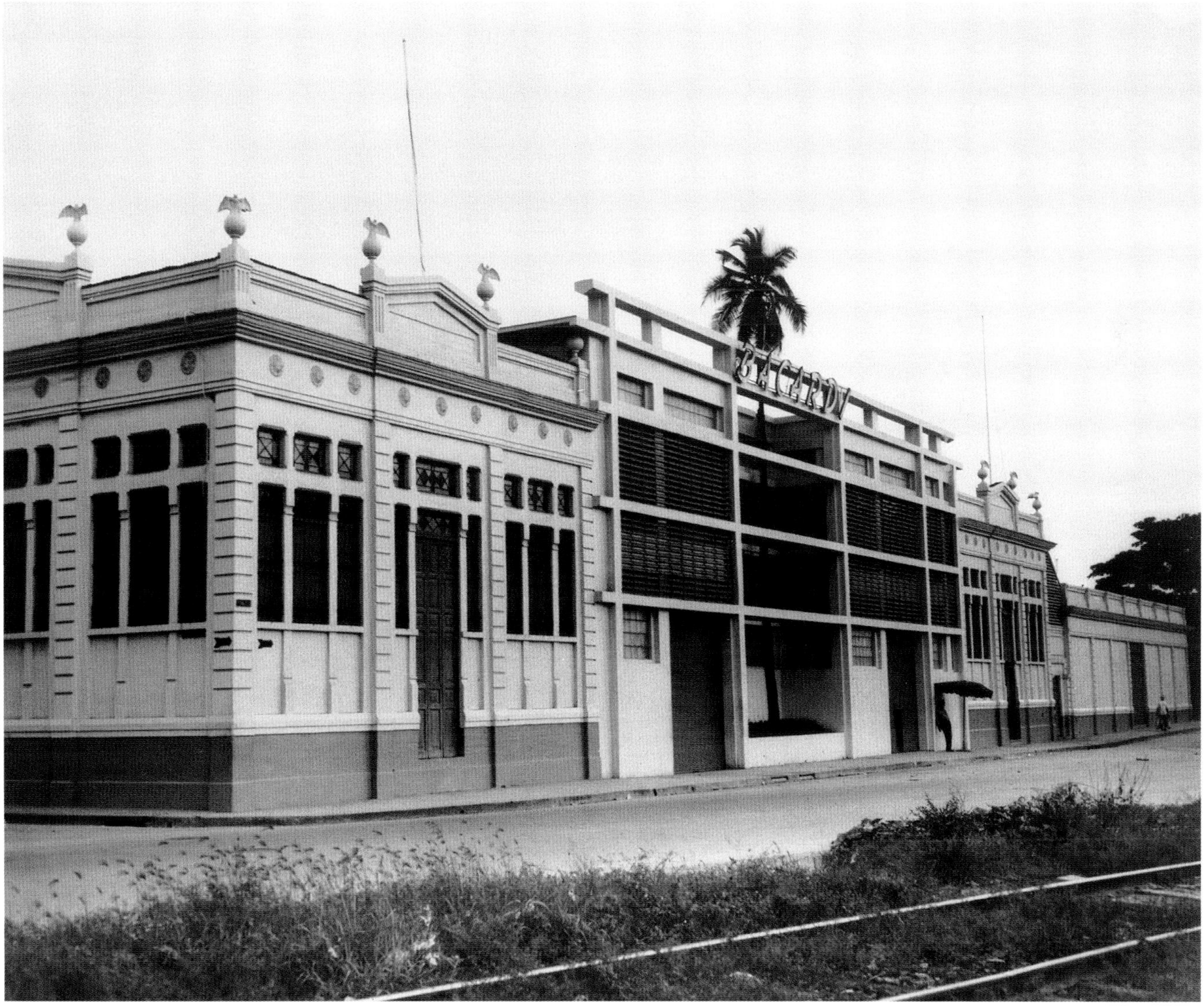

Left: Ron Bacardi Blending Building, including laboratories and technical offices, Santiago de Cuba.
Enrique Luis Varela, architect, 1940s. Courtesy of The Bacardi Archive.

Above: Addition to the Ron Bacardi plant on Matadero Street, preserving *El Coco*, Santiago de Cuba.
View from railroad. Ermina Odoardo-Ricardo Eguilior Arquitectos, 1950s.
Courtesy of The Bacardi Heritage Foundation.

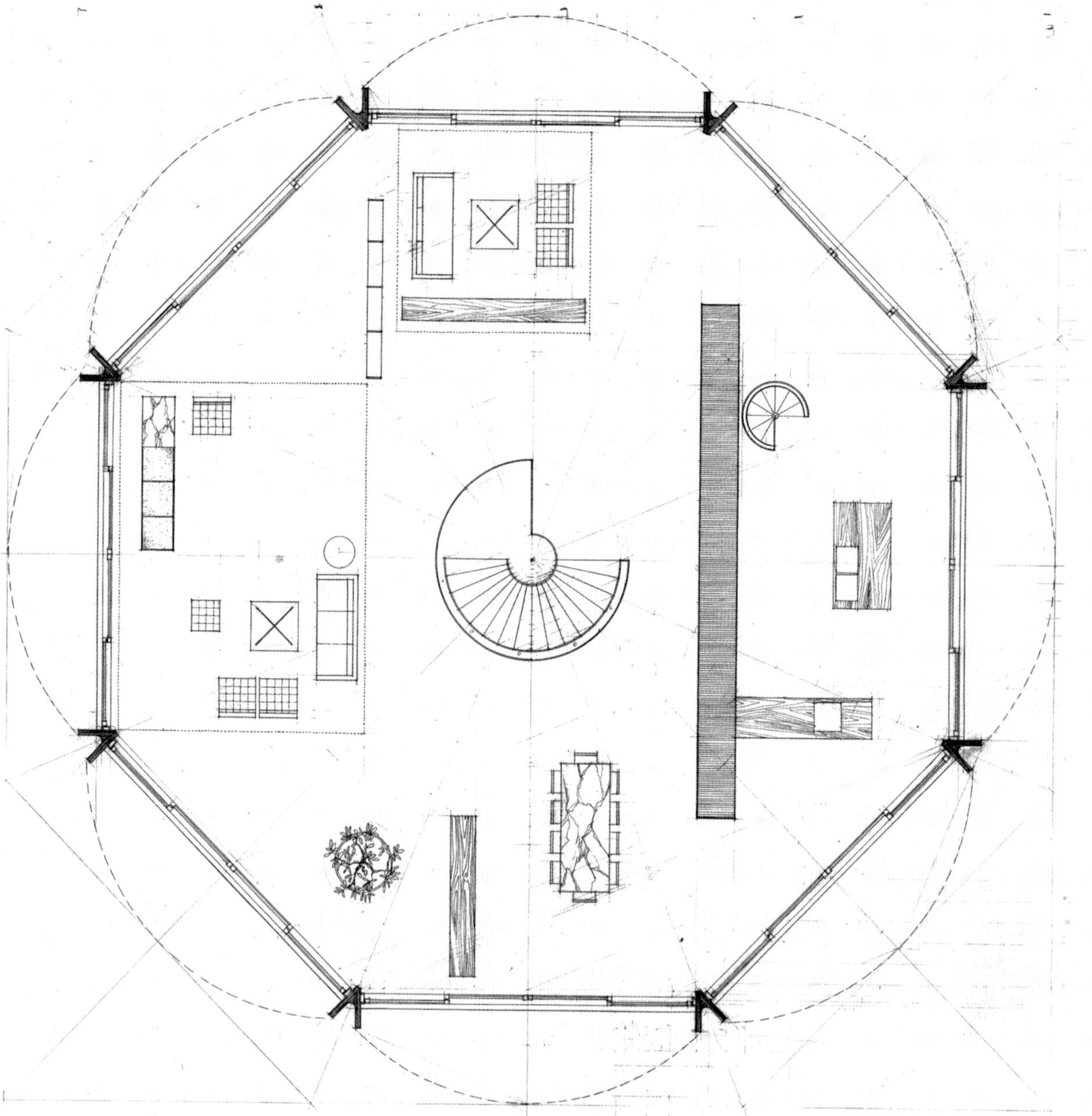

BOSCH HOUSE

PHILIP JOHNSON ARCHITECT

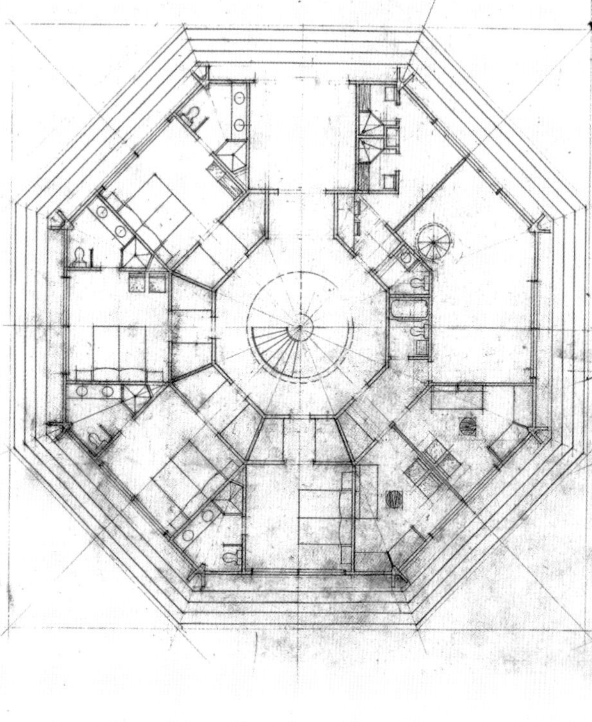

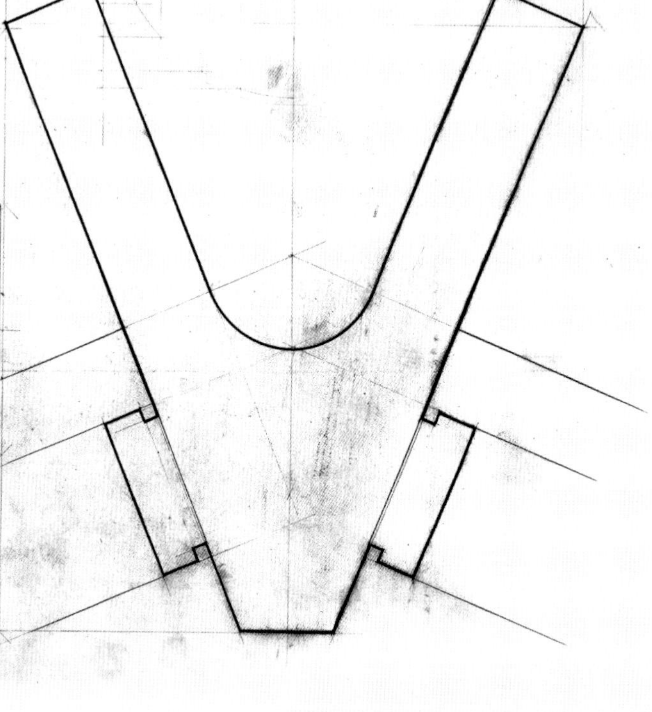

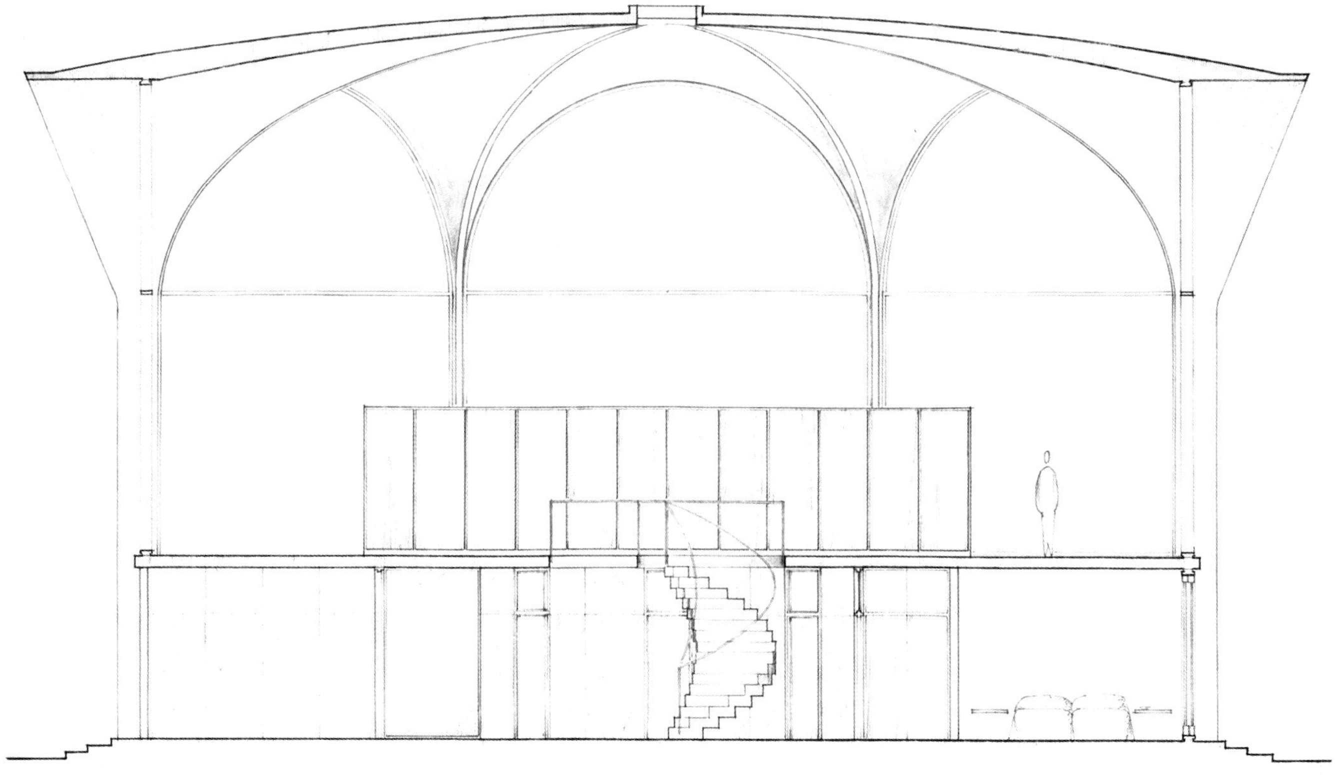

Left: Beach House for José "Pepin" Bosch, Varadero, Cuba. Floor plans and column detail. Philip Johnson, architect with Saenz-Cancio-Martin, engineers, 1956-57 (unbuilt). Drawings and Archives, Avery Architectural and Fine Arts Library, Columbia University.

Right: Beach House for José "Pepin" Bosch, Varadero, Cuba. Section. Philip Johnson, architect with Saenz-Cancio-Martin, engineers, 1956-57 (unbuilt). Drawings and Archives, Avery Architectural and Fine Arts Library, Columbia University.

Overleaf: Beach House for José "Pepin" Bosch, Varadero, Cuba. Model. Philip Johnson, architect, with Saenz-Cancio-Martin, engineers, 1956-57 (unbuilt). Photograph by Louis Checkman, The Getty Research Institute, Los Angeles.

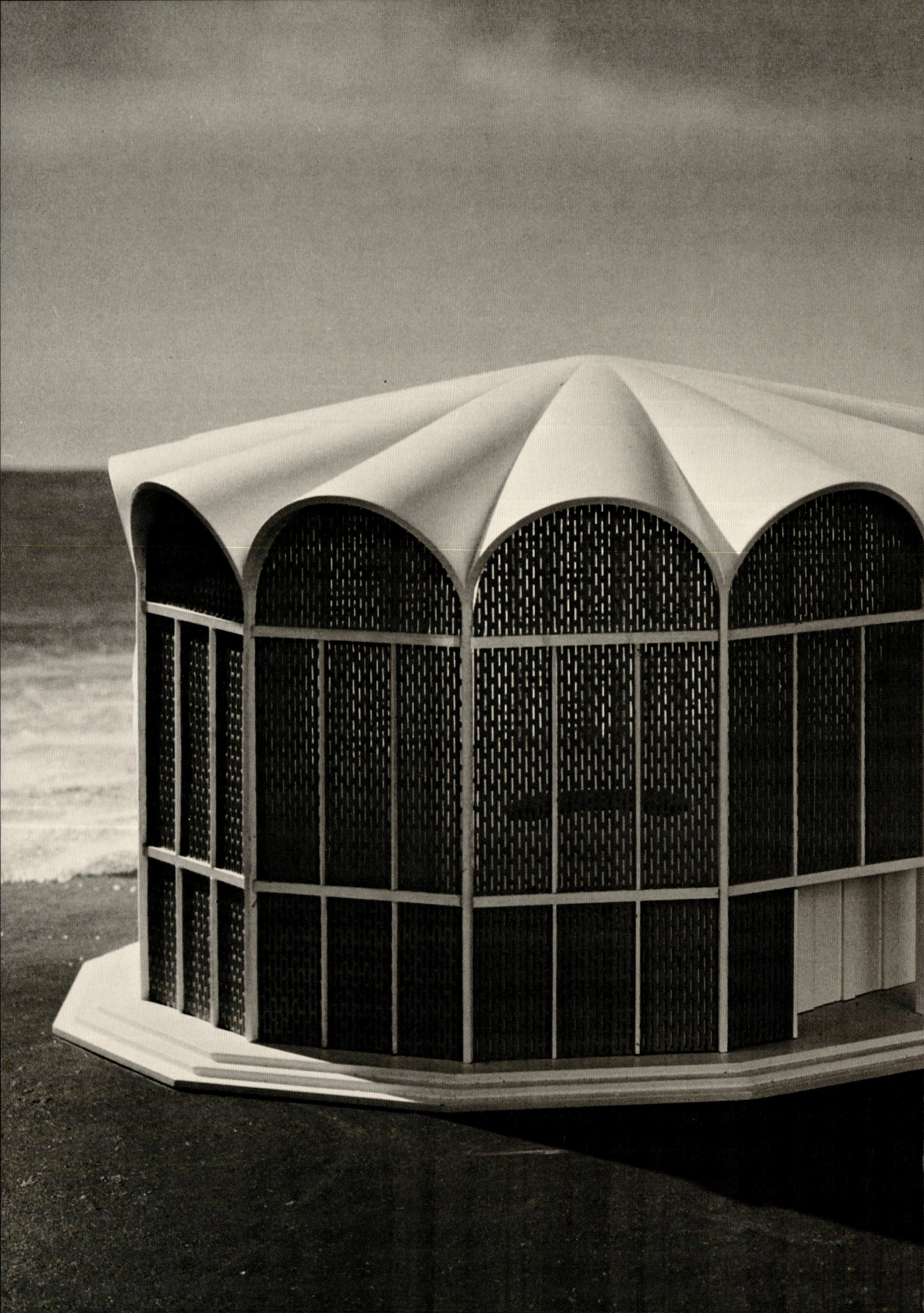

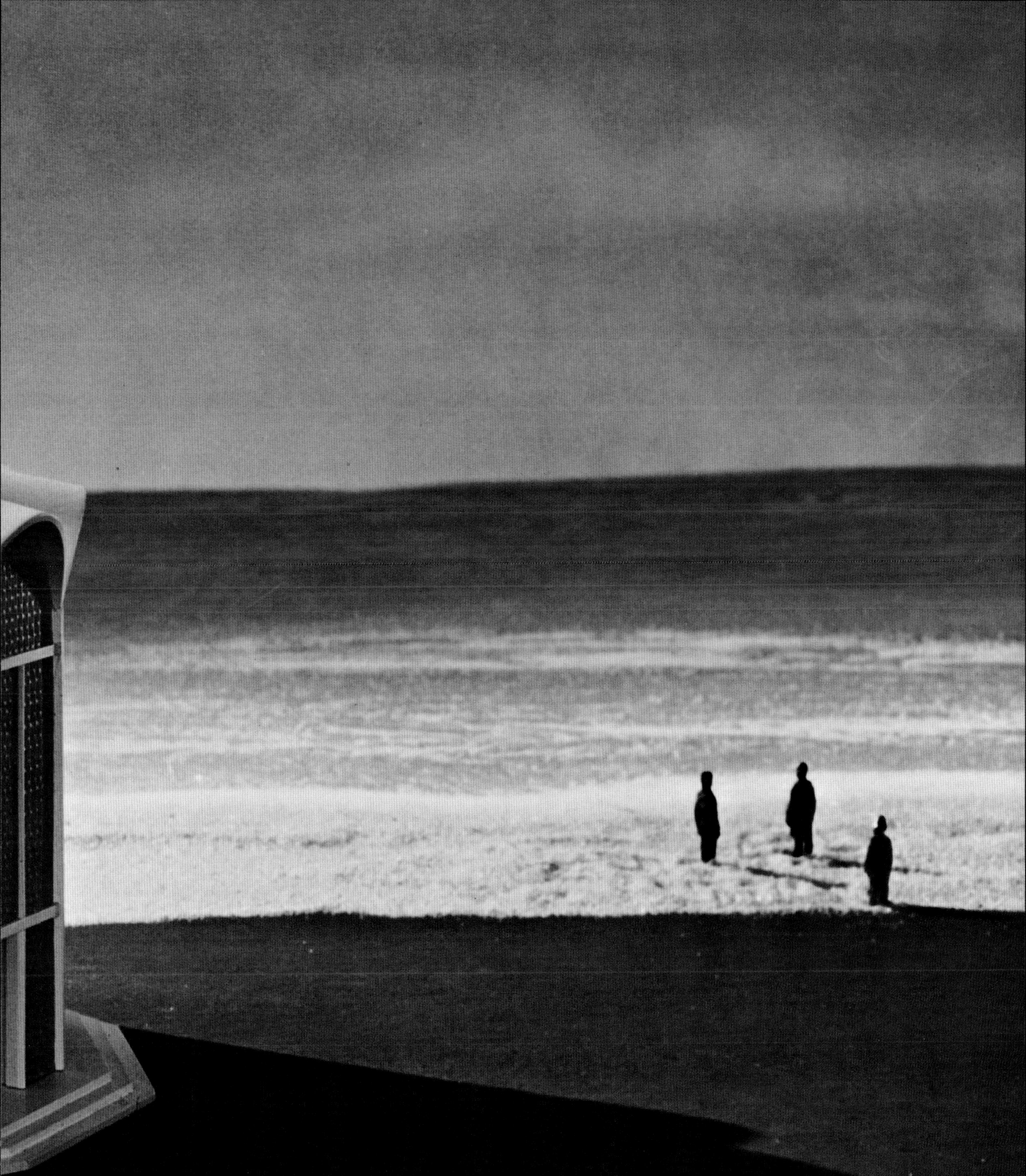

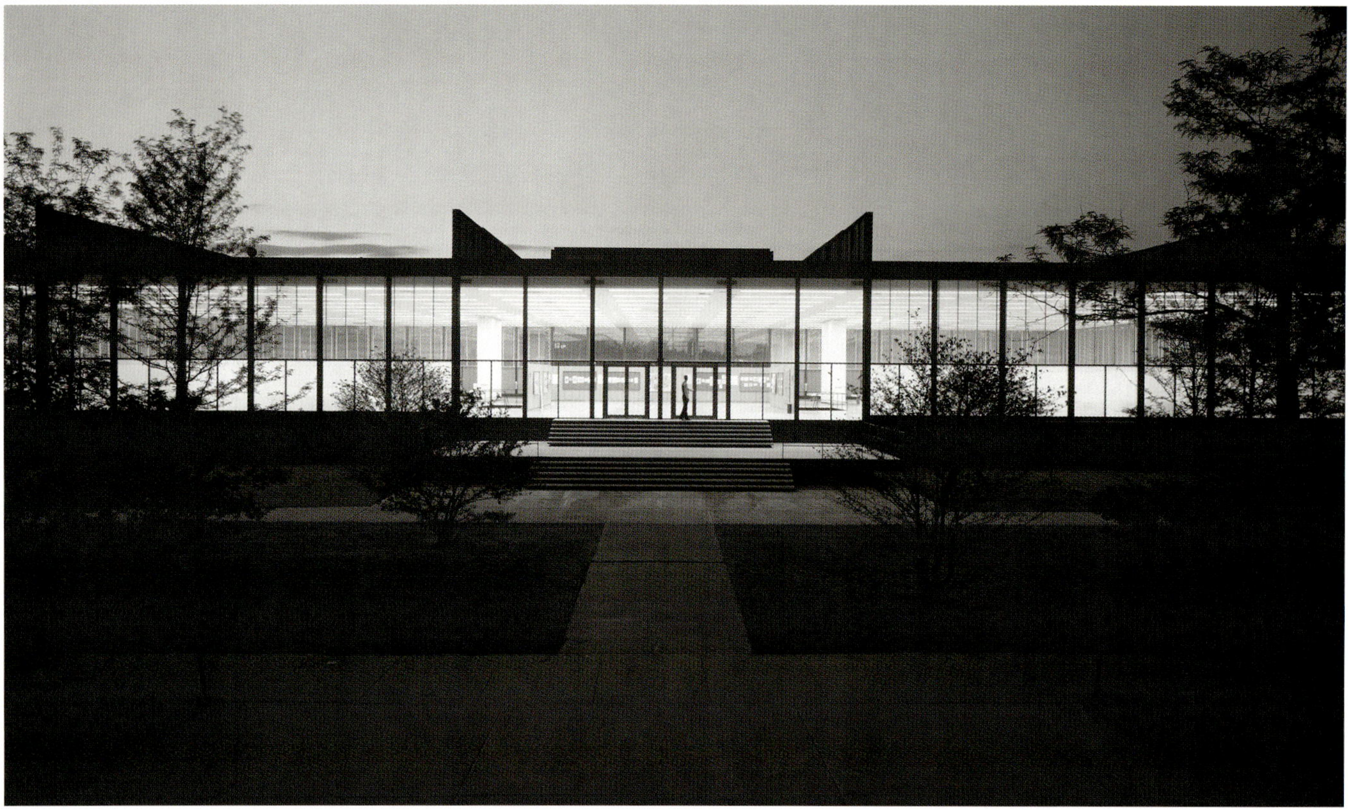

Mies designed a glass and concrete pavilion in the guise of a modern corporate temple for Bacardi. The physiognomy of this temple emphasized power, precision, transparency and order, corporate principles that Bosch and Bacardi wished to transmit to a global audience. The first sketches, drawn by Mies and Project Architect Gene Summers in Havana, offered the seed of the idea: a single square roof plate, five-foot deep, supported on eight perimeter columns and set atop a broad plinth. The service spaces were to be concealed in the plinth, providing the open space on top with maximum clarity. As a response to the tropical climate, the structure would be constructed of concrete and its glass enclosure set deeply inside the projecting roof.

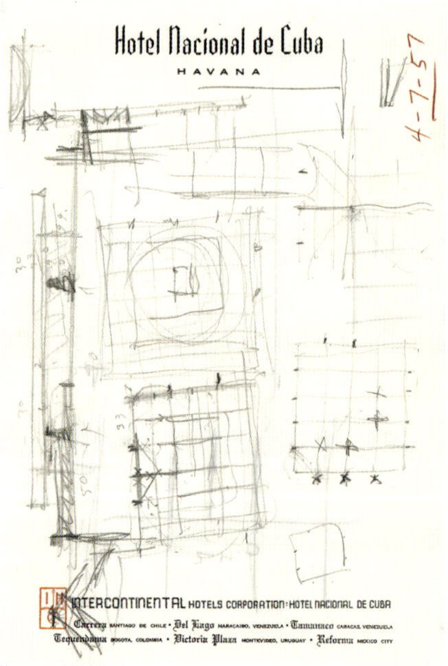

The clarity of the design derived partly from its reductive interpretation of Bosch's primary directive to Mies, to create a space without enclosures.[70] Mies used the singular, column-free volume beneath the roof to advance the concept of "universal space"—open rooms that were inherently flexible and adaptable.[71] The 20-foot high interior space was not entirely open, however; it was subdivided by low walls, a stair, and by the building's mechanical core. The dynamic planning of these interior elements floating in open space hewed to the compositional pattern Mies had cultivated since at least the Barcelona Pavilion in 1928. The character of this space was captured in two remarkable images produced by Mies's office. The first, an iconic and widely published perspective view, depicted the building's structural concept – a square roof plate supported on eight perimeter columns. The second, a photo-collage, assembled the transparency of the open office space, the marble and wood textures of the floating walls, the sea, and mountains, into vivid juxtapositions.[72]

The building is particularly notable for its structural artistry, developed in conjunction with SACMAG's Saenz, which allowed each component of the building, plinth, columns, roof and walls, to be understood separately and in terms of their construction. The single roof plane was particularly audacious: a two-way lattice of

Top: Crown Hall, Illinois Institute of Technology, Chicago. Ludwig Mies van der Rohe, architect, 1956. Photograph by Hedrich Blessing. Courtesy of Chicago History Museum.

Above: Ron Bacardí y Compañia, S.A. Administration Building, Santiago de Cuba. Sketch sections and plans by Gene Summers. Ludwig Mies van der Rohe, 1957 (unbuilt). © 2015 Artists Rights Society (ARS), New York / VG Bild-Kunst, Bonn.

Right: Ron Bacardí y Compañia, S.A. Administration Building, Santiago de Cuba. Model. Ludwig Mies van der Rohe, architect, 1957 (unbuilt). Photograph by Hedrich Blessing. Courtesy of the Chicago History Museum.

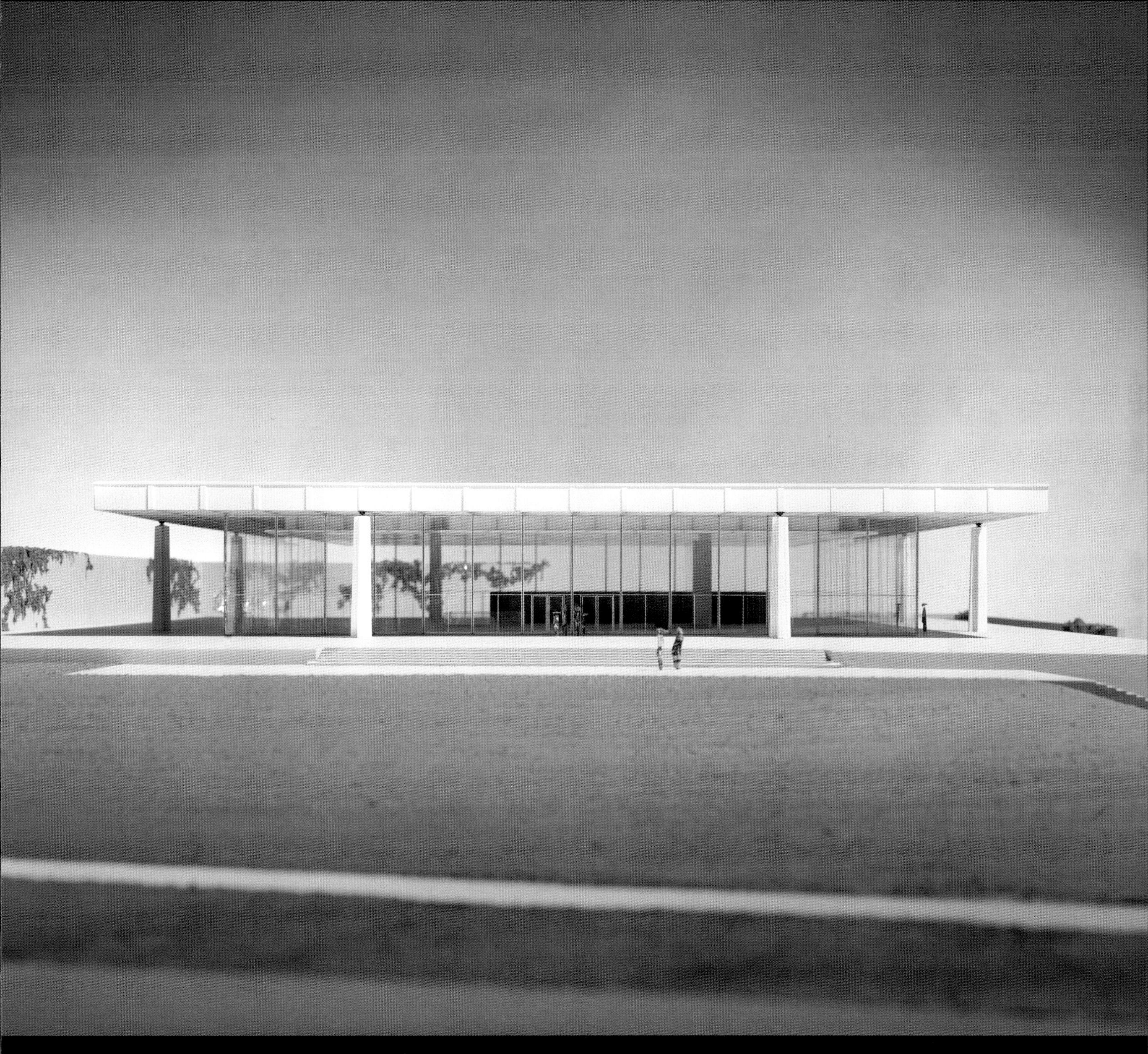

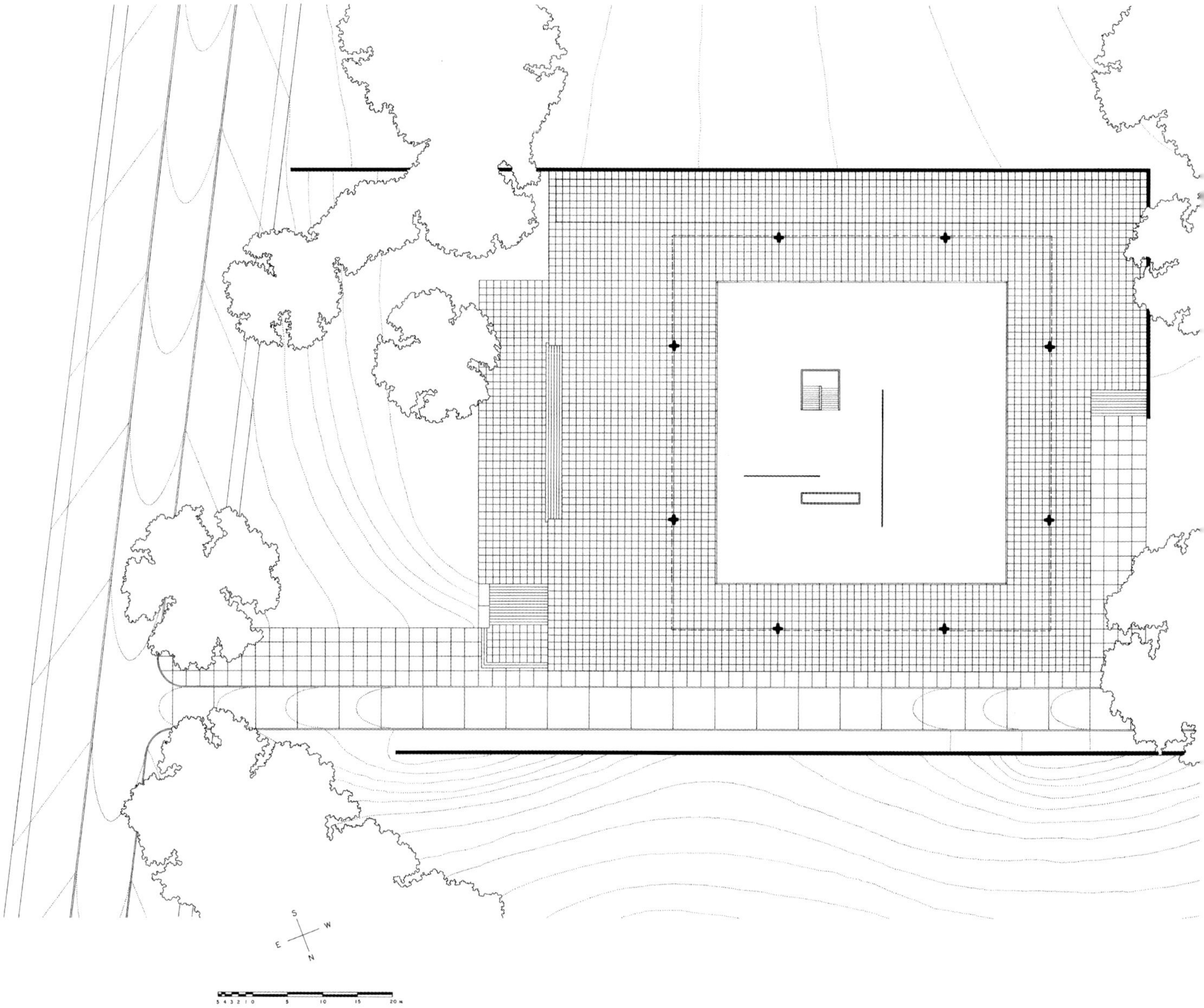

Above: Ron Bacardí y Compañia, S.A. Administration Building, Santiago de Cuba. Site Plan. Ludwig Mies van der Rohe, architect, 1957 (unbuilt). © 2015 Artists Rights Society (ARS), New York / VG Bild-Kunst, Bonn.

Right: Ron Bacardí y Compañia, S.A. Administration Building, Santiago de Cuba. Section. Ludwig Mies van der Rohe, architect, 1957 (unbuilt). © 2015 Artists Rights Society (ARS), New York / VG Bild-Kunst, Bonn.

tapered post-tensioned concrete beams spanning almost 180 feet in both directions. The frank exposition of structure, combined with the roof's primal evocation of shelter and the complete independence of the glass skin, made the Bacardi building a leading case study of modern building tectonics.[73]

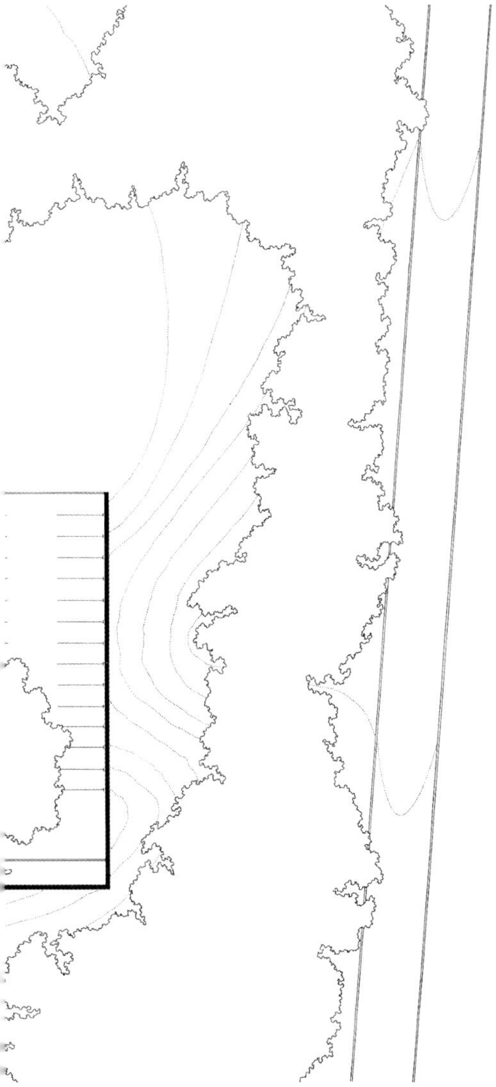

Cast in concrete to precise and monumental effect, the power of the Bacardi project rested partly in sober classical sensibilities. Like the nearby Museo Emilio Bacardi, it sat on a tall plinth, accessed by broad steps that augmented its civic presence. Atop the plinth, brick walls and a reflecting pool shaped a precinct that curator James Speyer has likened to a "miniature acropolis."[74] Mies envisioned the building to be painted white, not to express machine age sensibilities but rather a classical unity. Indeed, Mies's classicism was one translated to modern values, of proportions, of material integrity.[75] The translation was specifically evident in the cruciform, tapering profile of the concrete columns, which suggested the classical orders in their fluting and entasis; even the structural pin linking column and roof plate can be understood as a column capital. Similarly, the concrete roof plate seemed a proper entablature, decorated by classical "metopes" that were in fact precast concrete caps covering the terminations of the post-tensioning rods. The architects even discussed the incorporation of a slight curve, or camber, in both roof and floor to compensate for visual effects, a technique used in the construction of Greek temples.[76] The Bacardi headquarters' dual character—modern and classical—would have a strong influence on later architects, making the building one of Mies's most influential building types, and a virtual trope of modern architecture.

Mies's Santiago opus was never built (in Santiago, anyway). Friction between Bacardi and the regime of president Fulgencio Batista, and later the Cuban Revolution, doomed the proposal.[77] By 1960, the Bacardi enterprise was exiled from Cuba. Nonetheless, the Bacardi commission had advanced a vital new type in Mies's work. The architect reiterated its fundamental diagram for the (unbuilt) Schafer Art Museum in Schweinfurt, Germany, 1960–1963, and then at the Neue Nationalgalerie (New National Gallery) in Berlin, completed in 1967. Both projects adopted the building's spatial and structural diagram, albeit using steel frames more appropriate in Germany. Equally, the Mies design had also advanced an important new model for Bacardi, which in 1972 re-appropriated its form at both the Bacardi International Limited Building in Hamilton, Bermuda, and the proposed administrative building for the company's Puerto Rican operations.[78]

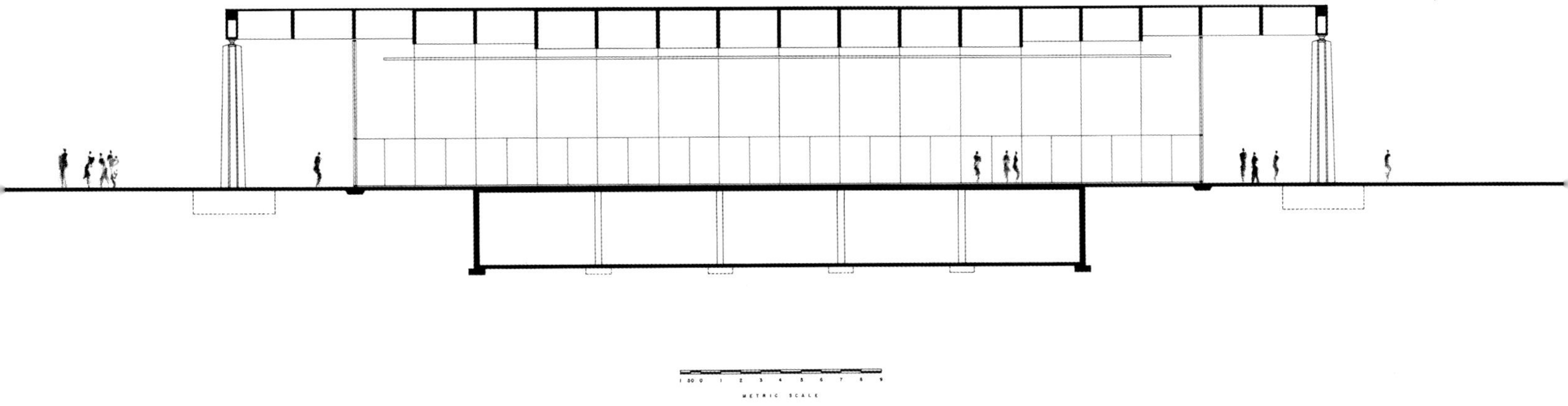

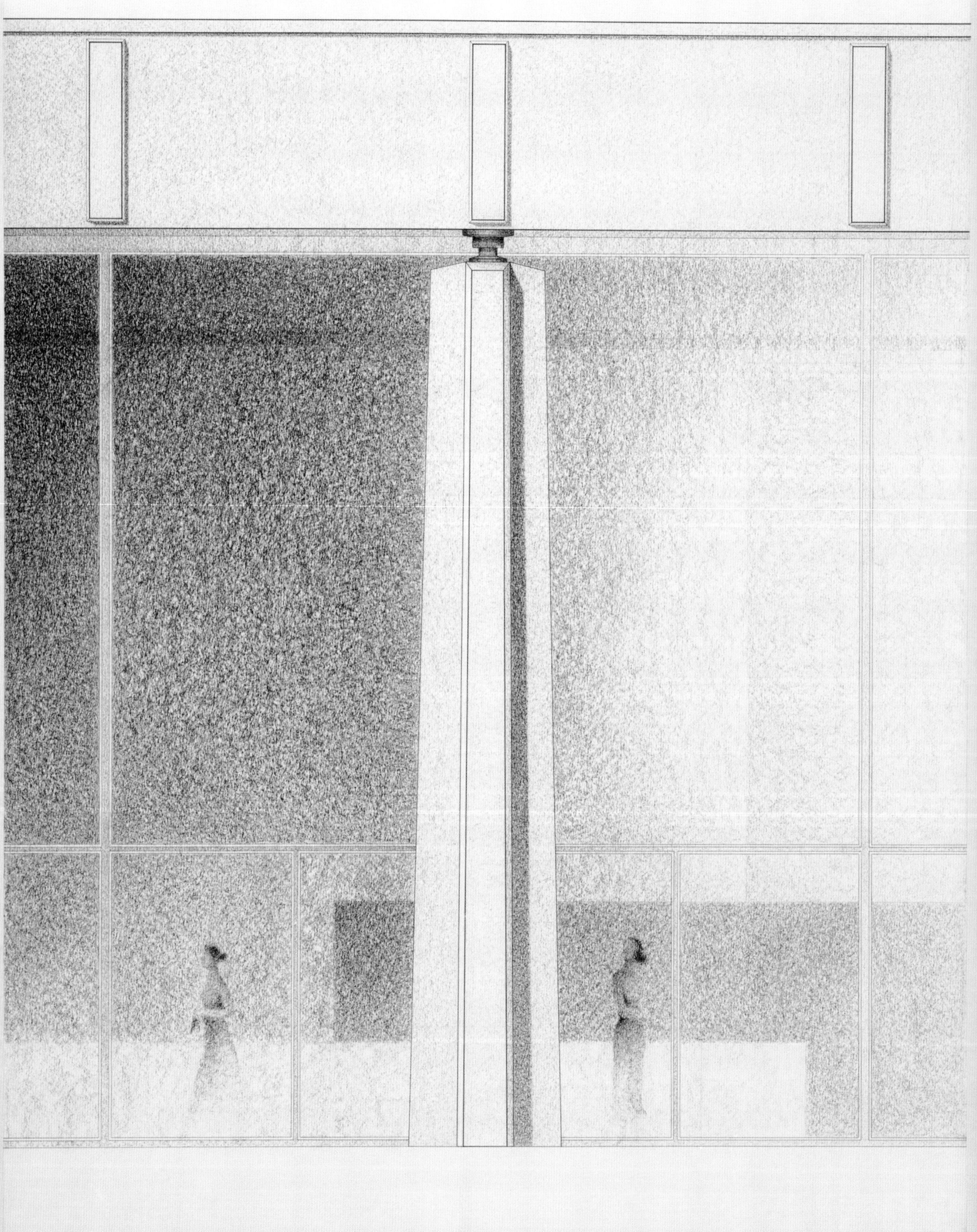

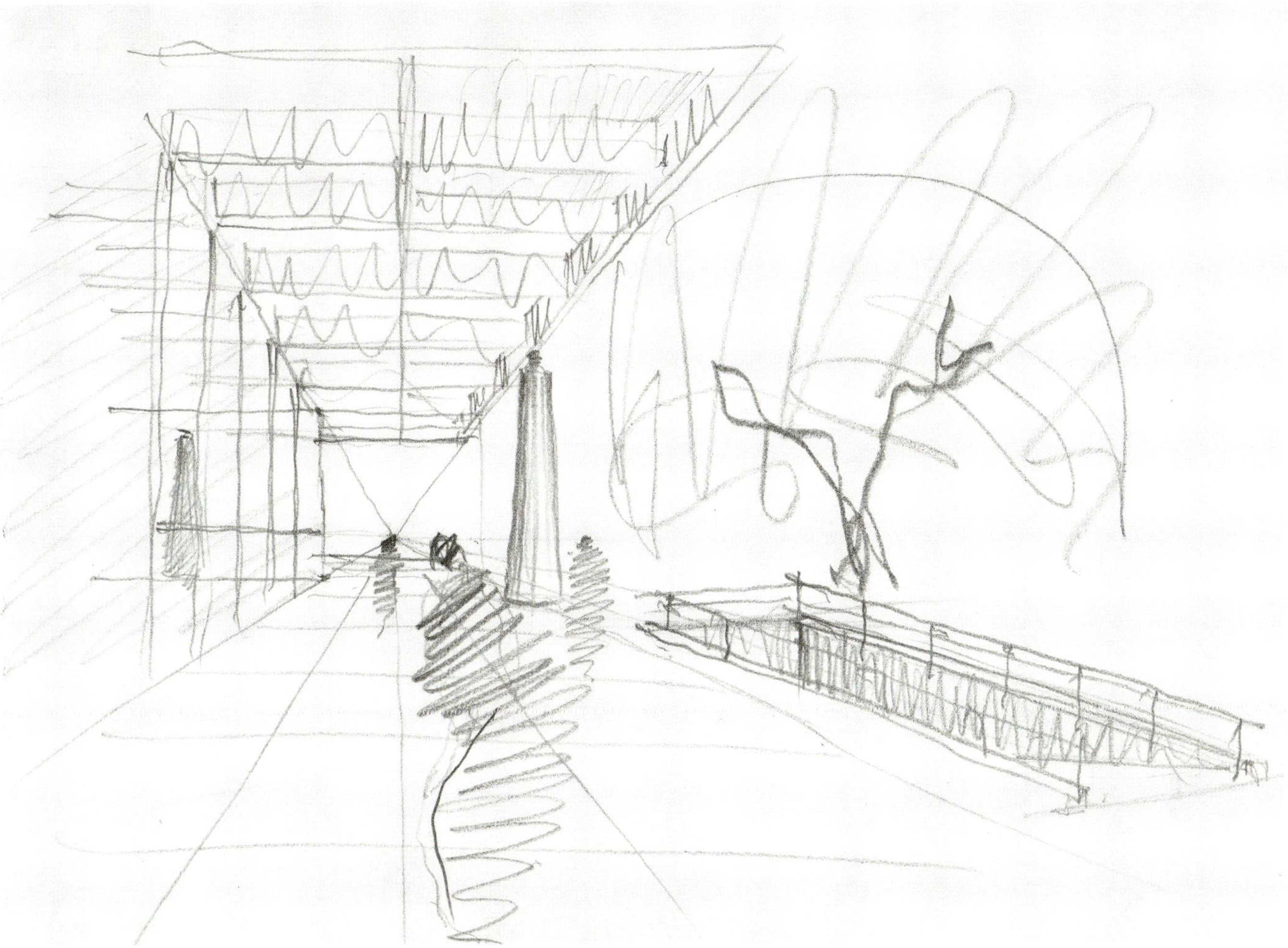

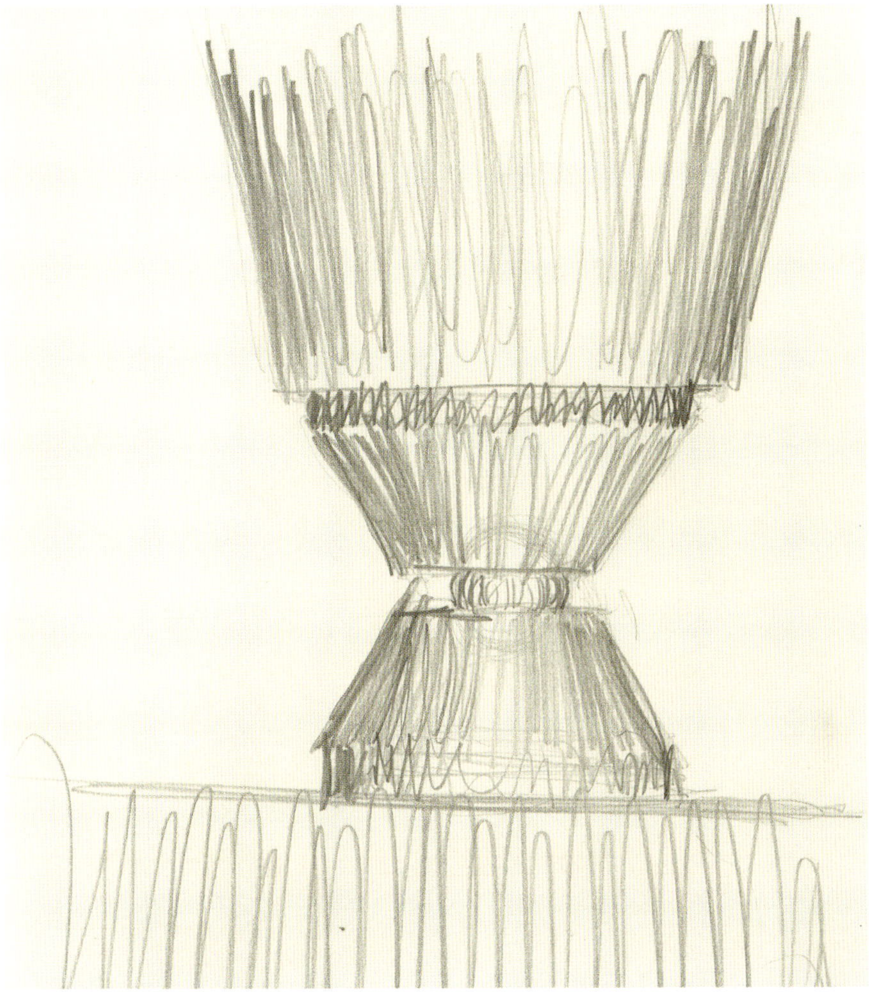

Far Left: Ron Bacardí y Compañia, S.A. Administration Building, Santiago de Cuba. Hand-drawn elevation. Ludwig Mies van der Rohe, architect, 1957 (unbuilt). © 2015 Artists Rights Society (ARS), New York / VG Bild-Kunst, Bonn.

Above: Ron Bacardí y Compañia, S.A. Administration Building, Santiago de Cuba. Hand-drawn perspective sketch showing conical column and pin connection to gridded roof plate. Ludwig Mies van der Rohe, architect, 1957 (unbuilt). © 2015 Artists Rights Society (ARS), New York / VG Bild-Kunst, Bonn.

Bellow: Ron Bacardí y Compañia, S.A. Administration Building, Santiago de Cuba. Hand-drawn detail of column. Ludwig Mies van Rohe, architect, 1957(unbuilt). © 2015 Artists Rights Society (ARS), New York / VG Bild-Kunst, Bonn.

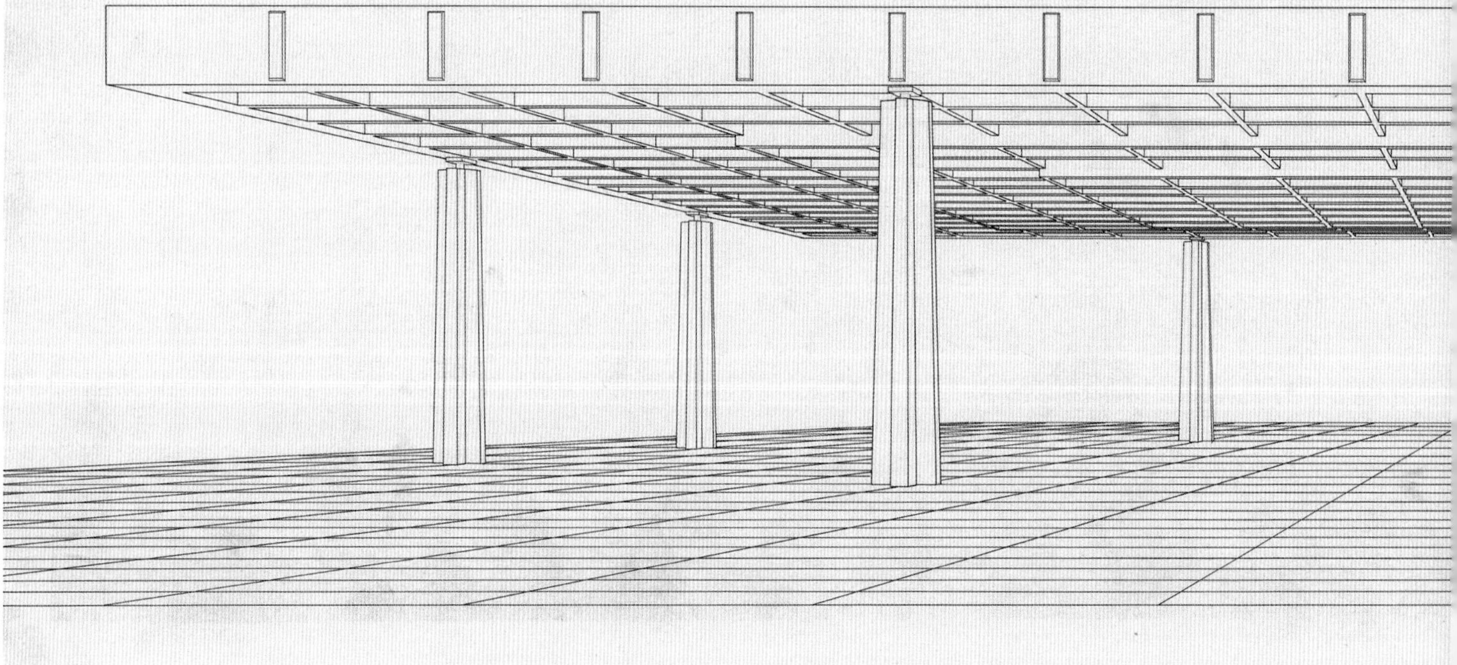

Ron Bacardi y Compañía, S.A. Administration Building, Santiago de Cuba. Hand-drawn perspective showing columns and roof plate.
Mies van der Rohe, architect, 1957 (unbuilt). © 2015 Artists Rights Society (ARS), New York / VG Bild-Kunst, Bonn.

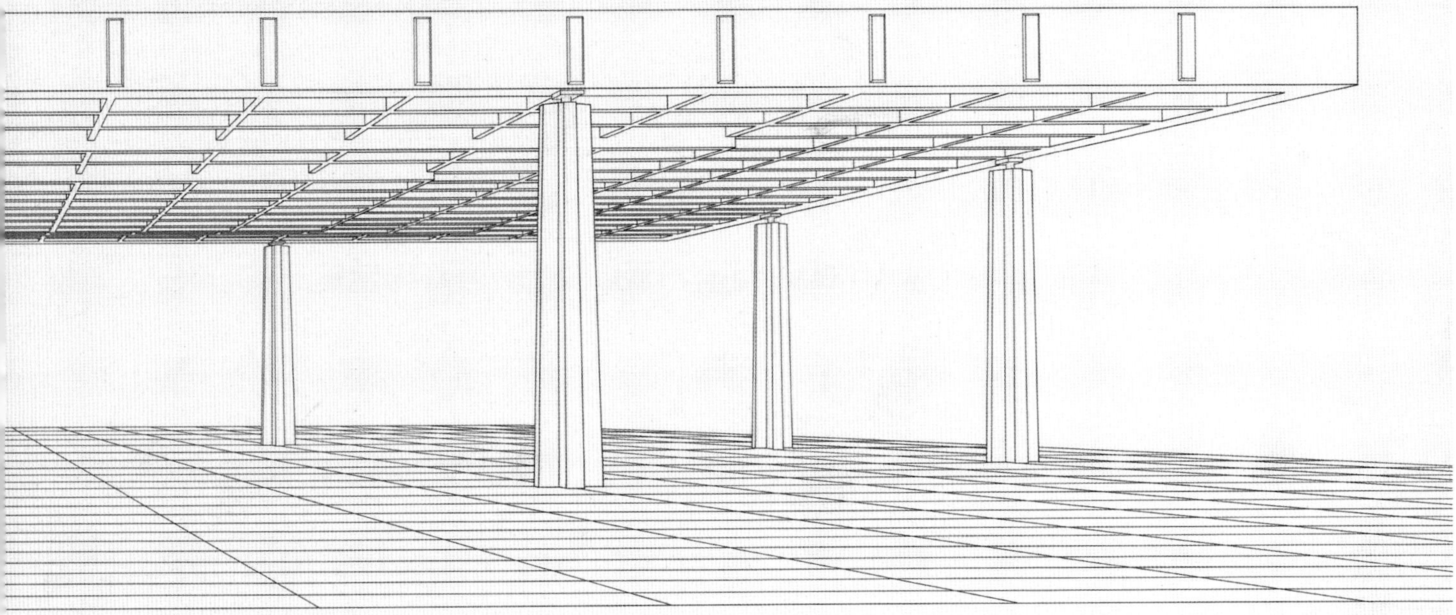

77

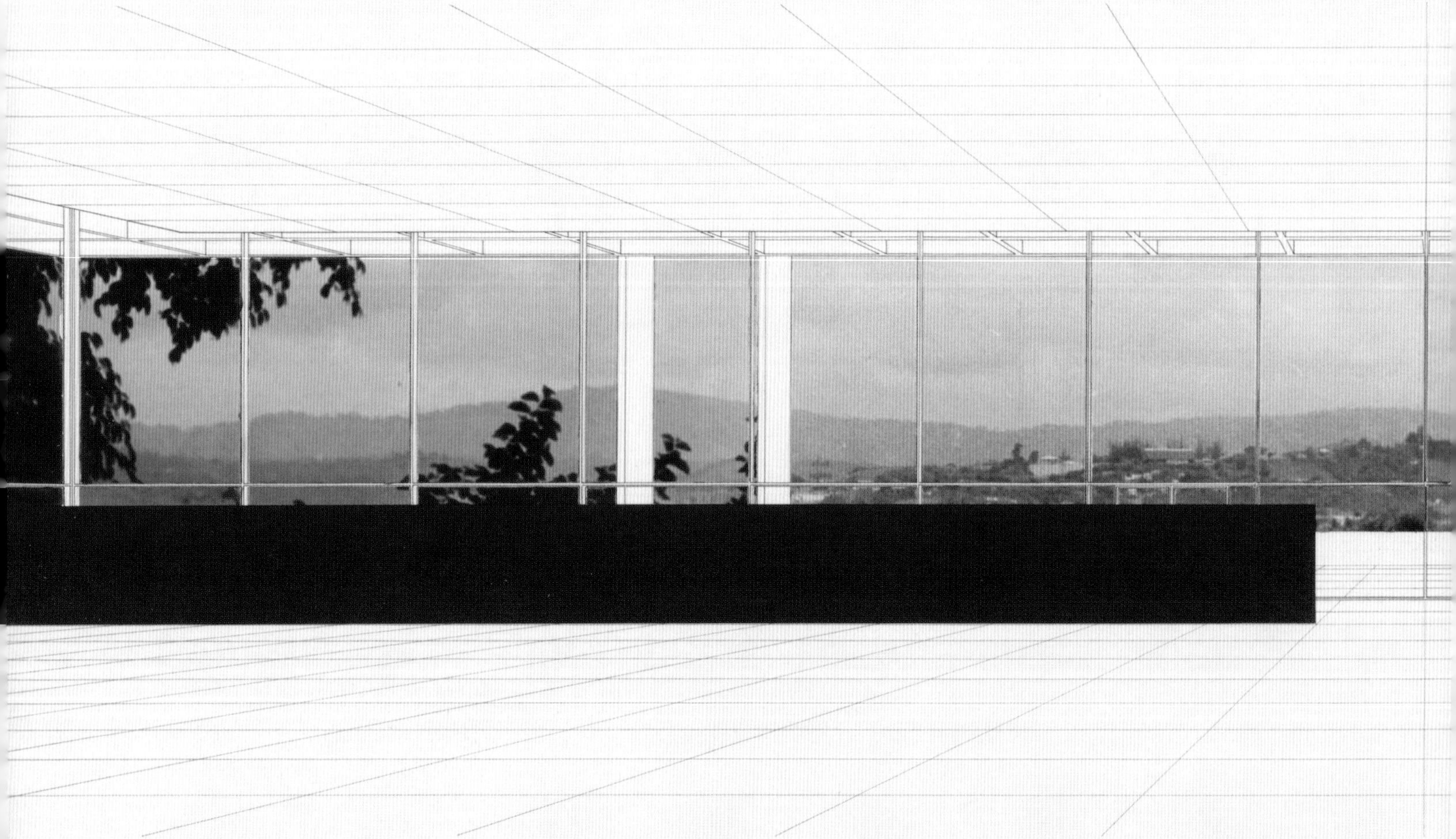

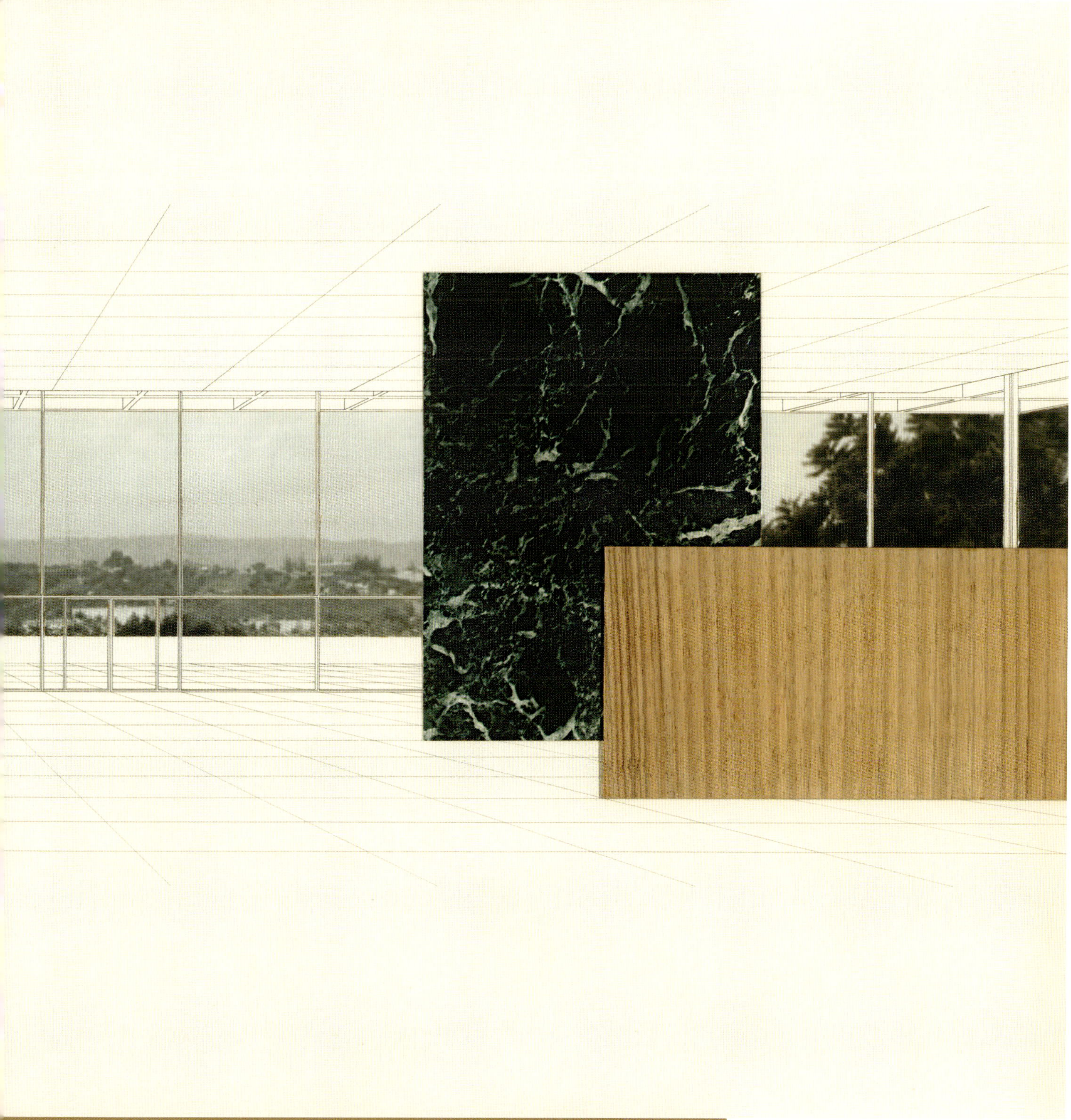

Ron Bacardí y Compañia, S.A. Administration Building, Santiago de Cuba. Multimedia collage showing interior. Ludwig Mies van der Rohe, 1957 (unbuilt). © 2015 Artists Rights Society (ARS), New York / VG Bild-Kunst, Bonn.

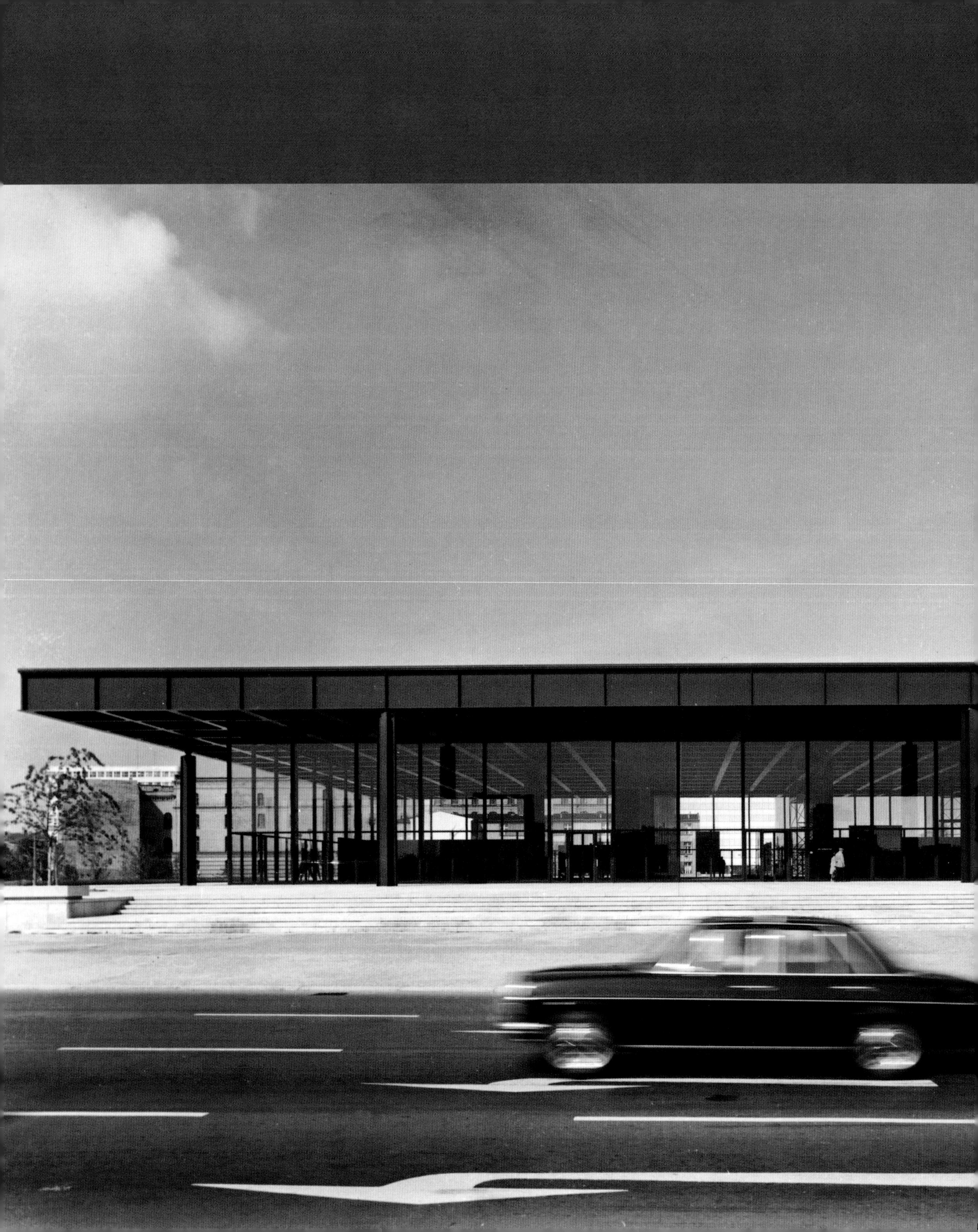

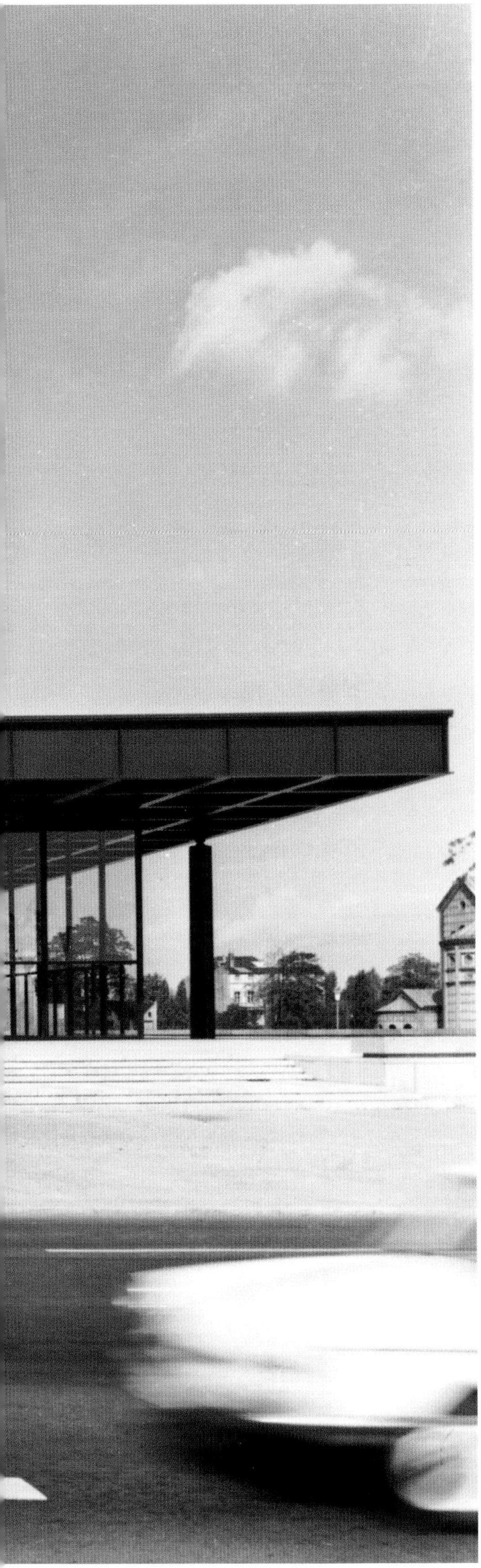

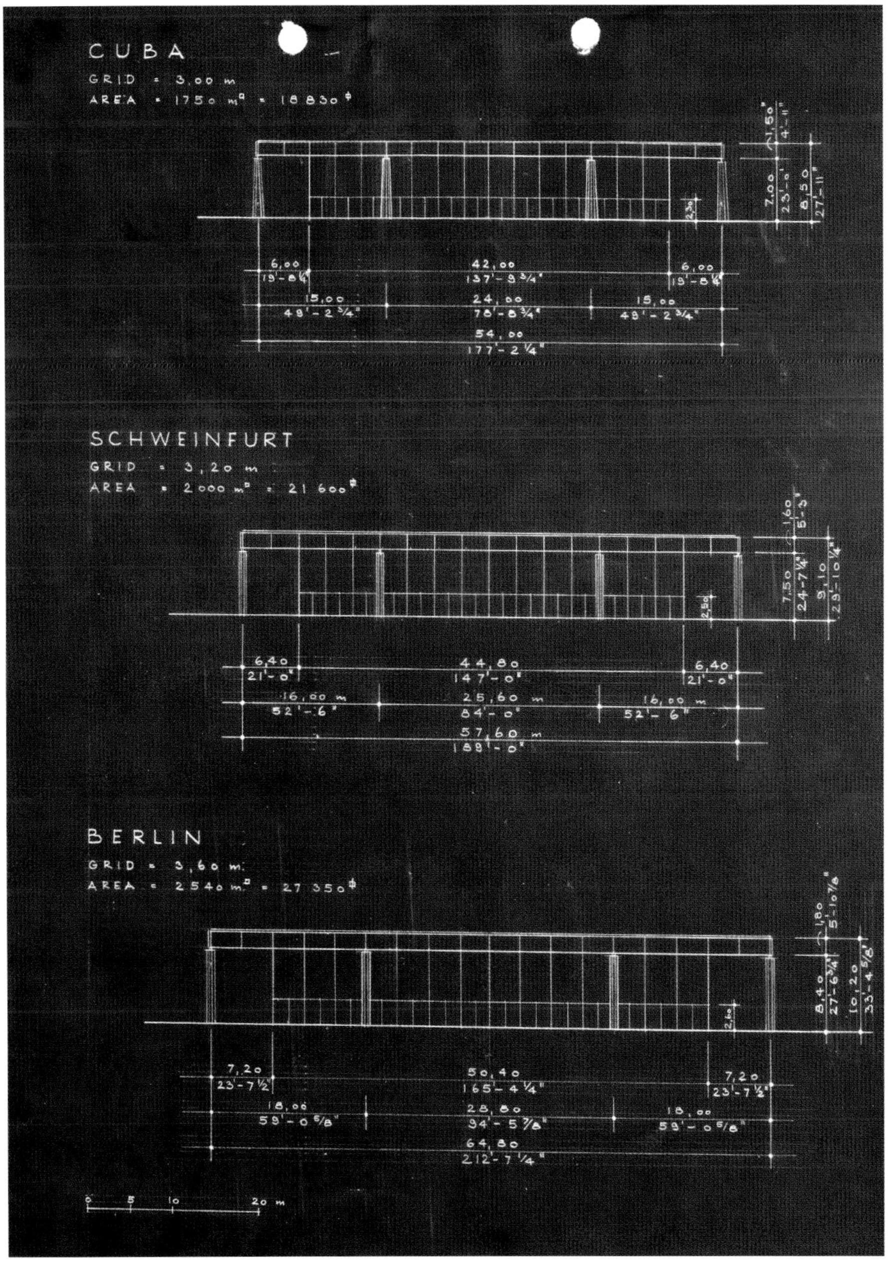

Left: Neue Nationalgalerie, Berlin. Ludwig Mies van der Rohe, architect, 1968. Photograph by Reinhard Friedrich, 1968. Courtesy of bpk, Berlin/Neue Nationalgalerie/ Reinhard Friedrich/ Art Resource, NY. © 2015 Artists Rights Society (ARS), New York / VG Bild-Kunst, Bonn.

Above: Composite elevations of the Ron Bacardi y Compañia, S.A. Administration Building, Schafer Art Museum in Schweinfurt, Germany and Neue Nationalgalerie in Berlin. Photostat. Ludwig Mies van der Rohe, architect. © 2015 Artists Rights Society (ARS), New York / VG Bild-Kunst, Bonn.

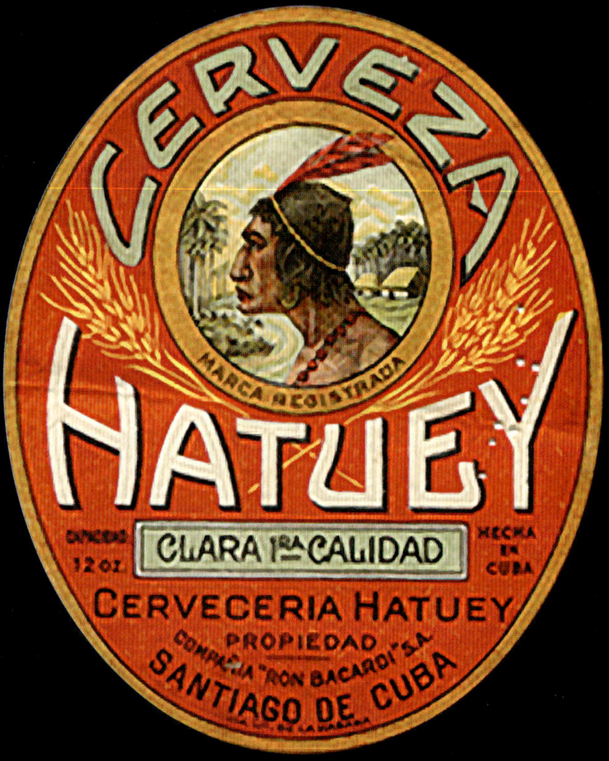
CERVEZA
MARCA REGISTRADA
HATUEY
12 oz.
CLARA 1RA CALIDAD
HECHA EN CUBA
CERVECERIA HATUEY
PROPIEDAD
COMPAÑIA "RON BACARDI" S.A.
SANTIAGO DE CUBA

BACARDI'S CUBAN BREWERIES

American writer Ernest Hemingway famously ordered Papa Doble daiquiris at El Floridita bar in Havana, but Santiago, the Cuban protagonist of Hemingway's *The Old Man and the Sea*, drank the Bacardi-brewed beer *Hatuey*.[79] Bacardi president Enrique Schueg launched Hatuey in Santiago de Cuba in 1927. After World War II, the company embarked on a national expansion of Hatuey, directed by Bosch and Joaquín Bacardi (Hatuey technical director and master brewer). The expansion largely consumed Bacardi from the late 1940s until the mid-1950s, as two new state-of-the-art plants transformed Hatuey into the leading beer producer in Cuba. Each plant was a demonstration project that supported Hatuey's brand emphasis on national identity, up-to-date technology, and conspicuously modern structures, and so offered tantalizing clues to Bacardi's subsequent development. The two plants, completed within a few years of each other, are quite different in approach, demonstrating an experimental approach that took the specific value of site and context into account.

Named for the sixteenth-century Taíno tribal chief and Cuban national hero who defied the Spaniards, the Hatuey brand underscored the anti-colonial, republican politics of Bacardi. Hatuey's distinctive red elliptical label showed the hero's stern profile silhouetted against a map of Cuba,[80] or against one of the island's characteristic landscapes. Bacardi built the Hatuey brand into a symbol of Cuban pride, as evidenced by innovative advertising that featured its breweries under the banner: "a national honor." [81]

Hatuey's first postwar brewery, *Cervecería Modelo*, was completed in 1948 outside Havana, in El Cotorro. Though it was positioned over a natural spring, the location was not purely dictated by water quality.[82] Modelo sat on a prominent corner facing the *Carretera Central*, a 700-mile highway built in 1927 connecting Havana with its provinces. At the entrance to the capital, only 20 years after the completion of the metropolitan Bacardi Building, Modelo offered a new suburban-industrial icon for Havana.

Bacardi commissioned Enrique Luis Varela, concurrently designing Bacardi's Santiago laboratories, to design Modelo.[83] Varela created a distinct monumentality for the building influenced by the commercial architecture of Streamlining and the design of world fairs.[84] Its focal point was a smooth and cylindrical hinge that joined the two box-like wings of the facility and addressed the highway. It was a gesture calibrated for the automotive era, celebrating movement and attracting the attention of motorists. The ensemble was also remarkable for its bold austerity and monumental abstraction. Crisp openings perforated the building's smooth walls, providing light to the multi-story machine rooms behind.

Modelo was promoted as a model brewery, with emphasis on technical advancement and modern hygiene. "Everything is made of glass, stainless steel and copper luster," noted *Bacardi Grafico*. "The temperature and humidity are controlled scientifically. Everything is surgically clean. The storage tanks, pipes, walls, floors and ceilings shine like mirrors." [85] The facility was designed, however, for more than efficiency; it was an attraction. The cylindrical hinge visible from the highway was touted as a silo that stored Hatuey's primary ingredient: malt harvested from barley fields in the Midwestern United States and Canada. Throughout the facility, signs indicated equipment and processes and uniformed workers performed their tasks as if on-stage for tourists.

The exposition and identity politics continued in Modelo's extensive beer garden, available for tastings and events such as the now legendary celebration of Ernest Hemingway's Nobel Prize in 1954.[86] Set in a lavish tropical landscape, the garden's *merenderos*, pavilions and kiosks explored contradictory images of Cuban identity. In one area, ehtereal white concrete canopies perforated by Royal Palms represented tropical modernism. Elsewhere, native Cuban bohíos, the

Hatuey label, 1920s. Courtesy of The Bacardi Archive.

thatched-roof indigenous huts of pre-colonial Cuba, but also perhaps a sideways nod to the Tiki in postwar American drinking culture, provided rustic shelter. "Beautiful and *Cubanisimo*," as an advertisement suggests, the brewery and its garden follies defined a comprehensive setting that not only symbolized Hatuey, but allowed visitors to engage with the brand through direct observation, tastings and participation in events. Such attention to "experience marketing," a consistent theme in Bacardi brand strategems, found a new postwar expression at Modelo.

Cervecería Central in Manacas, completed in 1953, was also designed for visibility, although it was 30 miles from Santa Clara, the nearest city. Like Modelo, it was sited, along the *Carretera Central*. Bacardi made the 1920s-era highway, symbol of modernity, mobility and connectedness, the central axis of its operations in Cuba. At one end, outside Havana, was the Modelo Brewery; at the other was Bacardi's home, Santiago. The company planned its new corporate headquarters in Santiago alongside the highway as well, emphasizing the important role tourism would play in planning.

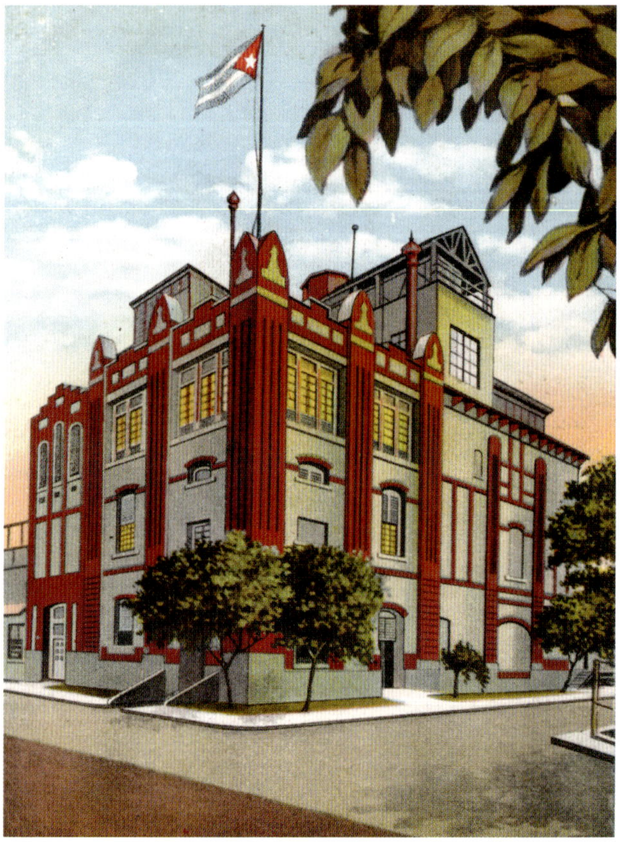

The view of *Central* from the highway functioned differently from that of Modelo. A vertical pylon sign announced the complex, initiating a landscape of low-slung production buildings parallel to the road that unfolded in a sequence of windshield views from the highway.[87] This rhythmic unfolding was articulated by an unusual structural feature: exoskeletal concrete arches designed by engineer Luis Saenz of Saenz-Cancio-Martin that spanned the building width and created interior spaces without any columns. The clear-span rooms were just one of the brewery's functional innovations. Its linear plan was conceived for rapid expansion from 100,000 to 1,000,000 barrels a year.[88] When the building opened in November 1953, it was presented in Havana's *Diaro de la Marina* as the most modern brewery in the world, *"un edificio modernisimo."*[89] 15,000 guests arrived for the inauguration, which was celebrated in the spirit of a political rally.

Across the *Carretera Central* from the plant, Bacardi developed another long low structure: El Cacique Motel. With 25 air-conditioned rooms, this Cuban adaptation of a fixture of American highway culture was conceived as an adjunct facility to the plant. Partly designed to serve visiting company executives, it affirmed the company's ambition that, like Modelo, the site function as tourist destination in its own right.

Modelo's austere monumentalism and *Central's* highway-inspired horizontalism illustrated how Bacardi used contradictory languages of modern architecture to elaborate the company's breweries as landmarks of modern industry. Each approach, however, was only the leading edge of a strategy designed to entice visitors and create a bond with consumers. A generation after Bacardi offered signature cocktail bars and its emblematic office building in central Havana as tourist attractions, Bacardi made these open breweries into destinations for newly mobile Cubans.

Above: Original Hatuey Brewery (former Santiago Brewing Company), Santiago de Cuba. Hand-tinted postcard, 1930s. Courtesy of The Bacardi Archive.

Right: Ron BACARDI de lo bueno lo mejor / Cerveza HATUEY apaga la sed y satisface a todos (Bacardi rum—the best of the best / Hatuey beer quenches thirst and satisfies all). Advertisement. Courtesy of The Bacardi Archive.

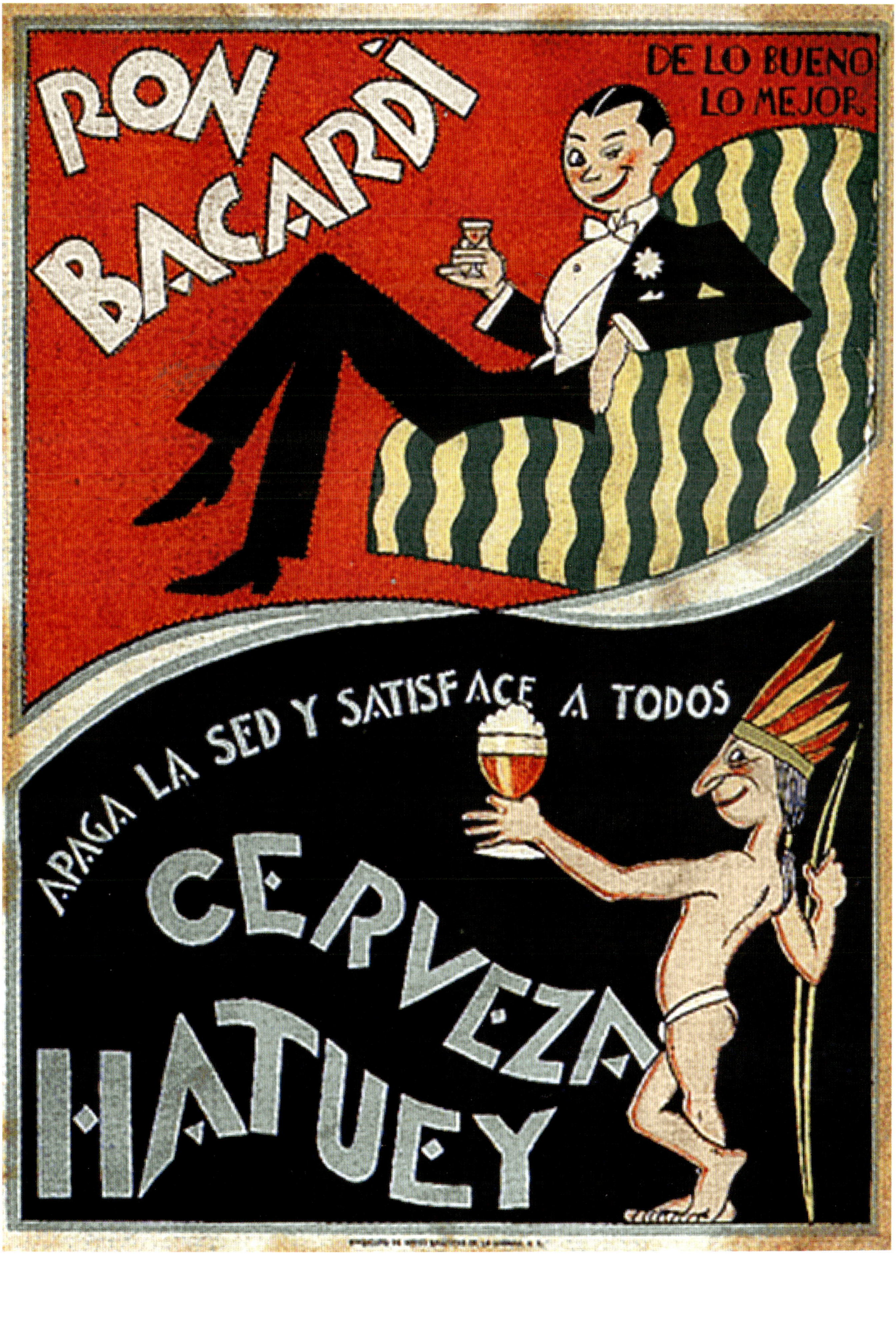
RON BACARDÍ
DE LO BUENO LO MEJOR
APAGA LA SED Y SATISFACE A TODOS
CERVEZA HATUEY

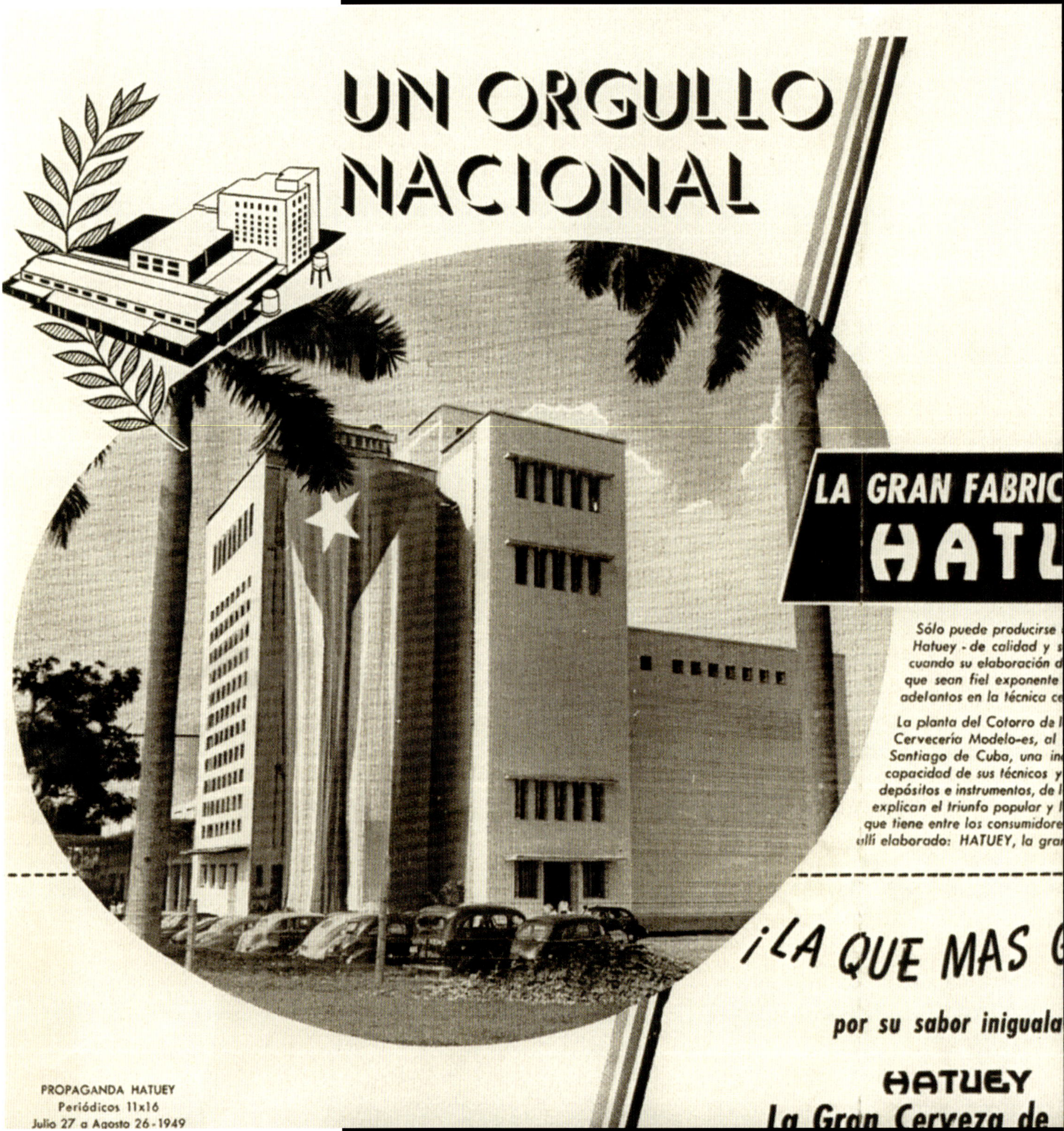
UN ORGULLO NACIONAL
LA GRAN
Sólo puede producirse
Hatuey - de calidad y
cuando su elaboración
que sean fiel exponente
adelantos en la técnica
La planta del Cotorro de
Cervecería Modelo-es, al
Santiago de Cuba, una
capacidad de sus técnicos
depósitos e instrumentos, de
explican el triunfo popular y
que tiene entre los
allí elaborado: HATUEY, la
¡LA QUE MAS
por su sabor
HATUEY
PROPAGANDA HATUEY
Periódicos 11x16
Julio 27 a Agosto 26-1949

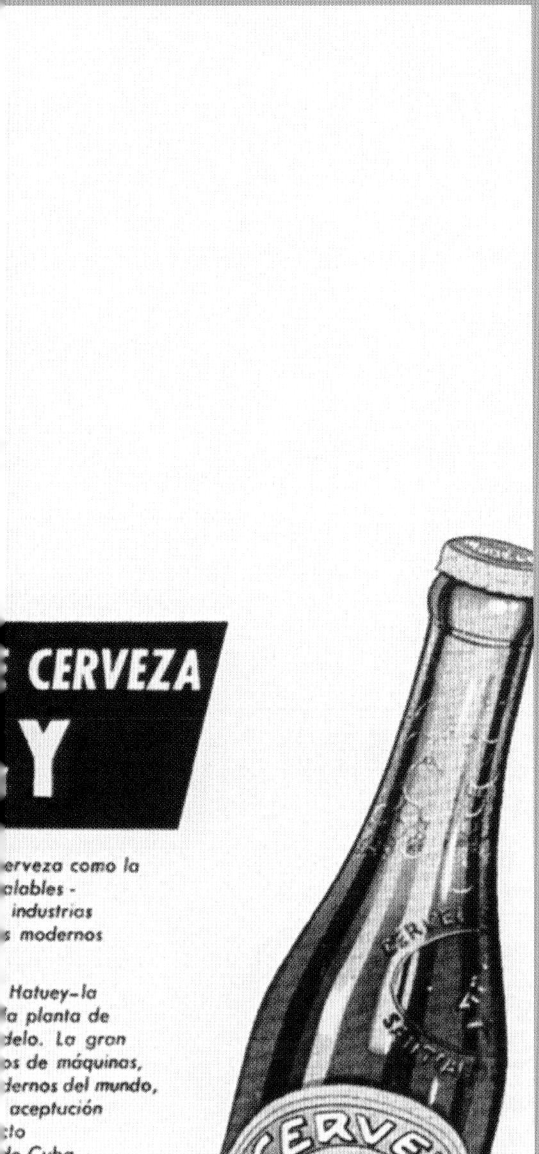

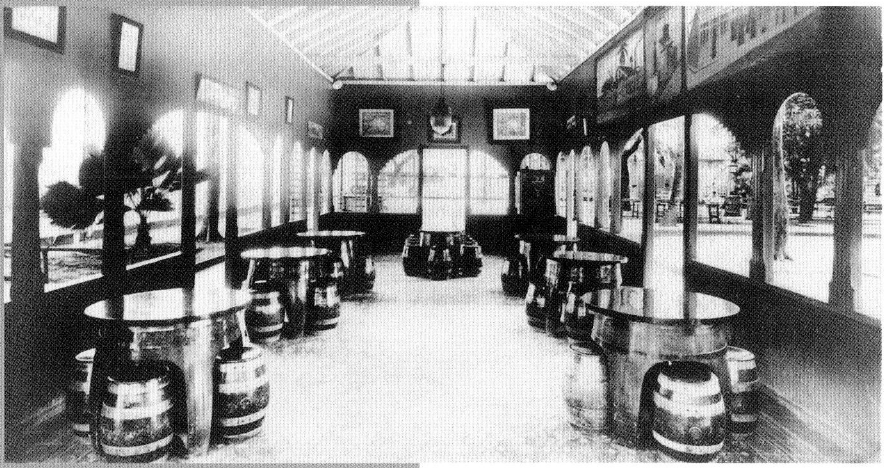

Left: Un Orgullo Nacional (A National Pride). Advertisement celebrating the opening of the Modelo Brewery, El Cotorro, Cuba. Enrique Luis Varela, architect, 1953. Courtesy of The Bacardi Archive.

Above: Kiosk in the gardens of the Hatuey Brewery, Santiago de Cuba. Postcard, 1920s. Courtesy of The Bacardi Archive.

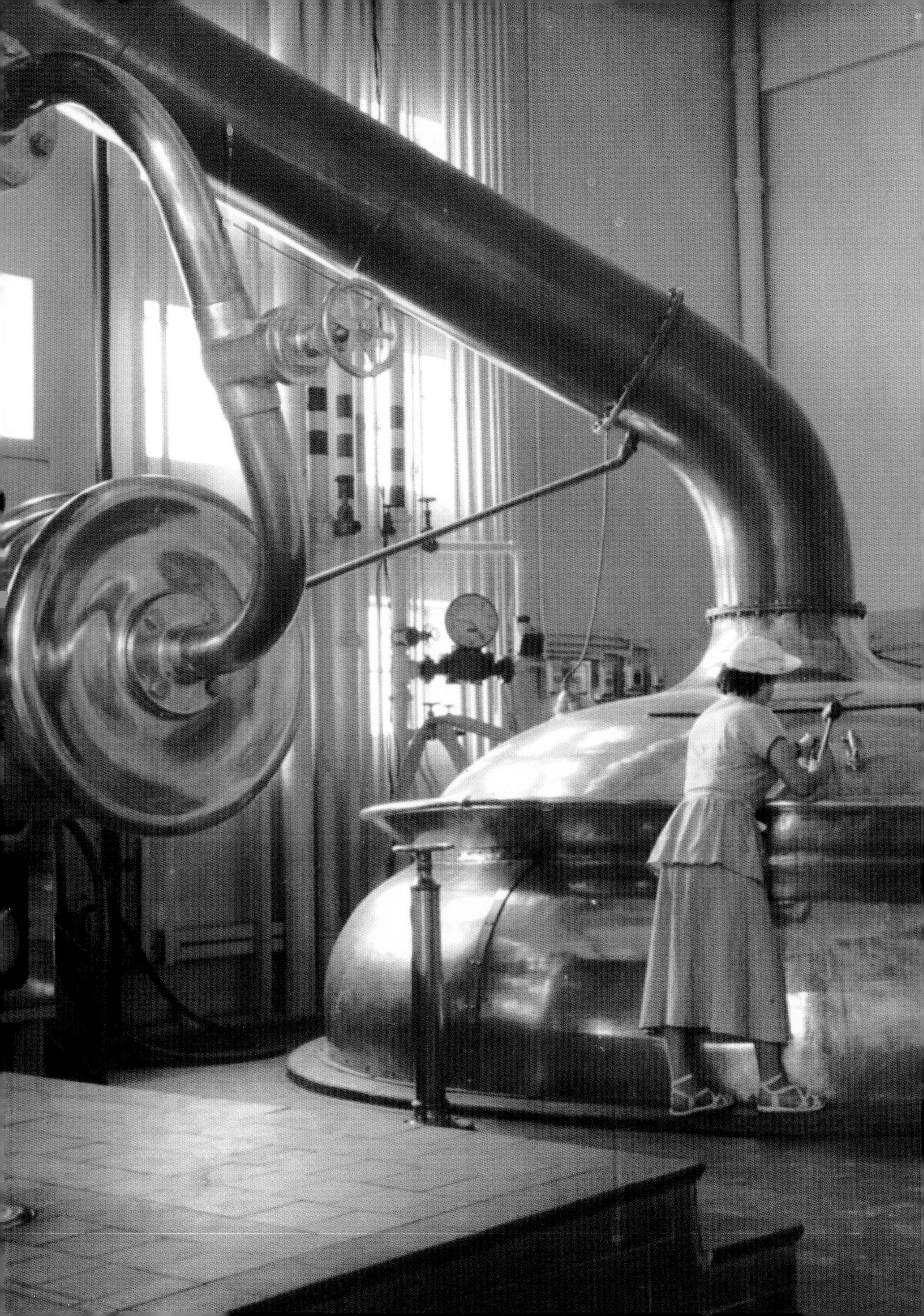

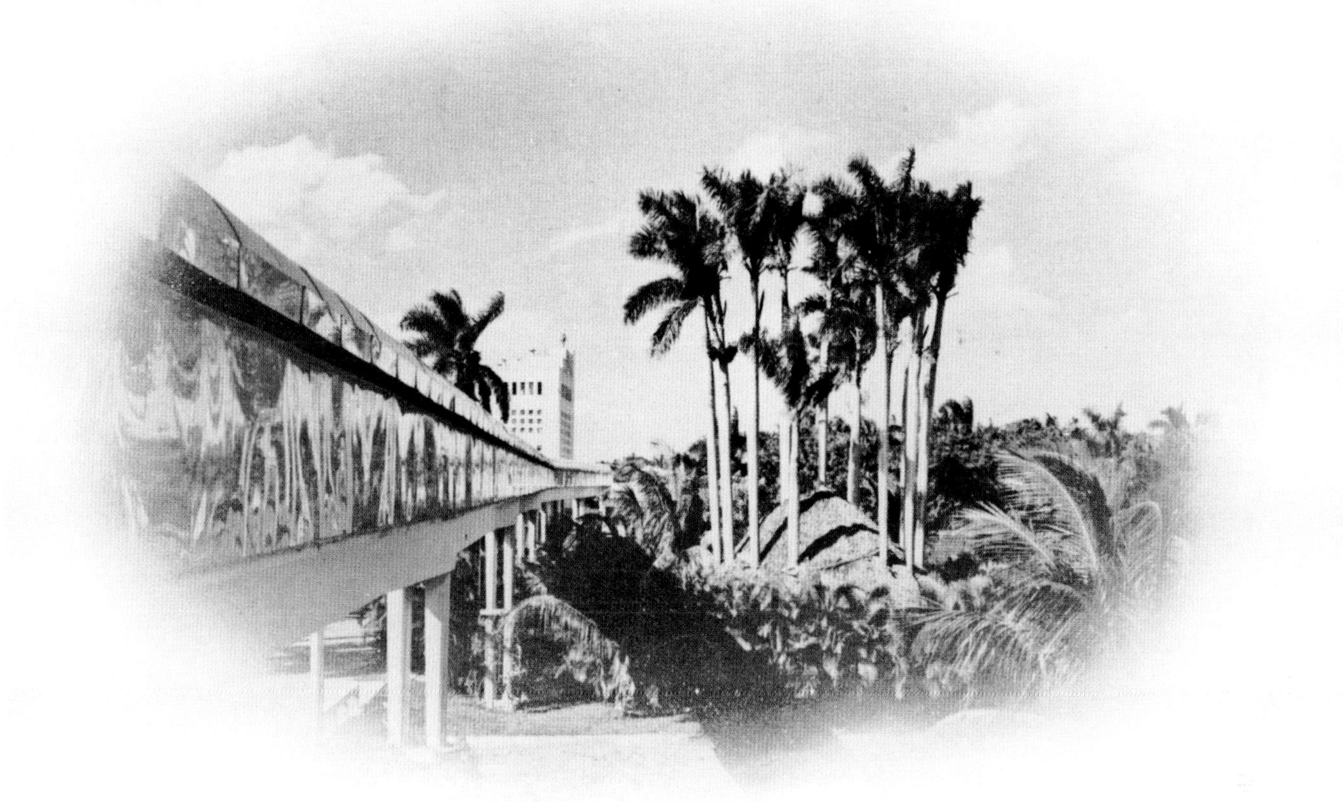

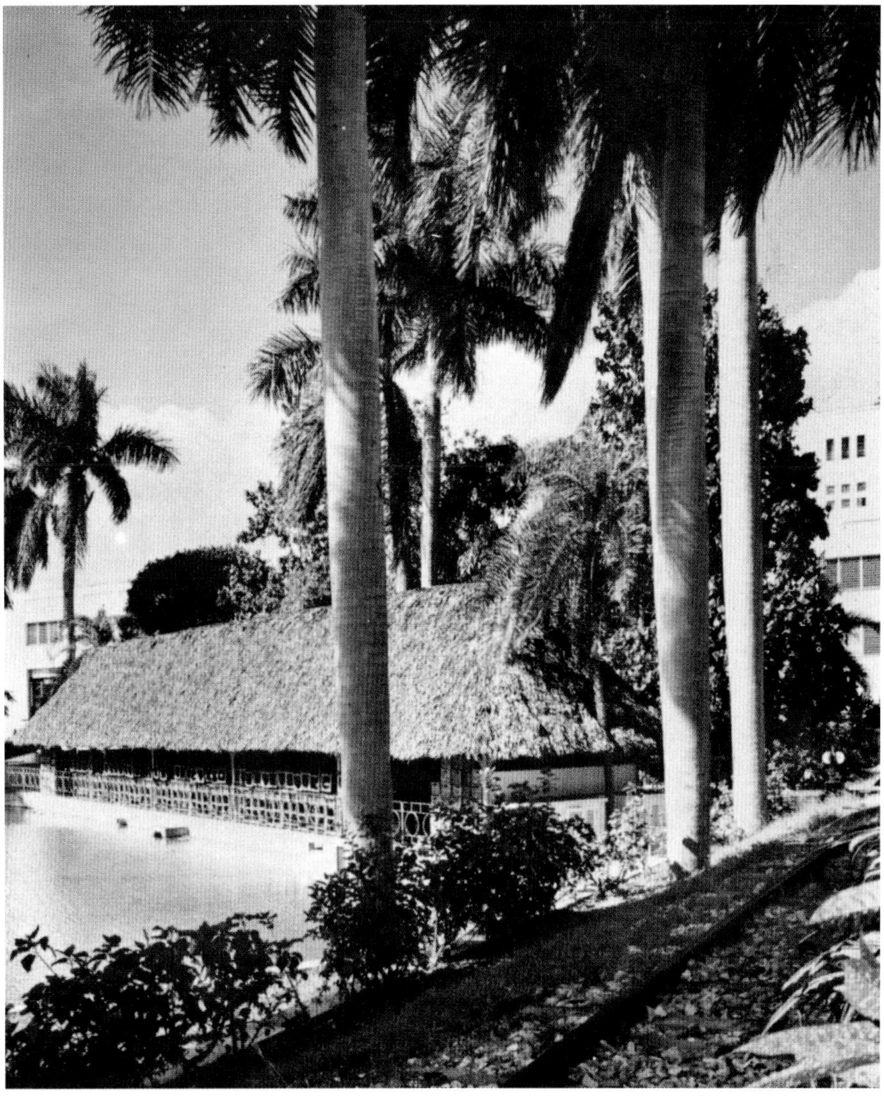

Left: Modelo Brewery, El Cotorro, Cuba. Brewing kettle. Enrique Luis Varela, architect, 1953. Courtesy of The Bacardi Archive.

Top: Modelo Brewery, El Cotorro, Cuba. Hospitality Pavilion (center right) in the gardens of the brewery. The traditional Cuban *bohío* is built around a circular stand of Royal Palms, 1953. From promotional brochure. Courtesy of The Bacardi Archive.

Right: Modelo Brewery, El Cotorro, Cuba. Cuban *bohío* facing the pool in the gardens of the brewery. From promotional brochure. Courtesy of The Bacardi Archive.

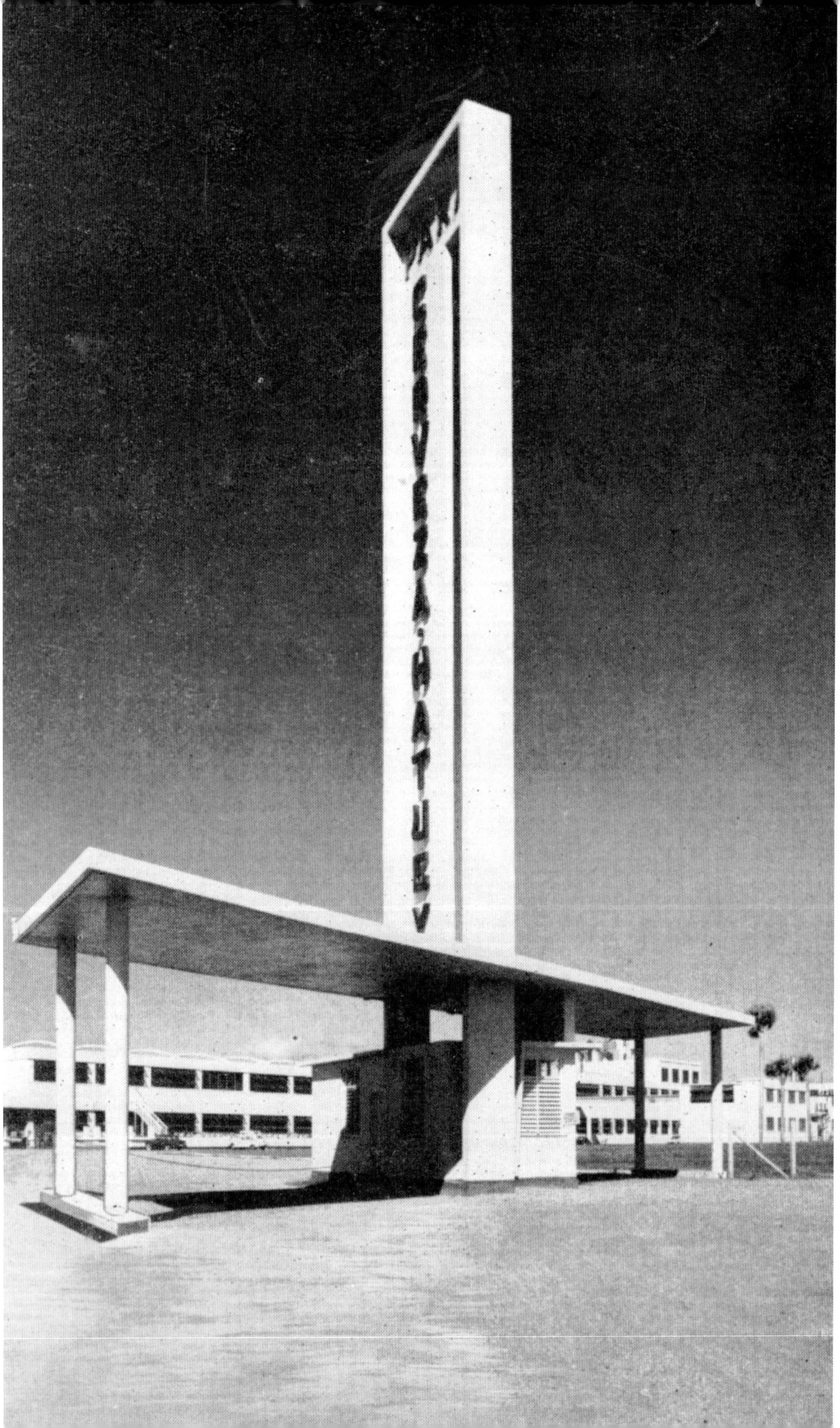

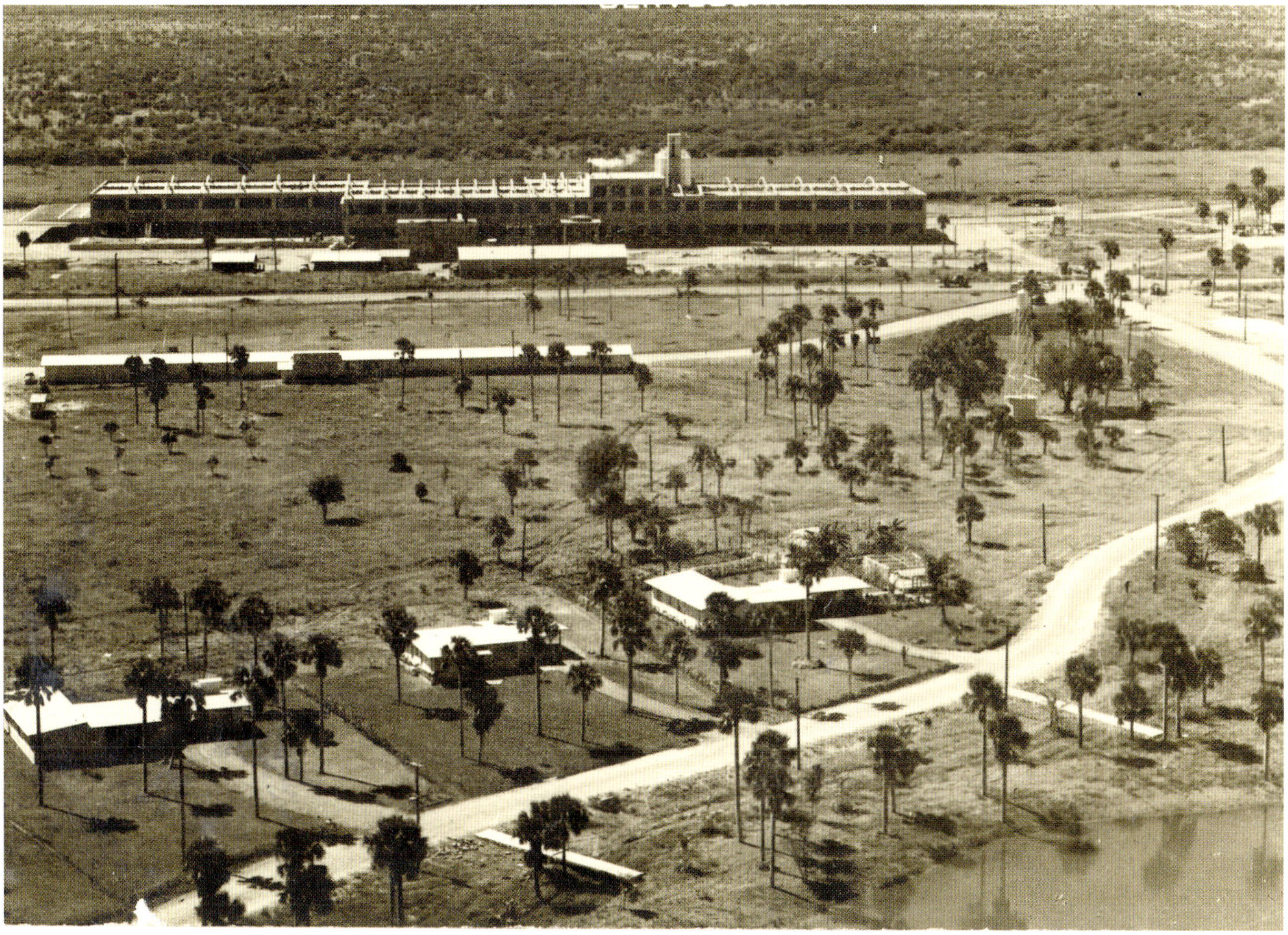

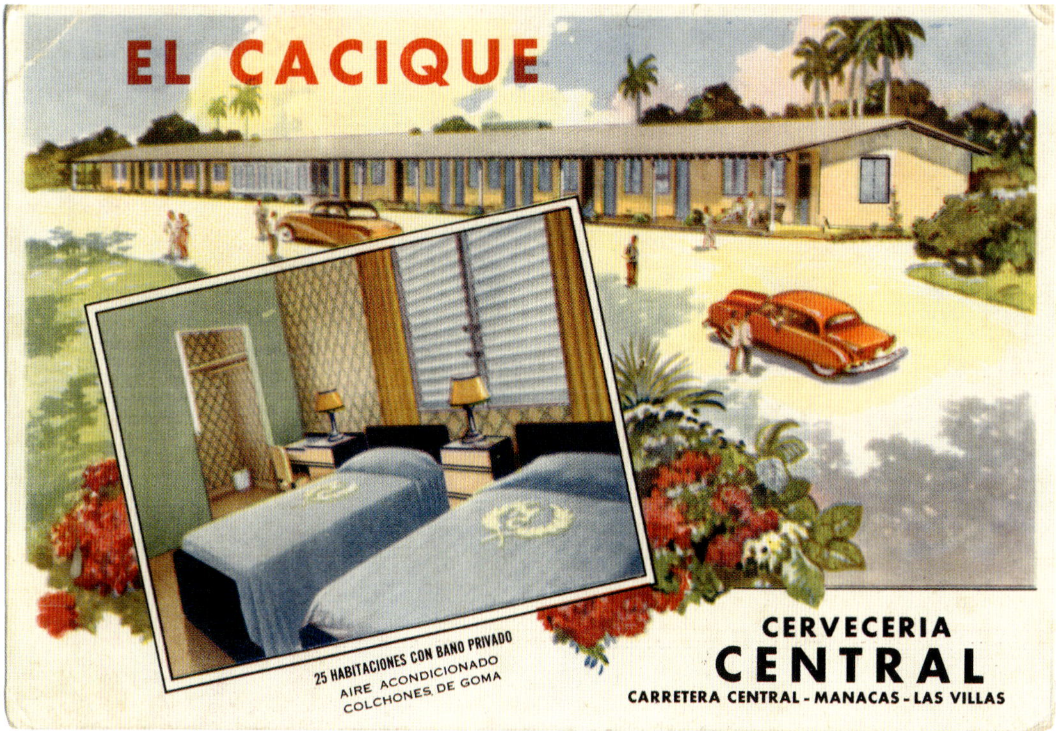

Left: Central Brewery, Manacas, Cuba. Entrance pylon. Enrique Luis Varela, architect with Saenz-Cancio-Martin, engineers (unconfirmed), 1953. From "Tercer Aniversario de la Cerveceria Central," *Bacardi Grafico* 4 (January 1957): 22. Courtesy of The Bacardi Archive.

Top: Central Brewery, Manacas, Cuba. Aerial view of brewery showing highway (Carretera Central), adjacent motel and housing. Enrique Luis Varela, architect with Saenz-Cancio-Martin, engineers (unconfirmed), 1953. Postcard. Courtesy of Cuban Heritage Collection, University of Miami.

Bottom: El Cacique Motel, Manacas, Cuba. Postcard. Courtesy of Cuban Heritage Collection, University of Miami.

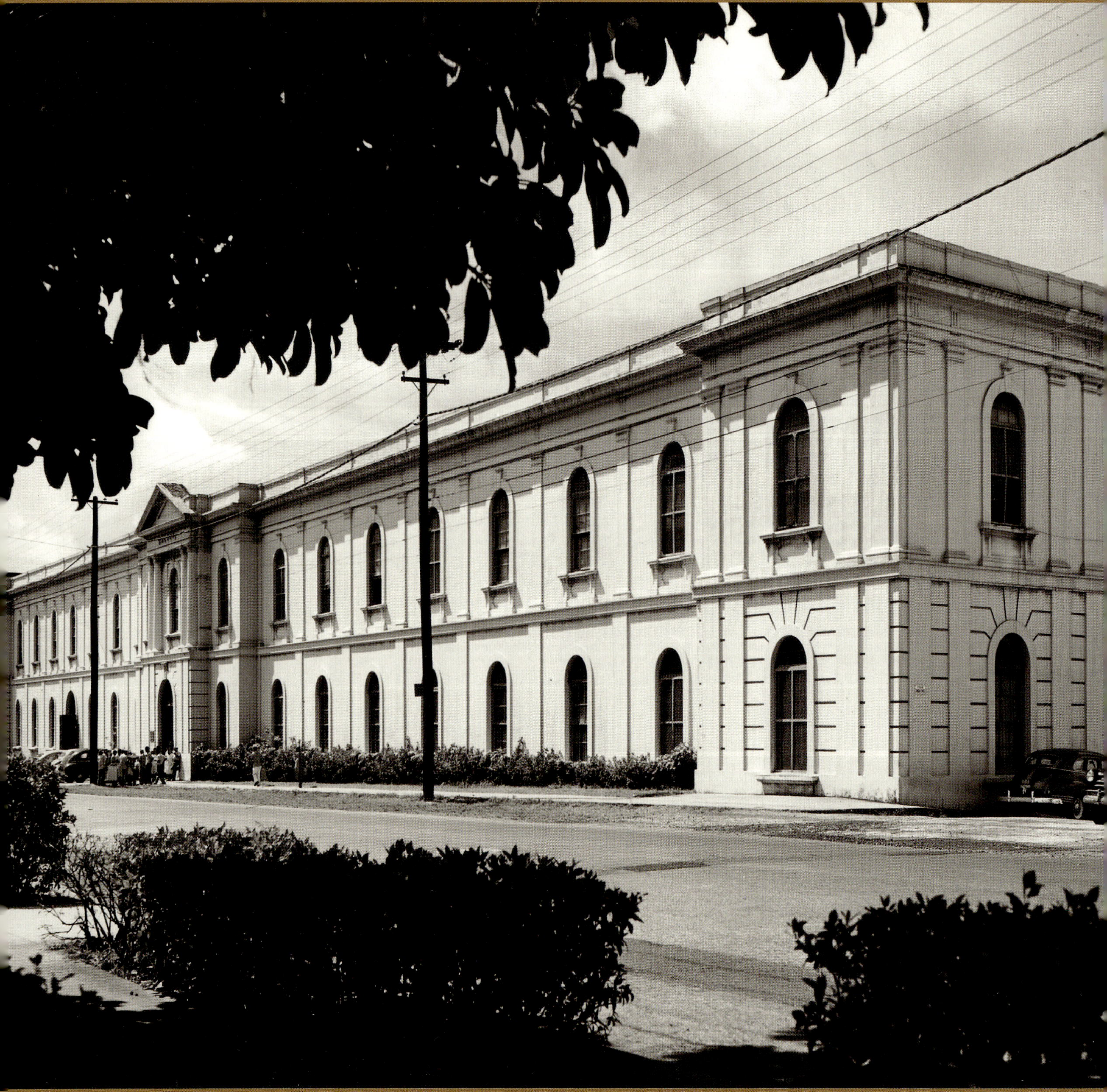

BACARDI IN PUERTO RICO

Beginning in the early 1930s Bacardi developed a strategy of overseas expansion through a network of distilleries in the sugar-producing lands of the American tropics. The plan, developed under Enrique Schueg, was executed first in Mexico and Puerto Rico, then after World War II in northern Brazil, Martinique, and the British West Indies. Advanced by Schueg's successor, Pepín Bosch, one culmination of this effort was the development of an entirely new campus outside San Juan, Puerto Rico. Collaborating closely with the Puerto Rican government, Bosch promised investment and the development of major industry on the island in exchange for more direct access to the lucrative American market. Indeed, American sales skyrocketed as Bacardi developed the world's largest premium rum distillery complex as well as one of the island's biggest tourist magnets on a picturesque bayfront site. The significance of this campus, Bacardi's first planned distillery complex, lies in its evolutionary development, which recorded changing design paradigms, development strategies and cultural identity during the company's rapid globalization.

Bacardi established itself in Puerto Rico in 1936, spurred by the end of Prohibition in the U.S., and the trade benefits of planting its flag directly on U.S. territory, Perhaps to assuage Puerto Ricans concerned about the rival presence of the well-known Cuban rum distiller, the company promptly represented itself to the island as a Puerto Rican institution. In 1939 Bacardi inserted itself into one of San Juan's most highly visible locations, the monumental *Hospital Civil* in Puerta de Tierra. Designed by Domingo Sermero and constructed between 1877 and 1887, the hospital was the last facility built in Puerto Rico by the Spanish colonial government.[90] A neoclassical symbol of the first urbanization outside the city's historic walls,[91] its broad arched walls transmitted a commanding civic prominence enhanced by the completion of the Luis Muñoz Rivera Park across the tree-lined Avenida Juan Ponce de León in 1925. The park improvements, by the Chicago planning firm Bennett, Parsons and Frost, which also designed the grounds of the new capitol framing the other side of Puerta de Tierra, helped transform this area into San Juan's metropolitan core. Framing one end of this core, the Hospital Civil's urban and historical prominence eventually attracted the interest of the newly founded Institute of Puerto Rican Culture (ICP),[92] the agency tasked with identification and preservation of Puerto Rican landmarks. An agreement with Bacardi led the ICP to purchase the building in 1960, and convert its arcaded and vaulted rooms into the General Archives of Puerto Rico in 1973.[93]

Soon after it installed in Puerta de Tierra, however, Bacardi began development of a new home, a 95-acre suburban campus on the Palo Seco peninsula, opposite San Juan on the west side of San Juan Bay.[94] The move reflected an undocumented but nonetheless crucial evolution of thinking about Bacardi facilities. By the 1940s suburban industrial campuses were already recognized for their positive effect on workers, on the culture of the organization, and on surrounding communities, as well as for the advertising value they delivered.[95] The Palo Seco site was set into an open area of broad lawns surrounded by pines with plenty of room to grow. The waterfront campus, equipped with modern buildings and machinery, accessible and picturesque (with scenic views toward El Morro and Old San Juan), soon became the new face of Bacardi in Puerto Rico.

The centerpiece of the Palo Seco plant was the distillery building. Designed in 1945, this marker of industrial transformation in Puerto Rico had a noble character that transposed industrial needs in monumentalizing architectural terms.[96] Specifically, the distillery was influenced by the Modern Classicalism of interwar civic works, particularly the architecture of the Depression-era Works Progress Administration (WPA). The building's central architectural feature was a five-story tower that incorporated the important distillery columns. A great vertical window alternating panels of glass and glass block rose to the top of the tower, where the company's name was spelled in chiseled letters. Flanking each side symmetrically, lower wings housing fermentation tanks and other plant equipment were disguised

Bacardi Corporation headquarters (former Hospital Civil), Puerta de Tierra, San Juan, Puerto Rico.
Domingo Sermero, architect, 1877-87. Courtesy of The Bacardi Archive.

by tall windows and continuous glass block clerestories. Puerto Rico's Governor Luis Muñoz Marin christened the ascetic, monumental structure *La Catedral del Ron* (The Cathedral of Rum).

The distillery created an axial figurehead for the Palo Seco campus, its imposing character denoting the industrial colonization of the once remote peninsula. The facility was then organized around a greensward that connected the distillery's main facade to the bay. Evocative of an American university campus, this central quadrangle became the informal but honorific repository of principal buildings, gardens and artwork collected over the history of the plant.[97]

The WPA-influenced classicism of the "rum cathedral" had little resonance with subsequent builders. A more frank, modern architecture was emerging in Puerto Rico, influenced as much by political events as by international trends. The New Deal administration of Governor Rexford G. Tugwell had set the stage for an important transformation of the island with *Operación Manos a la Obra* (Operation Bootstrap), which promoted industrial development via access to U.S. markets with no tariffs or import duties. Industrialization was also the agenda of Puerto Rico's PPD, or Partido Popular Democratico, founded in 1938, and headed by Luis Muñoz Marin. Muñoz-Marin, elected governor in 1948, as well as Teodoro Moscoso, president of Puerto Rico's Industrial Bank, would prove important partners for Pepín Bosch in the development of Bacardi's plans in Puerto Rico.

Bosch chose architects intimately involved in the postwar modernization and industrialization of Puerto Rico to direct the early development of the campus. Henry Klumb, the German émigré architect and protégé of Frank Lloyd Wright, a friend of the governor and member of the important Committee on the Design of Public Works, was commissioned to design a home for the Bacardi president at the most privileged position on the grounds.[98] Klumb used the commission to develop the residential vocabulary that historian Luz Marie Rodríguez called his "functional, ethical and conceptual idea of the tropics."[99] In this first home in Puerto Rico executed with his partner Stephen Armesen, Klumb expressed the idea of minimal shelter in a linear home with projecting butterfly roof planes and porous louvered walls, and a distinct and separate zone of service areas he would call the "living core." Building in wood and concrete block, Klumb structured an organic tropical home that was the private face of the plant for Pepín Bosch.

Toro, Ferrer Arquitectos, another important agent of modern architecture in Puerto Rico, was commissioned in 1954 to design the main plant building on the north side of the greensward.[100] The rambling complex featured concrete post and beam frames filled with lightweight louvers and awning-type windows that promoted ventilation. It translated into industrial terms the tropicalist syntax of the firm's landmark work in San Juan, like the Supreme Court of Puerto Rico (1952). In Klumb and Toro Ferrer, Bosch chose architects fundamentally different in approach, yet equally committed to the construction of Puerto Rico's modern identity.

Bacardi also commissioned Felix Candela, working concurrently on Bacardi's plants in Mexico, to design an open warehouse for aging rum. The cavernous vaulted structure

Right: Muñoz Rivera Park, San Juan, Puerto Rico. Plan. Bennett, Parsons and Frost, Planners, 1925. Courtesy of The Art Institute of Chicago, Edward H. Bennett Collection, Ryerson and Burnham Archives.

Overleaf: 'Cathedral of Rum' (Bacardi Corporation Distillery), Palo Seco, Puerto Rico. W. Donald Christie, engineer, 1946. Courtesy of The Bacardi Archive.

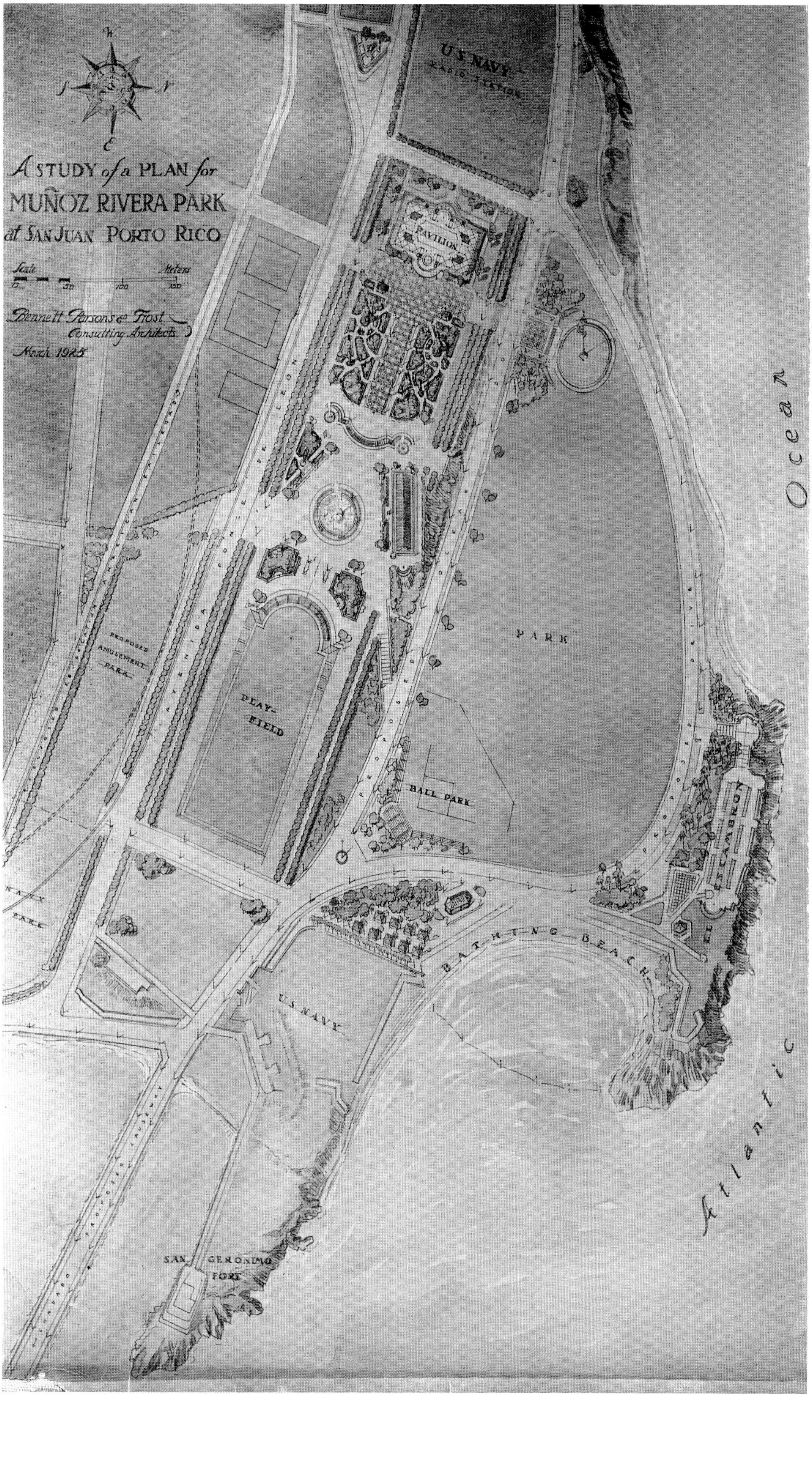
A STUDY of a PLAN for
MUÑOZ RIVERA PARK
at SAN JUAN PORTO RICO
Scale
Meters
Bennett Parsons & Frost
Consulting Architects
March 1925
U.S. NAVY
RADIO STATION
PAVILION
PARK
PROPOSED
AMUSEMENT
PARK
PLAY-FIELD
BALL PARK
BATHING BEACH
EL ESCAMBRON
U.S. NAVY
SAN GERONIMO
FORT
Atlantic
Ocean

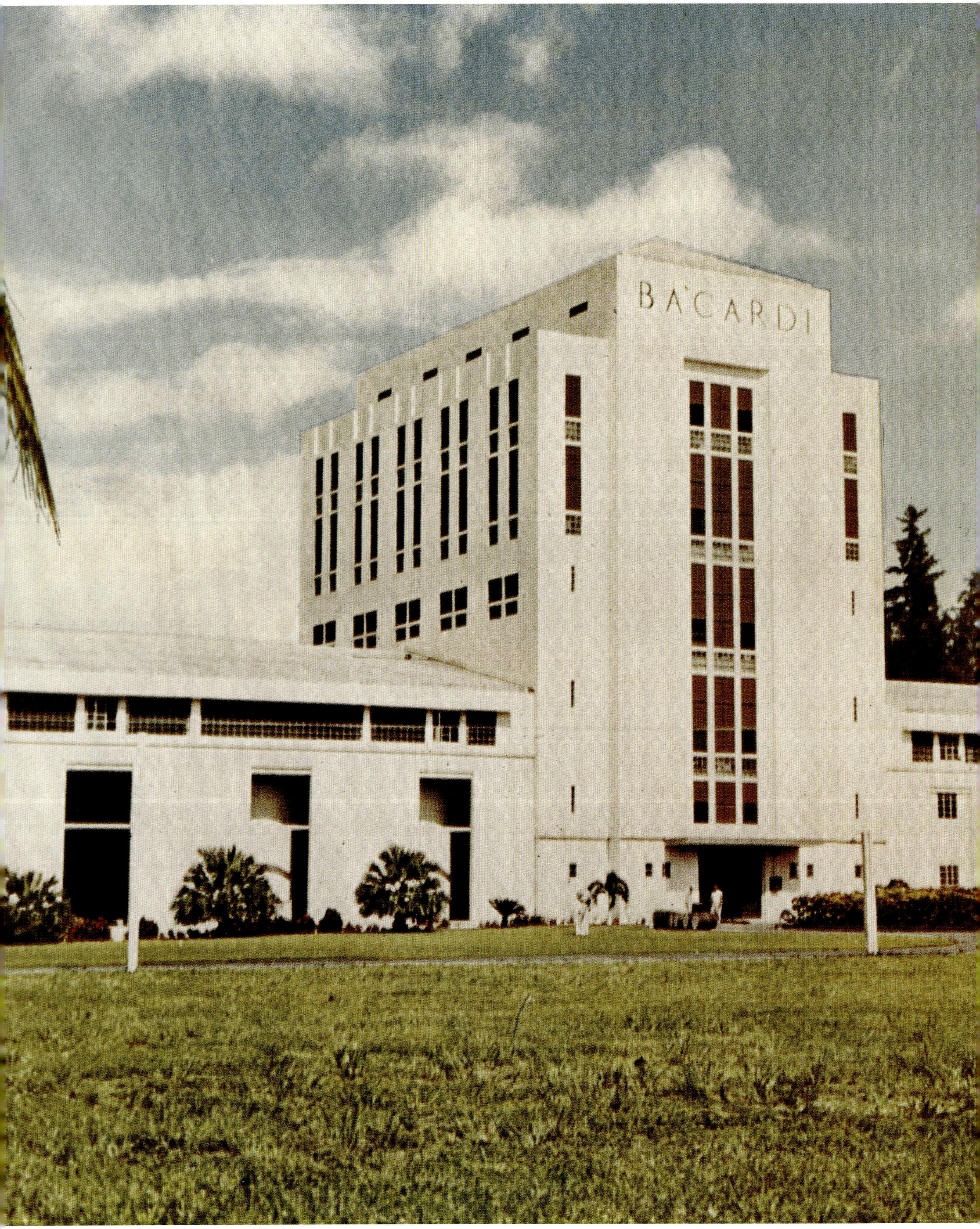
BACARDI

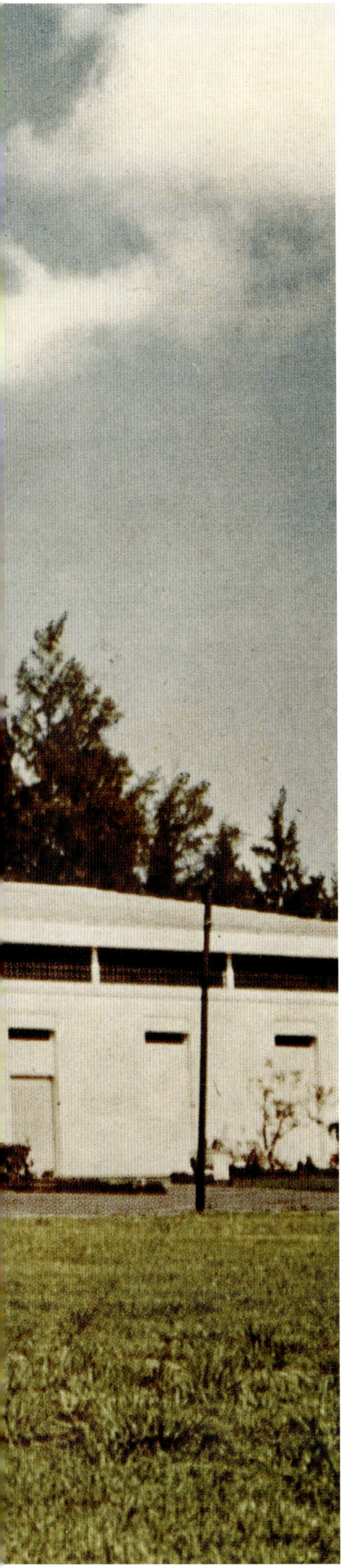

was designed to span 110 feet using a series of hyperbolic paraboloid arches joined along a principal 270-foot long nave. The pleated and gabled structure, resembling the carapace of an armored sea creature, was never built. Curiously, though, all the warehouses at the campus would employ a similar type of pleating, or corrugation, to achieve long span roofs with no intermediate supports. These undulating rooftops, executed by architects like SACMAG, Capacete-Martin-Gutierrez, Miguel Rosich and Ramon Benitez, unify the distillery complex.

By the early1960s, corresponding with Bacardi's exile from Cuba, expressive concrete structures indicative of modernist Latin American influences and the work of Felix Candela in particular grew around the axial center of the Cathedral of Rum. Most striking was the bat-winged *merendero* (pavilion), designed by Enrique Gutiérrez and Luis Saenz of SACMAG of Puerto Rico.[101] Visible from Old San Juan, it comprised a single hyperbolic paraboloid concrete shell, only one and one-quarter inch thick, whose soaring pointed wings were supported on just four concrete piers. Designed to celebrate the centennial of the company and completed in 1961, only a year after the confiscation of the company's Cuban assets, the *merendero* boldly transmited a sense of freedom and optimism (a sensibility Gutiérrez would echo two years later at the Bacardi Imports tower in Miami). Moreover, the canopy denoted the swelling imprint of tourism on the site. Its fanciful concrete shell was just the type of hospitality pavilion popping up in the great resort hotels of the period (for instance Candela and Juan Sordo Madaleno's El Jacaranda nightclub at the Hotel Presidente in Acapulco, 1957). Indeed, the *merendero* made a striking yet efficient shelter for parties and events and a way station for tourists arriving at the site.

Opposite the *merendero*, architects Miguel Rosich and Ignacio Carerra-Justiz added a museum, bottling plant and offices in 1965. The "Foyer Museum," Bacardi's first purpose-built museum since Elvira Cape's Museo Emilio Bacardi Moreau in 1927, featured a fan of post-tensioned conical vaults that opened toward the greensward. The structural system, nearly identical to Philip Johnson's recent design for Bosch's Varadero beach house, established a diagonal relationship across the green to the *merendero*, tying the concrete pieces visually.[102] Opposite this visual line, a curved ramp led from the museum floor to a catwalk that allowed tourists to inspect the adjacent bottling plant from above, transforming the ensemble into an ad-hoc visitors center.

Rich wall treatments were a design corollary to the sculptural building forms on the Palo Seco campus. Under the vaults of the museum, artist Homer Hill's 17 by 39 foot full-wall mural told the story of the company and family in a painted collage of photos, documents, medals, flags and a family tree. Outside, the broad walls of the bottling plant were adorned with large format ceramic murals of fantasy flowers, insects and other creatures. Created by Barcelona artist Rosalía Pujó and executed by the Catalan ceramic leader Industrial Cerámica Vallvés S.A.,[103] the murals evoke Francisco Brennand's inventive floral murals at the Bacardi Imports Tower in Miami, and their underlying premise of synthesis of the arts.

Postwar corporate and industrial campuses are most often admired as indications of a singular vision. In contrast, the Bacardi campus in Palo Seco is an eclectic landscape. The cathedral of rum, bat-winged *merendero*, vaulted Foyer Museum, bottling plant, and more recently the Casa Bacardi visitors' center, are grouped freely around the plant's greensward, which holds these diverse components in a loose assemblage. The assembled diversity offers a type of authenticity true to the company's essence. Far from random, each idiosyncratic piece represents a public face of the company.[104]

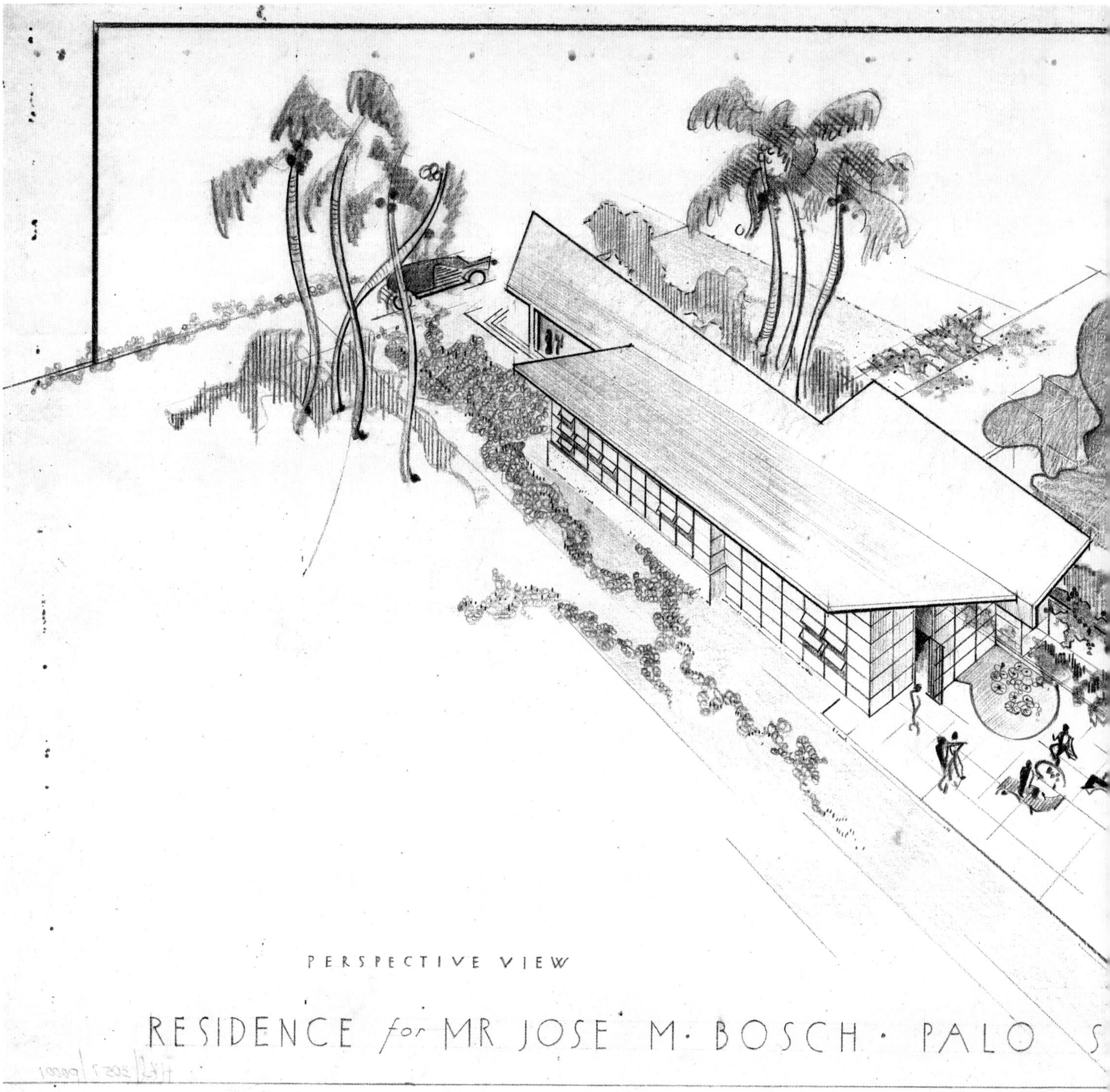

Residence for Mr. Jose M. Bosch at Bacardi Corporation Plant, Palo Seco, Puerto Rico. Perspective. Stephen V. Arneson and Henry Klumb, architects with Hunter Randolph, landscape architect, 1944. Colección Henry Klumb, Archivo de Arquitectura y Construcción de la Universidad de Puerto Rico.

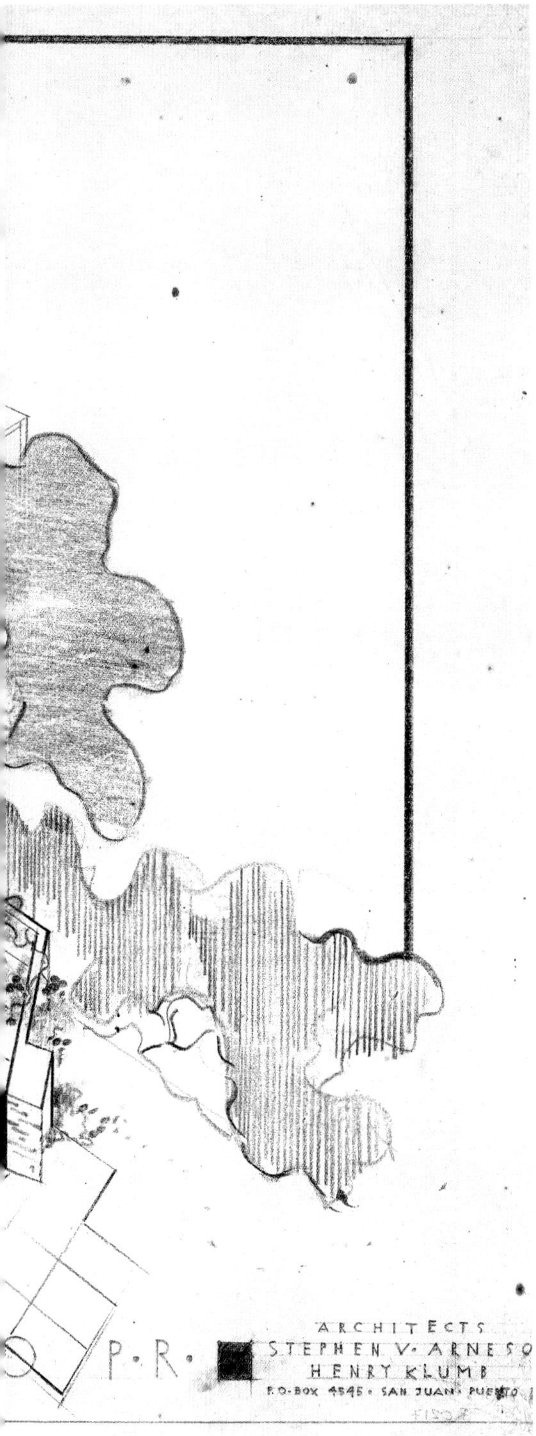

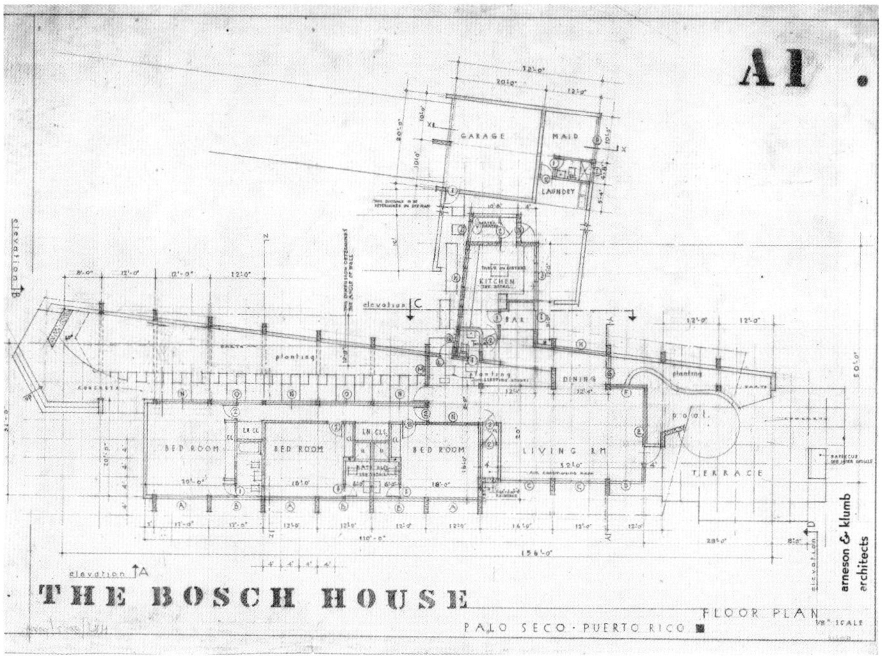

Residence for Mr. Jose M. Bosch at Bacardi Corporation Plant, Palo Seco, Puerto Rico. Plan. Arneson and Klumb, architects with Hunter Randolph, landscape architect, 1944. Colección Henry Klumb, Archivo de Arquitectura y Construcción de la Universidad de Puerto Rico.

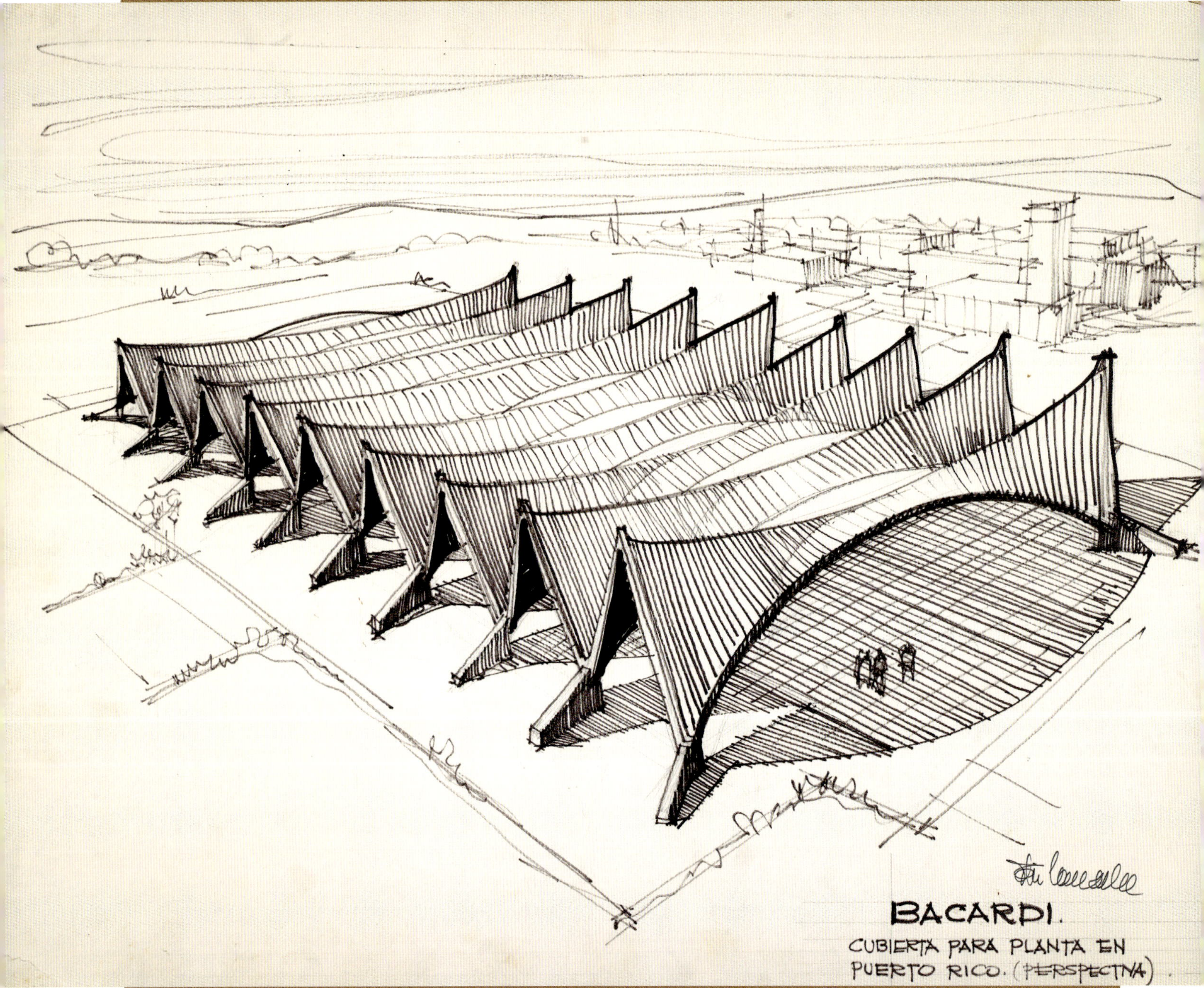
BACARDI.
CUBIERTA PARA PLANTA EN
PUERTO RICO. (PERSPECTIVA).

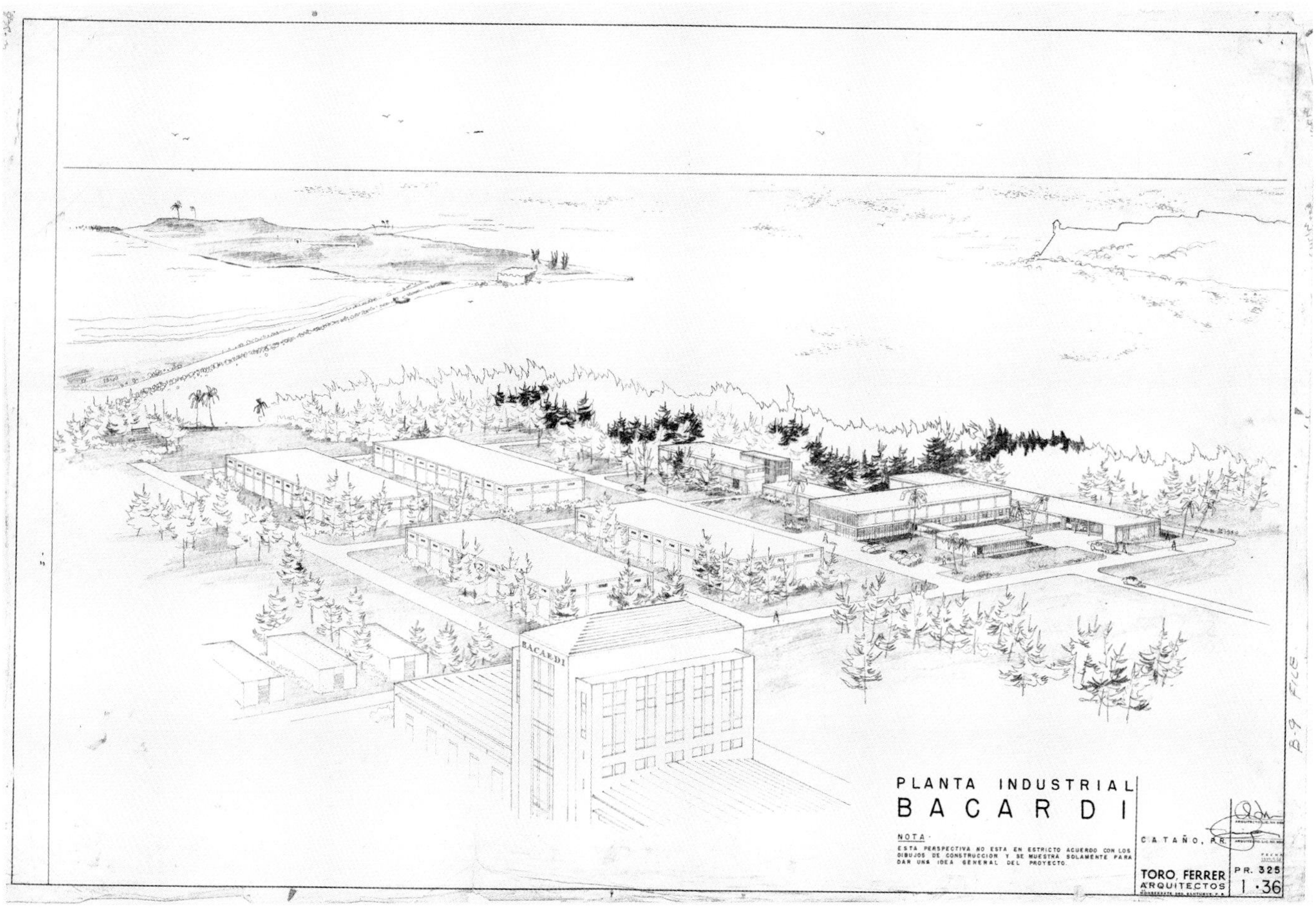

Left: Bacardi Corporation Plant, Palo Seco, Puerto Rico. Open warehouse for ageing rum, aerial perspective. Félix Candela, architect, 1950s (unbuilt). Drawings and Archives, Avery Architectural Fine Arts Library, Columbia University.

Above: Bacardi Corporation Plant, Palo Seco, Puerto Rico. Main plant building, aerial perspective. Toro y Ferrer Arquitectos, 1954. Colección Toro, Ferrer y Torregrosa Arquitectos, Archivo de Arquitectura y Construcción de la Universidad de Puerto Rico.

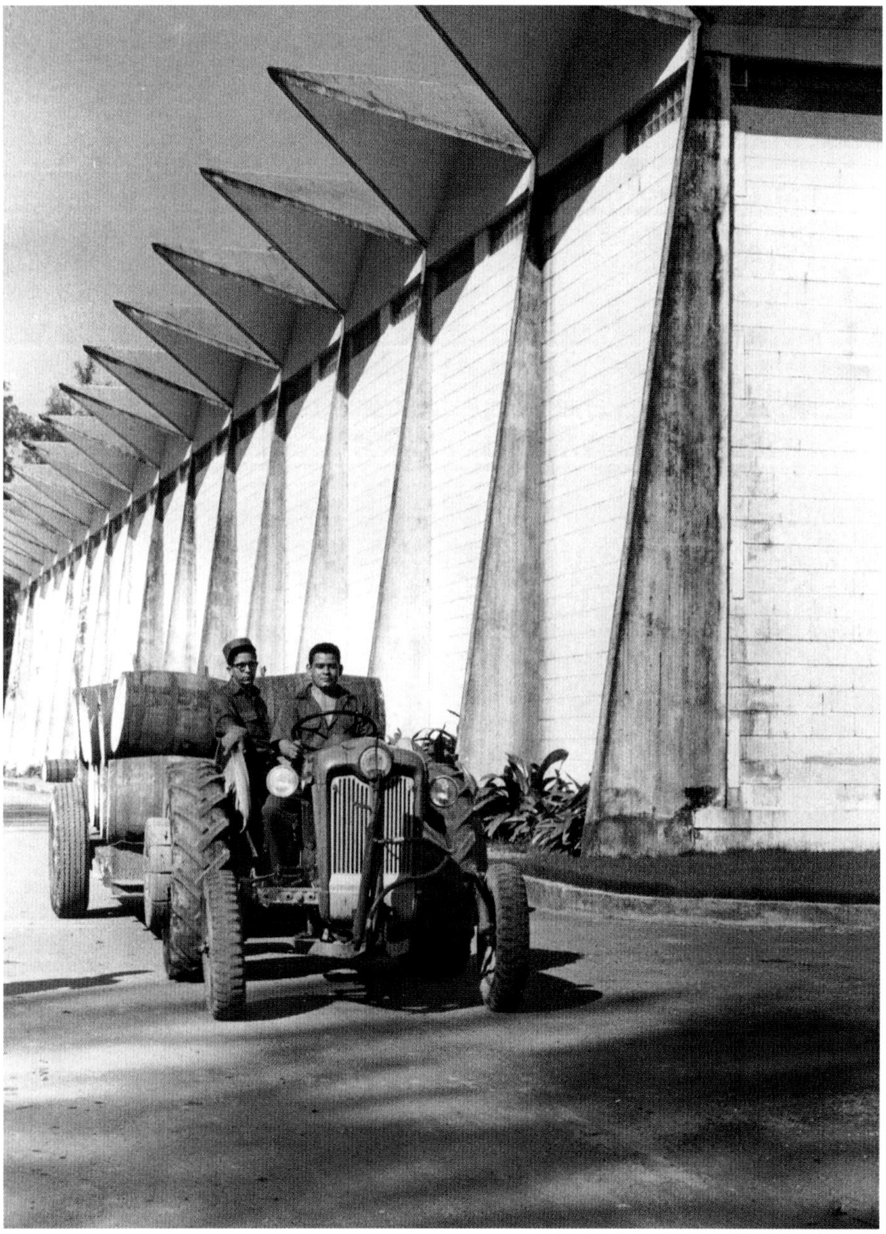

Above: Bacardi Corporation Plant, Palo Seco, Puerto Rico. Warehouse No. 1, Ramon M. Benitez, architect, 1959. Courtesy of The Bacardi Archive.

Right: Bacardi Corporation Plant, Palo Seco, Puerto Rico. *Merendero* (Centennial Pavilion) with view of El Morro and Old San Juan beyond. SACMAG, architects, 1962. Courtesy of The Bacardi Heritage Foundation.

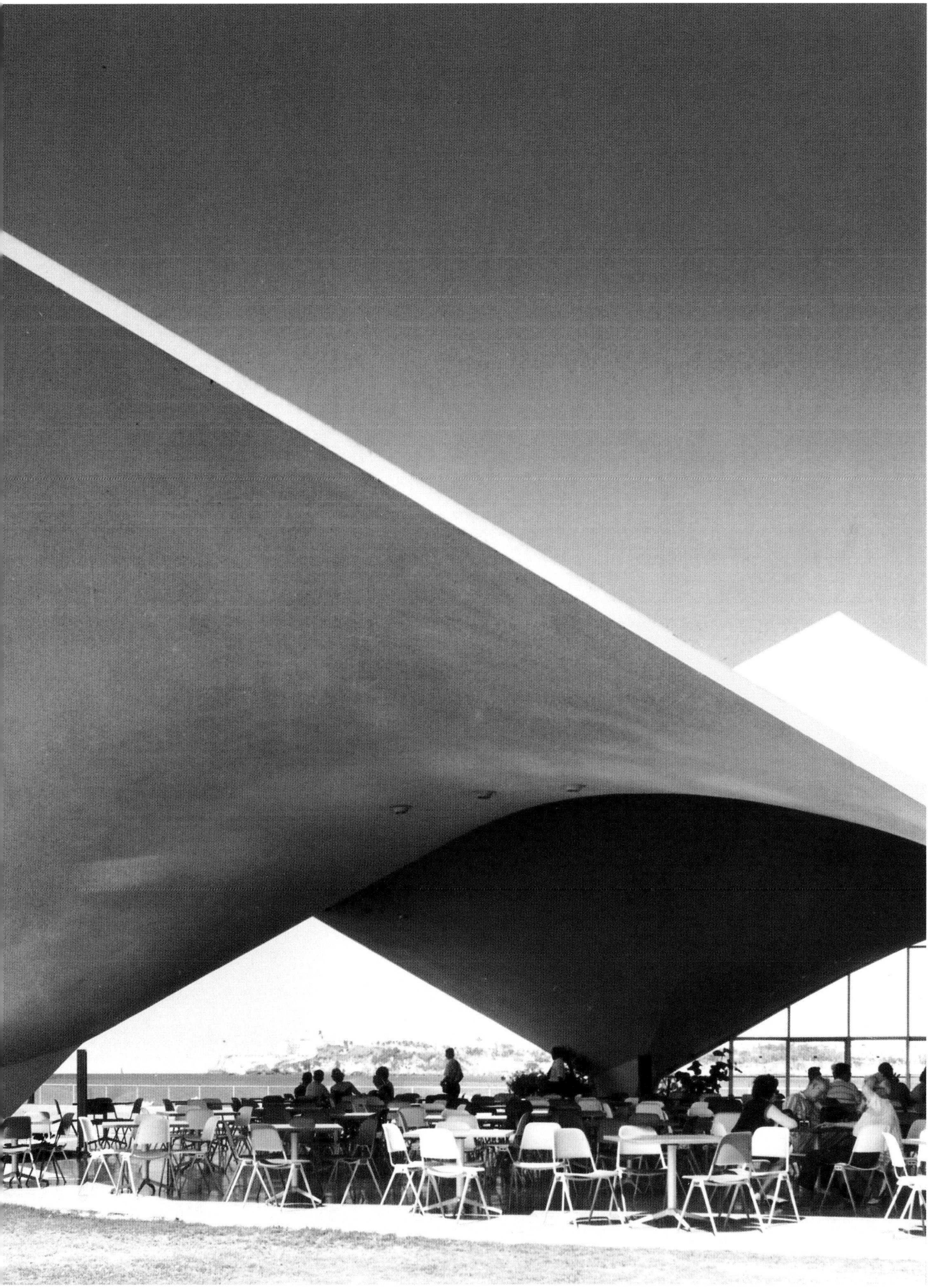

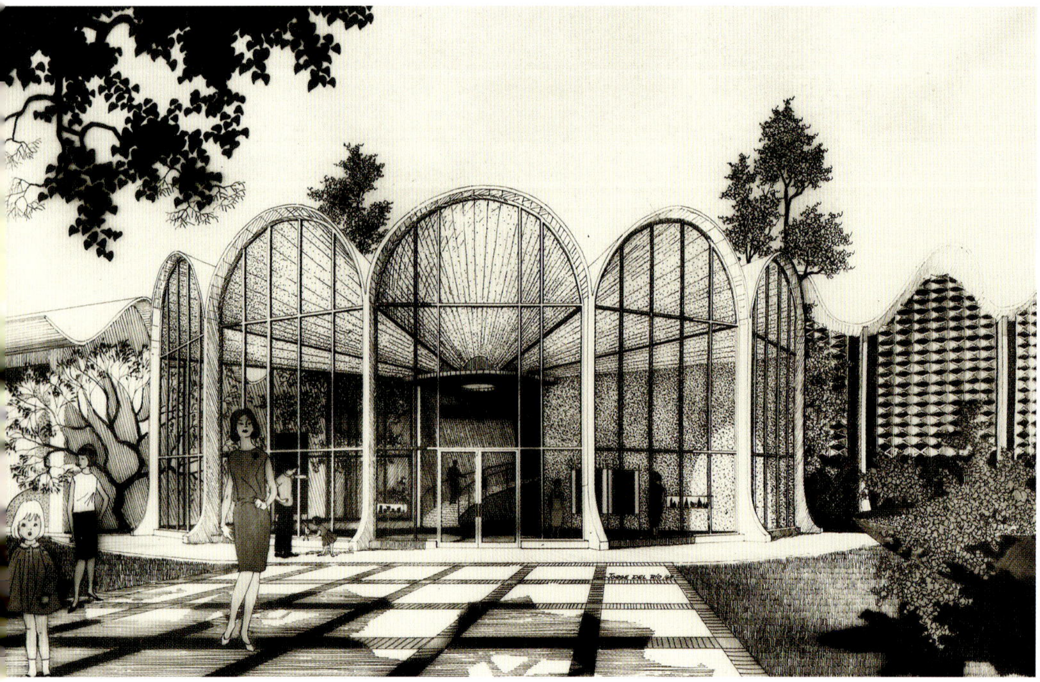

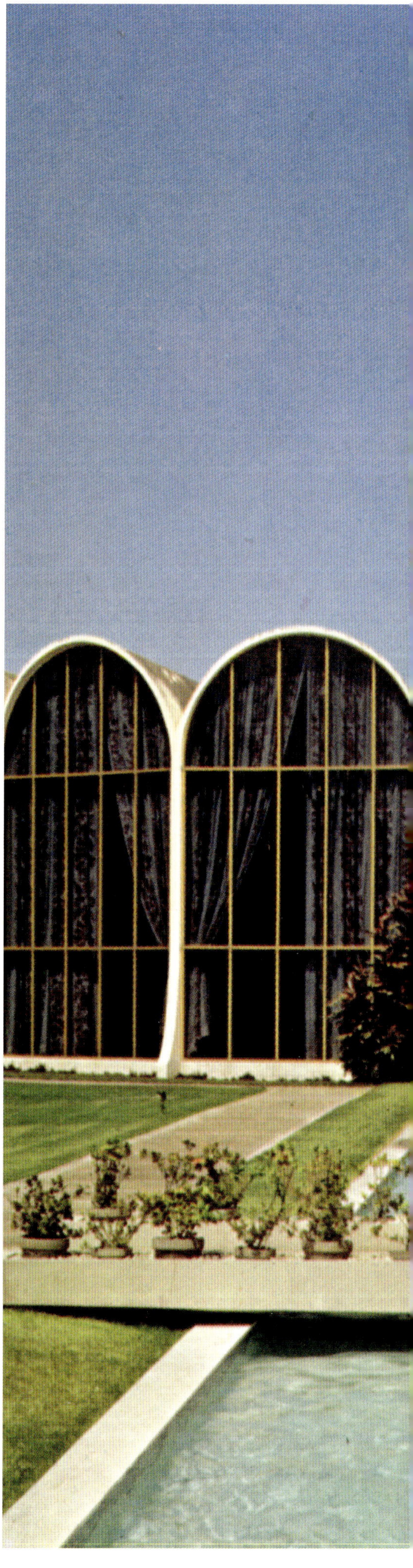

Above: Bacardi Corporation Plant, Foyer Museum and Bottling Plant, Palo Seco, Puerto Rico. Perspective. Miguel Rosich and Ignacio Carerra-Justiz, architects, 1965. Courtesy of The Bacardi Heritage Foundation.

Right: Bacardi Corporation Plant, Foyer Museum and Bottling Plant, Palo Seco, Puerto Rico. Miguel Rosich and Ignacio Carerra-Justiz, architects, 1965. Courtesy of The Bacardi Heritage Foundation.

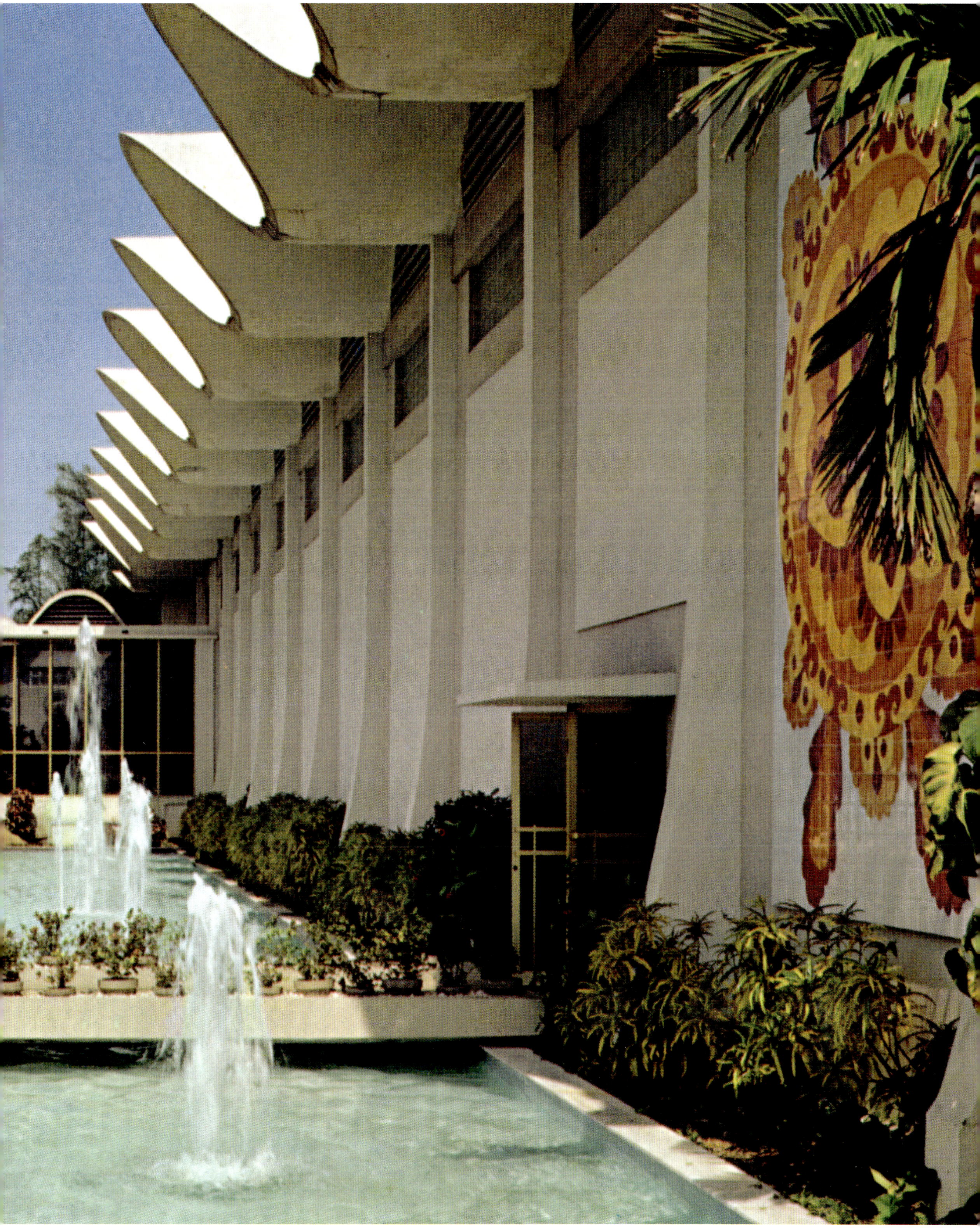

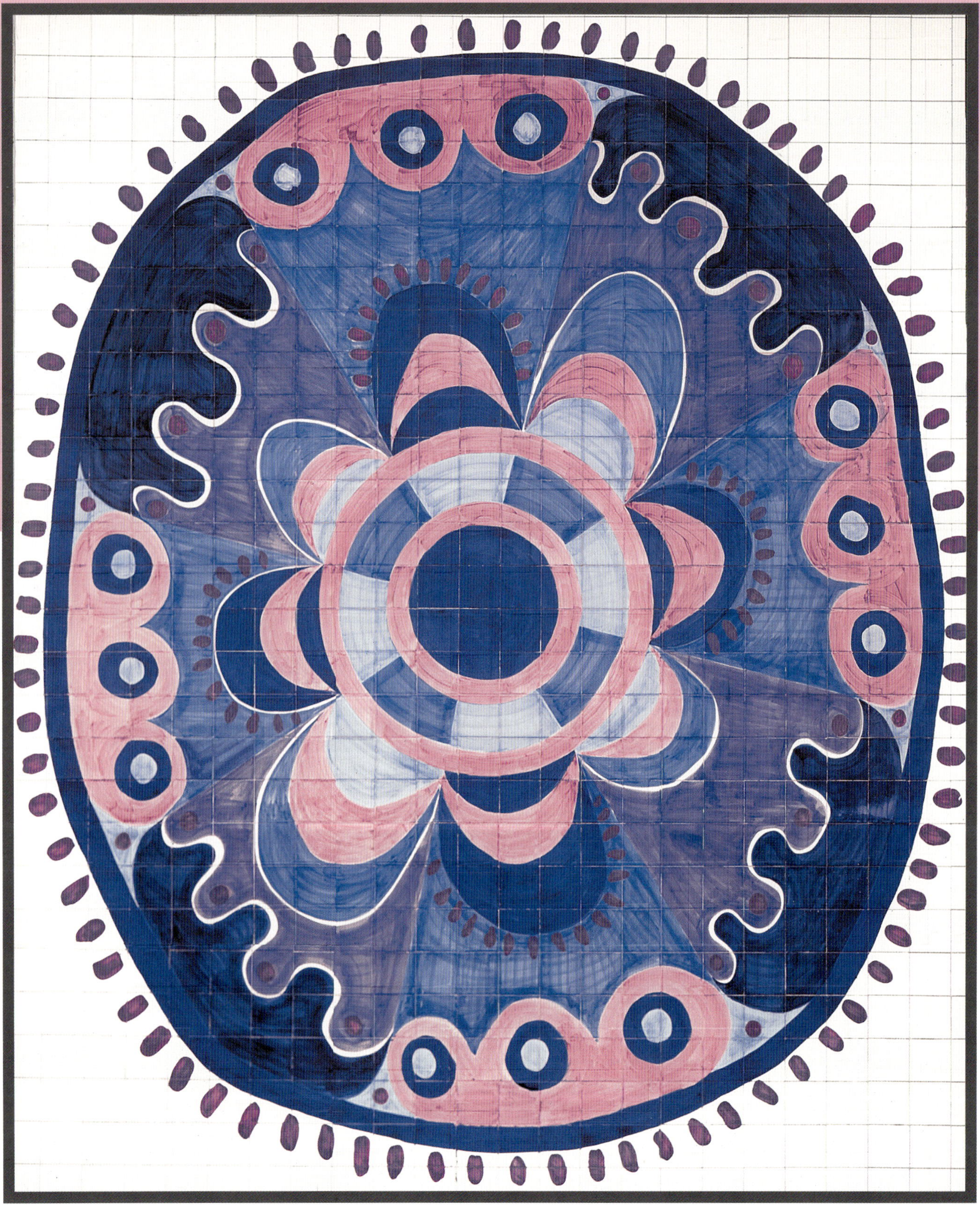

Excerpts from the fantasy flower tile mural series facing the Bottling Plant, Palo Seco, Puerto Rico.
Rosalía Pujó, painter. Courtesy of The Bacardi Archive.

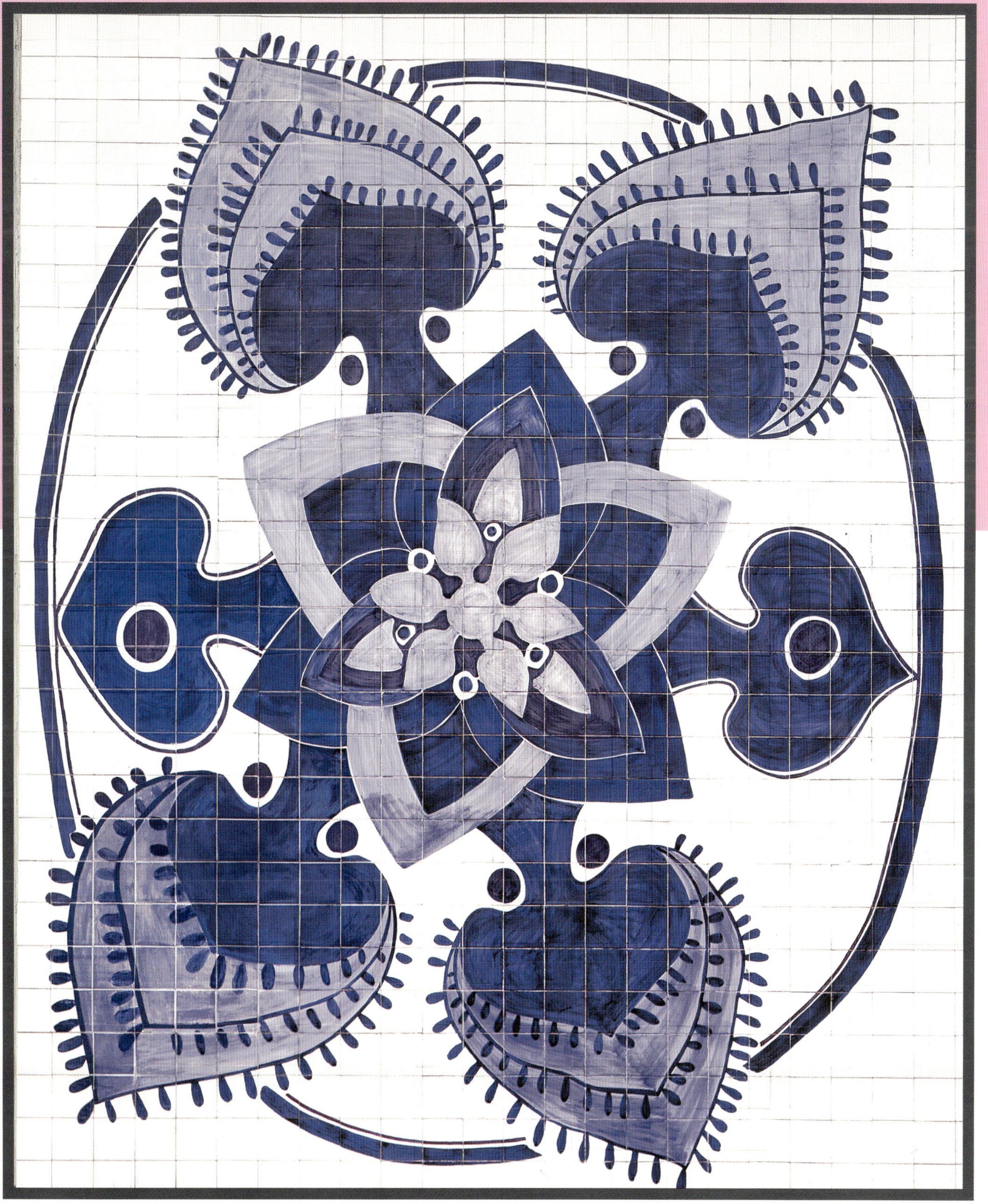

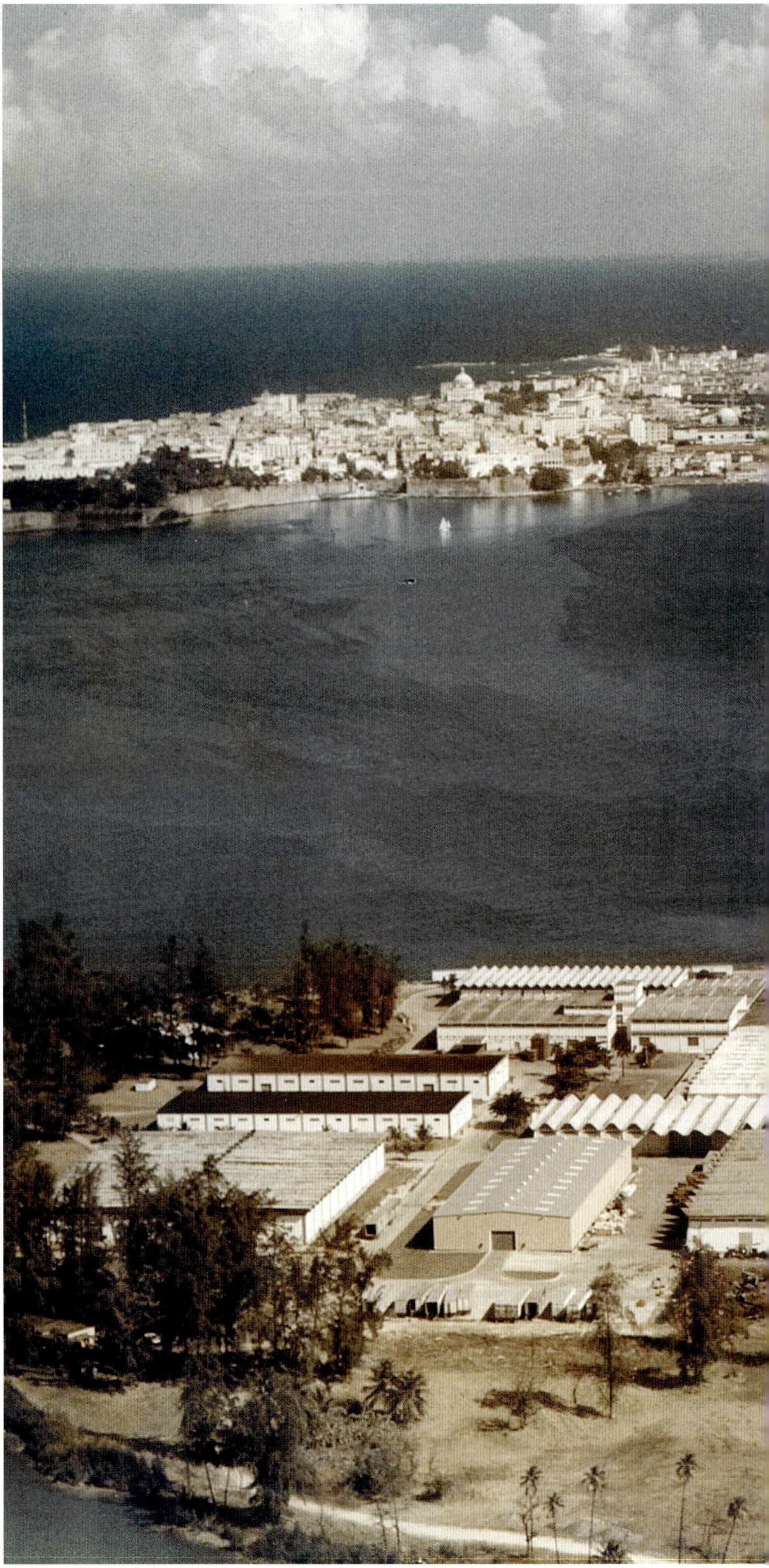

Bacardi Corporation Plant. Palo Seco, Puerto Rico.
Aerial view of buildings with Old San Juan beyond.
Courtesy of The Bacardi Archive.

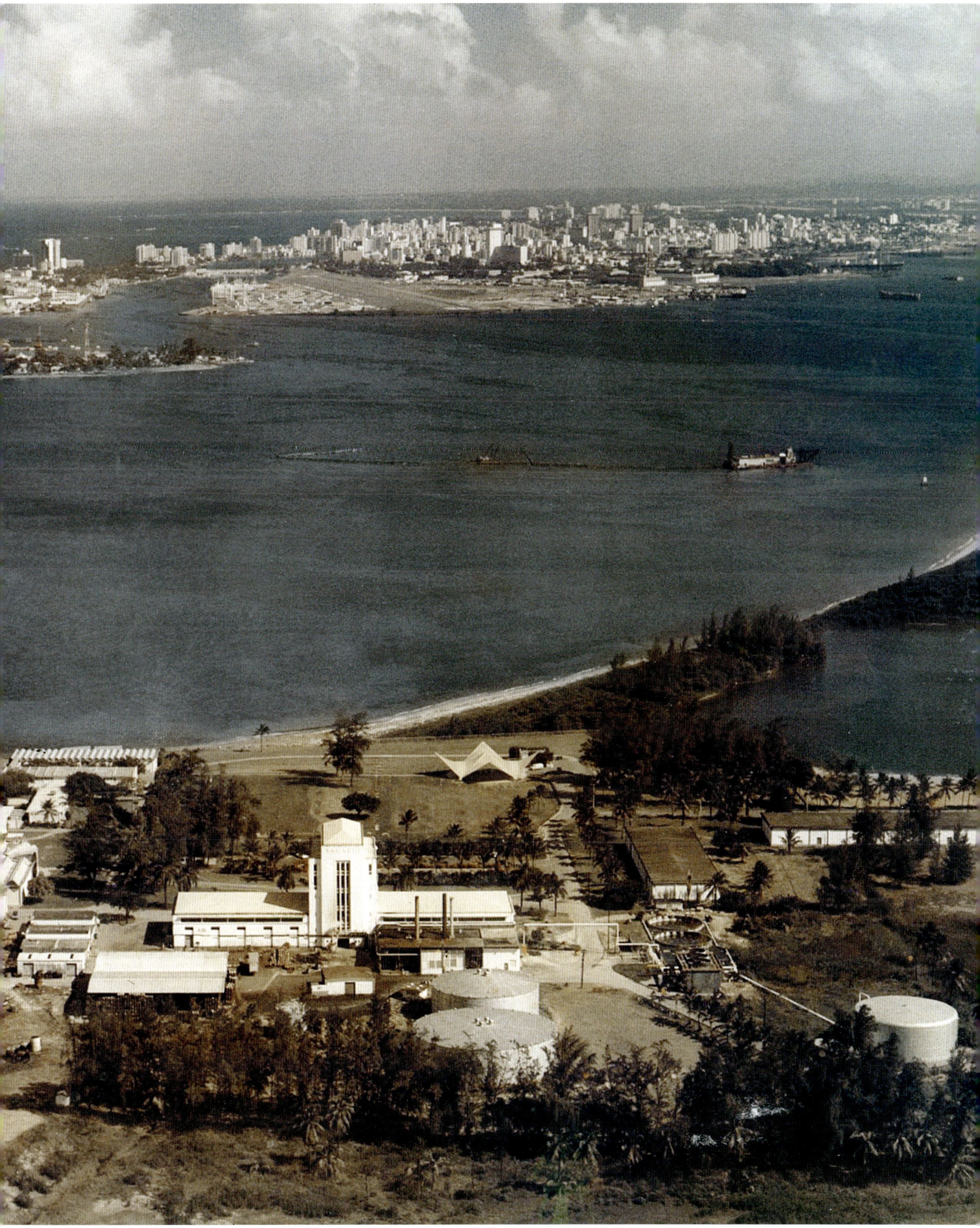

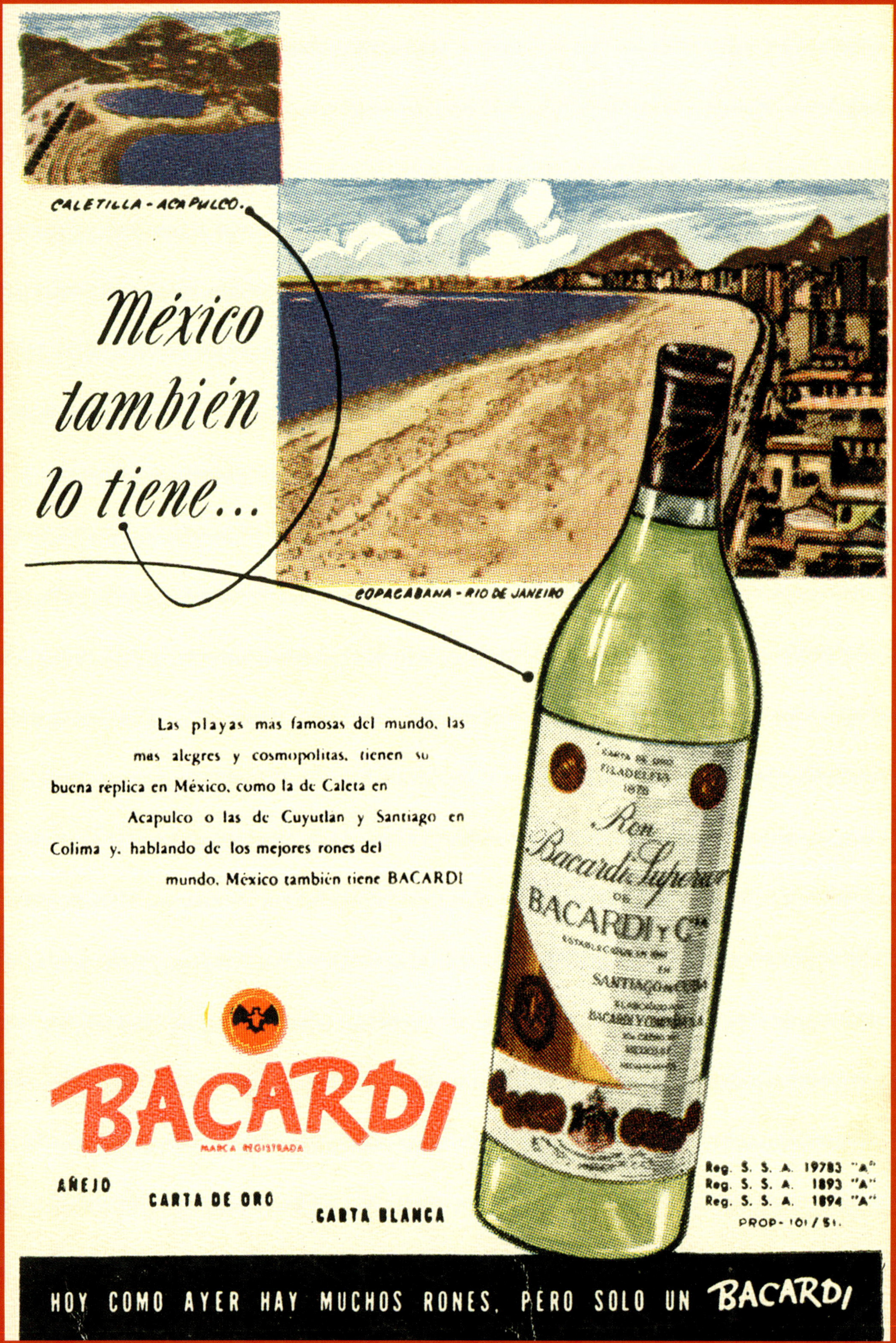
CALETILLA - ACAPULCO.
México
también
lo tiene...
COPACABANA - RIO DE JANEIRO
Las playas mas famosas del mundo, las
mas alegres y cosmopolitas, tienen su
buena réplica en México, como la de Caleta en
Acapulco o las de Cuyutlan y Santiago en
Colima y, hablando de los mejores rones del
mundo, México también tiene BACARDI
Ron
Bacardi Superior
BACARDI y Cia
SANTIAGO DE CUBA
BACARDI
MARCA REGISTRADA
AÑEJO
CARTA DE ORO
CARTA BLANCA
Reg. S. S. A. 19783 "A"
Reg. S. S. A. 1893 "A"
Reg. S. S. A. 1894 "A"
PROP- 101 / 51.
HOY COMO AYER HAY MUCHOS RONES, PERO SOLO UN BACARDI

BACARDI IN MEXICO

The development of new Bacardi campuses accelerated throughout the 1950s. If the company's first modern campus in Puerto Rico was ad hoc, new developments, principally in Mexico, were decisively scripted. Bacardi's Mexican operations had begun in 1931, in Atlampa, an industrial area of Mexico City. A young Pepín Bosch acculturated Bacardi to the Mexican context in part by permitting the Mexican unit to represent the company in progressive and adventurous ways. Bacardi Mexico became a demonstration unit for the company, tapping new markets, testing new management practices, and building state-of-the-art facilities.[105] Bosch's keen sense of marketing, paired with Mexico's own emerging culture of modernism, shaped the development of two remarkable and very different industrial plants: the fermentation and distillation plant at La Galarza, completed in 1956, and the bottling plant in Tultitlán, completed in 1959.

Whereas the Bacardi campus in San Juan was created *ex nihilo* on open terrain, Bacardi chose an ancient site for its Mexican distillery.[106] In 1955, Bacardi purchased La Galarza, a former hacienda in the picturesque Matamoros Valley. The valley stretches southwest from Puebla, the colonial capital of the state of Puebla, toward the city of Izucar de Matamoros. The climate at an altitude of 4,500 feet is subtropical, and the hills frame views of the Popocatepetl volcano. The waters of this volcano irrigate an important sugar producing and refining area where haciendas, like the *ingenios* (sugar mills) of eastern Cuba, were once concentrated.[107] The redevelopment of La Galarza tied Bacardi to Mexican landscape and history, establishing roots in an adopted land.

Mexican architects Hector Mestre and Manuel de la Colina, and the Cuban engineer Luis P. Saenz (Saenz-Cancio-Martin), collaborated with Felix Candela on the redevelopment of the hacienda. Candela was responsible for the new plant buildings, a tightly-knit complex of vaulted concrete structures erected in front of the old hacienda. The Spanish émigré had experimented with concrete vaults as early as 1949. With Cubiertas Ala, the company he cofounded in 1950, Candela parlayed the efficiency and natural economy of concrete shells into his position as a preeminent architect of industrial buildings and warehouses in Mexico. By hiring Candela, Bacardi embarked on a new adventure, using shell construction as a medium of design.

Acting as architect, engineer and contractor, Candela produced a variety of purpose-built structures, ascetic solutions to covering pumps, boilers and other functional requirements of a distillery. Most of the new structures were concrete barrel vaults that echoed the ancient brick structures of the adjacent hacienda. The most unusual was the 1 ½ inch–thick handkerchief dome that spanned 65 feet to cover the fermentation tanks, its spherical vault braced only by thin concrete ties. The open-air dome and vaults put Bacardi's plant equipment on display (even if the rum formula remained secret). Candela biographer Colin Faber found the baring of industry invigorating: "There are few walls but many colors. Concrete surfaces are exposed except for the shell roofs, which are waterproofed with orange paint… The complex of pipes, vats, tubes and mechanical components were painted according to their functions. The blacks, dark greens, whites, reds, and bronze hues are in fine contrast with the concrete."[108]

Beside Candela's vaulted plant structures was Saenz's distilling tower, a new type comparable, visually, to the rocket and gantry of a spaceport. Its concrete scaffold of vertical piers, circular catwalks and spiraling stairways ringed gleaming stainless steel distilling columns that rose almost 60 feet. Bacardi's Juan Grau had engineered this distilling apparatus to allow perfect taste matching with Bacardi's Cuban rum, and Saenz translated its purpose into naked industrial imagery that embodied the company's postwar faith in chemical science.[109] The tower combined purpose

Mexico tambien lo tiene… BACARDÍ (Mexico also has it… *BACARDÍ*). Advertisement, 1956.
Courtesy of The Bacardi Archive.

and symbol, creating a prototype industrial landmark for the modern age that would mark Bacardi distilleries built over the next decade.

The remainder of the plant was built within the stone and brick vestiges of the seventeenthth century hacienda. Architects de la Colina and Mestre, a native of Puebla, were probably responsible for the overall transformation of the antique structures.[110] Just a few years before they established a highly successful practice of modern corporate architecture in Mexico City, the architects judiciously outfitted La Galarza's brick vaults with offices, demonstration spaces and boardrooms, as well as plant equipment. A portion of the hacienda, located on high ground, was developed as a guesthouse, including meeting rooms and a bar. Here, a patio, retrofitted with a lawn, swimming pool and an outdoor bar, served as a retreat for family members and executives.

In fact, all of La Galarza's renovation seems designed with the visitor-tourist in mind, organized to fulfill expectations of an authentic Mexican experience. Former work precincts were transformed into scenic commons marked by tree-lined allées and plazas. A small private chapel, built in 1693, was restored as the focal point for a picturesque network of groves, gardens, lawns, canals and lagoons. The divergent imagery of the agrarian hacienda and the concrete plant structures was juxtaposed in sublime contrast at the Plaza Don Facundo, a small landscaped square that sat inbetween.

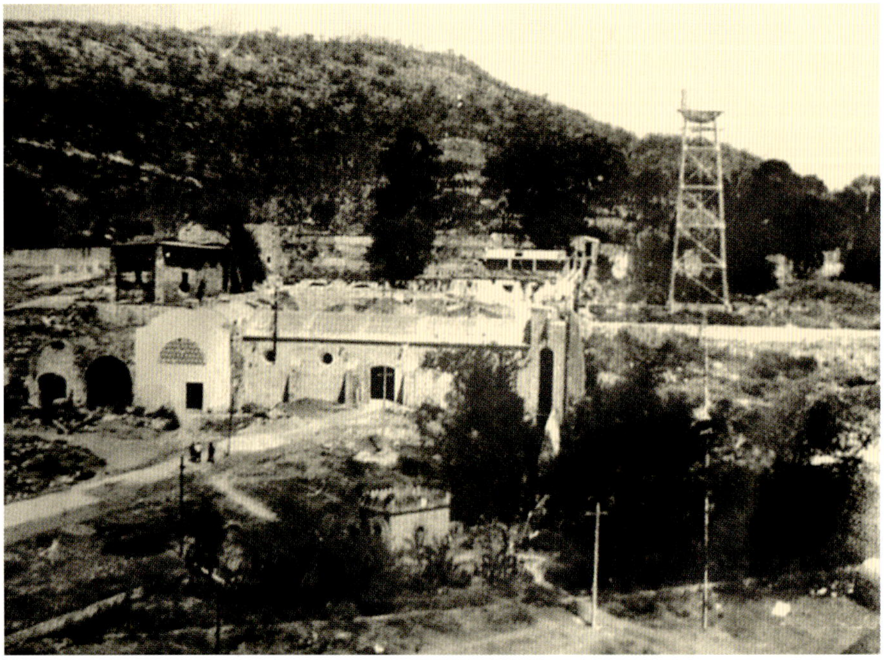

Upon the ruins of a colonial past, La Galarza's scenery was indeed integrated as a conscious act of brand development: a sugar mill recast as distillery and retreat. The encounter of old and new, picturesque and industrial was everywhere raised to a thematic level. Restored arcades, buttressed stonework, oculi, brick vaulting and battlements achieved new prominence when the stucco finishes of the colonial structures were removed. The stripping of stucco revealed stone and brick construction with roots in Roman masonry construction, reinterpreting the structures as a type of romantic ruin. The hacienda, reinterpreted and aestheticized as historic artifact, now functioned as a pastoral domain. Its rustic walls served as dramatic foil to the new concrete and steel industrial plant.

Within the context of the 1950s industrial transformation of Mexico, La Galarza represented a peculiar, anti-heroic model distinct from the international modern industrial and commercial architecture proliferating in Mexico (such as Guillermo Rossell y Lorenzo Carrasco's Automex plant). At La Galarza, industry symbolized not only progress, but also continuity and commitment. Bacardi mixed state-of-the-art production and historic artifacts with touristic spaces and models of hospitality to create an efficient and glamorous facility.

Hacienda La Galarza, Matamoros, Puebla, Mexico, c. 1950. Courtesy Bacardi Mexico.

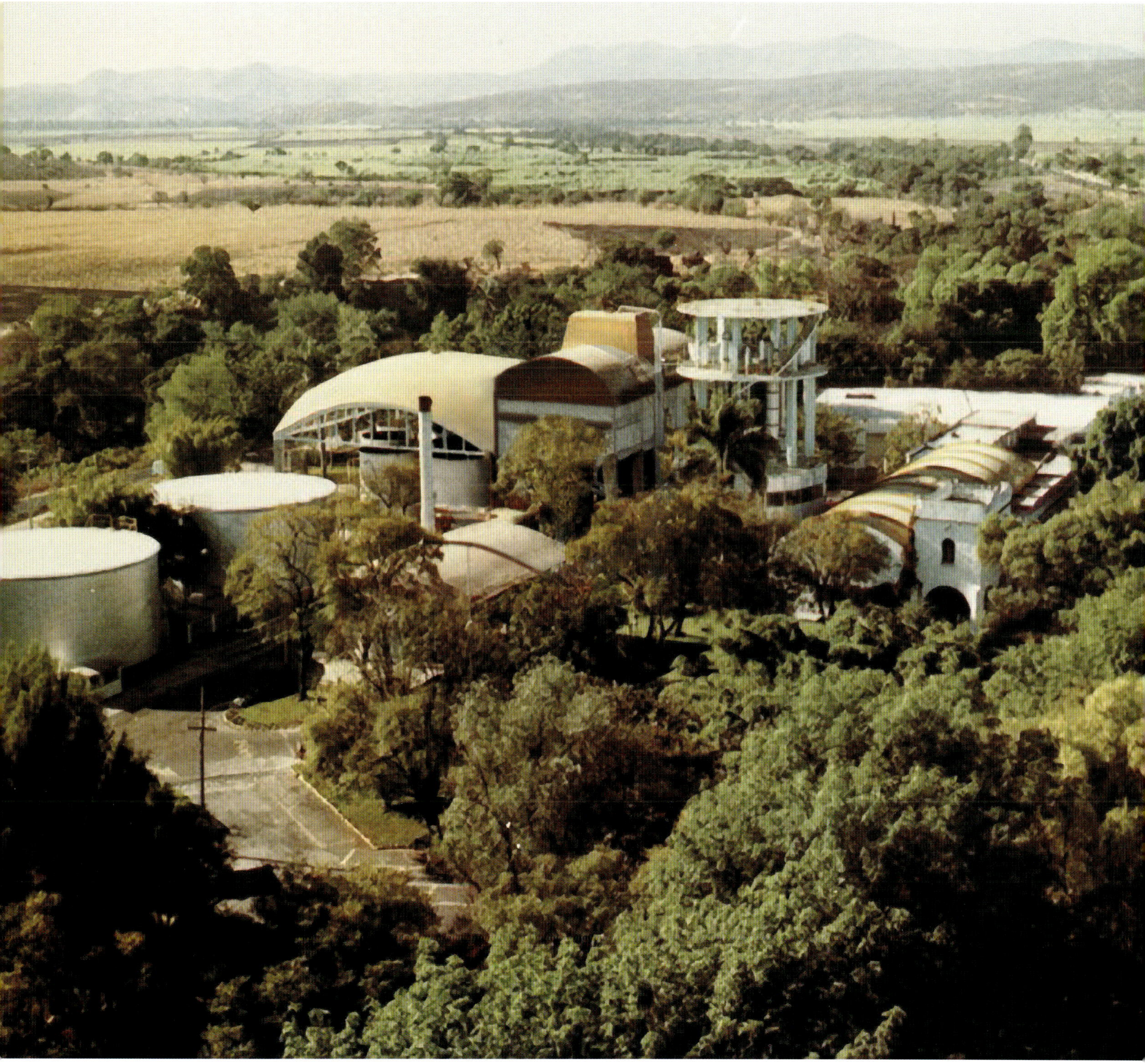

Bacardi y Compañía ,S.A. Distillery, La Galarza, Matamoros, Puebla, Mexico. Aerial view.
Félix Candela (Cubiertas Ala) with Héctor Mestre y Manuel de la Colina, architects;
distillation tower by Luis Saenz, engineer, 1954-55. Courtesy of The Bacardi Archive.

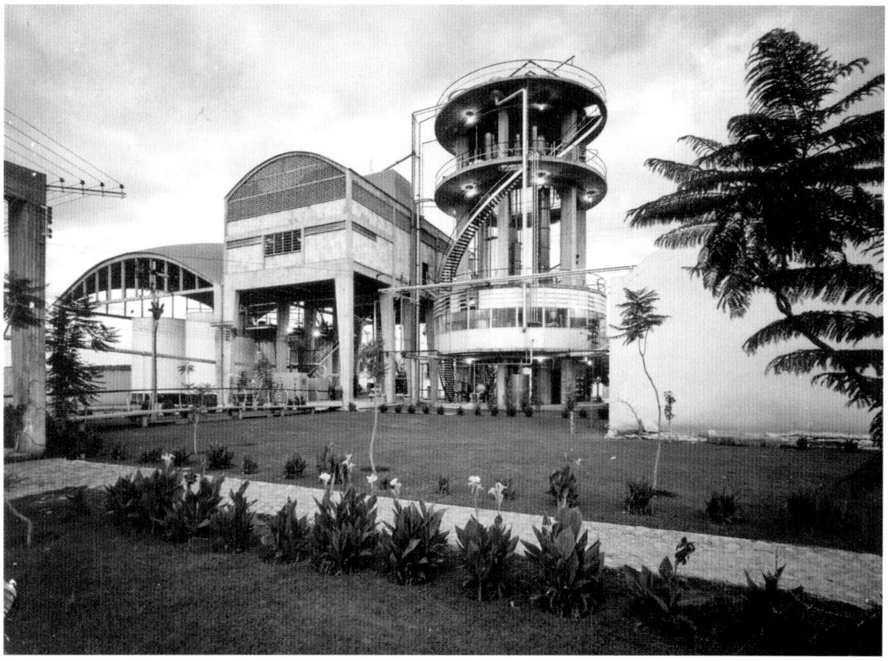

To complement the distillery at La Galarza, Bacardi developed a bottling plant and administration building along the Central Highway leading north out of Mexico City toward Queretaro. The site, surrounded by volcanoes, mountains and lakes, was in proximity to the ancient pyramid city of Teotihuacan. The site's Aztec name, *Tultitlán*, spoke to Mexico's history, but the highway and incipient industrial districts provided a modern context for the facility, which was planned along functionalist lines.

Tultitlán's planning stands in contrast to the romantic landscape of the distillery in La Galarza. Felix Candela, again paired with Saenz-Cancio-Martin (now SACMAG), and with Luis Torres Landa, a Mexican engineer, was responsible for most of the plant design. Candela produced a variety of concrete shell structures at Tultitlán—groin vaults, barrel vaults, umbrellas, and folded plate concrete slabs—a mix nearly emblematic of his career. In the open plain of Tultitlán's industrial outlands, the peaks and valleys of the facility's varied roof forms produced their own extraordinary landscape.

The lead figure among Candela's various shell forms was the cavernous groin-vaulted bottling plant, which was invested with a sense of monumentality. According to Candela, the hall was partly inspired by Minoru Yamasaki and Anton Tedesko's recently completed Lambert–St. Louis Airport Terminal (and by extension the Roman tradition of groin-vaulted spaces, like the Baths of Caracalla). Candela re-interpreted Lambert's intersecting barrel vaults using hyperbolic paraboloid (hypar) shells, double-curved surfaces whose shell-like structural membranes achieved elegance and ultra-thinness. The design called for nine bays covering an area of almost 90,000 square feet with only four intermediate supports;[111] each vault, only 1½-inches thick, spanned 85 feet and rose 32 feet off the floor.[112] The vaulted bays also stood independently, allowing for bat-winged sky-lit slots between the shells that illuminated the building interior. The vault surfaces were fluidly contoured, sculpting space and light.

The spacious bottling hall, completed in 1959, produced an extraordinary series of lofty rooms, more akin to the main hall of a railway station than to a factory. As Carlos Brillembourg notes, "The beauty of the solution asks us to consider these

Left: Bacardi y Compañia, S.A. Distillery, La Galarza, Matamoros, Puebla, Mexico. New plant buildings. Félix Candela (Cubiertas Ala) with Héctor Mestre y Manuel de la Colina, architects; distillation tower by Luis Saenz, engineer, 1954-55. Drawings and Archives, Avery Architectural and Fine Arts Library, Columbia University.

Right: Bacardi y Compañia, S.A. Distillery, La Galarza, Matamoros, Puebla, Mexico. Site plan. Félix Candela (Cubiertas Ala) with Héctor Mestre y Manuel de la Colina, architects; distillation tower by Luis Saenz, engineer, 1954-55. Drawings and Archives, Avery Architectural and Fine Arts Library, Columbia University.

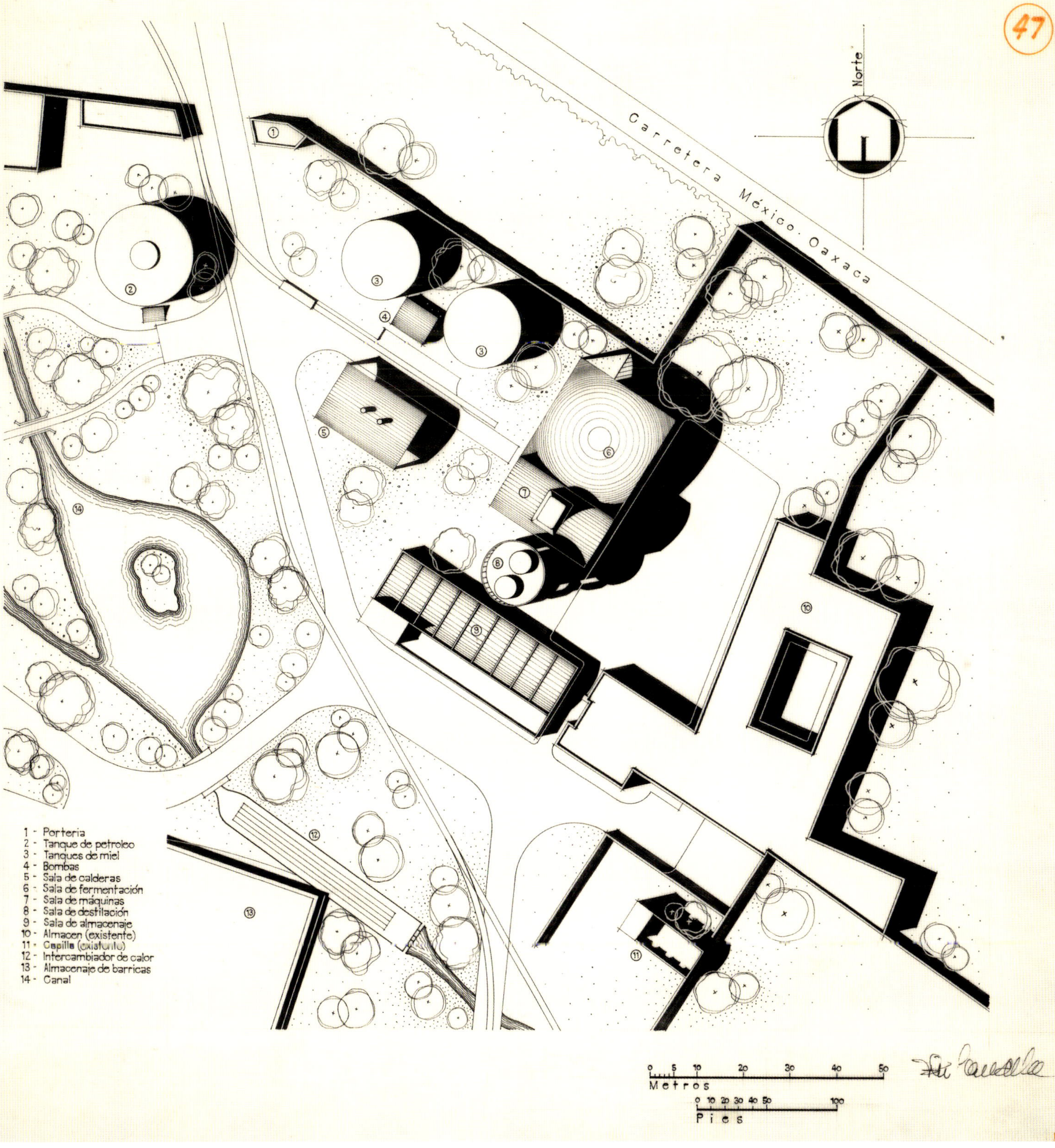
Carretera México Oaxaca
Norte
1 - Porteria
2 - Tanque de petroleo
3 - Tanques de miel
4 - Bombas
5 - Sala de calderas
6 - Sala de fermentación
7 - Sala de máquinas
8 - Sala de destilación
9 - Sala de almacenaje
10 - Almacen (existente)
11 - Capilla (existente)
12 - Intercambiador de calor
13 - Almacenaje de barricas
14 - Canal
0 5 10 20 30 40 50
Metros
0 10 20 30 40 50 100
Pies

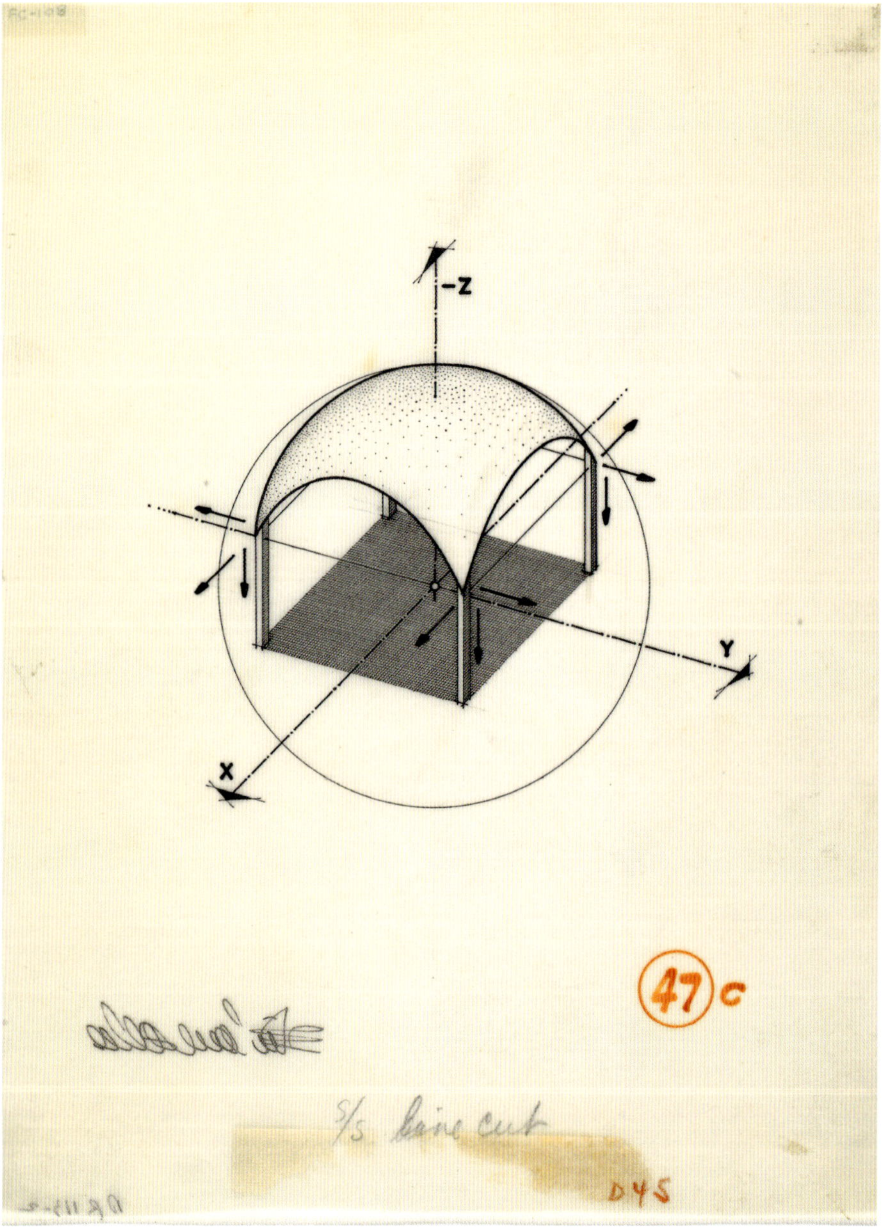

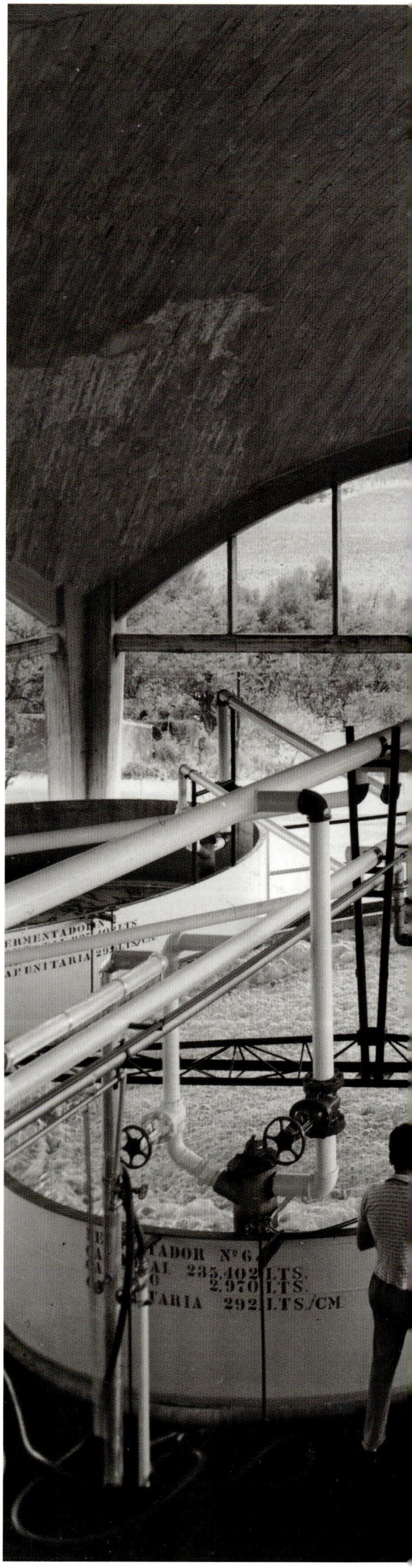

Above: Bacardi y Compañía, S.A. Distillery, La Galarza, Matamoros, Puebla, Mexico. Isometric drawing of handkerchief dome signed by Félix Candela. Drawings and Archives, Avery Architectural and Fine Arts Library, Columbia University.

Right : Bacardi y Compañía, S.A. Distillery, La Galarza, Matamoros, Puebla, Mexico. Fermentation tanks beneath the handkerchief dome. Félix Candela (Cubiertas Ala) with Héctor Mestre y Manuel de la Colina, architects, 1954-55. Courtesy of The Bacardi Archive.

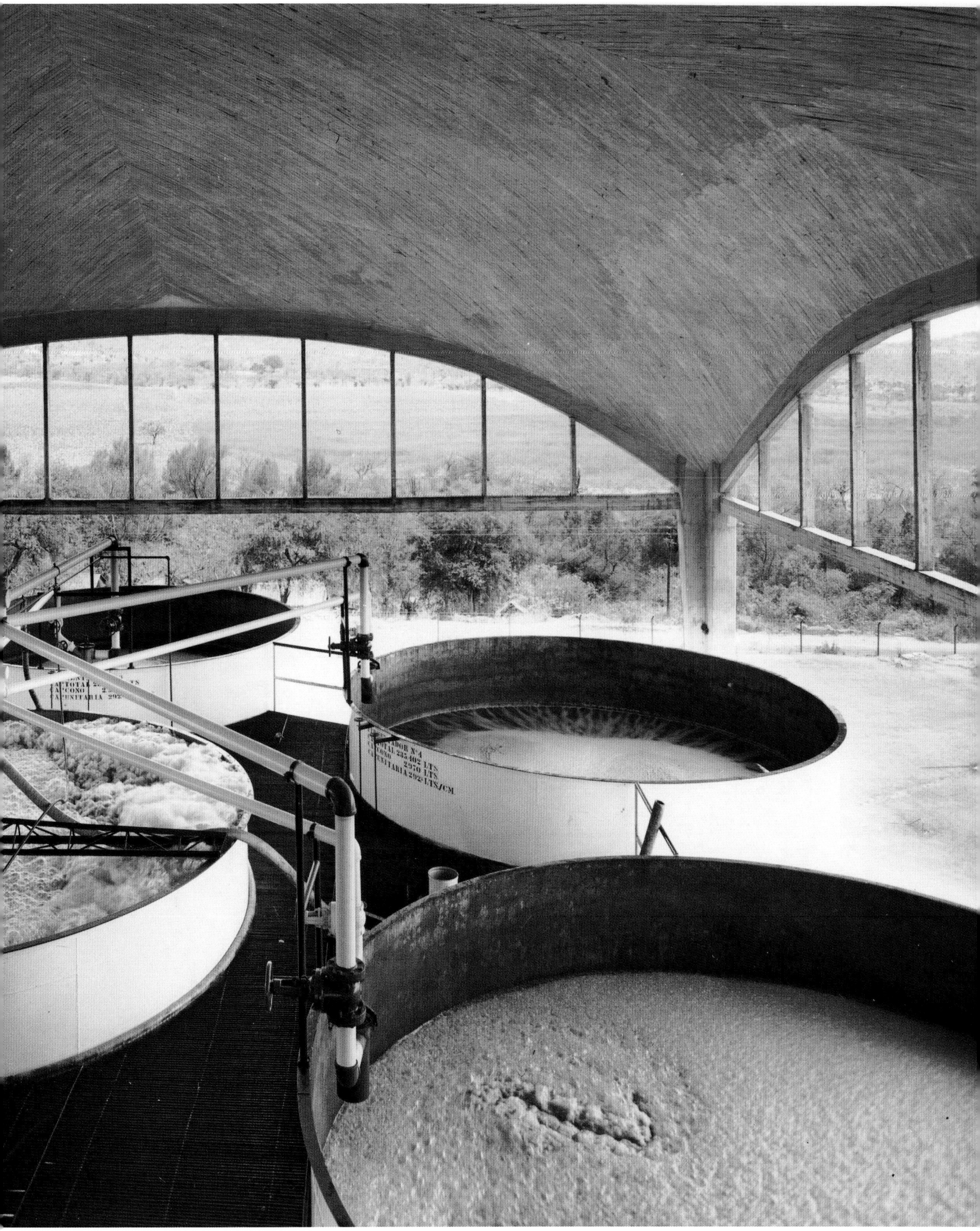
ADOR N°4
235 402 LTS
2970 LTS
292 LTS/CM

spaces independent of their original use, inhabited by art and people rather than by industry."[113] Candela had previously demonstrated the spatial power of hypars in projects like the church of San Antonio de las Huertas (1956), and the Los Manantiales restaurant in Xochimilco (1958). The Bacardi vaults, however, were novel in that they demonstrated how the efficiency of hypars could be translated to industrial uses. [114] By using modern techniques to reinterpret ancient forms, and applying these forms to versatile industrial uses, Candela made concrete relevant in new ways. *Architectural Forum's* photo essay "Four Great Pours," juxtaposed the Bacardi vaults with three prominent concrete works—Eero Saarinen's Dulles Terminal, Pier Luigi Nervi's International Labor Exposition hall and Riccardo Morandi's International Auto Exhibition hall – in order demonstrate "the return of concrete as the confident spanner of great spaces."[115]

Around the bottling hall, Candela developed warehouses, parking shelters and even housing using row upon row of straight-edged umbrellas, a modular construction system that employed a different type of hypar shell. As developed and promoted by Cubiertas Ala, umbrellas were inverted square or rectangular canopies that incorporated their own structure as well as an integrated drainage system. Capable of efficient and endless repetition, umbrellas were easily adapted to the needs of industry.[116] The umbrellas covering the warehouses for aging rum, for instance, were stretched along one axis to achieve larger column-free spans. In the six worker houses Candela produced at the Bacardi plant, each comprising a single umbrella supported on a central column, the shells were downturned in order to shed water.

Candela's landscape of vaults was not, as at La Galarza, showcased along the highway. Instead, a prominent office building for Bacardi Mexico was planned to mark the façade of the campus. SACMAG developed early plans for a single-story steel and glass box whose solid end walls, along with the vertical projection of the utility core, were to be covered with murals. SACMAG partner Ignacio Martin characterized the muralized walls as a solution "closer to the present trend of Mexican artistic expression, which integrates really native painting and sculpture in the architectural concept."[117] Although never built at Tultitlán, the notion of such murals must have intrigued Bosch; SACMAG employed a similar idea at the Bacardi Imports Tower in Miami only four years later.

With turmoil in Cuba, and an exiled Bosch spending much of his time in Mexico, developments at Tultitlán moved quickly. In 1959, Bosch commissioned Mies van der Rohe to take over the design of the administration building and surrounding landscape. Mies's master plan, developed in 1960, shows a grouping of steel and glass pavilions set within a park-like setting. In addition to the administration building, there was a gatehouse, a restaurant pavilion, and a bar pavilion, each deploying the same modular planning and the same syntax of structural steel members and plate glass. Anchored by the raised volume of the administration building, the smaller pavilions were positioned loosely to create dynamic relationships across a park-like landscape. The planning recalls not only the compositional freedom of Mies's interior planning, but also the architect's early 1940s design for the campus of the Illinois Institute of Technology (IIT), in Chicago.[118] Of this small complex, only the administration building would be built, and it remains Mies's only completed work in Latin America.[119]

Plan, section of main structures

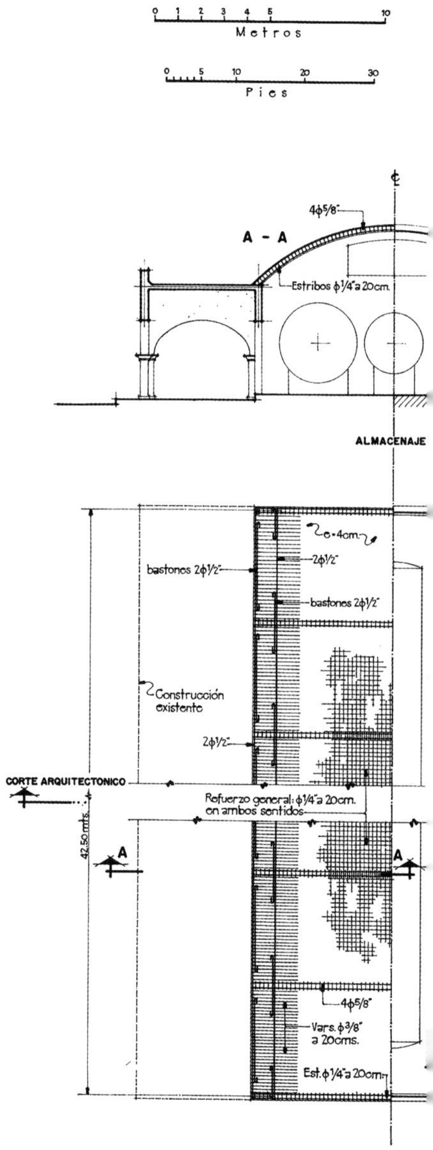

110

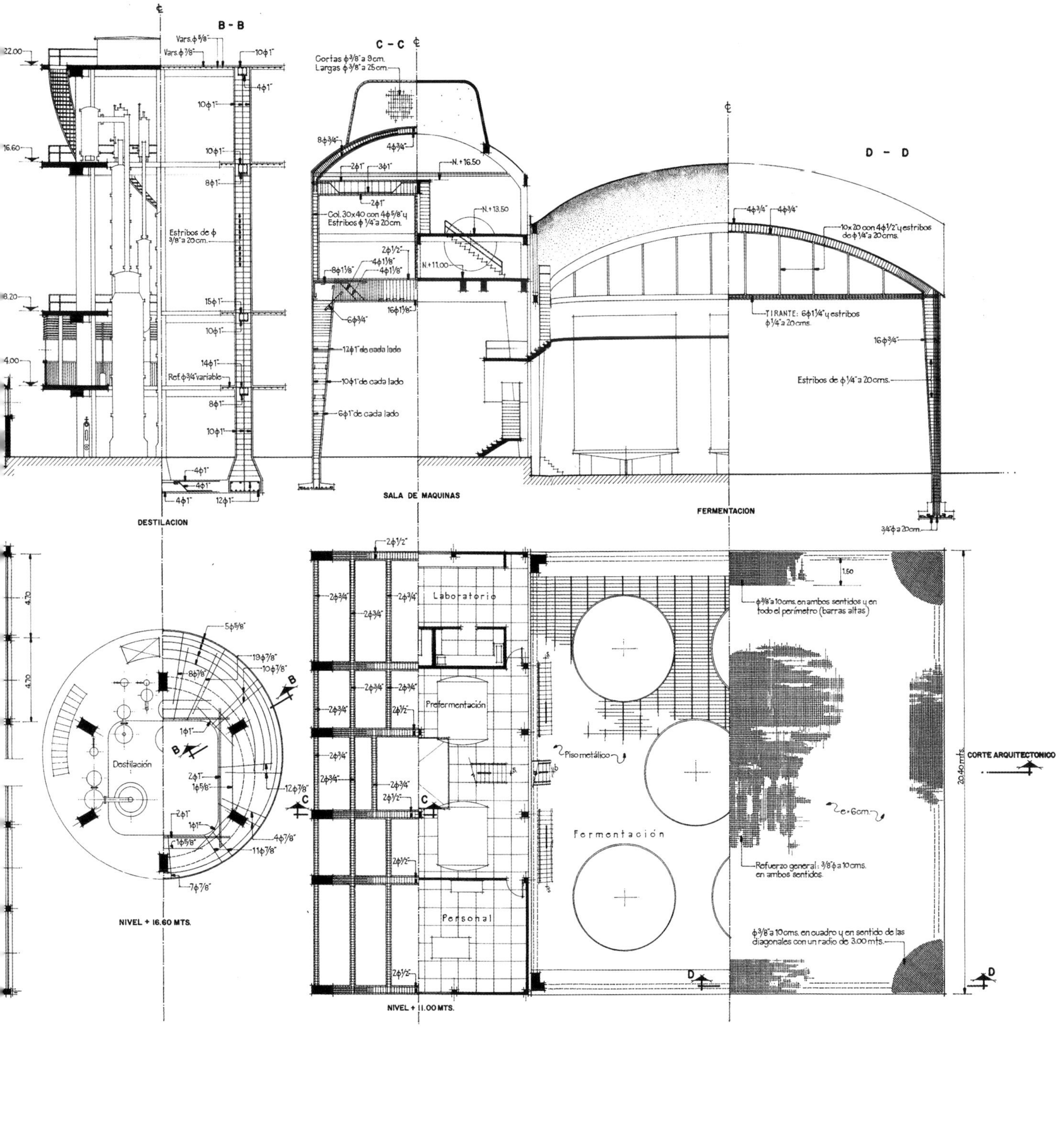

Bacardi y Compañia, S.A. Distillery, La Galarza, Matamoros, Puebla, Mexico. Sections of main plant buildings. Félix Candela (Cubiertas Ala) with Héctor Mestre y Manuel de la Colina, architects; distillation tower by Luis Saenz, engineer, 1954-55. From Colin Faber, *Candela: The Shell Builder* (Reinhold, 1963): 110-111.

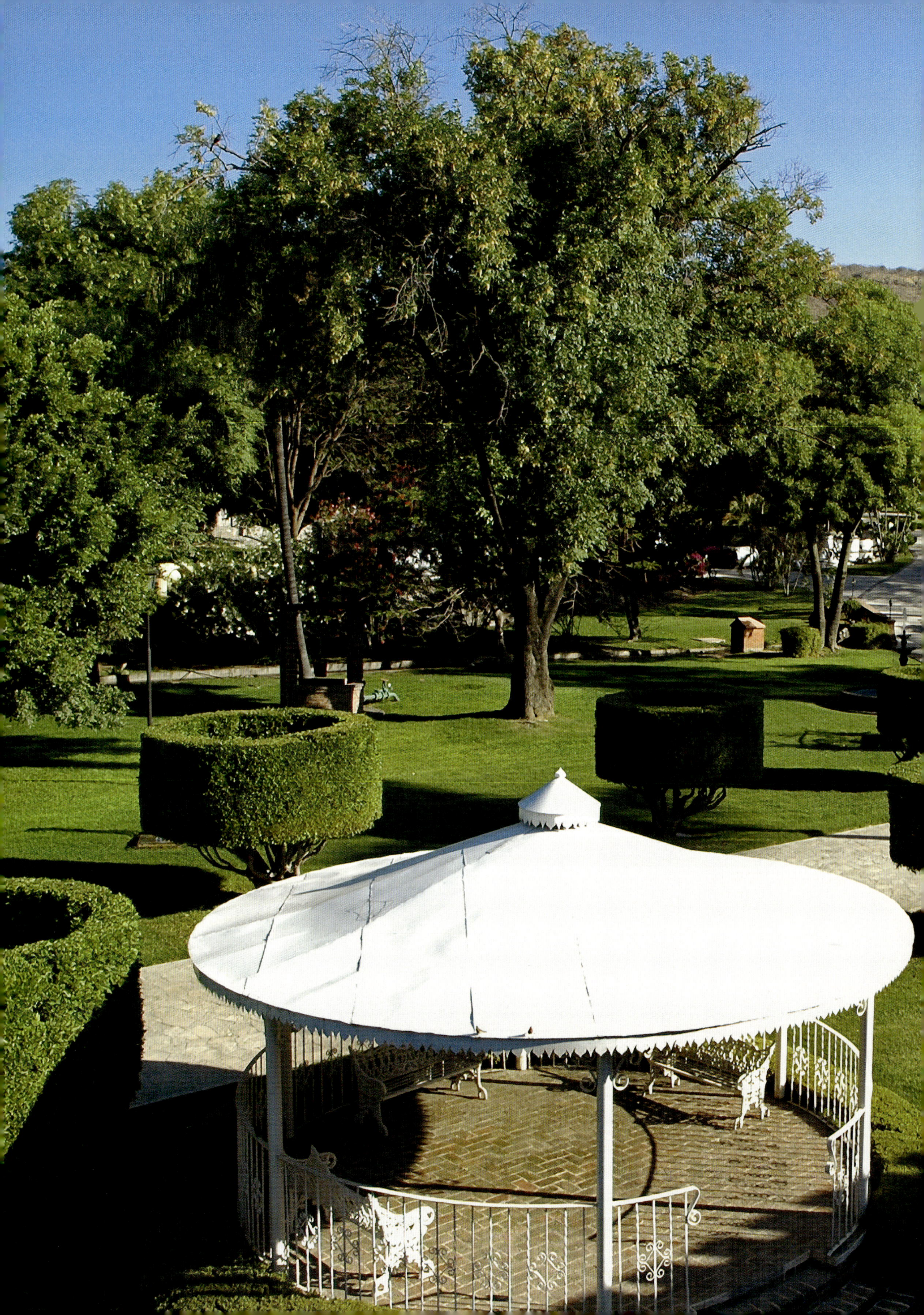

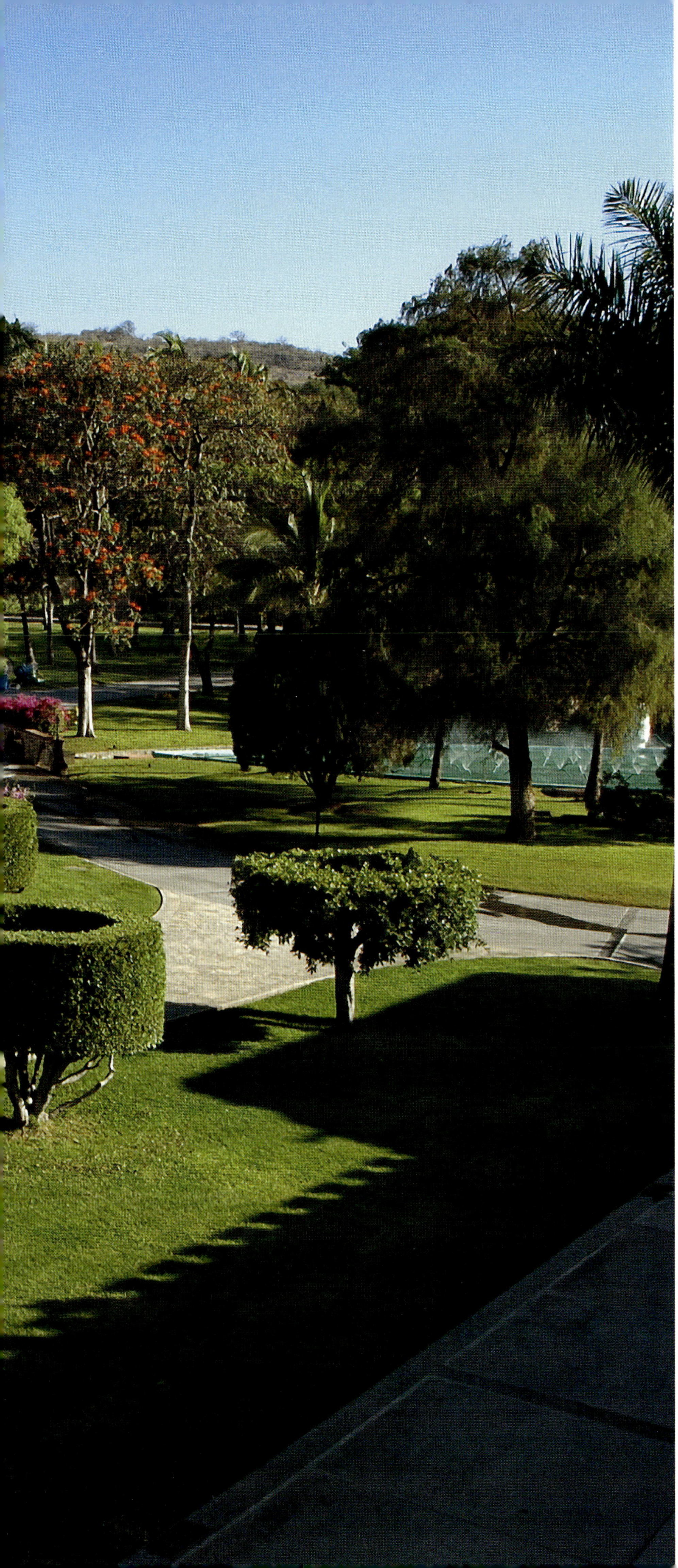

Bacardi y Compañía, S.A. Distillery, La Galarza,
Matamoros, Puebla, Mexico. Gardens.
Courtesy of The Bacardi Archive.

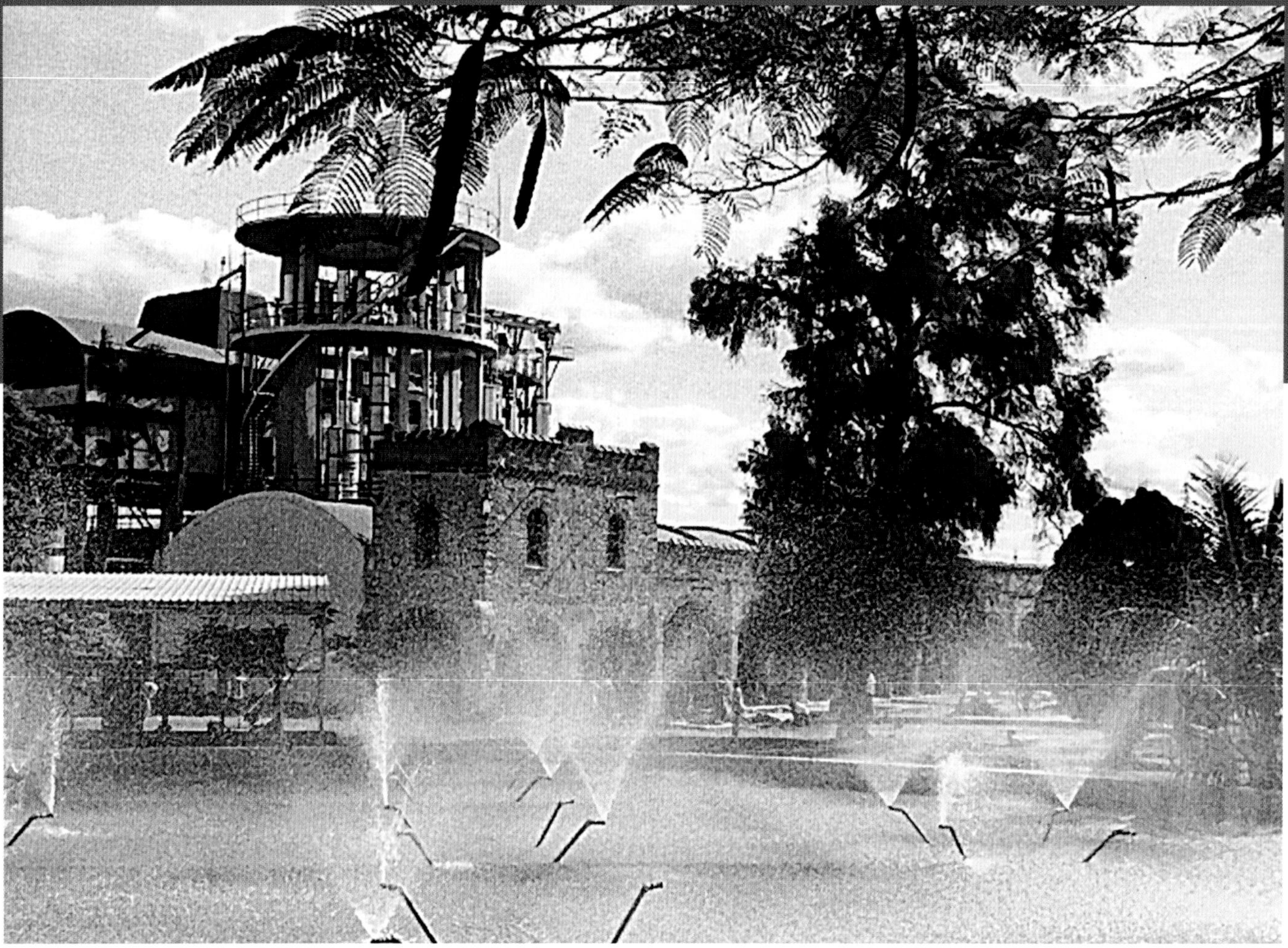

Bacardi y Compañía, S.A. Distillery, La Galarza, Matamoros, Puebla, Mexico. New plant buildings and distillation tower rising above the historic hacienda buildings. Photograph, 1950s. Courtesy of The Bacardi Archive.

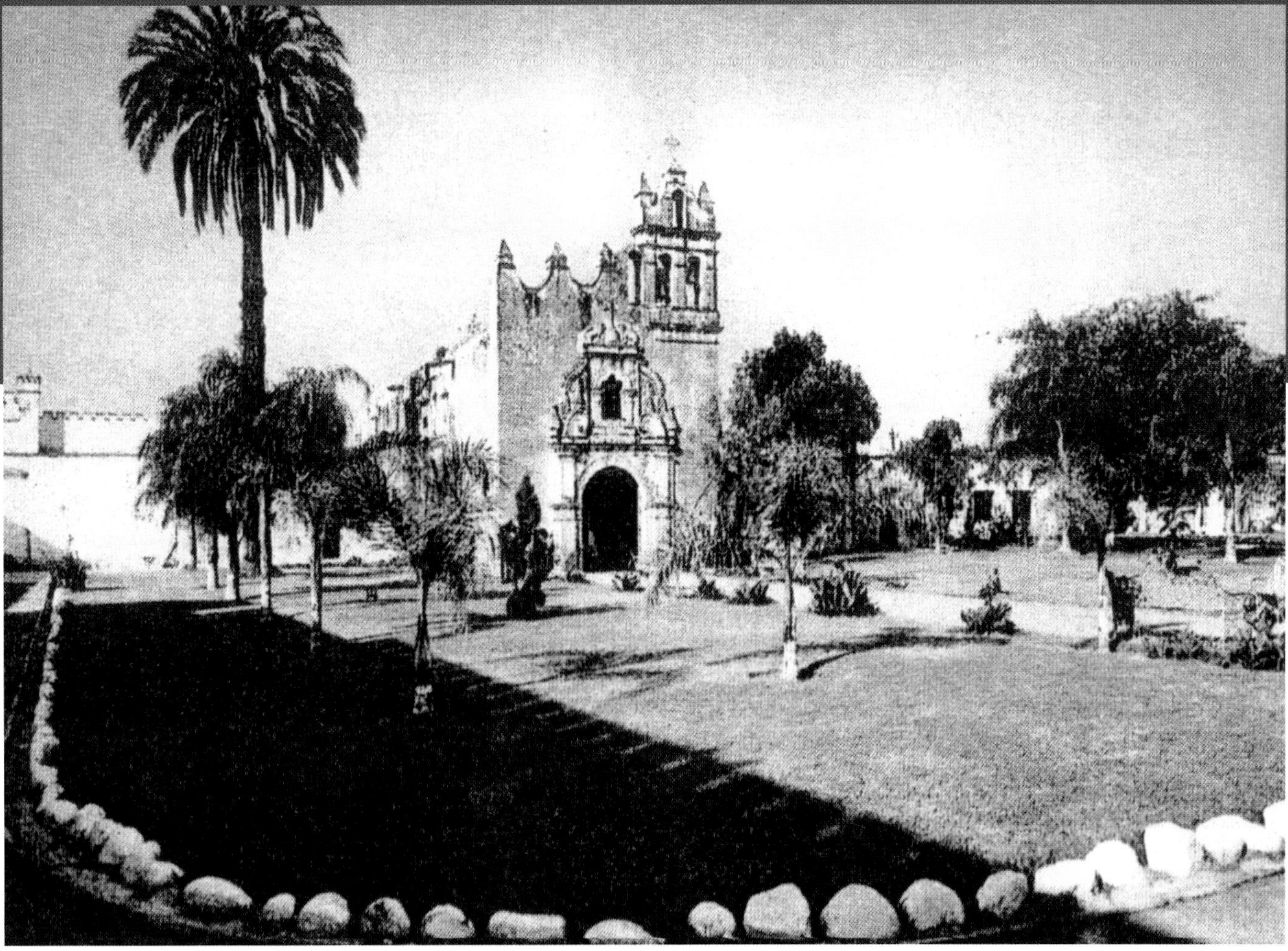

Bacardi y Compañia, S.A. Distillery, La Galarza, Matamoros, Puebla, Mexico. Chapel, 1693, on the grounds of La Galarza. Photograph, 1950s. Courtesy of The Bacardi Archive.

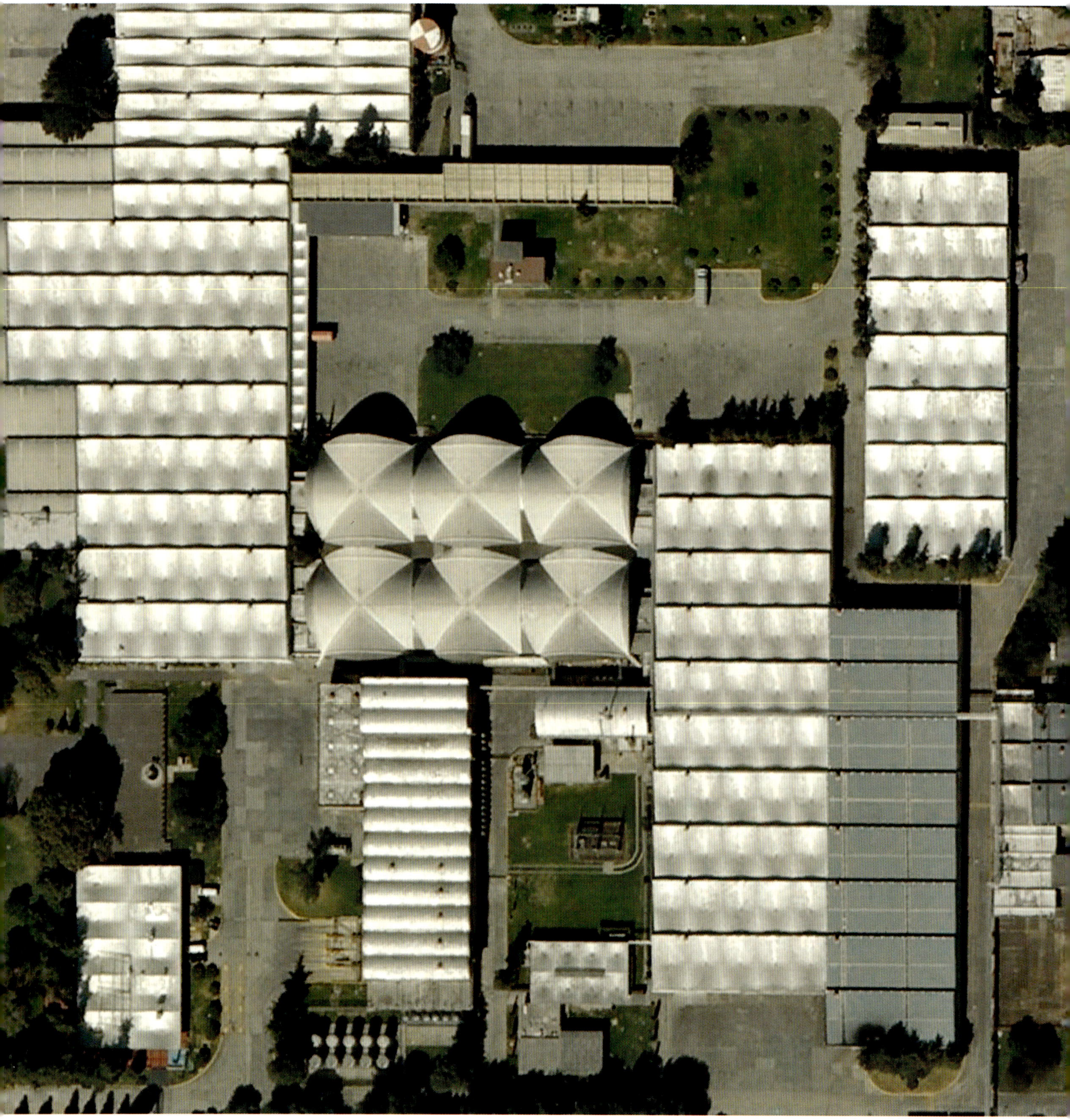

Bacardi y Compañía, S.A. Bottling Plant, Tultitlán, Mexico. Aerial view of concrete shells.
Google Earth: © 2015 INEG/© 2015 Google/Image © 2015 DigitalGlobe.

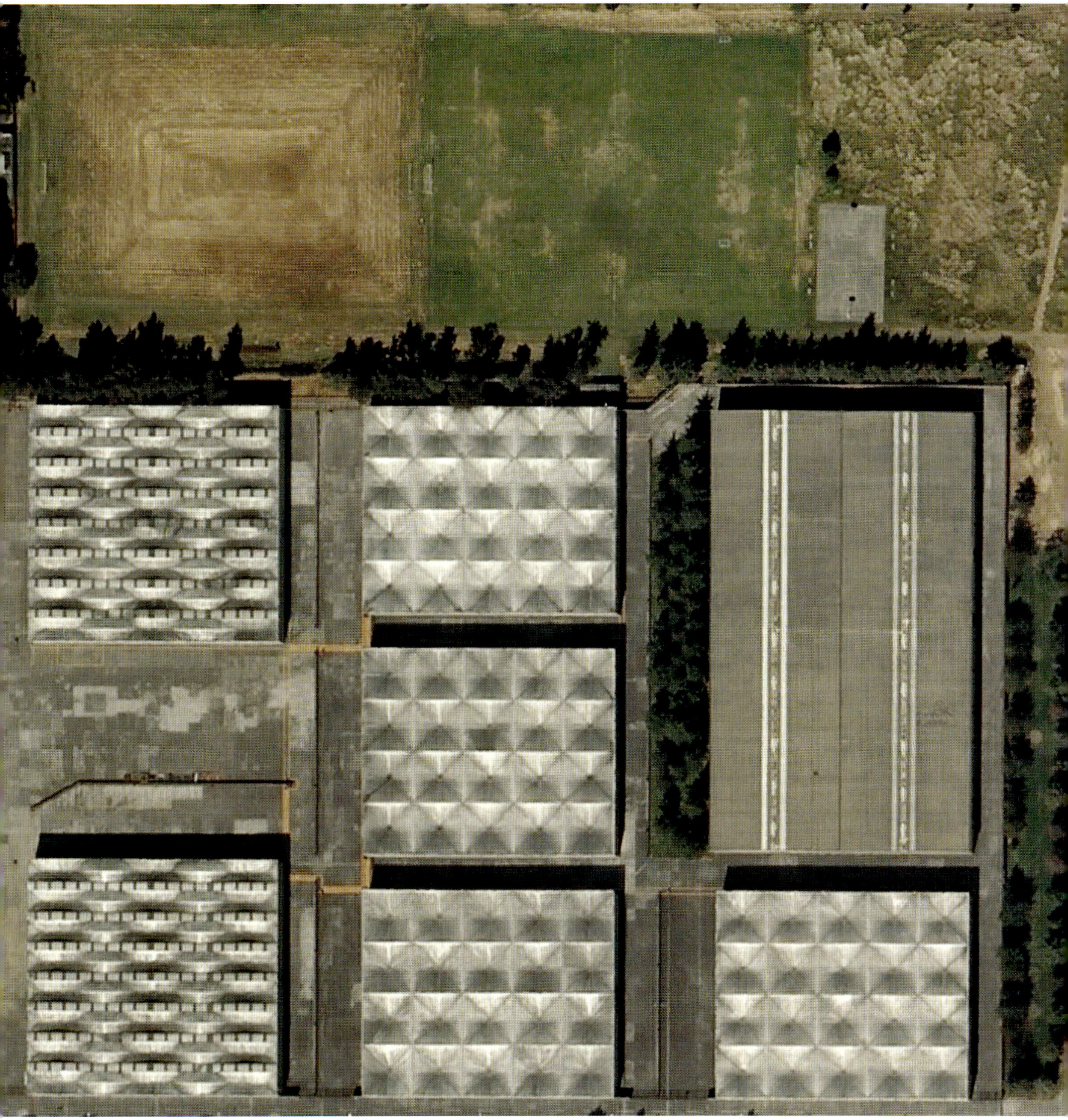

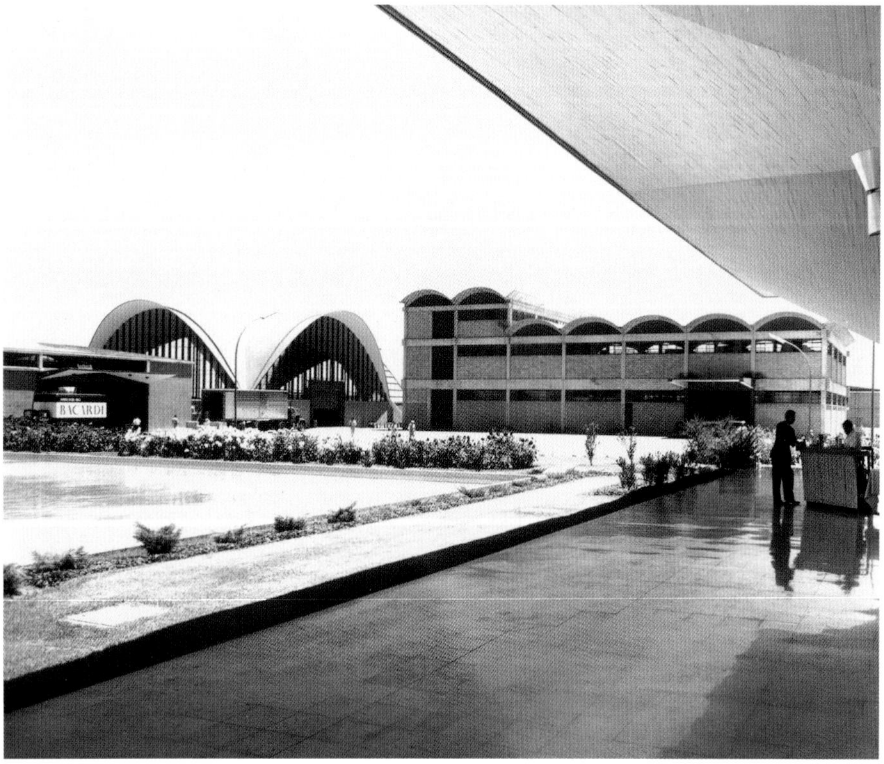

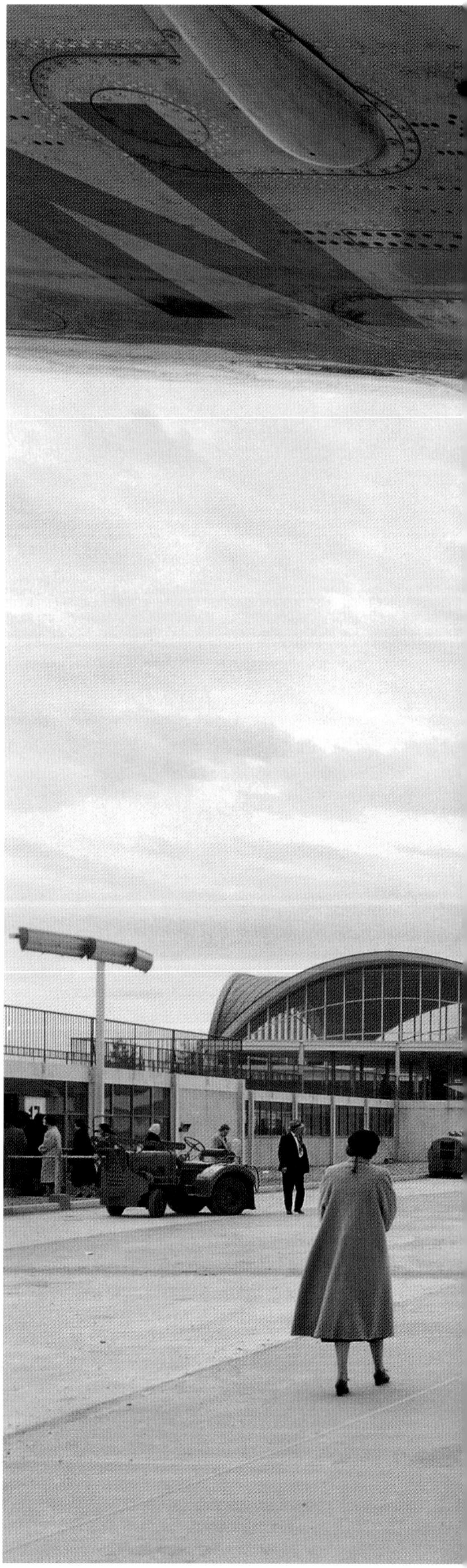

Above: Bacardi y Compañía, S.A. Bottling Plant, Tultitlán, Mexico. Félix Candela (Cubiertas Ala) with SACMAG, architects and Luis Torres Landa engineers, 1960-61. Courtesy of The Bacardi Archive.

Right: Lambert St. Louis Airport. Minoru Yamasaki, architect, 1956. © Ezra Stoller/ESTO.

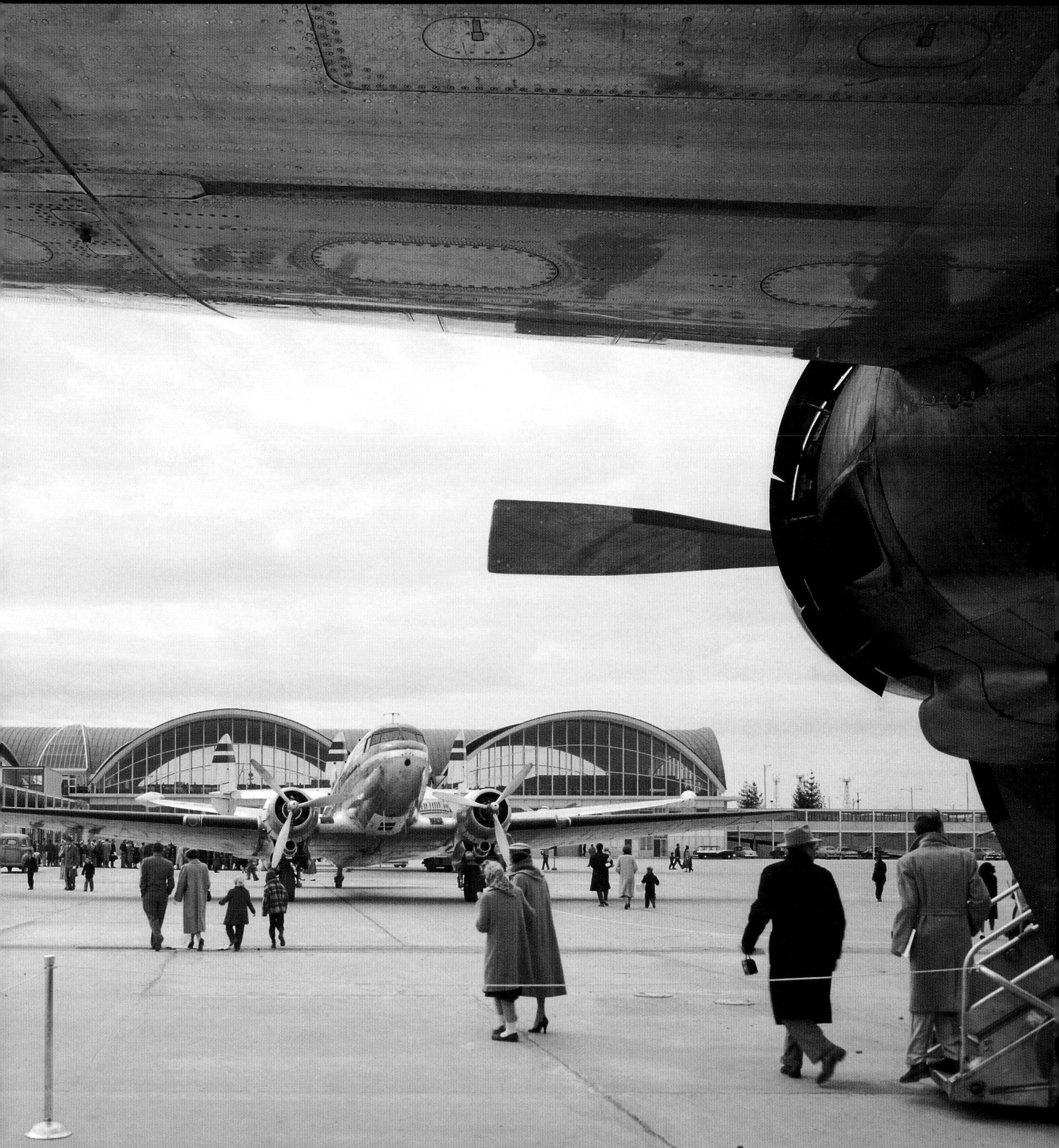

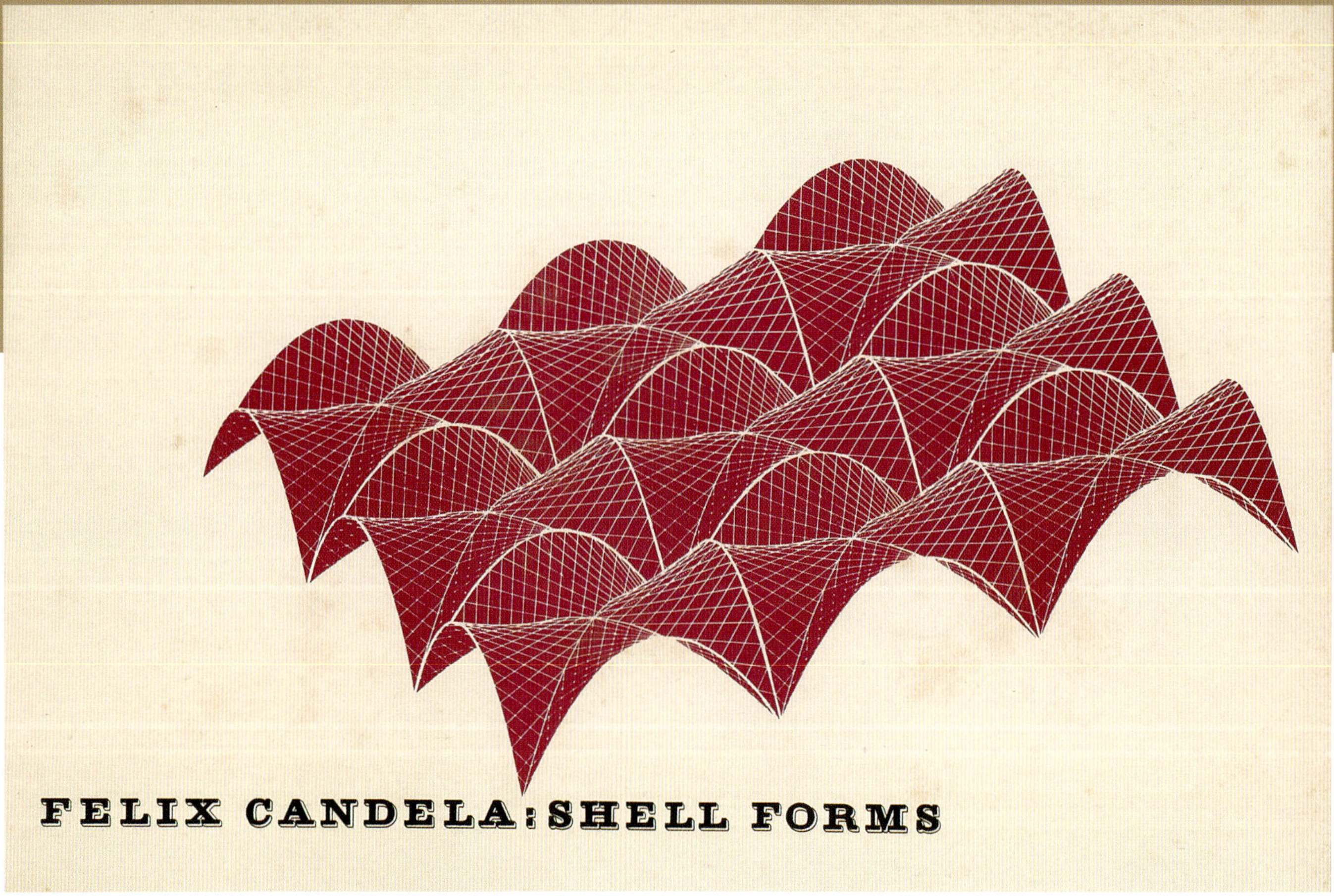

Félix Candela: Shell Forms (Los Angeles: University of Southern California, May 1957).
Esther McCoy papers, Archives of American Art, Smithsonian Institution.

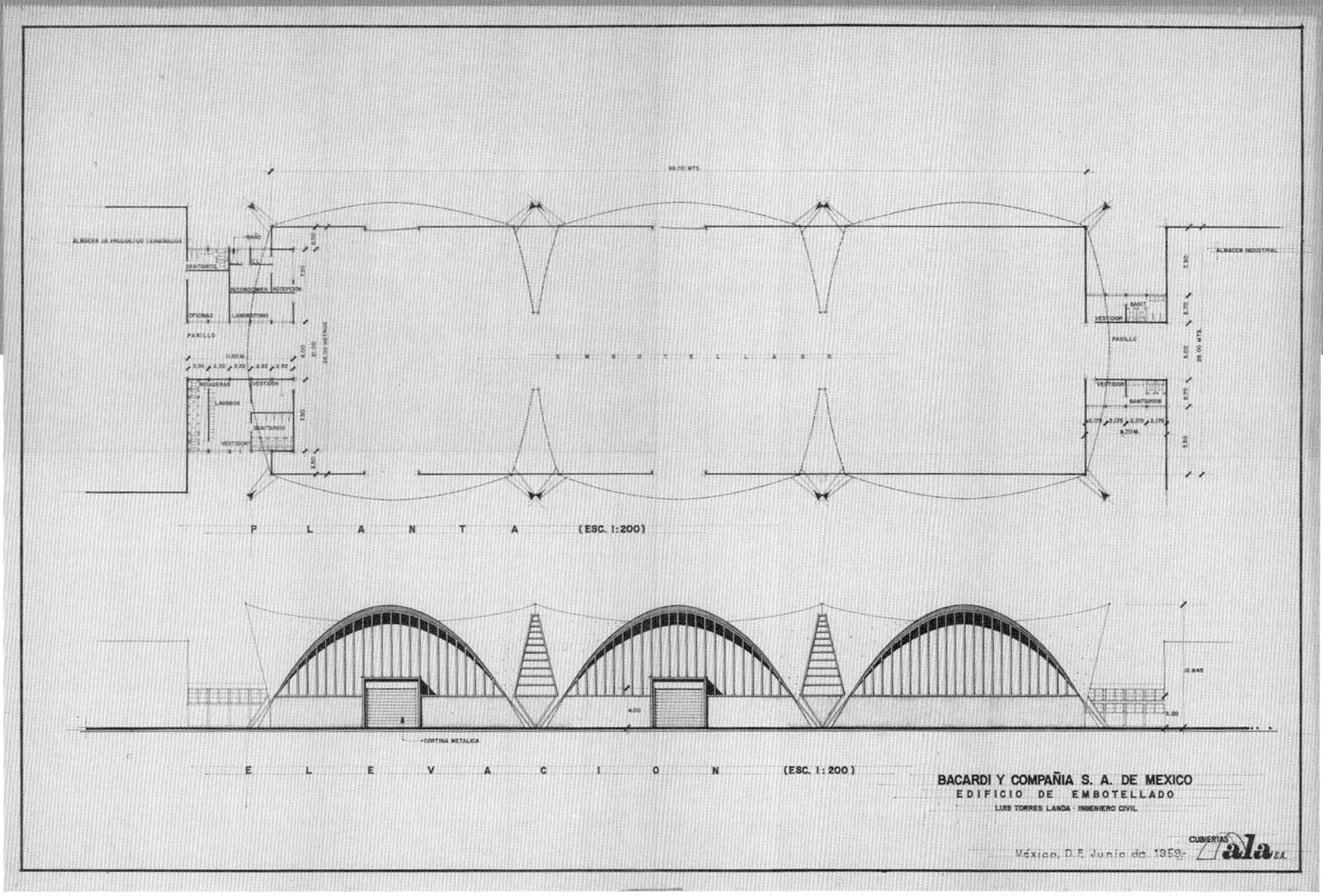

Bacardi y Compañía, S.A. Bottling Plant, Tultitlán, Mexico. Plan and Elevation.
Félix Candela (Cubiertas Ala), architect, with SACMAG and Luis Torres Landa, engineers, 1960-61. Archivo Candela Martín, Archivo de Arquitectos Mexicanos, FA-UNAM.

MEMORIA de CALCULOS PARA LA
AMPLIACION DE LA PLANTA DE EMBOTELLADO
BACARDI y COMPAÑIA S.A. de MEXICO. (1)

<u>Descripción de las edificaciones.</u>

En la zona de embotellado se proyecta construir tres bóvedas por arista en forma de paraboloide hiperbólico de planta cuadrada, de 31.00 x 31.00 mts con lucernarios desde 2.50 hasta disminuir en cero en la parte superior de las bóvedas.

Las bóvedas están formadas por cuatro mantos de paraboloide hiperbólico cortados por dos planos verticales y un tercer plano inclinado. Cada uno de estos gajos (de planta pseudotriangular) queda formado por 2 rectas a 45° y una curva, que es una hipérbola, en la parte exterior. (figuras 1a y 1b).

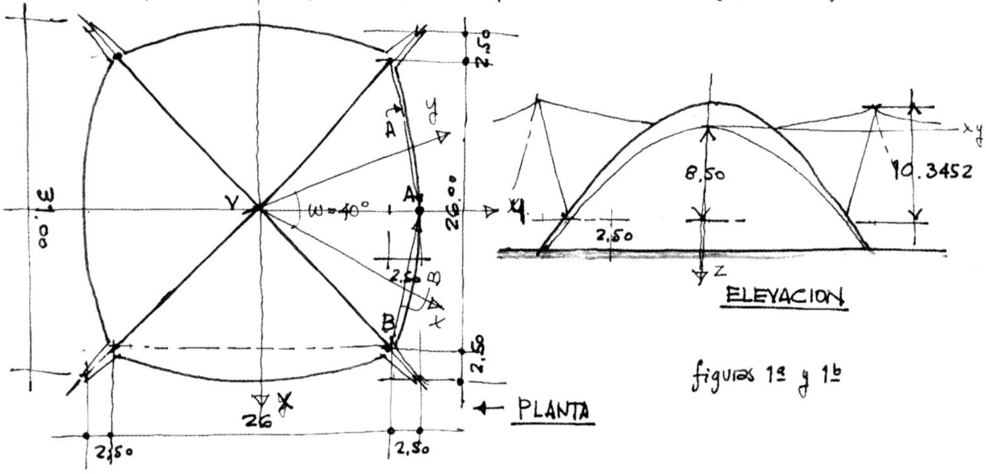

figuras 1a y 1b

<u>Bóveda por arista</u>. La cubierta está constituida por 4 gajos de paraboloide hiperbólico de eje z vertical y angulo de los ejes xy, ángulo $\omega = 40°$. El valor de la constante se puede obtener de la siguiente forma; calculando las coordenadas oblicuas del punto más alto (A) de la cubierta.

Conocida la altura respecto al vértice V del paraboloide

$$z_A = 10.3452 - 8.50 = -1.8452$$

$$x_A = y_A = \frac{15.50}{2\cos\frac{\omega}{2}} = \frac{15.50}{2 \cdot 0.939693} = 8.247374 \quad \text{luego } k = \frac{z}{xy} = -0.027127 \, \frac{1}{m}$$

Memória de Calculos para la Ampliacion de la planta de Embotellado Bacardi y Compañia S.A. De Mexico
(Calculus for the expansion of the Bacardi y Compañia S.A. Mexico bottling plant). Handwritten notes by Félix Candela.
Archivo Candela Martín, Archivo de Arquitectos Mexicanos, FA-UNAM.

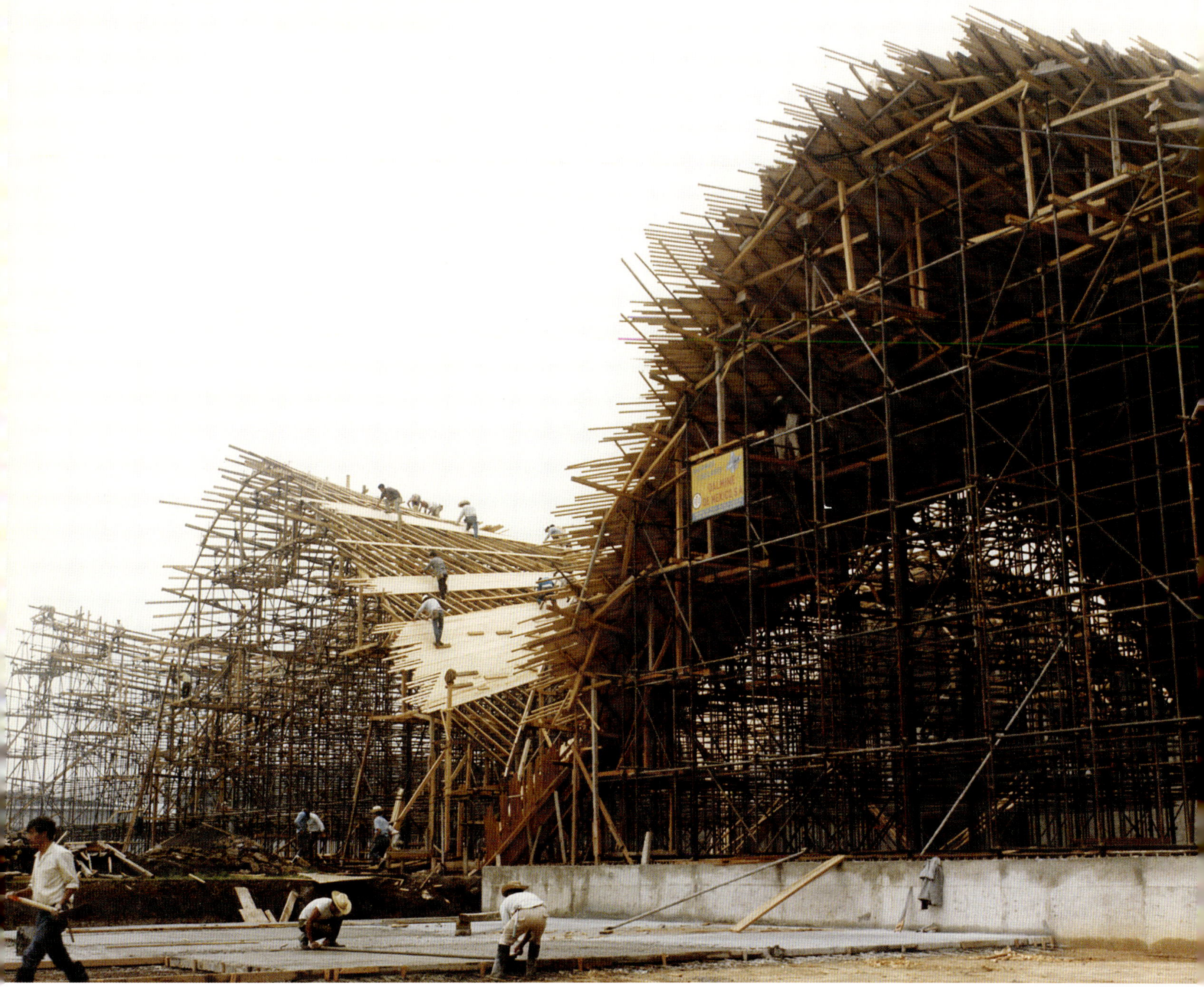

Bacardi y Compañía, S.A. Bottling Plant, Tultitlán, Mexico. Scaffolding and formwork for the concrete shell construction. Félix Candela (Cubiertas Ala), architect, with SACMAG and Luis Torres Landa, engineers, 1960-61. Courtesy of Bacardi Mexico.

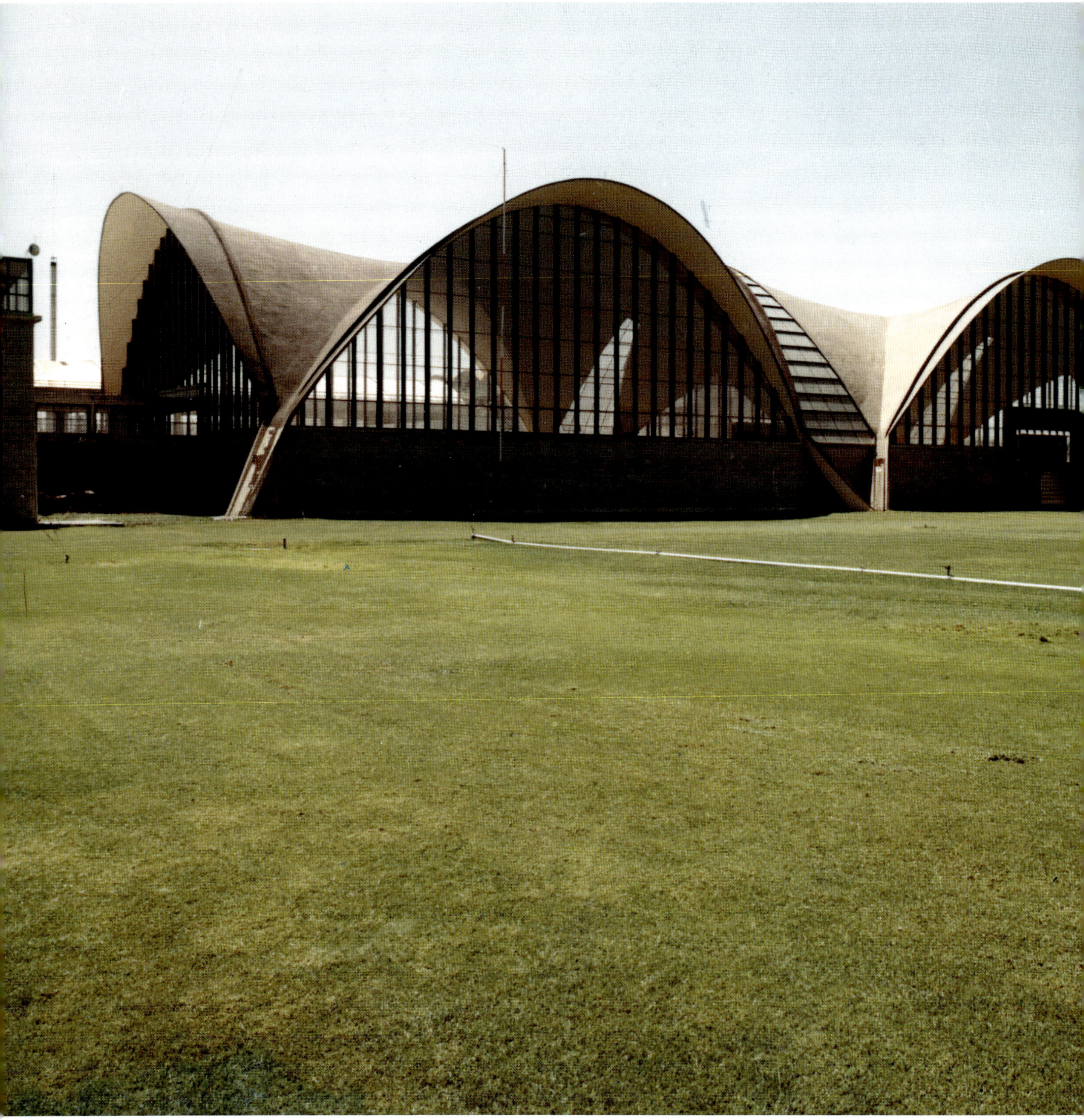

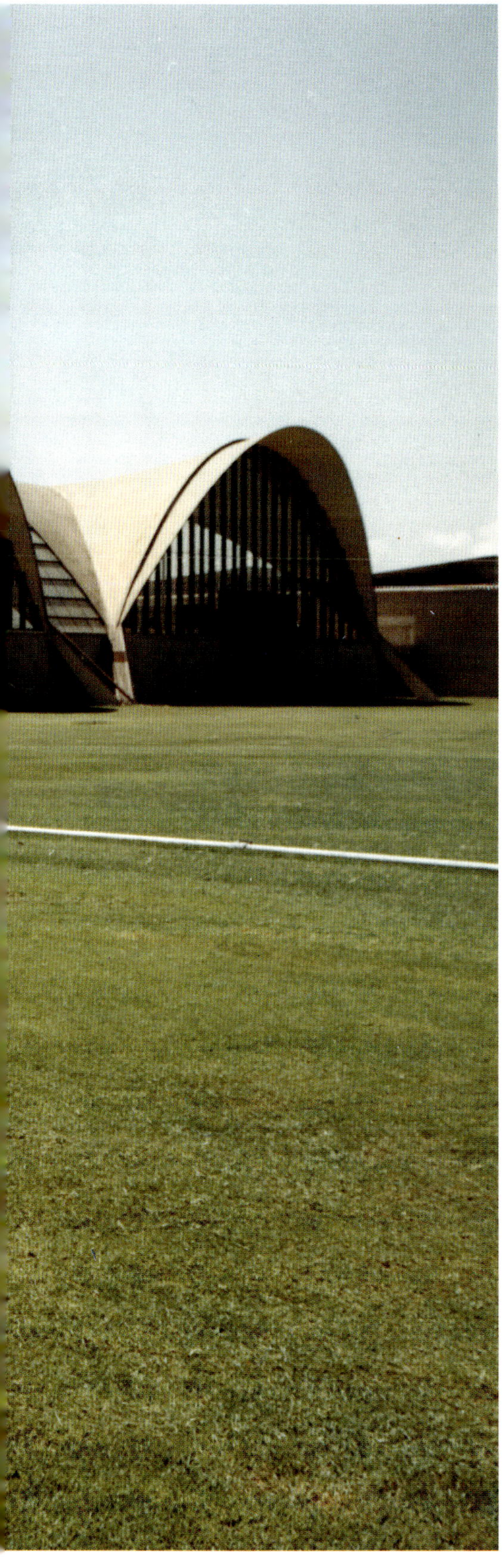

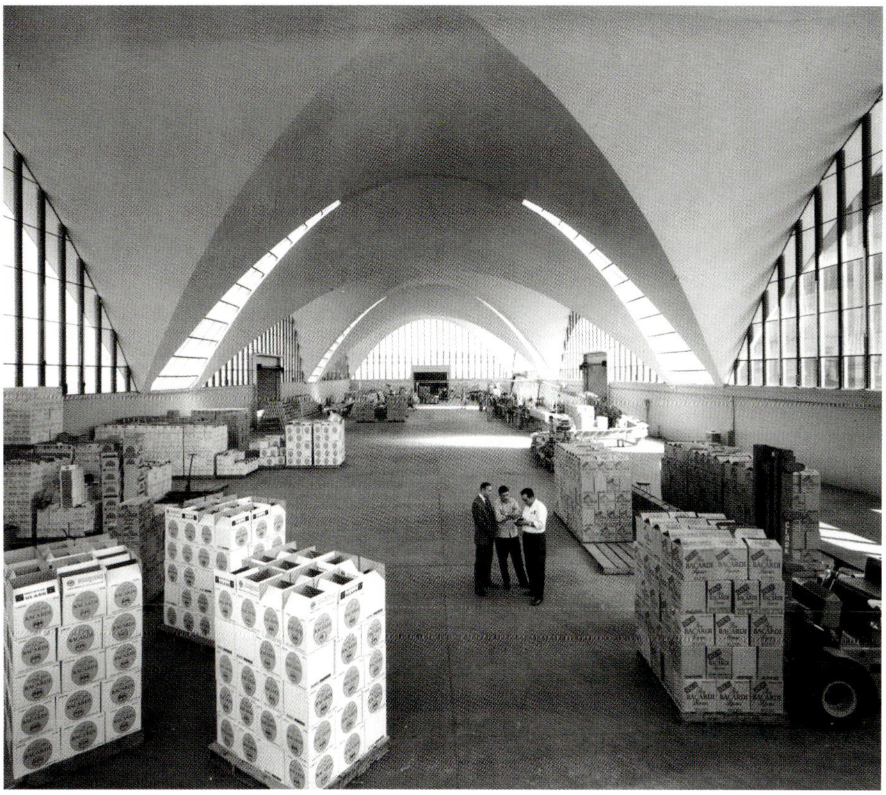

Left: Bacardi y Compañía, S.A. Bottling Plant, Tultitlán, Mexico. Bottling Hall. Félix Candela (Cubiertas Ala), architect with SACMAG and Luis Torres Landa, engineers, 1960-61. Courtesy of The Bacardi Archive.

Above: Bacardi y Compañía, S.A. Bottling Plant, Tultitlán, Mexico. Interior of Bottling Hall. Félix Candela (Cubiertas Ala), architect, with SACMAG and Luis Torres Landa, engineers, 1960-61. Courtesy of The Bacardi Archive.

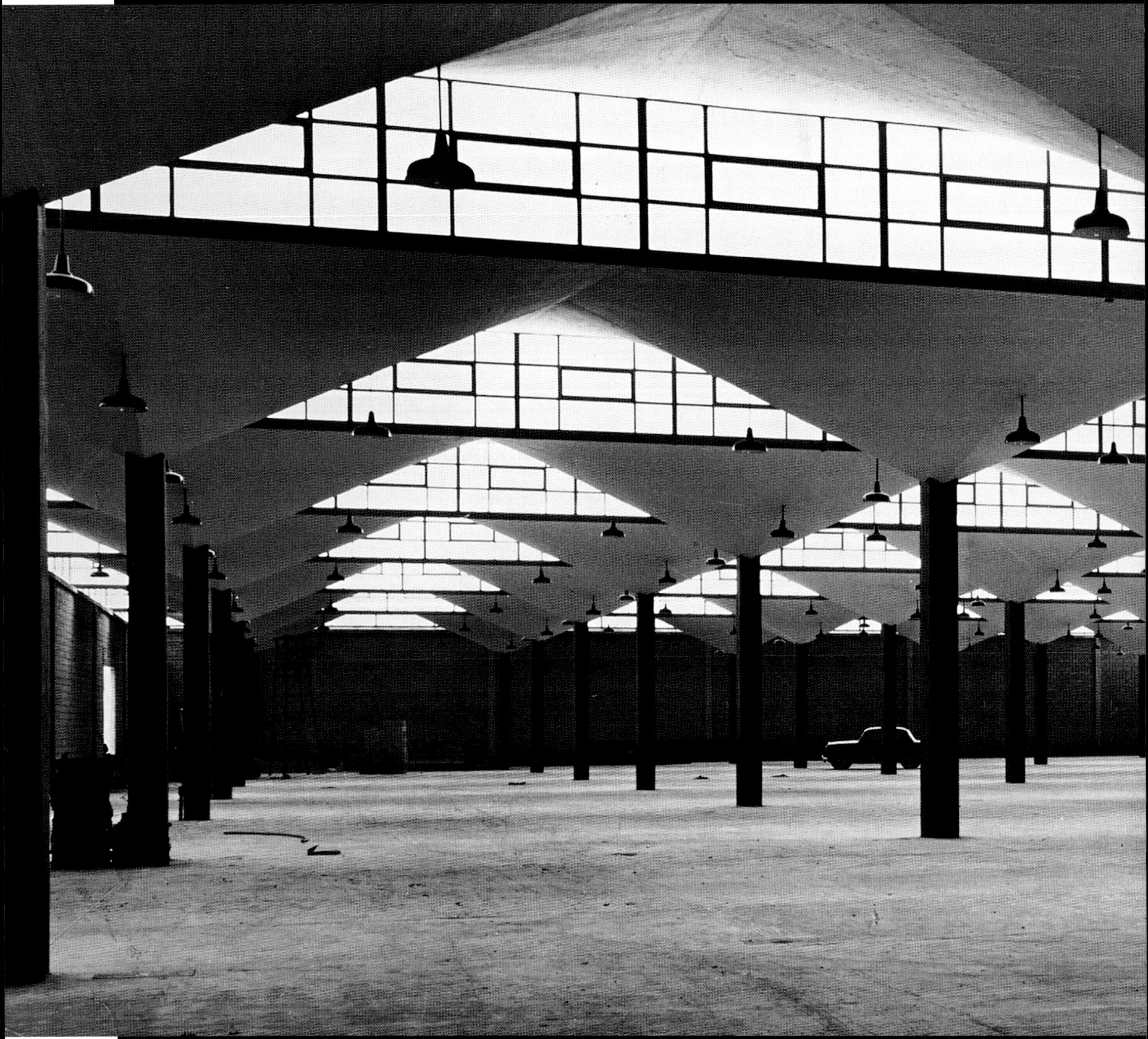

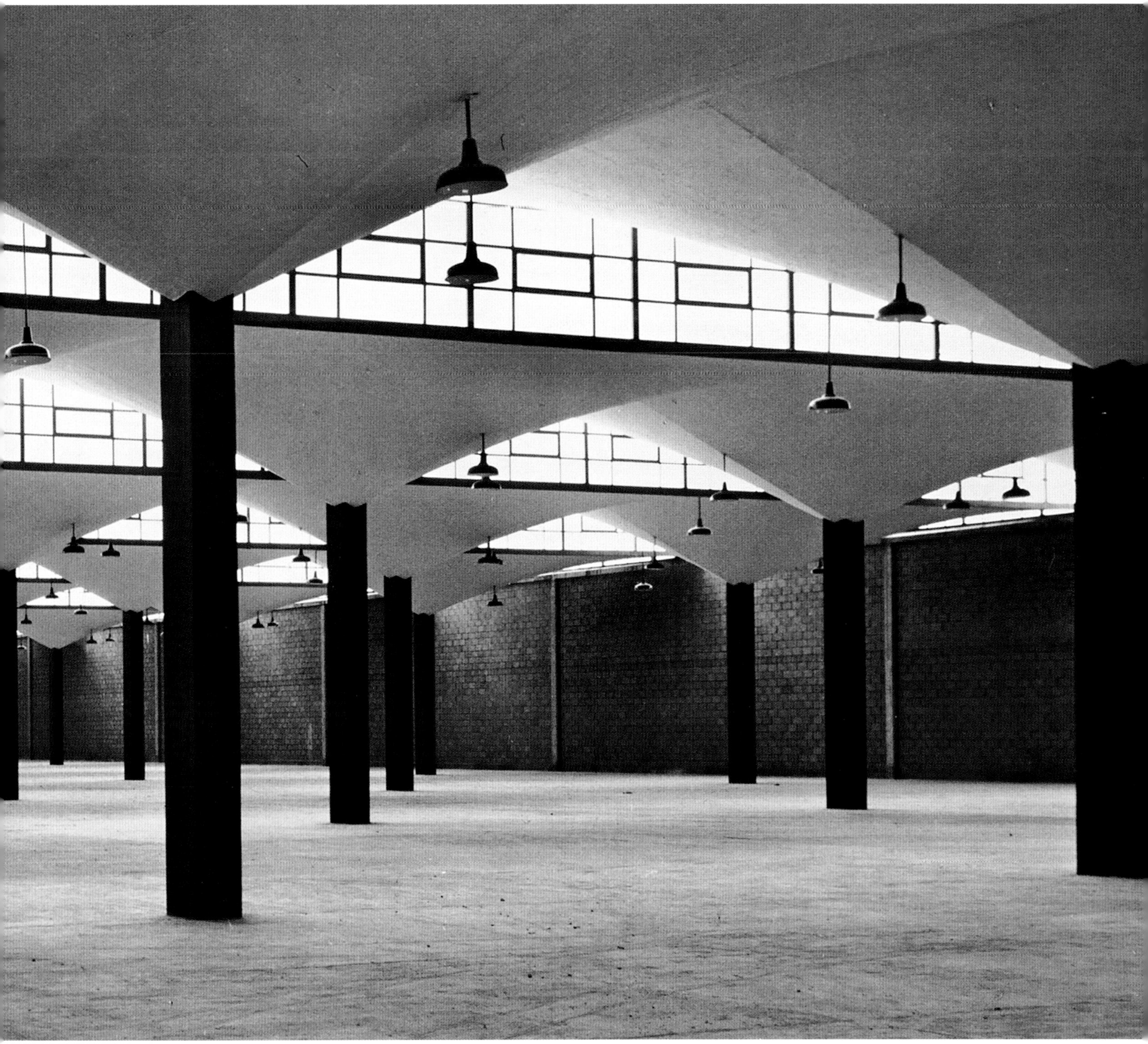

Bacardi y Compañía, S.A. Bottling Plant, Tultitlán, Mexico. Warehouse with umbrella roofs and clerestories.
Félix Candela (Cubiertas Ala), architect, with SACMAG and Luis Torres Landa engineers, 1960-61.
Drawings and Archives, Avery Architectural and Fine Arts Library, Columbia University.

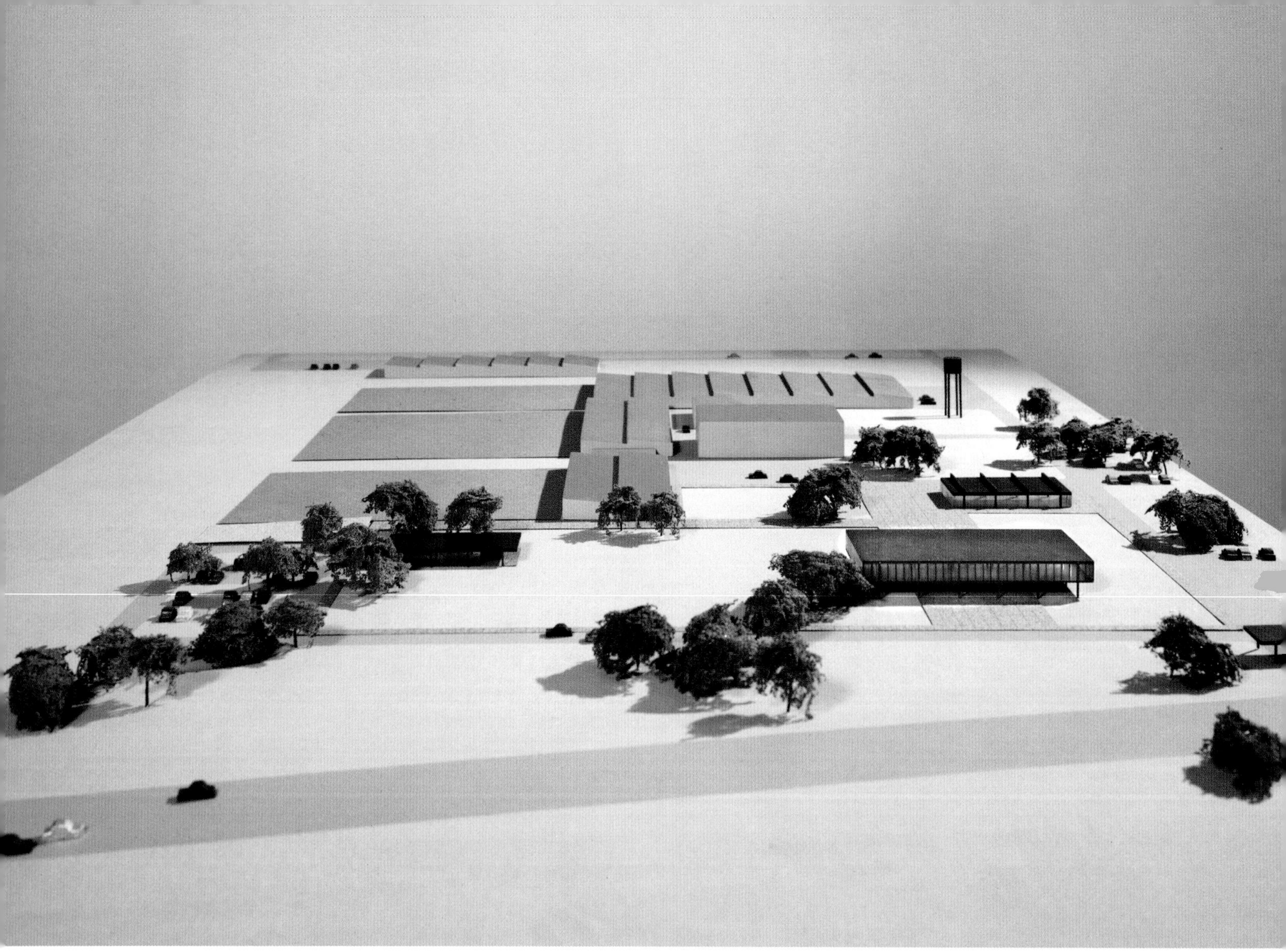

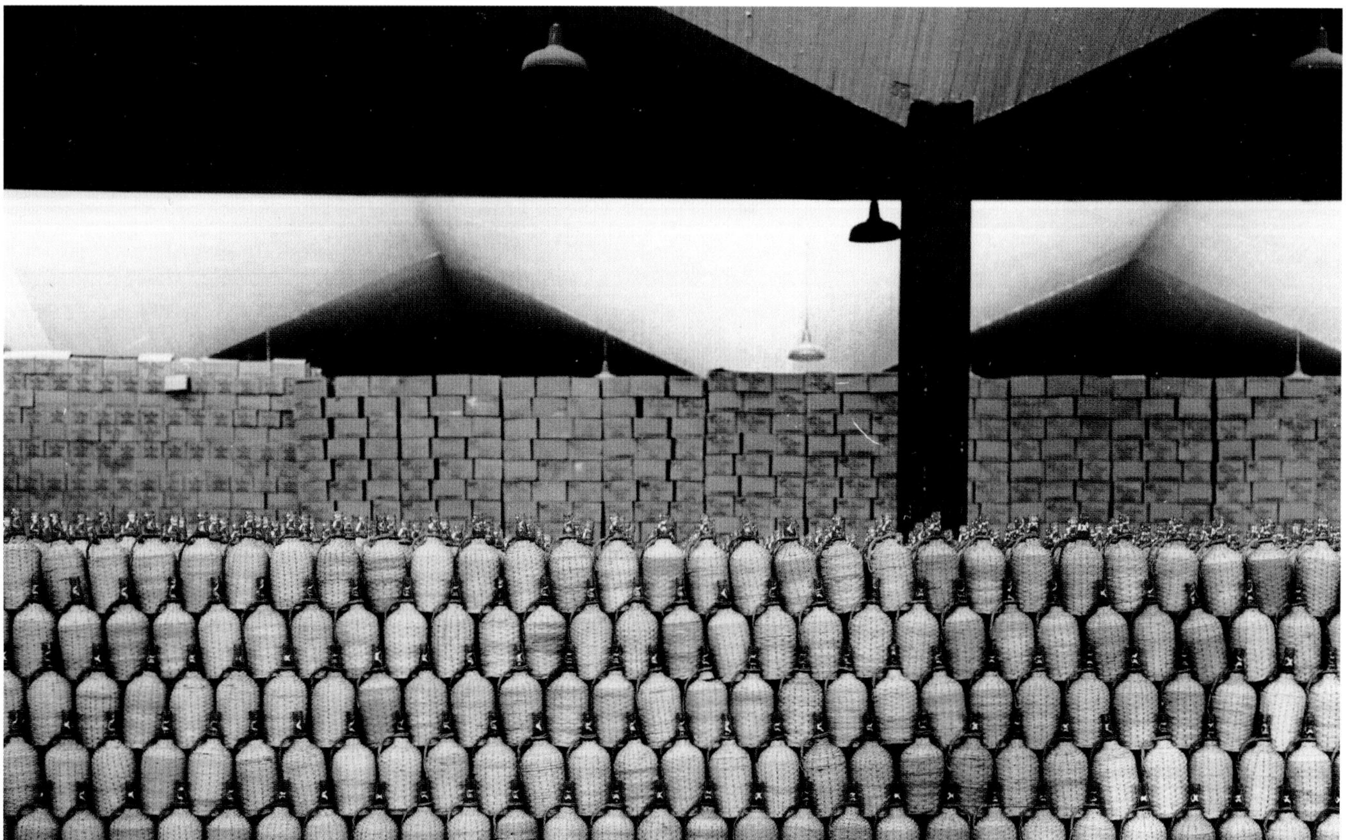

In contrast to the Santiago project, for which the Mies office prepared supporting diagrammatic studies, rendered details and photomontages of the interior, the archives of the Mexico project are spare. Only a detailed model was prepared, suggesting a less expository approach. Indeed, Mies and his associate Gene Summers had returned to the firm's more classic formulation of exposed steel skeleton (painted black), gray-tinted plate glass and travertine flooring. The shift has formed the basis for a critique, that Mies's Mexican opus is merely a reiteration, or even a repeated fragment, of the architect's glass-and-steel work in Chicago.[120] Yet the building's specific instrumentation of structure, form and space show a progression from the architect's previous work. The main office volume was set on pilotis, a design solution apparently inspired by the proximity and raised profile of the Mexico–Queretaro Highway. The long, low volume appeared to float, an impression strengthened by the building's cantilevered ends and inset ground-floor lobby. An open void connected the offices to the ground level, in essence a new synthesis of the open-plan idea articulated for Bacardi by Mies in Santiago. Support and utility spaces were elegantly assembled into wood-paneled cores at either end of the main space. Historian Sigfried Giedion, for one, argued that the Tultitlan building's space and façade effects were "achieved by an extremely subtle knowledge of how to arrive at perfection through the smallest alterations of position and proportion."[121]

In contrast to the rambling bottling facility and warehouses, where Candela's expressive concrete forms were repeated in crystalline rows, Mies's black pavilion stood in monumental singularity and cool corporate abstraction. Candela's suave concrete curves contrasted with Mies's web of steel. The two architectures, at the antipodes of midcentury architectural discourse, find an uneasy proximity at Tultitlán, joined under the patronage of Bacardi, for whom such divergences were simply the byproduct of its own complex agenda.

Top Left: Bacardi y Compañía, S.A. Administration Building, Tultitlán, Mexico. Model of proposed administration area buildings. Ludwig Mies van der Rohe, architect with Saenz, Cancio, Martin, Alvarez y Gutierrez, engineers, 1960. Photograph by Hedrich Blessing, c. 1960. Courtesy of Chicago History Museum.

Bottom Left: Bacardi y Compañía, S.A. Bottling Plant, Tultitlán, Mexico. Ageing barrels beneath umbrella roofs. Félix Candela (Cubiertas Ala), architect with SACMAG and Luis Torres Landa engineers, 1960-61. Courtesy of The Bacardi Archive.

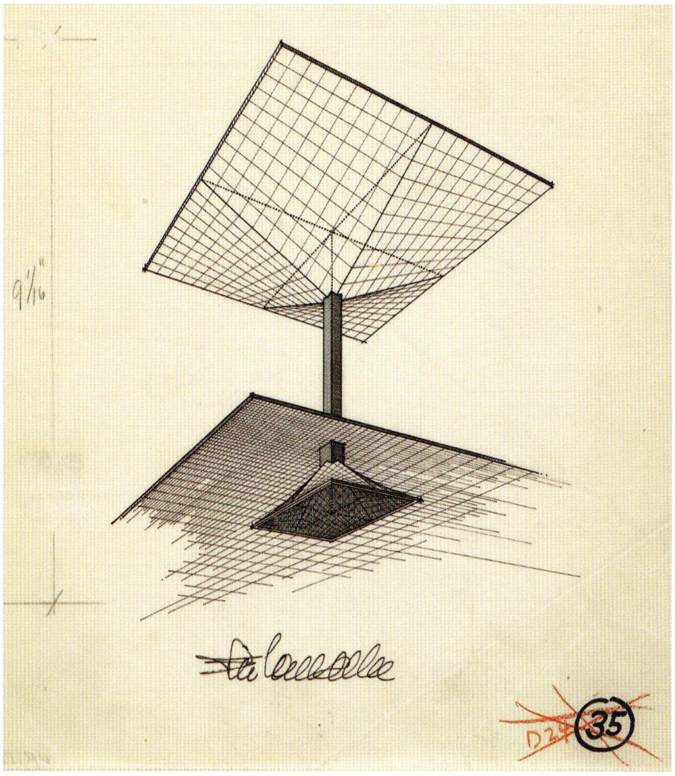

Right: Bacardi y Compañía, S.A. Bottling Plant, Tultitlán, Mexico. Mole's eye view of the umbrella system, including foundation, column and canopy details signed by Félix Candela, architect. Drawings and Archives, Avery Architectural and Fine Arts Library, Columbia University.

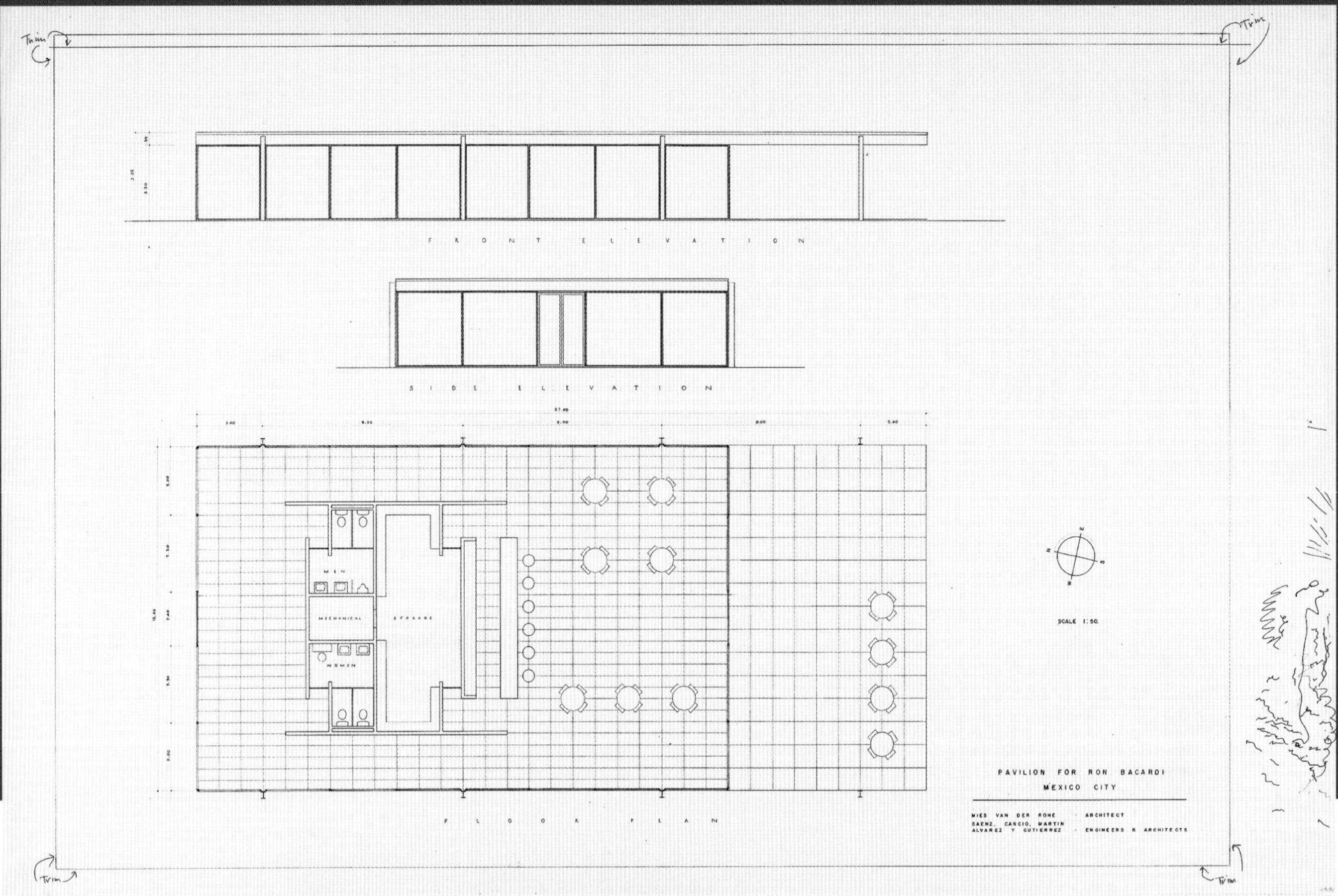

FRONT ELEVATION
SIDE ELEVATION
MEN
MECHANICAL
WOMEN
SCALE 1:50
PAVILION FOR RON BACARDI
MEXICO CITY
MIES VAN DER ROHE · ARCHITECT
SAENZ, CANCIO, MARTIN
ALVAREZ Y GUTIERREZ · ENGINEERS & ARCHITECTS
FLOOR PLAN
Trim

138

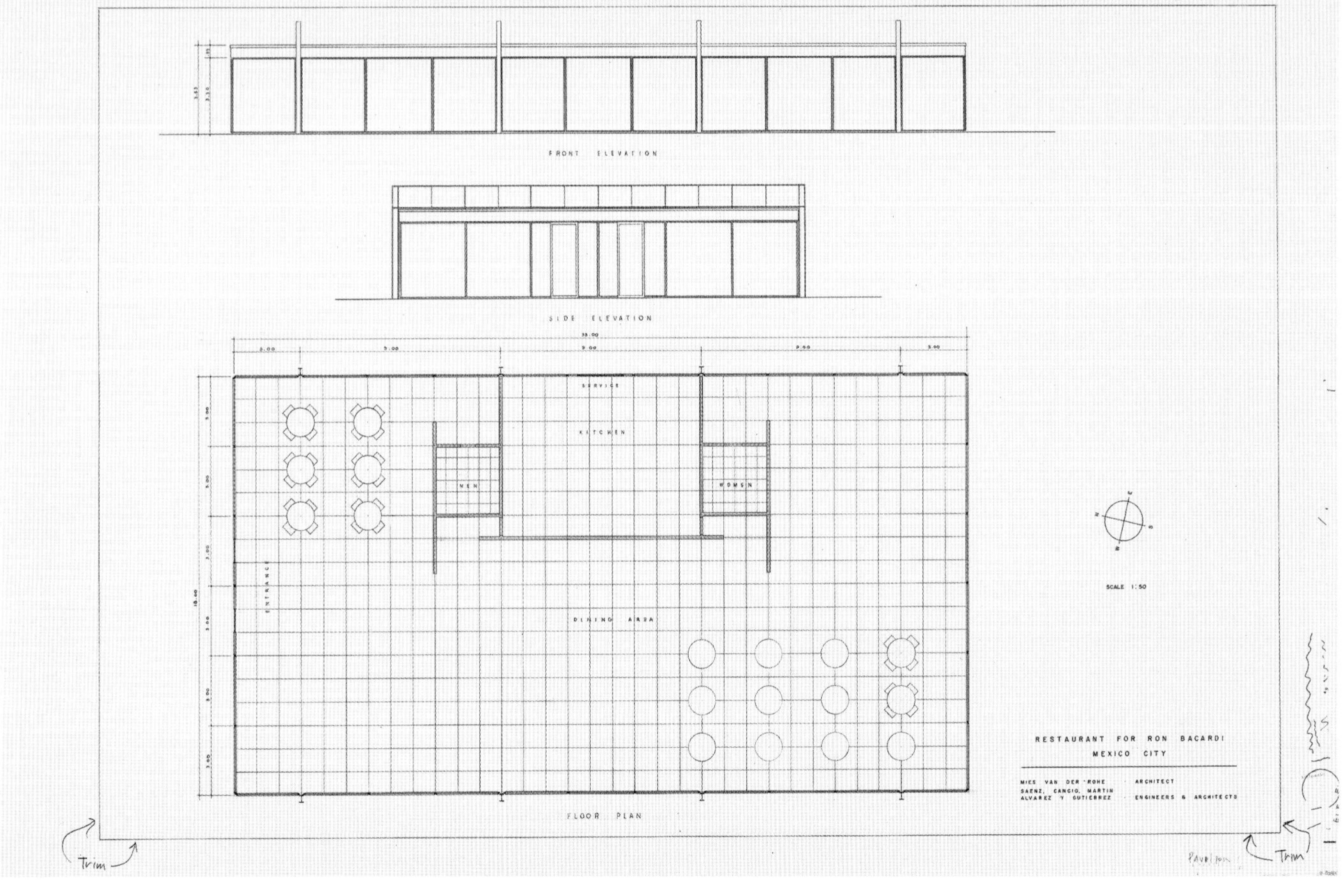

FRONT ELEVATION
SIDE ELEVATION
SERVICE
KITCHEN
MEN
WOMEN
ENTRANCE
DINING AREA
SCALE 1:50
RESTAURANT FOR RON BACARDI
MEXICO CITY
MIES VAN DER ROHE · ARCHITECT
SAENZ, CANCIO, MARTIN
ALVAREZ Y GUTIERREZ · ENGINEERS & ARCHITECTS
FLOOR PLAN
Trim

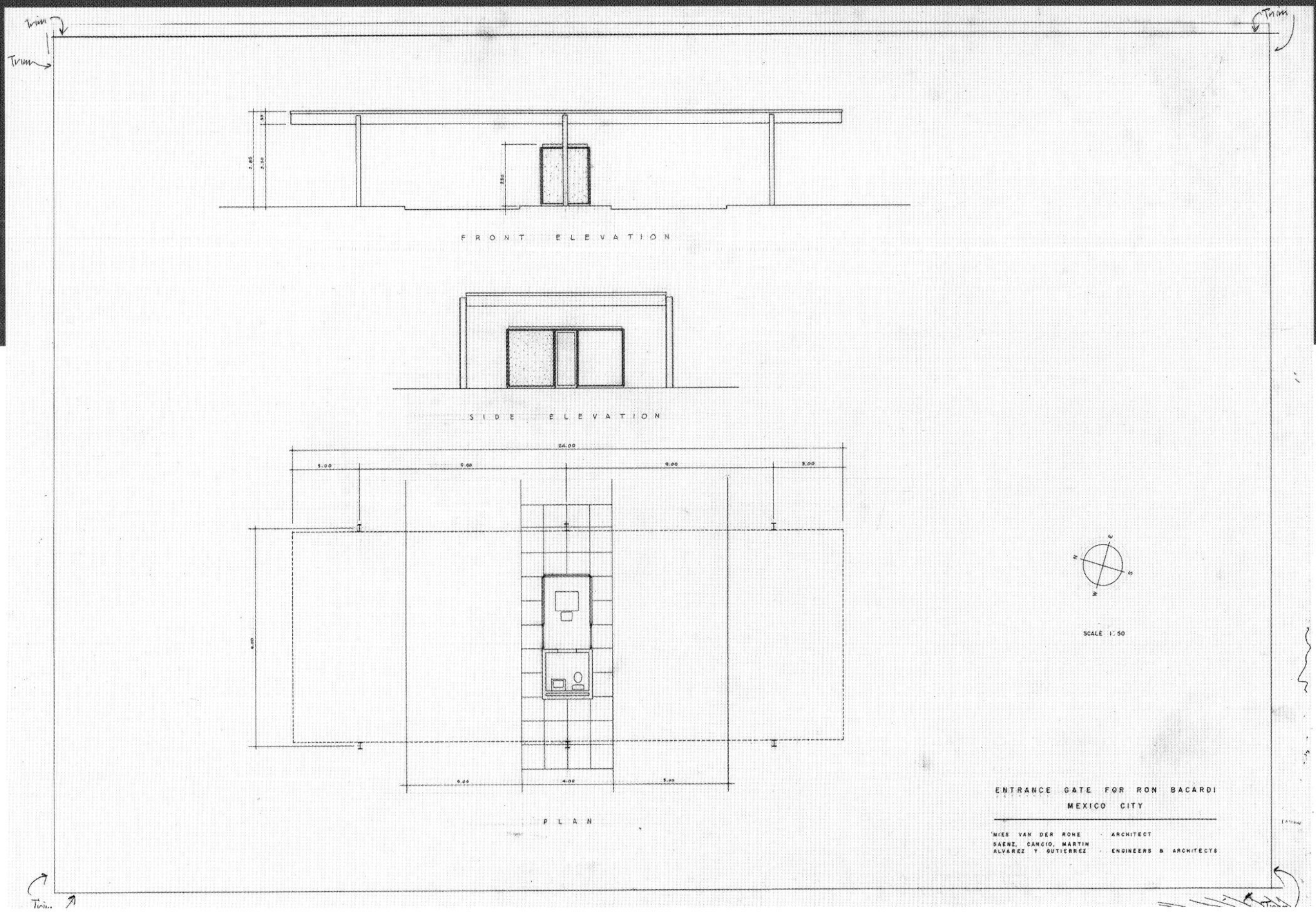

Top Left: Bacardi y Compañia, S.A. Administration Building, Mexico City, Mexico. Bar, floor plan and elevations. Ludwig Mies van der Rohe, architect with Saenz, Cancio, Martin, Alvarez y Gutierrez, engineers, 1958.

Bottom Left: Bacardi y Compañía, S.A. Administration Building, Mexico City, Mexico. Cafeteria, floor plan and elevations. Ludwig Mies van der Rohe, architect with Saenz, Cancio, Martin, Alvarez y Gutierrez, engineers, 1958.

Above: Bacardi y Compañia, S.A. Administration Building, Mexico City, Mexico. Entrance gate, floor plan and elevations. Ludwig Mies van der Rohe, architect with Saenz, Cancio, Martin, Alvarez y Gutierrez, engineers, 1958.

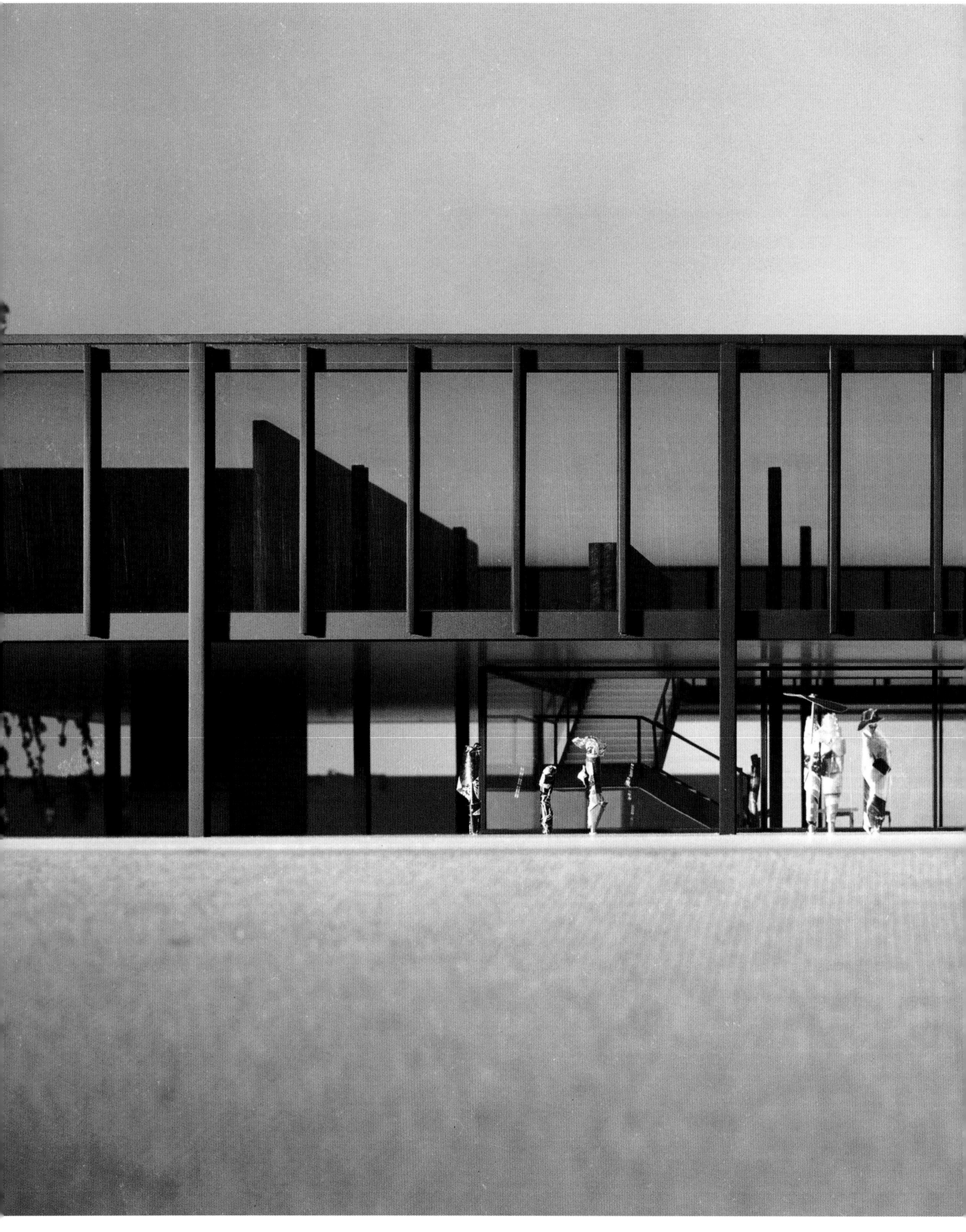

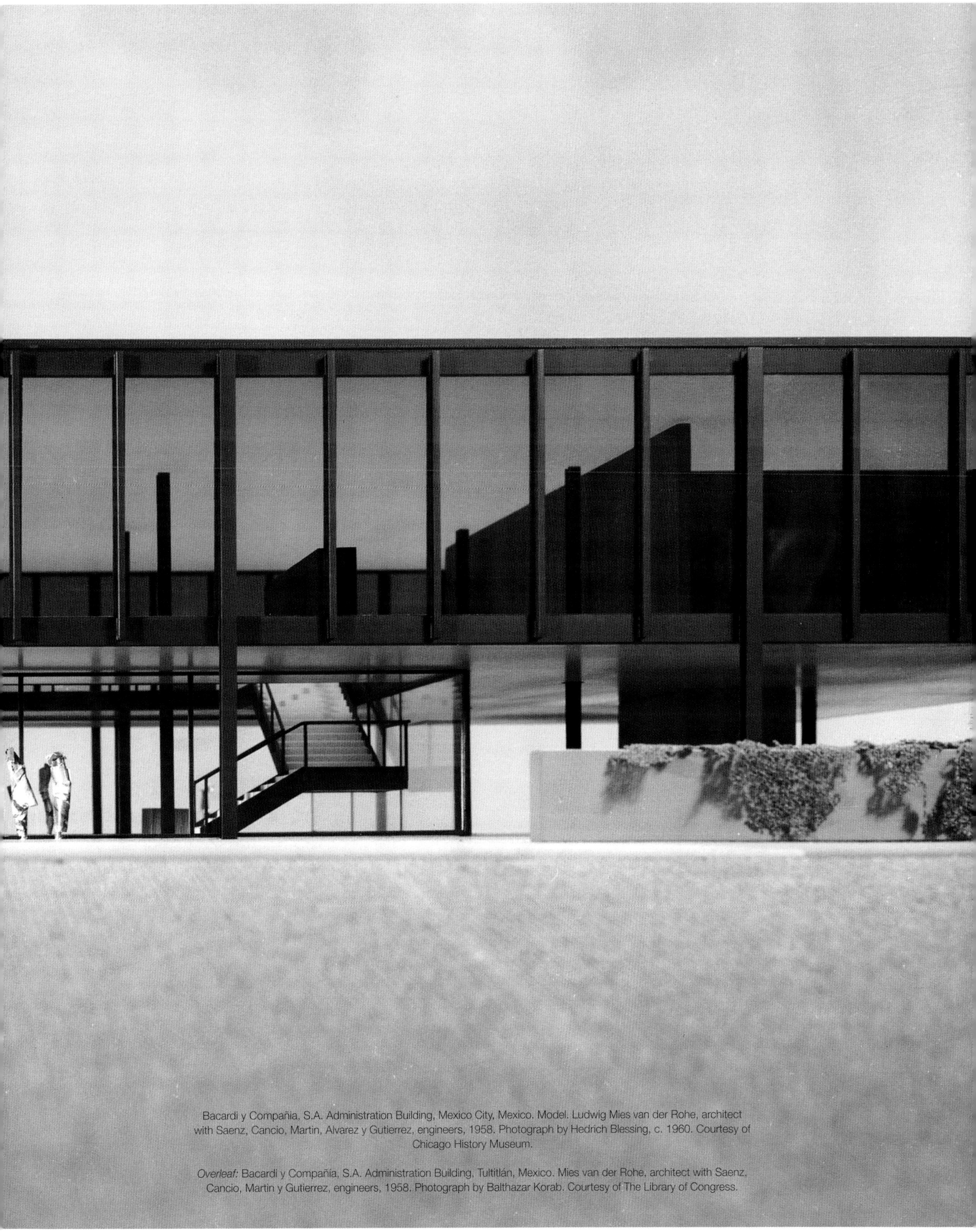

Bacardi y Compañia, S.A. Administration Building, Mexico City, Mexico. Model. Ludwig Mies van der Rohe, architect with Saenz, Cancio, Martin, Alvarez y Gutierrez, engineers, 1958. Photograph by Hedrich Blessing, c. 1960. Courtesy of Chicago History Museum.

Overleaf: Bacardi y Compañía, S.A. Administration Building, Tultitlán, Mexico. Mies van der Rohe, architect with Saenz, Cancio, Martin y Gutierrez, engineers, 1958. Photograph by Balthazar Korab. Courtesy of The Library of Congress.

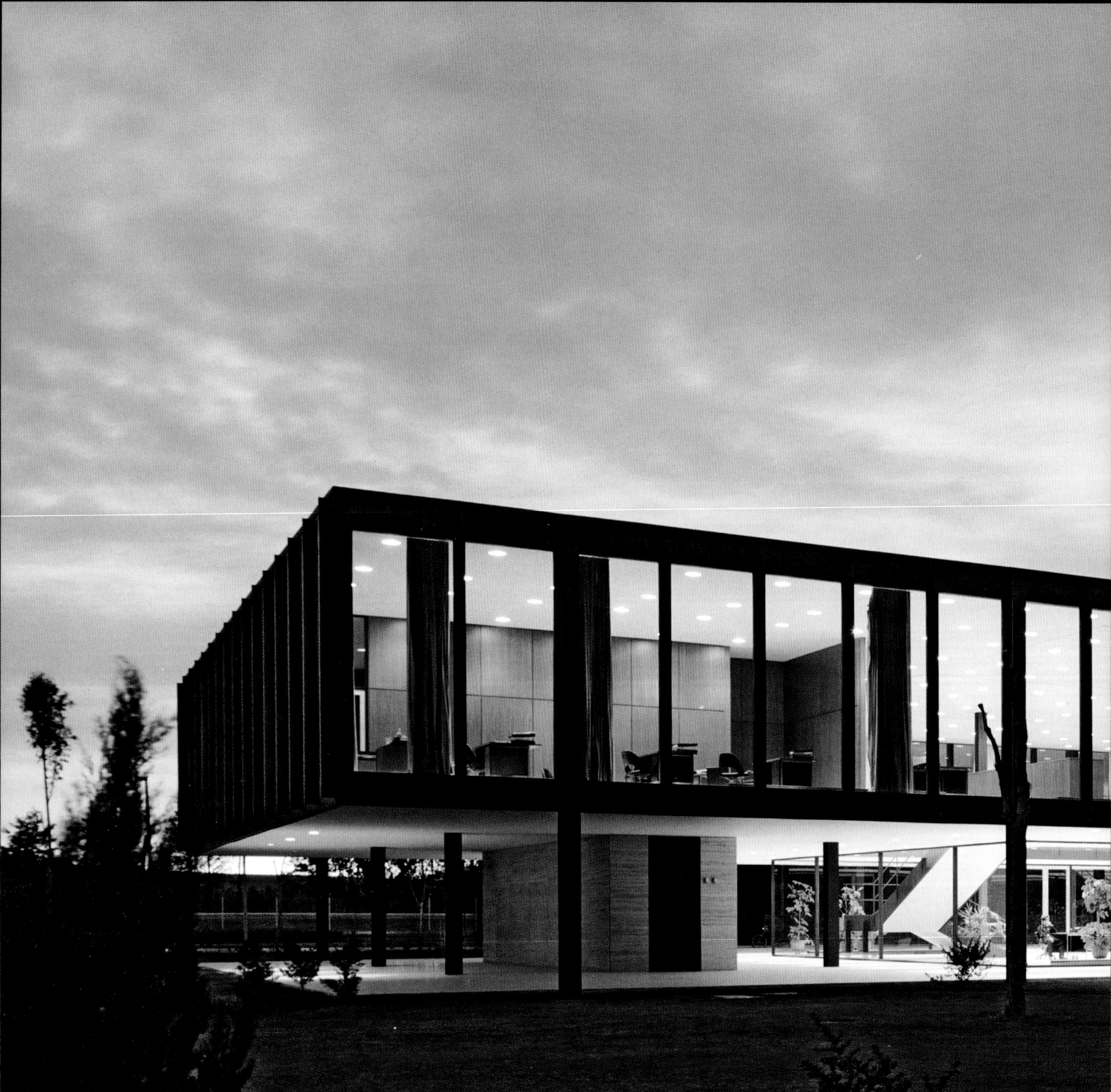

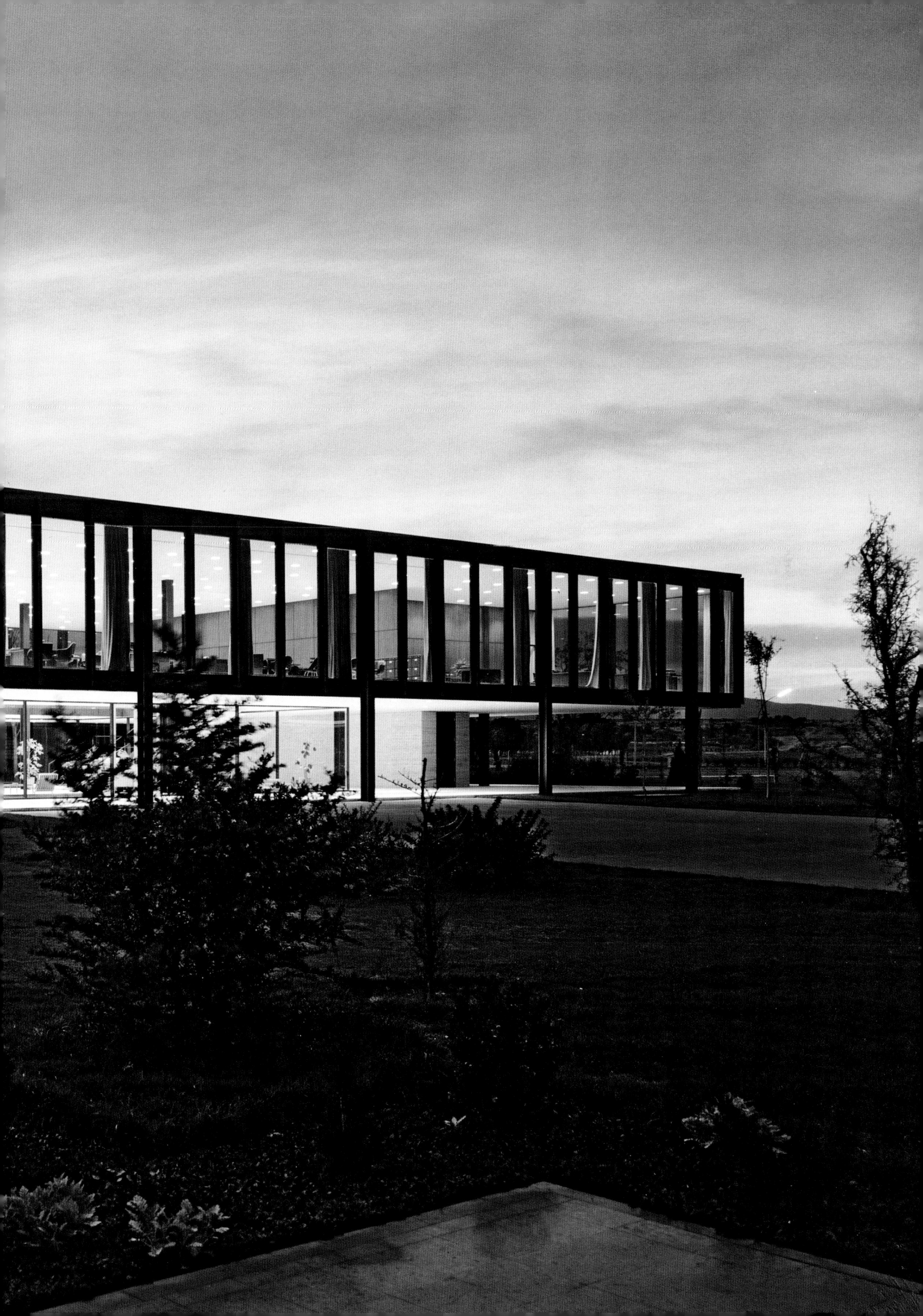

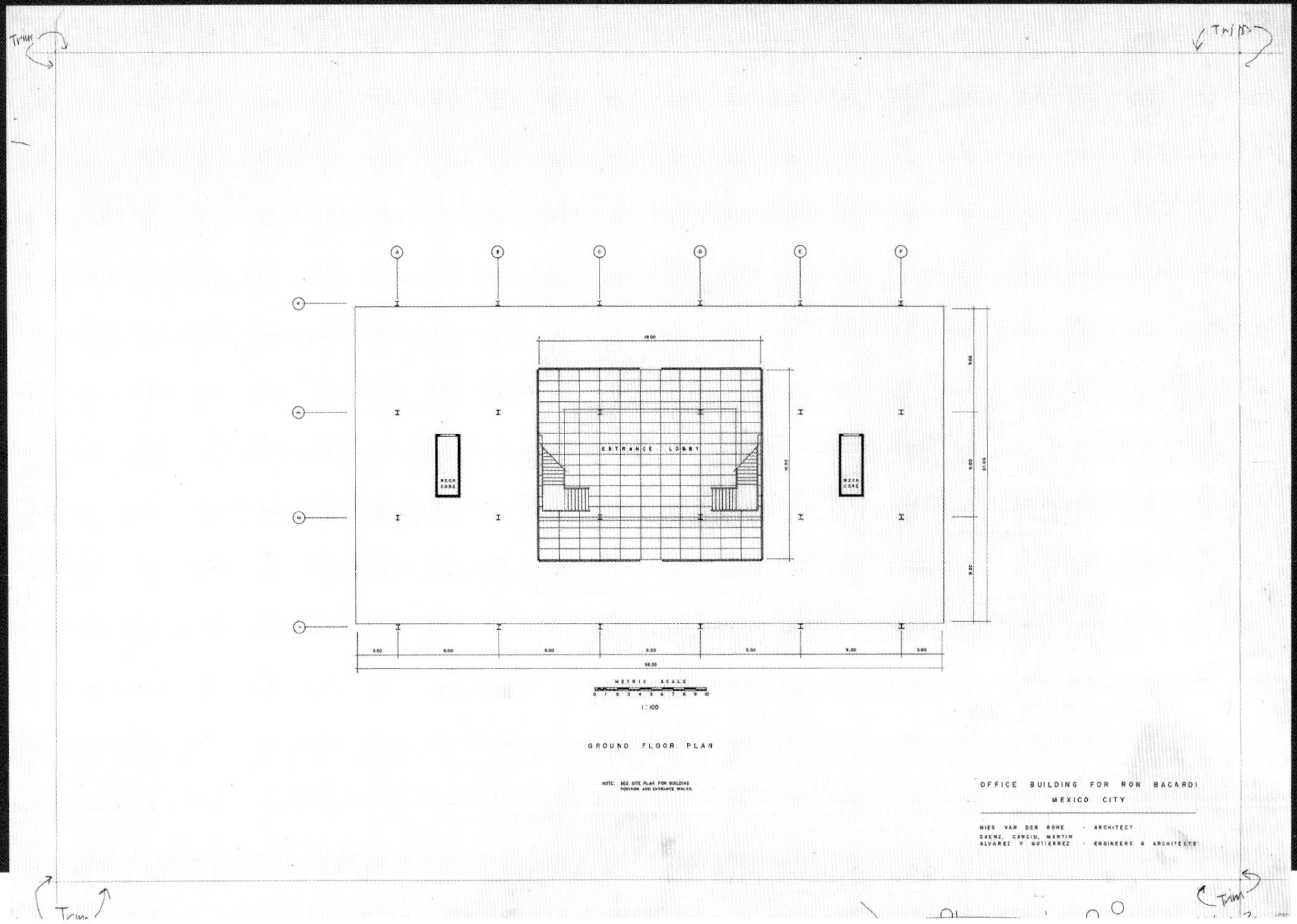
ENTRANCE LOBBY
MECH CORE
MECH CORE
METRIC SCALE
1:100
GROUND FLOOR PLAN
NOTE: SEE SITE PLAN FOR BUILDING POSITION AND ENTRANCE WALKS.
OFFICE BUILDING FOR RON BACARDI
MEXICO CITY
MIES VAN DER ROHE · ARCHITECT
SAENZ, CANCIO, MARTIN
ALVAREZ Y GUTIERREZ · ENGINEERS & ARCHITECTS
Trim

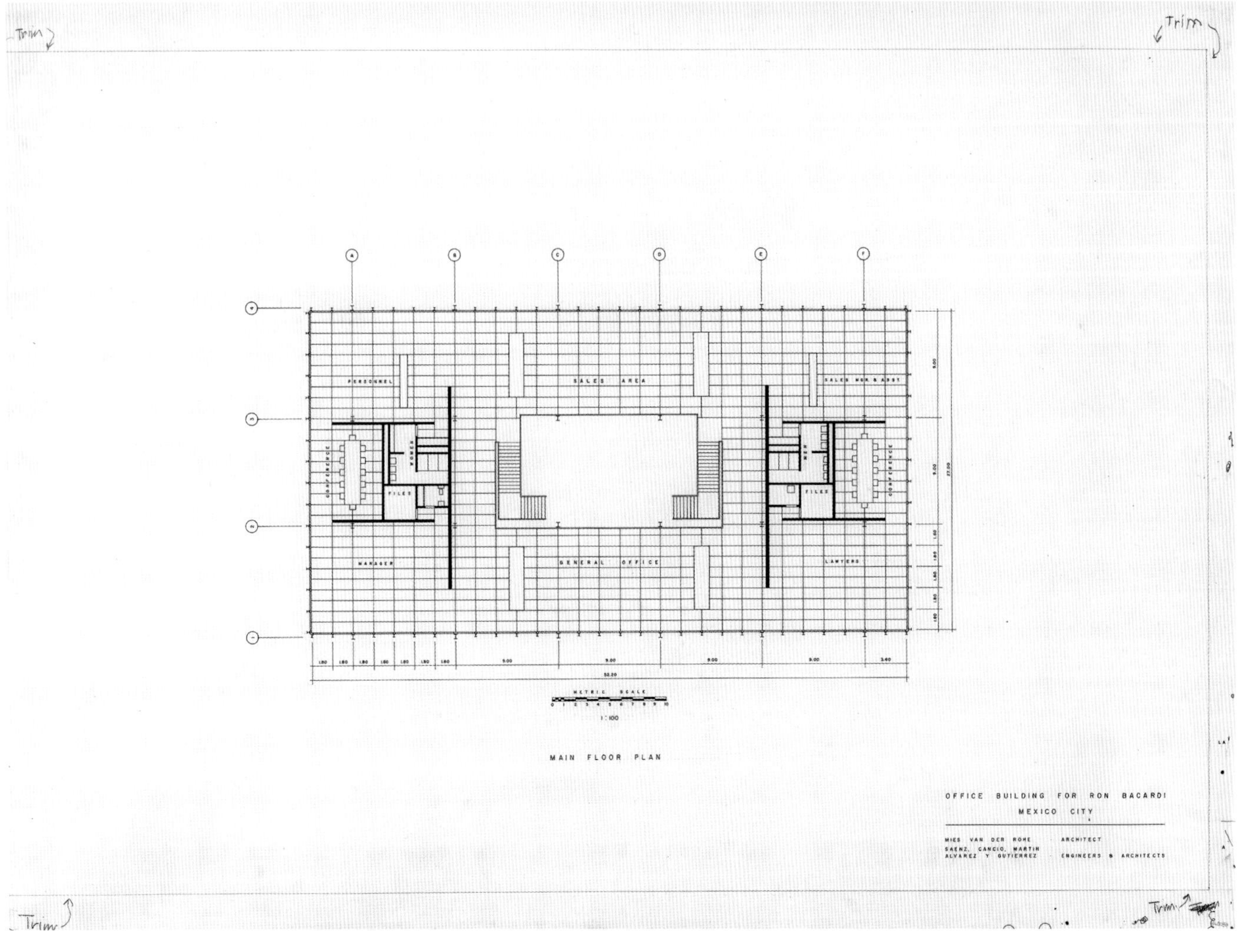
PERSONNEL
SALES AREA
SALES MGR & ASST
CONFERENCE
FILES
MANAGER
GENERAL OFFICE
LAWYERS
METRIC SCALE
1:100
MAIN FLOOR PLAN
OFFICE BUILDING FOR RON BACARDI
MEXICO CITY
MIES VAN DER ROHE · ARCHITECT
SAENZ, CANCIO, MARTIN
ALVAREZ Y GUTIERREZ · ENGINEERS & ARCHITECTS
Trim

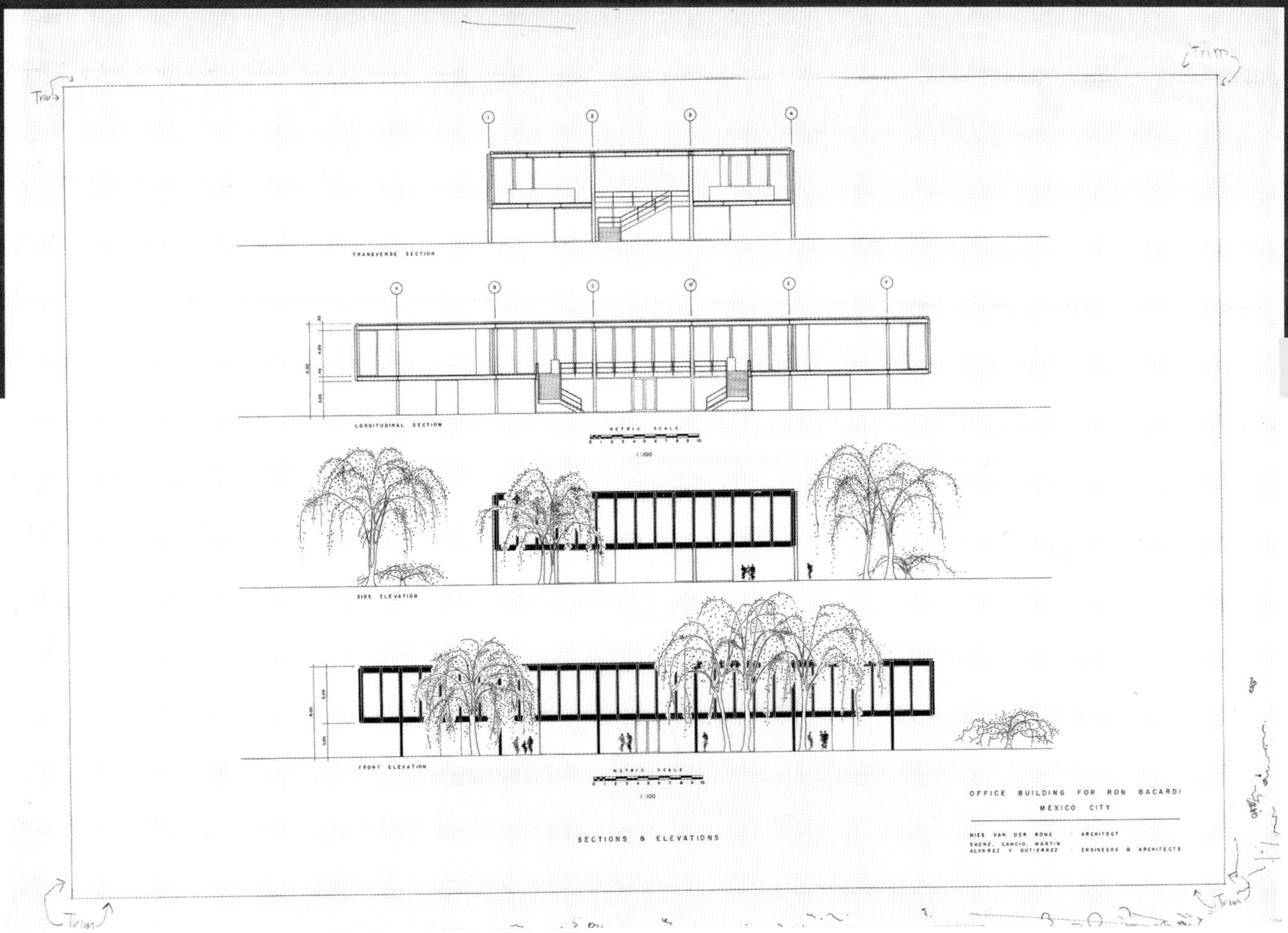

Top Left: Bacardi y Compañia, S.A. Administration Building, Tultitlán, Mexico. Ground floor plan. Ludwig Mies van der Rohe, architect with Saenz, Cancio, Martin, Alvarez y Gutierrez, engineers, 1958.

Bottom Left: Bacardi y Compañia, S.A. Administration Building, Tultitlán, Mexico. Main floor plan. Ludwig Mies van der Rohe, architect with Saenz, Cancio, Martin, Alvarez y Gutierrez, engineers, 1958.

Above: Bacardi y Compañia, S.A. Administration Building, Mexico City, Mexico. Sections and elevations. Ludwig Mies van der Rohe, architect with Saenz, Cancio, Martin, Alvarez y Gutierrez, engineers, 1958.

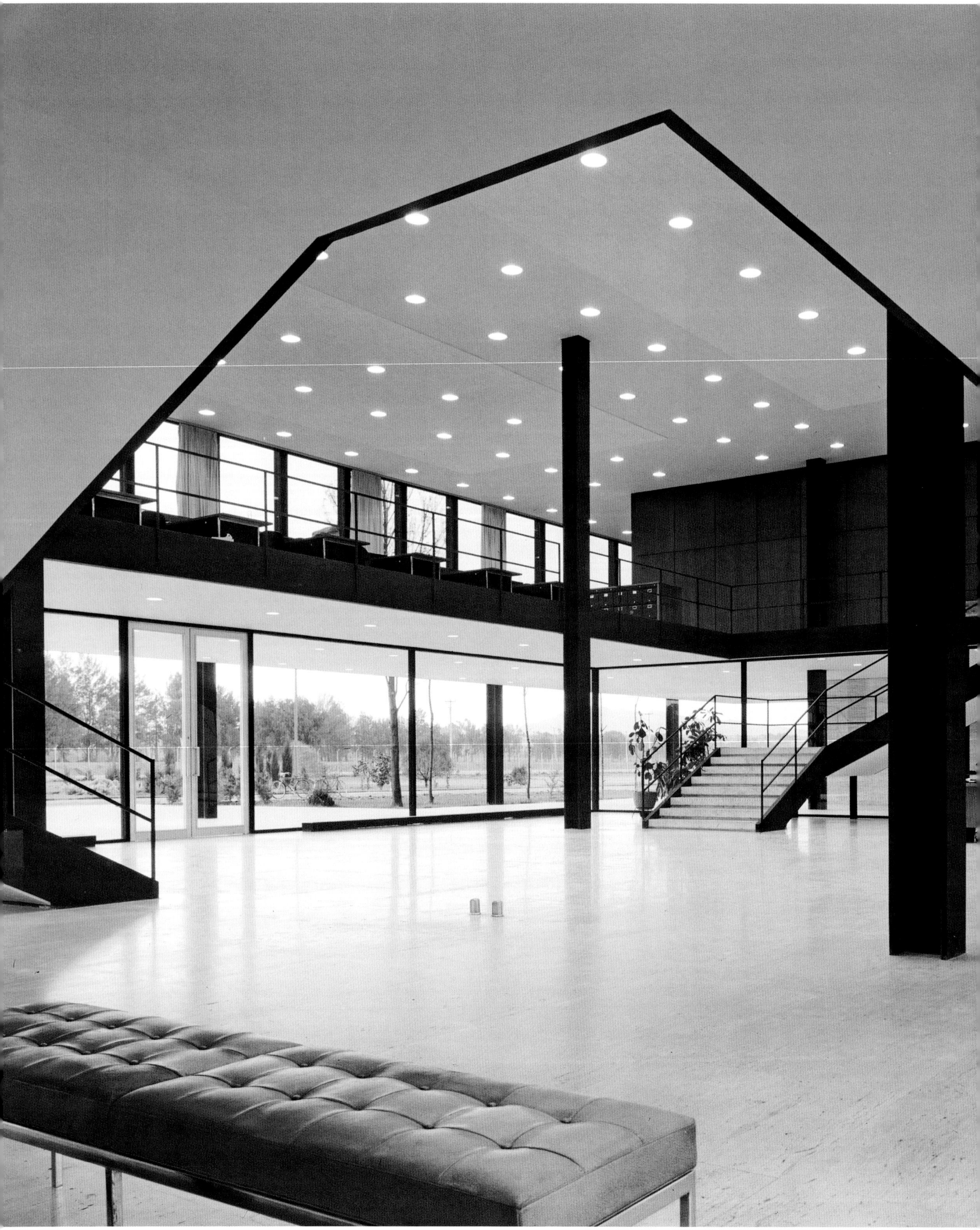

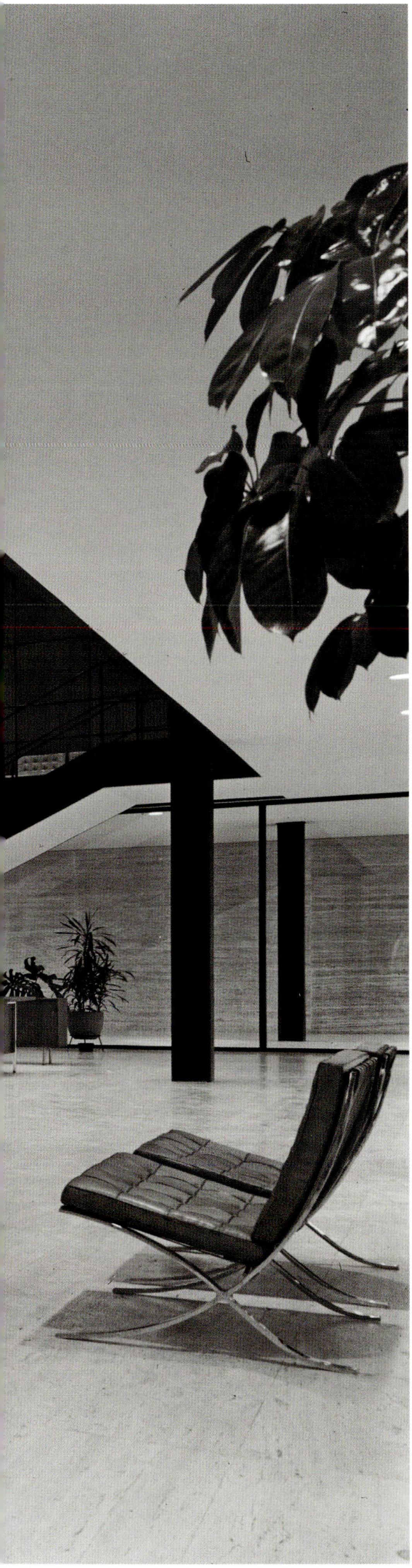

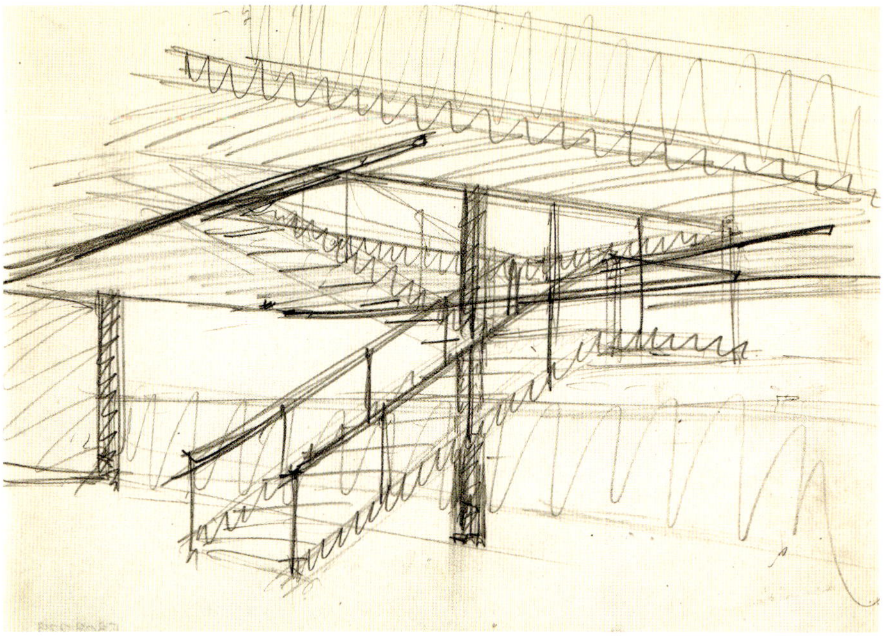

Left: Bacardi y Compañia, S.A. Administration Building, Tultitlán, Mexico. Interior view at entrance area. Ludwig Mies van der Rohe, architect, with Saenz, Cancio, Martin, Alvarez y Gutierrez, engineers, 1958. Photograph by Balthazar Korab, 1960. Courtesy of The Library of Congress.

Above: Bacardi y Compañia, S.A. Administration Building, Tultitlán, Mexico. Perspective sketch of stairway. Ludwig Mies van der Rohe, architect, with Saenz, Cancio, Martin, Alvarez y Gutierrez, engineers, 1958. © 2015 Artists Rights Society (ARS), New York / VG Bild-Kunst, Bonn.

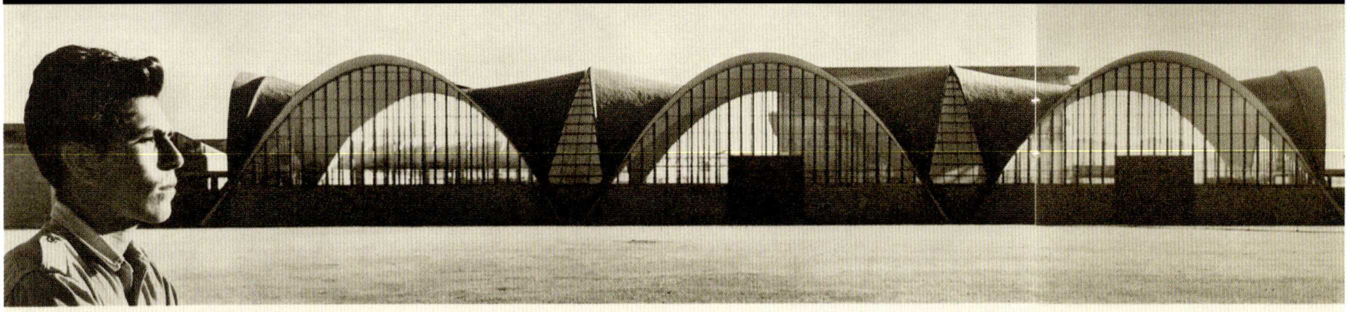

BACARDI IN MEXICO

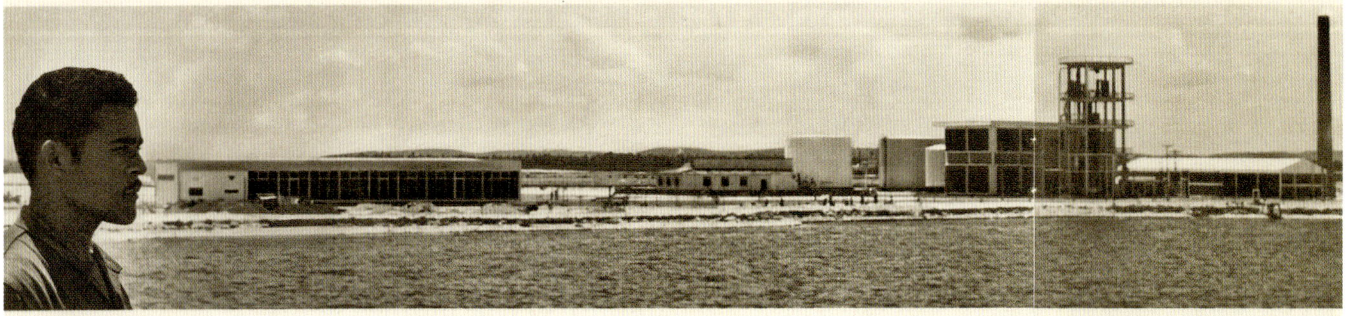

BACARDI IN BRAZIL

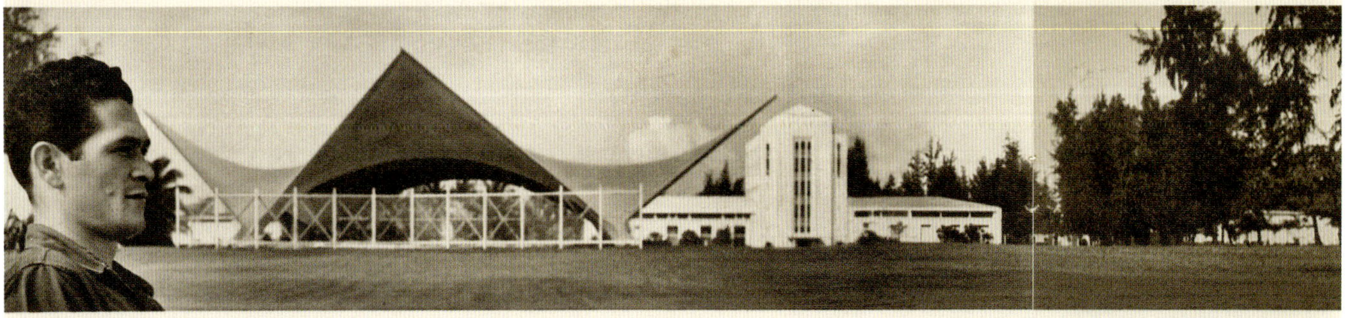

BACARDI IN PUERTO RICO

BACARDI IN EXILE

When Cuban rebels entered Havana in January 1959, banners thanking Fidel Castro ("Gracias, Fidel!") adorned the walls of the Modelo brewery. Less than two years after Bacardi and Bosch aligned themselves with the Revolution, however, the company's Cuban assets—including its plant in Santiago, its network of Hatuey breweries, and the Bacardi Building in Havana—were nationalized. The crisis triggered the exile of the company and its leaders and a reimagining of Bacardi in the Cuban diaspora.

One consequence of diaspora was a diffusion of identity and initiatives and the achievement of a new brand synthesis. Leaving Cuba, Bacardi became a transnational body with worldwide assets and a Pan-American identity: an archipelago of industry and administration that was a forerunner of today's globalized enterprises. When the company celebrated its centennial in 1962, it did so under a new motto: "Bacardi in many lands."[122] In fact, Bacardi doubled down on its international strategy, building more new centers spread throughout the American hemisphere. To build these centers, Bosch turned mainly to a cast of talented Cuban architects in exile who, in part, reinterpreted (and memorialized) the paradigms Mies and Candela had established for the company. Yet they also challenged the polemical certainties and formal obsessions of these architect giants with a flexible, eclectic approach, and with new vitality in the decoration of architectural surfaces. Collaborating with artists, they attempted to communicate a sense of Bacardi's tropical and Pan-American identity, and in so doing to achieve a broader cultural synthesis.

The first iterations of a new brand synthesis emerged in Miami. In 1963 Bacardi Imports, the company's U.S. distribution arm, moved from New York to this subtropical city just across the Florida Straits from Havana. Four years after the Cuban Revolution, and a year after the Cuban Missile Crisis, Miami had become home to hundreds of thousands of exiled Cubans. With its own recent exile, Bacardi's move was a statement of endurance and social solidarity. The Bacardi Imports Tower in Miami, designed by Enrique Gutiérrez of SACMAG of Puerto Rico,[123] boldly rendered the angst confronting Miami's Cuban community into a cutting edge yet playful landmark. The tower combined technical virtuosity, artistic brio, and touches of irony and parody, to pitch a powerful counter-narrative for the company in exile.

Bacardi's arrival coincided with, and symbolized, Miami's rise as a hub city for the Americas.[124] Bosch chose a site along Biscayne Boulevard, in a developing corridor of modern corporate offices rising north of downtown: mainly low-scale commercial blocks wrapped in tropicalist concrete eggcrates and louvered brises-soleil. Within this modernist corporate milieu, the Bacardi Building was strikingly tall and statuesque. The slender seven-story tower sprung from a broad paved plaza, the verticality of the one accentuated by the horizontality of the other. The tower-plaza association was full of references to Mies van der Rohe—not the architect's Bacardi work, but rather the Seagram Building in New York, completed five years earlier. The relationship dignified the building, a principal aim of Bosch who, like Seagram's Sam Bronfman, saw himself in the role of patron of architecture rather than client.[125]

In most every other way, the Bacardi tower subverted expectations of the tall building type. Rising from its plaza, the Bacardi Imports Tower defied gravity. It employed an exoskeletal structure in which the floors were hung using a system of cables and pulleys from trusses supported on four marble-clad piers. The resulting 24-foot cantilevers at either end transmitted a sense of daring, accentuated by delicate stairs that hung below these cantilevers. SACMAG's engineering virtuoso Luis Saenz extrapolated the structural strategy from work done in Cuba nearly a decade earlier at the Enriqueta Fernandez Apartment Building in Havana, similarly slung from four piers.[126] In Miami Saenz and Gutiérrez refined the hanging tower to emphasize simplicity, and exploit the exceptional transparency of the box-like glass space

"Bacardi in Many Lands," from Samuel Gallo, *Bacardi: 1862-1962* (S.l.: Bacardi Co.) 1962. Courtesy of The Bacardi Archive.

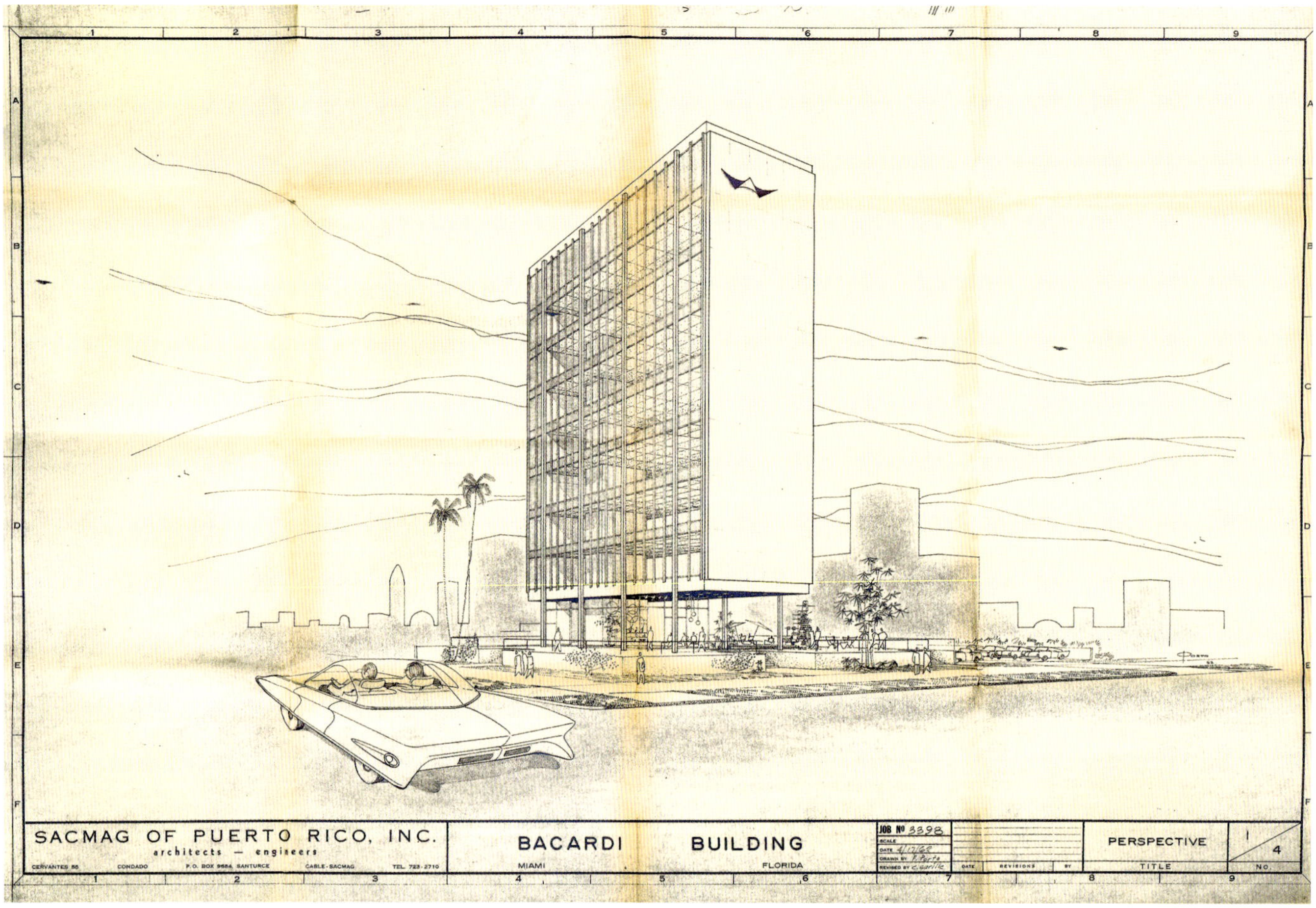

at its base. In this box—another ode to Mies, here the crystalline lobby of the 860-880 Lake Shore Drive Apartments in Chicago (1951)—the company replaced the customary tower lobby with a public art gallery known as The Bacardi.[127]

The tower was most remarkable, however, for its contrasting surface effects. It had a Janus-like skin that alternated finely tailored glass curtain walls with the flamboyant use of stone and azulejo tiles. The building's main east façade comprised a thin and taut skin of smoke-tinted plate glass stretched between piers dressed in carrara marble and vertical aluminum tendrils. The glass extended all the way to the top of the building, where it gave way to metal screens that gloriously exposed the building's powerful trusses. As Reinhold Martin has shown, such curtain wall systems, often dismissed as symbols of corporate conformity, could also be engineered to communicate the visual identity of the company.[128] Against the blue Miami sky, the Bacardi Building's impassive smoked-glass skin stood as a statement of corporate purpose, a testament to the controlled technique of rum production, and of course a signal of connection to Mies's earlier Bacardi work.

The tall, narrow sidewalls that brace the tower laterally were contrastingly graphic. Indicative perhaps of the company's own hemispheric transience, Pepín Bosch directed the development of narrative murals inspired by the Mexican mural movement, and specifically by the recently completed Central Library of the National Autonomous University of Mexico (1956), where hieroglyphic walls were illustrated by architect and muralist Juan O'Gorman.[129] Bosch commissioned the Brazilian artist Francisco Brennand to develop analogous murals, which were originally conceived to cover the north, south and west walls of the building.

Above: Bacardi Imports Tower, Miami. Perspective view. Enrique Gutierrez (SACMAG of Puerto Rico), c. 1962. Courtesy of The Bacardi Archive.

Right: Bacardi Imports Tower, Miami. Enrique Gutierrez (SACMAG of Puerto Rico) and Francisco Brennand, muralist, 1963. Photograph, 1972. Courtesy of The Bacardi Archive.

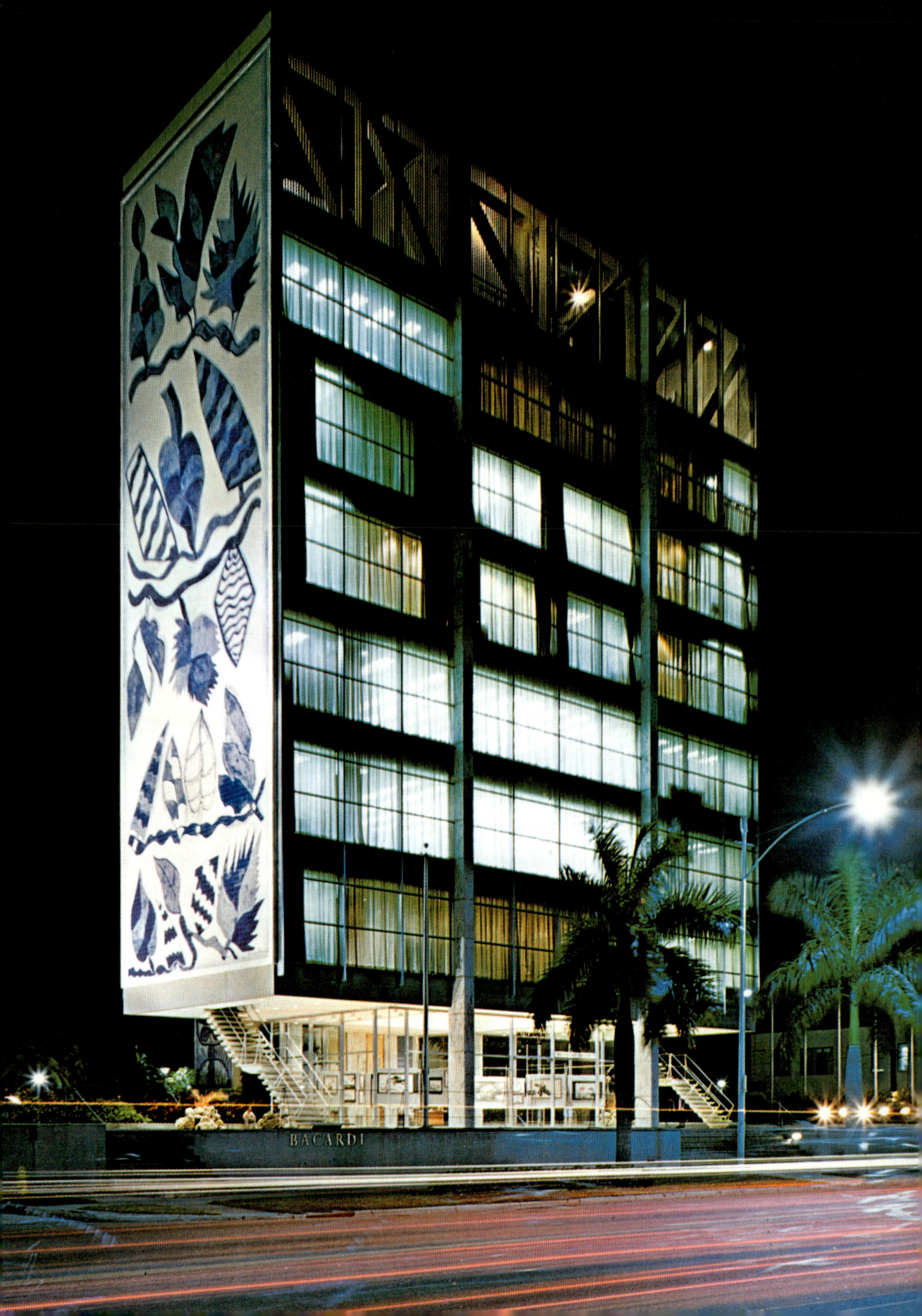
BACARDI

Miami was the first foreign commission for Brennand,[130] and he used the work to advocate for a closer integration of art and architecture.[131] In fact, the murals signified more than synthesis; they represented a new, postmodern approach to iconography in which applied decoration delivered messages that could compound, or contradict, the primary architectural idea. Brennand's murals featured flora that signified, in the words of the artist, "the discovery by Europeans of the South American continent."[132] The gigantic enlargements of exotic plant forms idealized the forests encountered by the conquistadores. Brennand placed the vegetal forms against a white surfaces framed by marble borders, free from any sense of perspective and loose in space, as if they were flying. The artist used colors that recalled the Portuguese tradition of azulejo painting, signifying the blue skies for which both Miami and the artist's native Recife were famous.[133] He employed a cobalt oxide tint in different gradations to create a subdued palette, concerned that too many colors would diminish the striking form of the building.

The "tropical, baroque sensuality"[134] of the murals, indeed the very presence of the murals, [135] captured the rising Latin American influence in Miami, a city that in the 1960s was searching for its own artistic and economic place in the hemisphere. Brennand's work displeased some, especially among Miami's modernist architects. Architect Lester Pancoast asked, "Should the Bacardi Building wear blue-and-white pajamas on Biscayne Boulevard every day of the year?"[136] However, the murals were popularly understood to represent both tropical Miami and Bacardi, and they paved the way for Miami artists to explore similar collaborations that helped to define a distinct regional modernism in the Magic City.[137] Whether, as noted in the press, the Bacardi Tower was the first "muralized" building in the United States,[138] it was clearly a sensation. Visible along Biscayne Boulevard, and even along flight paths into Miami International Airport, it was for a time Miami's newest tourist attraction.

As with the facades, modernist interiors by Adela Estrada and Alberto Fernandez-Pla fused corporate atmospherics with cocktail flair. The subdued tones of the offices, combining modular walnut wall panels, gray-green carpet, and modern furniture by Knoll, Dunbar and Macey Fowler, were splashed with intense colors. In the building's second-floor lobby, Fernandez-Pla designed a wall tapestry woven with abstracted symbols of a Bacardi cocktail in gray, white, purple, yellow and lime. The hand-tufted tapestry, produced by the famed carpet house V'Soske, combined cubist and Op Art tendencies to produce an emblem for the building and the company. [139] At the top of the building, in the seventh-floor "entertainment suite," Antonio Gattorno's mural *Waiting for Coffee*, relocated from the Empire State Building, was re-installed. Yet its meaning had changed; originally conceived to transform corporate space into an exotic and illusionary setting, this marker of Cuban identity, now neatly framed on a floating wall panel, functioned as an artifact of Bacardi's own history.

In 1973, a mushroomlike addition sprouted from the plaza behind the tower. The four-story Annex Building comprised two square blocks, arranged one atop the other, "as a reverse classical pyramid."[140] Designed by Cuban-émigré architect Ignacio Carrera-Justiz, the building had an unusual structure close in character to that of the adjacent tower. The Annex's upper block, comprising two office

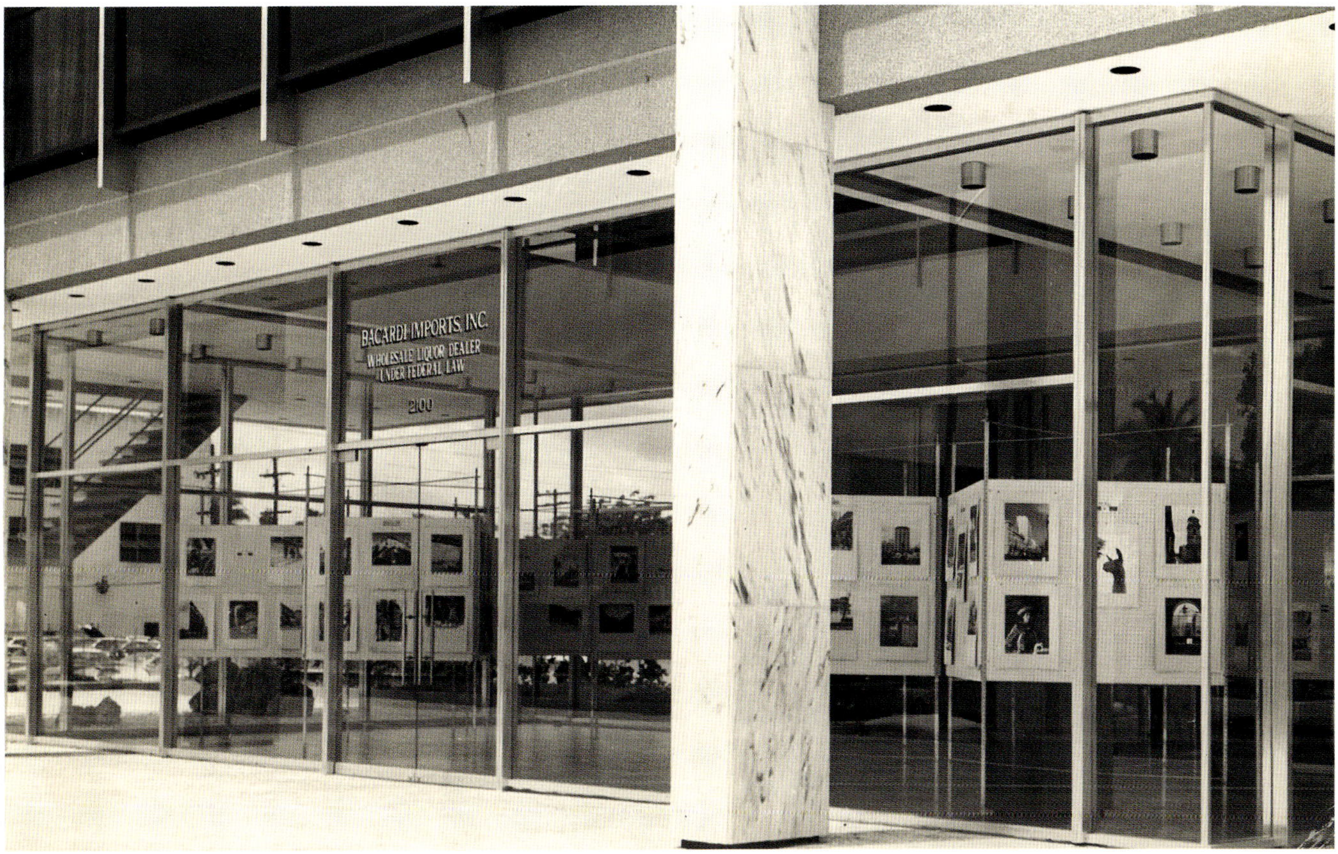

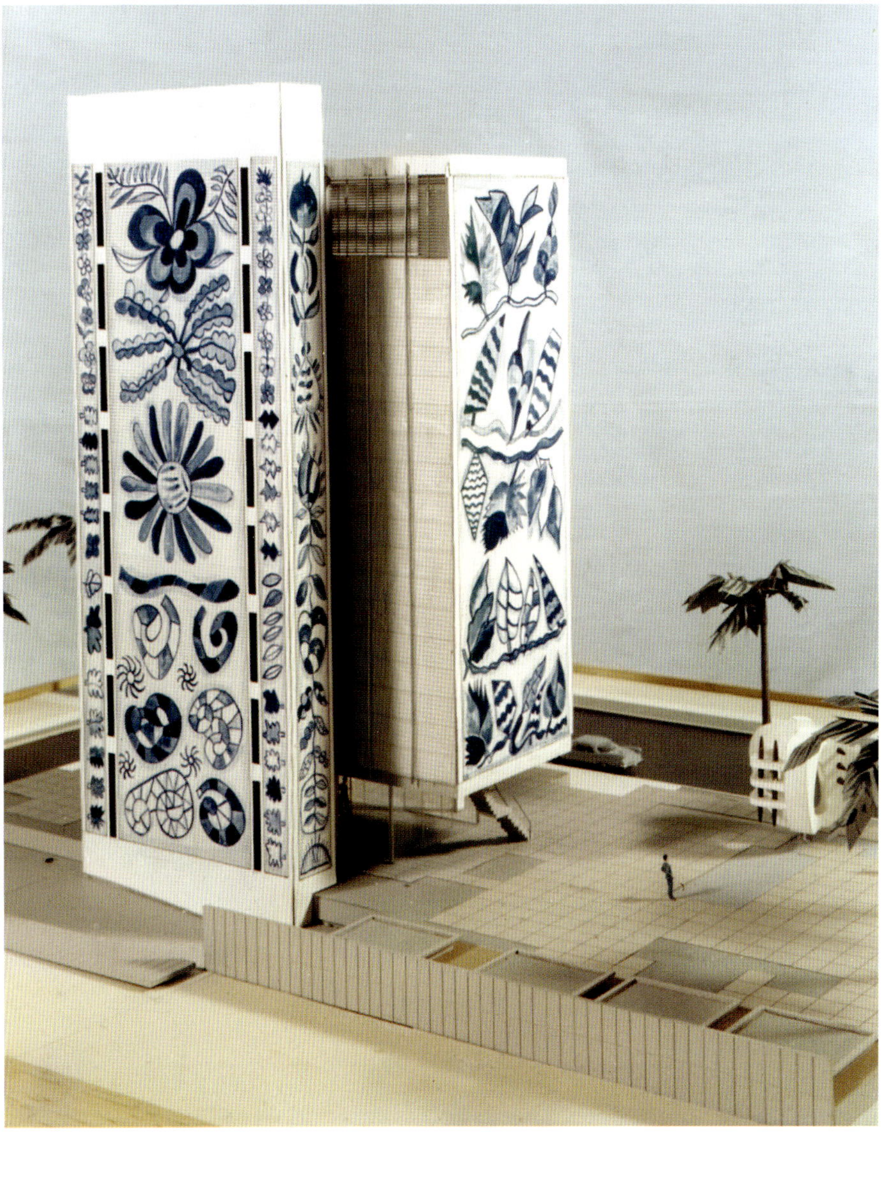

Top: Bacardi Imports Tower, Miami. Ground-floor gallery. Enrique Gutierrez (SACMAG of Puerto Rico), architect; Francisco Brennand, muralist; Adela Estrada and Alberto Fernandez-Pla, interior designers, 1963. Courtesy of The Bacardi Archive.

Bottom: Bacardi Imports Tower, Miami. Model. Enrique Gutierrez (SACMAG of Puerto Rico), architect, and Francisco Brennand, muralist, 1963. Courtesy of The Bacardi Archive.

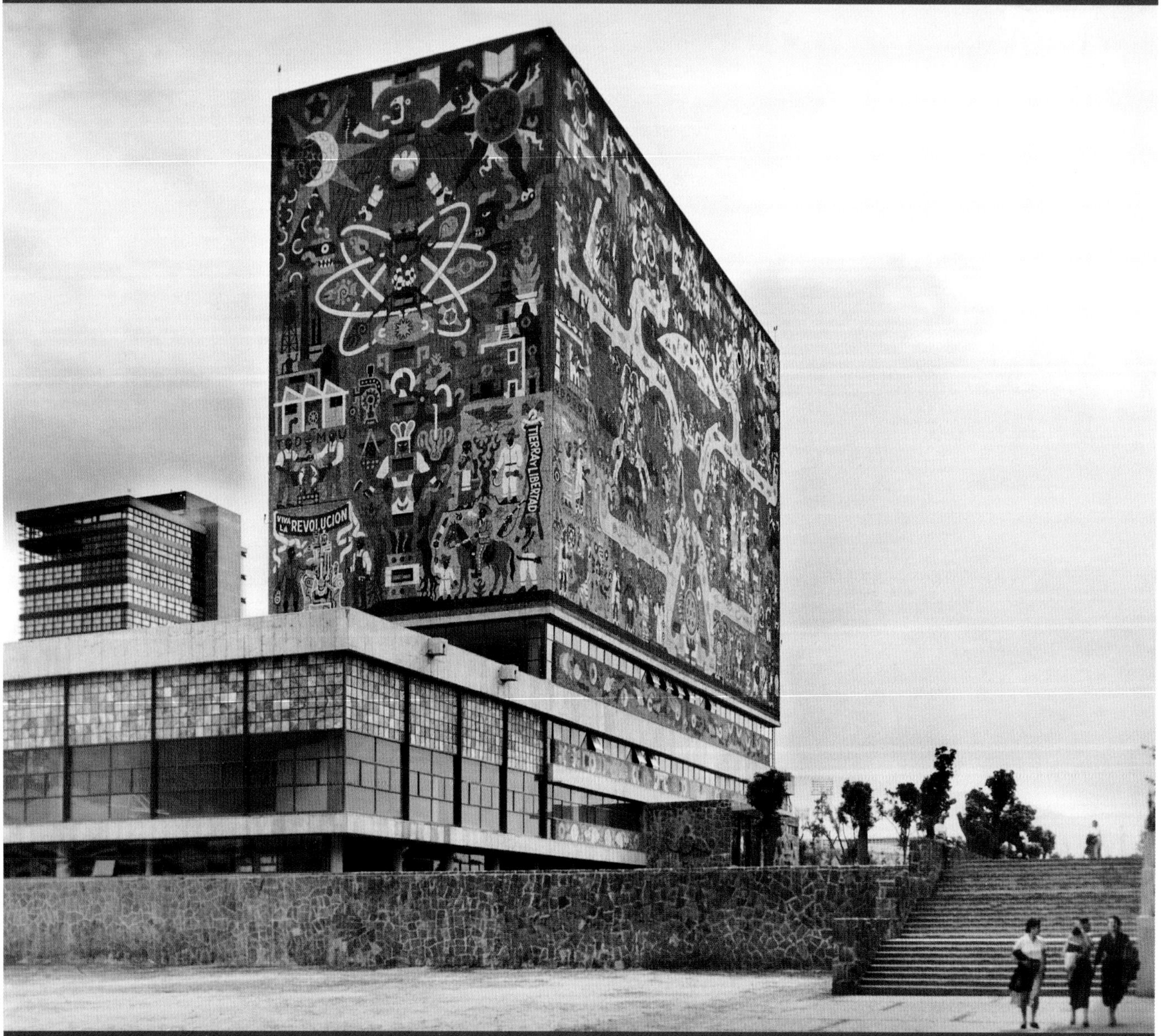
VIVA LA REVOLUCION
TIERRA Y LIBERTAD

floors, was hung by steel rods from a grid of deep, post-tensioned roof beams that cantilevered from the building's trunk-like core. The Annex also had, like the adjacent tower, an extraordinary skin. The four equal walls of the square pavilion were wrapped in tapestries of colored glass that translated commissioned artwork by the German artist Johannes Maria Dietz into a curtain wall. These vitreous tapestries, made from one inch-thick colored hammered glass pieces set into epoxy compound, portray Dietz's studies of the conversion of sugarcane into rum and include the prominent figures of bats. The graphic walls eschewed the transparent character of the tower, by contrast mysterious and opaque. At night the vitreous walls glowed, transforming the building into a colorful lantern, its horizontal tableaux an alluring counterpoint to the tower's landmark vertical walls.

A close reading of the Bacardi Imports Tower and its annex suggests no singular dogma behind the architecture, but rather a series of approaches, inventions and opportunities. These were just the sort of complex motivations bubbling up in contemporary architectural culture, celebrated in works like Robert Venturi's *Complexity and Contradiction in Architecture* (1966). The fusion of these motivations, like the tower's blending of modernist curtain wall and sensuous, larger-than-life floral tile work, emblematized in a new way the company's pluralism, a quality already evoked in classic Bacardi cocktail formulations like the Cuba Libre, and more recently in the company's contemporary, Saatchi & Saatchi–designed advertising campaign: "Bacardi: The Mixable One."

Left: Central Library of the Ciudad Universitária campus, National Autonomous University of Mexico (UNAM), Mexico City, Mexico. Juan O'Gorman, architect and muralist, with Gustavo Saavedra and Juan Martinez de Velasco, 1952. Courtesy of Archivos de Arquitectos Mexicanos, UNAM.

Below: Batalha dos Guararapes (Battle of Guararapes). Recife, Brazil. Francisco Brennand, artist. Photograph by Fred Jordão, 1978. Courtesy of Fred Jordão.

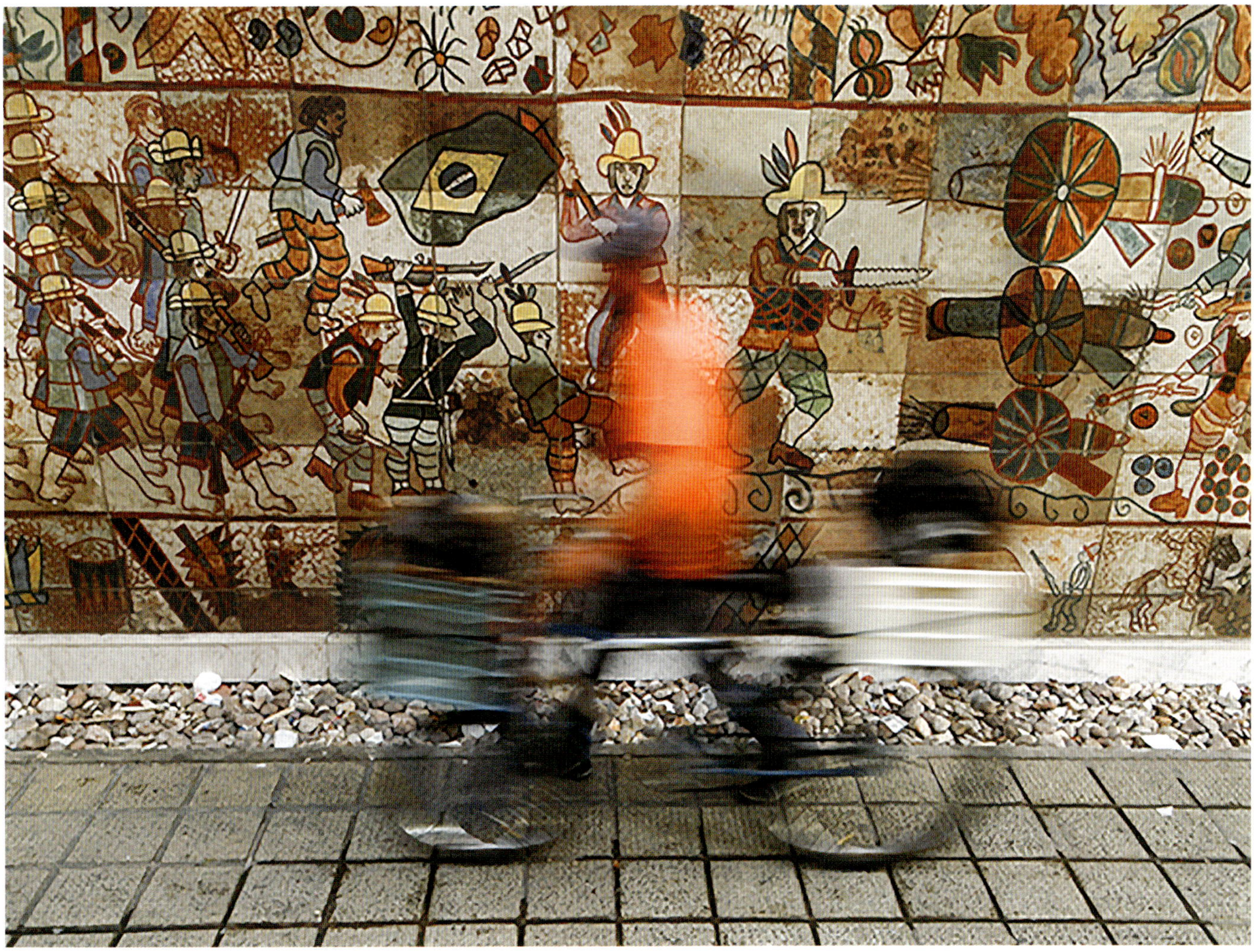

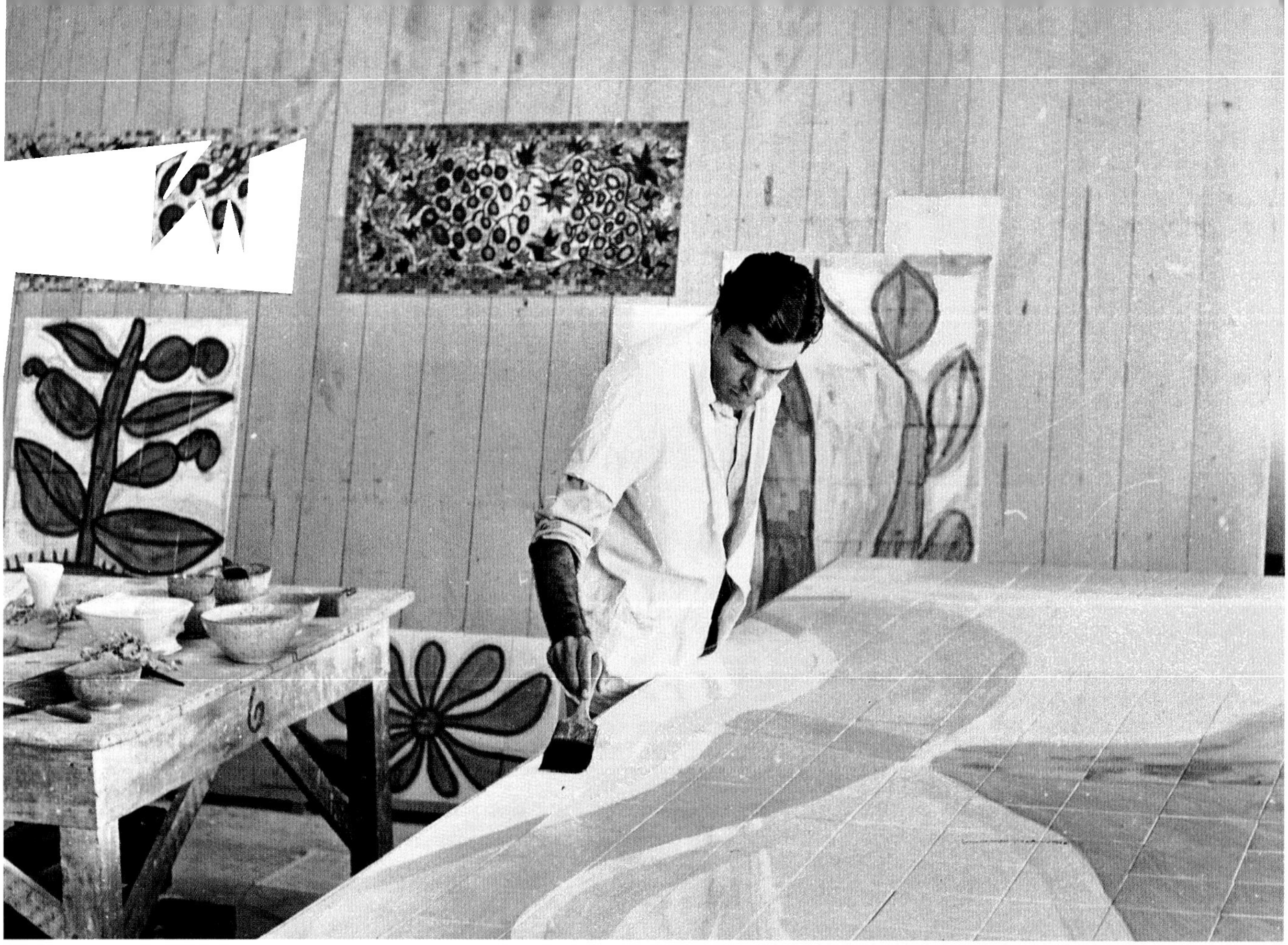

Francisco Brennand in his studio working on the *azulejos* for the Bacardi Imports Tower in Miami. Undated.
Courtesy of The Bacardi Archive.

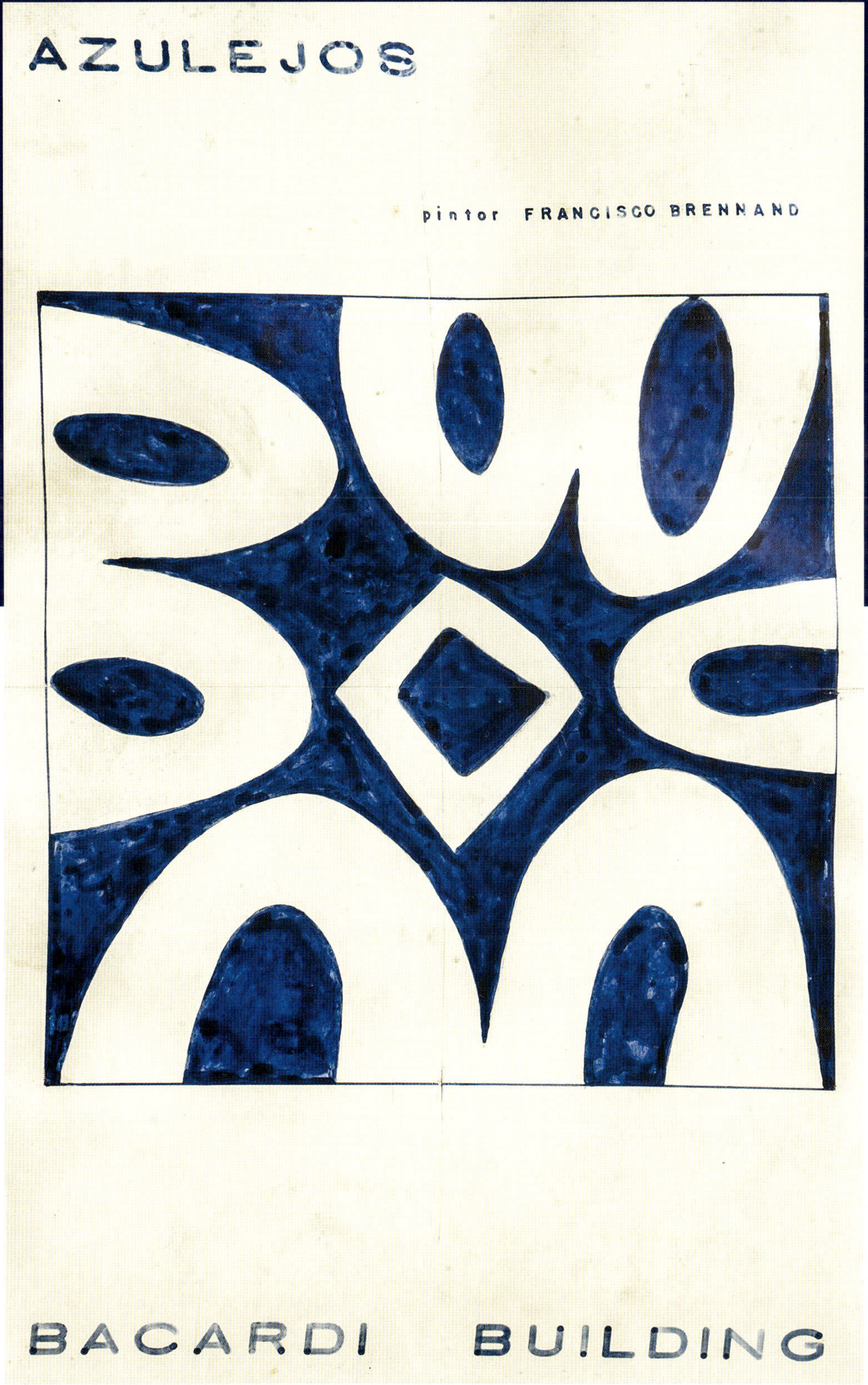

Study for Miami *azulejos*, Francisco Brennand, artist. Courtesy of Francisco Brennand.

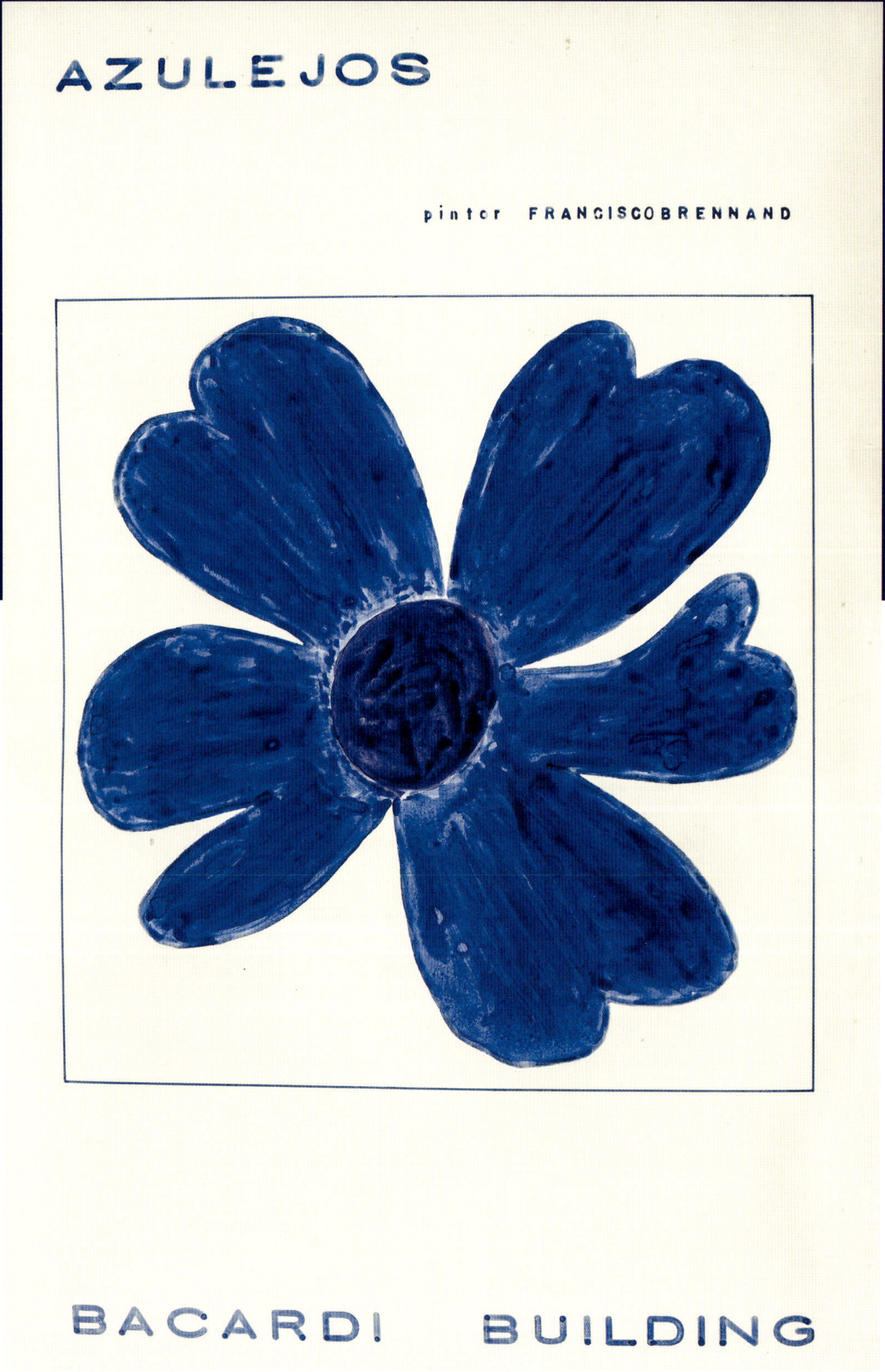

Study for Miami *azulejos*. Francisco Brennand, artist.
Courtesy of Francisco Brennand.

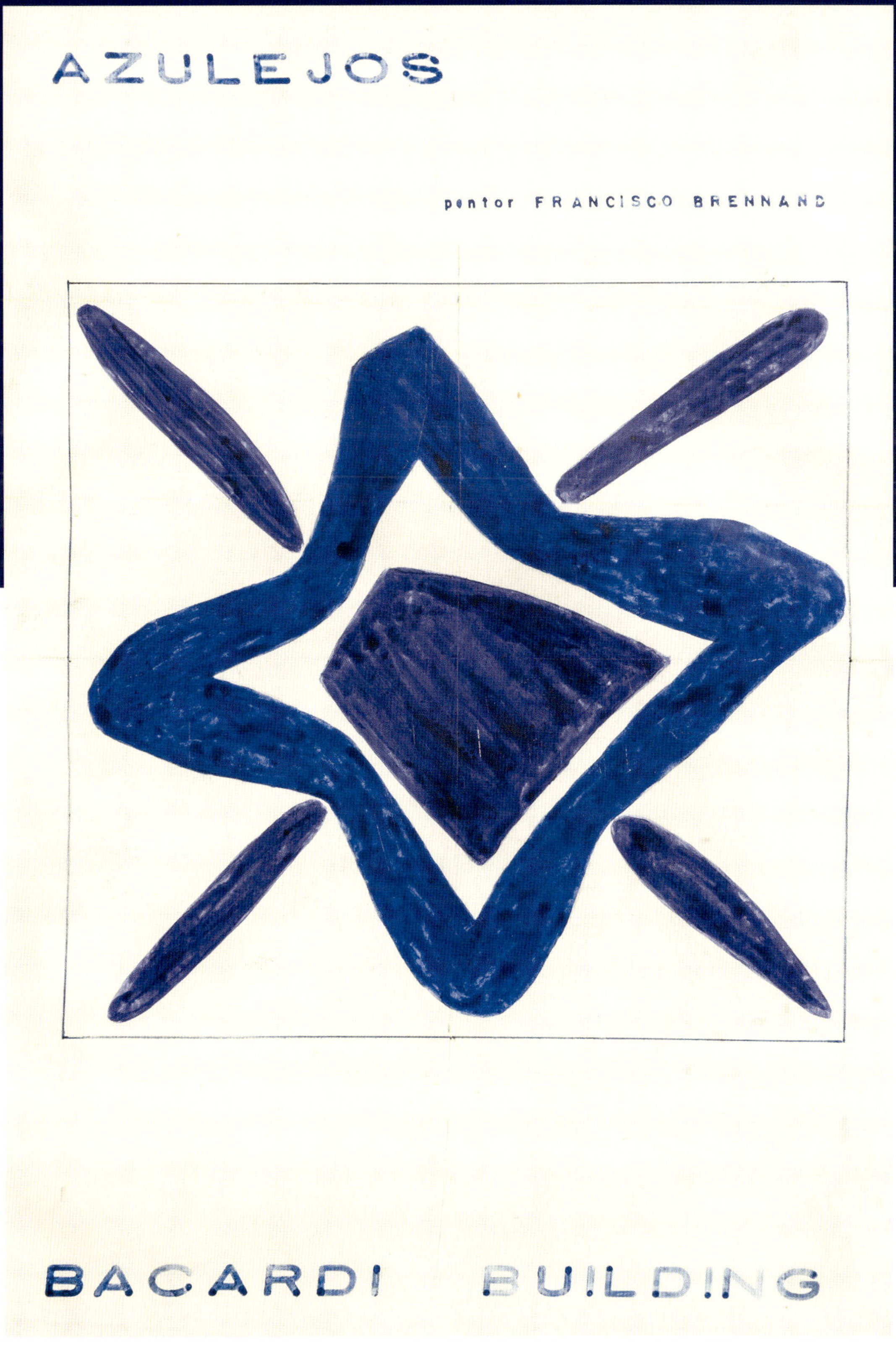
AZULEJOS
pentor FRANCISCO BRENNAND
BACARDI BUILDING

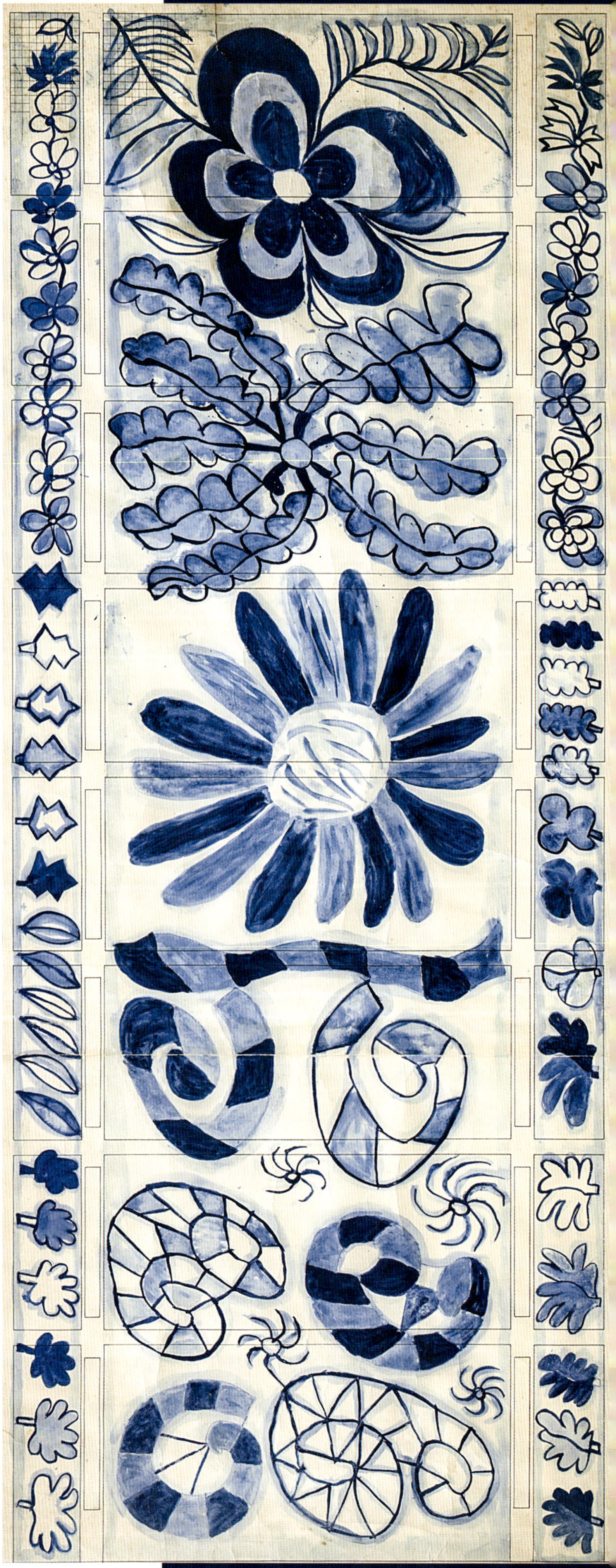

This Page: Bacardi Imports Tower, Miami.
Study panel for west facade mural.
Francisco Brennand, artist, 1963.
Courtesy of Francisco Brennand.

Opposite Page: Bacardi Imports Tower, Miami.
Study panels for North and South facades.
Francisco Brennand, artist, 1963.
Courtesy of Francisco Brennand.

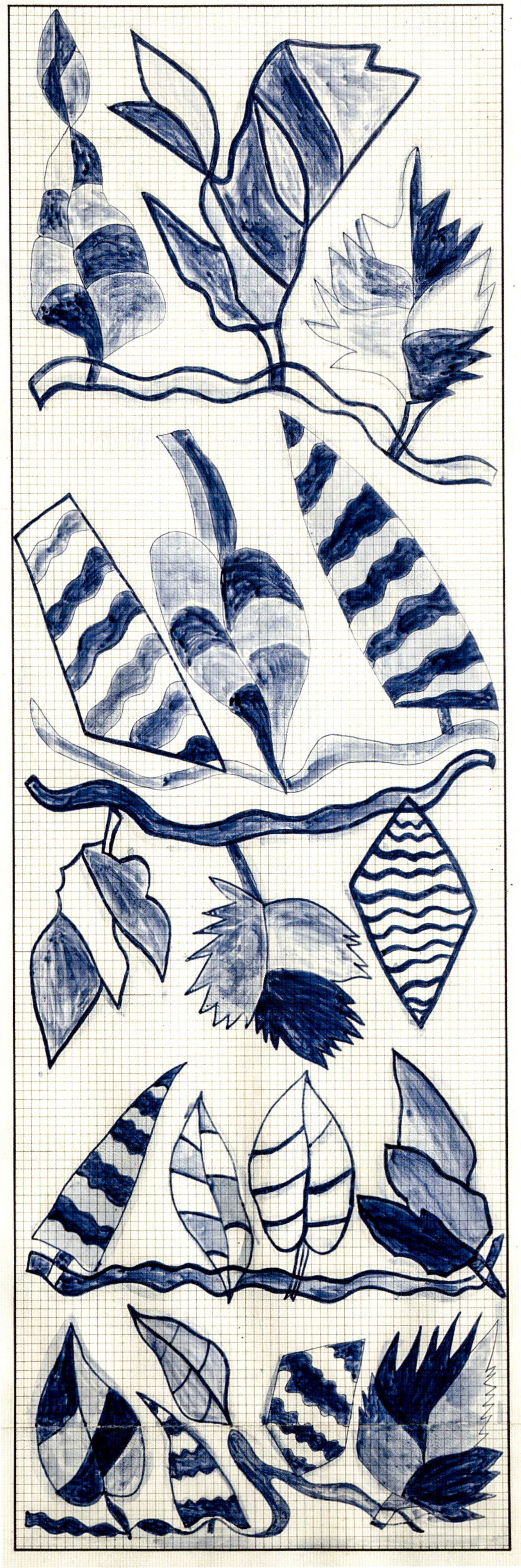

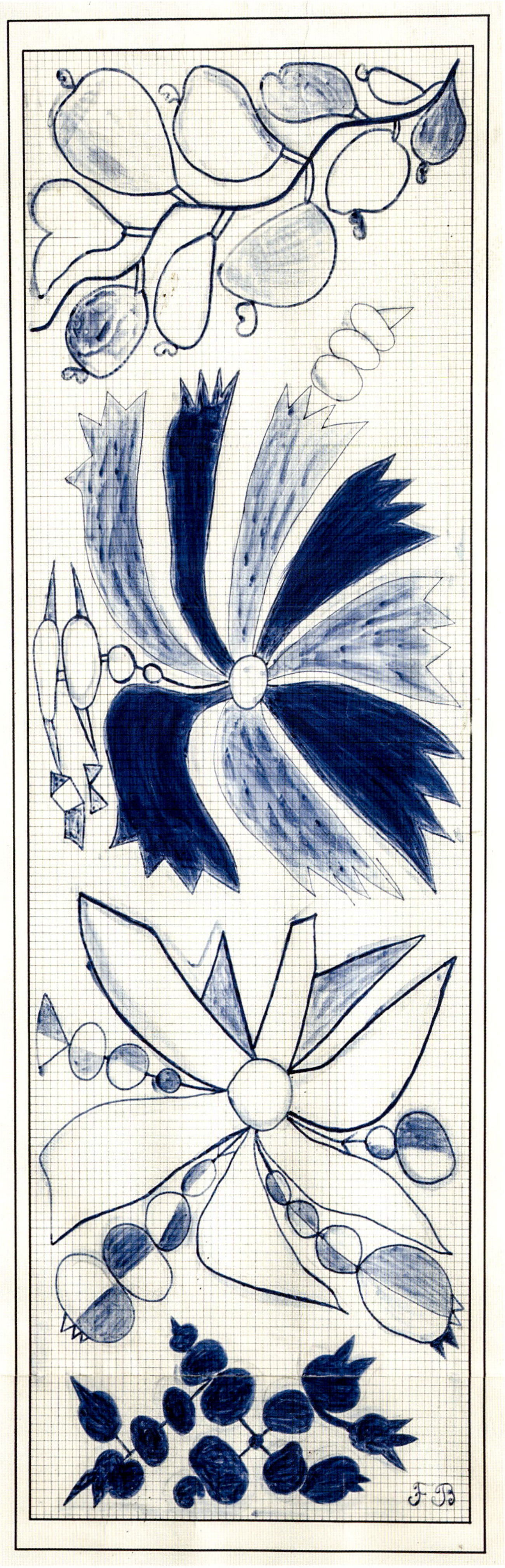
F B

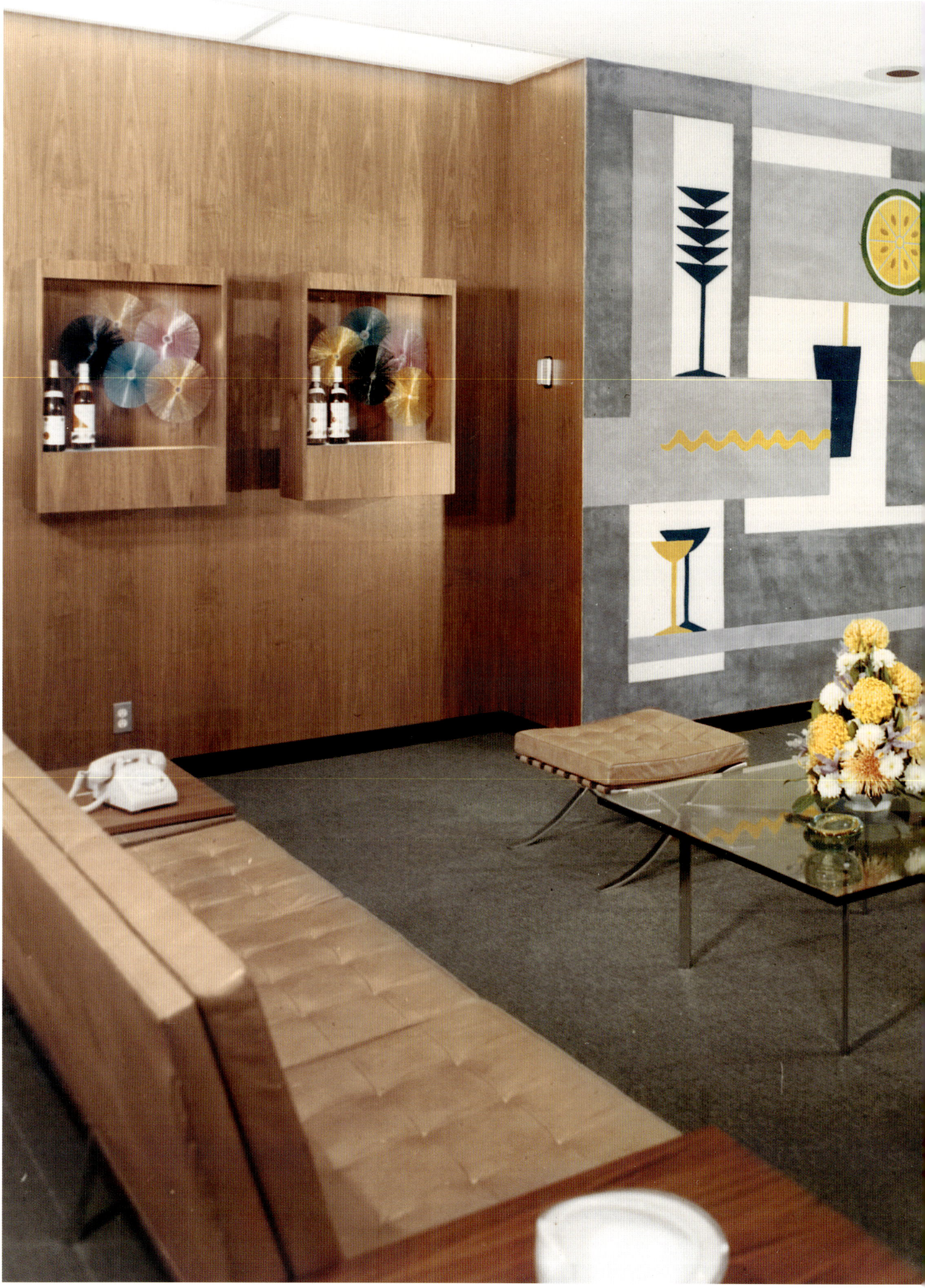

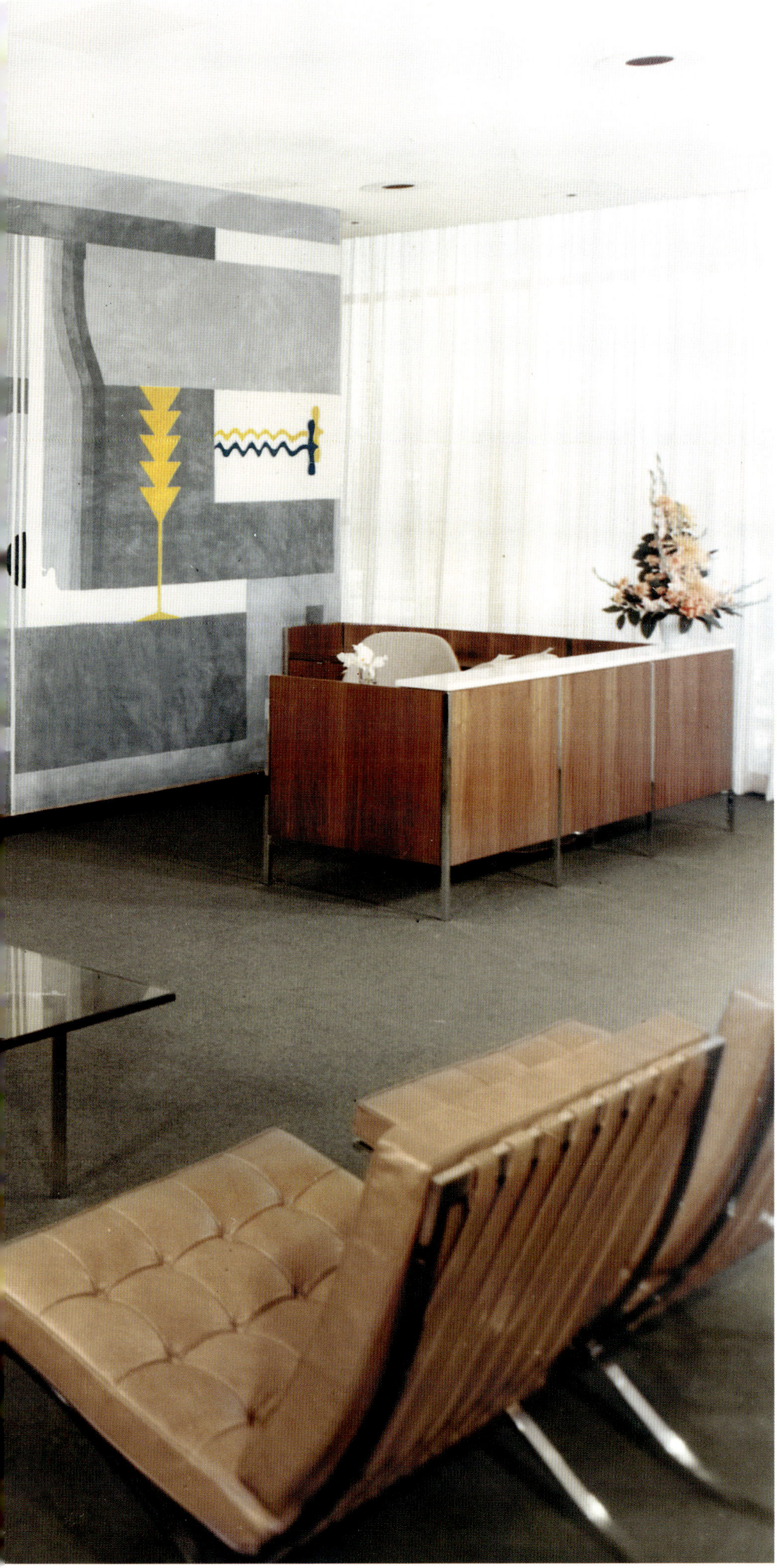

Bacardi Imports Tower, Miami. Main lobby. Enrique Gutierrez (SACMAG of Puerto Rico), architect; Adela Estrada and Alberto Fernandez-Pla, interior designers, 1963. Photograph by Ernest Graham, 1964. Courtesy of The Bacardi Archive.

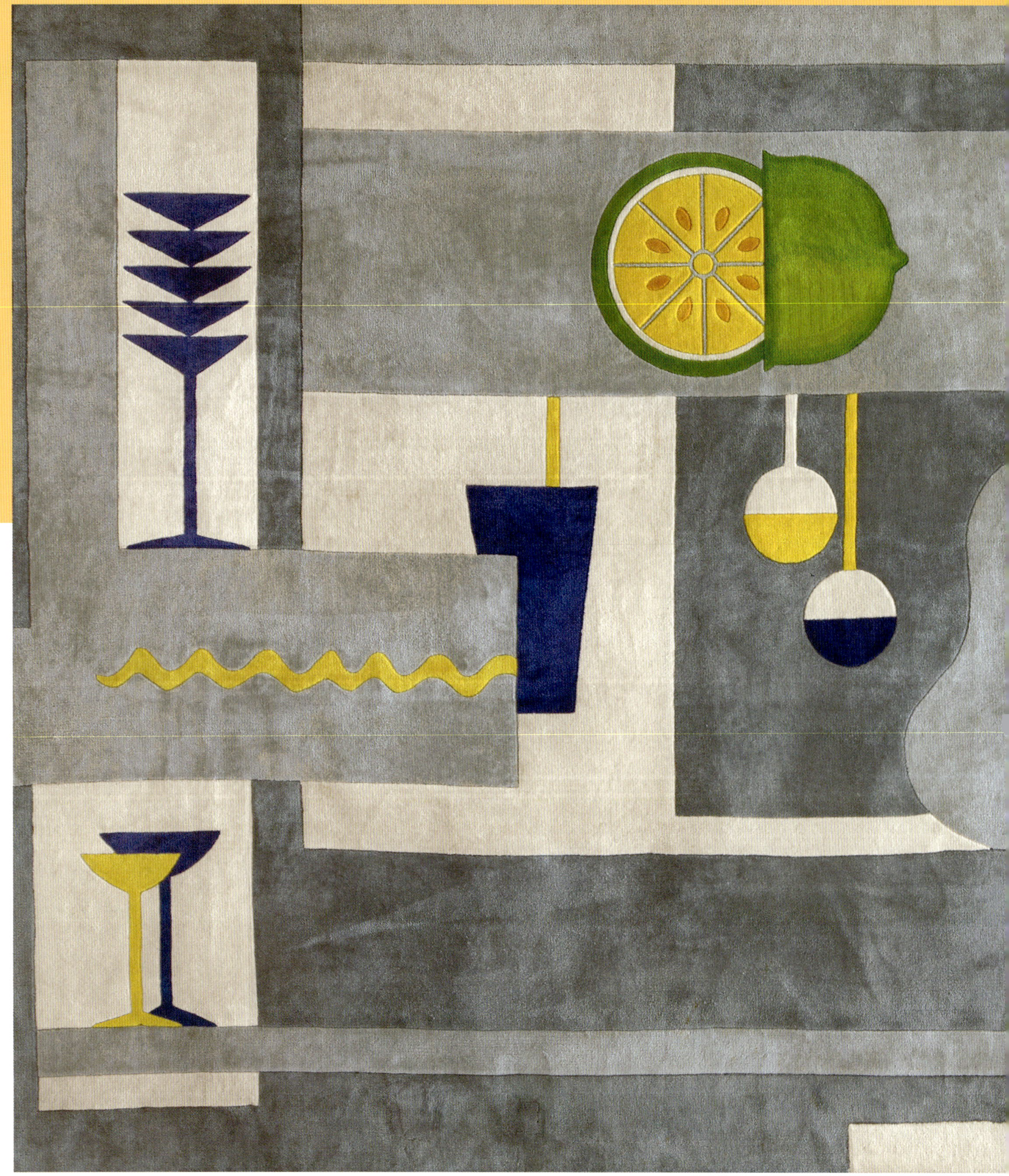

Bacardi Imports Tower, Miami. Carpet mural. Alberto Fernandez-Pla, designer, 1963. Courtesy of The Bacardi Archive.

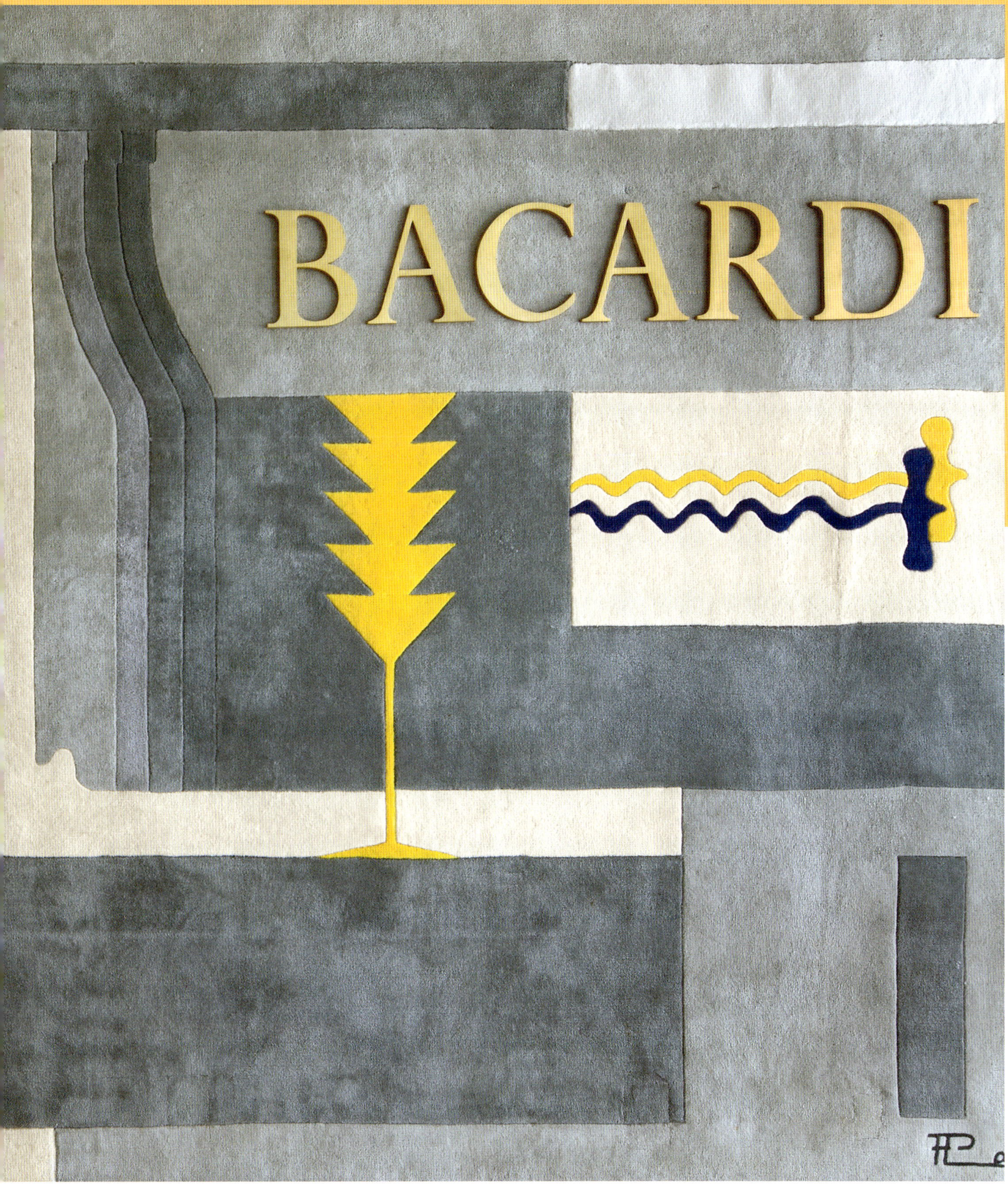
BACARDI

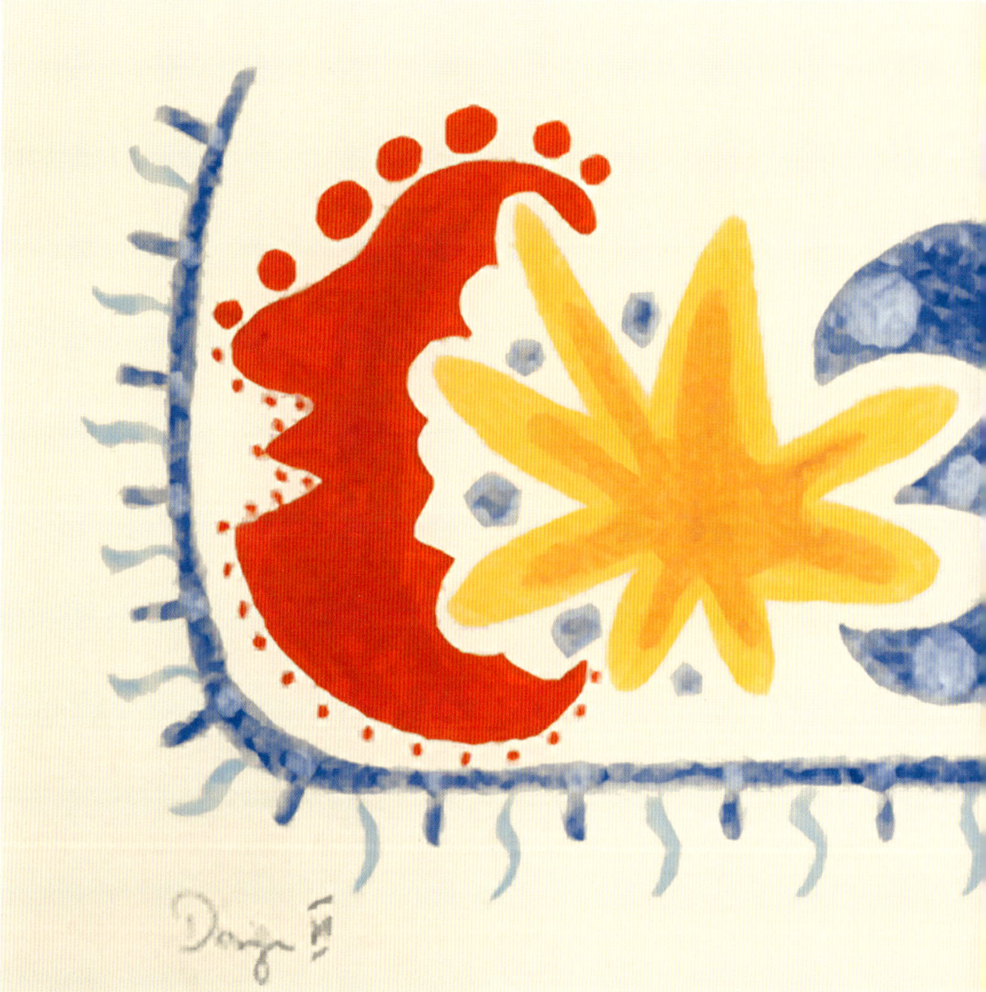

Annex Design IV. Johannes Maria Dietz, artist, 1972.
Study for the Bacardi Imports Tower.
Courtesy of The Bacardi Archive.

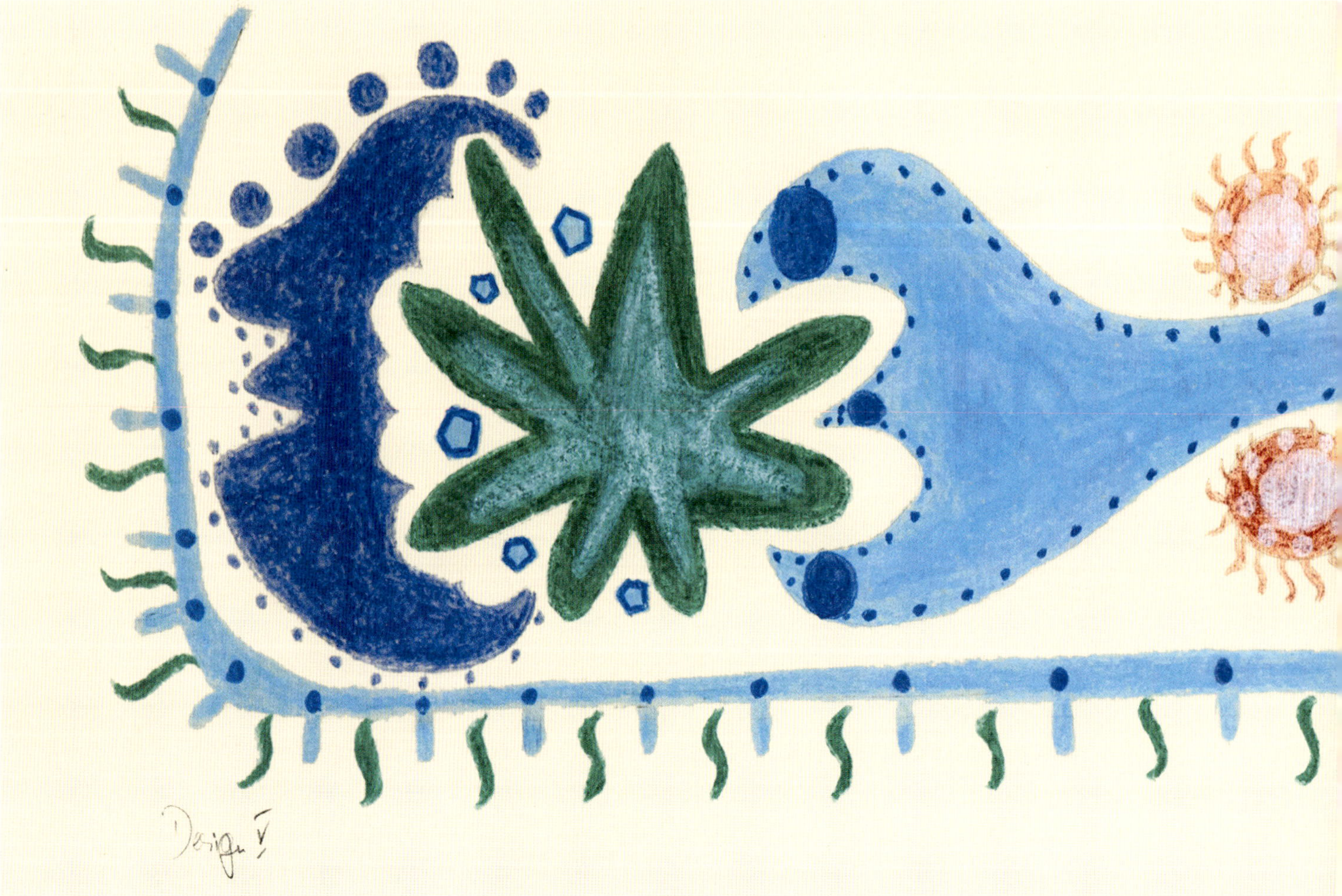

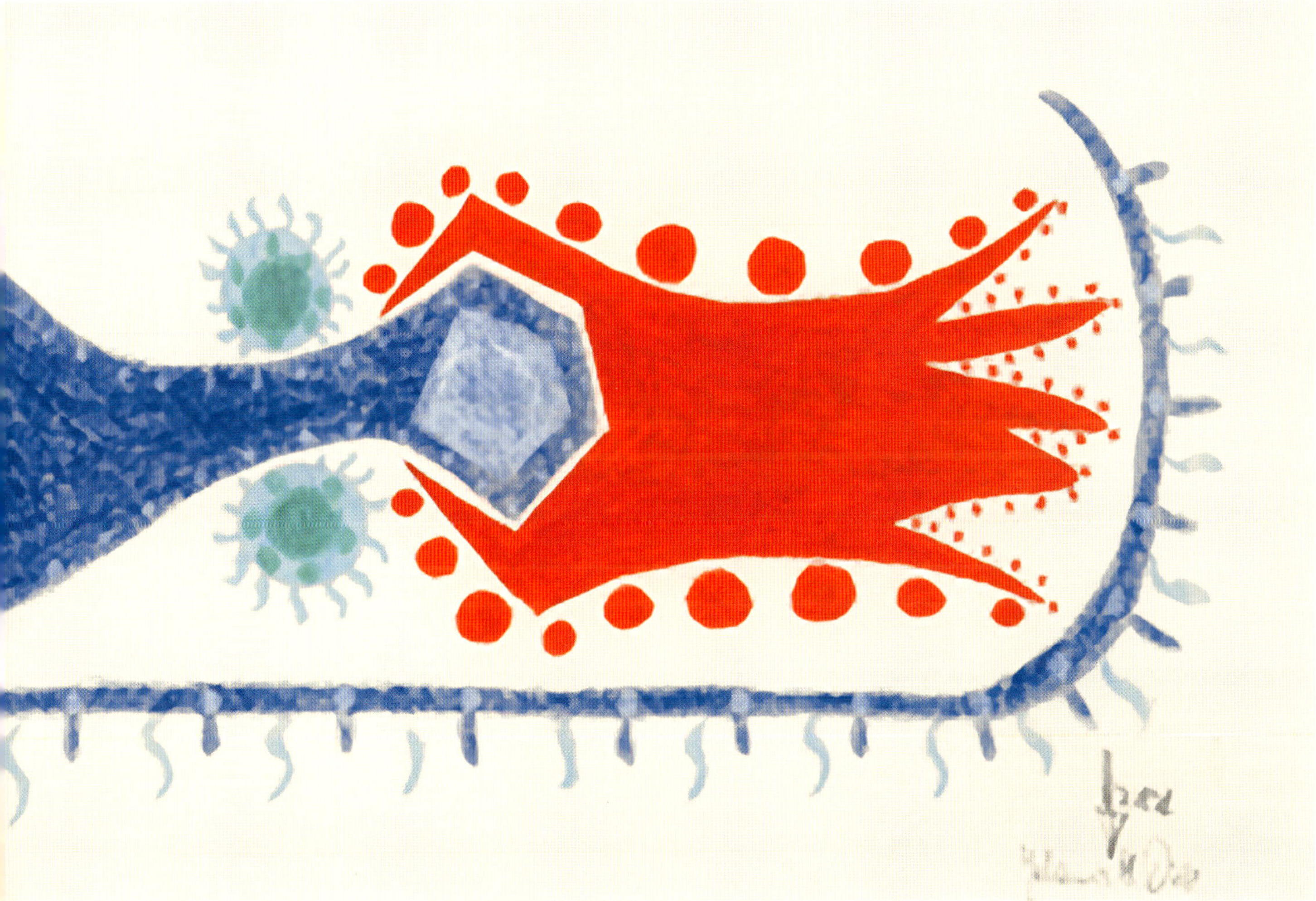

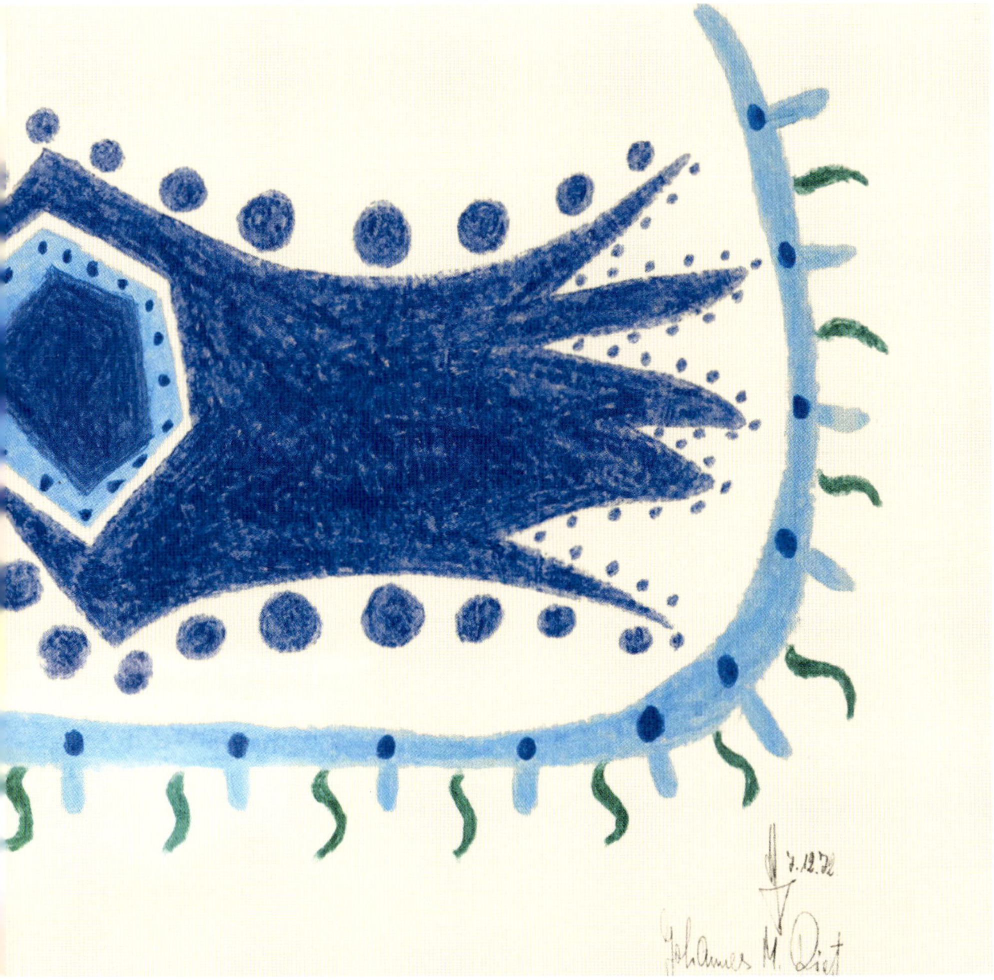

Annex Design VI. Johannes Maria Dietz, artist, 1972.
Study for the Bacardi Imports Tower.
Courtesy of The Bacardi Archive.

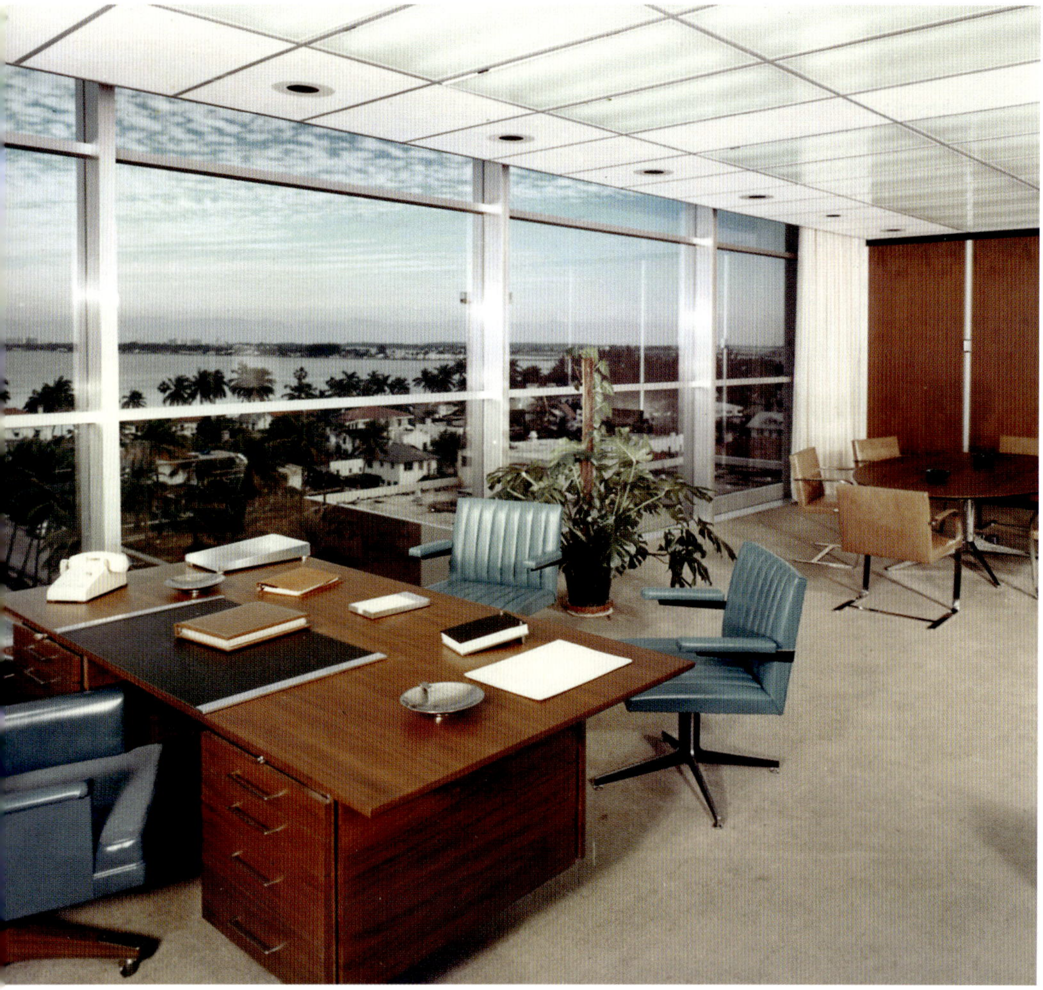

Left: Bacardi Imports Tower, Miami. Office of José "Pepin" Bosch. Enrique Gutierrez (SACMAG of Puerto Rico), architect; Adela Estrada and Alberto Fernandez-Pla, interior designers, 1963. Photograph by Ernest Graham, 1964. Courtesy of The Bacardi Archive.

Bottom: Bacardi Imports Tower, Miami. Seventh-floor dining room with relocated Gattorno mural. Enrique Gutierrez (SACMAG of Puerto Rico), architect; Adela Estrada and Alberto Fernandez-Pla, interior designers, 1963. Photograph by Ernest Graham, 1964. Courtesy of The Bacardi Archive.

Right: Bacardi Imports Administration Annex, Miami. Model. Ignacio Carerra-Justiz, architect. Stained-glass works by Gabriel and Jacques Loire based on designs by Johannes Maria Dietz, 1973. Courtesy of The Bacardi Archive.

Overleaf: Bacardi Imports Administration Annex, Miami. Ignacio Carerra-Justiz, architect. Stained glass works by Gabriel and Jacques Loire based on designs by Johannes Maria Dietz, 1973. Courtesy of The Bacardi Archive.

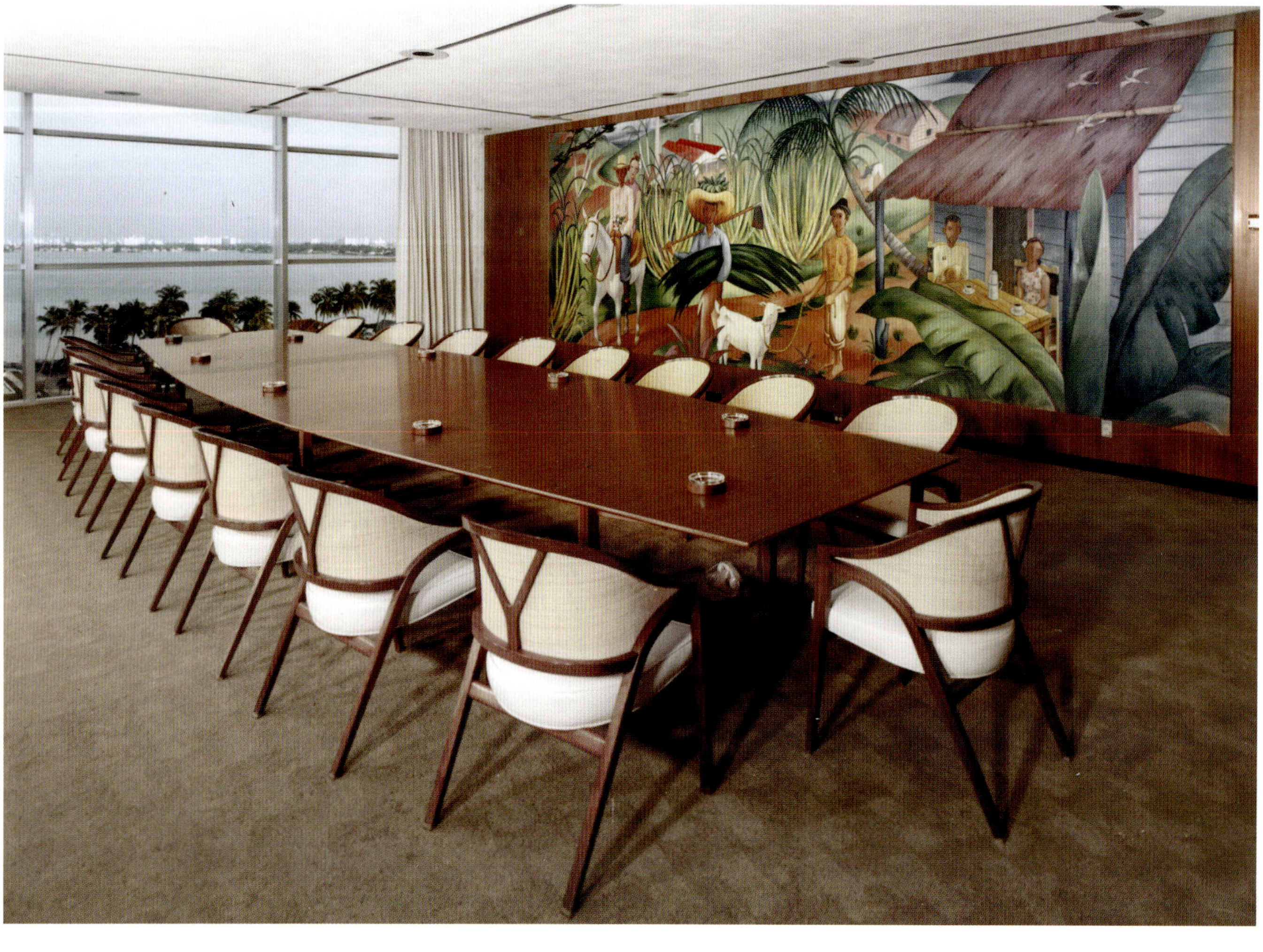

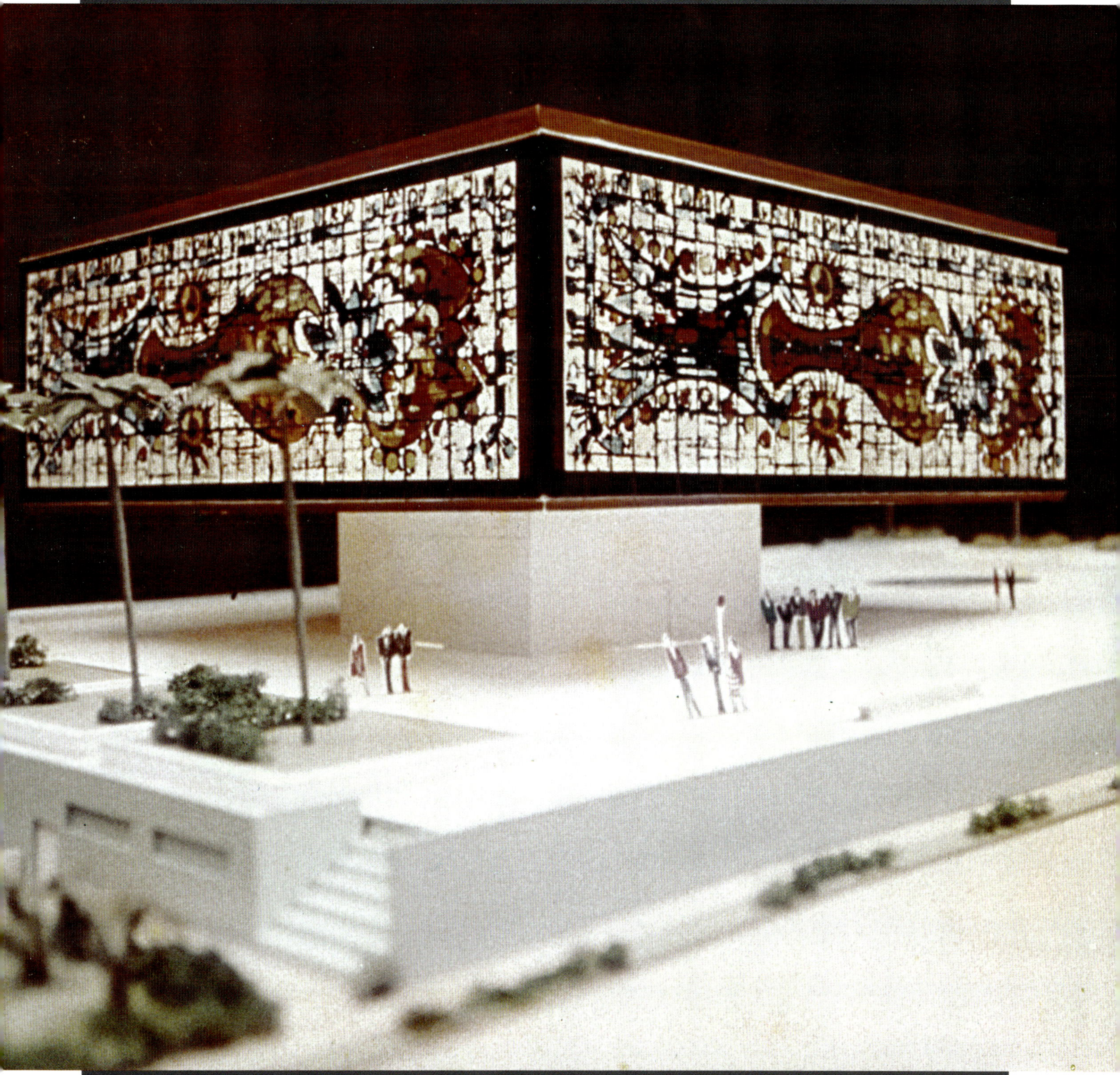

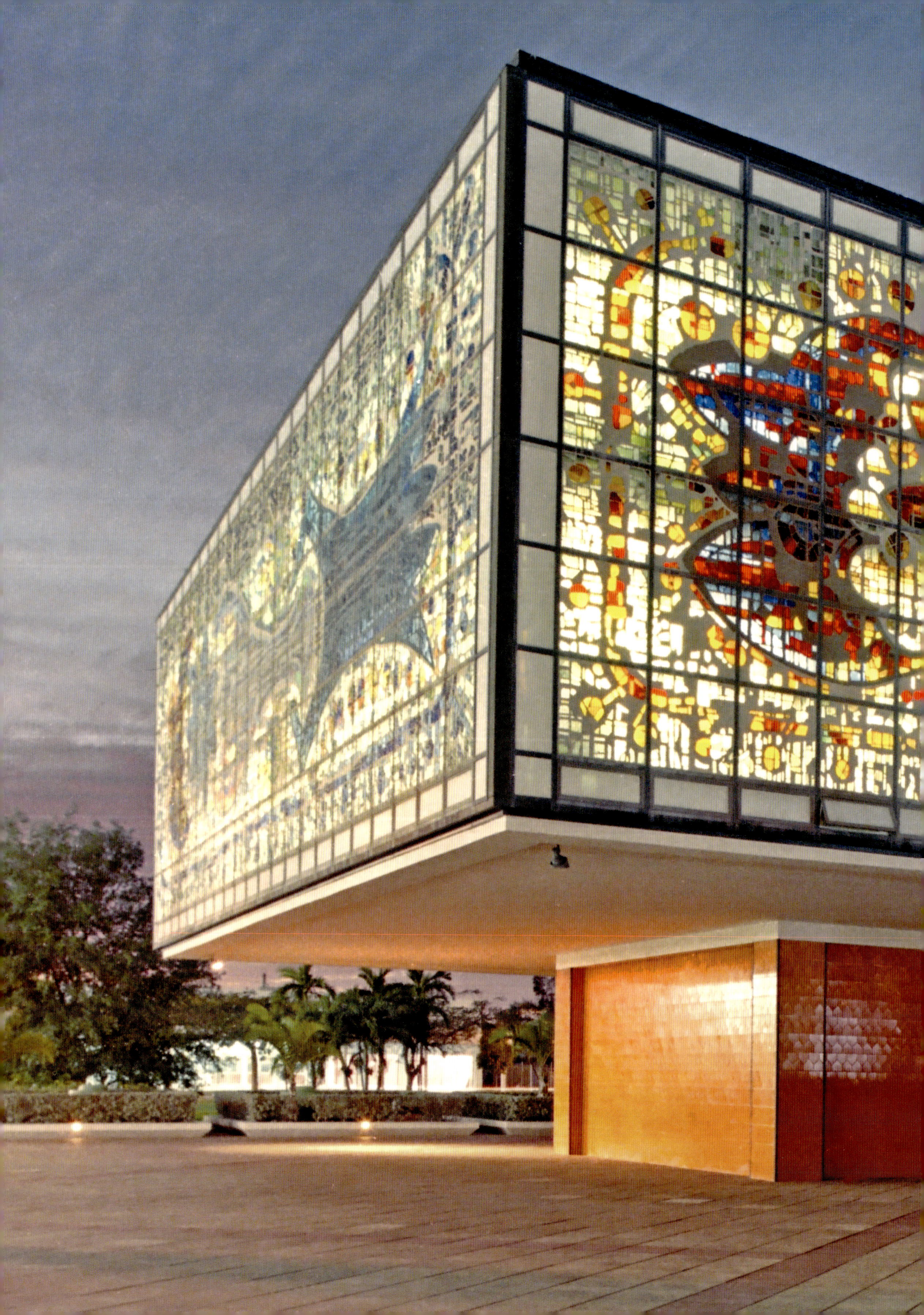

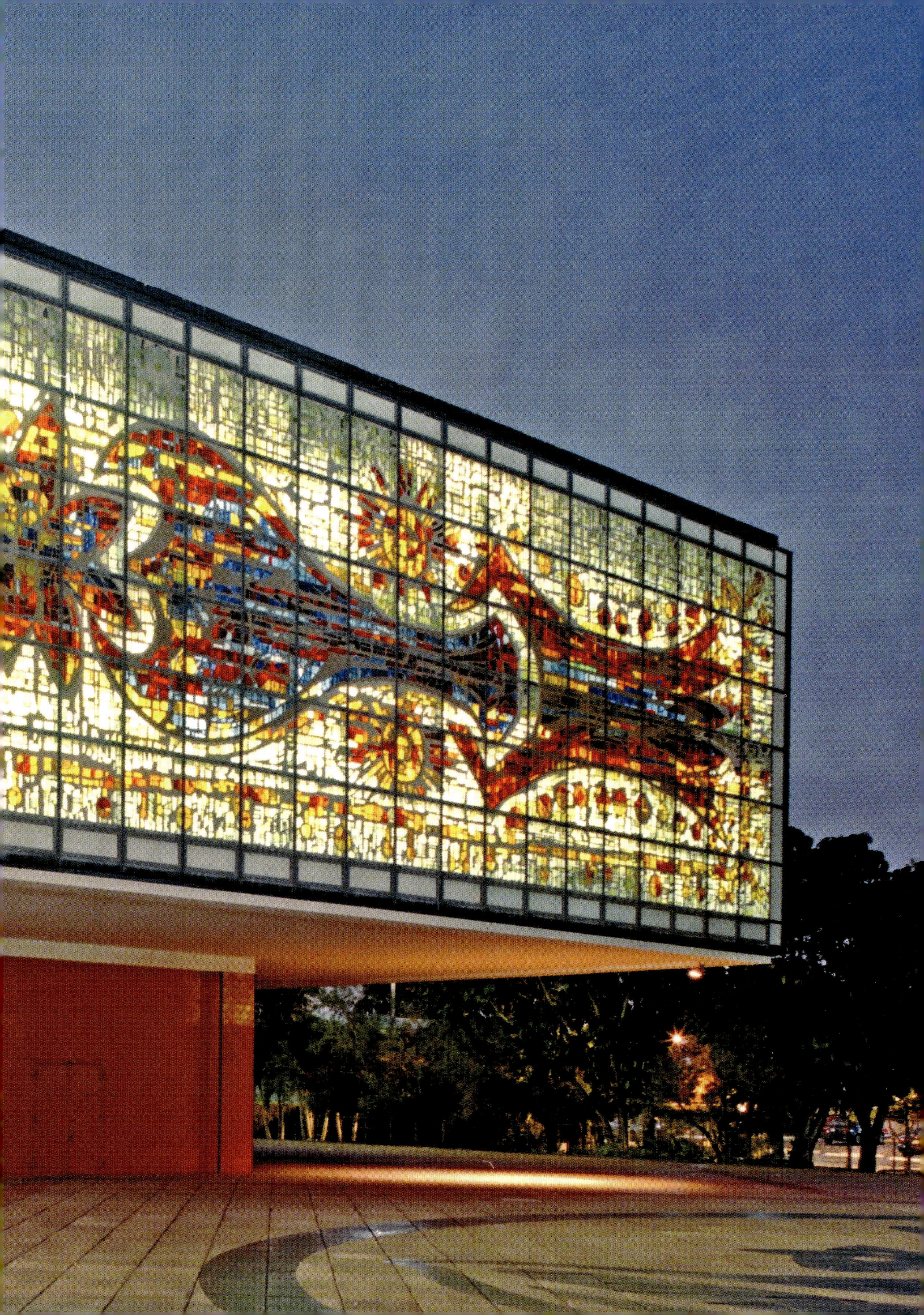

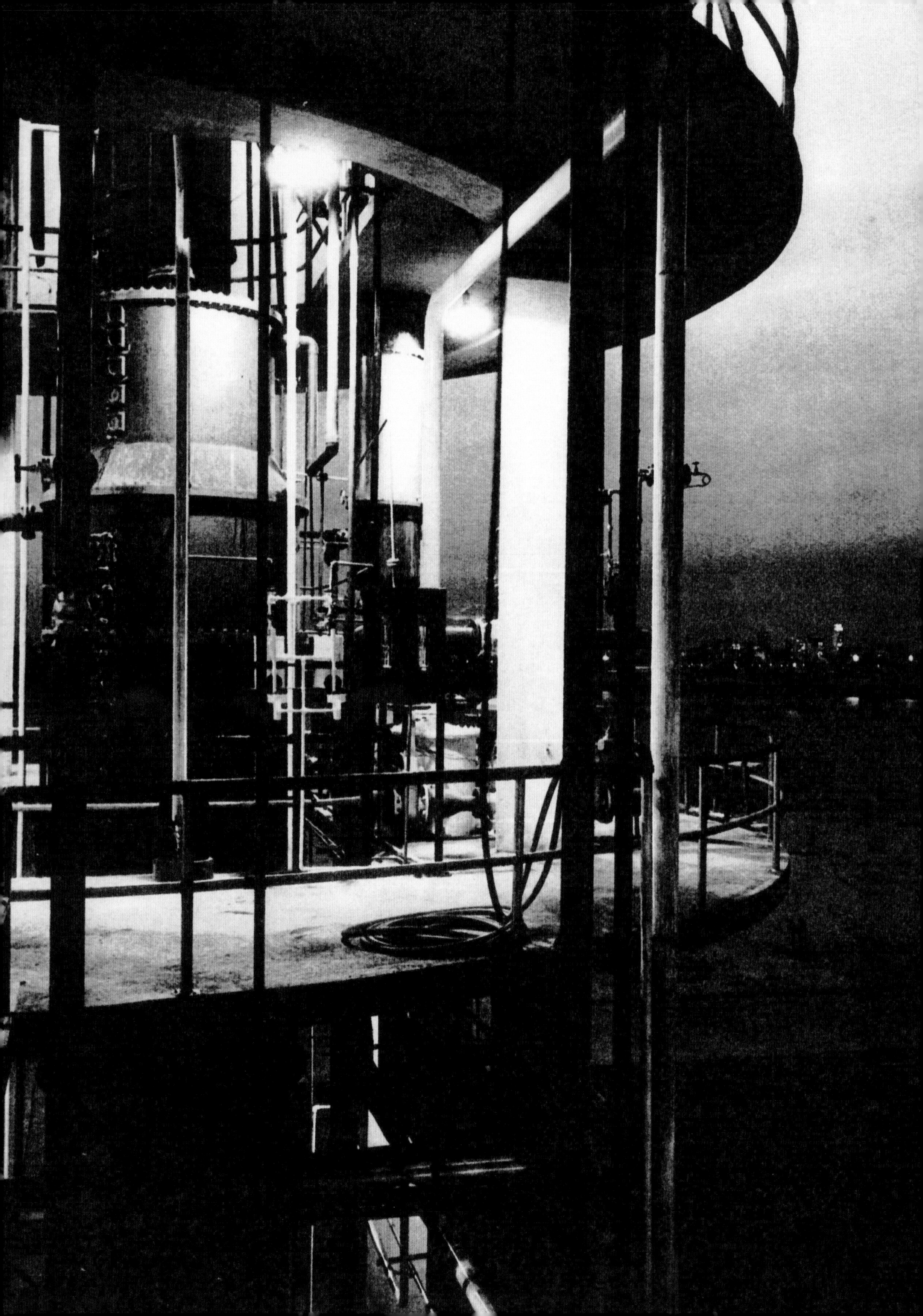

A LARGER ARCHIPELAGO

Miami was one node in a corporate network that, in the 1960s, stretched across sugar-producing regions from Brazil to Spain. In 1961, a new distillery was completed in Recife, Brazil, followed by another on New Providence Island, British West Indies (Bahamas), in 1964. Pepin Bosch stepped down as Bacardi president in 1967, but remained in charge of a robust expansion that included a new headquarters in Bermuda, and plants in Valencia, Venezuela (1970), Jacksonville, Florida (1972), Brampton, Ontario (1972), Fort de France, Martinique (1974), Malaga, Spain (1975), and Panama City, Panama (1979). Careful scientific control allowed BACARDI rum to be copied faithfully as the company expanded. Architecturally, though, formulas had to be continuously re-mixed to balance Cuban traditions with contemporary needs and diverse national identities. As Bosch developed these varied works, he turned largely to a single firm, Ermina Odoardo–Ricardo Eguilior Arquitectos, Santiago architects now based in Miami.

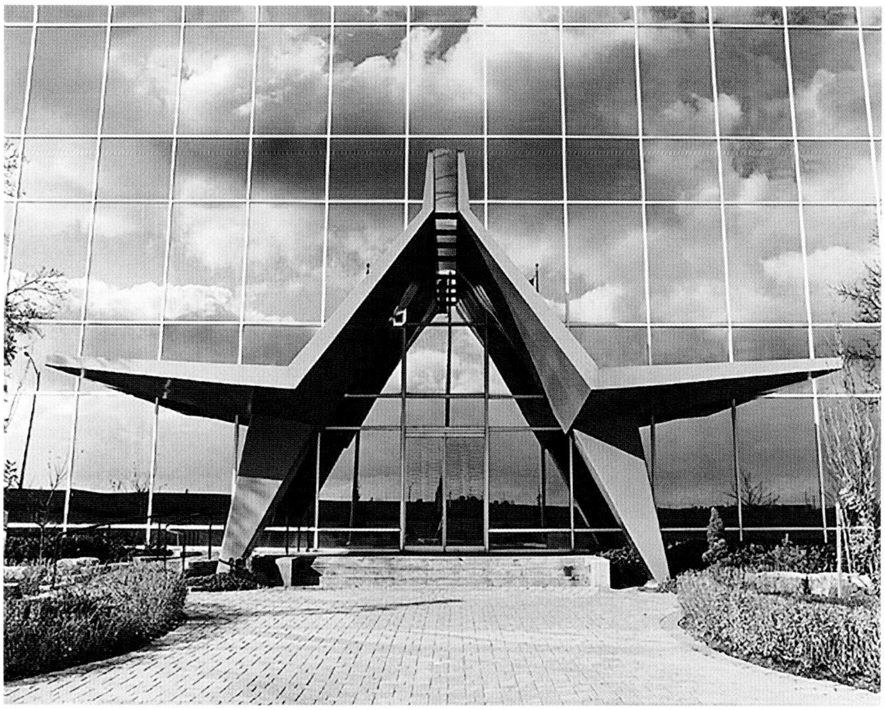

Bosch's qualities as arts patron and idea man were increasingly balanced by a new sense of pragmatism. The Recife distillery's steel sheds and tank farms, as well as a boiler and fermentation house clad with perforated terra-cotta facades, demonstrated little attention to architectural exposition of any kind. Only the distilling tower, a copy of the model inaugurated at La Galarza, as well as a colossal sky sign facing the harbor, were used to striking effect. Similarly, the laconic architecture of the campus in New Providence Island, British West Indies, included all-metal buildings designed and built by the Stran-Steel Corporation of Detroit, a leader in pre-engineered metal building systems.[141] Stran-Steel was famous for its technologically advanced cold-formed steel structures utilizing color-coated panels attached to nail-able metal channels. Completed in 1964, the ten-building complex of low gabled industrial sheds colored light blue and beige was built in only thirteen weeks. Both Recife and New Providence Island echoed the company interest in efficiently produced models of industrial architecture, exemplified in the concrete umbrellas and shells Felix Candela previously developed for Bacardi in Tultitlán, Mexico.

The Cortijó Bacardi, in Malaga, Andalucía, Spain, stands as a counterargument to this functional imperative. The renovation of a seventeenth-century Franciscan monastic compound (*cortijó*), as a conference center and Bacardi museum accompanied the construction of a new plant in 1975 by Bacardi y Cía. S.A. España. Like the hacienda at La Galarza, the Baroque-styled Cortijó offered the company a poignant tie to local heritage in this onetime sugar-producing region. Its buttressed stuccoed walls, tiled roofs, loggias, and corner tower formed a picturesque profile against the pastoral

Left: Bacardi & Company, Ltd., Recife, Brazil. Distillation tower at night. Ricardo Eguilior, architect, 1961. Courtesy of The Bacardi Archive.

Above: Bacardi Canada, Inc., Brampton, Ontario. Bat-winged entrance. Ermina Odoardo-Ricardo Eguilior Arquitectos, 1972. Courtesy of The Bacardi Archive.

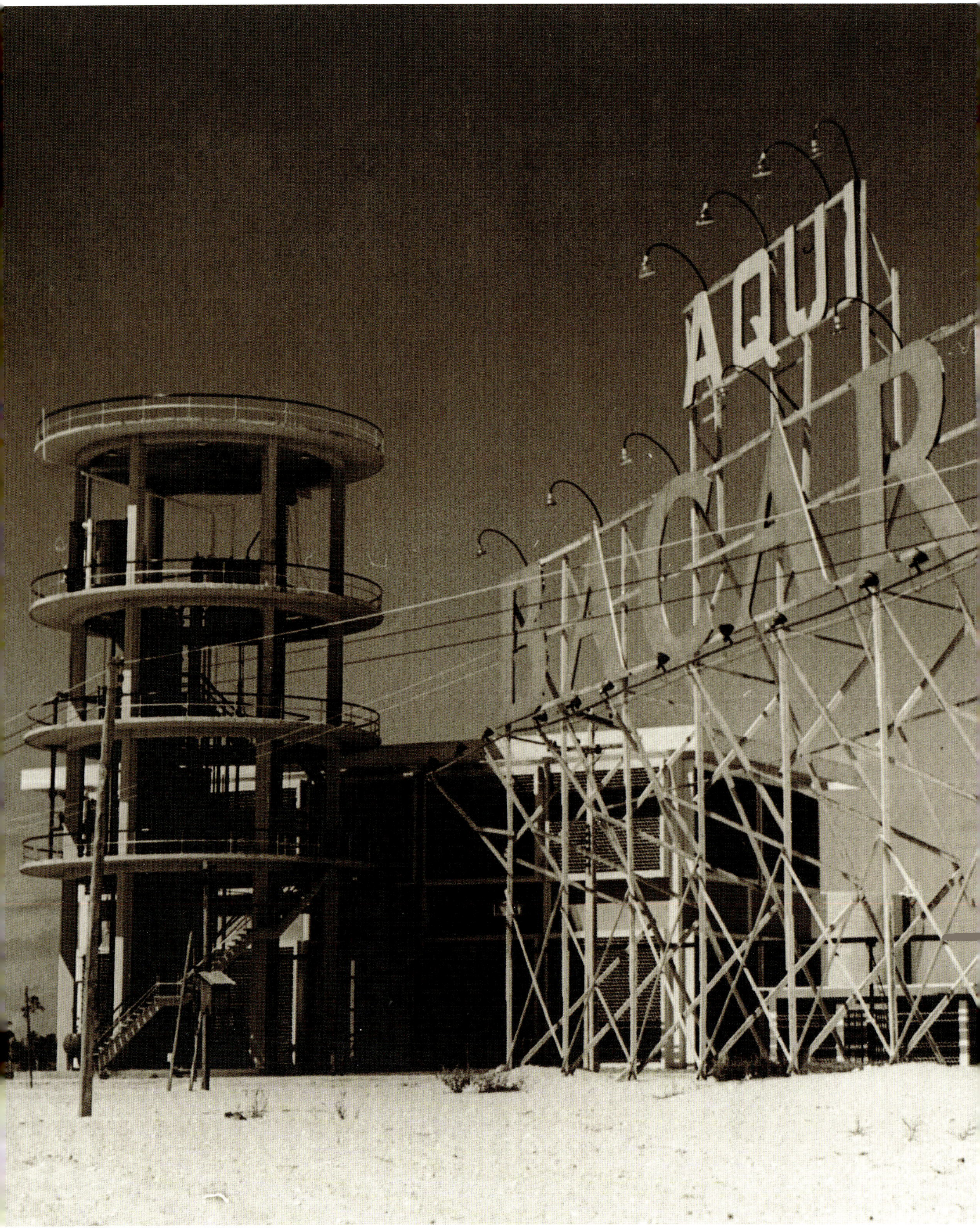
AQUI

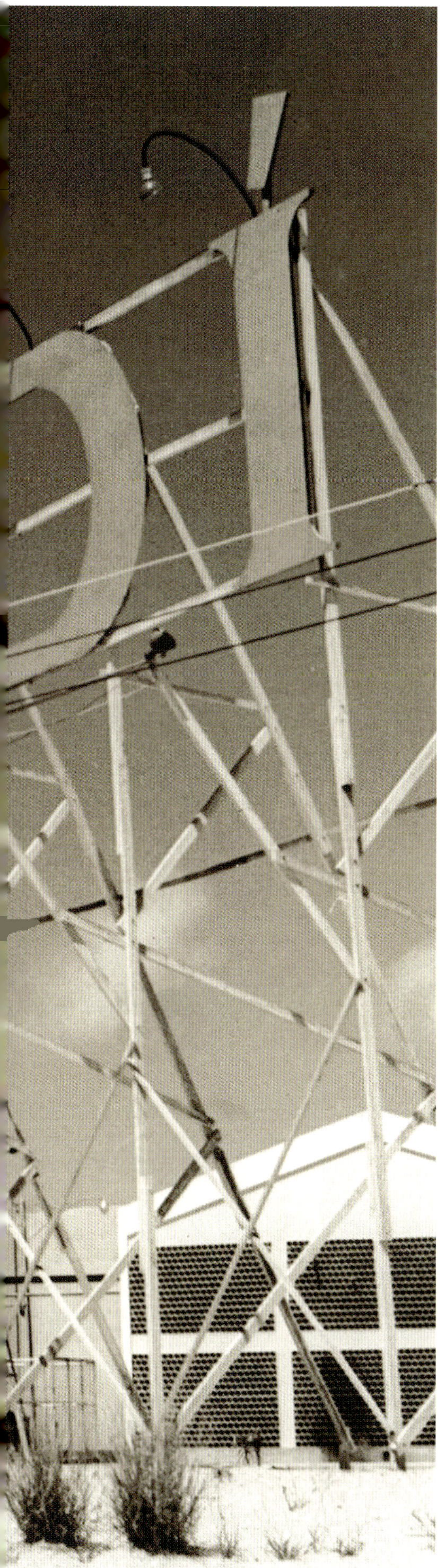

Left: Bacardi & Company, Ltd., Recife, Brazil. Distillation tower and sign. Ricardo Eguilior, architect, 1961. Courtesy of The Bacardi Archive.

Below: Stran-Steel solves another building problem. Advertisement featuring Daniel Bacardi overlooking the Bacardi facility on New Providence Island, Bahamas. From *The Bahamian Review*, October 1965: 41. Courtesy of The Bacardi Archive.

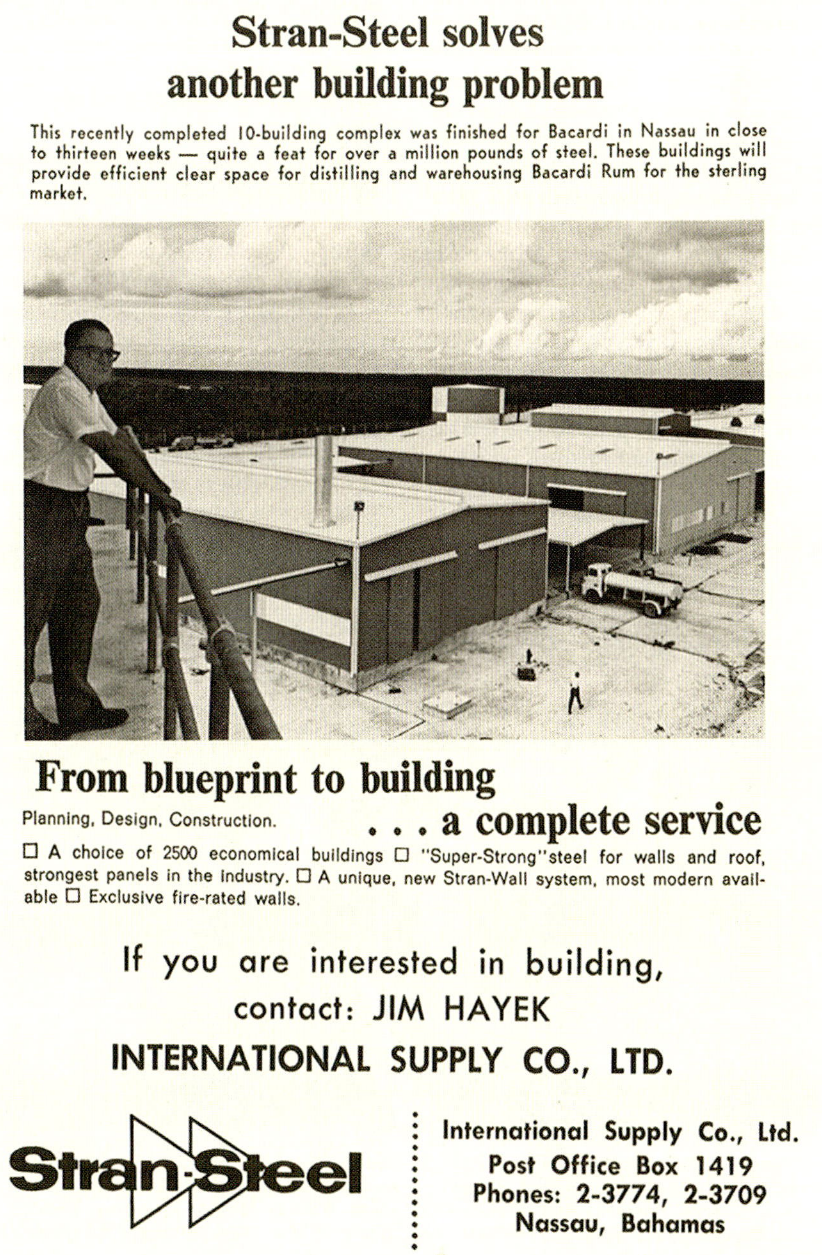

landscape of the Guadalhorce River valley, layering the modern industrial installation with the air of an attraction.

A final chapter of the company's post-exile transformation occurred in Bermuda.[142] The British overseas territory, an important way station for spirits during U.S. Prohibition, had developed in the 1960s as an offshore financial center—a by-product of the island's business-friendly legal and tax structures. Bacardi moved its headquarters to Bermuda in 1965, envisioning the island as the administrative hub for its future growth; it subsequently planned a prominent new building behind the waterfront in the capital Hamilton. As originally proposed by Ricardo and Ermina Eguilior, the five-story Bacardi International Limited Building had glass curtain walls and exposed columns on its long facades and solid walls at each end—much like the Bacardi Imports Tower in Miami. The Eguiliors conceived the end walls decorated with tile murals of abstracted Easter lilies, the flower of Bermuda, but the effort to "localize" the modern building proved insufficient. The design stirred local controversy, a backlash against the pervasive slab-type international business headquarters rising there.[143]

What happened next must have at least to some degree been instigated by changes in Bacardi itself. The Eguiliors redesigned the project as a square pavilion, reaching back to Mies van der Rohe's unbuilt 1957 project for Santiago for inspiration. That project had already become a powerful trope in the later work of Mies, as well as for other modernist architects. As later developments would show, the unbuilt Santiago headquarters had evolved as a powerful figure for Bacardi as well, a high point of representation for a global corporation; adapting the type to the verdant landscape of Bermuda, the Eguiliors incorporated collective memory into a physical symbol for the company.

Completed in 1972, the Hamilton headquarters materialized Mies's Santiago opus while defying the singular structural model on which it was based. Indeed, everywhere the building exhibited an overt tension between fidelity and innovation. The floating square roof plate set on eight cruciform steel columns, the inset glass volume sheltered beneath it, and the solid plinth were all there. Though, surrounded by lawn and set off by a broad fountain, the subtropical corporate citadel took on a more suburban flavor. Eguilior used continuous sheets of plate glass supported by glass struts, a technical achievement that emphasized not the virtual transparency envisioned by Mies, but a kind of continuous reflectivity. As Ricardo Eguilior explained to Bermudan officials, "this building, with 20-foot side walls of clear glass, puts Bermuda on display, the way it should always be."[144] The seamless glass was transformed at night by bold strokes of color and pattern in the curtains designed by Johannes Dietz, whose parallel work for Bacardi in Miami also involved transforming art into building skin. On the interior, an even larger transformation: Mies and Bosch's vision of an open universal space morphed into a more traditional diagram. Glass walled private offices along the building exterior were organized around a common open work area, creating a protected interior atrium.

The interiors, orchestrated by designer Maria Bergson, demonstrated an even larger departure from Mies's principles. Bergson, the onetime Austrian actress and leader in the interior design world (Prudential, Leo Burnett, U.S. Steel), swapped

Top: Bacardi y Cía, S.A. España El Cortijo, Malaga, Andalucía, Spain. Courtyard view, 1975. Courtesy of The Bacardi Archive.

Bottom: Bacardi y Cía, S.A. España El Cortijo, Malaga, Andalucía, Spain. Main hall, 1975. Courtesy of The Bacardi Archive.

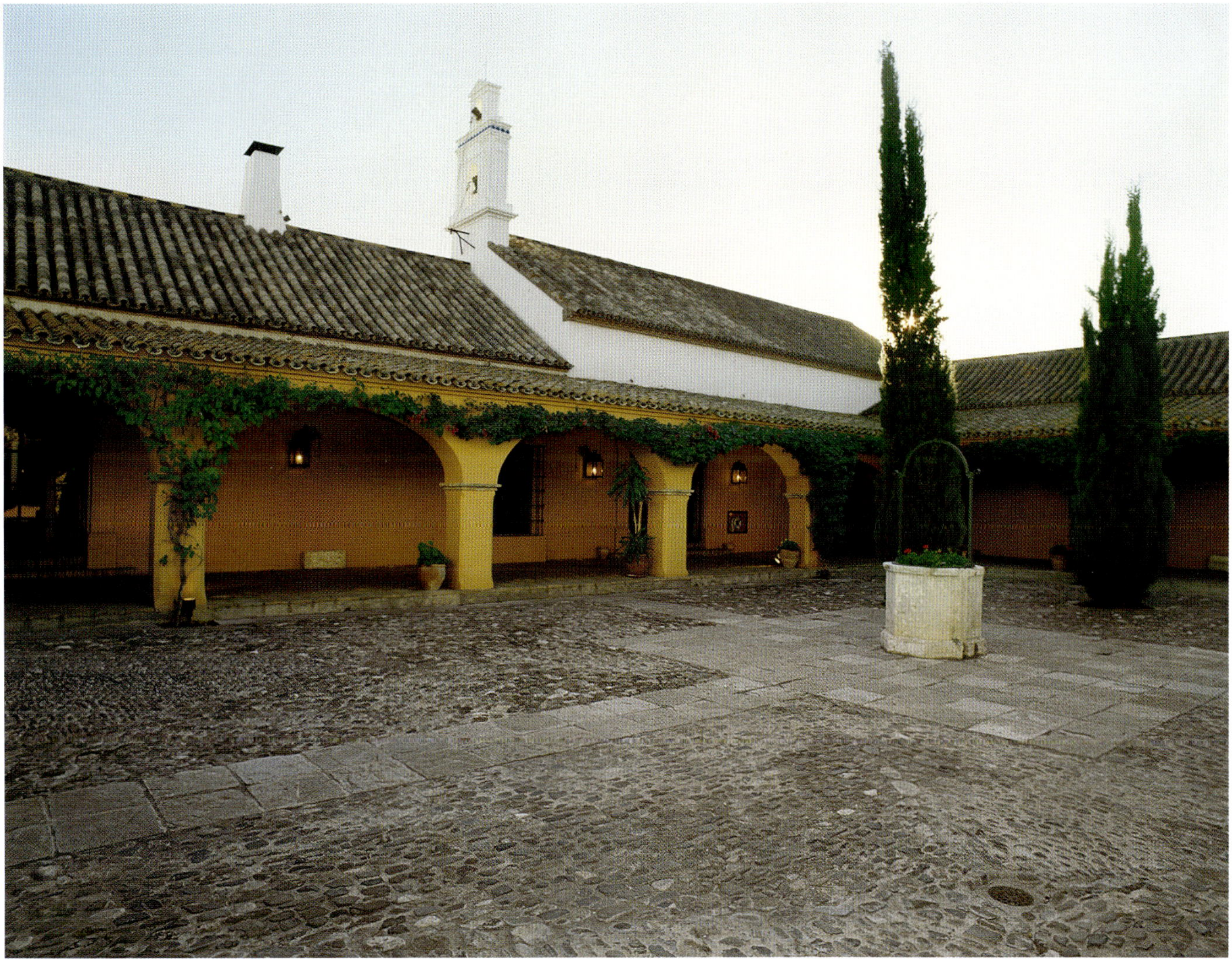

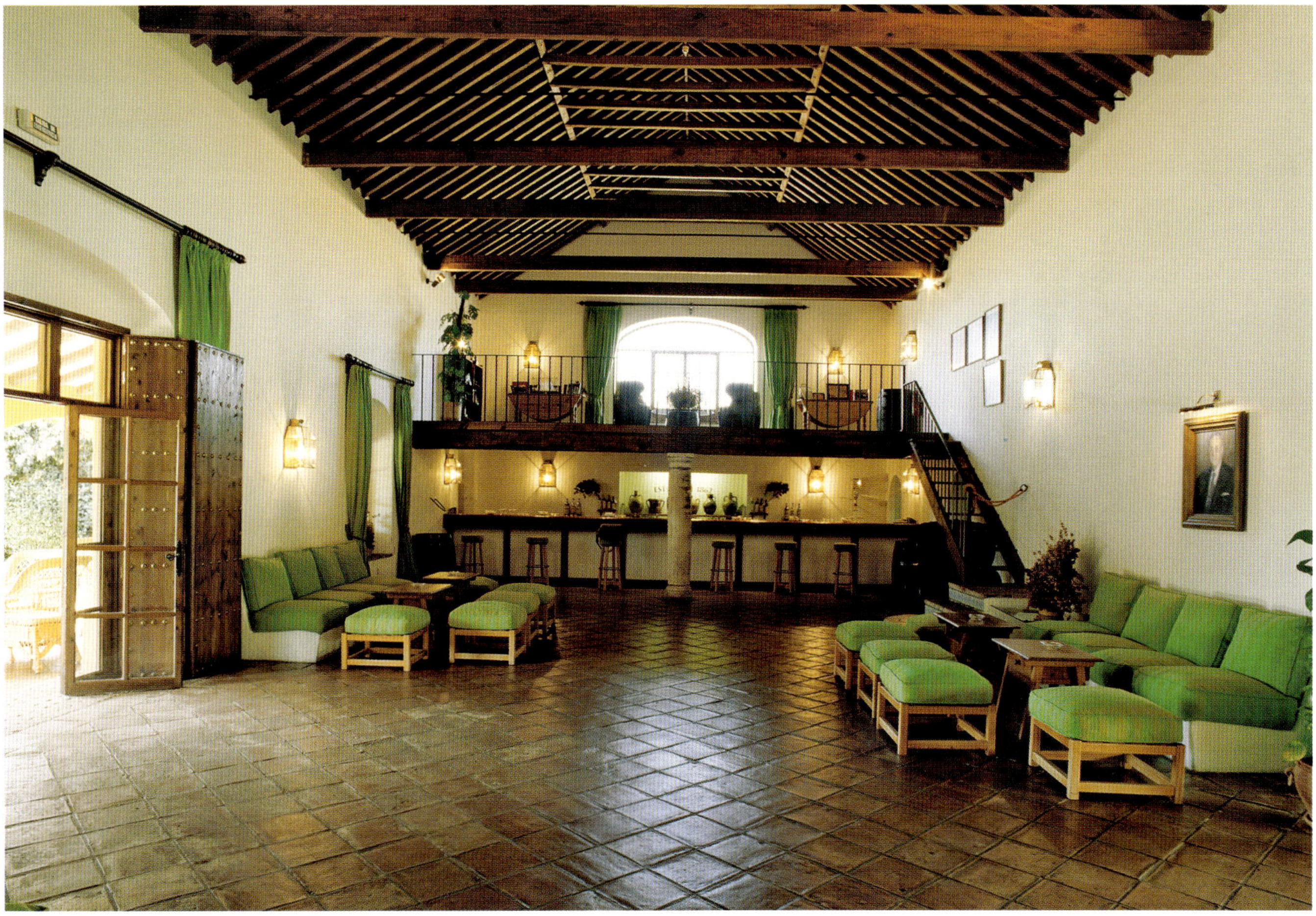

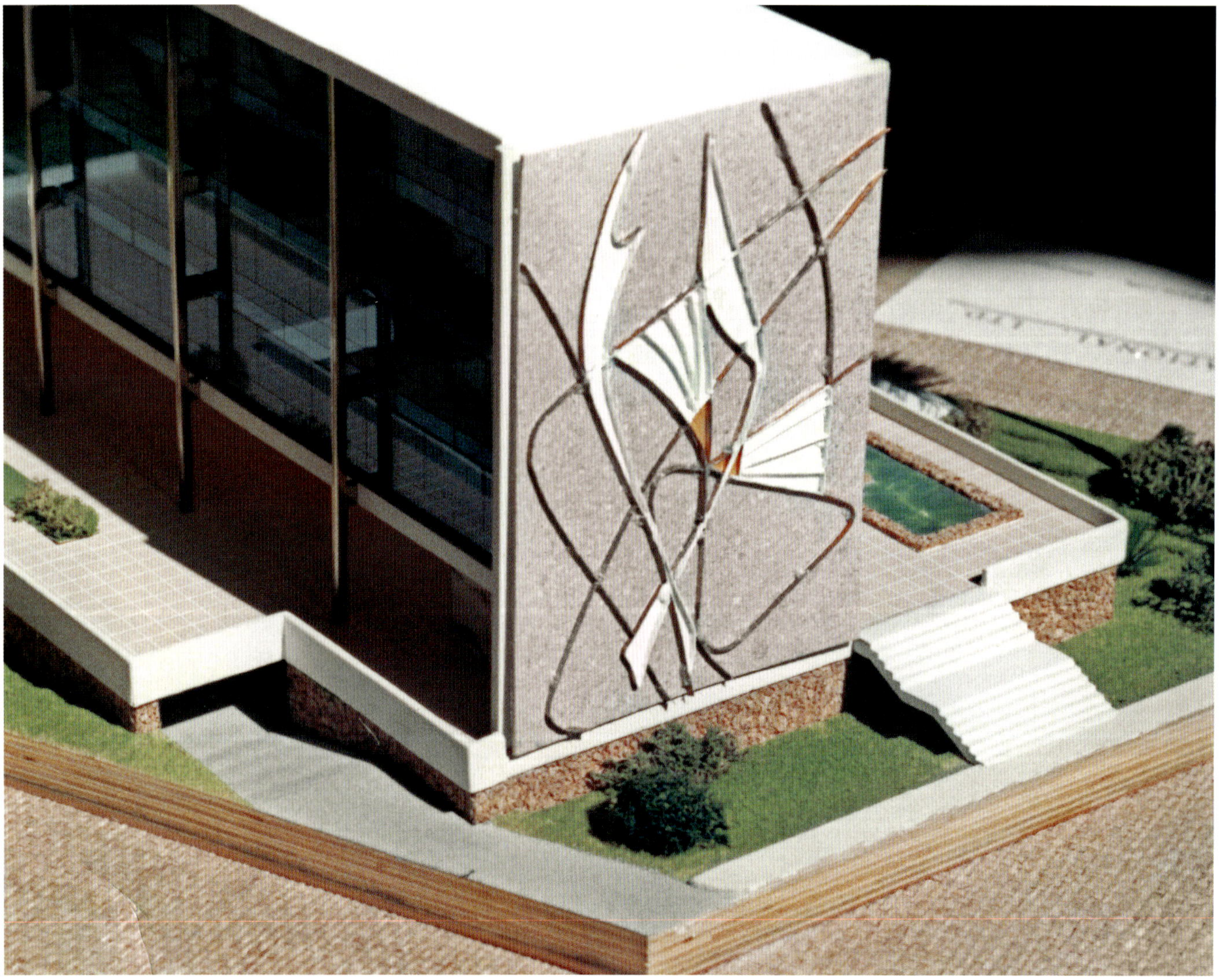

Above: Bacardi International Limited Building, Hamilton, Bermuda. Model of first proposal. Ermina Odoardo–Ricardo Eguilior Arquitectos, c. 1965 (unbuilt). Courtesy of Ermina O. Eguilior.

Right: Bacardi International Limited Building, Hamilton, Bermuda. Facade mural study of first proposal. Ermina Odoardo–Ricardo Eguilior Arquitectos, c. 1965 (unbuilt). Courtesy of Ermina O. Eguilior.

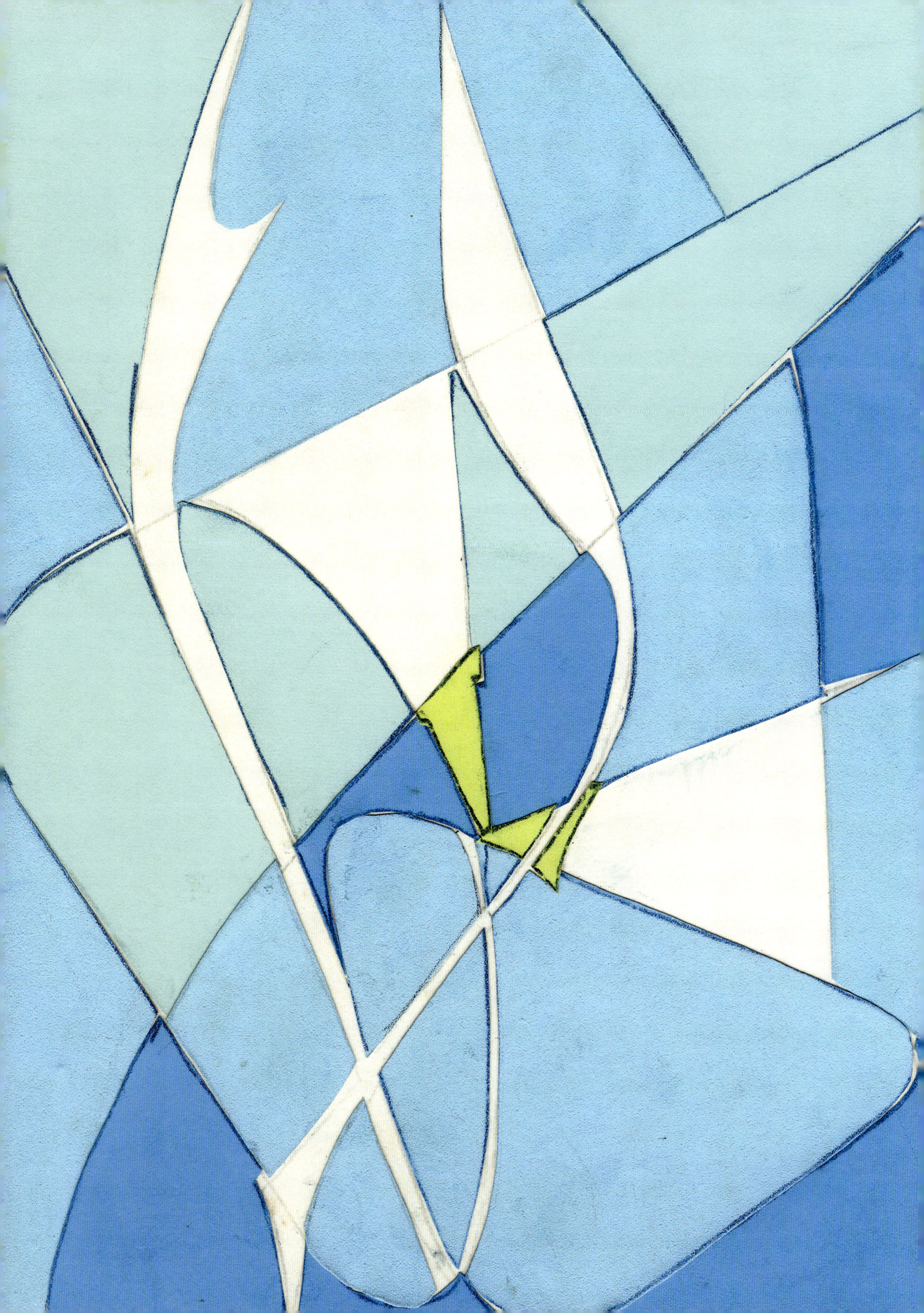

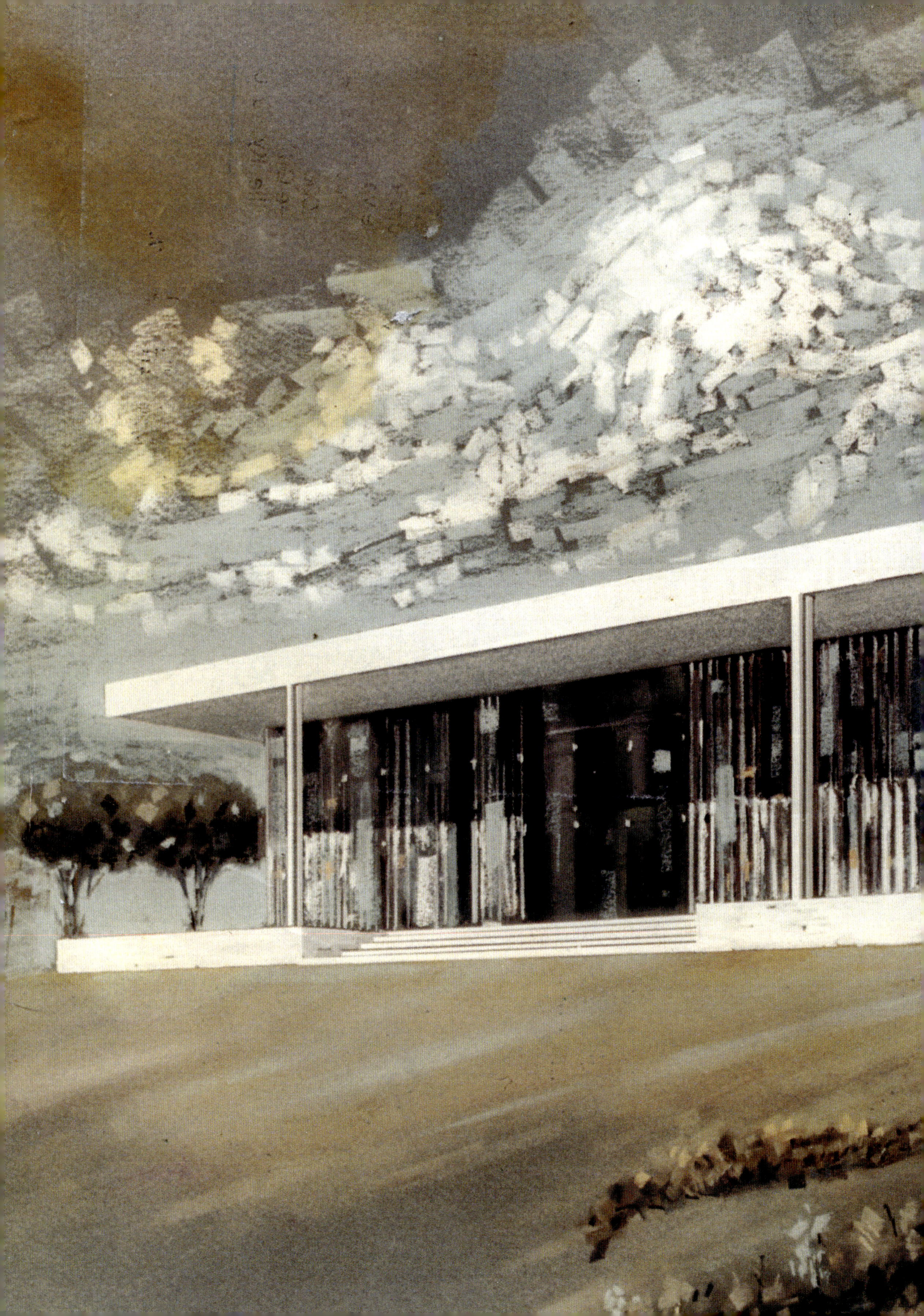

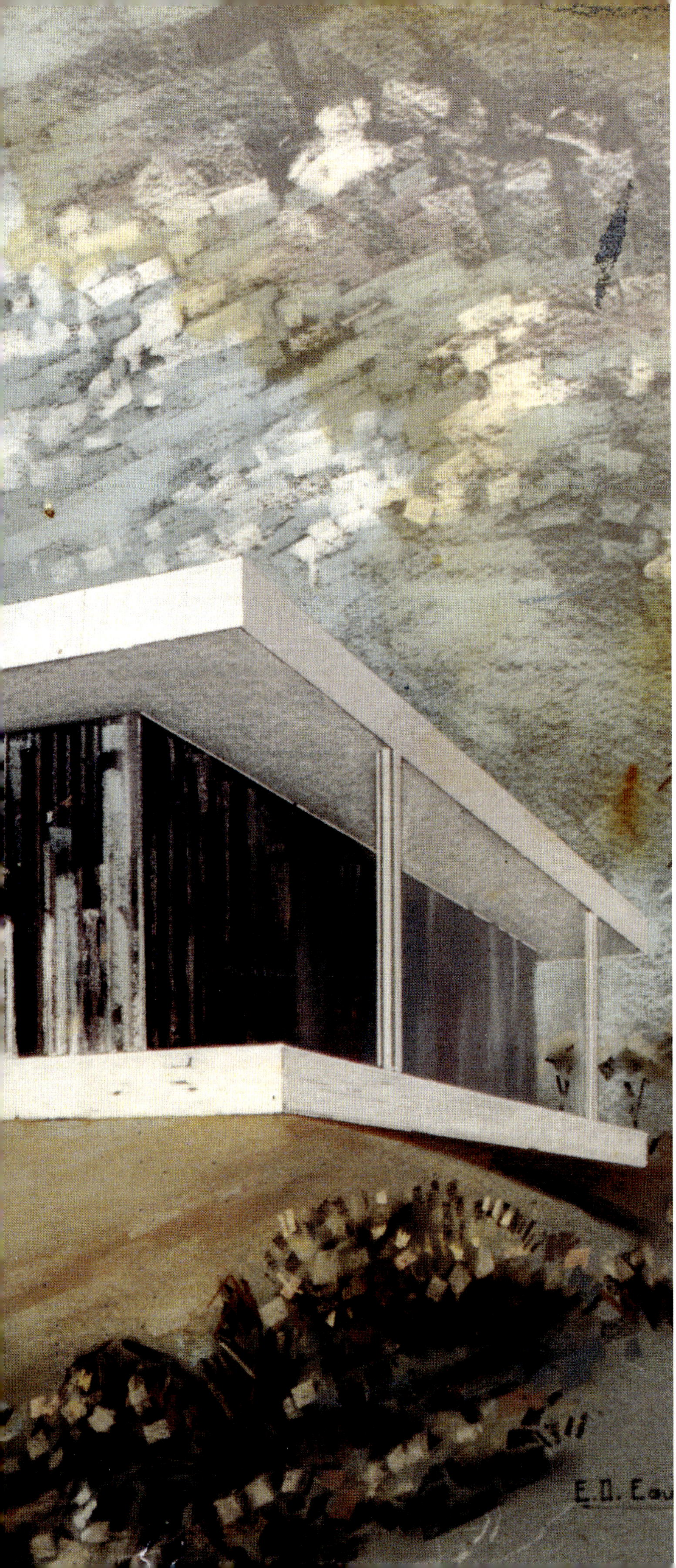

Bacardi International Limited Building, Hamilton, Bermuda. Rendering of final proposal. Ermina Odoardo–Ricardo Eguilior Arquitectos, c. 1970. Courtesy of The Bacardi Archive.

the luxe austerity of the German-émigré for a delirious collage of memory, tradition and geographic association. Visitors were greeted by Felix Ramos's hand-painted Cuban landscape, a twenty-two-foot-high mural that stretched across the front of the building like a marquee, transmitting the company's Cuban heritage all the way to the street. In the atrium, a luminous blue-and-white ceiling made of Plexiglas Luna cubes translated in Pointillist terms the positioning of stars in the skies over Santiago on February 4, 1862, the date of the founding of Bacardi. Bergson mixed contemporary and traditional furniture and fixtures, agitating the sensibilities resident in the modernist concept of the building. In the conference room, Platner Arm Chairs by Knoll contrasted with heavy wood paneling, a brass chandelier and Dietz's Op Art curtains. The theme of "Bacardi in many lands" was woven into the fibers of the building's handmade V'Soske rugs: each office and major space was identified in indigenous heraldic designs with a region of the world where Bacardi had a facility.

The Bermuda project might seem an outlier, a nostalgic detour following the expressive achievement of the company's Miami tower. However, as Bermuda was nearing completion, Bacardi proposed another Mies-inspired work, an executive office building for its Puerto Rico campus. Designed by J. Walter Severinghaus in the New York office of Skidmore, Owings & Merrill (SOM) with the Puerto Rican firm Reed, Torres, Beauchamp, Marvel, the Bacardi Executive Office Building remarkably amalgamated the physiognomy of the unbuilt Santiago building—the plinth, the platonic square shape, and the deep coffered roof plate supported on tapered cruciform columns—with a floor plan similar to the completed Bacardi offices in Tultitlán, Mexico. The plinth is pyramidal, formed by a distortion of the flat site that recalls pre-Columbian earth-mound structures found in Puerto Rico, as well as the contemporary earth-mound architecture made popular by architect William Morgan in Florida.[145] Above this plinth, an open landscape of offices divided by service islands ringed a central, sky-lit atrium where landscape architect Hunter Randolph elaborated a tropical oasis of canopy trees and stepped patios set around a winding water piece. The building's essence reflected the character of SOM's own neo-Miesian practice, which not only pioneered suburban office parks, but innovated translations of Bacardi's Santiago headquarters as a recurrent idea within its own work.[146] Nevertheless, 10 years after its exile from Cuba, the reflexive character of the executive office building transmitted a sense of longing for a golden era, as symbolized by Mies's singular modern syntax. Paradoxically, such reflexive structures were returning not to classical or vernacular traditions, but to a modernity tinged with memory and longing. While the executive office building was never built, one final recall of the unbuilt Santiago work came with the construction in 2003 of the Casa Bacardi visitors' center on the same site. At the entrance, tapered cruciform columns

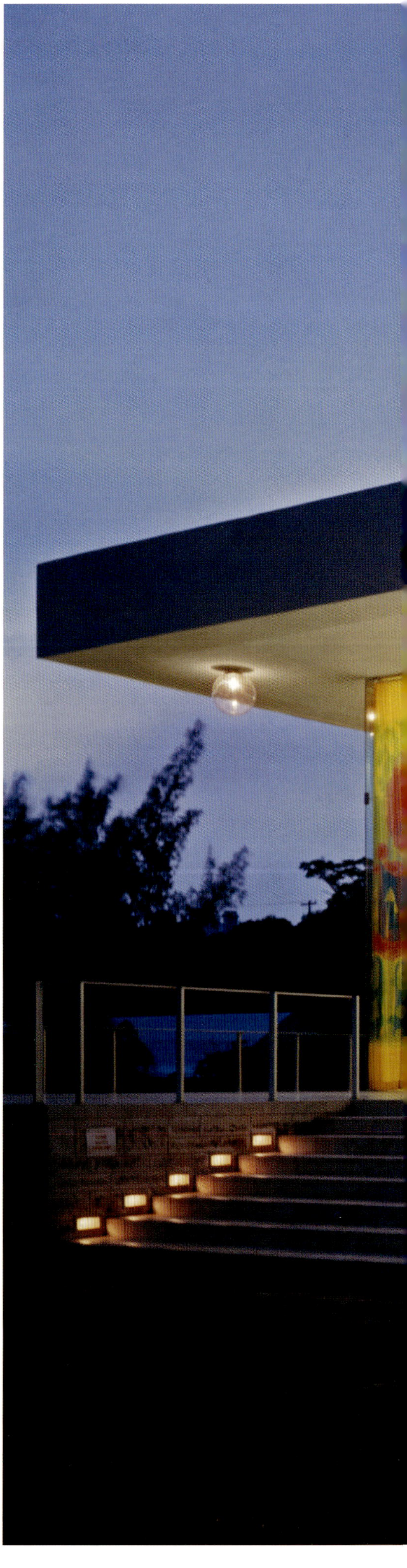

Right: Bacardi International Limited Building, Hamilton, Bermuda. Entrance. Ermina Odoardo–Ricardo Eguilior Arquitectos with Maria Bergson, interior designer, 1972. © Ezra Stoller/ESTO.

Overleaf: Bacardi International Limited Building, Hamilton, Bermuda. Night view. Ermina Odoardo–Ricardo Eguilior Arquitectos with Maria Bergson, interior designer, 1972. © Ezra Stoller/ESTO.

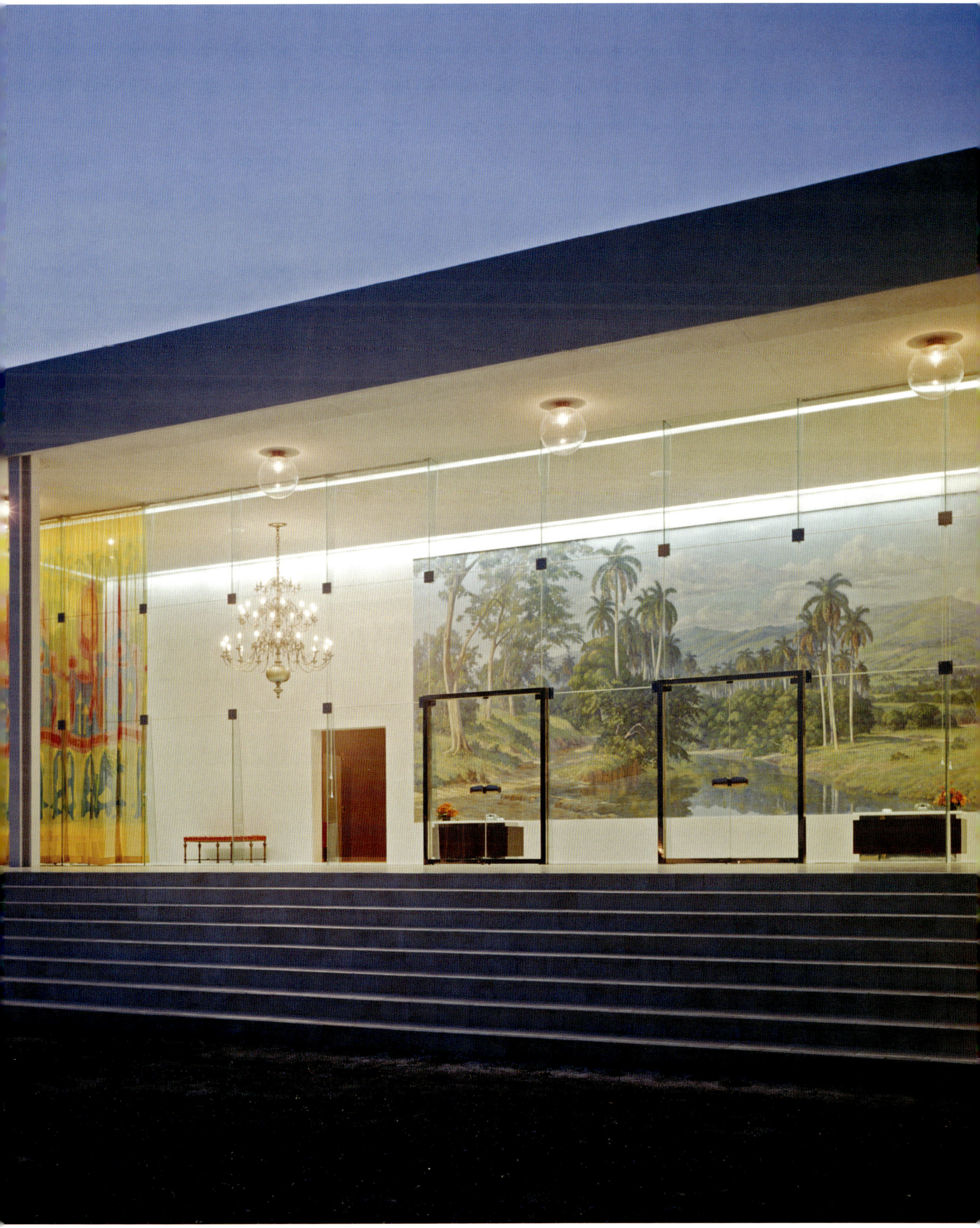

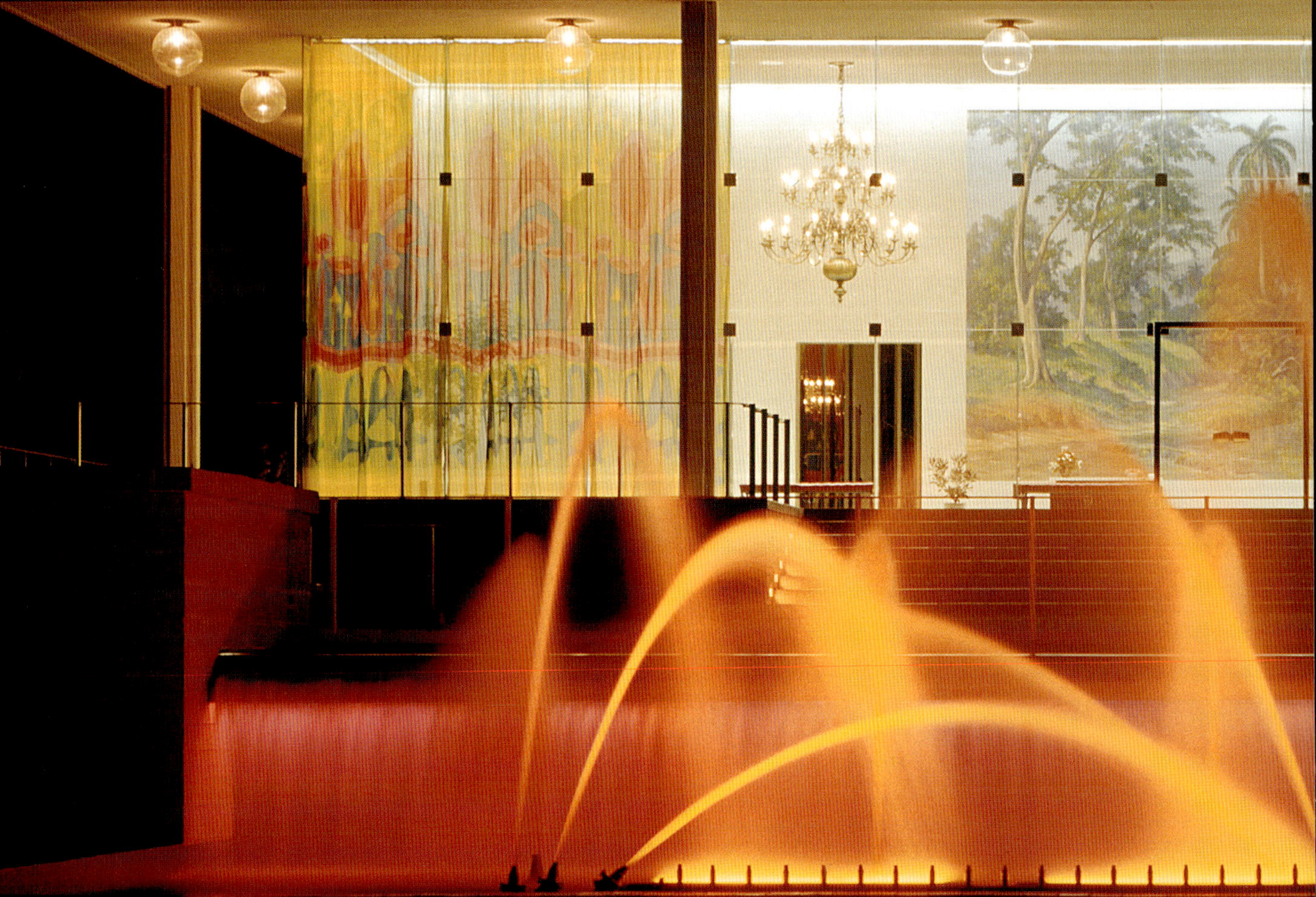

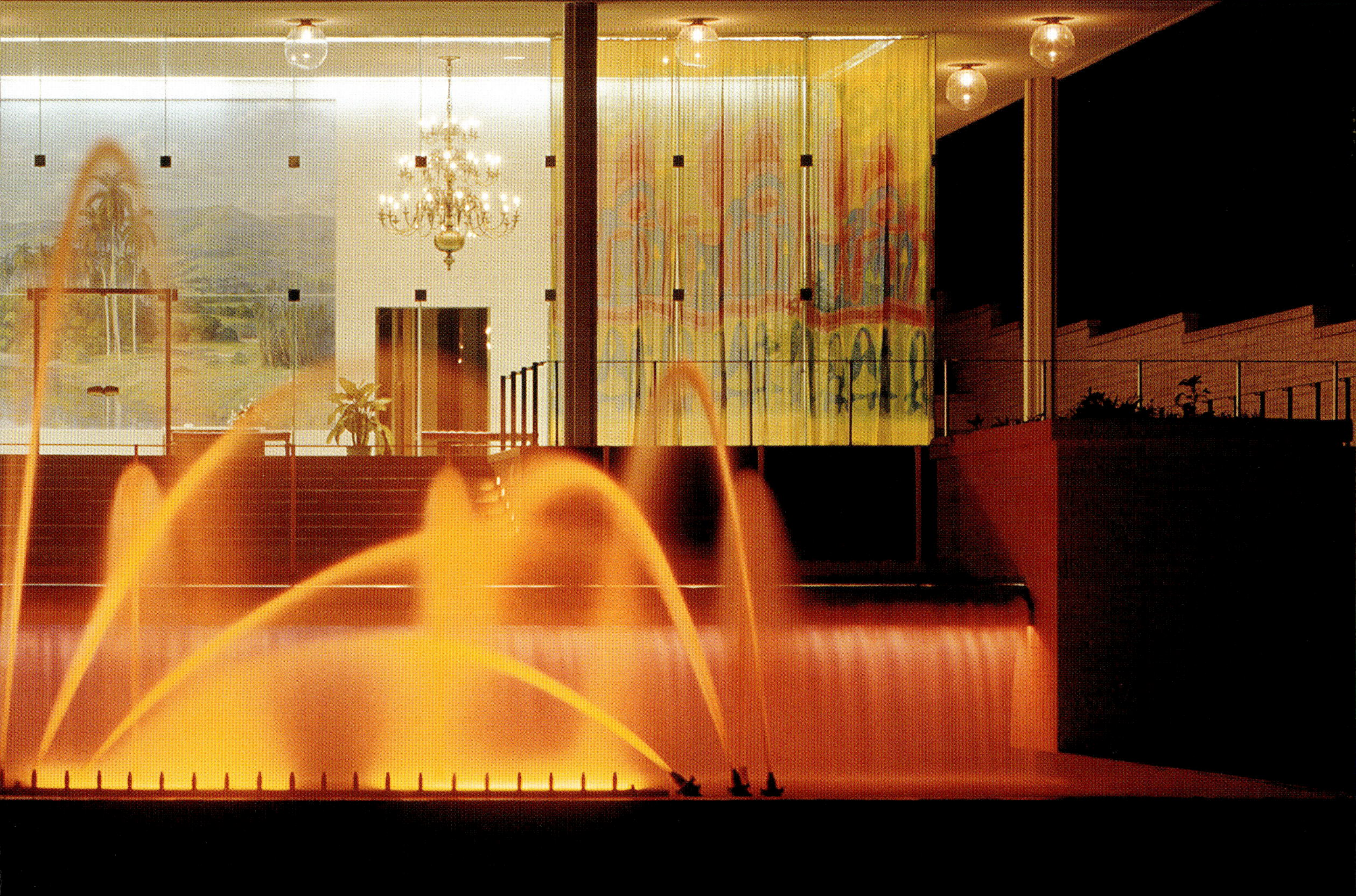

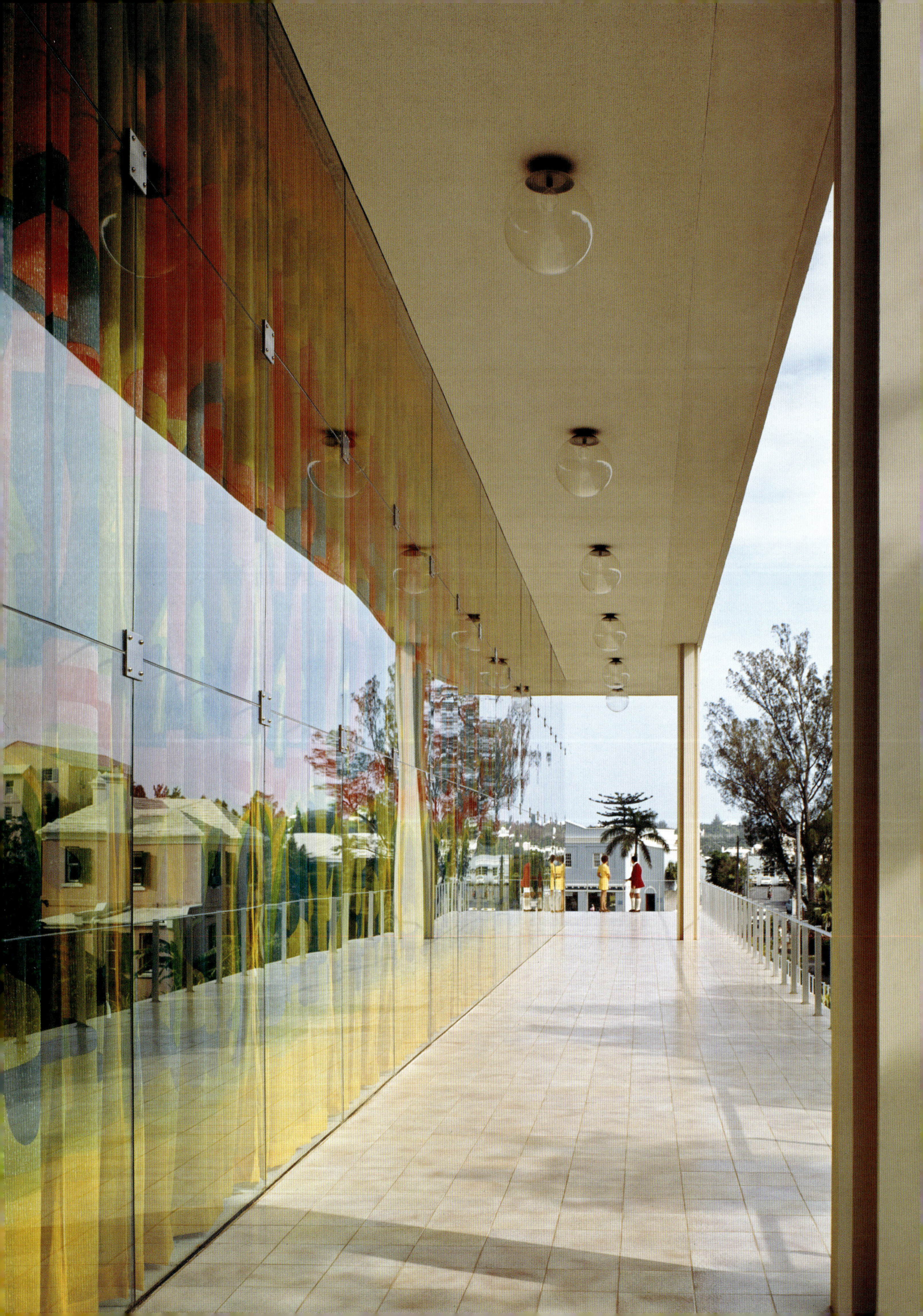

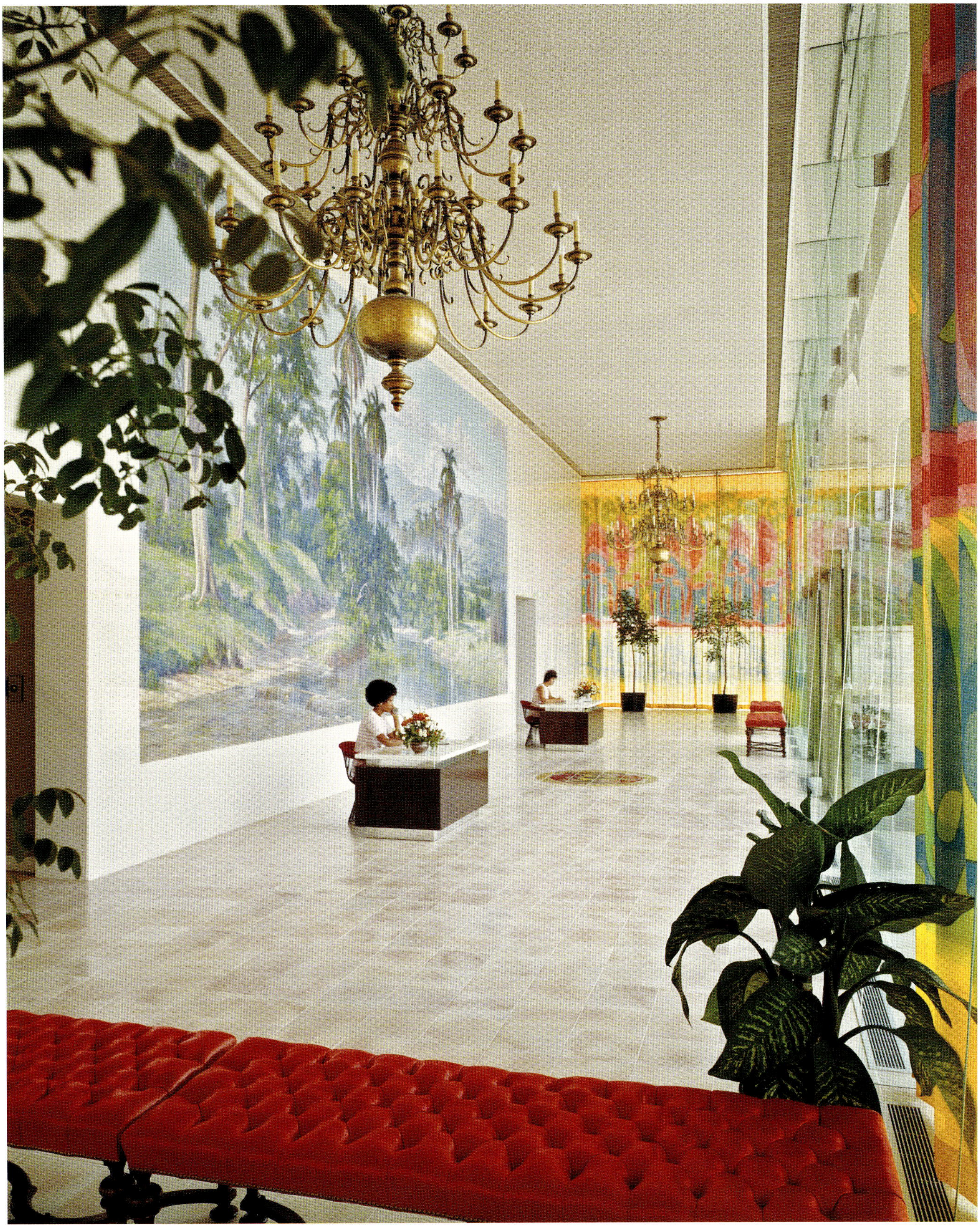

Left: Bacardi International Limited Building, Hamilton, Bermuda. Entrance portico. Ermina Odoardo–Ricardo Eguilior Arquitectos with Maria Bergson, interior designer, 1972. © Ezra Stoller/ESTO

Above: Bacardi International Limited Building, Hamilton, Bermuda. Entrance hall with painting by Felix Ramos. Ermina Odoardo–Ricardo Eguilior Arquitectos with Maria Bergson, interior designer, 1972. © Ezra Stoller/ESTO.

rise to support vaulted concrete canopies in the spirit of Candela (whose spirit has also thrives in the various concrete works executed on the campus).

From its exotic Miami complex to reiterations of Bacardi modern folklore in Bermuda and Puerto Rico, the exiled company reforged links to its Cuban identity as it identified as a Pan-American corporation. Pepín Bosch retired altogether in 1976, bringing to an end a heroic age of Bacardi construction. The numerous structures added to Bacardi's fantasy assemblage through the mid-1970s monumentalized the brand and told stories about the corporation's resilience and global reach. With growth and diversification, however, Bacardi began to reconceive its homes as representing separate brands, not just in terms of tourist potential but as well-defined tourist destinations.

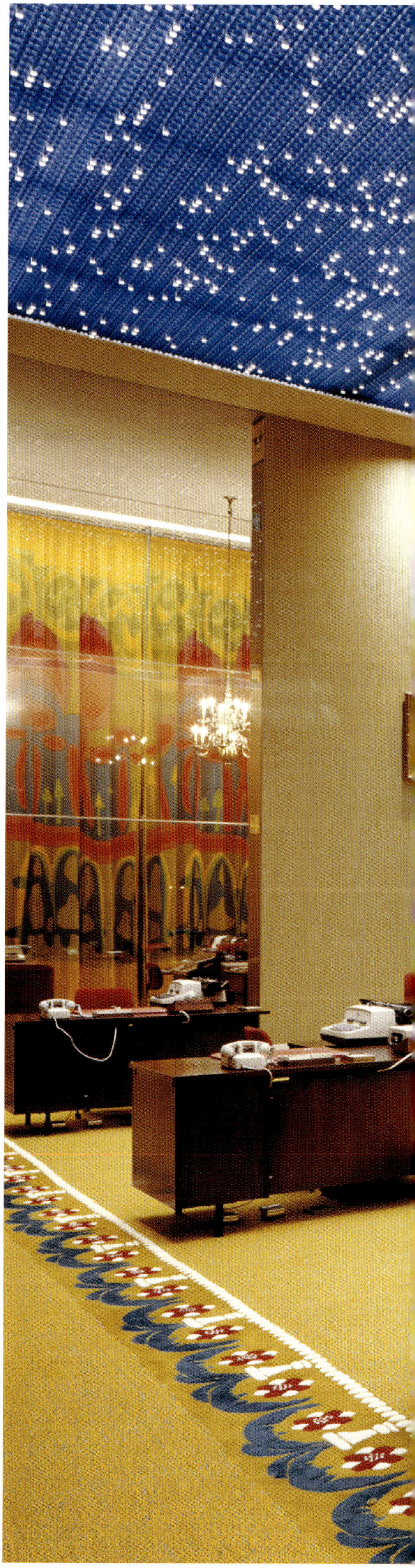

Right: Bacardi International Limited Building, Hamilton, Bermuda. Central office area. Ermina Odoardo–Ricardo Eguilior Arquitectos with Maria Bergson, interior designer, 1972.© Ezra Stoller/ESTO.

Page 190: Bacardi International Limited Building, Hamilton, Bermuda. Conference room. Ermina Odoardo–Ricardo Eguilior Arquitectos with Maria Bergson, interior designer, 1972. © Ezra Stoller/ESTO.

Page 191: Bacardi International Limited Building, Hamilton, Bermuda. Study for carpet design #5. Maria Bergson, interior designer, 1971. Carpet manufactured by V'Soske. Courtesy of V'Soske.

Page 192: Bacardi International Limited Building, Hamilton, Bermuda. Study for carpet design #6 and #16. Maria Bergson, interior designer, 1971. Carpets manufactured by V'Soske. Courtesy of V'Soske.

Page 193: Bacardi International Limited Building, Hamilton, Bermuda. Study for carpet design #4. Maria Bergson, interior designer, 1971. Carpets manufactured by V'Soske. Courtesy of V'Soske.

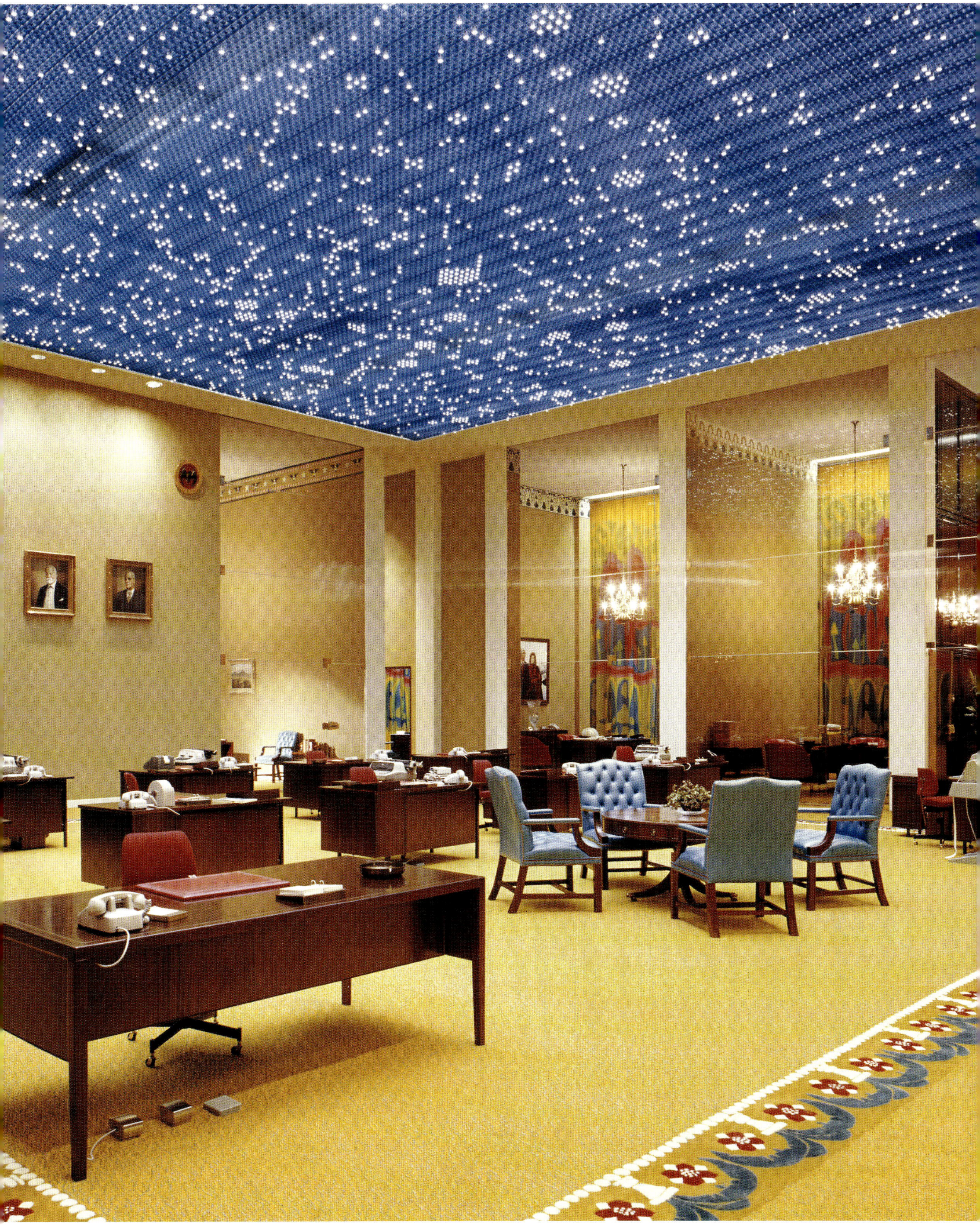

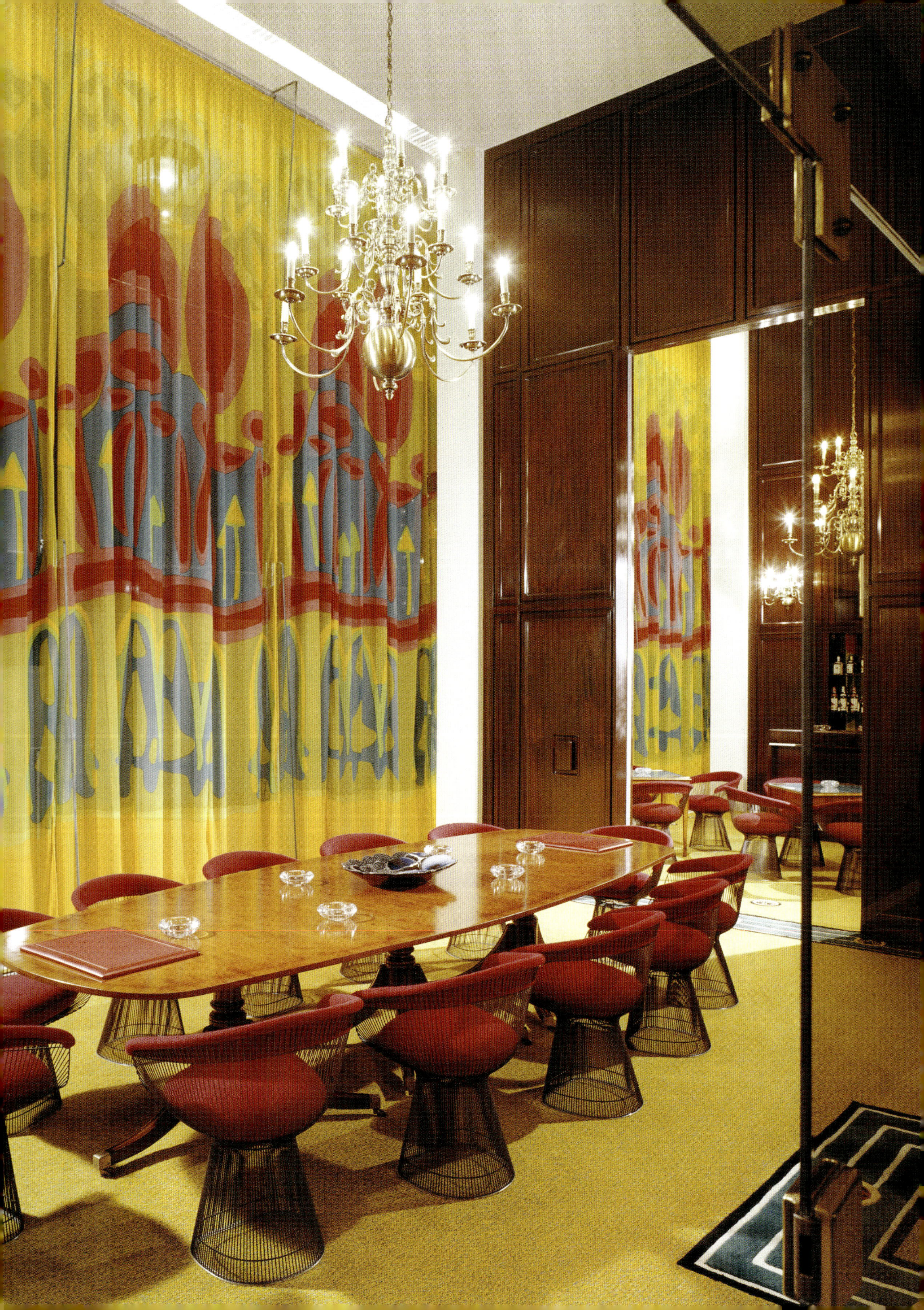

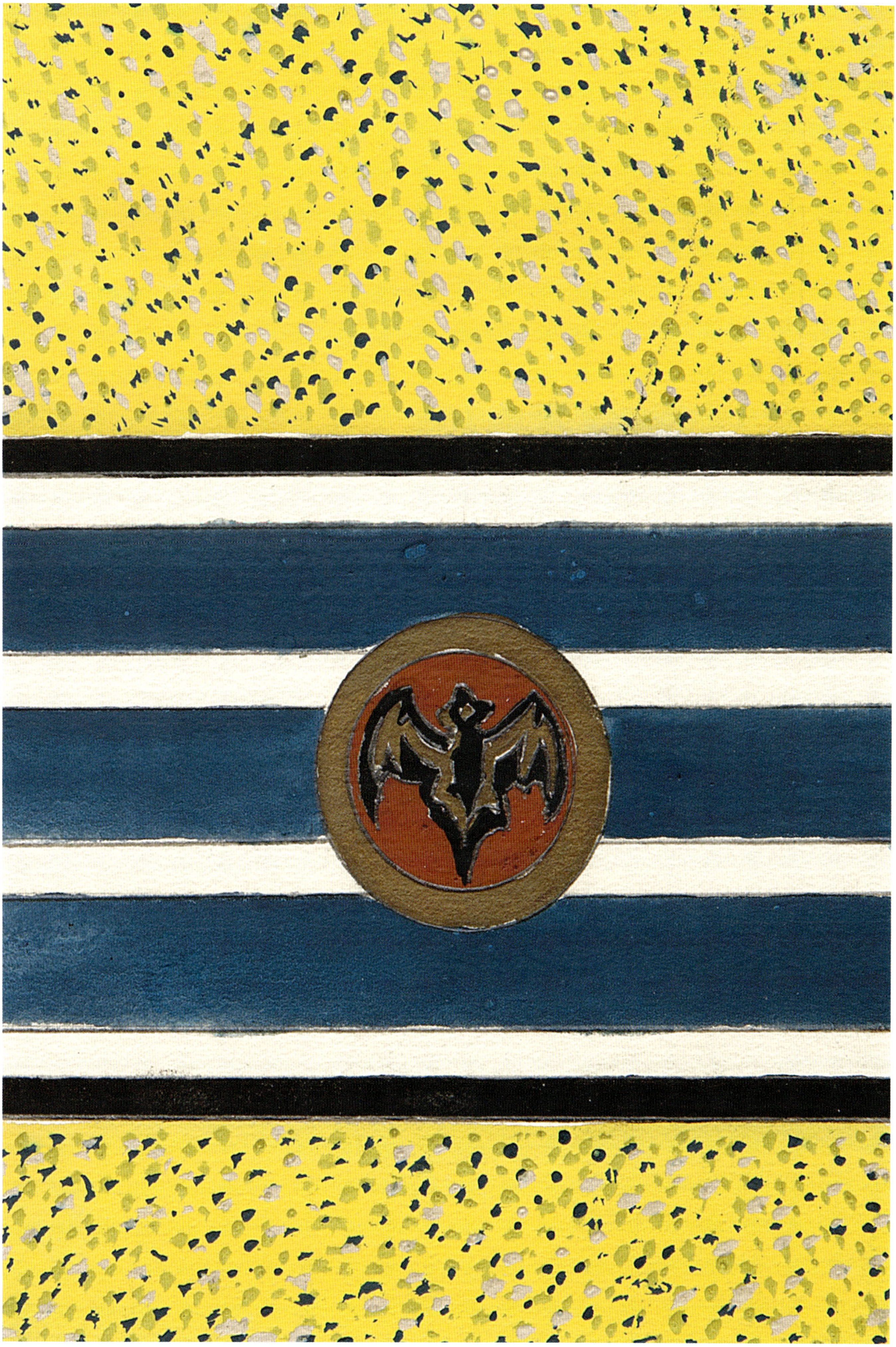

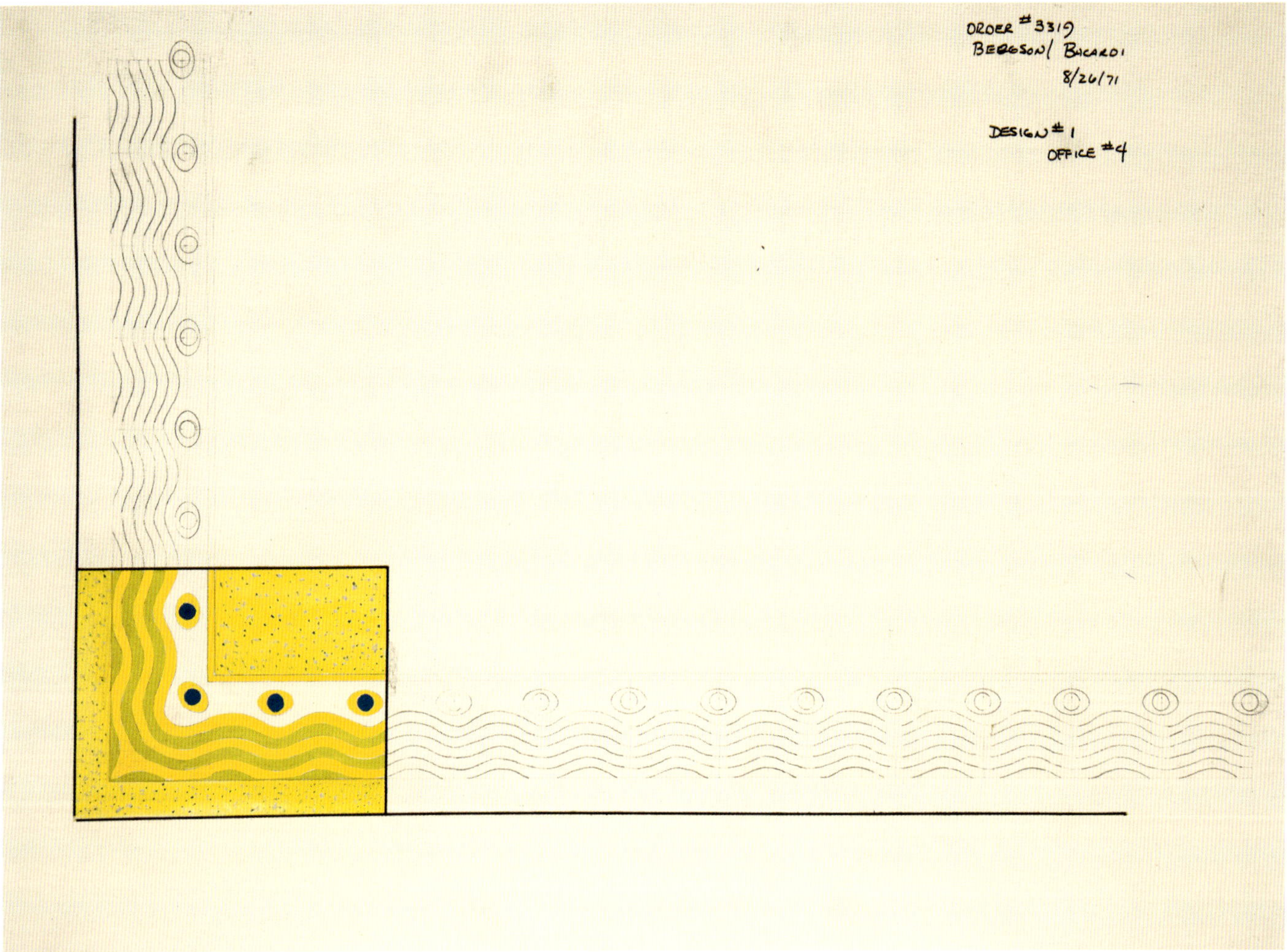
ORDER #3319
BERGSON/ BUCARDI
8/26/71
DESIGN #1
OFFICE #4

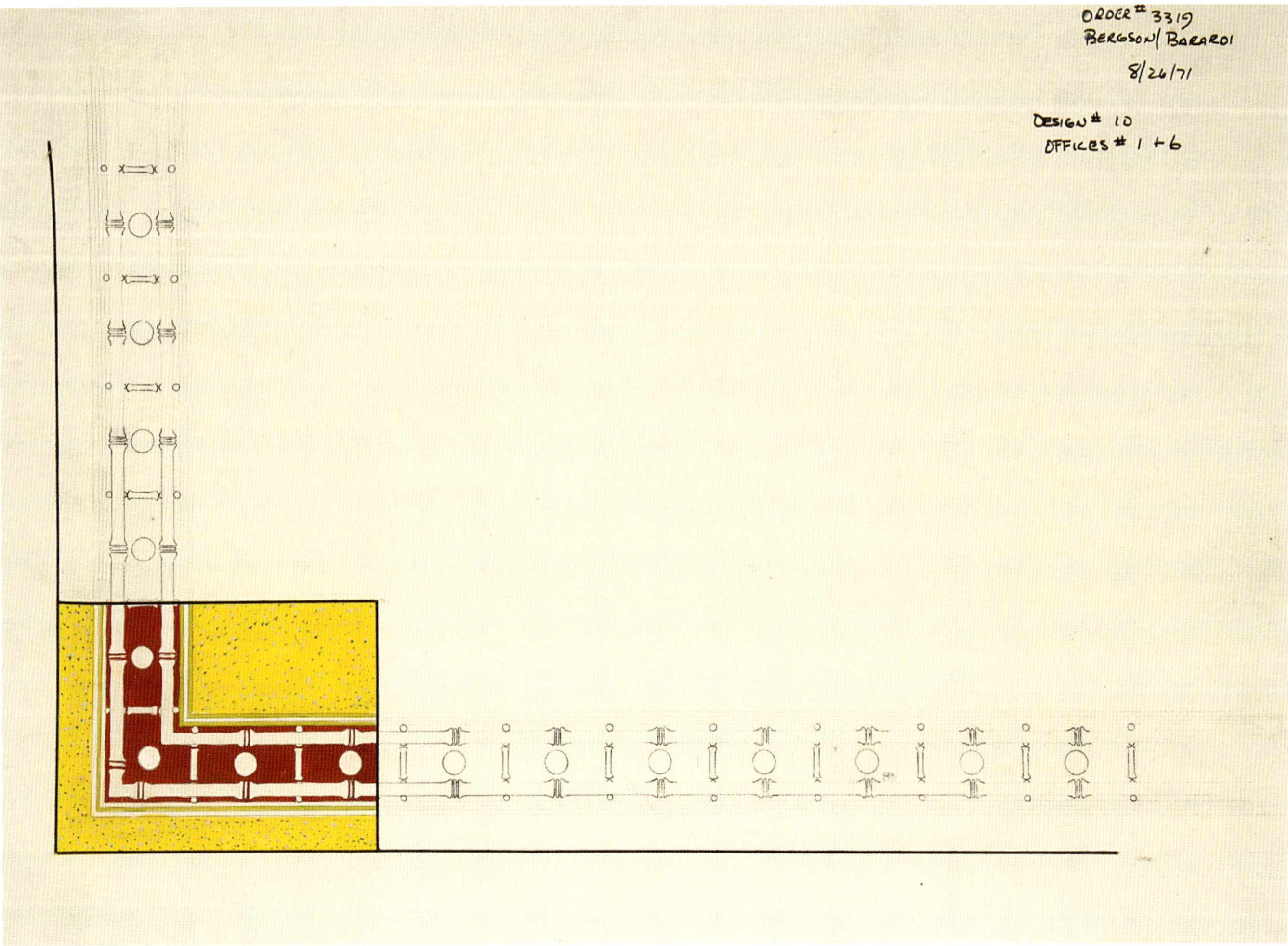
ORDER #3319
BERGSON/ BARARDI
8/26/71
DESIGN # 10
OFFICES # 1 + 6

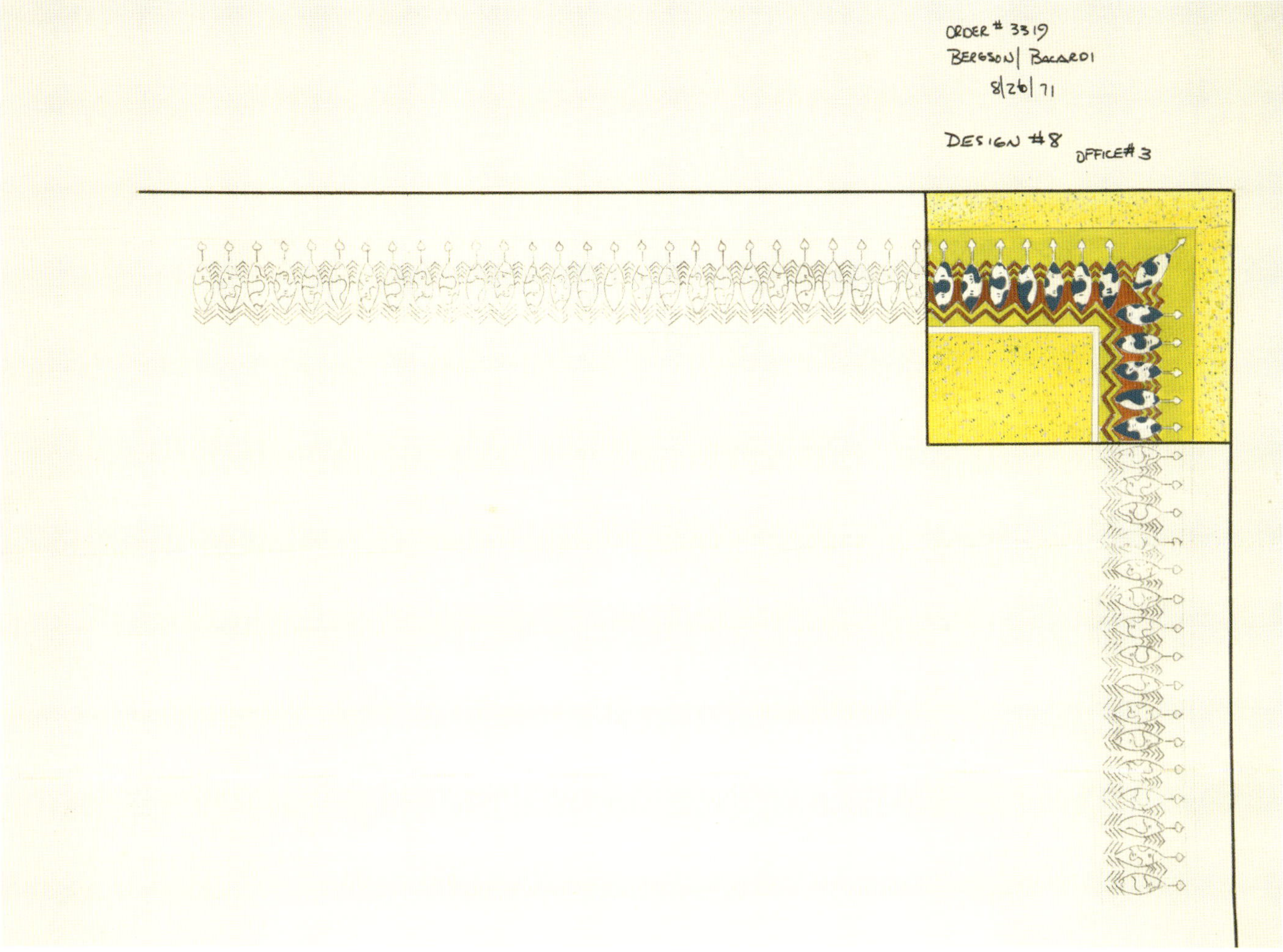
ORDER # 3319
BERGSON | BACARDI
8/26/71
DESIGN #8
OFFICE # 3

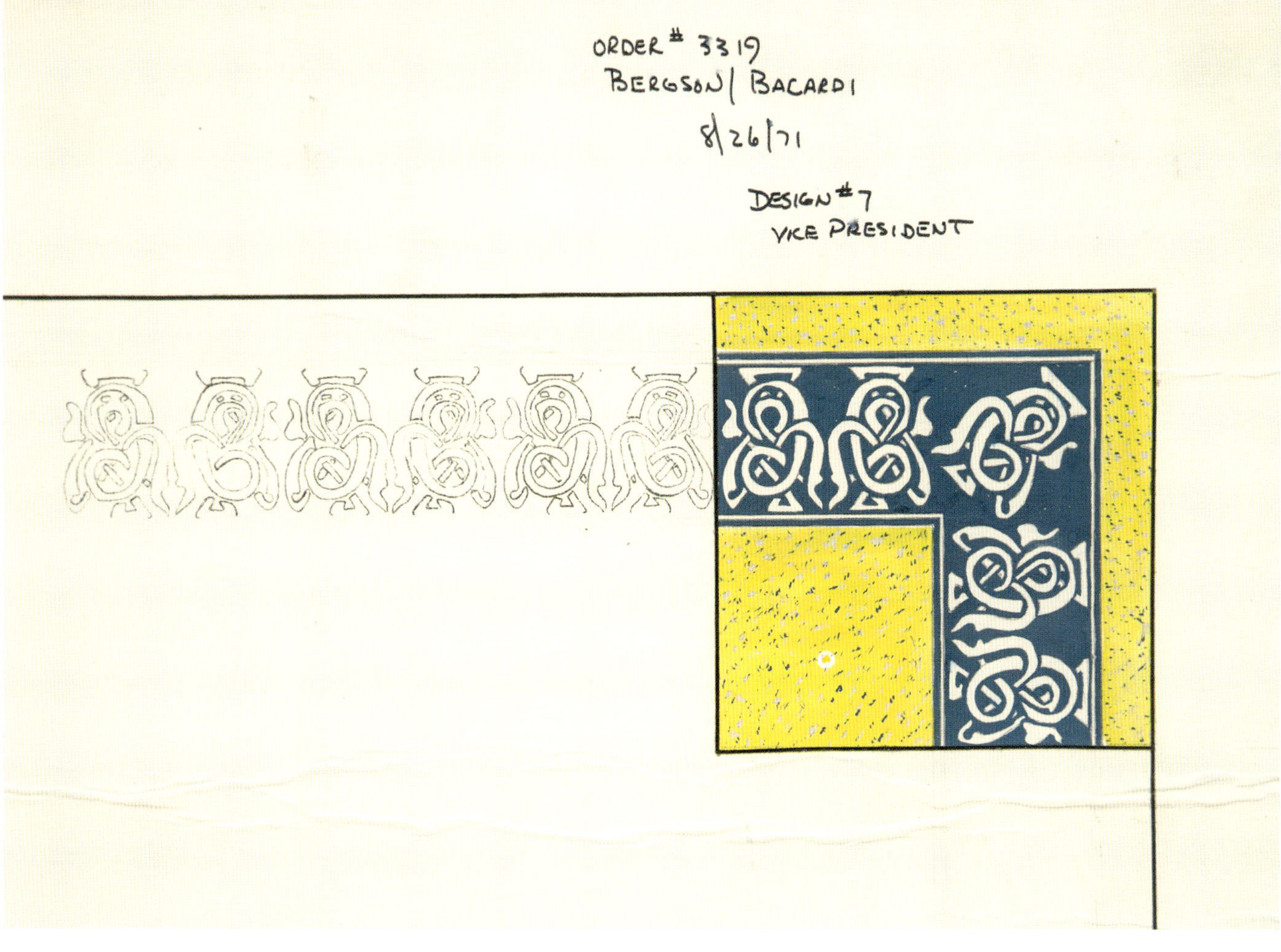
ORDER # 3319
BERGSON | BACARDI
8/26/71
DESIGN # 7
VICE PRESIDENT

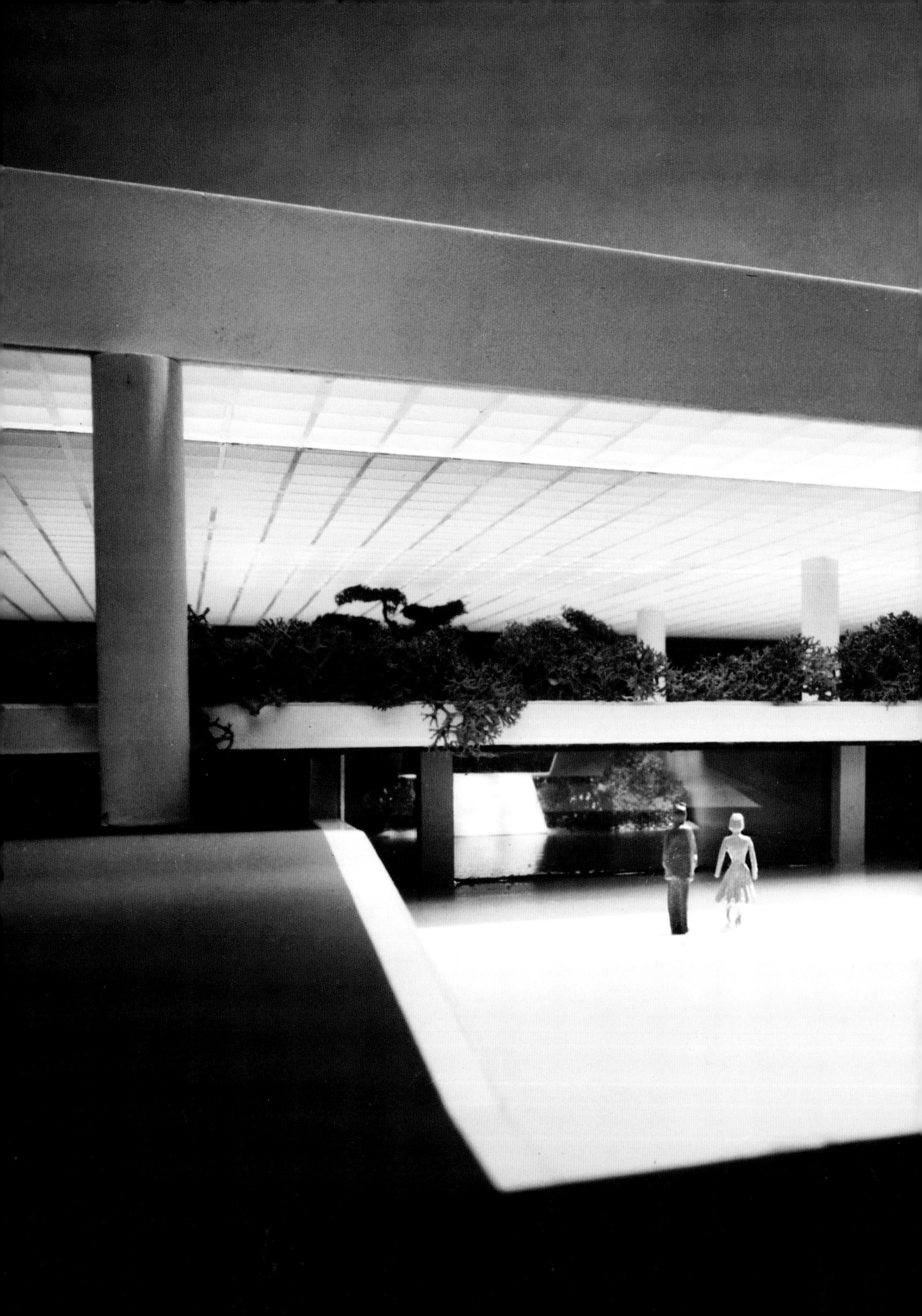

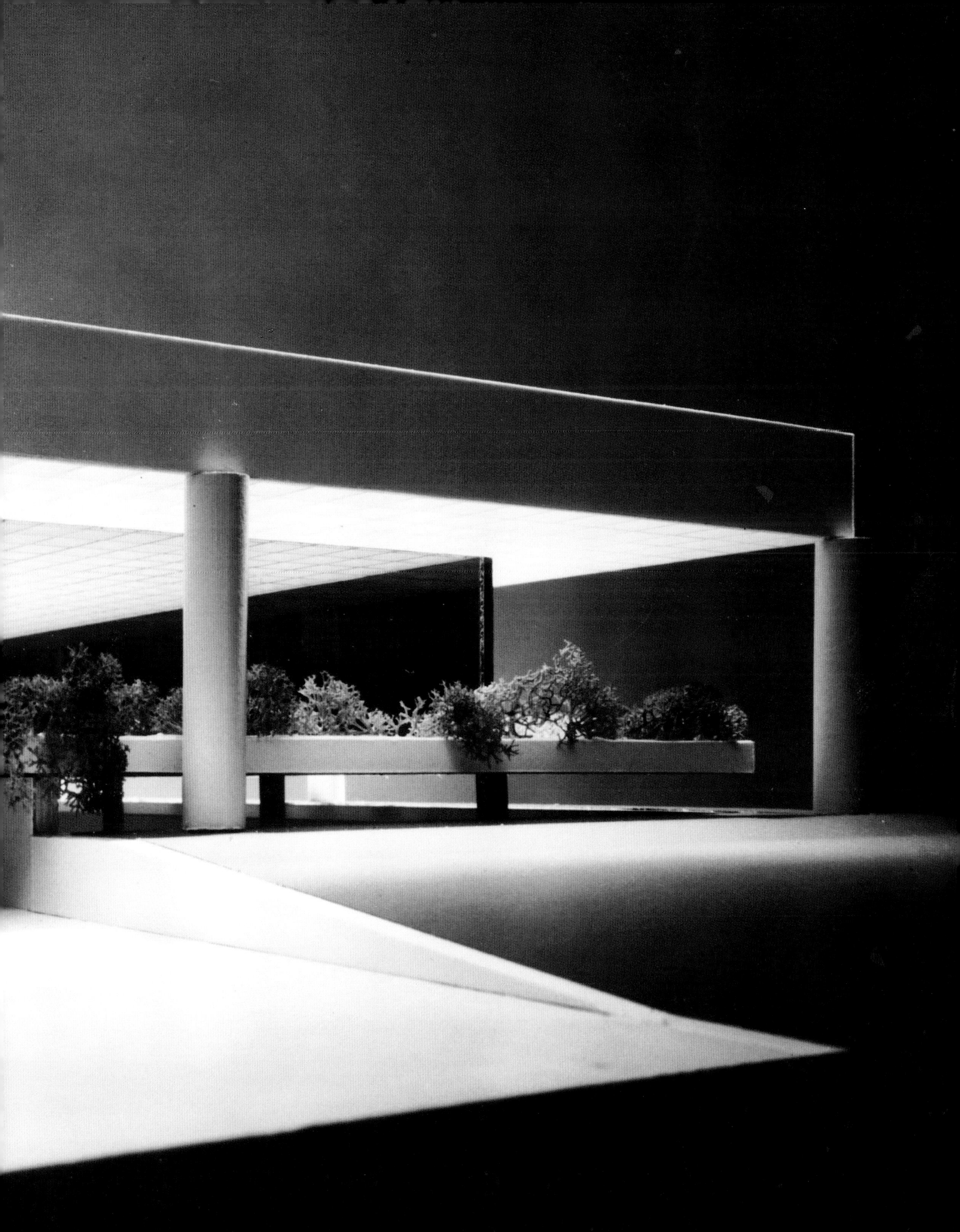

Bacardi Corporation Administration Building, Palo Seco, Puerto Rico. Photograph of model. Skidmore, Owings & Merrill LLP with Reed, Torres, Beauchamp y Marvel Arquitectos y Ingenieros, 1974 (unbuilt). Colección Thomas Marvel, Archivo de Arquitectura y Construcción de la Universidad de Puerto Rico.

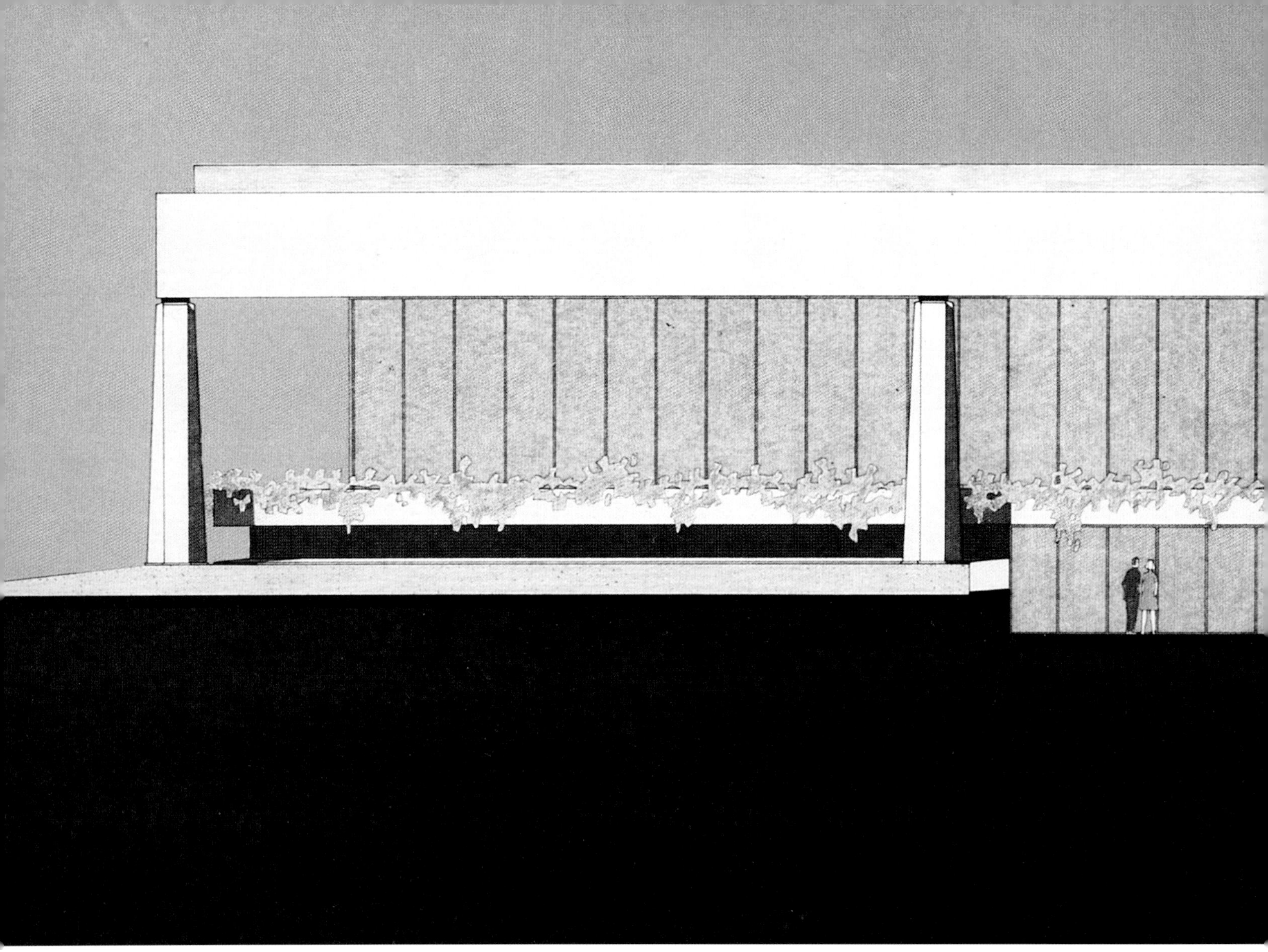

Top: Bacardi Corporation Administration Building, Palo Seco, Puerto Rico. Elevation. Skidmore, Owings & Merrill LLP with Reed, Torres, Beauchamp y Marvel Arquitectos y Ingenieros, 1974 (unbuilt). Colección Thomas Marvel, Archivo de Arquitectura y Construcción de la Universidad de Puerto Rico.

Right: Bacardi Corporation Administration Building, Palo Seco, Puerto Rico. Floor plan. Skidmore, Owings & Merrill LLP with Reed, Torres, Beauchamp y Marvel Arquitectos y Ingenieros, 1974 (unbuilt). Colección Thomas Marvel, Archivo de Arquitectura y Construcción de la Universidad de Puerto Rico.

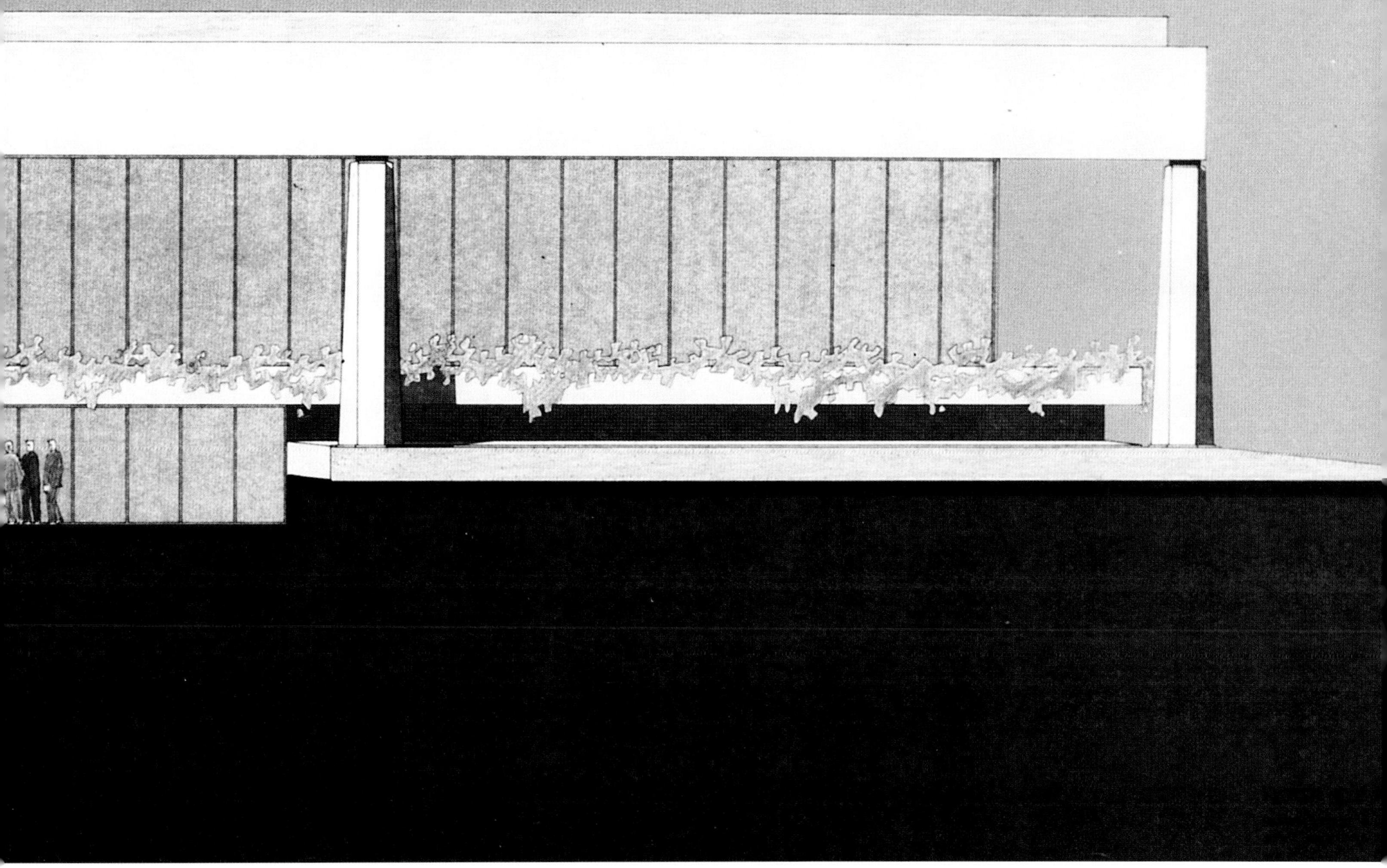

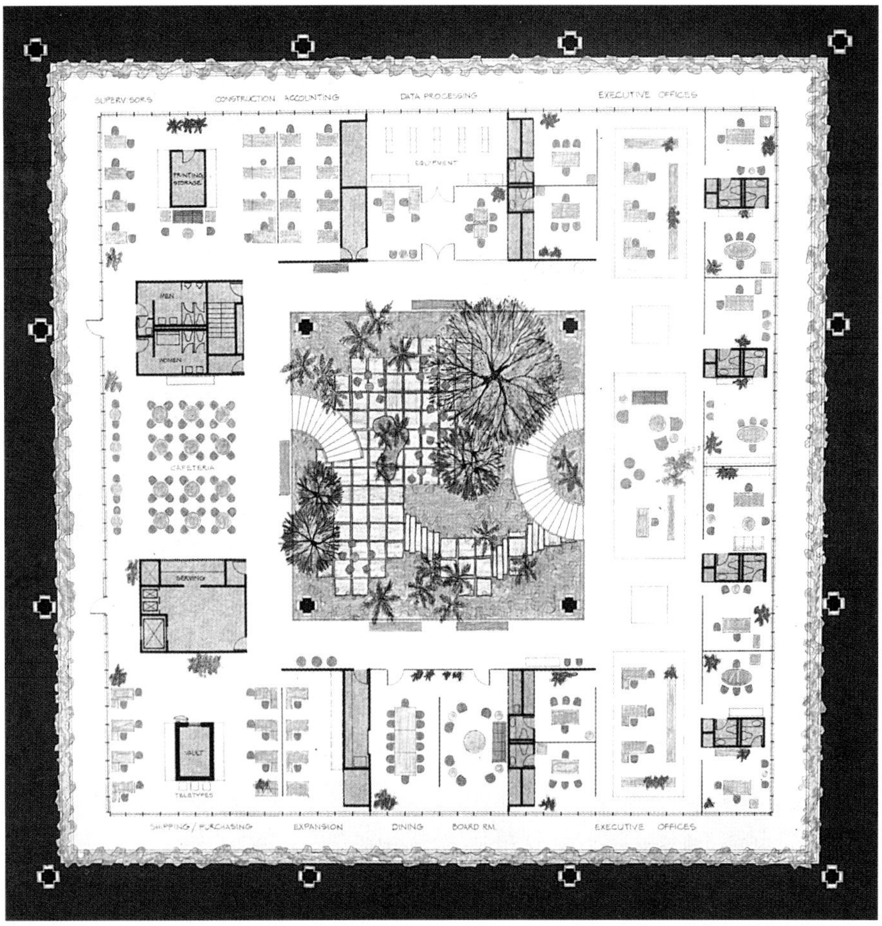

SUPERVISORS
CONSTRUCTION ACCOUNTING
DATA PROCESSING
EXECUTIVE OFFICES
PRINTING STORAGE
EQUIPMENT
MEN
WOMEN
CAFETERIA
SERVICE
VAULT
TELETYPES
SHIPPING / PURCHASING
EXPANSION
DINING
BOARD RM.
EXECUTIVE OFFICES

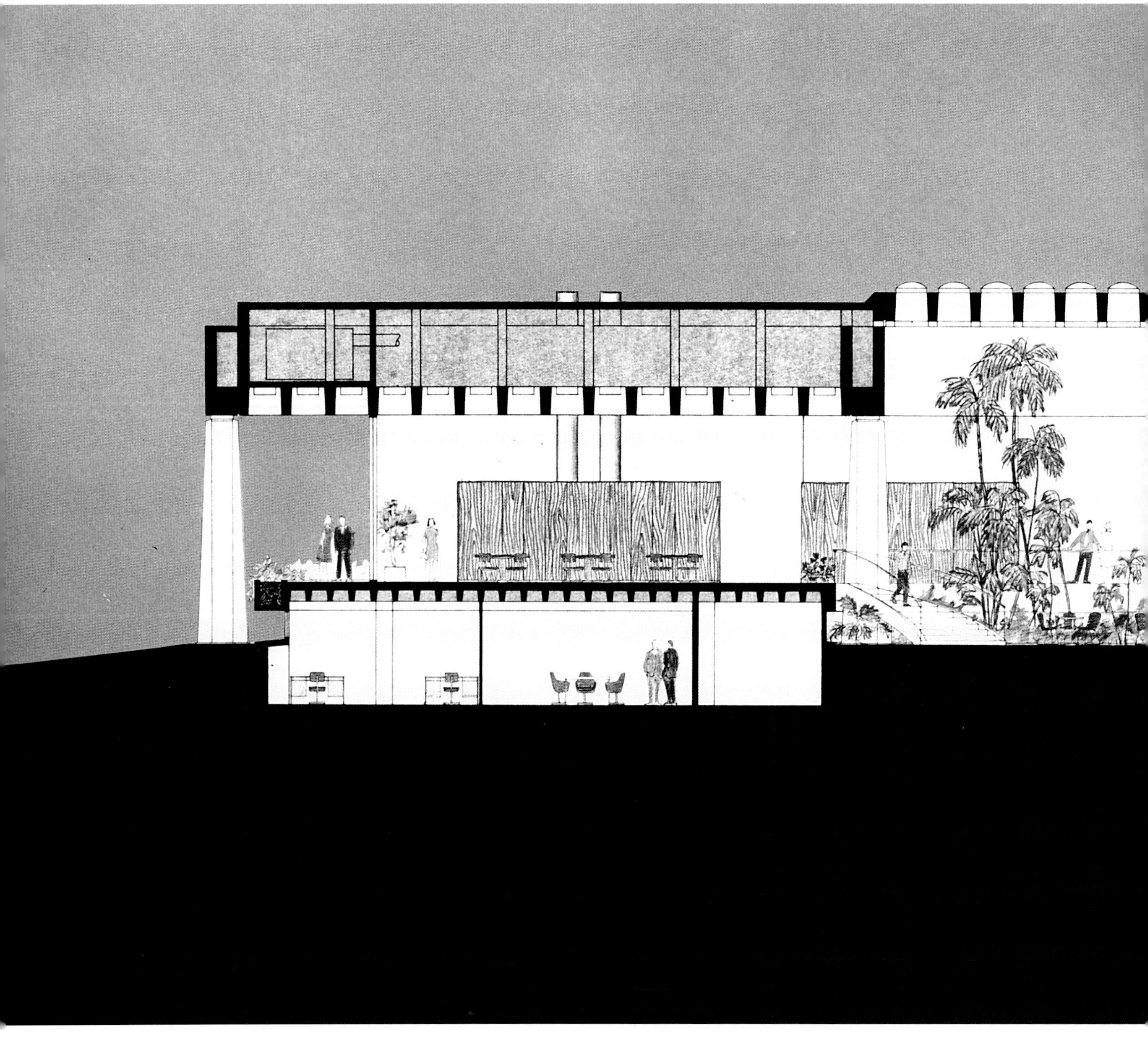

Bacardi Corporation Administration Building, Palo Seco, Puerto Rico. Elevation. Skidmore, Owings & Merrill LLP with Reed, Torres, Beauchamp y Marvel Arquitectos y Ingenieros, 1974 (unbuilt). Colección Thomas Marvel, Archivo de Arquitectura y Construcción de la Universidad de Puerto Rico.

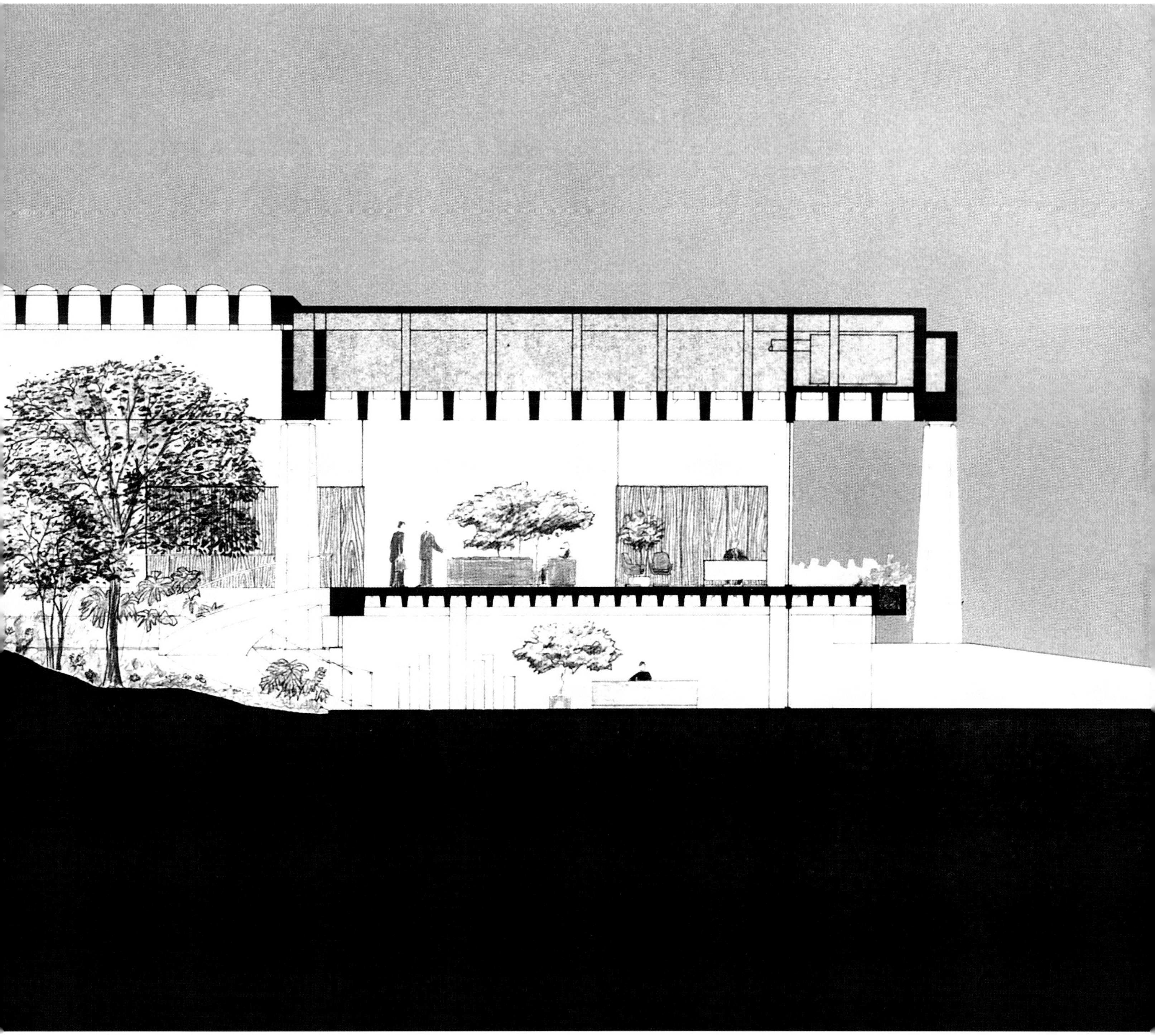

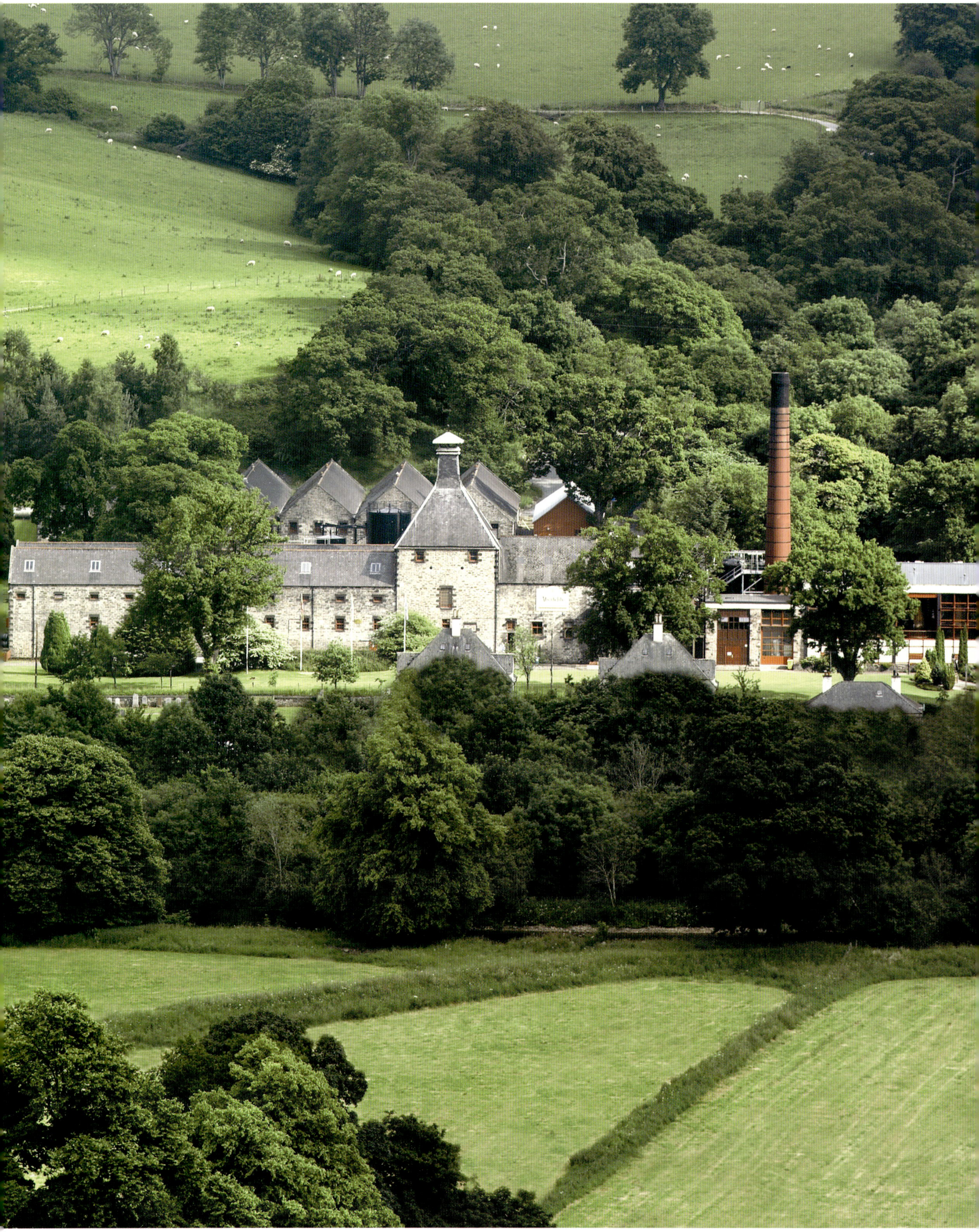

AT HOME EVERYWHERE

Until the early 1990s, Bacardi was a singular brand with multiple homes. In 1992, the company's intertwined corporate structures were reorganized as Bacardi Limited.[147] The next year, Bacardi completed the purchase of the Martini & Rossi group. More acquisitions followed. With a sprawling portfolio of brands new and old, Bacardi Limited now mixed rum with gin, tequila, vodka, vermouth and more.

As consumer preferences evolved, along with methods for tracking those preferences, so have the possibilities for precisely customizing the consumer experience at Bacardi's many facilities worldwide.[148] Building upon the emblematic architecture, museum displays and exhibition bars that represented the Bacardi experience for more than a century and a half, Bacardi Limited is currently focused on the development of "brand homes." Brand homes use place as a medium of the brand experience, delivering exclusive or in-depth experiences to visitors in order that they engage and establish an emotional bond with the brand.[149] While not exclusive to Bacardi, brand homes tie into the company's historic and current strengths using design to deliver key messages about product quality and process.

To build a home for each distinct brand, Bacardi demonstrates authenticity and craft in the manufacture of a spirit.[150] Bacardi locates these homes not in urban spaces, but at the imagined source of the raw materials, in the countryside, on the farm, at the distillery or at the château. The company currently operates nine brand homes, including the previously established rum distilleries at La Galarza in Mexico and Palo Seco in Puerto Rico.[151] At the latter, the company opened Casa Bacardi in 2003, a visitors' center that introduces visitors to the sight, smell, taste, and of course history, of BACARDI rum. Reputedly the second largest tourist attraction in Puerto Rico, Casa Bacardi leads visitors through historical simulacra of the company's original Matadero Street distillery, introduces characteristic company artifacts, entertains and educates at a "bat theater," and merchandises brand-related products at a Bacardi shop. Tramway tours of the grounds and cocktails in the stylish bat-winged *merendero* complete the experience.

By contrast, recently developed Bacardi brand homes offer far more in-depth product encounters in working settings. Abandoning a model based on mass tourism, these facilities allow visitors intimate hands-on experiences with raw materials, the manufacturing process and the culture of the brand. They immerse visitors in an environment that is entertaining and adventurous, yet subtly didactic and even museological. The company reinforces the brand's provenance by adapting historic buildings and often hiring prominent designers to construct the atmospherics. Some brand homes expand the experience with training centers, conference spaces, and even boutique hotel-type lodging on-site. Except at its rum distilleries, by design there is no reference to the parent company, Bacardi.

Brand home development has provided a conceptual structure for exploiting the sense of place, history and values acquired in historic facilities over decades and repackaging them for contemporary tourists. At the Dewar's Aberfeldy Distillery in Scotland, Bacardi restored architect Charles Cree Doig's distinctive 1898 distillery buildings, as well as its fresh water source, the Pitilie Burn.[152] The refurbishments, combined with new facilities, highlight the uniquely Scottish characteristics of malt Scotch whisky for the Dewar's center's many foreign visitors. History is even more palpable at the home of the Baron Otard brand in Cognac, France. Here, the attraction is the Chateau de Cognac, the fifteenth-century birthplace of the French monarch François I, where barrels of cognac are aged in the cellars beneath Gothic stone vaults. The angel's share emanating from these cellars cause a curious type of mushroom to thrive on the ancient walls of the chateau.

Dewar's Aberfeldy Distillery. Aberfeldy, Scotland. Charles Cree Doig, architect, 1898.
Photograph by John Swannell. Courtesy John Dewar & Sons Ltd.

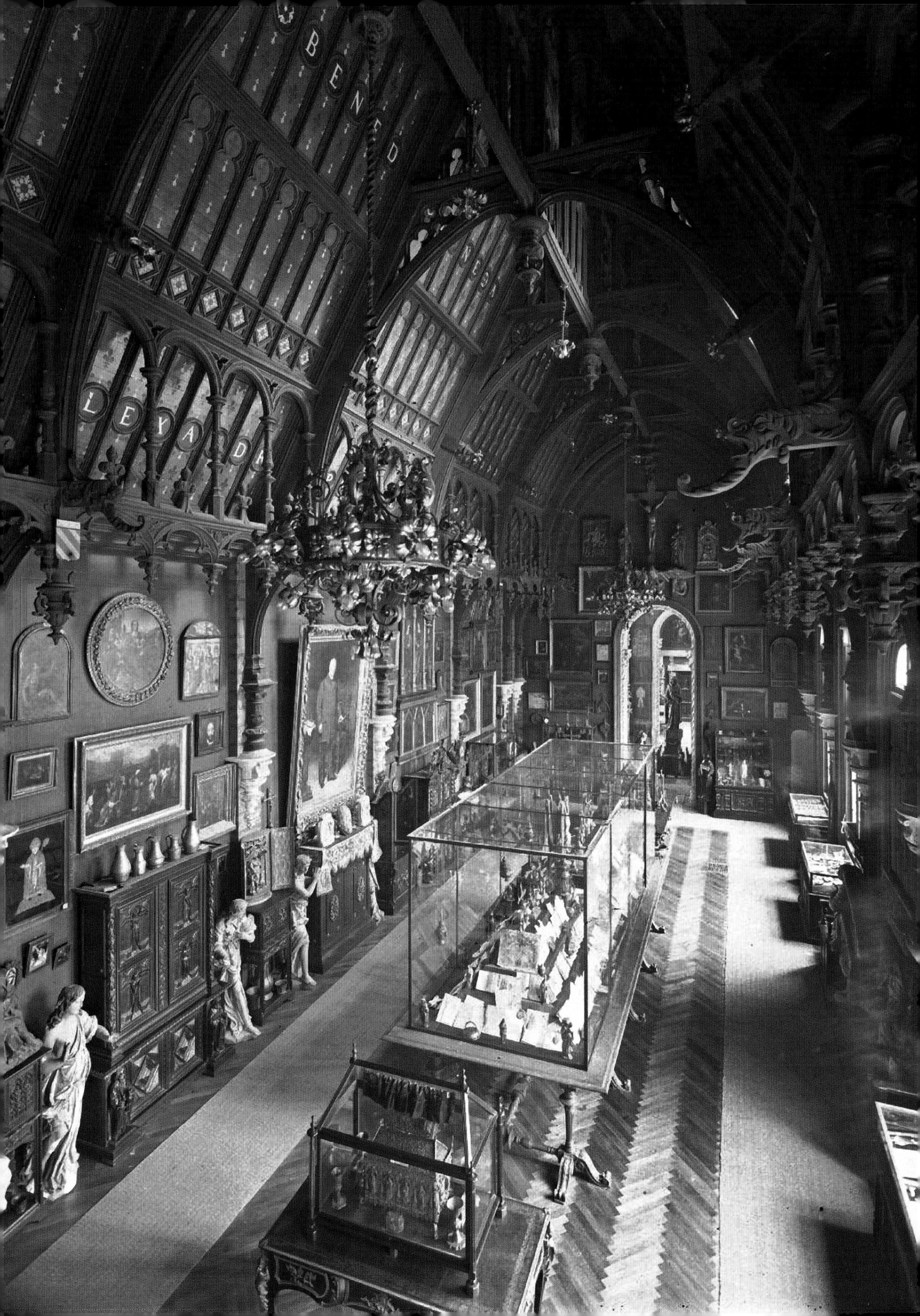
BENED
LEYADR

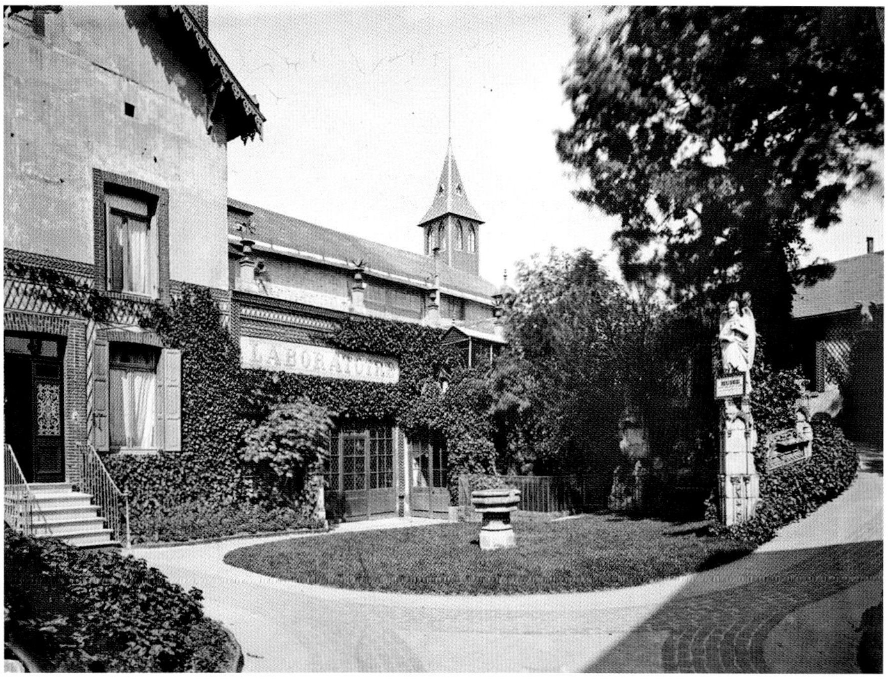

In some facilities, like the Palais Bénédictine in Fécamp, France, and Casa Martini in Pessione, Italy, long-standing cultural attractions are part of the brand experience. The distillery complex at Bénédictine, designed by architect Camille Albert and inaugurated in 1900, includes a neo-Gothic château that functions as a museum housing Bénédictine founder Alexandre le Grand's prolific collection of books, art and artifacts. At the home of Martini in Pessione, the winemaking complex has included a Museum of Enology since 1961. Contemporary offerings include the Martini Experience Room and the Mondo Martini exhibition, partly devoted to the brand's long history of publicity initiatives. At these homes, visitors are reminded of the intertwined role that wine and spirits, and creative design and marketing, play as ambassadors of national and regional cultures.

The most important efforts to date for Bacardi have been the entirely new brand homes for Grey Goose, in the heart of the Cognac region, and Bombay Sapphire, in the British county of Hampshire. In each, the company has taken an inventive approach to history, culture and tradition. In particular, facilities orchestrated by well-known designers are used to emphasize innovation, creative experiences, and experimentation.

Le Logis, the home Bacardi created for Grey Goose in the French village of Juillac-le-Coq, is most unusual. For one thing, it is not at the site of a distillery or plant, but rather in a seventeenth-century château purchased in 2012.[153] Open only to invited guests, the château is a center for training and accreditation as well as visits to the Grey Goose blending and bottling plant in nearby Gensac-la-Pallue. The chateau lends a sense of history to a brand invented in 1997 and purchased by Bacardi in 2004.[154] The location is relevant to the character of the vodka, which builds its mystique around the viniculture of Cognac. The village, the château, and the wine cellar are romantic settings for telling the story of the brand, which includes the ingredients, process, tradition, expertise and people that define the vodka.[155]

The brand home is organized around a lifestyle concept, particularly evident in the redesign of the interiors by a Milan-based interior design studio. Bacardi chose

Left: Le Palais Bénédictine, Fécamp, France. Gothic Room. Camille Albert, architect, 1900. Photographer unknown. Courtesy John Dewar & Sons Ltd.

Above: Le Palais Bénédictine, Fécamp, France. Laboratory. Camille Albert, architect, 1900. Photographer unknown. Courtesy John Dewar & Sons Ltd.

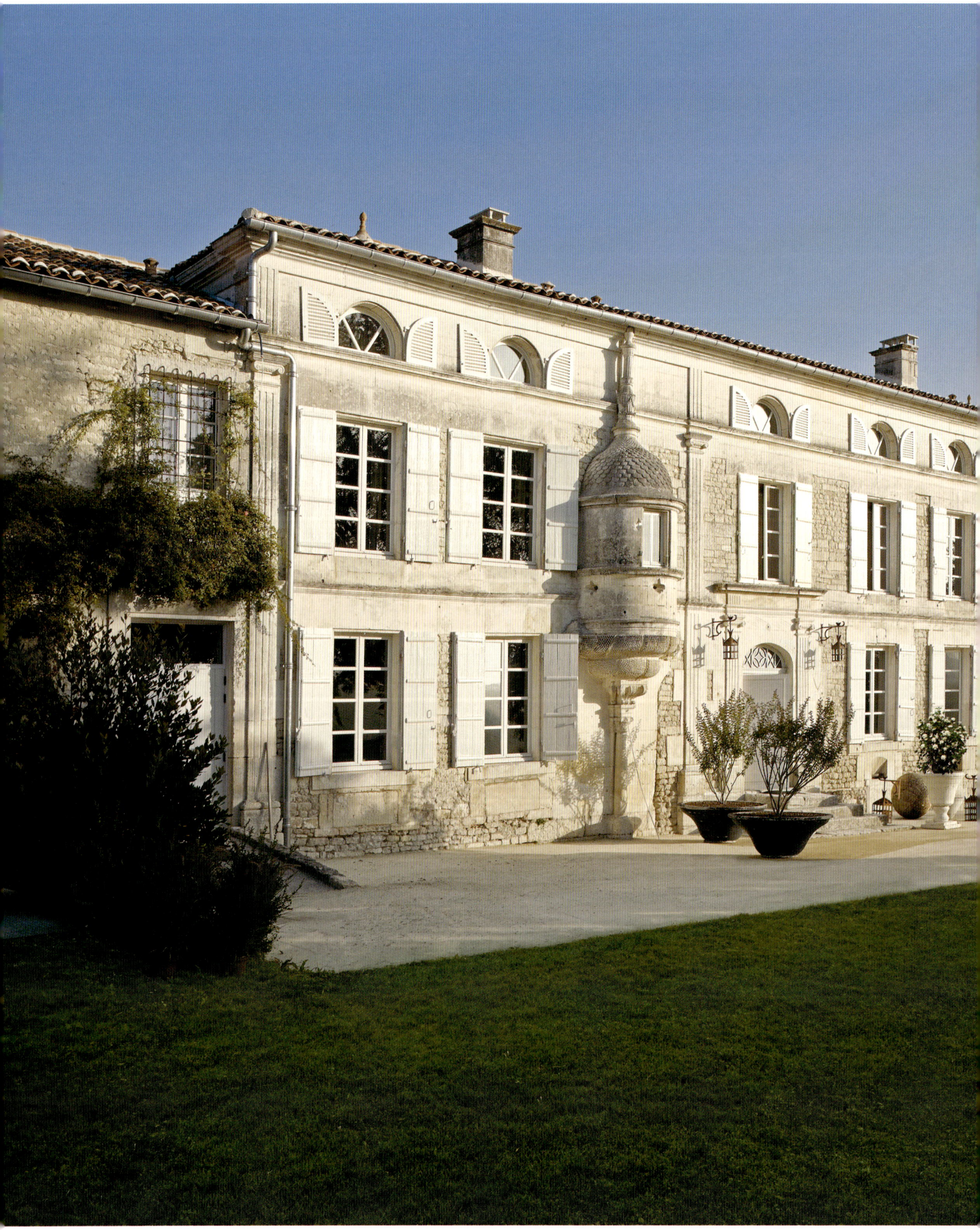

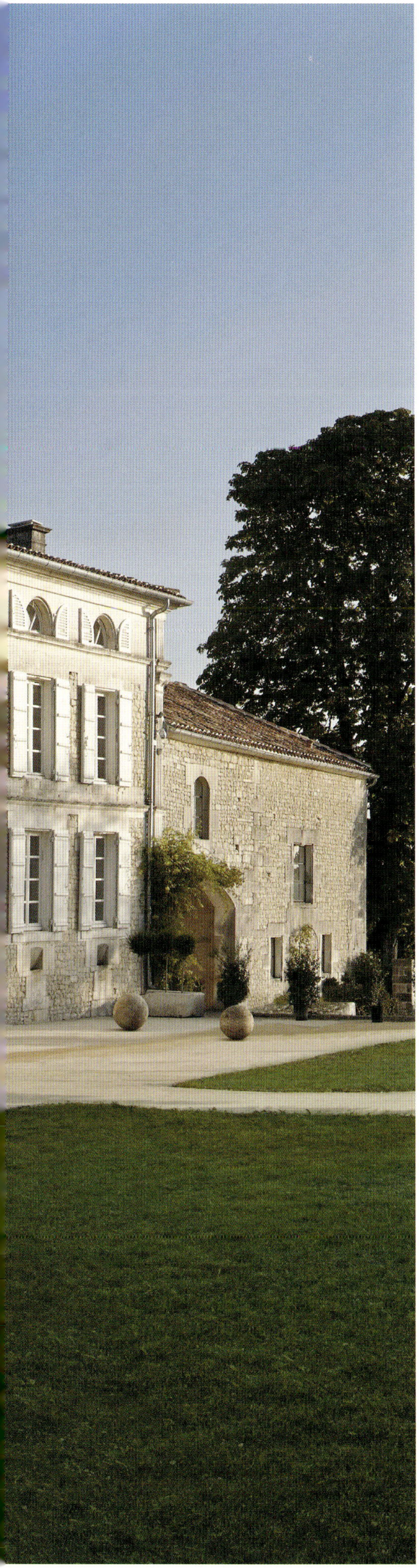

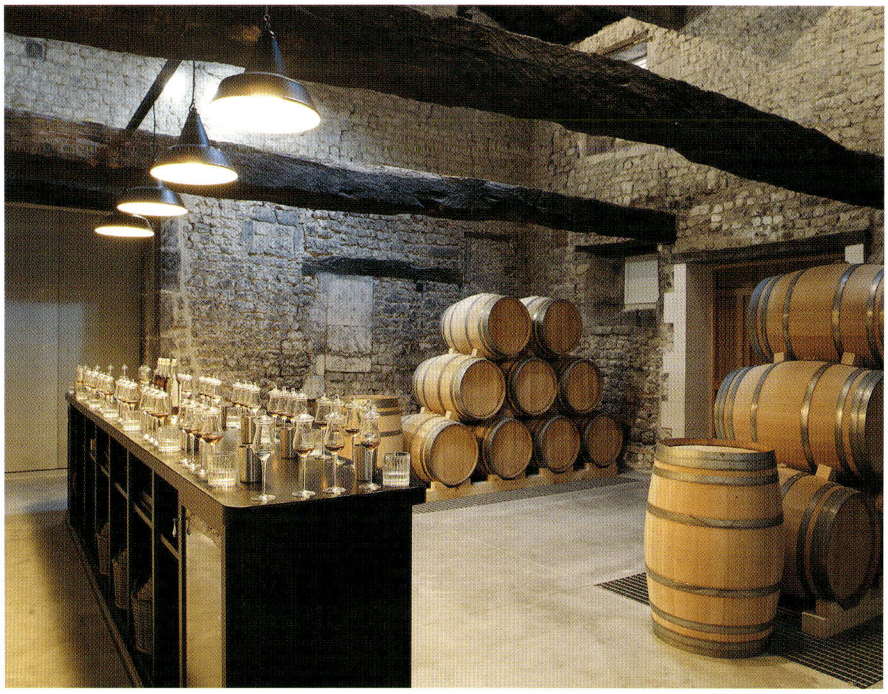

Left: Le Logis. Le Logis. Juillac-le-Coq, France. Facade of Le Logis, sixteenth century.
Renovation by local craftsmen and stonemasons to preserve architectural heritage of the property, 2012.
Photograph by Richard Moran. Courtesy of Ragged Edge.

Above: Le Logis. Juillac-le-Coq, France. Le Chai room where guests learn about
Grey Goose cellar master's blending of spirits. Photograph by Richard Moran. Courtesy of Ragged Edge

Overleaf: Le Logis. Juillac-le-Coq, France. Dining room.
Photograph by Richard Moran. Courtesy of Ragged Edge

Le Logis. Juillac-le-Coq, France. Pool area.
Photograph by Richard Moran. Courtesy of Ragged Edge

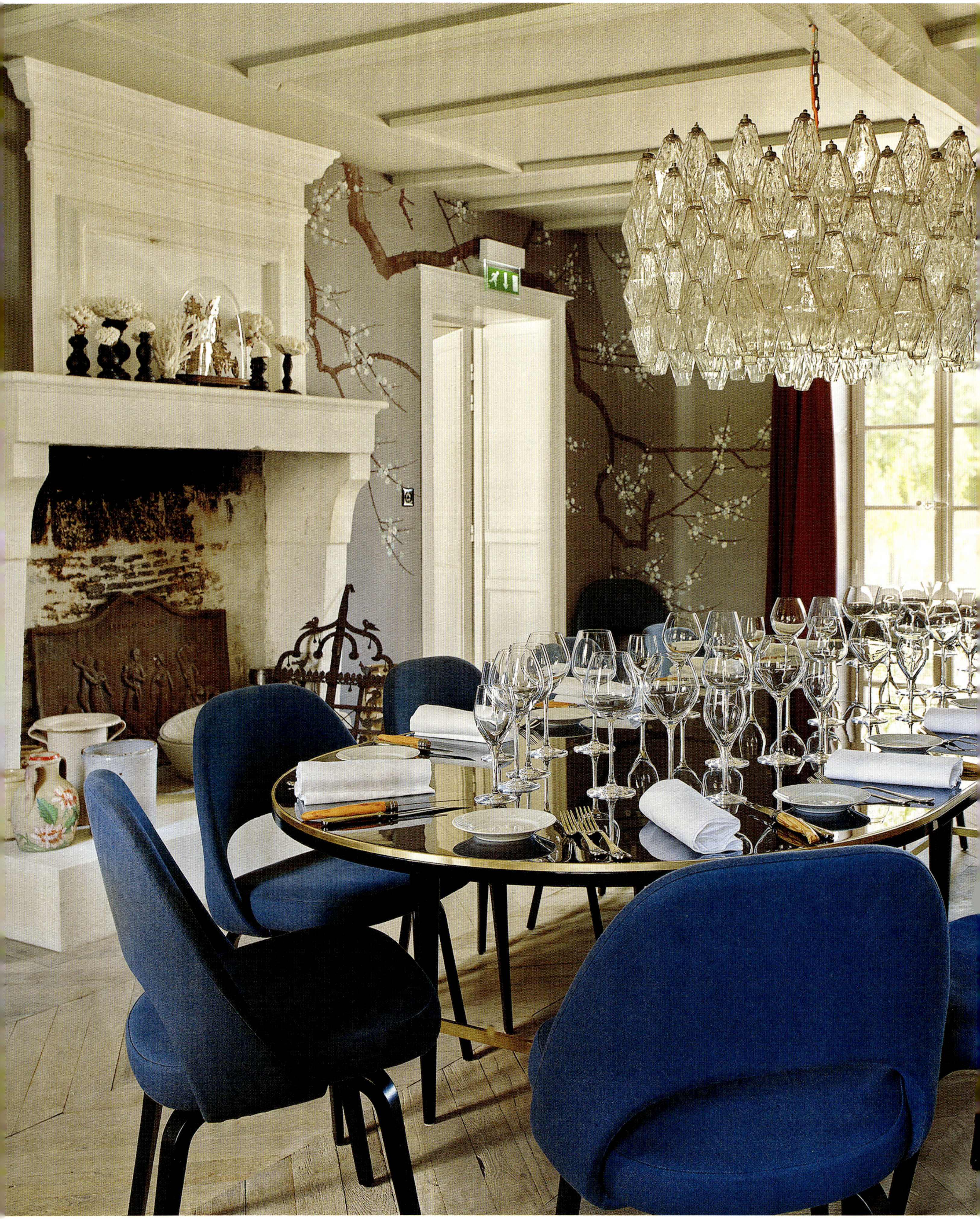

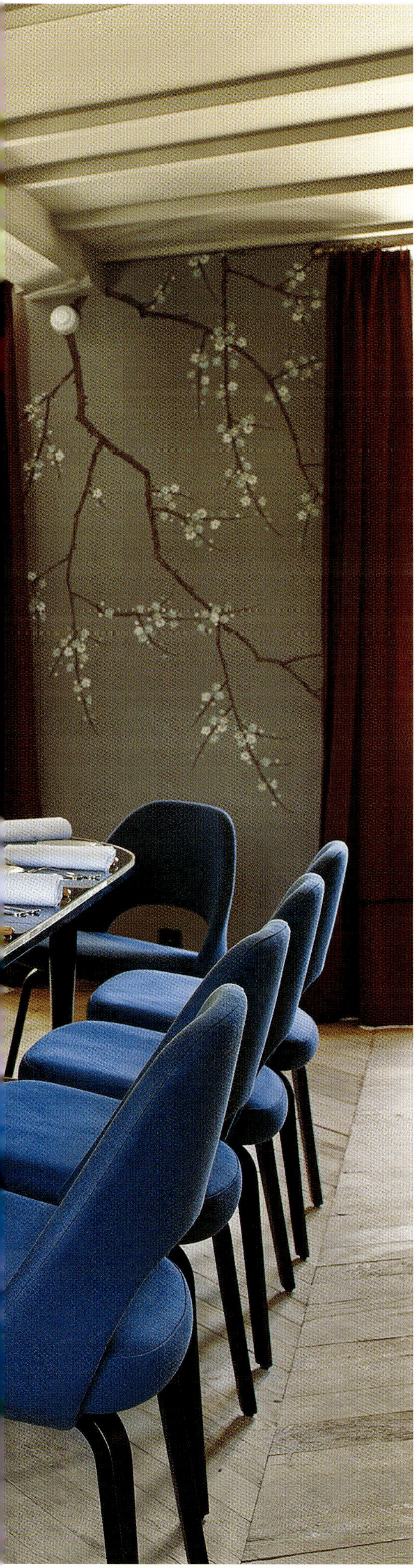

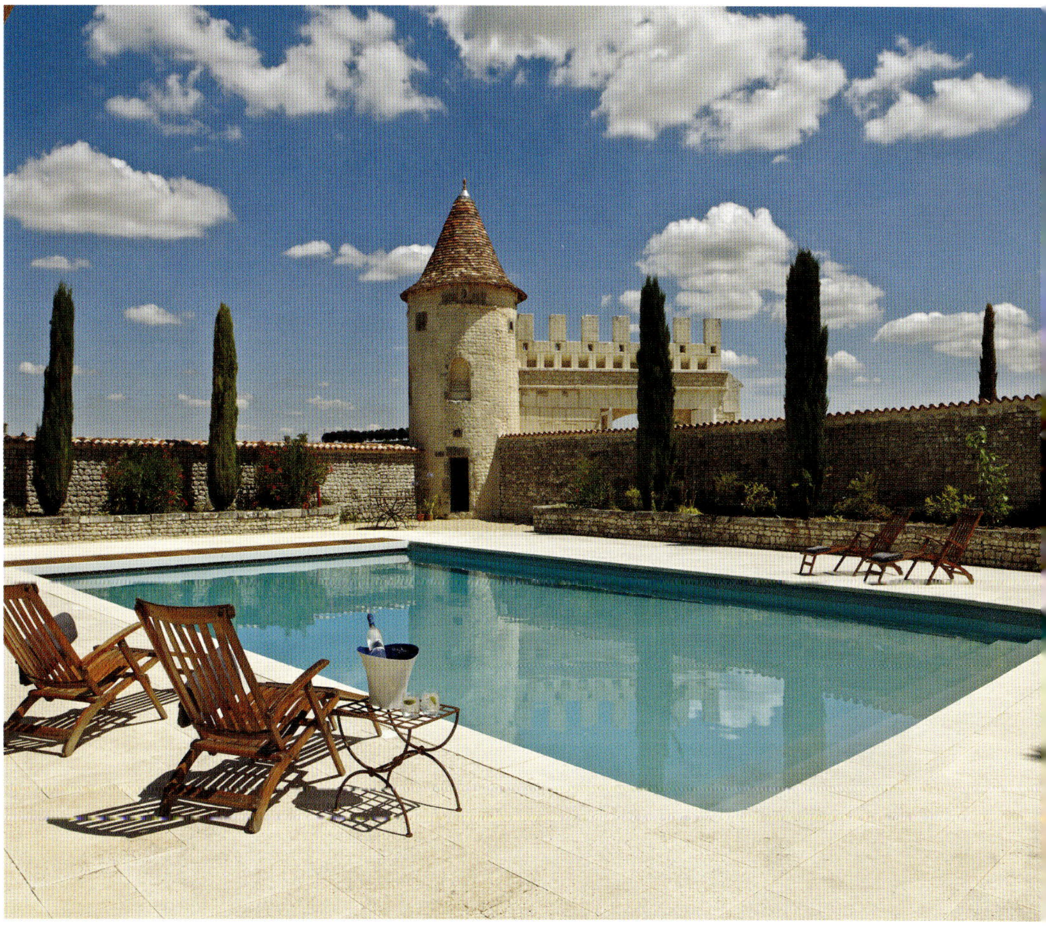

distinguished designers whose synthetic style, collaging old and new, comported perfectly with the invention of Grey Goose. In the main chateau building, a suite of smartly appointed rooms sets the stage for the visitors' meals and for informal social encounters. In these rooms, the character of Grey Goose is cultivated in the exposed wood beams and wood floors of the château, as well as in the warm gray walls and silk wall coverings and bespoke furnishings that outfit it.

Everything about Le Logis merges traditional and contemporary routines. The château's working vineyard, orchards, and potager garden form a backdrop to the deluxe swimming pool and barbecue pit. An open country kitchen combines stone hearth and rustic farm table with high-end appliances prepares French cuisine, linking Grey Goose to farm fresh ingredients and French culinaria. Spare but elegant guest rooms carved from the upper floors of the ancient chateau have the character of a high-end boutique hotel.

Educational facilities are housed in the eighteenth-century storehouse adjacent to the château. In this rustic setting, an interconnected suite of rooms trace the manufacture of Grey Goose vodka from raw materials to finished product. For instance, the brand's signature wheat is sampled and ground in a simulated granary, while in a bakery next door, visitors sample another French tradition by baking their own fresh bread from the wheat. In the barrel storage room, guests sip cognac, signifying the relationship between Grey Goose and the local industry. The sequence ends in the research and development atelier of the founding *Maître de Chai*, or cellar master, François Thibault. Later, vodka is sampled in a small but elegant on-site bar, mixed with fresh ingredients from the chateau's orchards and gardens.

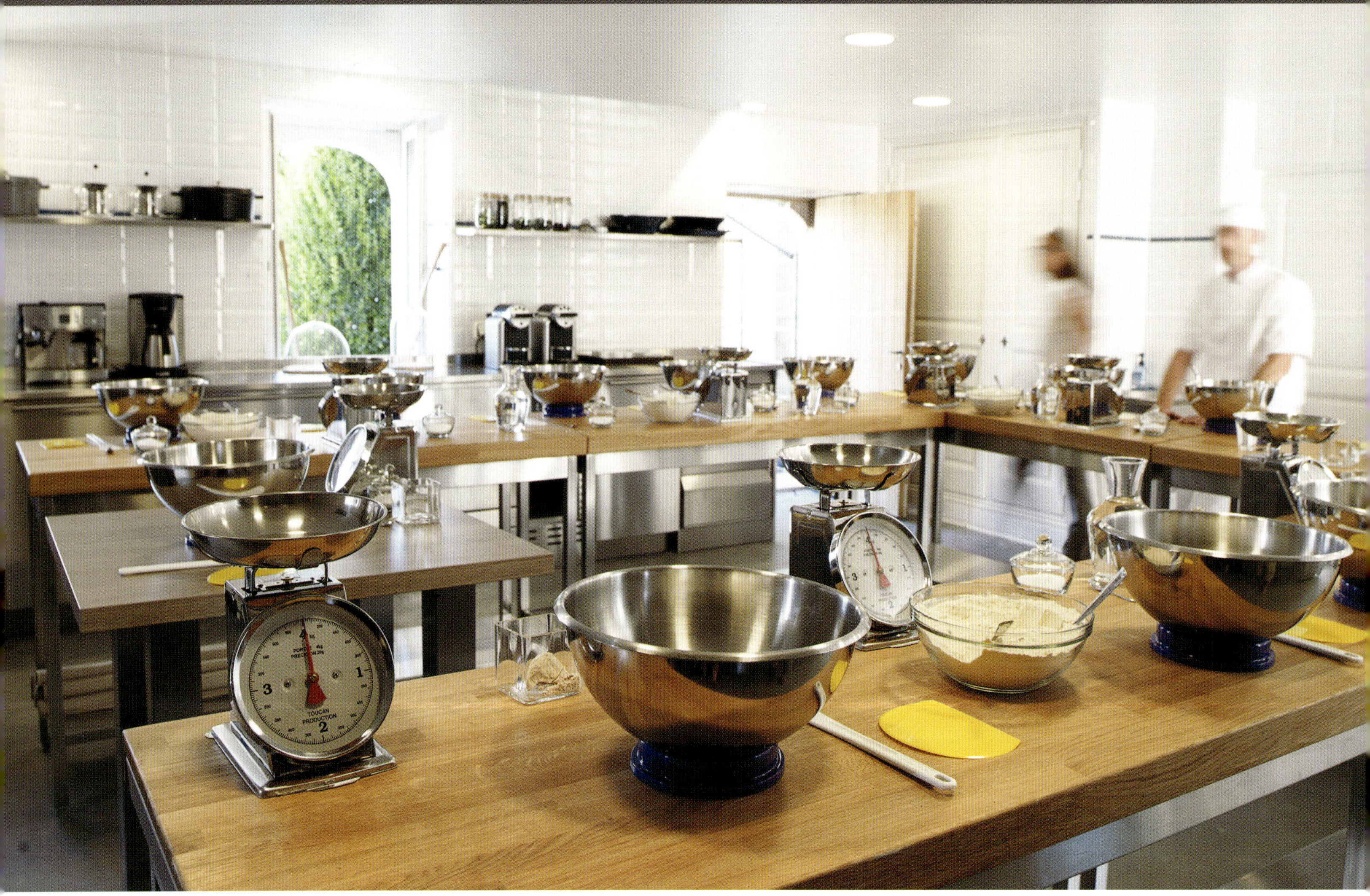

Le Logis. Juillac-le-Coq, France. La Boulangerie room where guests bake bread from the winter wheat used to make Grey Goose. Photograph by Richard Moran. Courtesy of Ragged Edge

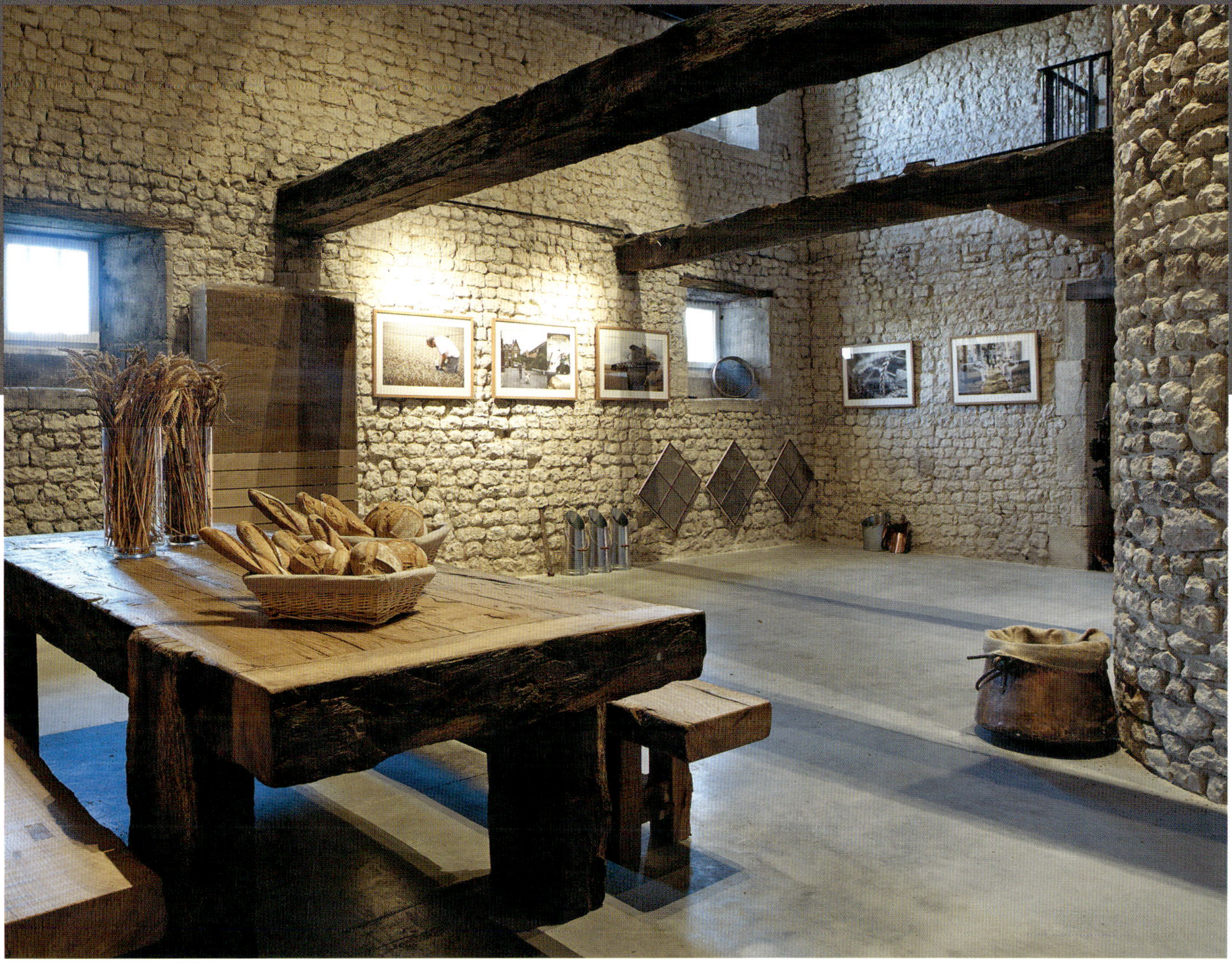

Le Logis. Juillac-le-Coq, France. La Picardie room celebrating wheat from Picardie, the breadbasket of France.
Photograph by Richard Moran. Courtesy of Ragged Edge

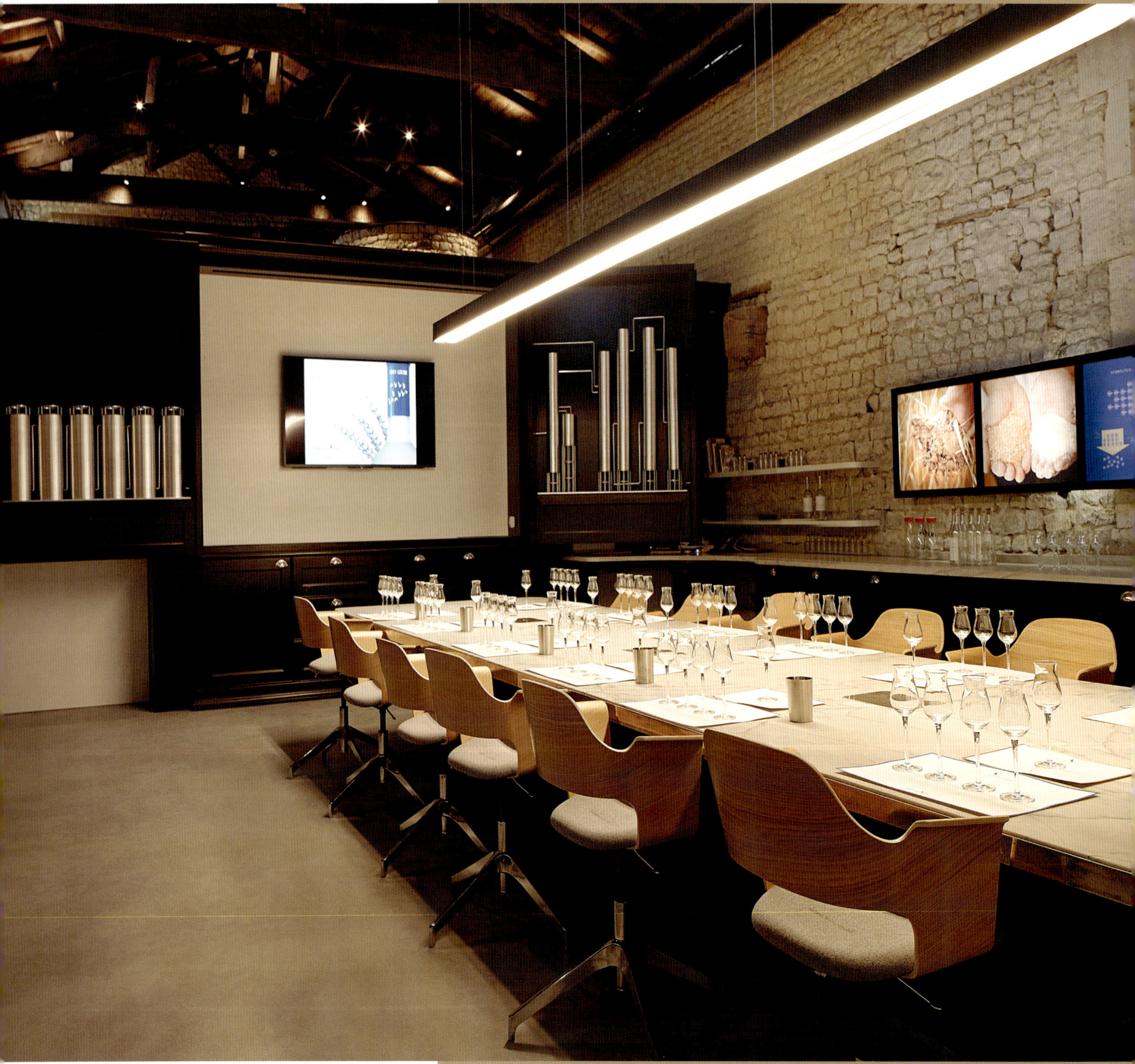

Le Logis. Juillac-le-Coq, France. Atelier of Maître de Chai François Thibault. Photograph by Richard Moran. Courtesy of Ragged Edge

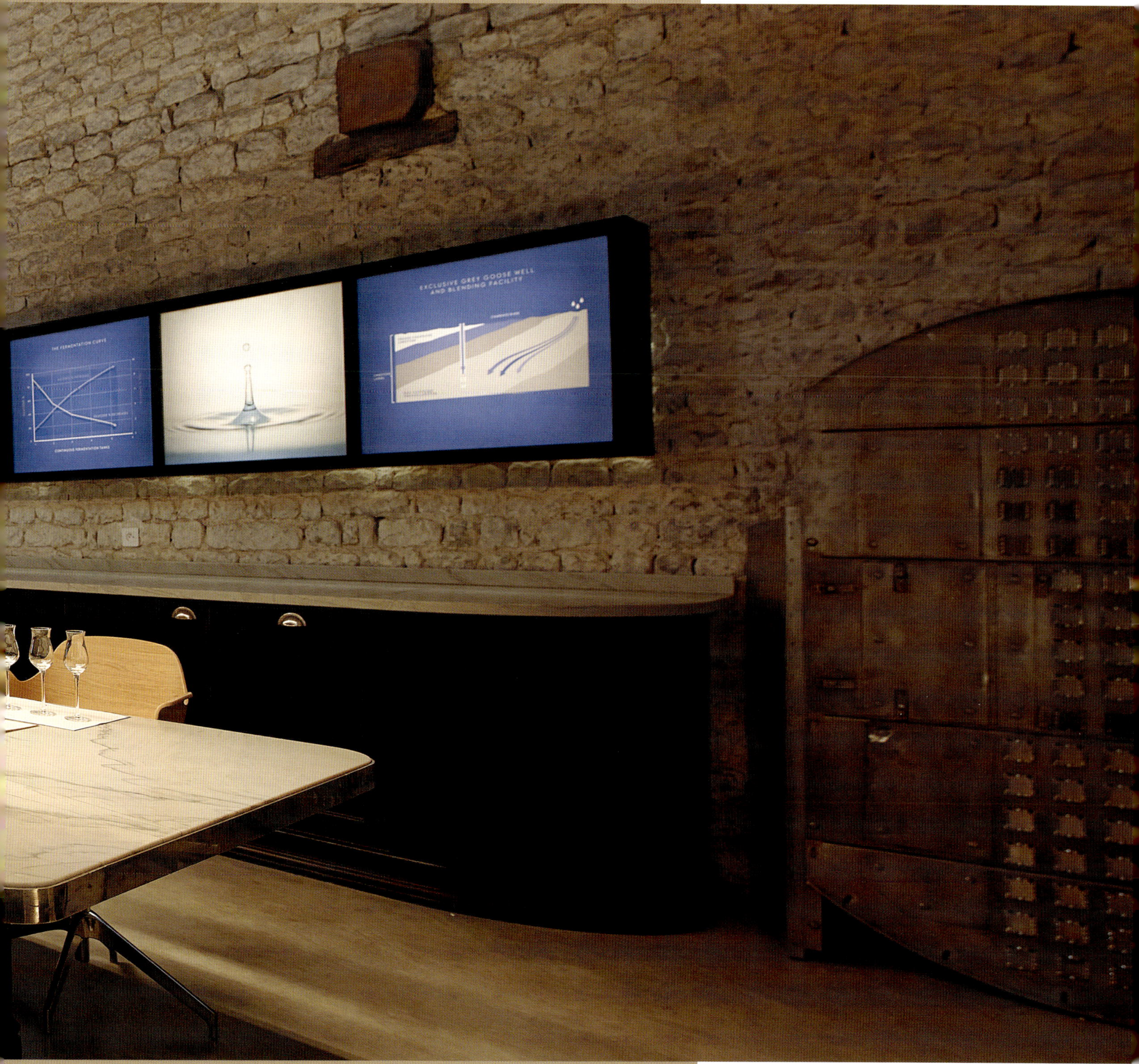
THE FERMENTATION CURVE
CONTINUOUS FERMENTATION TANKS
EXCLUSIVE GREY GOOSE WELL
AND BLENDING FACILITY

Le Logis promotes the idea of spirits brand as fashion house—the premium design and experience reinforcing the notion of premium brand. The stylish rooms and didactic exhibits allow visitors to understand the craftsmanship in the manufacture of Grey Goose, while the country setting, emphasis on French cuisine and historic château suggest a provenance the vodka would otherwise lack.

Bacardi conceived an even more ambitious brand-home development in the village of Laverstoke, England, where eighteenth- and nineteenth-century mills were converted into an adavanced gin distillery and visitors' experience for Bombay Sapphire. Like Grey Goose, Bombay Sapphire is a newer brand, launched in 1960 and purchased by Bacardi in 1997. The spirit takes its name from the Star of Bombay, a 182-carat gem on display at the Smithsonian Museum, connecting the brand with British Victorian lore and the popularity of gin during the British Raj. The Victorian-era Laverstoke Mill facility, reimagined as an attraction, is the embodiment of the Bombay Sapphire brand. In the design of the distillery, both the buildings and the brand were renovated.

Located in Hampshire, in countryside just 90 minutes southwest from London, the rolling green hills and hedgerows surrounding Laverstoke convey an authentic Britishness.[156] The extraordinary site had a mill long before the French Huguenot émigré Henry Portal founded a papermaking industry here in 1719. Over two centuries, the mill developed into a campus of 40 industrial buildings as it produced paper for the banknotes of the Bank of England and British Empire.[157] The pure waters of the River Test flowing through the complex, once critical to papermaking at the Laverstoke Mill, now provide a idyllic focus for the complex.

The principal opportunity of the site was its capacity to integrate the physical plant required to distill gin, while leveraging its historical structures and sylvan setting to provide that gin a provenance. The Laverstoke Mill complex would be assimilated creatively into a virtual theater of distilling. The project was initiated with an invited design competition, an arrangement that resonated with Bacardi's own history while it showcased the positioning Bombay Sapphire as a design-led product.[158] The London-based firms of Rogers Stirk Harbour + Partners (Richard Rogers) and Heatherwick Studios (Thomas Heatherwick) were invited to prepare preliminary designs for Laverstoke. Heatherwick Studio, who had first come to the attention of Bombay as the first winner of the Bombay Sapphire Prize, organized the working and tourist-oriented parts of the complex around a restored courtyard from which distilling equipment can be viewed through large industrial sash windows.

Heatherwick's winning design has a storybook quality that has turned the Victorian idea of industry on its head. This reinvention, from Dickensian factory to enchanted workshop, was choreographed through the transformative effects of heritage restoration, and in the careful addition of new elements. The natural riverbanks of the chalk stream were restored, surrounding the site in a lush wetland. Original brick mill buildings were polished and repackaged as industrial lofts, and historic engineering features, like an ancient water turbine, were revived as features of a more balanced ecology. The museological program includes a Laverstoke Mill Heritage Room near the entrance, which memorializes the plant's former function with artifacts and photographs.

Right: The Distillery at Laverstoke Mill, England. Aerial view. Heatherwick Studio, architect, 2014. Photograph by Iwan Baan.

Overleaf: The Bombay Sapphire Distillery at Laverstoke Mill, England. The River Test. Photograph by Iwan Baan.

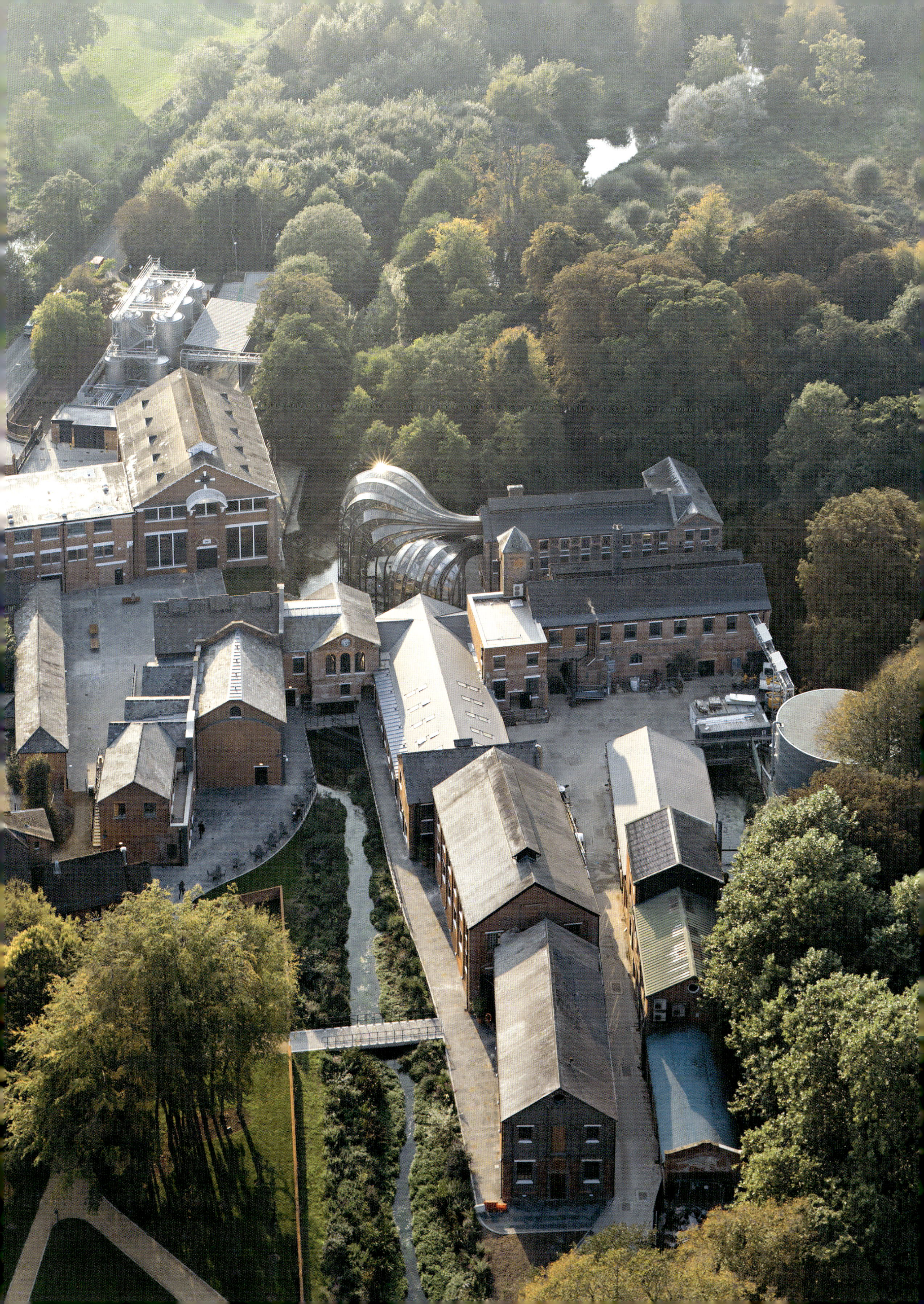

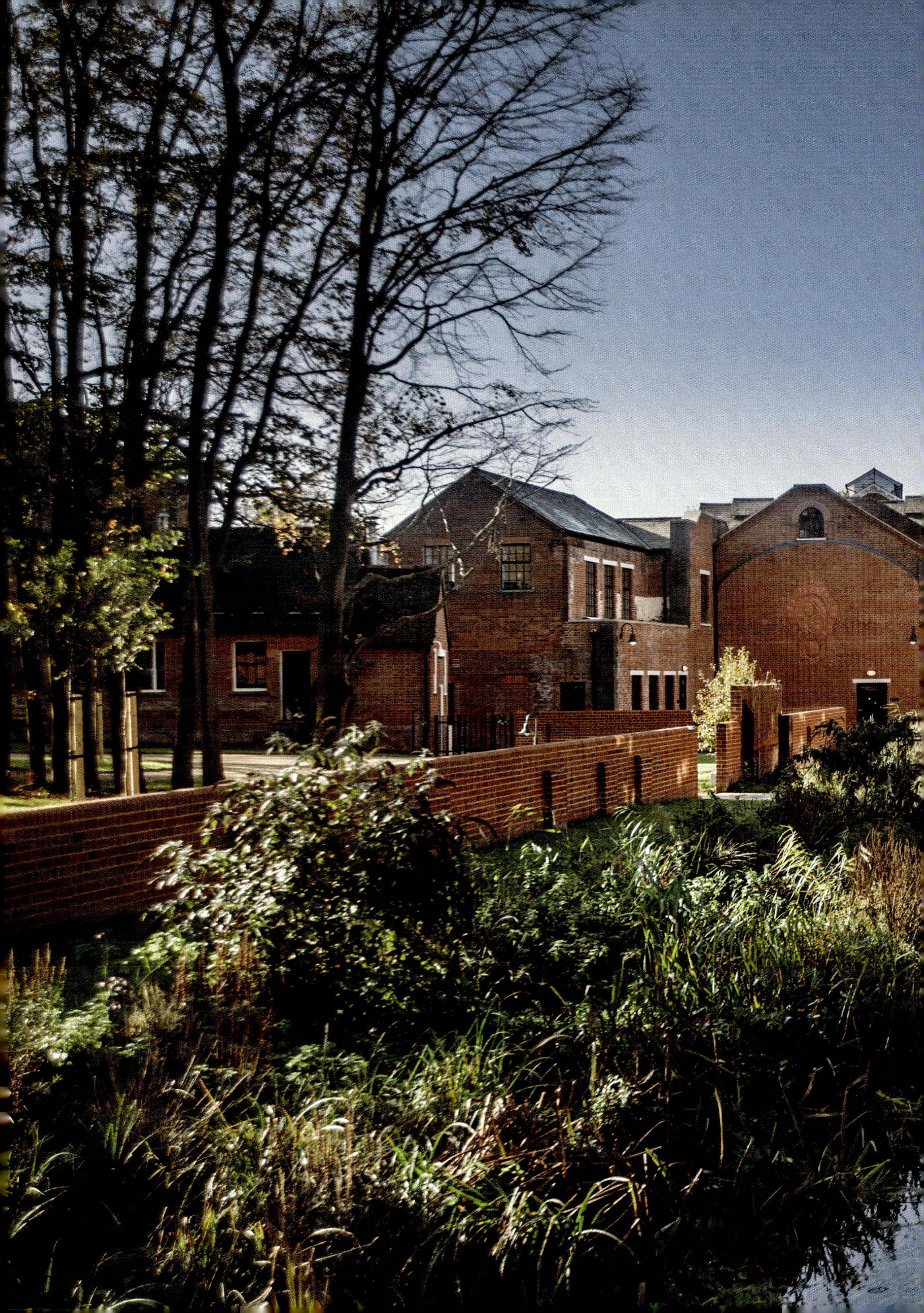

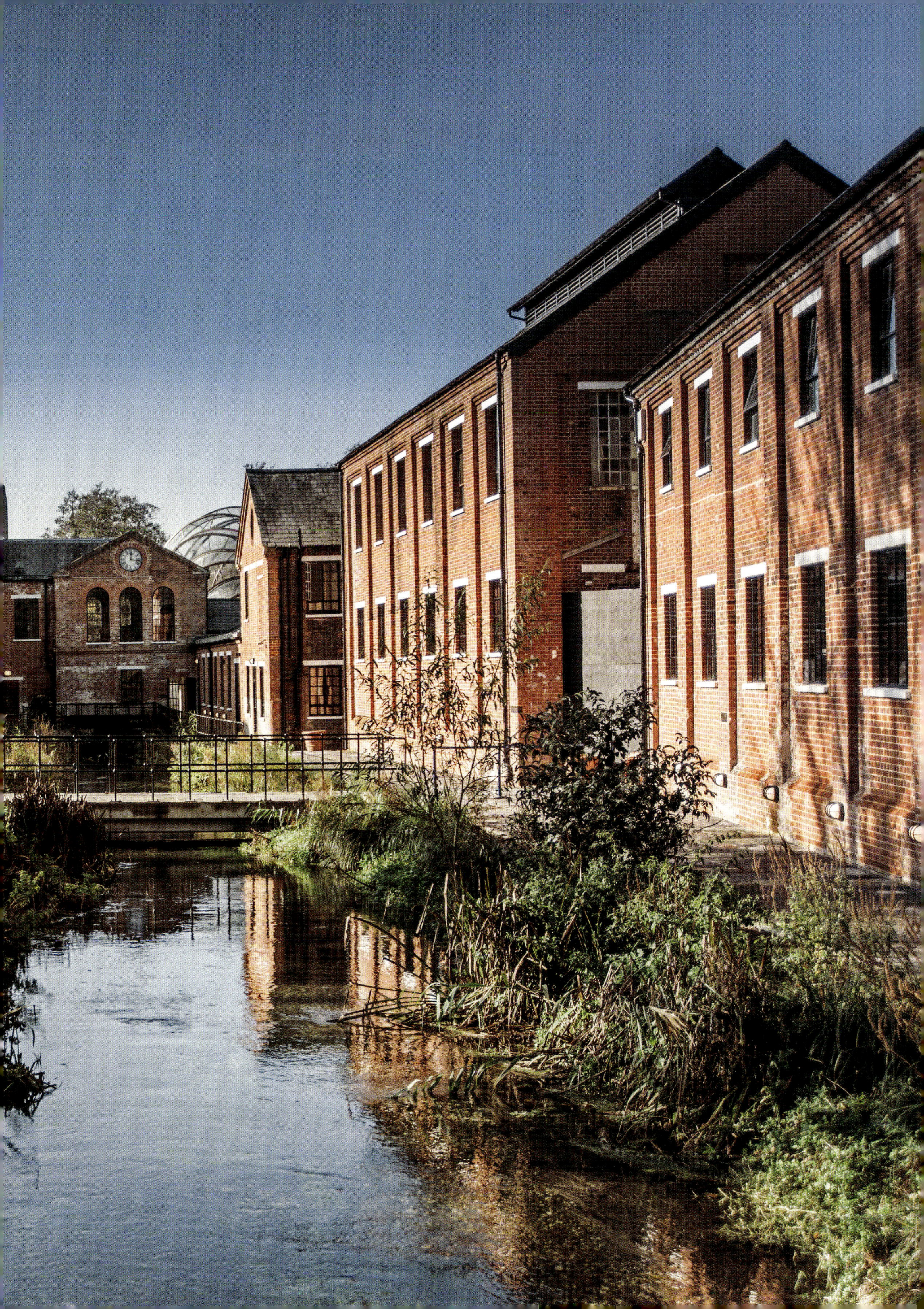

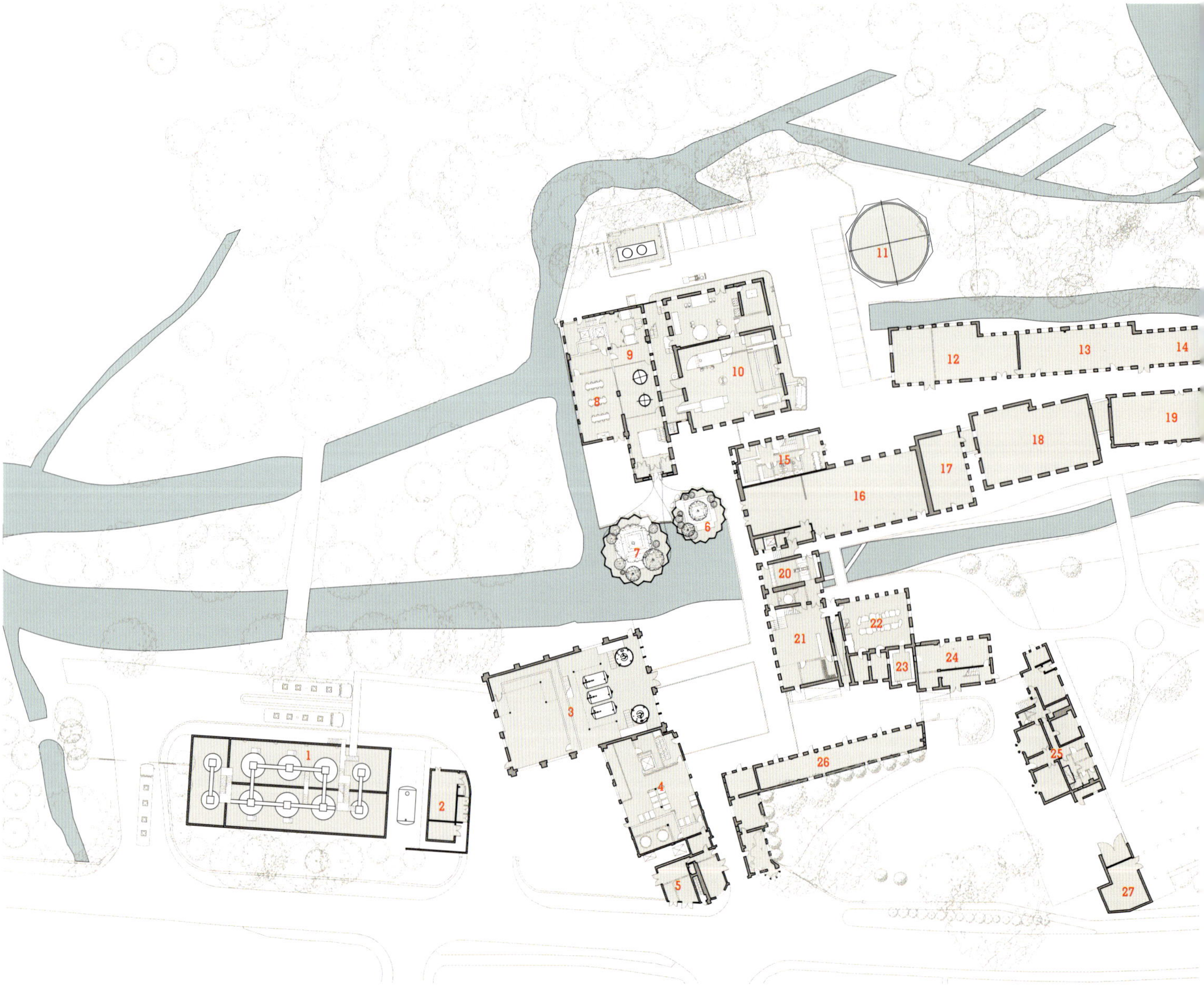

1 Tank Farm
2 MCC
3 India House
4 Botanical Store
5 Gatehouse
6 The Tropical Glass House
7 The Mediterranean Glass House
8 Dry Room
9 Daiken Still House
10 Energy Center
11 Sprinkler Tank
12 Pump House
13 Storage
14 Filter Room
15 Facilities
16 Gallery
17 Services
18 Restaurant
19 Cafe
20 Laverstoke Heritage Room
21 Entrance Hall
22 The Mill Bar
23 The Vault
24 The Gin Shop
25 Master Distillers House
26 Cottages
27 Coach House

The most striking additions to the plant are the two glasshouses, which embody the intended collision of old and new. Appearing to float in the stream that courses through the complex, the structures rise in folded glass pleats, converging and bending into the brick wall of an adjacent still house. Encompassing Mediterranean and tropical horticultures, the greenhouses showcase Bombay Sapphire's "botanicals," the plants that give gin its taste and aroma, allowing visitors "something to see and touch"[159] (visitors can inhale their essences in the neighboring Dry Room). The glasshouses appear both old-fashioned and futuristic. There is a stated allusion here to Britain's Victorian heritage of glass cloches, and more generally of glass houses,[160] while the rounded forms echo the historic copper stills visible inside the reconstructed brick shells of Laverstoke Mill. Yet the organic geometries of the structures, engineered through the use of digital parametric design to taper seamlessly into ducts, and assembled using 793 unique pieces of glass, are clearly a contemporary novelty, symbols of invention and innovation in glass design (a brand priority) writ large. Their funnel-like tops, which recirculate heat, are the most visible components of sustainability strategies devised by engineers Ove Arup & Partners, including state-of-the-art heat recovery, go-generation, a biomass boiler and photovoltaic roofs.

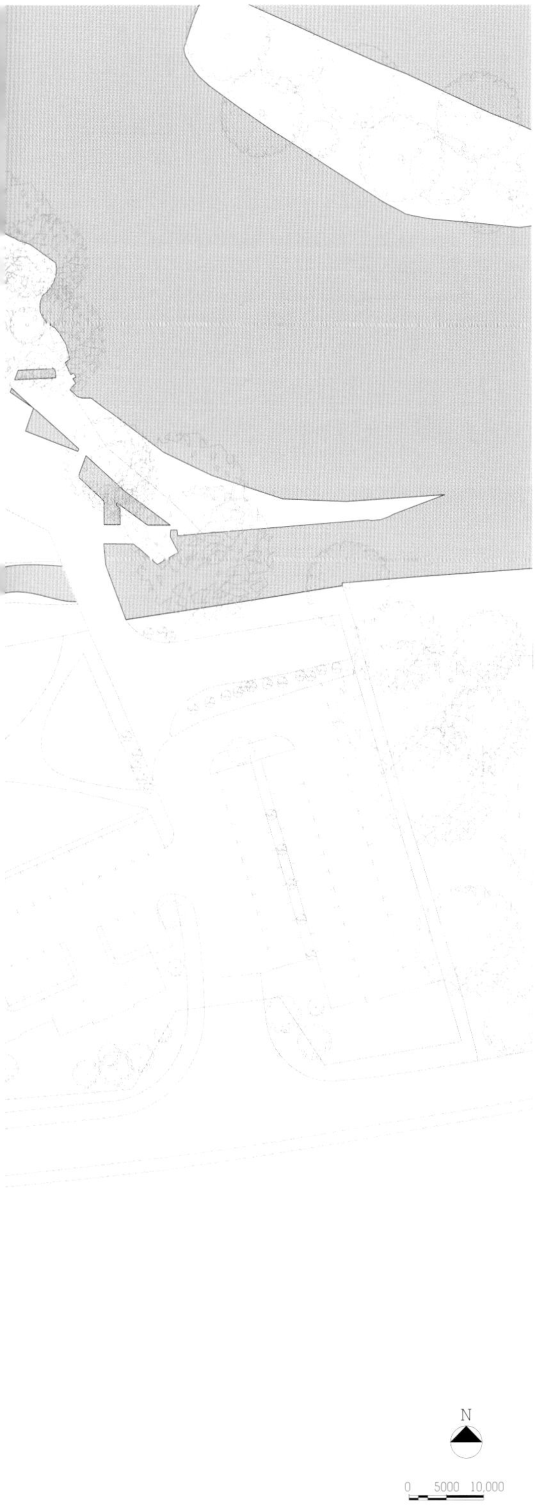

Visits to Laverstoke Mill are remarkably unstructured and relaxed. Guests are encouraged to develop an individualized experience, learning about the history of the mill and the gin by interacting with master distillers, plant managers, and knowledgeable brand ambassadors. A microchip embedded "passport" activates discreetly placed audio storytelling stations. At the center of the complex is a gallery furnished with historical displays and the company's glass art collection, and function rooms for special events. Visitors exit through a well-appointed Mill Bar, and the Gin Shop. Overall, the journey combines historic and environmental preservation and industrial technology into a new thematic experience, one that repositions Bombay Sapphire and, by extension, the always unmentioned Bacardi, as the enlightened custodians of national heritage, and reconstructs the distilling operation itself around the values of the tourist, who remains at the center of the action.

The company's inventive, measured development of brand homes throughout Europe marked a shift in Bacardi's self-perception through architecture. In the course of the twentieth century, Bacardi built iconic landmarks in steel and concrete; today such new structures are no longer the dominant strand of the story. Adaptive-use strategies, reflecting the global concern with sustainability and reusing resources, support the discrete authenticities of individual brands. The company is more focused on the low-impact strategy of merging into existing facts, supporting the idea, emergent throughout the twentieth century, that Bacardi can be at home anywhere.

The Bombay Sapphire Distillery at Laverstoke Mill, England. Courtesy Heatherwick Studio

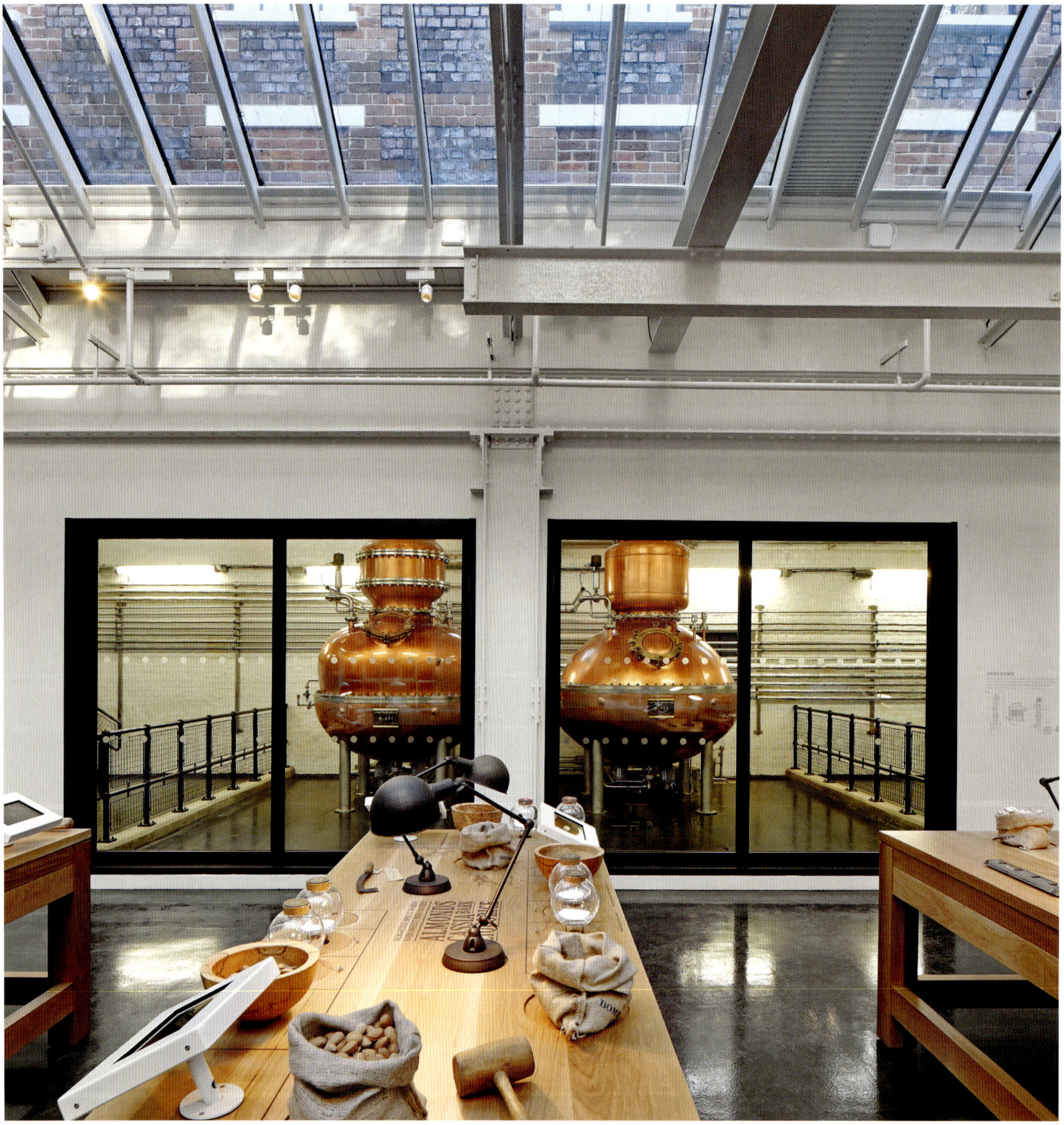

The Bombay Sapphire Distillery at Laverstoke Mill, England.
Botanical Dry Room with view of copper stills beyond. Photograph by Hufton + Crow.

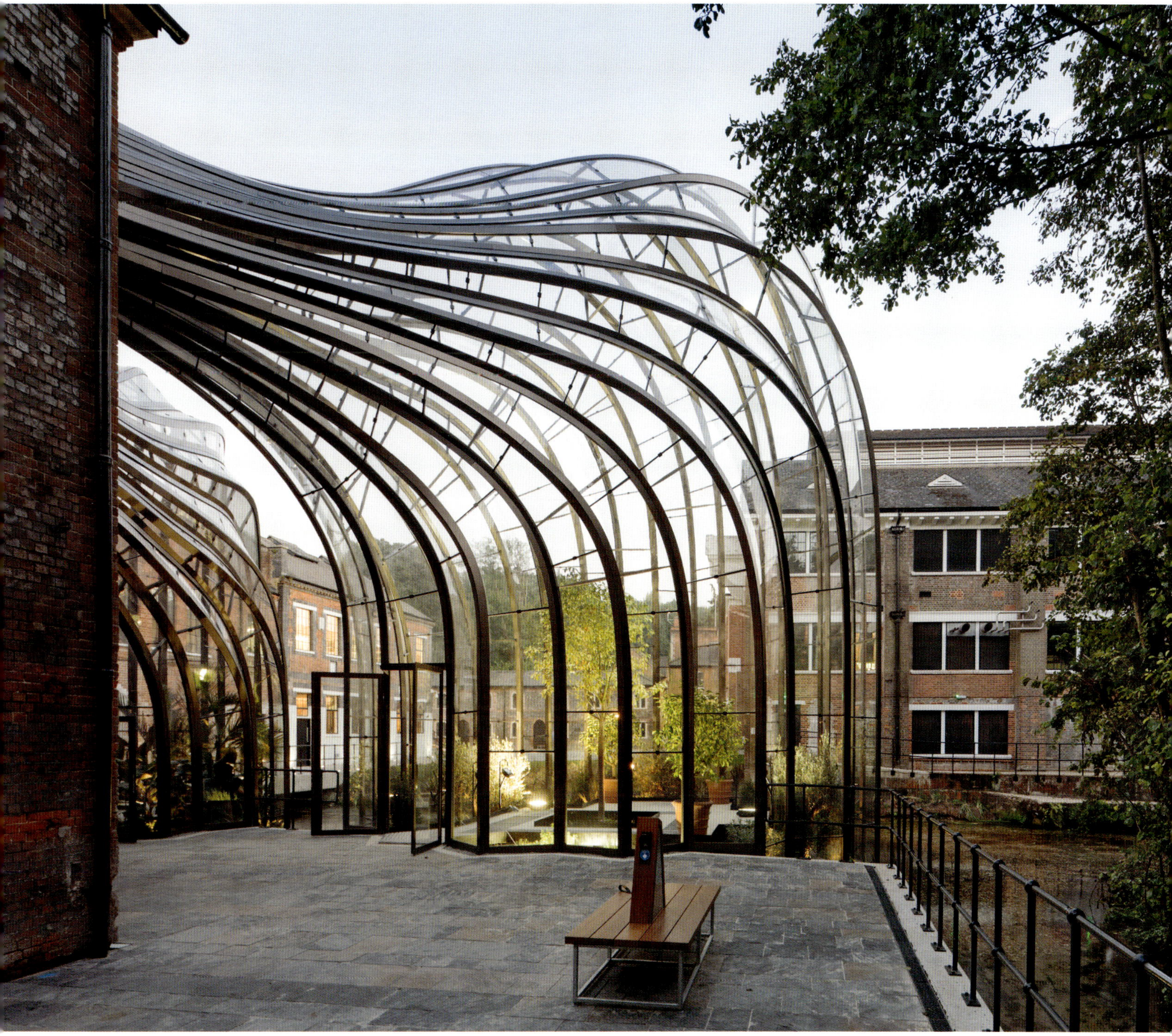

The Bombay Sapphire Distillery at Laverstoke Mill, England.
Glasshouses by Heatherwick Studio, architect, 2014. Photograph by Iwan Baan.

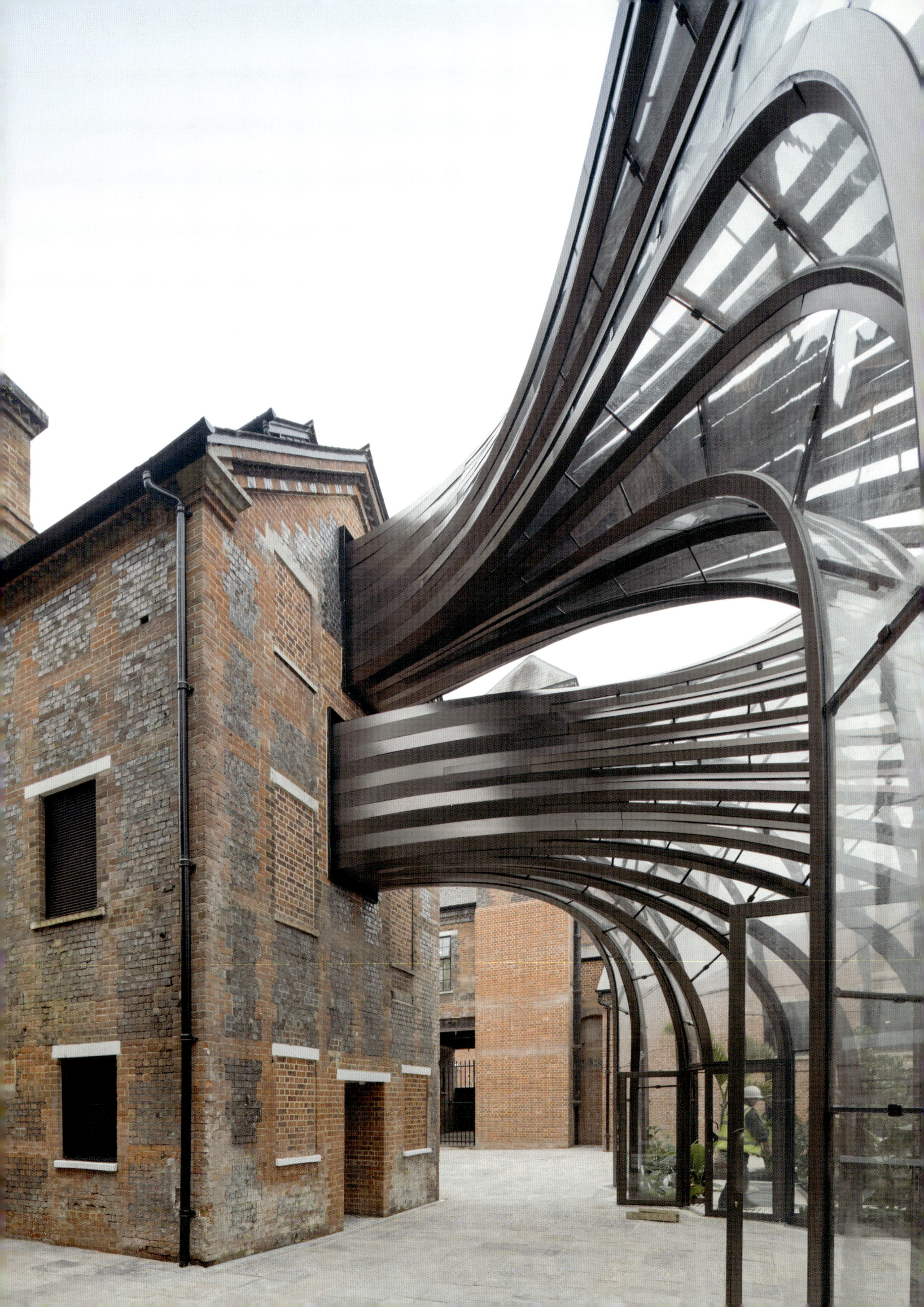

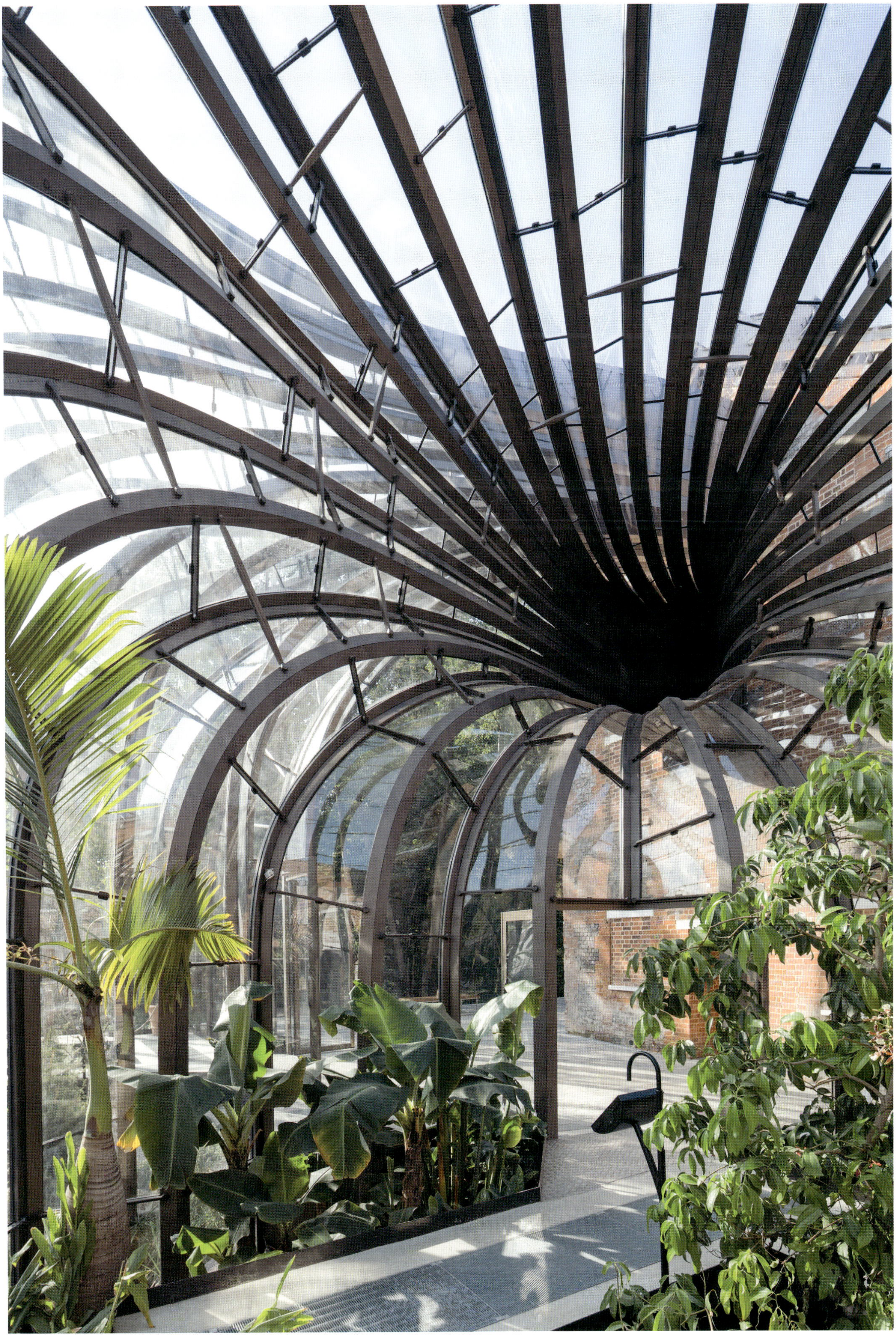

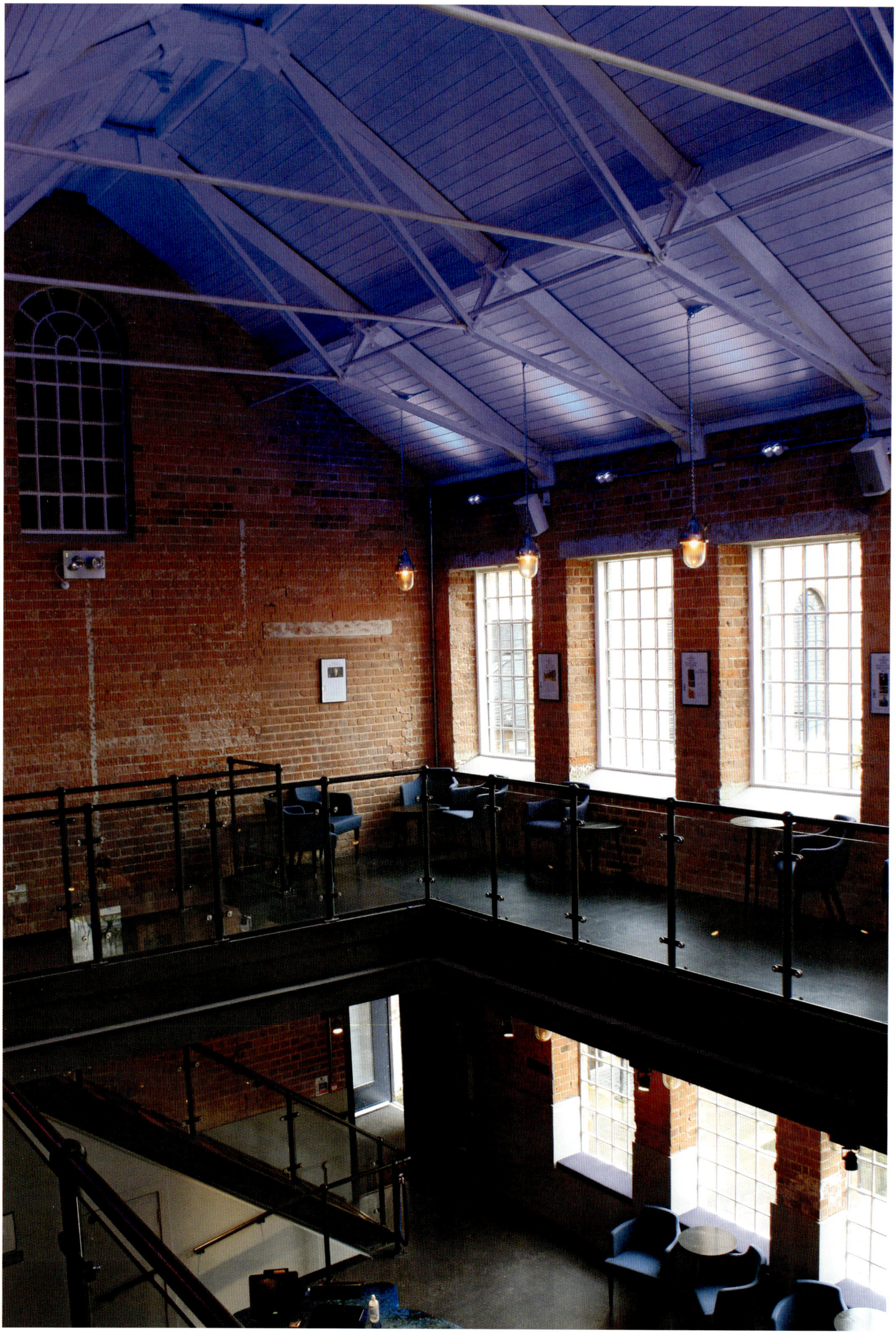

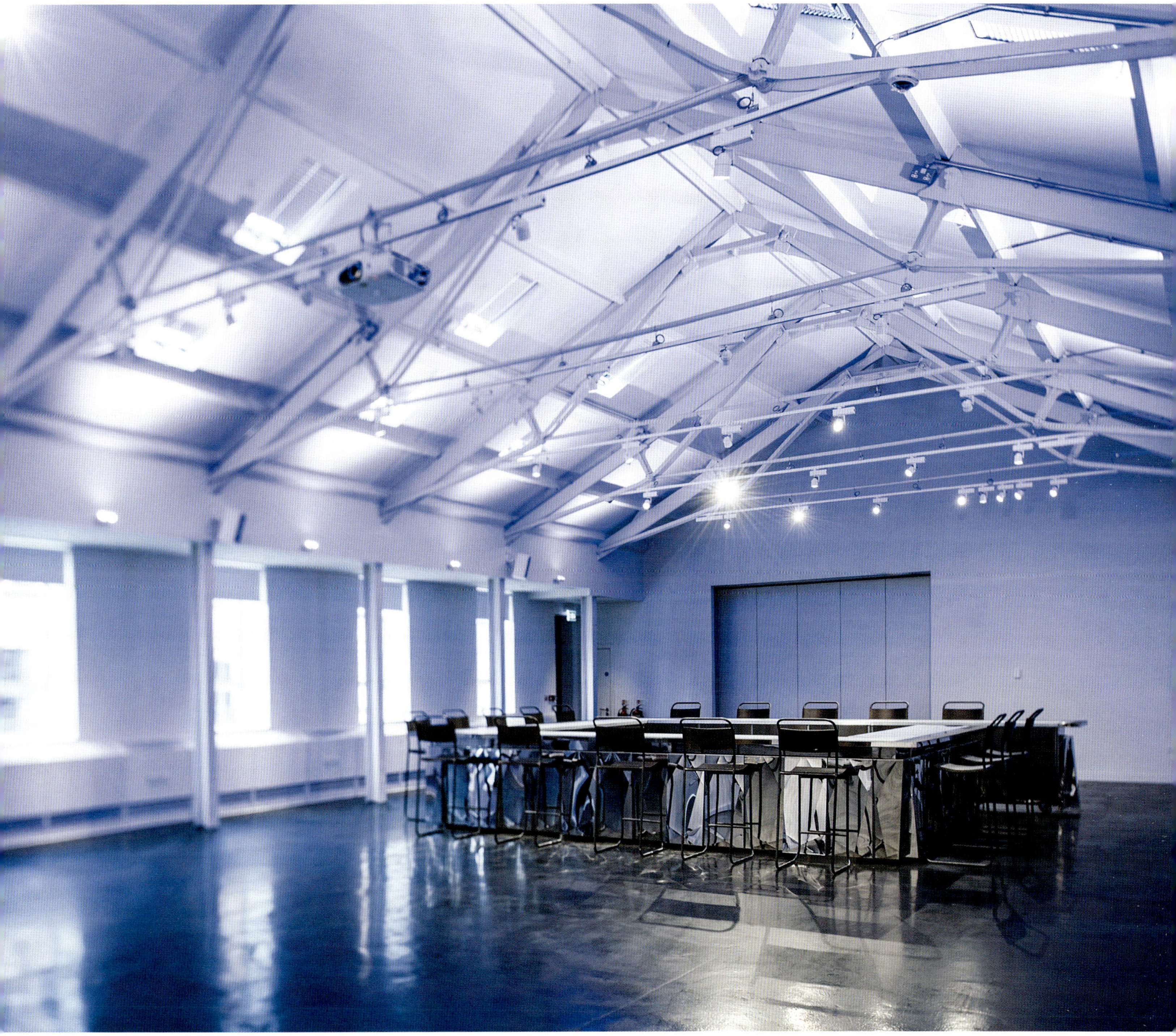

Overleaf: The Bombay Sapphire Distillery at Laverstoke Mill, England. Converging tendrils of the glasshouse duct into the walls of the adjacent Still House. Photograph by Iwan Baan.

The Bombay Sapphire Distillery at Laverstoke Mill, England. Glasshouse detail. Photograph by Iwan Baan.

Left: The Bombay Sapphire Distillery at Laverstoke Mill, England. Mill bar. Photograph by Will Brix.

Above: The Bombay Sapphire Distillery at Laverstoke Mill, England. The Gallery. Photograph by Iwan Baan.

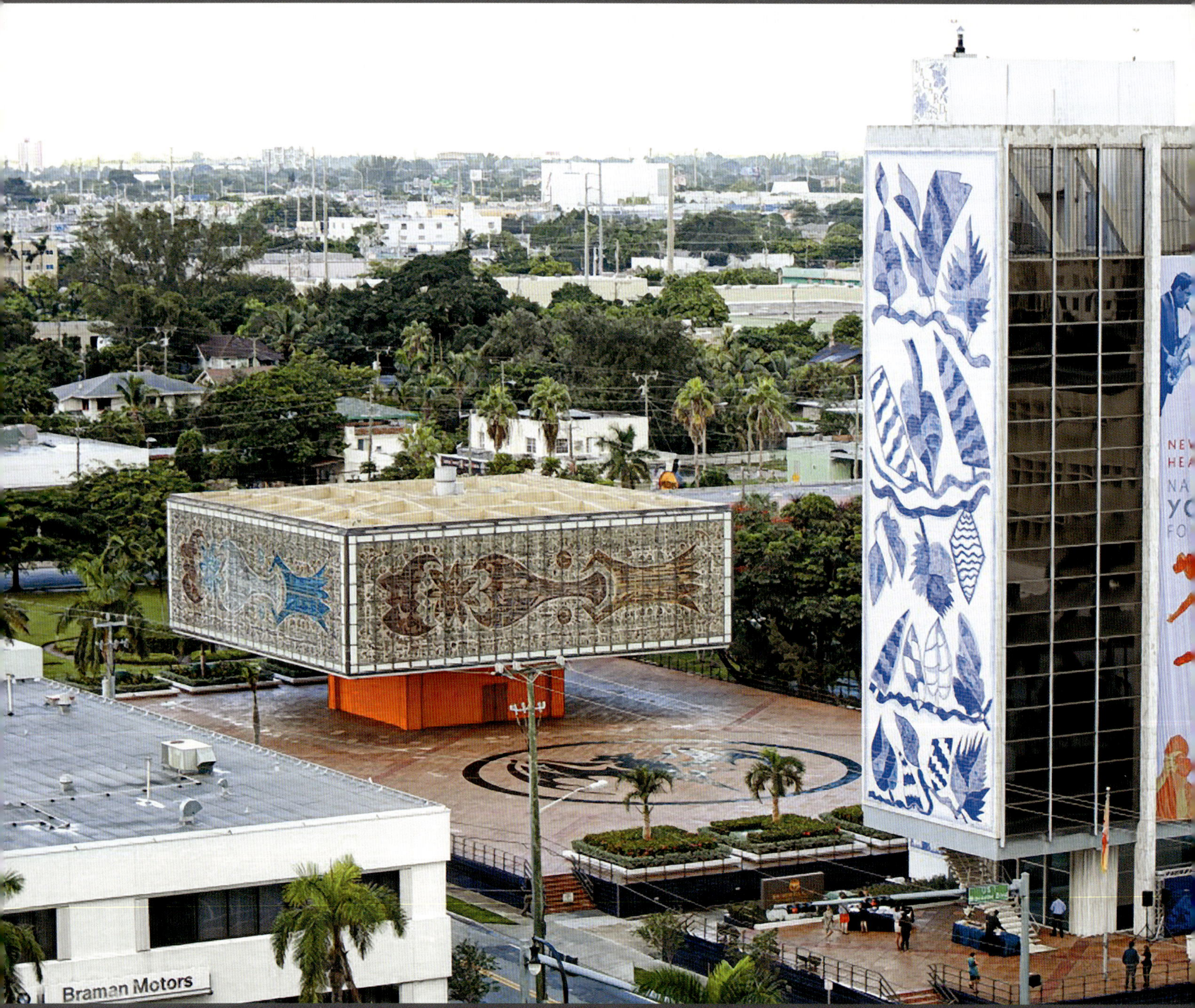
Braman Motors

BEYOND CORPORATE AMBITION

From the tin-roofed shed that housed its distillery in Santiago de Cuba to the historic châteaux and mills adapted as homes for the company's newest brands, Bacardi buildings are a record of transformation through architecture. The company is a principle custodian of this record, yet today the relevance of this history is interpreted, and perhaps even reappropriated, by players outside the corporate family. An early effort to preserve Bacardi architecture involved, curiously, the Edificio Bacardí in Havana. Defying Cold War narratives that have separated the company from its Cuban roots, the landmark was restored in 2003 under the care of the Office of the Historian of Havana. The preservation of this landmark attests that the meanings of the building go beyond Bacardi's own uses.

In establishing architectural significance, institutions and organizations around the world have taken the lead, validating Bacardi's built work through documentation and publication. The former Hatuey Brewery in El Cotorro, Cuba, and Bacardi's campus in Tultitlán, Mexico were documented by the Netherlands-based preservation movement DoCoMoMo. Tultitlan also is a UNESCO World Heritage Cultural site. The Palo Seco campus in Puerto Rico has been listed on the National Register of Historic Places (as has the company's previous headquarters in Puerta de Tierra). In the designation report of the former, Puerto Rico's Historic Preservation Officer highlights Bacardi's role as "an extremely significant representative of Hispanic Caribbean heritage within the United States' social and cultural network."[161]

In 2009, Bacardi left the Bacardi Imports Tower and surrounding campus in Miami for larger quarters in nearby Coral Gables, Florida. Although entirely new, the Bacardi Americas Building is a repository of corporate memory, comprising a substantial archive and museum and echoing artistic themes from several epochs of the company's development while also reflecting its multibrand identity.[162] Meanwhile, the original Miami Bacardi campus, now a locally designated historic structure, was repurposed in 2012 with the participation of Bacardi as the headquarters of the National YoungArts Foundation.[163] Its adaptive use echoes the type of layered identity Bacardi has created at its own homes. Public spaces and administration occupy the tile-clad hanging tower, while dance and visual arts studios are located in the lower Annex Building, behind the iconic glass tapestry that describes the conversion of sugarcane into molasses. Architect Frank Gehry, responsible for developing YoungArts' master plan, has proposed additions that will transform the complex with a new performing arts building and an outdoor park with audiovisual capabilities.

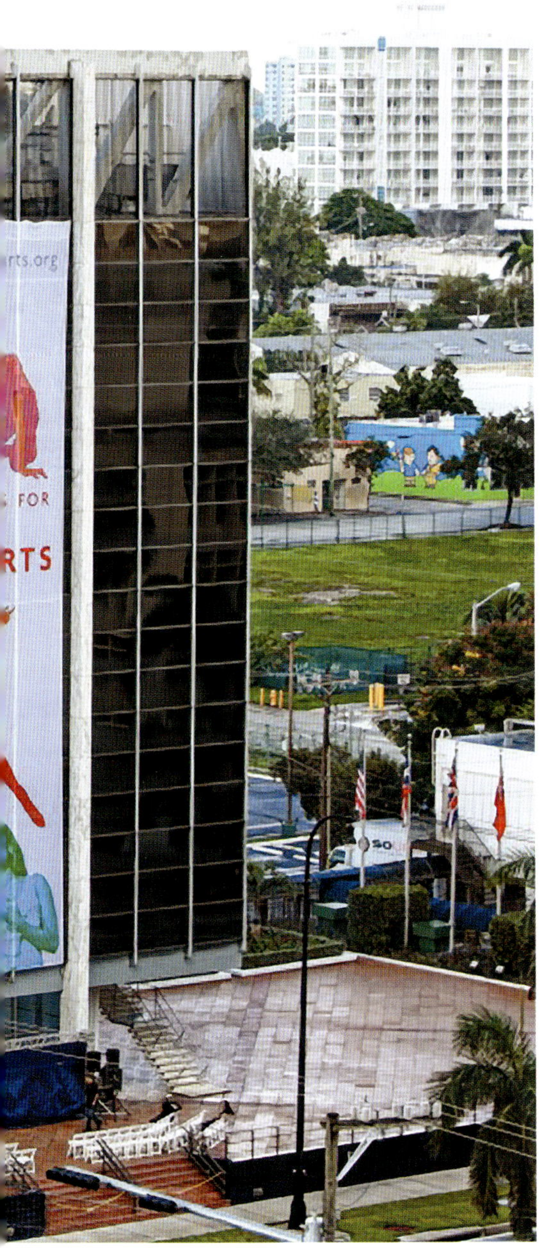

The iconic landmark Bacardi Tower and Museum building complex in Miami, Florida. In an act of civic and cultural philanthropy, Bacardi conveyed the property in 2012 to the National YoungArts Foundation at a significant reduction of its market value, ensuring that an important part of Miami's architecture and social and cultural fabric will be preserved and honored. Photography by Tomas Loewy.

According to Facundo L. Bacardi, a fifth-generation family member and current chairman of Bacardi Limited, "These buildings represented our home—they helped keep us unified coming out of Cuba.... So we wanted to make sure they ended up with someone who could extend that legacy of community."[164] As Bacardi's own history has illustrated, home is something that can unfold in surprising and adventurous ways.

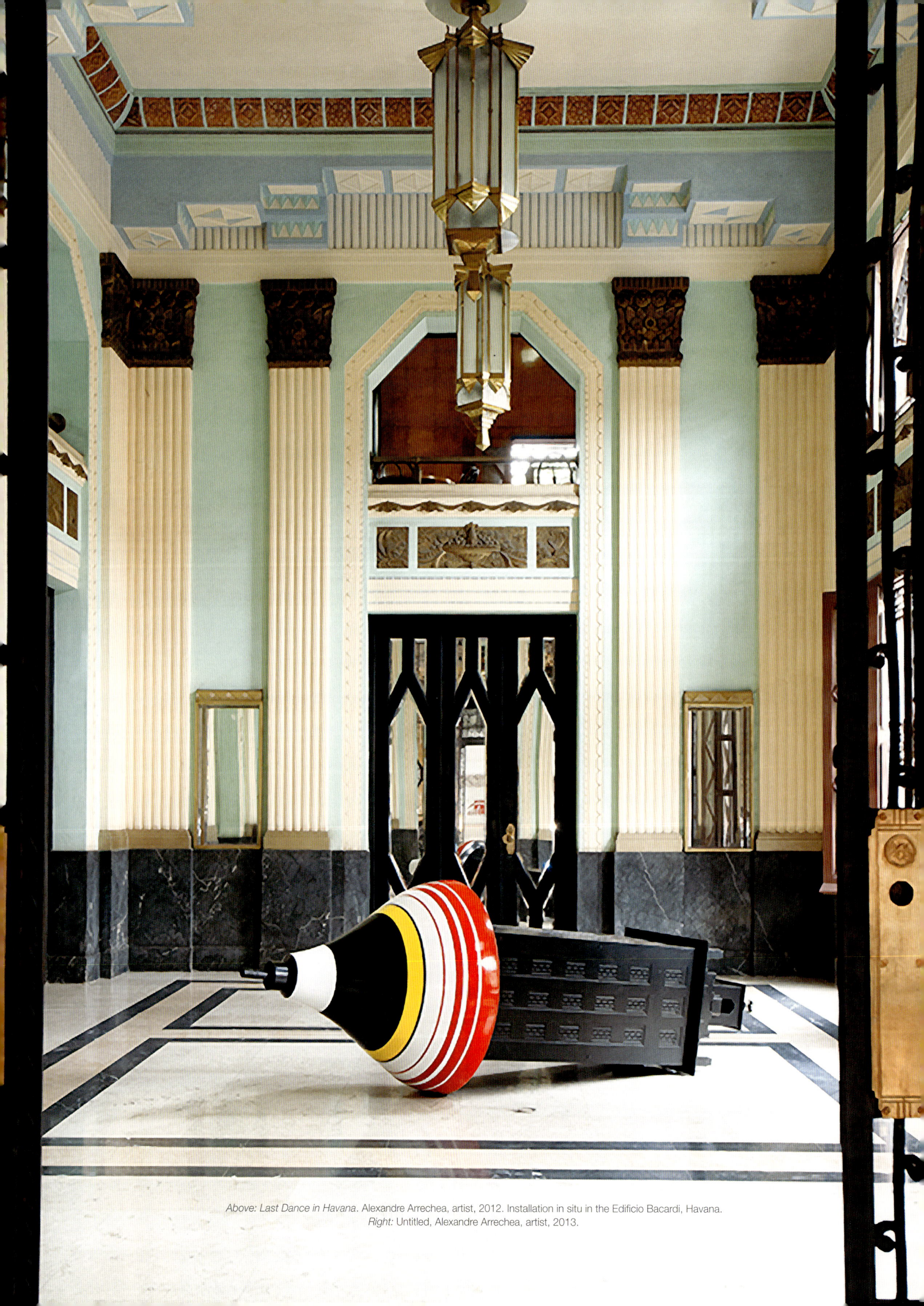

Above: Last Dance in Havana. Alexandre Arrechea, artist, 2012. Installation in situ in the Edificio Bacardi, Havana.
Right: Untitled, Alexandre Arrechea, artist, 2013.

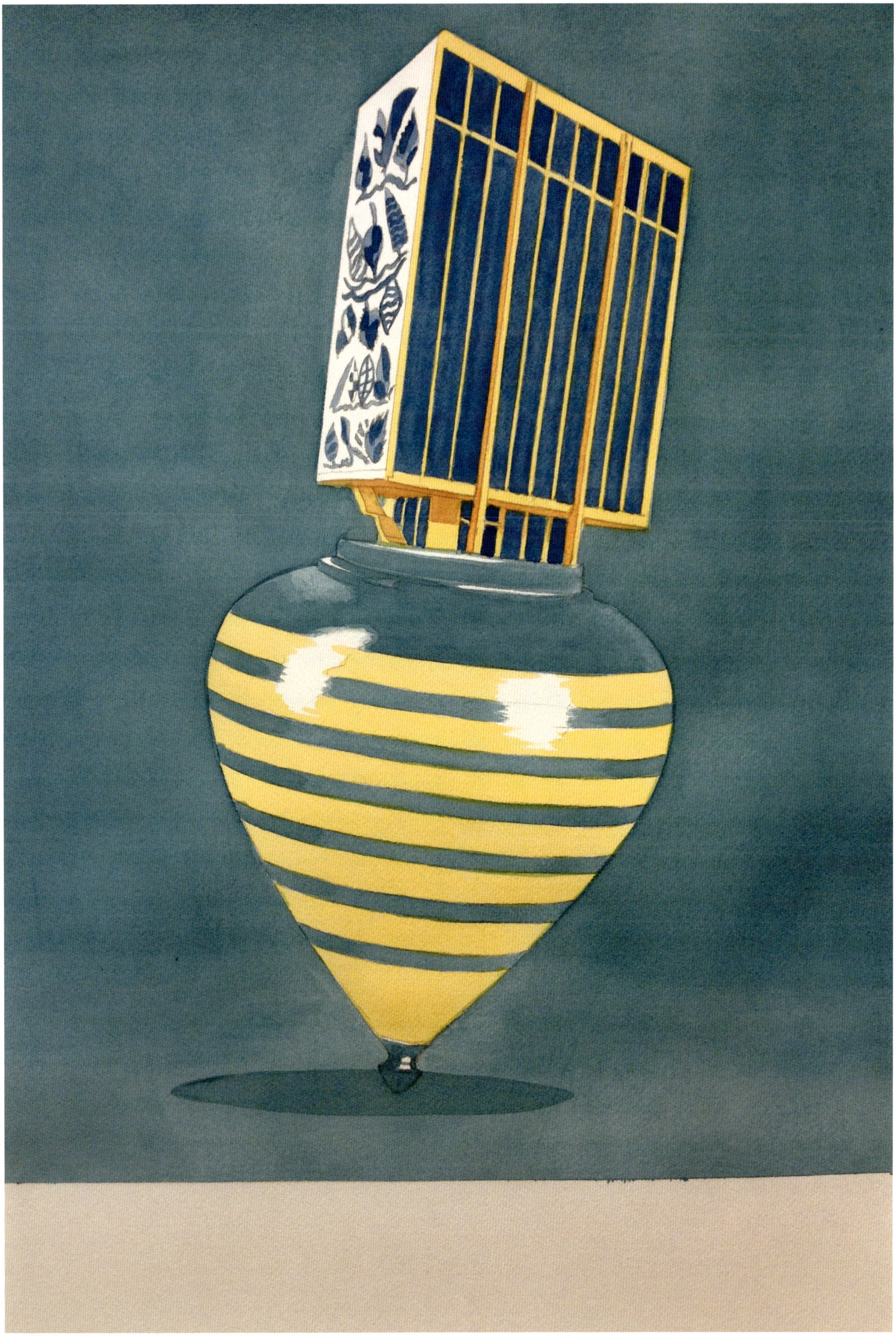

ENDNOTES

1. The research for this book was originally commissioned by the Coral Gables Museum for the 2012 exhibition *Building Bacardi: Architecture, Art and Identity*. The author was guest curator of the exhibition, and prepared an eponymous catalogue published the same year.
2. According to Bernd Schmitt and Alex Simonson, the concept of branding and brand management date back to the 1930s. They were reinvigorated in the 1980s with concepts like brand equity, brand extensions, brand image, cobranding, concept branding, brand recognition, brand awareness, and brand associations, among others. Bernd Schmitt and Alex Simonson, *Marketing Aesthetics: The Strategic Management of Brands, Identity and Image,* (New York: Free Press, 1997), 17. See also Anna Klingmann, *Brandscapes: Architecture in the Experience Economy* (Cambridge, Mass.: MIT Press, 2007) 55.
3. *Santiago de Cuba*, pamphlet, Santiago: Santiago Tourist Commission, c. 1930. Bacardi Archive.
4. The relationship between Bacardi buildings and corporate principles was a recurrent theme of *Bacardi Grafico,* the company magazine. Describing the completion of the main plant building at the Palo Seco campus by SACMAG, for instance, *Grafico* notes: "It was intended, and it has achieved that this factory could worthily be located adjacent to the remaining industrial links of Bacardi… Nor can we forget that all this installation is the product of those principles established by the founders of this organization, that if they had failed to seat any of this would have been possible." "Como se plasmó una realidad," *Bacardi Grafico* 8 (January 1958): 8.
5. The term *Creole* has various referents in Latin America. I intend the word to represent the mixing of peoples, traditions, and languages, as well as the adaptation of European cultures to American shores. It may also denote a local-born person of pure Spanish extraction, or it may refer more restrictively, as in the case of Santiago de Cuba, to members of old-line families of predominantly Spanish descent who have roots in the colonial period. "Creole," *Encyclopedia Britannica* online. Accessed March 2, 2015. http://www.britannica.com/EBchecked/topic/142548/Creole.
6. The application of chemical science to distilling flourished in the nineteenth century, especially the development of the theory of fermentation and the theory of heat. Robert James Forbes, *Short history of the art of distillation, from the beginnings up to the death of Cellier Blumenthal* (Leiden: E. J. Brill, 1948).
7. Rum was Cuba's third national product, after sugar and tobacco. Emilio Roig de Leuchsenring ed., *El Libro de Cuba: historia, letras, artes, ciencias, agricultura, industria, comercio, bellezas naturales* (Habana: Talleres del Sindicato de Artes Gráficas, 1925).
8. The term "Good Neighbor" was coined by nineteenth-century politician Henry Clay. The Good Neighbor Policy, initiated by U.S. President Franklin Delano Roosevelt in an address March 4, 1933 emphasized non-interference in the domestic affairs of Latin America, as well as reciprocal trade. "Good Neighbor Policy," *Wikipedia,* accessed February 28, 2015. http://en.wikipedia.org/wiki/Good_Neighbor_policy. See also "The AMERICAS Agree on BACARDÍ: The Good Neighbors are good mixers—and know the priceless formula for international amity and understanding," Bacardi advertisement, artist unknown, 1930s. Magazine clipping in the Bacardi Archive.
9. Bacardi marketed to, and through the agency of, American troops stationed in Santiago in the wake of the Spanish American war. In 1927, Facundo E. Bacardi noted that the American Navy "was more responsible than any other single agency for the widespread sale of the rum manufactured by his company… our greatest advertiser." "American Judges of Rum Must Bow to Navy, Cuban Manufacturer Tells L.A.: Inferior Liquor Has Spoiled Nation's Taste For Good Spirits, Bacardi Declares," *The San Bernardino County Sun*, November 2, 1927, 3.
10. See Peter Foster, *Family Spirits: The Bacardi Saga*, (Toronto: Macfarlane Walter & Ross, 1990), 24.
11. Emilio Bacardi's civic works were the result of close collaboration with the American governor Leonard Wood. They include the Calle Padre Pico steps, in Santiago (1899–1903), an urban staircase connecting the El Tivoli neighborhood to the center city. Yuniel Calzadilla-Cruz, "The Provincial Museum Emilio Bacardi Moreau: A Labyrinth to Unknown Treasures," *Ciencia en su PC* 4 (October–December 2010): 145, accessed September 7, 2012.
12. Calzadilla-Cruz, "The Provincial Museum Emilio Bacardi Moreau," 145.
13. de Leuchsenring, *El Libro de Cuba*, 755.
14. "Convinced Dry Law will Stay," *Miami Daily News-Record*, December 30, 1928, 8.
15. The terms "flying to heaven with BACARDI" and "flying from the desert with BACARDI" are borrowed from Bacardi postcard advertisements, c.1920s. The importance of the Bacardi Building as a Prohibition-era destination for American tourists is supported in numerous literary accounts. For example, in *Action in Havana*, Elinor Rice writes of the building's famous Bacardi Bar: "We couldn't go back to New York and admit we hadn't been there. It defies convention." Elinor Rice, *Action in Havana* (New York, Duell, Sloan and Pearce, 1940), 151.
16. For an excellent description of Bacardi involvement in Cuban national politics, see Tom Gjelten, *Bacardi and the Long Fight for Cuba: The Biography of a Cause* (New York: Viking) 2008. The role Bacardi played in modern Cuban culture requires further research. Certainly, the company commissioned some of Cuba's most important artists and illustrators, as well many of its great architects.
17. "Bacardi became synonymous with rum itself," as Alfredo José Estrada writes. Alfredo José Estrada, *Havana: Autobiography of a City* (New York: Palgrave Macmillan 2008). During the 1930s Bacardi defended its brand in advertisements and in the courts, asserting that in cocktail formulations, Bacardi meant BACARDI, not rum.
18. See Eduardo Luis Rodriguez, *La Habana: arquitectura del siglo XX* (Barcelona: Art Blume, 1998), 224.
19. See Jean-Francois Lejeune, "The City as Landscape: Jean Claude Nicolas Forestier and the Great Urban Works of Havana, 1925–1930" in *The Journal of Decorative and Propaganda Arts* 22, Cuba Theme Issue (1996): 150–185.
20. Architectural competitions were an important method of selecting design teams in 1920s Havana (although few competitions were devoted to commercial buildings). Prominent competitions of the period included the Colegio de Belen (1924), the Liceo de Villaclara (1924), the Consejo Nacional de Veteranos (1926), the Circulo Familiar de Guirade Melena (1926), and the Esplanada del Maine (1928). Esteban Rodriguez Castells and Pedro Martinez Inclan, *Discurso de ingreso como miembro de número de la Sección de arquitectura* (La Habana: Imprenta Molina y cía. 1936).
21. See Roberto Segre, "La Habana. Ortoxia y digresiones de la Primera Modernidad," in Carlos Sambricio and Roberto Segre, *Arquitectura en la ciudad de La Habana: primera modernidad* (Madrid: Sociedad Editorial Electa España, 2000), 80.
22. Leading Cuban architects like Manuel Copado, Manuel de Tapia Ruano, Rafael de Cárdenas, Moenck y Quintana, Rafael Goyeneche, Eugenio Cosculluela y Barreras, Hernández y Compañia, Esteban Rodriguez Castells and Rafael Fernández Ruenes, submitted entries. The jury included professors of architecture Emilio de Soto and Pedro Martínez Inclán, architects Leonardo Morales and Enrique Gil, and Bacardi president Enrique Schueg. "Concurso para el Edificio Bacardi," *El Arquitecto* (Cuba) 3:22 (January 1928): 65.
23. "Edificio cooperativo de la Habana," Catalogue. Havana: Instituto de Artes Gráficas de la Habana, 1925. The young architects Mario Romañach and Carlos Tapia are listed as delineators of the project.
24. Manuel Gallego, "El primer edificio cooperativo de la Habana (Cuba)," *La Construcción Moderna* (Madrid) 20:18 (September 30, 1923): 275–282.
25. Rafael de Cárdenas won third place. "Concurso para el Edificio Bacardi," *El Arquitecto,* 67 and "Concurso para el Edificio Bacardi: Segundo Premio," *Revista del Colegio de Arquitectos* 12:2 (February 1928): 24–30.
26. See Francisco Mujica, *History of the Skyscraper* (Paris: Archaeology & Architecture Press, 1929).
27. The Bavarian contractor Grasyma supplied stone for the Bacardi Building from sources in Germany, Sweden, Norway, Italy, France, Belgium and Hungary. From "Edificio Bacardi: Arquitectura e Ingenieria, Cuba," http://www.encaribe.org/es/article/edificio-bacardi/561.
28. The 2 Park Avenue Building in New York City by Ely Jacques Kahn, with Leon Victor Solon as colorist, exemplified the rising popularity of polychromy in commercial architecture.
29. Although outlawed during Prohibition, bars flourished as speakeasies. The speakeasy evolved a novel character, closer to a clubroom than a saloon. Abroad, similar establishments were known as "American Bars." Joseph Lanza, *The Cocktail: The Influence of Spirits on the American Psyche* (New York, St. Martin's Press, 1997), 28.
30. Contemporary press reviews contrasted the glamorous Edificio Bacardi and Bacardi Bar with the humble wood distillery of Bacardi's origins, dramatizing the company's rapid growth.

"Bacardi Rum was First Made in Old Barn," *Mount Carmel Item*, September 26, 1931, 2.

31. Massaguer, the Cuban illustrator, caricaturist, was founder and director of publications like *Social* and *Carteles*, which depicted the aspirations of modern Cubans. He also collaborated with *Life, The New Yorker, Collier's, Vanity Fair, American Magazine, Redbook, Cosmopolitan, Literary Digest, Sunday World* and *Town and Country*." "Conrado W. Massaguer," Lambiek Comiclopedia, accessed March 1, 2015, http://www.lambiek.net/artists/m/massaguer_conrado.htm.

32. Exhibition bars developed by distillers, such as the ones developed for Bacardi in Havana and New York, are today found around the world. In Havana, for example, Bacardi competitor Havana Club developed an exhibition bar in the eighteenth-century Casa del Conde de Bayona on the main cathedral square in Havana in the 1950s. In this traditional setting, American visitors were invited to "admire the handsome Old Cuban 'Patio,' the mahogany ceilings, marble floors, antique crystal chandeliers, etc." Postcard for Havana Club Rum, undated. In a similar effort, for Martini & Rossi, as many as eight Terrazze Martini were built starting in 1958, including seven in Europe and one in São Paulo, Brazil.

33. Calvert Whiskey and Seagram were located in the Chrysler Building. Schenley was located in the New York Club building; in 1937 the company moved to the Empire State Building.

34. The big four American distillers included National Distillers Products Corporation, Schenley Products Company, Seagram (Distillers Corporation), and Hiram Walker-Gooderham & Worts Ltd. The concentration of distilling was a result of post-Prohibition Federal regulations, as provided under the National Industrial Recovery Act (NIRA). "Whiskey: Newest U.S. business, oldest U.S. problem. The companies which will run it and the conditions under which it will be run. Such a subject needs a preface." *Fortune* 8:2 (November 1933), 28–29. From "Whiskey and America: A post-prohibition reunion," *Fortune* (June 24, 2012), http://fortune.com/2012/06/24/whiskey-and-america-a-post-prohibition-reunion-fortune-1933/.

35. "Name, Schenley; Age, Three … Occupation, biggest Whiskey seller in the U. S. Its brief honeymoon with Golden Wedding and the Dreary Morning After. The Success of its cheap brands; its $8,000,000 net," *Fortune* 13:2 (May 1936): 102.

36. Procuring New York's grand, but faded clubhouses was one way distillers polished their reputation in the aftermath of Prohibition. Before the construction of its iconic tower on Park Avenue, Seagram explored the purchasing either the Metropolitan Club or the Racquet and Tennis Club. Phyllis Lambert, *Building Seagram* (New Haven: Yale University Press, 2013), 17.

37. At the time the Bacardi Bar was built, Morris Sanders directed Schenley's art department. Carolyn Gray Lemaster, *Corner of the Tapestry: A History of the Jewish Experience in Arkansas, 1820s–1990s* (Little Rock: University of Arkansas Press, 1994),132, 214.

38. E.A.J. "Arresting New Murals," *New York Times*, November 25, 1934.

39. The face of the Cuban overseer in the mural was that of Grover A. Whalen, Schenley Chairman. Schenley later had the mural edited to remove the faces. Joseph Anthony Gahn, "The America of William Gropper, Radical Cartoonist," PhD Diss., Syracuse University, 1966.

40. Gropper had recently come to notice with biting caricatures in the 1932 inaugural exhibition at the Museum of Modern Art. Gahn, "The America of William Gropper," 124.

41. Lewis Mumford, *Mumford on Modern Art in the 1930s* (Berkeley and Los Angeles: University of California Press, 2008), 191.

42. The Bacardi Bar's subtle balance of colors, new materials and mural art belonged, according to Walter Rendell Storey, to the emerging and individual style of metropolitan cocktail lounges in New York, comparable to contemporary bars by Alexander Rodchenko and Russel Wright. Walter Rendell Storey, "The Cocktail Bar Creates a Décor," *New York Times*, December 23, 1934.

43. Although Lapidus used modern styling at the Seagram executive bar, he designed the adjacent Seagrams executive offices in a more traditional Tudor style. Phyllis Lambert, *Building Seagram* (Yale University Press, 2013), 6.

44. Robert A.M., Stern, Gregory Gilmartin, and Thomas Mellins, *New York 1930: Architecture and Urbanism Between the Two World Wars,* (New York: Rizzoli, 1987), 327.

45. Bacardi likely sponsored other BACARDÍ Rooms. The author has located at least one other: the BACARDÍ Room in the Biltmore Hotel, Providence, R.I.

46. In coordination with Schenley, Bacardi moved to the 35th floor of the Empire State Building in 1937. "Schenley Company Takes Offices in Empire State Building," *Altoona Tribune*, April 3, 1937, 9.

47. Houck, Bertha A. "The Root of All Art" *The Spur* 61 (February 1938): 40.

48. Everything in the Bacardi Room related to the sensibility of Gattorno's mural, which served as the backdrop for countless photos. Gleaning from the mural, Hughes selected twelve colors "typical of the Cuban countryside" that were repeated in the carpet, the ceiling, the furniture fabrics, and according to one report, the fabric of a line of dresses designed by the Havana-based Salas sisters. "Architect Turns Tables on Noted Dress Designers," *The Paris News*, February 9, 1938, 3.

49. "Goat Hunt Stirs Office Building," *Charleston Daily Mail*, January 11, 1938, 1.

50. Sarah Driscoll, "Deconstructing Hemingway's America: The Hemingway-Gattorno Relationship in the U.S.–Cuban Imagination." MA Thesis, Arizona State University, May 2011, 17.

51. The power of the corporation as the leading institution in postwar American society is explored in Peter F. Drucker, *Concept of the Corporation* (New York, The John Day Company, 1946).

52. Biographic references of Bosch invariably mention that he was a onetime Minister of Finance in Cuba. The reference seems important, as Bosch cultivated an enlightened, business-minded approach in all aspects of his tenure as president of Bacardi.

53. "Retired? Not Chief of Bacardi," *The New York Times*, March 8, 1970.

54. Enrique Varela was notably involved in at least two major projects for the Plaza Civica in Havana (later Centro Civico Martí; today Plaza de la Revolution), where he advocated for the development of a monumental core of "grandeur and magnitude." His projects included planning for an international exposition (1947–48), and the design of the Jose Martí memorial (with Jean Labatut and Juan José Sicre), completed in 1959. His work for Bacardi spanned the period between two stints as Minister of Public Works under Fulgencio Batista (1940–44, and 1952–59), and includes concurrent work on a new bottling plant for Bacardi in Santiago. "La Exposicion Internacional de la Habana de 1948," *Arquitectura Cuba* 13:146 (September 1945): 304.

55. Email from Ermina Eguilior Bosch to Allan Shulman, October 2, 2014.

56. The Havana-based engineering firm Saenz-Cancio-Martin was founded in 1948, by Luis P. Sáenz, Edilberto R. Cancio and Ignacio Martín. SACMAG left Cuba in 1960. In the following years SACMAG developed its own diaspora: SACMAG de México, S.A. de C.V. and Grupo SACMAG in Mexico; SACMAG of Puerto Rico, Inc. and SACMAG International in Puerto Rico; SACMAG Recife; and SACMAG Miami.

57. Telephone interview with Hilario Candela, July 12, 2012.

58. Letter from Jeanne Davern, Assistant to the Editor of *Architectural Record*, to Gene R. Summers, office of Mies van der Rohe, June 17, 1959. Folder 9, Mies van der Rohe Archive, Museum of Modern Art.

59. Letter from José Mario Bosch to Jeanne Davern, Assistant to the Editor of *Architectural Record*, August 31, 1959. Ron Bacardi Office Building folder 10, Mies van der Rohe Archive, Museum of Modern Art.

60. See Brett Steele, "Absolut® Mies™, Absolute Modern: Building Good Copy," *AA Files* 48 (Winter 2002), 2–14.

61. As Stover Jenkins and David Mohney point out, Johnson developed a great interest in sculptural canopies in the 1950s. Stover Jenkins and David Mohney, *The Houses of Philip Johnson* (New York: Abbeville Press Publishers, 2001), 167. The vaults in the Bosch home were, perhaps, a further development of the butterfly vaulting Johnson used in the ceilings of his own Guest House (1953) and at the Kneses Tifereth Israel Synagogue (1957). In Cuba, however, Johnson goes beyond a "decorated ceiling." Johnson's turn to plasticity finds full expression in the Roofless Church in New Harmony, Indiana (1957), and the Nahal Soreq nuclear reactor, Rehovot, Israel (1960).

62. Phyllis Lambert has demonstrated the influence of Pier Luigi Nervi on Philip Johnson's design for the Monaco Hotel in Havana. Phyllis Lambert, "Philip Johnson: Breaking with Modernism—The 'Whence & Whither' of It." in Emmanuel Petit ed., *Philip Johnson: The Constancy of Change* (New Haven: Yale University Press, 2009).

63. Although the Bosch home was never completed, Johnson reiterated elements of the home two years later in the design for a water folly on his New Canaan, Connecticut estate. Jenkins and Mohney, *The Houses of Philip Johnson*, 167.

64. Although it is unclear to what degree the decision to commission Mies can be attributed to

Philip Johnson, Enrique Gutierrez, architect with SACMAG, notes that Johnson accompanied Mies on his visits to Cuba. Interview with Enrique Gutierrez, October 17, 2014. By contrast, notes by Gene Summers of a January 21, 1957 telephone conversation with Philip Johnson attributes the commission to the recommendation of SACMAG's Luis Saenz. Ron Bacardi Office Building Folder 1, Mies van der Rohe Archive, Museum of Modern Art.

65. Georgina George, "Report on Bacardi Office Building." April 1954 (on Saenz Cancio Martin letterhead). Ron Bacardi Office Building Folder 1, Mies van der Rohe Archive, Museum of Modern Art.

66. See Brynnar Nelson Swenson, "The Corporate Form: Capital, Literature, Architecture." PhD Diss., University of Minnesota, 2008, 225.

67. *Fortune* identified American corporate headquarters as the "architecture that most vividly reveals the life of its time." Francis Bello, "Architecture's New Technology," *Fortune* 53:1 (March 1956): 128–130, quoted in Benjamin Sitton Flowers, *Skyscraper: The Politics and Power of Building New York City in the Twentieth Century* (Philadelphia: University of Pennsylvania Press, 2009), 141.

68. The site chosen for the Bacardi Headquarters was at the eastern terminus of Avenida General Wood, a broad paseo that connected via the Paseo Marti to the Bacardi factories along Carretera Bacardi.

69. "My ideal office is one where there are no partitions, where everybody, both offices and employees, are seeing each other." Letter from José Maria Bosch to Ludwig Mies van der Rohe, February 14, 1957. Ron Bacardi Office Building Folder 1, Mies van der Rohe Archive, Museum of Modern Art.

70. Mies van der Rohe called the single big room "the most economical and most practical way of building today… The purposes that the building serves change continually, and we can't afford to knock down the building every time. Therefore we revised Sullivan's formula 'form follows function' and constructed a practical and economical room, and we fitted its function in." C. Norberg-Schulz, "Ein Gespräch mit Mies van der Rohe," *Baukunst und Werkform* 11, (1958): 615–616. From Immo Boyken and Hans J. Oestmann, "Ludwig Mies van der Rohe and Egon Eiermann: The Dictate of Order," *Journal of the Society of Architectural Historians* 49:2 (June 1990): 133–153. Mies's prior investigation of structural models for universal space included projects like the Fifty x Fifty House (1950–52) and IIT's Crown Hall (1956). The Bacardi project, done collaboratively with Havana-based engineers and architects SACMAG, brought the idea into a new synthesis, using refinements of technique, proportions and materials. Phyllis Lambert has described Mies's process of working through and improving a single structural type as "the slow unfolding of architecture. Phyllis Lambert, "Mies Immersion: Introduction," in Phyllis Lambert, *Mies in America* (New York: H.N. Abrams, 2001), 482, 490.

71. As Brett Steele has pointed out, Mies had a career-long interest in highly realistic project simulations, and used the technique of photo-collage extensively. These collages, along with the hyper-realistic model he developed for the project, were part of a strategy to depict characteristics like transparency, materiality, and contrast. Brett Steele, "Absolut® Mies™, Absolute Modern: Building Good Copy." *AA Files* 48 (Winter 2002): 2–14. Mies personally selected the Bacardi photo-collage for the cover of the July 1958 issue of *Architectural Design*, which featured the Bacardi's Santiago offices.

72. The constructive art of the Bacardi Headquarters building has been analyzed in relation to traditional building practices, particularly those made popular in the nineteenth-century theories of architect Gottfried Semper. Most recently, Martino Doimo's *Arte muraria, spazio, tettonica…* (Building Art, Space, Tectonics) dissects the Bacardi headquarters in terms of its tectonic elements. Martino Doimo, *Arte muraria, spazio, tettonica, Mies, Bacardi Building Cuba, elementi della costruzione—figure della composizione,* (Treviso, Canova, impr., 2009).

73. James Speyer, *Mies van der Rohe,* (Chicago: Hillison & Etten Company, 1968).

74. Alfred Neumeyer, describing Berlin's Neue Nationalgalerie, a successor to the unbuilt Bacardi project, called the structure "classical" without Greece and without the Renaissance, merely by the purity of its materials and the visualization of its proportionate relations." Alfred Neumeyer, "Berlin's New National Gallery," *Art Journal* 29:1, (Autumn 1969): 92–93.

75. Letter from Ignacio Martin to MVDR office, July 16, 1959. Ron Bacardi Office Building Folder 9, Mies van der Rohe Archive, Museum of Modern Art.

76. In 1958, a proposal was advanced in Santiago de Cuba expanding the Avenida de los Olivos directly through Bacardi's site. Postcard from José Maria Bosch to Gene Summers, MVDR office. June 17, 1958. Ron Bacardi Office Building, Folder 2, Mies van der Rohe Archive, Museum of Modern Art.

77. The common heritage of Bacardi and the Neue Nationalgalerie (New National Gallery) in Berlin was observed in an exhibition titled "There is a Reason," opened September 2010, at the Neue Nationalgalerie.

78. Ernest Hemingway, *The Old Man and the Sea* (New York, Scribner, 1952).

79. Hatuey was known popularly as "un indio con dos canoas." According to Estrada, it was "the quintessential lager of Havana." Estrada, 26.

80. "Un Orgullo Nacional," print advertisement for Hatuey featuring "La Gran Fabrica de Cerveza Hatuey: Modelo," 1949. Bacardi Archive.

81. Email from Ermina Eguilior Bosch to Allan Shulman, September 26, 2014.

82. The Mira Rosich firm, well known for the Art Deco Lopez-Serrano Building in Havana, included architects Ricardo Mira, Miguel Rosich and Ana Maria Relano *Rosich*. Miguel Rosich later completed many projects at the Bacardi distillery in Puerto Rico.

83. The cylindrical corner at El Cotorro can be compared to American commercial projects like the May Co. at Wilshire and Fairfax by architects Albert C. Martin & S.A. Marx, 1940; the NBC's studio at Hollywood Radio City by architect John Austin, 1938; and the Canada Dry Building by architect Walter M. Cory, 1940.

84. "Fascinante Proceso de la Elaboracion," *Bacardi Grafico*8 (January 1958): 21.

85. A vivid account of the lunch to celebrate Hemmingway's Nobel Prize can be found in Guillermo Cabrera Infante, "El Viejo y La Marca," *Ciclón* 2:5 (September 1956), republished in Guillermo Cabrera Infante and Stephen D. Gingerich, *The New Centennial Review* 2:2, Origins of "Postmodern" Cuba (Summer 2002): 110–115.

86. "Windshield views" of roadside architecture were explored a decade later in British art critic Lawrence Alloway's 1959 photo documentation of the General Motors Technical Center, published in "City Notes," *Architectural Design* 29:1 (1959): 34–35. See also Kevin Lynch Donald Appleyard and John R. Myer, *The View from the Road* (Cambridge: M.I.T. Press for the Joint Center for Urban Studies of the Massachusetts Institute of Technology and Harvard University, 1964.

87. Samuel C. Beesch and G. M. Shull, "Fermentation," *Industrial & Engineering Chemistry* 48:9 (1956): 1585–1603.

88. "Más de 15,000 personas en la inauguración de la Cerveceria Central de Manacas, en Las Villas." *Diario de la Marina,* November 17, 1953. Also "Cerveceria Central Manacas Recuerdo de la Inauguracion Nov. 15, 1953 HATUEY, la gran cerveza de Cuba, abre su tercera cerveceria en Manacas." Postcard. Accessed at Cubalabella.com

89. Gustavo F. Araoz, Jr., "Statement of Significance," National Register of Historic Places Registration Form for Carcel de Puerta de Tierra. NPS Form 10-300, (July 12, 1976): 8.

90. Roberto Segre, *Arquitectura antillana del siglo XX* (La Habana: Arte y Literatura, 2003), 76.

91. The ICP's purchase of the Bacardi Building was not without controversy. When the Institute of Puerto Rican Culture's director Ricardo Alegria communicated his intention to purchase the building, Bosch reportedly replied, "You are worse than Fidel." Eric Wills, "Guarding the Glories of San Juan: Preservationists are saving sites in and around Puerto Rico's capital city," *Preservation* 61:1, (January–February 2009). Accessed March 2, 2015. http://www.preservationnation.org/magazine/2009/january-february/san-juan.html

92. The ICP's renovation and adaptive use of the Hospital Civil/Bacardi Building was executed by architect Jesus Amaral of Amaral y Morales Arquitectos (Puerto Rico), based on preliminary drawings by Spanish architect Manuel Fernández Huidobro. It was completed in 1973. "Detalle Archivo: Archivo General de Puerto Rico," *Censo-Guía de Archivos de España e Iberoamérica*. http://censoarchivos.mcu.es/CensoGuia. Accessed February 6, 2015.

93. Bacardi acquired the 95-acre tract in 1937.

94. George C. Nimmons quoted in Louise A. Mozingo, *Pastoral Capitalism,* (Cambridge, Massachussetts & London, England: MIT Press, 2011), 28.

95. The design of the distillery building remains un-attributed. W. Donald Christie, M.E. Consulting Engineer, of New York City, remains the only name associated with the development of the building. Christie's drawings in the archives of the Palo Seco plant described the distillery's structure and plant equipment.

96. Enriqueta Schueg de Bosch reputedly designed the gardens at Palo Seco (as well as those at La Galarza and Miami. It is likely her landscape aesthetic influenced countless other Bacardi facilities as well). Such gardens, apparently undocumented, were an important component of the Bacardi image. Pepin Bosch emphasized the value of such beautification, for instance in José Mario Bosch, "Como se plasmó una realidad," *Bacardi Grafico* 8 (January 1958): 7.

97. Concurrent to the development of the home in Palo Seco, Bosch commissioned Klumb & Armesen to design a cinema and music hall in Santiago de Cuba. The cinema, never completed, comprised a fan-shaped hall, vaguely reminiscent of the recently completed Teatro Warner Radiocentro (cinema Yara) in Havana by Emilio de Junco (1945–47). The site planning includes gardens and a pond, and tropicalist canopies that connect parking areas to the theater. Klumb drawings in the collection of the Archivo de Arquitectura y Construcción de la Universidad de Puerto Rico.

98. Luz Marie Rodriguez, "Klumbumbus descubre el Trópico: Henry Klumb, Puerto Rico y la modernidad en lo existente," *Arquitextos* 120:4 (May 2010), Vitruvium.com.br

99. The main plant building, as completed in 1958, appears only loosely based on the project by Toro Ferrer. Construction Documents, dated 1956, were prepared by the Cuban firm Saenz-Cancio-Martin with Puerto Rican engineers Jose Benitez Gautier-Jose L. Capacete. Archives of the Bacardi Distillery, Puerto Rico.

100. SACMAG of Puerto Rico was a successor to the Havana-based architecture and engineering firm SACMAG.

101. In addition to the Pepin Bosch beach house design by Philip Johnson, conical vaults were also used by Felix Candela, for instance at the Chemical Sciences Auditorium at the Ciudad Universitaria (UNAM), México DF (Felix Candela with Guillermo Rosell and Enrique Yanez, 1952).

102. Enrique Vivoni, Aileen Castañeda, and Daniel Expósito Sánchez collaborated to identify the mural artist. Email message to author. October 14, 2014.

103. The Bacardi distillery in Palo Seco was listed on the National Register of Historic Places in 2010. Carlos A. Rubio Cancela, State Historic Preservation Officer, Puerto Rico State Historic Preservation Office. "National Register of Historic Places Registration Form for Bacardi Distillery," June 17, 2010. NPS Form 10-900: 8.

104. An analysis partly based on Lynn A. Isabella and Ted Forbes, "Grupo Bacardi de Mexico S.A.," (Charlottesville, VA: University of Virginia Darden Business Publishing, 1994).

105. Bacardi acquired the La Galarza hacienda in 1955, likely with the assistance of the Mexican president Adolfo Ruiz Cortines. As in Puerto Rico, new plant developments were facilitated by strategic relationships with the government of Mexico, managed by Ernesto Robles-Leon, president of Grupo Bacardi de Mexico, S.A., from the mid-1950s. The management style of Ernesto Robles-León is described well in Isabella and Forbes, "Grupo Bacardi," 4–5.

106. Historically, such haciendas combined plantation and factory enterprises under a single feudal system, but this practice had been mostly abandoned by the 1920s. David F. Ronfeldt, *Atencingo; the politics of agrarian struggle in a Mexican ejido* (Stanford, Calif., Stanford University Press, 1973).

107. Colin Faber, *Candela, the shell builder* (New York, Reinhold Pub. Corp., 1963), 113–114.

108. The facilities at La Galarza, based on a novel plant design by Bacardi engineer Juan Grau, included an on-site laboratory. La Galarza's technologically advanced equipment, like its distillery tower, set the tone for new Bacardi plants, like those in Recife and Nassau. The Bacardi laboratory subsequently moved to New Providence Island, Bahamas, then to Jacksonville, Florida. Foster, *Family Spirits*, 117.

109. Architects de la Colina and Mestre are noted for their work for private corporations in Mexico City. Examples include Seguros La Comercial (1964) and COMERMEX (1970).

110. Only three of the originally projected nine vaults were completed in 1959. Antonio Candela and Juan Antonio Tonda added three matching vaults in 1971.

111. Maria Garlock, and D.P. Billington, *Félix Candela: Engineer, Builder, Structural Artist* (Yale University Press, 2008), 154.

112. Carlos Brillembourg, "Great Curves," *Architects Newspaper*, April 20, 2012.

113. *Arts & Architecture* described Felix Candela's concrete shells as "the most provocative structural type in Mexico in the 50s-60s … evoking connection to the ancient temple and church builders." Félix Candela, "The shell as space enclose," *Arts & Architecture* 72

114. (January 1955): 12.

115. "Four Great Pours," *Architectural Forum* 115 (September 1961): 104-115.

116. According to Candela biographer Colin Faber, Cubiertas Ala constructed 3,000,000 square feet of umbrellas in Mexico. Maria Garlock, and D.P. Billington, *Félix Candela: Engineer, Builder, Structural Artist* (New Haven: Yale University Press, 2008). In 1958, Candela noted: "Although we have built almost all known forms and some original, the most perfect and economical solution has been the rectangular umbrella." Letter from Felix Candela to José Benitez Gautier, November 4, 1958. Felix Candela Collection; Avery Architectural and Fine Arts Library, Columbia University.

117. Letter from Ignacio Martin (SACMAG) to MVDR, October 7, 1958, Folder 9, Mies van der Rohe Archive, Museum of Modern Art.

118. Franz Schulze and Edward Windhorst, *Mies van der Rohe: A Critical Biography, New and Revised Edition* (Chicago: University of Chicago Press, 2012), 196–201. Accessed online February 13, 2015. www.library.miami.edu.

119. Beside the Bacardi projects, Mies planned one other building in Latin America: the United States consulate in São Paulo, Brazil (1957), although it was never built.

120. The critique, as Salvador Lizárraga Sánchez notes, centers on the suspicion that the Tultitlán is "either a second-rate copy of a larger unbuilt project for Bacardi in Cuba or that it is at best an average, late-Miesian building mechanically reproduced from the architect's Chicago office alongside many others in the last years of his career." Salvador Lizárraga Sánchez, "Bacardi Breezer," *AA Files* 62 (2011): 104.

121. Sigfried Giedion, *Space, Time and Architecture* (Cambridge: Harvard University Press, 1967), quoted in quoted in Salvador Lizárraga Sánchez, "Bacardi Breezer," *AA Files* 62 (2011): 104–107.

122. The Bacardi Centennial was marked by the publication *Bacardi, 1862 1962*. Samuel Gallo, *Bacardi, 1862–1962*, (S.l.: Bacardi Co., 1962).

123. In the aftermath of the Cuban Revolution, SACMAG of Puerto Rico became a successor firm to SACMAC.

124. TJ Hils, "What's New? That Building in Miami," *Construction Craftsman* 4:1 (January 1965): 14-16.

125. Arthur Drexler has explored civic considerations in the development of the Seagram Building. He has noted that the Seagram tower's reduced footprint was indicative of the project's independence from commercial considerations. Arthur Drexler, "The Seagram Building," *Architectural Record* 124 (July 1958): 139.

126. Antonio Quintana of Quintana, Rubio and Pérez Beato Arquitectos with Luis Saenz of Saenz-Cancio-Martin designed the Enriqueta Fernandez Apartment Building in Havana (1950–55). Predicting the strategy Gutiérrez and Saenz used in Miami, the core of the building — comprising stairs, elevators, and bathrooms—was located in an independent tower to permit the exceptional lightness of the main structure. See description of the building in Eduardo Luis Rodriguez, *The Havana Guide: Modern Architecture 1925–1965* (New York: Princeton Architectural Press, 2000). 130.

127. Pepin Bosch's longtime friend, the architect and painter Alberto Fernández-Pla was the inaugural curator of the Bacardi art gallery.

128. Reinhold Martin, *The Organizational Complex: Architecture, Media, and Corporate Space* (Cambridge, Massachusetts: The MIT Press, 2003), 163-164.

129. According to Francisco Brennand, Bosch referred to the tiled panel finish of the National Library of Mexico as an example of what he intended to do." Interview with Francisco Brennand, Oct. 22, 2012, by e-mail.

130. At the time of the Bacardi commission, Brennand's major completed works in Brazil included the 32-meter mural of the Battle of Guararapes for the Banco da Lavoura de Minas Gerais in Belo Horizonte; the School of Itanhaem in Sao Paulo; and the interior of a ballroom for the Sao Domingos Hotel in Recife.

131. As described by the *Brazilian Bulletin*: "In referring to the use of murals and other objet d'arts in building design, Brennand stresses the word 'overlay' rather than 'decorate' to underscore his belief in the combined unity of the final work." "Brazilian Art on Miami Building," *Brazillian Bulletin*, Aug 15, 1963. See also Hils, "What's New? 14–16. See also "Tiles Tell Sensual Tale of Tropics," *Miami News*, February 3, 1964.

132. Brennand interview, Oct. 22, 2012.

133. The Bacardi Imports Tower was described by Brazilian poet Ariano Suassuna in stanzas published for the opening of the building: The Americans call her Flórida, But her name is Florida: flowered peninsula, of the Spanish Roses, that the Salt purifies and eats / White of the Clouds, blue of the Sky, and now the blue and white of the Floral / Yes! The naves of [Brazilian] Northeastern churches, The Walls of clay, Stone and / lime, there the winged Form flew, from Fire and brazier, of the Blue marine and / Portuguese; White Sun of the Brazilian Northeast / The Land is other; The same is the Clear Sky / and the same is that Blue of fire and gold; the Gold of Honey. Ariano Suassuna, "Mural de Brennand em Miami" (Mural of Brennand in Miami). Published in brochure celebrating the opening of the Bacardi Imports Tower. Recife: Sociedades Cultural Brasil-Estados Unidos, 1963. Translation by Angela Pedrao.

134. Emanoel Araujo, museum director, critic and curator in São Paulo, quoted in Larry Rohter, "In Brazil, Iconoclast Is Bearded In His Den; A Controversial Sculptor Revels in His Menagerie," *The New York Times*, April 22, 2004.

135. According to historian Henry Russell Hitchcock, "tiled surfaces became one of the key character-defining elements of the international style in Latin America." Tile murals were also, as Hitchcock affirmed, an indicator of Latin influence in the U.S. Henry Russell Hitchcock, *Latin American Architecture Since 1945*, (New York: The Museum of Modern Art, 1955).

136. Lester Pancoast, architect with the Miami firm Pancoast, Ferendino, Grafton and Skeels, quoted in "An Architect on End," *The Miami News*, May 29, 1965.

137. Miami artists Al Vrana and Kay Pancoast, for example, collaborated extensively with local architects.

138. Hils, "What's New?" 14–16.

139. V'Soske's carpet design collaborations were the subject of a 1942 exhibition at the Museum of Modern Art, featuring floor coverings by artists like Stuart Davis and Arshile Gorky. A recent exhibition at the Center for Architecture in New York, "V'Soske Rugs by Architects: Architecture in Transition, 1979–1993," featured the work of Michael Graves, Charles Gwathmey, Steven Holl, Richard Meier, Lee F. Mindel and Peter Shelton. Founder Stanislav V'Soske, "the dean of American rug design, died in 1983. Dan Shaw, "V'Soske's Stunning Rugs go on Display," *Architectural Digest* 69:6 (June 2012): 48.

140. "The New Bacardi Office Building at Miami," press release by SACAM & Associates, Inc., engineers, (undated): 1. Bacardi Archive.

141. Stran-Steel was a division of the National Steel Corporation (Pittsburgh).

142. Interview with Ermina Eguilior Bosch, September 25, 2014.

143. According to Ermina Eguilior Bosch, Bermudan planning authorities rejected the initial Bacardi design for a five-story slab building. Interview with Ermina Eguilior Bosch.

144. Celia Musson-Nzabalinda, "Legacy of a Premium Company," *Bermuda Sun*, Bacardi 150th Anniversary Special Edition 2012 supplement, February 3, 2012.

145. Robert McCarter notes that earth berm architecture connects to ancient sources like pyramidal structures, often in tropical climates. According to McCarter, "Almost all of Morgan's designs involve a dialogue—rarely equal—between massive heavy anchorage and linear light-weight frame, a weaving of attributes of earth and sky to form the space of dwelling between." Robert McCarter, *William Morgan Architects: Master Architect Series VI: Selected and Current Works*, Images Publishing Dist Ac (July 24, 2006).

146. The relationship between the Mies firm and Skidmore Owings & Merrill (S.O.M.) has been suggested in many publications. For instance, see Blair Kamin, *Why Architecture Matters: Lessons from Chicago* (Chicago: University of Chicago Press) 2001. S.O.M. buildings, like The Upjohn Company in Kalamazoo, Michigan (1959–61), and the U.S. Air Force Academy Dining Hall in Colorado Springs, Colorado (1956–62), seem to interpret and innovate the Bacardi Santiago model.

147. Before its 1992 reorganization, the five essential parts of Bacardi were Grupo Bacardi de Mexico, S.A., Mexico City; Bacardi Imports Inc., Miami; Bacardi & Company, Nassau; Bacardi Corporation, San Juan; Bacardi International Ltd., Bermuda. The holding company created by the reorganization was Bacardi Limited.

148. Each year, approximately 500,000 people visit Bacardi brand homes worldwide. Interview with Simon Taylor, Global Brand Centre Strategy Development Manager at Bacardi Global Brands, in London. November 28, 2014. Other well-known brand homes include Heineken in Amsterdam, Guinness in Dublin, and Jack Daniel's in Lynchburg, Tennessee.

149. Although the literature on brand homes is thin, I refer to Mark Weiner's analysis of corporate food displays. Mark Weiner, "We Are What We Eat; or, Democracy, Community, and the Politics of Corporate Food Displays." Review of the Jack Daniel Distillery; Hershey's Chocolate World; the World of Coca-Cola in *American Quarterly* 46:2, (June 1994): 227–250.

150. Interview with Simon Taylor, Global Brand Centre Strategy Development Manager at Bacardi Global Brands, in London. November 28, 2014.

151. The nine brand homes include two for Bacardi: La Galarza in Mexico and the Palo Seco Puerto Rico campus; other brand homes include the Cazadores Distillery in Arandas, Jalisco, Mexico; Dewar's at the Aberfeldy Distillery in Scotland; the Bombay Sapphire Distillery at Laverstoke Mill, Hampshire, UK; the Palais Bénédictine in Fécamp, France; Le Logis du Fresne (Grey Goose) in Cognac, France; Maison Noilly Prat in Marseillan, France; and Casa Martini in Pessione, Italy.

152. Charles Cree Doig, architect and engineer of the Aberfeldy distillery, is responsible for the kiln's signature pagoda roof. Doig is said to have designed almost 100 whisky distilleries in Scotland and Northern Ireland.

153. Le Logis du Fresne functioned, as early as 2006, as an inn. Previously, it was a rural estate, tied to surrounding lands in what is now the village of Juillac-le-Coq. Bacardi and Grey Goose have compiled an exhaustive history of the property and its owners, dating from its founding as the domain of Fresne in the fourteenth century. "Logis du Fresne research," March 11, 2014. Benedictine.

154. Grey Goose was developed by Maître de Chai Francois Thibault and spirits entrepreneur Sidney Frank in 1997.

155. Grey Goose Manifesto from "A Vision For Our Home." August 2011. Pdf file.

156. Hampshire, on the southern coast of England, is acclaimed as home to the ancient English capital of Winchester, as the birthplace of the British Navy and cultural icons like Jane Austen and Charles Dickens, and for its hogs..

157. Geraint Franklin, "Laverstoke Mill, Whitchurch, Hampshire. An Assessment by the Architectural Investigation London and Southeast Team," Reports & Papers Series B/001/2006 London: English Heritage (January, 2006). See also Charles Dickens "Story of a Banknote."

158. Bacardi initiated the *Concurso para el Edificio Bacardi* in 1927 in order to select a design for its new office building in Havana, Cuba. More recently, Bombay Sapphire has sponsored an annual glass design competition, and the Bombay Sapphire Prize. Bombay Sapphire Prize winners include designers such as Marcel Wanders, Yves Behar, and Karim Rashid. Glass works produced in design competitions sponsored by the Bombay Sapphire Foundation are featured in the Laverstoke Mill gallery.

159. Ivano Tonutti, Bombay's Master of Botanicals, quoted in Ellie Stathaki. "Bombay Sapphire's new distillery by Thomas Heatherwick is unveiled at Laverstoke Mill" *Wallpaper* (September 22 2014) Accessed online February 17, 2015. www.wallpaper.com/architecture/bombay-sapphires-new-distillery-by-thomas-heatherwick-is-unveiled-at-laverstoke-mill.

160. Janelle Zara, "First Look: Thomas Heatherwick's Bombay Sapphire Distillery," *Architectural Record* (October 13, 2014), Accessed online February 17, 2015. http://archrecord.construction.com/news/2014/10/141013-Bombay-Sapphire-Thomas-Heatherwick-Gin-Laverstoke-Mill.asp.

161. Cancela, "Bacardi Distillery," 8.

162. HOK was interior designer for the buildout of the Bacardi Americas Building in Coral Gables, for which Gensler designed the environmental brand experience & graphic design, 2009

163. National Young Arts Foundation, formerly the National Foundation for Advancement in the Arts, was "established in 1981 by Lin and Ted Arison to "identify and support the next generation of artists, and to contribute to the cultural vitality of the nation by investing in the artistic development of talented young artists in the visual, literary, and performing arts." http://www.youngarts.org/sites/default/files/YoungArts-New-Headquarters-Brochure.pdf "

164. Robin Pogrebin "Gehry to turn Bacardi complex into arts campus." *The New York Times*, October 3, 2012.

BIBLIOGRAPHY

1. General works

Adam, Nicholas. *Skidmore, Owings & Merrill: SOM since 1936*. Milan: Electa Architectura, 2007.

Alonso, Alejandro G., Contreras, Pedro and Fagiuoli, Martino. *Havana Deco*. New York: W.W. Norton, 2007.

Araoz, Jr., Gustavo F. "Statement of Significance," National Register of Historic Places Registration Form for Carcel de Puerta de Tierra. NPS Form 10–300, July 12, 1976.

"Bacardi Opening Office in New York," *The Brooklyn Daily Eagle*. October 14, 1933: 19.

"Bacardi says brand's future is in Puerto Rico, not Cuba," *Cuba News*. v. 17 (April 2009): 6.

Bedingfield, Robert E. "Personality: From Sugar to Banking to Rum: Bacardi's President Lost a Fortune in His Twenties," *New York Times*. June 9, 1963: 141.

Beesch, Samuel C. and Shull, G. M. "Fermentation." *Industrial & Engineering Chemistry* 48 (9) (September 1956) 1585–1603.

Bello, Francis. "Architecture's New Technology," *Fortune* (March 1956): 128–130.

Blaser, Werner. *Mies van der Rohe: Die Kunst der Struktur.* Zurich and Stuttgart: Verlag für Architektur, 1965.

Blaser, Werner. *West Meets East: Mies van der Rohe*. Basel and Boston: Birkhäuser-Publishers for Architecture, 2001.

Blocker, Jack S., Fahey, David M. and Tyrrell, Ian R. ed. *Alcohol and Temperance in Modern History: An International Encyclopedia*. Santa Barbara, California: ABC-CLIO, 2003.

Bounds, John H. "Industrialization in the Bahamas," *Revista Geográfica* 77 (December 1972): 95-113.

Boyken, Immo and Oestmann, Hans J. "Ludwig Mies van der Rohe and Egon Eiermann: The Dictate of Order," *Journal of the Society of Architectural Historians*, Vol. 49, No. 2 (June 1990), 133–153.

Brillembourg, Carlos. "Great Curves," *Architects Newspaper* (April 20, 2012).

"Bringing the tropics to latitude 40 40' longitude 73 50'," *Interior design* 17 (August 1, 1941): 34–37, 54.

Candela, Félix. "Stress analysis for any hyperbolic paraboloid," *Architectural Record* 124 (August 1958): 205–207.

Candela, Félix. "The shell as space enclosed," *Arts & Architecture* 72 (January 1955): 29.

Candela, Félix. "Understanding the hyperbolic paraboloid," *Architectural Record* 124 (July 1958): 191–195.

Castells, Esteban Rodriguez and Martinez Inclan, Pedro. *Discurso de ingreso como miembro de número de la Sección de arquitectura*. La Habana: Imprenta Molina y cía., 1936.

"City Notes," *Architectural Design* 29:1 (1959) 34–35.

"Convinced Dry Law will Stay," *Miami Daily News-Record*, December 30, 1928.

Cullen, Deborah. *Nexus New York: Latin/American artists in the modern metropolis*. New York: Museo del Barrio and New Haven: Yale University Press, 2009.

Danz, Ernst Ed. *Architecture of Skidmore, Owings & Merrill, 1950–1962*. New York: Praeger, 1963.

Dawson, Mari Aixala and Argamasilla, Pepin R. *Bacardi: A Tale of Merchants, Family, and Company*. Miami: Facundo and Amalia Bacardi Foundation Inc., 2006.

"Designer Bergson," *Architectural Forum* 120 (February 1964): 108–111.

Drexler, Arthur. "The Seagram Building" *Architectural Record* 124 (July 1958): 139.

Driscoll, Sarah. "Deconstructing Hemingway's America: The Hemingway-Gattorno Relationship in the U.S.-Cuban Imagination," M.A. thesis diss. Arizona State University, 2011.

Drucker, Peter F. *Concept of the Corporation*. New York: The John Day Company, 1946.

"El Nuevo Ministro de Obras Publicas," *Arquitectura Cuba* 10:53 (June 1942): 206.

Estrada, Alfredo José. *Havana: Autobiography of a City*. New York: Palgrave Macmillan, 2008.

Faber, Colin. *Candela: The Shell Builder*. New York, Reinhold Pub. Corp., 1963.

"Félix Candela: Shell Forms," Catalogue of exhibition (Los Angeles: University of Southern California) May 1957. Esther McCoy papers, Archives of American Art, Smithsonian Institution.

Flowers, Benjamin Sitton. *Skyscraper: The Politics and Power of Building New York City in the Twentieth Century*. Philadelphia: University of Pennsylvania Press, 2009.

Forbes, Robert James. *Short History of the Art of Distillation, From the Beginnings up to the Death of Cellier Blumenthal*. Leiden: E. J. Brill, 1948.

Foscue, Edwin J. "The Central Highway of Cuba." Economic Geography, 9 (October 1933): 406–412.

Foster, Peter. *Family Spirits: the Bacardi Saga*. Toronto: Macfarlane Walter & Ross, 1990.

Gahn, Joseph Anthony. "The America of William Gropper, Radical Cartonist," PhD diss., Syracuse University, 1966. Accessed online at http://www.aaa.si.edu/collections/container/viewer/Dissertation-on-Gropper—205340

Gallo, Samuel. *Bacardi, 1862–1962*. S.l. : Bacardi Co., 1962.

Garlock, Maria and Billington, D.P. *Félix Candela: Engineer, Builder, Structural Artist*. Princeton: Princeton University Art Museum and New Haven: Yale University Press, 2008.

"Genial Arquitecto," *Bacardi Grafico* 12 (January 1959): 16–19.

George, Georgina. "Report on Bacardi Office Building," Study for Saenz Cancio Martin, April 1954. Mies van der Rohe Archive, MoMa. (Ron Bacardi Office Building Folder 1).

Gewen, Barry. "Cuba Libre: Rum, Revolution and a Family Tale," Review of *Bacardi and the Long Fight for Cuba: The Biography of a Cause* by Tom Gjelten. *New York Times*, September 24, 2008.

Giedion, Sigfried. *Space, Time and Architecture*. Cambridge: Harvard University Press, 1967.

Gjelten, Tom. *Bacardi and the Long Fight for Cuba: The Biography of a Cause*. New York: Viking, 2008.

"Glamor … for your Summer Sipping." *Harrisburg Telegraph*, August 26, 1936.

Gordon, John. "Exhibition Preview: Business Buys American Art," *Art in America* 48:1 (1960): 89.

Grimes, William. *Straight Up or on the Rocks: A Cultural History of American Drink*. New York: North Point Press, 2001.

Hemingway, Ernest. *Gattorno: With 38 Reproductions and a Few Critical Opinions*. Catalogue: Habana: Impresores Ucar, García, 1935.

Hemingway, Ernest. *The Old Man and the Sea*. New York: Scribner, 1952.

Hitchcock, Henry Russell, *Latin American Architecture Since 1945*. New York: The Museum of Modern Art, 1955.

"Homer Hill, Artist, Depicted Air Bases," *The New York Times*, April 4 1968.

"Hot Fifty - Bombay Sapphire Foundation," *Design Week*, February 14, 2008. Accessed on line from http://www.designweek.co.uk/features/hot-fifty-bombay-sapphire-foundation/1137589.article.

Infante, Guillermo Cabrera, "El Viejo y La Marca," *Ciclón* 2:5 (September 1956). From Guillermo Cabrera Infante and Stephen D. Gingerich, *The New Centennial Review* 2:2, Origins of "postmodern" Cuba (Summer 2002): 110–115.

Insera, Magda Isabel de la y Gonzalez, Marta María. "El Art Deco en la Arquitectura de Autor de la Habana en las decadas de los años 30 y 40," *Fac. Arq. ISPYAE*, 1981 or 1987, Tuf Roberto Segre.

Isabella, Lynn A. and Forbes, Ted. *Grupo Bacardi de Mexico S.A.* Charlottesville: University of Virginia Darden Business Publishing, 1994.

Janz, Wesley. "Theaters of Power: Architectural and Cultural Productions," *Journal of Architectural Education* 50:4 (May, 1997): 230–243.

Jenkins, Stover and Mohney, David. *The Houses of Philip Johnson*. New York: Abbeville Press Publishers, 2001.

"Just Make it Beautiful," *Miami News*, February 3, 1964.

Knight, Franklin W. "Origins of Wealth and the Sugar Revolution in Cuba, 1750–1850," *The Hispanic American Historical Review* 57:2 (May 1977): 231–253.

Knowles, Scott G. and Leslie, Stuart W. "Industrial Versailles: Eero Saarinen's Corporate Campuses for GM, IBM, and AT&T," *Isis* 92:1 (March 2001): 1–33.

Lambert, Phyllis. *Building Seagram*. New Haven: Yale University Press, 2013.

Lambert, Phyllis. *Mies in America*. New York: H.N. Abrams, 2001.

Lambert, Phyllis. "Philip Johnson: Breaking with Modernism—The 'Whence & Whither' of It," in *Philip Johnson: The Constancy of Change*, edited by Emmanuel Petit. 190–207. New Haven: Yale University Press, 2009.

Lanza, Joseph. *The Cocktail: The Influence of Spirits on the American Psyche*. New York, St. Martin's Press, 1997.

Lejeune, Jean-Francois. "The City as Landscape: Jean Claude Nicolas Forestier and the Great Urban Works of Havana, 1925–1930," *The Journal of Decorative and Propaganda Arts* 22, Cuba Theme Issue (1996): 150–185.

Lemaster, Carolyn Gray. *Corner of the Tapestry: A History of the Jewish Experience in Arkansas, 1820s–1990s*. Little Rock: University of Arkansas Press, 1994.

Lipietz, Alain. "The Local and the Global: Regional Individuality or Interregionalism?" *Transactions of the Institute of British Geographers* 18:1 (1993): 8–18.

Lora, Marta Elena. "La Arquitectura de Carlos Segrera Patrimonio de Santiago de Cuba," *Arquitectura y Urbanismo*, 23:2 (2002): 40–47.

Lynch, Kevin, Appleyard, Donald and Myer, John R. *The View from the Road*. Cambridge: M.I.T. Press for the Joint Center for Urban Studies of the Massachusetts Institute of Technology and Harvard University, 1964.

Maingot, Anthony P. "The 'Global' and the 'Local' in the Caribbean." Review of *Culture and Customs of Cuba* by William Luis; *Culture and Customs of Haiti* by J. Michael Dash; Culture and Customs of Jamaica by Martin Mordecai and Pamela Mordecai in *Caribbean Studies* 31:1, Garveyism and the Universal Negro Association in the Hispanic Caribbean (January–June 2003): 267.

"Maria Bergson Associates," *Contract Interiors* 120 (April 1961): 84–103

Martin, Reinhold. *The Organizational Complex: Architecture, Media, and Corporate Space*. Cambridge, Massachusetts: The MIT Press, 2003.

"Mayor Approves Cuban's Caricature: It Shows Him Playing Maracas as Rhumba Dancer Sways," *New York Times*, June 7, 1939.

"Memos of a Midnighter," *The Scranton Republican*, 15 August 1935.

Mertins, Detlef. "Mies's Event Space," *Grey Room* 20 (Summer, 2005): 60–73.

"Mies, Genio de la Arquitectura: Bacardi le confia la construccion de su nueva sede en Santiago de Cuba. Sus revolucionarios diseños." *Bacardi Grafico* 6 (July 1957): 6–9.
"Morris B. Sanders Studio & Apartment," Report of the Landmarks Preservation Commission; November 18, 2008; Designation List 407; LP-2267.
Mozingo, Louise A. *Pastoral Capitalism.* Cambridge, Massachussetts & London, England: MIT Press, 2011.
"Mr. Bacardi," *New Yorker* (February 9, 1929): 14–15.
Mujica, Francisco. *History of the Skyscraper.* Paris: Archaeology & Architecture Press, 1929.
Mumford, Lewis. *Mumford on Modern Art in the 1930s,* Berkely and Los Angeles: University of California Press, 2008.
Muñoz Hernández, Ruslan y Peñate Diaz, Florencia. "Modern architecture and industrial heritage in the Havana municipality of Rancho Boyeros," *Arquitectura y Urbanismo* 35:2, Con Criterio/ Arquitectura moderna y patrimonio industrial en el municipio Rancho Boyeros, La Habana (2014).
"Name, Schenley; Age, Three ... Occupation, biggest Whiskey seller in the U. S. Its brief honeymoon with Golden Wedding and the Dreary Morning After. The Success of its cheap brands; its $8,000,000 net," *Fortune* 13 (May 1936): 98–104.
Neumeyer, Alfred. "Berlin's New National Gallery." *Art Journal* 29:1 (Autumn 1969): 92–93.
Norberg-Schulz, Christian. "Ein Gespräch mit Mies van der Rohe," *Baukunst und Werkform* 11 (1958): 615–616, in Boyken, Immo and Oestmann, Hans J. "Ludwig Mies van der Rohe and Egon Eiermann: The Dictate of Order," *Journal of the Society of Architectural Historians* 49:2 (June 1990): 133–153.
"Now, Señor, the Highball," *Harrisburg Telegraph*, April 28, 1937.
"Nuestros Objetivos," *Bacardi Graphico* 1 (April 1956): 2–3.
O'Rourke, Kathryn E. "Mies and Bacardi: Mixing Modernism, c. 1960," *Journal of Architectural Education* 66:1 (October 2012): 57–71.
Palma, Rojo. Rodolfo. *Bacardi Mexico.* Guadalajara, Jalisco: Bacardi y Compania / Lindero Ediciones, 2003.
"Paper Trail: The Esther McCoy Papers," *Archives of American Art Journal* 45:3/4 (2005): 55–60
Perez Firmat, Gustavo. *The Havana Habit.* New Haven: Yale University Press, 2010.
Poole, Sean M. *Gattorno: A Cuban Painter for the World.* Miami: American Art Corporation, 2004.
Redman, Chris. "Flying Sky High: Grey Goose Vodka," *France Today*, February 20, 2011. Accessed online February 14, 2015. http://www.francetoday.com/articles/2011/02/20/flying_sky_high_grey_goose_vodka.html.
"Retired? Not Chief of Bacardi," *The New York Times*, March 8, 1970.
Rice, Elinor. *Action in Havana.* New York: Duell, Sloan and Pearce, 1940.
Rodríguez, Eduardo Luis. *La Habana: arquitectura del siglo XX.* Barcelona: Art Blume, 1998.
Rodríguez, Eduardo Luis. "The Architectural Avant-Garde: From Art Deco to Modern Regionalism," *The Journal of Decorative and Propaganda Arts* 22, Cuba Theme Issue (1996): 254–277.
Rodriguez, Eduardo Luis. *The Havana Guide: Modern Architecture 1925–1965.* New York: Princeton Architectural Press, 2000.
Rodríguez, Luz Marie. "Klumbumbus descubre el Trópico: Henry Klumb, Puerto Rico y la modernidad en lo existente." *Arquitextos* 120:4 (May 2010) Vitruvium.com.br
Rohter, Larry. "In Brazil, Iconoclast Is Bearded In His Den; A Controversial Sculptor Revels in His Menagerie," *The New York Times*, April 22, 2004.
Roig de Leuchsenring, Emilio ed., *El Libro de Cuba: historia, letras, artes, ciencias, agricultura, industria, comercio, bellezas naturales.* Habana: Talleres del Sindicato de Artes Gráficas, 1925.
Ronfeldt, David F. *Atencingo: The Politics of Agrarian Struggle in a Mexican Ejido.* Stanford: Stanford University Press, 1973.
Rossi, Aldo. *Architettura della città.* Padua: Marsilio Editori, 1966.
Salfrán, Heriberto Duverger and Ramirez Moreno, Nicolás ed. *Oriente de Cuba : guía de arquitectura: Santiago de Cuba, Guantánamo, Holguín, Las Tunas, Granma.* Sevilla: Junta de Andalucía, Consejería de Obras Públicas y Transportes and Cuba: Asamblea Provincial del Poder Popular de Santiago de Cuba, 2002.
Schmitt, Bernd and Simonson, Alex. *Marketing aesthetics: the strategic management of brands, identity and image.* New York: Free Press, 1997.
Schulze, Franz and Danforth, George E., ed. "Volume 17: Ron Baccardí y Compañía, S.A., administration building (Cuba) and other buildings and projects," *The Mies Van Der Rohe Archive Series: An Illustrated Catalog of the Mies Van Der Rohe Drawing in the Museum of Modern Art: Part II, 1938–1967, The American Work.* New York and London: Garland Publishing, Inc., 1992.
Schulze, Franz and Danforth, George E., ed. "Volume 18: Ron Bacardi Y Compañia, S. A., Administration Building (Mexico) and other buildings and projects," *The Mies Van Der Rohe Archive Series: An Illustrated Catalog of the Mies Van Der Rohe Drawing in the Museum of Modern Art: Part II, 1938–1967, The American Work.* New York and London: Garland Publishing, Inc., 1992.
Schulze, Franz and Windhorst, Edward. *Mies van der Rohe: A Critical Biography, New and Revised Edition.* Chicago: University of Chicago Press, 2012.
Segre, Roberto. *Arquitectura antillana del siglo XX.* La Habana: Arte y Literatura, 2003.
Segre, Roberto. "La Habana. Ortodoxia y digresiones de la Primera Modernidad," In *Arquitectura en la ciudad de La Habana: primera modernidad, edited by* Carlos Sambricio and Roberto Segre, 66–228. Madrid: Sociedad Editorial Electa España, 2000.
Shaw, Dan. "Ground swell: the V'Soske rug studio's architectural collaborations get a red-carpet salute." *Architectural Digest* 69:6 (June 2012): 48.
Shulman, Allan T. "Building Bacardi: Architecture, Art & Identity (catalogue to exhibition)." Coral Gables: Coral Gables Museum, 2012.
Shulman, Allan T. "Hormigón y transparencia: Bacardi en las Américas," *Summa+* 138 (September 2014): 94–101.
Shulman, Allan T. "The Mixable One: Two Projects for Compañia Ron Bacardi," X Seminário DOCOMOMO Brasil, Arquitetura Moderna e Internacional: conexões brutalistas 1955–75 Curitiba. 15–18.out.2013 - PUCPR
Speyer, A. James. *Mies van der Rohe.* Chicago: Hillison & Etten Company, 1968.
Steele, Brett. "Absolut® Mies™, Absolute Modern: Building Good Copy," *AA Files* 48 (Winter 2002): 2–14.
Stern, Robert A.M., Gilmartin, Gregory and Mellins, Thomas. *New York 1930: Architecture and Urbanism Between the Two World Wars.* New York: Rizzoli, 1987.
Sugden, Derek, "Candela: Shell Builder," *Architectural Association Journal* 80 (December 1964): 136–137.
Swenson, Brynnar Nelson. "The Corporate Form: Capital, Literature, Architecture. PhD Diss., University of Minnesota, 2008.
"The Bacardi Rum Company Celebrates Its Hundredth Anniversary with New Offices, Bottling Plant and Warehouse on the Outskirts of Mexico City," *Financial Times*, March 15, 1962.
Varela, Enrique Luis. "La Exposicion Internacional de la Habana en 1948," *Arquitectura Cuba* 13:146 (September 1945): 304–306.
Varela, Enrique Luis. "Filosofia de la Arquitectura Moderna o Contemporanea," *Arquitectura Cuba,* 15 (June 1947): 194–199.
Weiner, Mark. "We Are What We Eat; or, Democracy, Community, and the Politics of Corporate Food Displays," Review of the Jack Daniel Distillery; Hershey's Chocolate World; the World of Coca-Cola in *American Quarterly* 46:2 (June 1994): 227–250.
Werner, Claudia Sans. "Designing the Hyphen: Linking Identity and Architecture in Bacardi's Former Miami Headquarters," M.A. thesis diss. Corcoran College of Art and Design, 2013.
"Whiskey: Newest US Business, Oldest US Problem; the companies which will run it, and the conditions under which it will be run; such a subject needs a preface; this is it," *Fortune* Vol 7, Number 11 (November 1933): 28.
"Wizard of the shells," *Architectural Forum* 111 (November 1959): 154–159.
"Work of Felix Candela," *Progressive Architecture* 36 (July 1955): 106–115.
Wright, Gwendolyn. *USA.* London: Reaktion Books, 2008.
"Brand Homes: Ties that bind: brands lay down social roots," *Marketing Event* (May 15, 2012): 16. Accessed online at http://iiiprxy.library.miami.edu:2183/itw/infomark/148/731/37270189w16/purl=rc1_GBFM_0_A289765049&dyn=3!xrn_1_0_A289765049?sw_aep=miami_richter

2. Bacardi Buildings: Selected Works

Museo Emilio Bacardi Moreau, Santiago de Cuba

Calzadilla-Cruz, Yuniel. "The Provincial Museum Emilio Bacardi Moreau: A Labyrinth to Unknown Treasures," *Ciencia en su PC* 4 (October–December 2010): 144–156. http://cubanartsconnection.blogspot.com/2013/03/el-museo-provincial-emilio-bacardi.html

Edificio Bacardi, Havana, Cuba

"El Concurso para el Edificio Bacardi," *El Arquitecto* 3:24–25 (January 1928): 65–77.
"Concurso para el Edificio Bacardi: Segundo Premio," *Revista del Colegio de Arquitectos de la Habana* 12:2 (February 1928): 24–30.
"El Edificio 'Bacardi' por Esteban Rodrigues Castells, José Menendez y Menendez, Rafael Fernández Ruenes. Arq. Ing. Arellano y Mendoza, Ing. y Arq. Contrastistas," *Revista del Colegio de Arquitectos de la Habana* 15:4 (April 1931): 10–19.

Bacardi Bar and Import Lounge (House of Schenley), New York City

"Bacardi Bar and Import Lounge," *American Architect* 147 (December 1935): 29–34.

Gray, Christopher. "Demolished Club Casts a Long Shadow," *The New York Times*, April 10, 2014.

Storey, Walter Rendell. "The Cocktail Bar Creates a Décor: New Materials and Subtle Colors Contribute To an Effect That is Smartly Contemporary," *The New York Times*, December 23, 1934.

"The New York Club," *Architects and Builders Magazine* 39 (July 1907): 502–505.

Bacardi Room (Empire State Building), New York City

"Architect Turns Tables on Noted Dress Designers," *The Paris News*, February 9, 1938.

"Entertaining at Your Private Club," *Arts & Decoration* 48 (June 1938): 20-21.

"Goat Hunt Stirs Office Building," *The Charleston Daily Mail*, January 11, 1938.

Houck, Bertha A. "The Root of All Art," *The Spur* 61 (February 1938): 40.

"Leases Four Floors in Empire State: Schenley Corp. and Affiliated Firms Will Move Offices Above May 1," *New York Times*, March 23, 1937.

"Schenley Company Takes Offices in Empire State Building," *Altoona Tribune*, April 3, 1937.

"The Bacardi Room," *The Brooklyn Daily Eagle*, February 4, 1938.

Ron Bacardi y Compañia S.A. Administration Building, Santiago de Cuba

"Bürogebäude der Ron Bacardi & Co. in Santiago, Cuba," *Bauen und Wohnen* 13:9 (September 1959): 313–315.

Doimo, Martino, *Arte muraria, spazio, tettonica, Mies, Bacardi Building Cuba, elementi della costruzione – figure della composizione*. Treviso, Canova, impr., 2009.

"Edificio para 'Ron Bacardi S.A.,' Santiago de Cuba," *Proa* 124 (February 1959): 10–11.

"Luz, más luz: los templos tardíos de la técnica," *AV monographs* 92 (November–December 2001): 48–51.

"Office building for Compania Ron Bacardi S.A., Santiago de Cuba." *Architectural Design* 28 (November 1958): 442–447.

Rogers, Ernesto Nathan. "Classicità di Mies van der Rohe," *Casabella Continuità* 228 (June 1959): 5–13.

"Sede en Santiago de Cuba," *Bacardi Grafico* 11 (October 1958): 2–3.

Bacardi Corporation Distillery, Palo Seco, Puerto Rico

"Bacardi Amplaria Actividades Aquí,'" El Mundo (Puerto Rico), January 28, 1956.

"Bacardi Celebra Apertura de Planta $8,000,000," *El Mundo* (Puerto Rico), January 18, 1958.

"Bacardi Inaugura Planta en Aldea de Palo Seco," *El Mundo* (Puerto Rico), January 16, 1958.

"Biografia de Una Industria." *El Mundo* (Puerto Rico), April 28, 1970.

Bosch, José Mario. "Como se plasmó una realidade," *Bacardi Grafico* 8 (January 1958): 2–9.

"Casa Bacardi," *Beverage Industry* 94:6 (June 2003): 11.

"Catedral del Ron," *Bacardi Grafico* 12 (January 1959): 15.

"La Casa Bacardi Establecera Sucursal en San Juan: Ocupara El Edificio de 'La Colectiva' Obreros Que Utilizara," *El Mundo* (Puerto Rico), March 8, 1936.

Panorama de San Juan, Bacardi Grafico 1, April 1956: 25.

Peñate Díaz, Florencia. "La obra de las arquitectas cubanas de la República entre los años 40 y fines de los 50 del siglo XX," *Arquitectura y Urbanismo* 33–3 (2012). http://www.google.com/url?sa=t&rct=j&q=&esrc=s&source=web&cd=1&ved=0CCIQFjAA&url=http%3A%2F%2Frau.cujae.edu.cu%2Findex.php%2Frevistaau%2Farticle%2Fdownload%2F213%2F208&ei=1Pf0VK-eBMK-ggT5jYCQCQ&usg=AFQjCNF7vFlkW1UaNQE5Bi5wgCUx7H_ATg&bvm=bv.87269000,d.eXY

Rubio Cancela, Carlos A. State Historic Preservation Officer, Puerto Rico State Historic Preservation Office. "National Register of Historic Places Registration Form for Bacardi Distillery," June 17, 2010. NPS Form 10-900: 8.

Bacardí y Compañía S.A. de C.V. Distillery, La Galarza, Puebla, Mexico

"Nuevo Ogullo de Bacardi," *Bacardi Grafico* 6 (July 1957): 12–18.

"Structure by Félix Candela," *Arts & Architecture* 73 (May 1956): 20–24.

Bacardí y Compañía S.A. de C.V. Bottling Plant, Tultitlán, Mexico

Candela, Félix. "Planta embotelladora Bacardí en Mexico." *Nuestra Arquitectura* 376 (March 1961): 43.

del Cueto Ruiz Funes, Juan Ignacio. "Félix Candela, el mago de los cascarones de concreto," *Arquine* 2 (December 1997): 46–57.

del Cueto Ruiz Funes, Juan Ignacio. "The Spirit of Candela in the Bacardi Mexico Bottling Company," in del Cueto, Juan Ignacio, ed. *That Creative Spring.... Reinforced Concrete Shells in Mexico.* Proceedings of the International Association for Shell and Spatial Structures symposium. México, D.F.: UNAM, Facultad de Arquitectura, 2008.

"Deux solutions pour des hall industriel," *Architecture d'aujourd'hui* 32:95 (April–May 1961): 50–51.

"Félix Candela: Bottling Plant, Bacardí de Mexico Headquarters, Mexico City, Mexico 1959–1971," *A & U: Architecture & Urbanism* 2:389 (February 2003): 54–59.

"Four Great Pours," *Archictectural Forum* 115 (September 1961): 104–115.

"Hall d'une usine à Cuantitlan près de Mexico," *Architecture d'aujourd'hui* 32–95 (April–May 1961): 48–49.

Joedicke, Jürgen. "Lagerhaus und Abfüllhalle der Rumfabrik Bacardi S.A., Tultitlán, Mexiko," *Bauen und Wohnen* 17 (September 1963): 396–398.

Tonda, J. A. "Bovedas de Cascaron para la Planta de Bacardí en Mexico," *Revista IMCYC* 10:60 (January–February 1973): 76.

Bacardí y Compañía S.A. de C.V. Administration Building, Tultitlán, Mexico

"Administration building," *Arts & Architecture* 79 (May 1962): 18–19, 32.

"An administrative building in Mexico," *Zodiac* 10 (1962): 182–187.

"Architectural Details: 1. Mies van der Rohe," *Architectural Record* 134:2 (October 1963): 149–164.

"Bacardi Building, Mexico City," *Architectural Design* 32 (October 1962): 470–473.

"Edificio para 'Ron Bacardi S.A.,' Santiago de Cuba," *Proa* 124 (February 1959): 10–11.

Lizárraga Sánchez, Salvador. "Bacardi Breezer," *AA Files* 62 (2011): 104–107.

"Mexican Headquarters for Bacardi Rum," *Architectural Record* 127 (April 1960): 178–179.

"Mies builds in Mexico," *Architectural Forum* 116 (January 1962): 92–95.

Piñón, Helio. "Economia, precisión, rigor y universalidade," *Quaderns d'arquitectura i urbanisme* 254 (Summer 2007): 130–135.

Rogers, Ernesto Nathan. "Classicità di Mies van der Rohe," *Casabella Continuità* 228 (June 1959): 5–13.

"Verwaltungsgebäude Ron Bacardi bei Mexico-City," *Bauen und Wohnen* 16 (October 1962): 407–411.

Cervecería Modelo, El Cotorro, Cuba

"Las Oficinas de la Modelo," *Bacardi Grafico* 4 (January 1957): 8–10.

"Fascinante Proceso de la Elaboracion," *Bacardi Grafico* 8 (January 1958): 20–23.

Zardoya, Maria Victoria and Álvarez, Ángel Manuel. "Theme: The Machine, Industry and Modern Architecture," Fiche prepared for docomomo (international working party for documentation and conservation of buildings, sites and neighborhoods of the modern movement, undated. Accessed http://rlicc.asro.kuleuven.ac.be/rlicc/docomomo/Registers/2008%20Machine/Cuba/Industry%20Selection%20overview%20and%20argumentation%20fiches.pdf

Cervecería Central, Manacas, Las Villas, Cuba

"Cerveceria Central Manacas Recuerdo de la Inauguracion Nov. 15, 1953 HATUEY, la gran cerveza de Cuba, abre su tercera cerveceria en Manacas," Postcard found on Cubalabella.com

"Más de 15,000 personas en la inauguración de la Cerveceria Central de Manacas, en Las Villas," *Diario de la Marina*, November 17, 1953.

"Un Valor Positivo en el Progreso Industrial," *Bacardi Grafico* 7 (October 1957): 12–17.

Bacardi & Company Distillery, New Providence Island, Bahamas

"Bacardi Moving to Bahamas," *New York Times*, September 13, 1961.

Bacardi Imports Inc. Tower, Miami, Florida

"A Cuban Painter for the World," *The Miami News*, February 3, 1964.

"An Architect on End," *The Miami News*, May 29, 1965.

Ash, Clarke. "A Study in Contrasts: Miami Architecture From Ornate Towers to Modernity," *New York Times*, Oct 27, 1968.
"Bacardi Buildings on the Boulevard," *Miami Herald*, September 16, 1962.
"Bacardi Builds on the Boulevard: Firm Readying Import Offices," *The Miami Herald*, August 31, 1962.
"Bacardi Companies Mark Their 102 Anniversary," *The Miami Herald*, February 3, 1964.
"Bacardi Home Newest Toast to Miami," *The Miami Herald*, February 3, 1964.
"Bacardi Moves to Miami," *Interior Design* (May 1964): 126–129.
"Bacardi Rum Moving Here," *The Miami Herald*, September 10, 1962.
"Bacardi to move office," *The New York Times*, Sep 1, 1962.
"Bacardi Tower Has Colorful Facade," *The New York Times*, Mar 15, 1964.
"Beauty on Stilts," *The Miami Herald*, February 10, 1963.
Bell, Jonathan. "Bacardi Pleaser: Bacardi Headquarters, Miami," *Wallpaper* 62 (October 2003): 112–113.
"Blue and White Ceramic Tile Murals Most Sticking Aspect," *The Miami Herald*, February 3, 1964.
"Brazilian Art on Miami Building," *Brazilian Bulletin*, Aug 15, 1963.

"Exposição De Brennand Aberta Ontem Na SCBEU," *Diario de Pernambuco*, November 30, 1963.
Fogarty, Fred. "A 28,000 Piece Puzzle!" *The Miami Herald*, September 22, 1963.
Hils, T.J. "What's New? That Building in Miami," *Construction Craftsman* 4:1 (January 1965): 14–16.
Laus, Harry. "Um pintor pernambucano," *Jornal do Brasil*, February 16, 1964.
Madia, Enrique. "Edificios Bacardi en Miami / Bacardi buildings in Miami," *Archivos de arquitectura antillana (AAA)* 32 (January 2009): 296–297.
Madia, Enrique and Lejeune, Jean Francois. "The Bacardi Building: Miami," DOCOMOMO-US. Chapter News, Spring 2009
Martin, Lydia. "Artistic office building promotes Art with Gallery," *Miami Herald*, August 23, 1987.
Pogrebin, Robin. "Gehry to Turn Bacardi Complex Into Arts Campus," *The New York Times*, October 3, 2012
Pogrebin, Robin. "Invenção Que Nasce da Memória," *O Estado de S. Paulo*, October 7, 2012.
"Painel Fantástico de Brennand Vai Mostrar Floral do Brasil em Miami," *Ultima Hora*, April 21, 1963.
Read, Gray. "The Bacardi Building: Architecture, Rum and Revolution," in Shulman, Allan and Castillo, Greg ed. *Aula: architecture & urbanism in las Americas* 3, Miami Tropical (2002): 28–35.
Sampson, Hannah. "Bacardi Landmark to House Art Hub," *Miami Herald*, October 3, 2012.
"Spirited Design Bacardi's Buildings Have Helped Define Miami," *Miami Herald*, January 22, 2005.
Suassuna, Ariano. "Mural of Brennand in Miami," Poem inscribed in the program of the building inauguration. Collection Francisco Brennand. 1963.
"The Bacardi Buildings, 2100 Biscayne Boulevard," Designation Report. Historic and Environmental Preservation Board, City of Miami. October 6, 2009.
"Tiles Tell Sensual Tale of Tropics," *Miami News*, February 3, 1964.
Youngarts New National Headquarters. Brochure (Miami: National Youngarts Foundation). Undated.

Bacardi, Recife, Brazil

"Otro Jalon Industrial," *Bacardi Grafico* 9 (April 1958): 6–9.

Bacardi Limited Administration Building, Hamilton, Bermuda

Musson-Nzabalinda, Celia. "Legacy of a Premium Company," *Bermuda Sun*, Bacardi 150th Anniversary Special Edition 2012 supplement, February 3, 2012.

Dewars Distillery, Aberfeldy, Scotland, United Kingdom

Jones, Adam. "The distilling industry is reshaped by deals," *Financial Times*, November 28, 2003. Accessed online http://iiiprxy.library.miami.edu:10038/docview/228801188?pq-origsite=summon

Bombay Sapphire Distillery, Laverstoke, Hampshire, United Kingdom

Birch, Amanda. "Bombay Sapphire Distillery: Heatherwick Studio's New State-of-the-Art Bombay Sapphire Distillery Assaults the Senses in Every Way," *Building Design* bdonline.co.uk (September 1, 2014).
McKenzie, Dominic. "Gin and Tectonics: Heatherwick Studio's Renovation of a Decayed Mill for Bombay Sapphire is as Remarkable for its Subtlety as its Set-pieces," *Architecture Today* 252 (October 2014): 16–18, 21.
Pritchard, Owen. "Gin fizz: Thomas Heatherwick's Hampshire distillery for Bombay Sapphire combines flamboyancy with thoughtfulness," *Architects' Journal* 240:12 (October 2014): 36–41.
Stathaki, Ellie. "Bombay Sapphire's New Distillery by Thomas Heatherwick is Unveiled at Laverstoke Mill," *Wallpaper* (September 22, 2014). Accessed online February 17, 2015. www.wallpaper.com/architecture/bombay-sapphires-new-distillery-by-thomas-heatherwick-is-unveiled-at-laverstoke-mill.
Tucker, Johnny. "Gin Palace: Gin brand Bombay Sapphire Has Sunk its Heritage Stake Deeper into the British Psyche by Establishing a Distillery in the Heart of the Hampshire Countryside," *Blueprint* 337 (November–December 2014): 88.
Zara, Janelle. "First Look: Thomas Heatherwick's Bombay Sapphire Distillery," *Architectural Record* (October 13, 2014). Accessed online February 17, 2015. http://archrecord.construction.com/news/2014/10/141013-Bombay-Sapphire-Thomas-Heatherwick-Gin-Laverstoke-Mill.asp.

BACARDI TIMELINE

1494 Christopher Columbus first explores the bay of Santiago de Cuba.

1514 Founding of Santiago de Cuba, which is declared the island's capital.
Havana becomes capital in 1607.

1793 Slave rebellion in Saint-Domingue (Haiti) spurs the migration of many French families to Santiago de Cuba.

1815 Facundo Bacardí Massó is born in Sitges, Spain.

1823 U.S. institutes the Monroe Doctrine, stating that European nations can no longer colonize or interfere with the newly independent nations of the Americas.

1830 Facundo Bacardí Massó arrives in Santiago.

1838 Matadero Street Distillery is built for John Nunes.

1844 Birth of Emilio Bacardí Moreau; Año del Cuero (Year of the Lash) slave revolt in Cuba

1850s Cuba the number one sugar producer in the world. Sugar the number one export of Cuba

1852 Earthquake in Santiago de Cuba

1859 Doña Amalia Bacardí inherits Marina (Baja) Street property, the first still and later offices of Bacardi in Santiago

1862 Bacardi Boutellier y Compañia is founded in Santiago de Cuba by Facundo Bacardí Massó and José León Bouteiller; Matadero Street distillery is purchased by Bacardi and Bouteiller

Mid-1800s *Mojito*

1868-78 Cuba's Ten Years' War. War ends with the Treaty of Zanjón and the abolition of slavery

1876 Centennial International Exposition, Philadelphia. BACARDÍ Ron Superior Extra-Secco takes first prize

1879 La Guerra Chiquita (the Little War); Emilio Bacardí Moreau exiled to Chaferine Islands

1895 Jose Marti leads resumption of the war of Cuban independence

1898 Spanish American War. Spain relinquishes Cuba in the Treaty of Peace in Paris; Emilio Bacardi Moreau is designated Mayor of Santiago de Cuba; *Daiquiri*

1899 Emilio Bacardí Moreau founds the Museo y Biblioteca Pública de Santiago de Cuba

1900 *Cuba Libre*

1901 Pan-American Exposition opens in Buffalo, New York. BACARDÍ rums are awarded a gold medal.

1902 Cuban Republic is established

1906 U.S. occupies Cuba; Emilio Bacardí Moreau becomes Cuban Senator

1908 Emilio Bacardí Moreau publishes *Cronicas de Santiago de Cuba*

1909 Bacardi bat trademark registered in Puerto Rico as "Ron Superior Bacardí & Compañía"

1910 Bacardi opens facility in Spain, becomes Cuba's first multi-national company; Bacardi begins use of illustration in advertising

1914 Panama Canal opens; World War I begins

1915 Panama-Pacific International Exposition opens in San Francisco, California to celebrate the opening of the Panama Canal; New distillery on Matadero Street, surrounding *El Coco*, is built by master builder Gerardo Vega Wright

1917 Cuba enters World War I

1918 World War I ends

1919 U.S. Congress passes the Volstead Act, initiates Prohibition; Bacardi re-organized as Compañia Ron Bacardi, S.A., a stock corporation. Emilio Bacardí Moreau is the company's first president; Bauhaus School is established in Weimar, Germany

1922 *Piña Colada*; Death of Emilio Bacardí Moreau; Enrique Schueg Chassin becomes second Bacardi president; New distillery in El Barrio San Pedrito, including a bottling plant, ice factory, laboratory and carpentry shop; Wrigley Building is completed in Chicago, Graham, Anderson, Probst & White, architects

1925 *El Libro de Cuba* (*The Book of Cuba*) is published; Gerardo Machado elected president of Cuba. Leaves island in 1933; Bacardi is largest industrial enterprise in Cuba; Roney Palace Hotel in Miami Beach and Miami News Tower in Miami are completed. Biltmore Hotel in Coral Gables is completed the following year, Schultze and Weaver, architects

1927 Architecture Competition for the Edificio Bacardi de la Habana, in Cuba

1929 Stock market crash in New York City—severe economic conditions follow; Mexican Revolution and Cristero War end. Creation of *Partido Nacional Revolucionario* (National Revolutionary Party, current PRI); Barcelona International Exposition. BACARDÍ rums awarded a grand prize. Ludwig Mies van der Rohe is the designer of the German Pavilion; Emilio Bacardi Moreau Municipal Museum, designed by architect Carlos Segrera Fernández, is completed; architects Esteban Rodriguez-Castells and Rafael Fernández Ruenes win the design competition for the Edificio Bacardi in Havana; Initiation of HATUEY Beer, which is brewed in the facilities of the former Santiago Brewing Company

1930 Smoot-Hawley Act raises tariffs on foreign imports; Beginning of *El Milagro Mexicano* (Mexican Economic Miracle); Completion of Edificio Bacardi in Havana; Esteban Rodriguez-Castells and Rafael Fernández Ruenes, architects with José Menéndez. Cocktail recipe booklet: *BACARDI: Algunos De Sus Muchos Usos* (*Bacardi and Its Many Uses*) published in Havana; Mies van der Rohe is appointed director of the Bauhaus in Dessau, Germany. The school is closed by the Nazi party in 1933

1931 Bacardi distillery in Mexico is opened (first Bacardi distillery outside Santiago)

1933 Volstead Act repealed; Prohibition ends; Fulgencio Batista assumes power in Cuba

1934 Bacardi partners with liquor importer, Schenley Distillers Corporation. Their office is established in New York City's Chrysler Building; Architect Morris Sander is appointed head of the art department at Schenley LiquorsLazaro Cardenas becomes president of Mexico, initiates major land redistribution and industrial expansion

1935 Schenley's Bacardi Bar and Imports Lounge in New York City is completed by Morris Sanders, architect

1936 José "Pepin" Bosch registers Bacardi Corporation in Puerto Rico. The first San Juan distillery is opened; The Seagram executive bar, designed by Morris Lapidus, opens in the Chrysler Building, New York City

1937 A "Bacardi Cocktail must be made with BACARDÍ Rum"—decision of the New York Supreme Court

1937 Ad campaign in U.S.: *Sí Señor*; Cuban artist Conrado Massaguer designs Bacardi ad: *"Cuba is Great"—there is a reason*; Ludwig Mies van der Rohe immigrates to the United States, where he is appointed head of the Armour Institute of Technology in Chicago (later Illinois Institute of Technology)

1938 Bacardi Room opens at the Empire State Building. Franklin Hughes, architect

1939 Architect Félix Candela immigrates to Mexico after fighting for the Republican cause during the Spanish Civil War; Bacardi moves its operations to a bigger facility in San Juan; Distilled Spirits Exhibit at the New York World's Fair. Morris Sanders, architect and Morris Lapidus, designer; World War II begins

1940s Ad campaign: *Que Suerte tiene el Cubano!* New bottling plant in Santiago opens, designed by Gerardo Vega Wright

1941 Pearl Harbor; Cuba enters World War II

1944 Jose "Pepin" Bosch becomes deputy-managing director, unofficially leader of Bacardi; Bacardi Imports opens in New York City, replaces Schenley as Bacardi distributor; Bacardi initiates development of Palo Seco campus near Cataño, Puerto Rico

1945 End of World War II

1946-47 Completion of the new Bacardi distillery at the company's Palo Seco campus, Cataño, Puerto Rico, W. Donald Christie architect. The distillery will soon be called the "Cathedral of Rum"

1947 U.S. grants Puerto Rico partial self-government, enabling Puerto Ricans to elect their own governor. Luiz Munoz Marin is elected Governor in 1948

1949 Ad campaign: *Rumbera*; Ad campaign: *All Nations Agree! Bacardi*; Philip Johnson completes the Glass House in New Canaan, Connecticut

1950s Addition to Matadero Street distillery, around *El Coco*, Santiago de Cuba, architect unknown

1950 Pepin Bosch becomes third president of Bacardi; Félix Candela founds Cubiertas Ala S.A., dedicated to the design and construction of industrial structures; Mies van der Rohe designs the 50 x 50 House, an unbuilt project considered the archetype for the Bacardi Administration Building in Santiago de Cuba

1952 Fulgencio Batista seizes power in Cuba; Puerto Rico becomes a Commonwealth of the U.S.

1953 Fidel Castro launches an attack on the Moncada

barracks in Santiago de Cuba. Castro imprisoned until 1955

1954 Pepin Bosch commissions a new home in Palo Seco, Puerto Rico, designed by Stephen Arneson and Henry Klumb, architects; "Report on Bacardi Office Building," prepared by Georgina George, architect, recommends constructing a new corporate headquarters that would serve as both model work environment and tourist attraction

1956 New distillery completed for Bacardi y Compañia S.A. de C.V., at La Galarza, Matamoros, Puebla, Mexico. Félix Candela with Hector Mestre and Manuel de la Colina, architects and Luis Saenz engineer; Philip Johnson commissioned to design the Hotel Monaco along the Malecon in Havana; Pepin Bosch commissions Philip Johnson to design Casa Pepin Bosch, Santa Maria del Mar, Habana del Este (unbuilt); Mies van der Rohe completes Crown Hall at the Illinois Institute of Technology in Chicago. Jose Pepin Bosch visits the iconic building, which is based on a principle of universal space; Lambert-St. Louis Airport Terminal, designed by Minoru Yamasaki, is completed. The building inspires Félix Candela's solution for the Bottling Plant at Tultitlán, Mexico; General Motors Technical Center in Warren, Michigan, is completed. The complex, designed by Eero Saarinen, is known as the "Versailles of Industry"

1957 Mies van der Rohe is commissioned to design Bacardi Administration Building, Santiago de Cuba (unbuilt); Raúl Alvarez and Enrique Gutiérrez join Saenz-Cancio-Martin Ingenieros; the resulting firm is called Saenz-Cancio-Martin-Alvarez-Gutiérrez, or SACMAG

1958 Bacardi expands its plant in Palo Seco with a new facility originally designed by architects Toro y Ferrer; Mies van der Rohe, with Philip Johnson, complete the Seagram Building in New York City; Raúl Alvarez, Enrique Gutiérrez and Richard Neutra win the gold medal from the Colegio de Arquitectos (Cuba) for the Alfred de Schulthess Residence in Havana (completed 1956)

1959 Fulgencio Batista flees Havana. Fidel Castro enters Santiago de Cuba and assumes power in Cuba. A large wave of Cuban exile migrations to the U.S. ensues; Mies van der Rohe is commissioned to design the Administration Building in Tultitlán, Mexico. Mies travels to Havana to present the design; SACMAG of Puerto Rico is formed

1960 Pepin Bosch departs Cuba for Mexico (July); foreign businesses in Cuba are nationalized (August); domestic businesses in Cuba are nationalized (October). These include Compañia Ron Bacardi, S.A., Cerveceria Modelo, S.A., and Cerveceria Central, S.A.

1960-61 President John F. Kennedy's Alliance for Progress aims to create economic cooperation between North and South America; New Bottling Hall and Aging Warehouses for Bacardi y Compañia S.A. de C. V. are completed in Tultitlán, Mexico; Felix Candela with Luis Torres Landa and SACMAG

1961 Bay of Pigs invasion

1961 Bat-winged Centennial Pavilion (*merendero*) and Entrance Gate completed at Palo Seco campus, Puerto Rico; Bacardi opens its new production facility in Recife, Brazil. In arranging for the manufacture of glass bottles, Pepin Bosch meets artist Francisco Brennand; IBM's Thomas J. Watson Research Center established in Yorktown Heights, N.Y. Eero Saarinen, architect

1963 Completion of Bacardi Imports Building, Miami. Enrique Gutierrez/SACMAG of Puerto Rico, architect; Opening of the public art gallery on the ground floor of the Bacardi Imports Building in Miami. Alberto Fernandez-Pla is inaugural curator

1964 Bacardi opens production facility in Nassau, The Bahamas. The ten building factory was completed in 13 weeks using metal buildings designed and built by the Stran-Steel Corporation (famous for its re-design of the Quonset Hut during World War II)

1965 Bacardi International Limited relocates from the Bahamas to Bermuda. Bottling Hall and Family Museum completed at Palo Seco campus, Puerto Rico

1966 Ad campaign: *Bacardi, The Mixable One*

1967 Pepin Bosch steps down as president of Bacardi, remains in charge of Bacardi's expansion program

1968 Cuban government stops using the Bacardi trademark

1973 Enrique Gutiérrez completes One Biscayne Tower, Miami's tallest office building. He is the architect and developer of the project

1972 Bacardi International Limited inaugurates new Administration Building in Bermuda; Bacardi Bottling Corporation opens Castleton Beverage Corporation in Jacksonville, Florida; Bacardi Canada Inc opens distillery and bottling plant in Brampton, Ontario

1974 Bacardi España S.A. opens distillery and bottling plant in Malaga, Spain

1975 Bacardi Building Annex is completed in Miami. Ignacio Carrera-Justiz, architect

1976 Jose Pepin Bosch retires from Bacardi

1978 BACARDÍ rum becomes leading spirit brand in the United States

1979 BACARDÍ rum becomes the world's top-selling premium spirit brand; Bacardi Centroamérica establishes a distillery in Panama City

1992 Bacardi Limited is formed, unifying five separate strategic operating units of the Company: Bacardi International Limited Bermuda; Bacardi & Company Limited—Bahamas; Bacardi Corporation—Puerto Rico; Bacardi Imports, Inc.—United States; and Bacardi y Compañia S.A. de C.V.—Mexico

1993 Bacardi completes acquisition of the Martini & Rossi Group

1993 Bacardi Deutschland opens in Buxtehude, Germany

1997 Bacardi Limited is established in Nanjangud, India

1998 Bacardi purchases DEWAR'S Scotch Whiskey and Bombay Sapphire Gin

2001 Bacardi Shanghai Limited opens in Shanghai, China

2002 Bacardi Limited acquires the Cazadores Tequila distillery in Arandas, Mexico

2004 Bacardi acquires GREY GOOSE Vodka

2009 New Bacardi Americas Headquarters is completed in Coral Gables, Florida. Gensler, Environmental Brand Experience & Graphic Design

2012 Bacardi transfers its iconic Administration complex on Biscayne Boulevard to the National YoungArts Foundation, a nonprofit organization that identifies and supports emerging young artists in the visual, literary, and performing arts.

INDEX